T0310705

Resource Management of Mobile Cloud Computing Networks and Environments

George Mastorakis
Technological Educational Institute of Crete, Greece

Constandinos X. Mavromoustakis
University of Nicosia, Cyprus

Evangelos Pallis
Technological Educational Institute of Crete, Greece

A volume in the Advances in Systems Analysis, Software Engineering, and High Performance Computing (ASASEHPC) Book Series

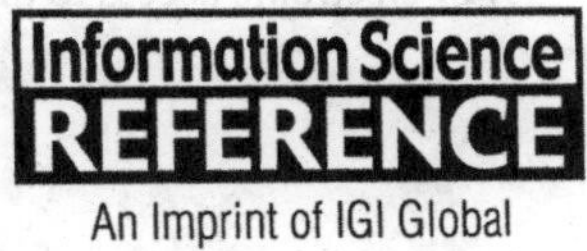

Managing Director: Lindsay Johnston
Managing Editor: Austin DeMarco
Director of Intellectual Property & Contracts: Jan Travers
Acquisitions Editor: Kayla Wolfe
Production Editor: Christina Henning
Development Editor: Brandon Carbaugh
Typesetter: Cody Page
Cover Design: Jason Mull

Published in the United States of America by
Information Science Reference (an imprint of IGI Global)
701 E. Chocolate Avenue
Hershey PA, USA 17033
Tel: 717-533-8845
Fax: 717-533-8661
E-mail: cust@igi-global.com
Web site: http://www.igi-global.com

Library of Congress Cataloging-in-Publication Data

Library of Congress Cataloging-in-Publication Data

Resource management of mobile cloud computing networks and environments / George Mastorakis, Constandinos X. Mavromoustakis, and Evangelos Pallis, editors.
pages cm
Includes bibliographical references and index.
ISBN 978-1-4666-8225-2 (hardcover) -- ISBN 978-1-4666-8226-9 (ebook) 1. Cloud computing. 2. Cloud computing--Management. 3. Mobile computing. I. Mastorakis, George, 1978- II. Mavromoustakis, Constandinos X., 1974- III. Pallis, Evangelos, 1971-
QA76.585.R38 2015
004.67'82--dc23

2015003298

This book is published in the IGI Global book series Advances in Systems Analysis, Software Engineering, and High Performance Computing (ASASEHPC) (ISSN: 2327-3453; eISSN: 2327-3461)

British Cataloguing in Publication Data
A Cataloguing in Publication record for this book is available from the British Library.

All work contributed to this book is new, previously-unpublished material. The views expressed in this book are those of the authors, but not necessarily of the publisher.

For electronic access to this publication, please contact: eresources@igi-global.com.

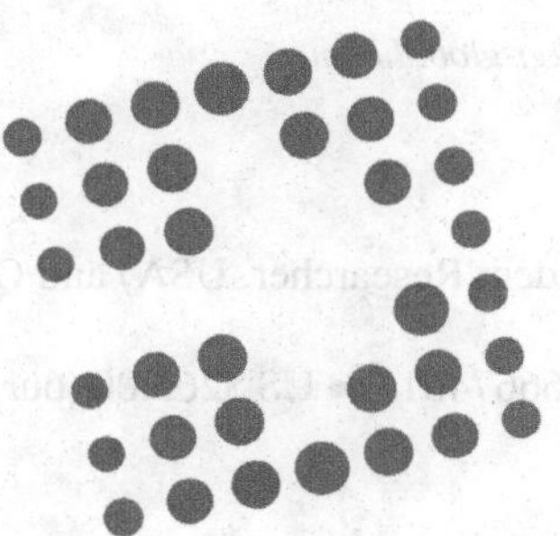

Advances in Systems Analysis, Software Engineering, and High Performance Computing (ASASEHPC) Book Series

Vijayan Sugumaran
Oakland University, USA

ISSN: 2327-3453
EISSN: 2327-3461

Mission

The theory and practice of computing applications and distributed systems has emerged as one of the key areas of research driving innovations in business, engineering, and science. The fields of software engineering, systems analysis, and high performance computing offer a wide range of applications and solutions in solving computational problems for any modern organization.

The **Advances in Systems Analysis, Software Engineering, and High Performance Computing (ASASEHPC) Book Series** brings together research in the areas of distributed computing, systems and software engineering, high performance computing, and service science. This collection of publications is useful for academics, researchers, and practitioners seeking the latest practices and knowledge in this field.

Coverage

- Performance Modelling
- Computer Networking
- Network Management
- Software Engineering
- Computer Graphics
- Virtual Data Systems
- Storage Systems
- Engineering Environments
- Parallel Architectures
- Enterprise Information Systems

IGI Global is currently accepting manuscripts for publication within this series. To submit a proposal for a volume in this series, please contact our Acquisition Editors at Acquisitions@igi-global.com or visit: http://www.igi-global.com/publish/.

The Advances in Systems Analysis, Software Engineering, and High Performance Computing (ASASEHPC) Book Series (ISSN 2327-3453) is published by IGI Global, 701 E. Chocolate Avenue, Hershey, PA 17033-1240, USA, www.igi-global.com. This series is composed of titles available for purchase individually; each title is edited to be contextually exclusive from any other title within the series. For pricing and ordering information please visit http://www.igi-global.com/book-series/advances-systems-analysis-software-engineering/73689. Postmaster: Send all address changes to above address.

Titles in this Series

For a list of additional titles in this series, please visit: www.igi-global.com

Research and Applications in Global Supercomputing
Richard S. Segall (Arkansas State University, USA) Jeffrey S. Cook (Independent Researcher, USA) and Qingyu Zhang (Shenzhen University, China)
Information Science Reference • copyright 2015 • 672pp • H/C (ISBN: 9781466674615) • US $265.00 (our price)

Challenges, Opportunities, and Dimensions of Cyber-Physical Systems
P. Venkata Krishna (VIT University, India) V. Saritha (VIT University, India) and H. P. Sultana (VIT University, India)
Information Science Reference • copyright 2015 • 328pp • H/C (ISBN: 9781466673120) • US $200.00 (our price)

Human Factors in Software Development and Design
Saqib Saeed (University of Dammam, Saudi Arabia) Imran Sarwar Bajwa (The Islamia University of Bahawalpur, Pakistan) and Zaigham Mahmood (University of Derby, UK & North West University, South Africa)
Information Science Reference • copyright 2015 • 354pp • H/C (ISBN: 9781466664852) • US $195.00 (our price)

Handbook of Research on Innovations in Systems and Software Engineering
Vicente García Díaz (University of Oviedo, Spain) Juan Manuel Cueva Lovelle (University of Oviedo, Spain) and B. Cristina Pelayo García-Bustelo (University of Oviedo, Spain)
Information Science Reference • copyright 2015 • 745pp • H/C (ISBN: 9781466663596) • US $515.00 (our price)

Handbook of Research on Architectural Trends in Service-Driven Computing
Raja Ramanathan (Independent Researcher, USA) and Kirtana Raja (IBM, USA)
Information Science Reference • copyright 2014 • 759pp • H/C (ISBN: 9781466661783) • US $515.00 (our price)

Handbook of Research on Embedded Systems Design
Alessandra Bagnato (Softeam R&D, France) Leandro Soares Indrusiak (University of York, UK) Imran Rafiq Quadri (Softeam R&D, France) and Matteo Rossi (Politecnico di Milano, Italy)
Information Science Reference • copyright 2014 • 520pp • H/C (ISBN: 9781466661943) • US $345.00 (our price)

Contemporary Advancements in Information Technology Development in Dynamic Environments
Mehdi Khosrow-Pour (Information Resources Management Association, USA)
Information Science Reference • copyright 2014 • 410pp • H/C (ISBN: 9781466662520) • US $205.00 (our price)

Systems and Software Development, Modeling, and Analysis New Perspectives and Methodologies
Mehdi Khosrow-Pour (Information Resources Management Association, USA)
Information Science Reference • copyright 2014 • 365pp • H/C (ISBN: 9781466660984) • US $215.00 (our price)

www.igi-global.com

701 E. Chocolate Ave., Hershey, PA 17033
Order online at www.igi-global.com or call 717-533-8845 x100
To place a standing order for titles released in this series, contact: cust@igi-global.com
Mon-Fri 8:00 am - 5:00 pm (est) or fax 24 hours a day 717-533-8661

Editorial Advisory Board

List of Reviewers

Table of Contents

Chapter 5
A Social-Oriented Mobile Cloud Scheme for Optimal Energy Conservation 97
Constandinos X. Mavromoustakis, University of Nicosia, Cyprus
George Mastorakis, Technological Educational Institute of Crete – Agios Nikolaos, Greece
Athina Bourdena, University of Nicosia, Cyprus
Evangelos Pallis, Technological Educational Institute of Crete – Heraklion, Greece
Dimitrios Stratakis, Technological Educational Institute of Crete – Heraklion, Greece
Emmanouil Perakakis, Technological Educational Institute of Crete – Agios Nikolaos, Greece
Ioannis Kopanakis, Technological Educational Institute of Crete – Agios Nikolaos, Greece
Stelios Papadakis, Technological Educational Institute of Crete – Agios Nikolaos, Greece
Zaharias D. Zaharis, Aristotle University of Thessaloniki, Greece
Christos Skeberis, Aristotle University of Thessaloniki, Greece
Thomas D. Xenos, Aristotle University of Thessaloniki, Greece

Chapter 6
Traffic Analyses and Measurements: Technological Dependability 122
Rossitza Goleva, Technical University of Sofia, Bulgaria
Dimitar Atamian, Technical University of Sofia, Bulgaria
Seferin Mirtchev, Technical University of Sofia, Bulgaria
Desislava Dimitrova, ETH Zurich, Switzerland
Lubina Grigorova, Vivacom JSCO, Bulgaria
Rosen Rangelov, Lufthansa Technik-Sofia, Bulgaria
Aneliya Ivanova, Technical University of Sofia, Bulgaria

Section 3
Content-Aware Streaming in Mobile Cloud

Chapter 7
Adaptation of Cloud Resources and Media Streaming in Mobile Cloud Networks for Media Delivery 175
Jordi Mongay Batalla, National Institute of Telecommunications, Poland & Warsaw University of Technology, Poland

Chapter 8
Context-Awareness in Opportunistic Mobile Cloud Computing 203
Radu-Corneliu Marin, University Politehnica of Bucharest, Romania
Radu-Ioan Ciobanu, University Politehnica of Bucharest, Romania
Radu Pasea, University Politehnica of Bucharest, Romania
Vlad Barosan, University Politehnica of Bucharest, Romania
Mihail Costea, University Politehnica of Bucharest, Romania
Ciprian Dobre, University Politehnica of Bucharest, Romania

Chapter 9
H.265 Video Streaming in Mobile Cloud Networks 238
Qi Wang, University of the West of Scotland, UK
James Nightingale, University of the West of Scotland, UK
Jose M. Alcaraz-Calero, University of the West of Scotland, UK
Chunbo Luo, University of the West of Scotland, UK
Zeeshan Pervez, University of the West of Scotland, UK
Xinheng Wang, University of the West of Scotland, UK
Christos Grecos, University of the West of Scotland, UK

Section 4
Network and Service Virtualization

Chapter 10
Virtualization Evolution: From IT Infrastructure Abstraction of Cloud Computing to Virtualization of Network Functions 279
Harilaos Koumaras, NCSR Demokritos, Greece
Christos Damaskos, NCSR Demokritos, Greece
George Diakoumakos, NCSR Demokritos, Greece
Michail-Alexandros Kourtis, NCSR Demokritos, Greece
George Xilouris, NCSR Demokritos, Greece
Georgios Gardikis, NCSR Demokritos, Greece
Vaios Koumaras, NCSR Demokritos, Greece
Thomas Siakoulis, NCSR Demokritos, Greece

Chapter 11
Towards Ubiquitous and Adaptive Web-Based Multimedia Communications via the Cloud 307
Spyros Panagiotakis, Technological Educational Institute of Crete, Greece
Ioannis Vakintis, Technological Educational Institute of Crete, Greece
Haroula Andrioti, Technological Educational Institute of Crete, Greece
Andreas Stamoulias, Technological Educational Institute of Crete, Greece
Kostas Kapetanakis, Technological Educational Institute of Crete, Greece
Athanasios Malamos, Technological Educational Institute of Crete, Greece

Chapter 12
A Resource Prediction Engine for Efficient Multimedia Services Provision 361
Yiannos Kryftis, University of Nicosia, Cyprus
George Mastorakis, Technological Educational Institute of Crete, Greece
Constandinos X. Mavromoustakis, University of Nicosia, Cyprus
Jordi Mongay Batalla, National Institute of Telecommunications, Poland & Warsaw University of Technology, Poland
Athina Bourdena, University of Nicosia, Cyprus
Evangelos Pallis, Technological Educational Institute of Crete, Greece

Detailed Table of Contents

Section 1
Introduction and Applications of Mobile Cloud Computing

This section comprises an introduction to cloud computing as a recently emerged technology in the wireless communication era. It elaborates on issues related to the mobile cloud computing concept, which has become an important research area due to the rapid growth of the applications in the mobile computing environments. It also presents research approaches associated with the prediction and the quantification of the technical debt in cloud software engineering. Finally, it provides insight and reports the results derived by particular methodologies that jointly consider cloud-specific properties and rely on the Empirical Mode Decomposition (EMD) approaches.

Mobile Cloud Computing (MCC) has become an important research area due to rapid growth of mobile applications and emergence of cloud computing. MCC refers to integration of cloud computing into a mobile environment. Cloud providers (e.g. Google, Amazon, and Salesforce) support mobile users by providing the required infrastructure (e.g. servers, networks, and storage), platforms, and software. Mobile devices are rapidly becoming a fundamental part of human lives and these enable users to access various mobile applications through remote servers using wireless networks. Traditional mobile device-based computing, data storage, and large-scale information processing is transferred to "cloud," and therefore, requirement of mobile devices with high computing capability and resources are reduced. This chapter provides a survey of MCC including its definition, architecture, and applications. The authors discuss the issues in MCC, existing solutions, and approaches. They also touch upon the computation offloading mechanism for MCC.

Predicting and quantifying promptly the Technical Debt has turned into an issue of significant importance over recent years. In the cloud marketplace, where cloud services can be leased, the difficulty to identify the Technical Debt effectively can have a significant impact. In this chapter, the probability of introducing the Technical Debt due to budget and cloud service selection decisions is investigated. A cost estimation approach for implementing Software as a Service (SaaS) in the cloud is examined, indicating three scenarios for predicting the incurrence of Technical Debt in the future. The Constructive Cost Model (COCOMO) is used in order to estimate the cost of the implementation and define a range of secureness by adopting a tolerance value for prediction. Furthermore, a Technical Debt quantification approach is researched for leasing a cloud Software as a Service (SaaS) in order to provide insights about the most appropriate cloud service to be selected.

Cloud environments compose unique operational characteristics and intrinsic capabilities such as service transparency and elasticity. By virtue of their exclusive properties as being outcomes of their virtualized nature, these environments are prone to a number of security threats either from malicious or legitimate intent. By virtue of the minimal proactive properties attained by off-the-shelf signature-based commercial detection solutions employed in various infrastructures, cloud-specific Intrusion Detection System (IDS) Anomaly Detection (AD)-based methodologies have been proposed in order to enable accurate identification, detection, and clustering of anomalous events that could manifest. Therefore, in this chapter the authors firstly aim to provide an overview in the state of the art related with cloud-based AD mechanisms and pinpoint their basic functionalities. They subsequently provide an insight and report some results derived by a particular methodology that jointly considers cloud-specific properties and relies on the Empirical Mode Decomposition (EMD) algorithm.

Section 2
Mobile Cloud Resource Management

This section examines the various types of resource management techniques that are available for the mobile clouds, such as resource offloading, mobile cloud infrastructure and mobile device power control, control theory, data mining, machine learning, radio spectrum management, and mobile cloud computing economic-oriented mechanisms. It also elaborates on issues related to the social-oriented context of the mobile cloud computing environments to support optimal energy conservation of the mobile devices. Finally, it elaborates on traffic analysis and measurement issues in emerging mobile computing systems.

Chapter 4
Mobile Cloud Resource Management...69
Konstantinos Katzis, European University Cyprus, Cyprus

Providing mobile cloud services requires seamless integration between various platforms to offer mobile users optimum performance. To achieve this, many fundamental problems such as bandwidth availability and reliability, resource scarceness, and finite energy must be addressed before rolling out such services. This chapter aims to explore technological challenges for mobile cloud computing in the area of resource management focusing on both parts of the infrastructure: mobile devices and cloud networks. Starting with introducing mobile cloud computing, it then stresses the importance of resource management in the operation of mobile cloud services presenting various types of resources available for cloud computing. Furthermore, it examines the various types of resource management techniques available for mobile clouds. Finally, future directions in the field of resource management for mobile cloud computing environment are presented.

Chapter 5
A Social-Oriented Mobile Cloud Scheme for Optimal Energy Conservation....................................97
Constandinos X. Mavromoustakis, University of Nicosia, Cyprus
George Mastorakis, Technological Educational Institute of Crete – Agios Nikolaos, Greece
Athina Bourdena, University of Nicosia, Cyprus
Evangelos Pallis, Technological Educational Institute of Crete – Heraklion, Greece
Dimitrios Stratakis, Technological Educational Institute of Crete – Heraklion, Greece
Emmanouil Perakakis, Technological Educational Institute of Crete – Agios Nikolaos, Greece
Ioannis Kopanakis, Technological Educational Institute of Crete – Agios Nikolaos, Greece
Stelios Papadakis, Technological Educational Institute of Crete – Agios Nikolaos, Greece
Zaharias D. Zaharis, Aristotle University of Thessaloniki, Greece
Christos Skeberis, Aristotle University of Thessaloniki, Greece
Thomas D. Xenos, Aristotle University of Thessaloniki, Greece

This chapter elaborates on energy usage optimization issues by exploiting a resource offloading process based on a social-oriented mobile cloud scheme. The adoption of the proposed scheme enables for increasing the reliability in services provision to the mobile users by guaranteeing sufficient resources for the mobile application execution. More specifically, this chapter describes the process to improve the energy consumption of the mobile devices through the exploitation of a social-oriented model and a cooperative partial process offloading scheme. This research approach exploits social centrality, as the connectivity model for the resource offloading, among the interconnected mobile devices to increase the energy usage efficiency, the mobile nodes availability, as well as the process of execution reliability. The proposed scheme is thoroughly evaluated to define the validity and the efficiency for the energy conservation increase of future mobile computing devices.

Resource management schemes in current data centers, including cloud environments, are not well equipped to handle the dynamic variation in traffic caused by the large diversity of traffic sources, source mobility patterns, and underlying network characteristics. Part of the problem is lacking knowledge on the traffic source behaviour and its proper representation for development and operation. Inaccurate, static traffic models lead to incorrect estimation of traffic characteristics, making resource allocation, migration, and release schemes inefficient, and limit scalability. The end result is unsatisfied customers (due to service degradation) and operators (due to costly inefficient infrastructure use). The authors argue that developing appropriate methods and tools for traffic predictability requires carefully conducted and analysed traffic experiments. This chapter presents their measurements and statistical analyses on various traffic sources for two network settings, namely local Area Network (LAN) and 3G mobile network. LAN traffic is organised in DiffServ categories supported by MPLS to ensure Quality of Service (QoS) provisioning. 3G measurements are taken from a live network upon entering the IP domain. Passive monitoring was used to collect the measurements in order to be non-obtrusive for the networks. The analyses indicate that the gamma distribution has general applicability to represent various traffic sources by proper setting of the parameters. The findings allow the construction of traffic models and simulation tools to be used in the development and evaluation of flexible resource management schemes that meet the real-time needs of the users.

Section 3
Content-Aware Streaming in Mobile Cloud

This section provides some novel applications that have been made possible by the rapid emergence of cloud computing resources and elaborates on content-aware streaming issues in mobile cloud computing environments. More specifically, it presents novel adaptation methods of cloud resources and media streaming techniques in mobile cloud networks for efficient media delivery. It then elaborates on context-awareness issues in opportunistic mobile cloud computing environments and context-aware adaptive streaming based on the latest video coding standard H.265 in the context of Internet-centric mobile cloud networking.

Multimedia content delivery is one of the use cases of Mobile Cloud Networks. Cloud Networks are then called Media Clouds. Since mobile devices are becoming increasingly important receptors of Multimedia content, Mobile Cloud Computing is undertaking an important role for delivering Multimedia content from the Cloud through the Internet towards the Mobile users. On the other hand, high requirements of Multimedia content streaming establish the necessity of crossp-layer mechanisms for avoiding or decreasing the effects of, for example, mobile network congestion or cloud congestion. This chapter introduces an exemplary solution, at the application layer, which takes into account the state of the network for efficient Media streaming in Mobile Cloud networks (Media Mobile Cloud). Concretely, the presented solution proposes a novel adaptation algorithm that adapts not only Media bitrate in the case when there is a congestion in Mobile last mille, but also adapts Media content source when the Cloud suffers from congestion.

Chapter 8
Context-Awareness in Opportunistic Mobile Cloud Computing 203
Radu-Corneliu Marin, University Politehnica of Bucharest, Romania
Radu-Ioan Ciobanu, University Politehnica of Bucharest, Romania
Radu Pasea, University Politehnica of Bucharest, Romania
Vlad Barosan, University Politehnica of Bucharest, Romania
Mihail Costea, University Politehnica of Bucharest, Romania
Ciprian Dobre, University Politehnica of Bucharest, Romania

Smartphones have shaped the mobile computing community. Unfortunately, their power consumption overreaches the limits of current battery technology. Most solutions for energy efficiency turn towards offloading code from the mobile device into the cloud. Although mobile cloud computing inherits all the Cloud Computing advantages, it does not treat user mobility, the lack of connectivity, or the high cost of mobile network traffic. In this chapter, the authors introduce mobile-to-mobile contextual offloading, a novel collaboration concept for handheld devices that takes advantage of an adaptive contextual search algorithm for scheduling mobile code execution over smartphone communities, based on predicting the availability and mobility of nearby devices. They present the HYCCUPS framework, which implements the contextual offloading model in an on-the-fly opportunistic hybrid computing cloud. The authors emulate HYCCUPS based on real user traces and prove that it maximizes power saving, minimizes overall execution time, and preserves user experience.

Chapter 9
H.265 Video Streaming in Mobile Cloud Networks... 238
Qi Wang, University of the West of Scotland, UK
James Nightingale, University of the West of Scotland, UK
Jose M. Alcaraz-Calero, University of the West of Scotland, UK
Chunbo Luo, University of the West of Scotland, UK
Zeeshan Pervez, University of the West of Scotland, UK
Xinheng Wang, University of the West of Scotland, UK
Christos Grecos, University of the West of Scotland, UK

Mobile video applications have started to dominate the global mobile data traffic in recent years, and both opportunities and challenges have arisen when the emerging mobile cloud paradigm is introduced to support the resource-demanding video processing and networking services. This chapter offers in-depth discussions for content- and context-aware, adaptive, robust, secure, and real-time video applications in mobile cloud networks. The chapter describes and analyses the essential building blocks including the state-of-the-art technologies and standards on video encoding, adaptive streaming, mobile cloud computing, and resource management, and the associated security issues. The focus is context-aware

future of mobile multimedia is that with the integration of these technologies one can shape a diversity of future pervasive and personalized cloud-based Web applications, where the client-server operations are obsolete. In particular, it is believed that in the future Web cloud-based Web applications will be able to communicate, stream, and transfer adaptive events and content to their clients, creating a fully collaborative and pervasive Web 3D environment.

Chapter 12
A Resource Prediction Engine for Efficient Multimedia Services Provision 361
Yiannos Kryftis, University of Nicosia, Cyprus
George Mastorakis, Technological Educational Institute of Crete, Greece
Constandinos X. Mavromoustakis, University of Nicosia, Cyprus
Jordi Mongay Batalla, National Institute of Telecommunications, Poland & Warsaw University of Technology, Poland
Athina Bourdena, University of Nicosia, Cyprus
Evangelos Pallis, Technological Educational Institute of Crete, Greece

This chapter presents a novel network architecture for optimal and balanced provision of multimedia services. The proposed architecture includes a central Management and Control (M&C) plane, located at Internet provider's premises, as well as distributed M&C planes for each delivery method, including Content Delivery Networks (CDNs) and Home Gateways. As part of the architecture, a Resource Prediction Engine (RPE) is presented that utilizes novel models and algorithms for resource usage prediction, making possible the optimal distribution of streaming data. It also enables for the prediction of the upcoming fluctuations of the network that provide the ability to make the proper decisions in achieving optimized Quality of Service (QoS) and Quality of Experience (QoE) for the end users.

Compilation of References 381

About the Contributors 419

Index 431

Preface

OVERVIEW

With the daily life becoming increasingly dependent on mobile technologies and wireless communications, novel challenges arise in the field of the resource management. Mobile users become incrementally dependent on applications that are capable to reliably support the 3A (Anything, Anytime, Anywhere) vision and seeming less likely to interact with external applications and services, claiming advanced capabilities. In addition, the enormous growth of cloud computing, together with the advances on mobile technology has led to the new era of mobile cloud computing. These technologies, emerged from cluster, grid, and now cloud computing, have all aimed at allowing access to large amounts of computing power in a fully virtualized manner by aggregating resources from remotely hosted terminals and offering a single system view. Within this framework a lot of open-ended issues are addressed in this book, like the efficient and reliable management of distributed resources in the mobile clouds, which becomes important due to the incremental trend in the number of users and devices and the available resources, through their running applications. Furthermore, this book focuses on a new communication paradigm, elaborating on modeling, analysis, and efficient resource management in mobile cloud computing environments. It explores the challenges in mobile cloud computing, including current research efforts and approaches. It provides technical/scientific information about various aspects of mobile cloud computing, ranging from basic concepts to research grade material, including future directions. The current state is defined over a digital cloud-oriented 'universe', in which different applications are not only serving as a base for improving our quality of communication and access to information but also play important roles in dictating the quality of our lives. This book captures the current state of resource management in such environments and acts as a solid source of comprehensive reference material on the related research field.

DESCRIPTION AND CHALLENGES

As an increasing number of people communicate and computationally collaborate over the Internet, via different accessing systems and mobile devices, the need for a reliable management of resources in such mobile cloud computing environments, facilitating ubiquitous availability and efficient access to large quantities of distributed resources, has become manifest. The mobile cloud computing paradigm is set to drive technology over the next decade and integrate the resources availability through the 3As (Anywhere, Anything, Anytime). Notwithstanding, there are a lot of challenges to meet, in order to have the mobile cloud computing paradigm applicable in all aspects and in an efficiently utilized manner. Itself, this poses a fertile ground and a hot research and development area for mobile cloud computing, as is being projected as the future growth area in both academia and industry. In addition, social networking is experiencing an exponential growth and is becoming part of our daily routines. The communications overlay it creates can be exploited by a number of applications and services. Users are connecting to social networks, by using small mobile devices, such as smart phones and tablets that are able to form opportunistic networks. Current trends in mining social communication among mobile users, present numerous research and technical challenges, as many of these application scenarios, serve to add more inefficiencies in the end-to-end communication and offer inconsistent and low-quality user-generated content. Social-oriented communication networks form a potential infrastructure for increased resource availability to all users in the network, especially to those that face reduced resource availability (e.g. energy, memory, processing resources, etc.). Opportunistic wireless networks exhibit unique properties, as they depend on users' behavior and movement, as well as on users' local concentration. Predicting and modeling their behavior is a difficult task but the association of the social interconnectivity factor may prove part of the solution, by successfully tapping into the resources they are offering. Resource sharing in the wireless and mobile environment is even more demanding as applications require the resource sharing to happen in a seamless and unobtrusive to the user manner, with minimal delays in an unstructured and ad-hoc changing system without affecting the user's Quality of Experience (QoE). This forms a highly ambitious objective as on one hand wireless environments cannot reliably commit to sharing resources for establishing reliable communication among users, since there is no way of guaranteeing resource allocation and on the other hand, if that was to be overcome their limited capabilities exacerbate further the problem. The mobility factor imposes additional constraints as network topology is constantly producing fluctuation in bandwidth usage and resource availability. The dependency on device capabilities restricts solutions to particular devices, lacking generality in its applicability.

As social platforms are used by a staggering majority of 87% of mobile users for communication and message exchange (Tang, 2010), they form an underlying Web, interconnecting mobile users and possibly enabling reliable resource sharing. Using social connectivity and interactivity patterns, it is possible to provide adaptability to device capabilities and operating environment, enabling devices to adapt to frequent changes in location and context. In addition, one of the ever lacking resources in the wireless mobile environment is that of energy. As energy is stored in batteries, it comprises of the only source for mobile device operation and as new and more power demanding applications are created every day, energy usage optimization forms a challenging field, approached by both hardware and software solutions. Furthermore, social networking started as an online tool for forming connections and information sharing. Its appeal and huge popularity primarily came from the fact that the social activity was enhanced in the online line environment with the use of multimedia, giving users instant access to information. Another aspect of the online environment was the ability of the social network users to share their location with others, instantly advertising their present coordinates, either using programs such as FourSquare, or having automatic tracking by exploiting the mobile devices GPS-enabled capabilities. The use of user mobility in opportunistic networks will help to realize the next generation of applications based on the adaptive behavior of the devices for resource exchange. The problem of energy usage optimization that considers energy as a finite resource, which needs to be shared among users, providing most processing power whilst maintaining group connectivity, will greatly benefit by using a socially-oriented centrality model. Opportunistic networks will greatly benefit from the capability of the mobile devices to gather information from any hosted application, in order to better utilize network resources. The task allocation and load balancing can be strictly or voluntarily associated with the social communication. Several research approaches propose architectures, which rely on the local information derived by the devices and their local views, in optimizing load balancing and energy management, as well as even some self-behaving properties, like self-organization.

In addition, it is undoubtedly true that over the past few decades, several research efforts have been devoted to device-to-device or Machine-to-Machine communication networks, ranging from physical layer communications to communication-level networking challenges. Wireless devices can exchange resources on the move and can become data "Prosumers," by producing a great amount of content, while at the same time as content providers devices can consume the content. The research efforts for achieving energy efficiency on-the-move for wireless devices, trades-off the QoS offered, by significantly reducing the performance with energy-hungry applications such as video, interactive gaming, etc. While energy-hungry applications are widely utilized by wireless devices, the explicit lifetime of devices should be extended, towards hosting and running the application in the device entire lifetime. In order to achieve resource management in wireless devices within the context of the cloud paradigm, efficient allocation of processor power, memory capacity resources, and network bandwidth should be considered. To this end, resource management should allocate resources of the users and their respected applications, on a cloud-based infrastructure, in order to migrate some of their resources on the cloud. Wireless devices are expected to operate under the predefined QoS requirements as set by the users and/or the applications' requirements. Resource management at cloud scale requires a rich set of resource and task management schemes that are capable to efficiently manage the provision of QoS requirements, whilst maintaining total system efficiency. However, the energy-efficiency is the greatest challenge for this optimization problem, along with the offered scalability in the context of performance evaluation and measurement. Different dynamic resource allocation policies targeting the improvement of the application execution performance and the efficient utilization of resources have been explored so far. Other research approaches related to the performance of dynamic resource allocation policies, had led to the development of a computing framework, which considers the countable and measureable parameters that will affect task allocation. Several authors address this problem, by using the CloneCloud approach of a smart and efficient architecture for the seamless use of ambient computation to augment mobile device applications, off-loading the right portion of their execution onto device clones, operating in a computational cloud. Other researchers statically partition service tasks and resources between client and server portions, whereas in a later stage the service is reassembled on the mobile device. This approach allows many vulnerabilities, as it has to take into consideration the resources of each cloud rack, depending on the expected workload and execution conditions (CPU speed, network performance). In addition, computation offloading schemes have been proposed to be used in cloud computing environments, towards minimizing the energy consumption of a mobile device, in order to be able to run certain/specified and under constrains application. Energy consumption has also been studied, in order to enable computation offloading, by using a combination of 3G and Wi-Fi infrastructures. However, these evaluations do not maximize the benefits of offloading, as they are considered as high latency offloading processes and require low amount of information to be offloaded. Cloud computing is currently impaired by the latency experienced during the data offloading through a Wide Area Network (WAN).

In this context and by considering all the above-mentioned issues, this book explores the mobile devices characteristics, as well as the social interactivity as a method for modeling and achieving resource sharing in the wireless mobile environment. It also combines the energy management issues with communication-level parameters and models, in order to optimize the energy management and the load sharing process. In addition, this book explores the challenges in mobile cloud computing and includes current efforts and cutting-edge technology approaches to address them. It provides detail technical information about various aspects of mobile cloud computing, ranging from basic concepts to research grade material, including future directions. As the topic is by nature novel, it demonstrates the different newly introduced approaches in the area of resource management in newly introduced mobile cloud computing technologies. It also provides sustained reflection on some of the ways, in which important recent technological advances in mobile cloud computing research might help to increase mobile network resources availability through the 3As.

TARGET AUDIENCE

This book adopts an interdisciplinary approach and reflects both theoretical and practical approaches in order to be targeted to multiple audiences. The intended audience includes college students, researchers, scientists, engineers, and technicians in the field of mobile networks, cloud computing, ad-hoc computing, body networks, sensor networks, cognitive radio networks, and content-aware networks. It can also be a reference for selection by the audience with multiple field backgrounds, such as college and university undergraduate or graduate students for potential use in their programmable computing courses, as well as researchers and scientists for exploitation in universities and institutions. Electrical, electronic, computer, software, and telecommunications engineers can also be included in the audience of this book, as well as members of professional societies, such as Computer and Communication Society of IEEE, ACM, and other related ones.

ORGANIZATION OF THE BOOK

The book is organized into 12 chapters. A brief description of each chapter follows below:

Chapter 1 elaborates on the Mobile Cloud Computing (MCC) paradigm that has become an important research area due to the rapid growth of mobile applications and the emergence of cloud computing. MCC refers to the integration of cloud computing into a mobile environment. It provides mobile users with processing and data storage services using a cloud computing platform. Cloud computing has widely perceived as the next generation computing infrastructure. Cloud providers (e.g. Google, Amazon, and Salesforce) support mobile users, by providing the required infrastructure (e.g. servers, networks, and storage), platforms, and software. Cloud computing facilitates users to utilize on demand resources as well. Mobile devices are rapidly becoming a fundamental part of human lives and these enable users to access various mobile applications through remote servers using wireless networks. However, mobile devices typically have limitations related to hardware and communication resources, thereby restricting the improvements in mobile computing services. Traditional mobile device based computing, data storage and large scale information processing is transferred to "cloud," and therefore, requirement of mobile devices with high computing capability and resources have been reduced. This chapter provides a survey of MCC including its definition, architecture and applications. The authors have discussed the issues in MCC, existing solutions and approaches. They also touch upon the computation offloading mechanism for MCC. Future research directions of MCC are also discussed.

Chapter 2 elaborates on the prediction and the quantification of the Technical Debt that has turned into an issue of significant importance over recent years. In the cloud marketplace, where cloud services can be leased, the difficulty to identify the Technical Debt effectively can have a significant impact. In this chapter, the probability of introducing Technical Debt due to budget and cloud service selection decisions is investigated. Therefore, the Technical Debt may originate from budget constraints during the software development process and the capacity of a cloud service. In this context, a cost estimation approach for implementing Software as a Service (SaaS) in the cloud is examined, indicating three scenarios for predicting the incurrence of Technical Debt in the future. The Constructive Cost Model (COCOMO) is used in order to estimate the cost of the implementation and define a range of secureness by adopting a tolerance value for prediction. Furthermore, a Technical Debt quantification approach is researched for leasing a cloud Software as a Service (SaaS) in order to provide insights about the most appropriate cloud service to be selected. Finally, a quantification tool was developed as a proof of concept linked to the research approach, implementing the formulas and aiming to predict, quantify and evaluate the Technical Debt in the cloud service level in order to be promptly managed.

Chapter 3 elaborates on the cloud environments that compose unique operational characteristics and intrinsic capabilities, such as service transparency and elasticity. By virtue of their exclusive properties as being outcomes of their virtualized nature, these environments are prone to a number of security threats, either from malicious or legitimate intent. By virtue of the minimal proactive properties attained by off-the-shelf signature-based commercial detection solutions employed in various infrastructures, cloud-specific Intrusion Detection System (IDS) Anomaly Detection (AD)-based methodologies have been proposed, in order to enable accurate identification, detection and clustering of anomalous events that could manifest. Therefore, in this chapter the author firstly aims to provide an overview in the state of the art related with cloud-based AD mechanisms and pinpoints their basic functionalities. He subsequently provides an insight and reports some results derived by a particular methodology that jointly considers cloud-specific properties and relies on the Empirical Mode Decomposition (EMD) algorithm.

Chapter 4 elaborates on mobile cloud issues, as a difficult complex task, involving various technologies all connected together and operating in a harmonized way to deliver optimum seamless services to mobile users. It requires that many fundamental problems such as bandwidth availability and reliability, resource scarceness and finite energy be addressed before rolling out these types of services. This chapter aims to explore technological challenges for mobile cloud computing in the area of resource management focusing on both parts of the infrastructure, which are mobile devices and cloud networks. It starts with the introduction into mobile cloud computing stating how resource management is vital for the operation of mobile cloud services. It then presents and analyses the various types of resources available for cloud computing. Furthermore, it examines the various types of resource management techniques available for mobile clouds such as resource offloading, cloud infrastructure and mobile devices power control, control theory, data mining, machine learning, radio spectrum management and finally mobile cloud computing economic mechanisms looking into the latest research publications available for keeping up with the latest trends. Finally, this chapter draws the picture for future directions in the field of resource management for the mobile cloud computing environment.

Chapter 5 elaborates on energy usage optimization issues by exploiting a resource offloading process based on a social network-oriented mobile cloud scheme. The adoption of the proposed scheme enables for increasing the reliability in services provision to the mobile users, by guaranteeing sufficient resources for the mobile applications execution. More specifically, this chapter describes the process to improve the energy consumption of the mobile devices, through the exploitation of a social oriented model, enabling for a cooperative partial process offloading scheme. This research approach exploits social centrality, as the connectivity model for the resource offloading among the interconnected mobile devices to increase the energy usage efficiency, the mobile nodes availability, as well as the process of execution reliability. The proposed scheme is thoroughly evaluated to define the validity and the efficiency for the energy conservation increase of future mobile computing devices.

Chapter 6 is associated with the technological and scalable dependability of the traffic in the cloud computing as a challenging problem. The capability of the users and services to move in time and space creates dynamic picture of the traffic that requires special attention in resource management. The lack of the flexibility of resource allocation, release and identification makes the data model static, unpredictable and incapable to adjust to the changes. In this chapter, traffic measurements in IP and 3G networks are presented. After careful analyses of different traffic models by statistical tools, gamma distribution applicability for inter-arrival times modeling is proved as a generic solution. The measured LAN traffic is combined with DiffServ and MPLS for better Quality of Service. Measurements in 3G core network demonstrate traffic changes in mobile environment. The open research topics mostly related to moving objects and data as well as distribution parameters mapping are described at the end.

Chapter 7 elaborates on multimedia content delivery as one of the use cases of mobile cloud networks. Cloud networks are referred to as media clouds. Since mobile devices are becoming increasingly important receptors of multimedia content, mobile cloud computing is undertaking an important role for delivering audiovisual content from the cloud through the Internet towards the mobile users. On the other hand, high requirements of multimedia content streaming establish the necessity of cross layer mechanisms for avoiding or decreasing the effects of, for example, mobile network congestion or cloud congestion. This chapter introduces an exemplary solution, at the application layer, which takes into account the state of the network for efficient media streaming in mobile cloud networks (media mobile cloud). Concretely, the presented solution proposes a novel adaptation algorithm that adapts not only media bitrate in the case when there is a congestion in mobile last mille, but also adapts media content source when the cloud suffers from a congestion.

Chapter 8 presets issues based on the smartphones that have shaped the mobile computing community by introducing cutting edge hardware, normally found in traditional computing systems, into everyday handhelds which are now able to run complex and rich applications. Unfortunately, these impressive features do not come cheap as the power consumption of such devices overreaches the limits of current battery technology. Most solutions for energy efficiency turn towards mobile cloud computing, where the power-hungry code is offloaded from the mobile device and executed in the cloud. Although mobile cloud computing inherits all the advantages of cloud computing, it is far from being the perfect solution for mobile energy efficiency, as it does not treat user mobility, the lack of connectivity, or the high cost of mobile network traffic. In this chapter, the authors introduce mobile-to-mobile contextual offloading, a novel collaboration solution for handheld devices, which takes advantage of an adaptive contextual search algorithm for scheduling mobile code execution over smartphone communities, based on predicting the availability and mobility of nearby devices. They present the HYCCUPS framework, which implements the contextual offloading model in an on-the-fly opportunistic hybrid computing cloud. They emulate HYCCUPS based on real user traces and they prove that it maximizes power saving, minimizes overall execution time of mobile applications and it preserves user experience. Furthermore, they analyze the impact of opportunistic networking and network usage to prove the feasibility of the HYCCUPS framework.

Chapter 9 elaborates on the mobile video applications that have started to dominate the global mobile data traffic in recent years and both opportunities and challenges have arisen when the emerging mobile cloud paradigm is introduced to support the resource-demanding video processing and networking services. This chapter offers in-depth discussions for content- and context-aware, adaptive, robust, secure and real-time video applications in mobile cloud networks. The chapter describes and analyses the essential building blocks, including the state-of-the-art technologies and standards on video encoding, adaptive streaming, mobile cloud computing, and resource management, and the associated security issues. The focus is context-aware adaptive streaming based on the latest video coding standard H.265 in the context of Internet-centric mobile cloud networking. Built upon selected building blocks underpinned by promising approaches and emerging standards, an integrated architecture is proposed, towards achieving next-generation smart video streaming for mobile cloud users, with future research directions in this field identified.

Chapter 10 discusses the evolution of the cloud computing paradigm and its applicability in various sections of the computing and networking/telecommunications industry, such as the cloud networking, the cloud offloading and the network function virtualization. The new heterogeneous virtualized ecosystem that is formulated creates new needs and challenges for management and administration also at the network part. For this purpose, the approach of Software Defined Networking is discussed and its future perspectives are further analyzed.

Chapter 11 at first surveys the Web technologies that can enable ubiquitous and pervasive multimedia communications over the Web and then reviews the challenges, which are raised by their combination. In this context, the relevant HTML5 APIs and technologies provided for service adaptation are introduced and the MPEG-DASH, X3Dom and WebRTC frameworks are discussed. What is envisaged for the future of mobile multimedia is that with the integration of these technologies one can shape a diversity of future pervasive and personalized cloud-based Web applications, where the client-server operations are obsolete. In particular, it is believed that in the future Web; cloud-based Web applications will be able to communicate, stream and transfer adaptive events and content to their clients, creating a fully collaborative and pervasive Web 3D environment.

Chapter 12 presents a novel network architecture for optimal and balanced provision of multimedia services. The proposed architecture includes a central Management and Control (M&C) plane located at Internet provider's premises, and distributed M&C planes for each delivery method, including Content Delivery Networks (CDNs) and Home Gateways. As part of the architecture, the authors present a Resource Prediction Engine (RPE) that utilizes novel models and algorithms for resource usage prediction that makes possible the optimal distribution of streaming data, and for prediction of the upcoming fluctuations of the network that provide the ability to make the proper decisions in achieving optimized Quality of Service (QoS) and Quality of Experience (QoE) for the end users.

George Mastorakis
Technological Educational Institute of Crete, Greece

Constandinos X. Mavromoustakis
University of Nicosia, Cyprus

Evangelos Pallis
Technological Educational Institute of Crete, Greece

REFERENCE

Tang, J., Musolesi, M., Mascolo, C., Latora, V., & Nicosia, V. (2010, April). Analysing information flows and key mediators through temporal centrality metrics. In *Proceedings of the 3rd Workshop on Social Network Systems* (p. 3). ACM Press.

Acknowledgment

Our sincere gratitude goes to the chapter authors who contributed their time and expertise to this book.

George Mastorakis
Technological Educational Institute of Crete, Greece

Constandinos X. Mavromoustakis
University of Nicosia, Cyprus

Evangelos Pallis
Technological Educational Institute of Crete, Greece

Section 1

Introduction and Applications of Mobile Cloud Computing

This section comprises an introduction to cloud computing as a recently emerged technology in the wireless communication era. It elaborates on issues related to the mobile cloud computing concept, which has become an important research area due to the rapid growth of the applications in the mobile computing environments. It also presents research approaches associated with the prediction and the quantification of the technical debt in cloud software engineering. Finally, it provides insight and reports the results derived by particular methodologies that jointly consider cloud-specific properties and rely on the Empirical Mode Decomposition (EMD) approaches.

Chapter 1
Mobile Cloud Computing:
An Introduction

Jyoti Grover
Global Institute of Technology, India

Gaurav Kheterpal
Metacube Software Private Limited, India

ABSTRACT

Mobile Cloud Computing (MCC) has become an important research area due to rapid growth of mobile applications and emergence of cloud computing. MCC refers to integration of cloud computing into a mobile environment. Cloud providers (e.g. Google, Amazon, and Salesforce) support mobile users by providing the required infrastructure (e.g. servers, networks, and storage), platforms, and software. Mobile devices are rapidly becoming a fundamental part of human lives and these enable users to access various mobile applications through remote servers using wireless networks. Traditional mobile device-based computing, data storage, and large-scale information processing is transferred to "cloud," and therefore, requirement of mobile devices with high computing capability and resources are reduced. This chapter provides a survey of MCC including its definition, architecture, and applications. The authors discuss the issues in MCC, existing solutions, and approaches. They also touch upon the computation offloading mechanism for MCC.

INTRODUCTION

People have always seen the dream of using the computing resources as a utility such as water, electricity, telephone and gas etc. ever since the first computer was developed. Cloud computing is the one of the most promising technology to convert these dreams into reality. Cloud computing is a technology that facilitates the delivery of services by providing hardware and software in data centers over the Internet. The market of mobile phone has grown rapidly. The number of mobile phones worldwide reached approximately 4.6 billion that is 370 times more than its number in year 1990 (Dinh, H.T & Lee, C. & Niyato, D. & Wang, W, 2012). With the increased use of mobile phone lead the dream "Information

DOI: 10.4018/978-1-4666-8225-2.ch001

at your fingertips anywhere, anytime" become true. But, due to inadequacy of computing and storage resources on mobile phones as compared to PCs and laptops, cloud computing brings opportunities for mobile phones.

Cloud computing provides on-demand, scalable, device-independent and reliable services to its users. The aim of mobile cloud computing (MCC) is to use cloud computing techniques for storage and processing of data on mobile devices, and hence to reduce their limitations. The term MCC was introduced just after the concept of cloud computing that was launched in mid-2007. Since then, it has been drawing attention of organizations to reduce the development cost of mobile applications. It provides the mobile users and researchers a variety of mobile services at low cost. Evolution of cloud computing is shown in Figure 1. Here, we discuss the technologies that have led to the development of MCC.

- **Utility Computing:** It is the process of providing computing and storage services through an on-demand, pay-per-use billing method. Utility computing is a model in which the provider owns, operates and manages the computing and storage infrastructure and the subscribers' access it as and when required on a rental or metered basis.
- **Computer Cluster:** A group of linked computers is called a computer cluster. This group works together closely such that in many respects these computers form a single computer.
- **Grid Computing:** Grid computing is a processor architecture that associates various computer resources to reach a main objective. In grid computing, the computers in a network work together like a supercomputer. A grid works on various scientific or technical tasks that are too big for a supercomputer and requires great number of computer processing power or access to large amount of data.
- **Cloud Computing:** It is a type of computing that relies on sharing computing resources rather than having local servers or personal devices to handle applications. It is a style of computing in which dynamically scalable and often virtualized resources are provided as a server over the Internet.

Figure 1. Evolution of cloud computing

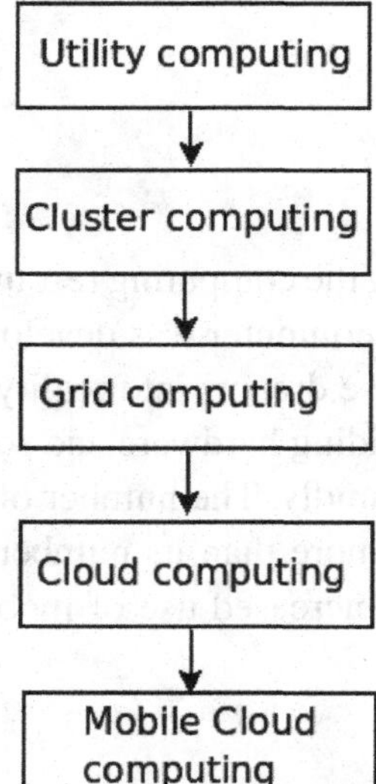

Cloud computing and grid computing are based on the concept of utility computing. A cluster of computer hardware and software that provide the services (generally paid) to general public, establishes a 'public cloud'. Cloud computing facilitates the computing as a utility much like electricity, gas, water etc. for which amount is paid as per its use. Some examples of public clouds available today are Microsoft's Azure platform, Google's App Engine, Amazon's Elastic Cloud and Salesforce etc. MCC is the combination of cloud computing and mobile networks to bring benefits for mobile users, network operators, as well as cloud computing providers (Abolfazli, Saeid & Sanaei, Zohreh & Ahmed, Ejaz & Gani, Abdullah & Buyya, Rajkumar, 2013 and Liu, Fangming & Shu, Peng & Jin, Hai & Ding, Linjie & Yu, Jie & Niu, Di & Li, Bo, 2013). The basic goal of MCC is to facilitate execution of rich mobile applications on multitude of mobile devices anywhere, anytime through Internet regardless of heterogeneous environments and platforms based on pay-as-we-need basis (Abolfazli, Saeid & Sanaei, Zohreh & Gani, Abdullah & Xia, Feng & Yang, Laurence T., 2013).

Mobile cloud computing (MCC) is a technique in which mobile applications are built, powered and hosted using cloud computing technology. It enables the programmers to design applications specifically for mobile users without being bound by the mobile operating system and computing or memory capacity of the mobile devices. Mobile cloud computing features are generally accessed via a mobile browser from a remote web server, without the need of installing a client application on the recipient phone.

MCC is supported by cloud-backed infrastructure and provides feature-rich applications to the mobile users. Most of the applications built for mobile users require extensive computation power and software platforms for application execution. Many low-end but browser-enabled mobile phones are unable to support such applications. MCC enables the execution of these applications using the computing, storage and platform resources available through the cloud. Therefore, greater number of mobile users can be supported. While there is much potential, development in this area is still in its infancy.

As mobile devices (such as smartphone, tablets etc.) have become an essential part of human lives, mobile users accumulate various services from mobile applications (e.g., iPhone apps, Google apps, etc.). Increasing the number of mobile applications demands more resources (storage, computation) and improved interactivity for better experience. Resources in cloud platforms such as Google AppEngine (Google app engine homepage), Microsoft Azure (Microsoft azure homepage), Amazon EC2 (Amazon elastic compute cloud EC2 homepage) and Salesforce can handle the lack of resources in mobile devices. Several definitions are proposed by different authors according to their views.

Marinell (Marinella, 2009) defines the MCC as an extension to cloud computing in which foundation hardware consists of mobile devices. According to this definition, MCC exploits the sensing, storage and computational capabilities of multiple network wireless devices to support variety of applications by creating distributed infrastructure.

Aepona (Aepona, 2010) describes MCC as a new standard for mobile applications where data processing and storage are moved from mobile devices to powerful and centralized computing platforms in clouds. These centralized applications are accessed through wireless connection using web browser on the mobile devices.

Mobile cloud computing forum (Mobile cloud computing forum homepage) defines MCC as an infrastructure where both data storage and data processing happen outside the mobile device. Mobile cloud applications pass the computing power and data storage away from mobile devices and into clouds.

Equivalently, MCC can be defined as a combination of mobile web and cloud computing (Christensen, Jacson H., 2009 and Liu,L. & Moulic, R. & Shea, D, 2011) that is the most popular tool for mobile users to access applications and services on the Internet.

According to the recent study from Juniper Research, the number of mobile cloud computing users is expected to grow rapidly in the next five years. Cloud-based mobile market (Perez, S., 2010) will generate annual revenue of $9.5 billion in 2014 from $400 million in 2009, at an average annual increase of 88%. This phenomenal growth is caused by increase in mobile broadband coverage and the need for always-available collaborative services for the enterprise. Fernando, N. & Loke, S. W. & Rahayu, W. (2013) explain the convergence of mobile and cloud computing, and distinguish it from the earlier domains such as cloud and grid computing.

Small businesses can expand their IT resources by leveraging cloud computing. The primary objective of MCC is to provide mobile users with enhanced resources such as extended battery life, computation time, communication etc. Therefore, both these technologies have different objectives and challenges. Table 1 shows the comparison between cloud computing and MCC. In MCC, issues such as network connectivity, mobility, bandwidth utilization cost, mobile device energy, amount of communication, location awareness are of paramount importance whereas such issues are not critical in cloud computing. In Table 1, N represents "Non-critical" and I represent "Important".

Need for a Mobile Cloud

MCC combines the advantages of mobile computing with the potential applications of cloud computing and therefore widens the range of MCC uses. In this section, we discuss the different areas such as image processing, natural language processing, sharing GPS and Internet access and multimedia search etc., where MCC is required.

- **Image Processing:** It is required in a real life mobile environment, where a foreign traveler takes an image of street sign, performs OCR (optical character recognition) to extract words and translates these words into a known language (as discussed by Cheng, J. & Balan, R. K. & Satyanarayan, M., 2005). For example in a scenario (Huerta-Canepa, G. & Lee, D., 2010), a traveler is visiting a museum in a country where he does not understand the description written in French language. He takes a picture of the text and starts an OCR App on his phone. But due to limited battery power and computing resources, he can request for sharing the resources of nearby mobile devices who are also interested in this common processing. This approach can be applied to many situations where a group is involved in performing the activity together.

Table 1. Comparison of cloud computing and mobile cloud computing

Issues	Cloud Computing	Mobile Cloud Computing
Device energy	N	I
Mobility	N	I
Network connectivity	N	I
Bandwidth utilization cost	N	I
Location awareness	N	I
Context awareness	N	I
Security	I	I

- **Natural Language Processing:** As discussed above, MCC can be used to translate a language to other language. For example, foreign travelers can communicate with local persons using natural language processing tool. Text to speech can also be converted for visually impaired persons where mobile users are having the file contents wanted to read.
- **Sharing GPS and Internet Access:** Data can be shared among group of users near to each other using LAN or peer-to-peer networks. Similarly, mobile devices can access file that can be downloaded from another mobile device of peer-to-peer network.
- **Multimedia Search:** Mobile devices are used to store multimedia data such as audio, video, pictures etc. In MCC context, multimedia data can be searched on the nearby mobile users.
- **Social Networking:** It is also an example of cloud computing where we can interact with our friends on social networks such as orkut, facebook, twitter etc. Integrating a mobile cloud with social network facilitates automatic sharing of P2P data; thereby reduce the need of backup.
- **Sensor Data Applications:** Most of the mobiles are equipped with sensors these days. Sensors reading such as Geographical Positioning System (GPS), light sensors, microphone, thermometer, clock etc. can be time stamped and linked with other phone readings. Based upon this sensor information, queries can be executed such as "what is the average temperature of nodes within two Kms of my location".

Architecture of Mobile Cloud Computing (MCC)

A typical architecture of MCC is shown in Figure 2. Mobile devices can access cloud services using two techniques, i.e. through mobile networks or using access points. Devices in mobile networks are connected via base stations (e.g. base transceiver station (BTS), satellite etc.) that establish the connections and functional interfaces between the network and mobile devices.

Figure 2. Mobile cloud computing (MCC) architecture

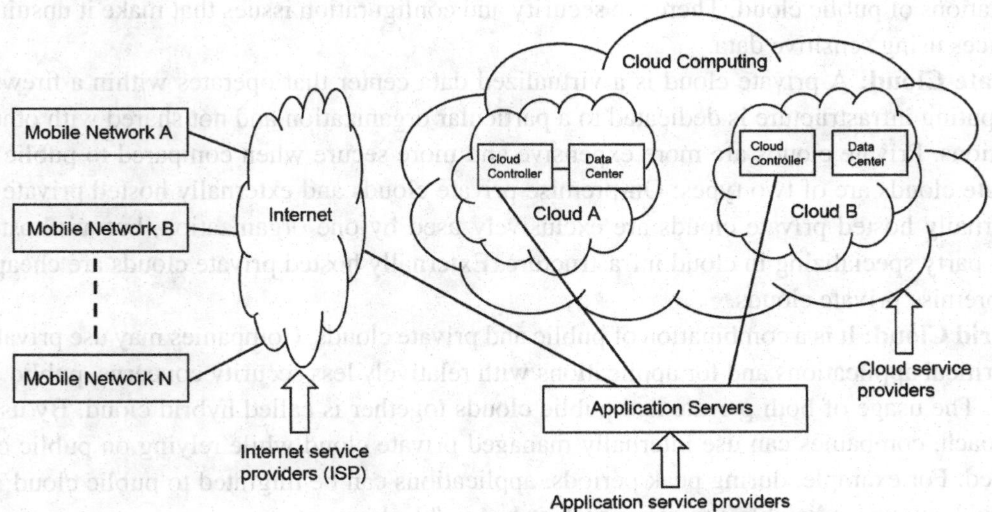

However, mobile users can connect to access points through Wi-Fi that is connected to Internet Service Provider (ISP) providing Internet connectivity to users. Mobile cloud users can access cloud services without using telecom services where data traffic is chargeable. Wi-Fi based connections provide low latency and consume less energy as compared to 3G. Additionally, mobile users can access Wi-Fi connections wherever the latter is available.

Mobile users' requests and information are sent to central processors that are connected to servers which provide mobile network services. Mobile users' requests are sent to cloud through the Internet. In the cloud, cloud controllers process the requests to provide mobile users with the corresponding cloud services. These services are actualized with the concept of utility computing, virtualization and service-oriented architecture (e.g. database, web and application servers). MCC can be referred in two perspectives: (a) Infrastructure based and (2) ad hoc MCC.

In infrastructure based MCC, static hardware infrastructure provides services to mobile users. In ad hoc MCC, group of mobile devices acts as a cloud and facilitates in providing local or Internet based cloud services to other mobile devices. It is difficult to design techniques for ad hoc MCC as compared to infrastructure based MCC.

Cloud computing is a large scale distributed network system based on the number of servers in data centers. Typically, cloud computing is classified based upon these two parameters: - a) Location of the cloud computing and b) Types of services offered.

Location of the Cloud

Generally, cloud computing is classified in the following three ways:

- **Public Cloud:** A public cloud is a cloud computing model in which applications (also known as software-as-a-service), computing and storage services are available for general use over the Internet. Public cloud services are provided based on a pay-per-usage mode or other purchasing models. Examples of public cloud are IBM's Blue Cloud, Amazon Elastic Compute Cloud (EC2), Google App Engine, Sun Cloud and Windows Azure Services Platform. However, there are some limitations of public cloud. There are security and configuration issues that make it unsuitable for services using sensitive data.
- **Private Cloud:** A private cloud is a virtualized data center that operates within a firewall. The computing infrastructure is dedicated to a particular organization and not shared with other organizations. Private clouds are more expensive and more secure when compared to public clouds. Private clouds are of two types: On-premise private clouds and externally hosted private clouds. Externally hosted private clouds are exclusively used by one organization, but are hosted by a third party specializing in cloud infrastructure. Externally hosted private clouds are cheaper than On-premise private clouds.
- **Hybrid Cloud:** It is a combination of public and private clouds. Companies may use private cloud for critical applications and for applications with relatively less security concerns, public cloud is used. The usage of both private and public clouds together is called hybrid cloud. By using this approach, companies can use internally managed private cloud while relying on public cloud as needed. For example, during peak periods, applications can be migrated to public cloud in order to avoid any unpredictable situations such as brown/blackouts etc.

Figure 3. Service based cloud computing architecture

SaaS (e.g., Salesforce, Google Apps)
PaaS (e.g., Google App engine, Windows Azure, force.com)
IaaS (e.g., EC2, S3, amazon web services)
Data centers

- **Community Cloud:** It is an infrastructure shared by several organizations which supports a specific community. For example, all government organizations within a state may share computing infrastructure on the cloud to manage data related to citizens residing in the state.

Classification Based Upon Service Provided

Cloud computing systems are regarded as a collection of different services. Therefore, the cloud services are categorized based on a layer concept as shown in Figure 3. These layers are named as data center layer, infrastructure as a Service (IaaS), Platform as a Service (PaaS) and Software as a Service (SaaS).

- **Data Centres Layer:** This layer is concerned with hardware facility and infrastructure for clouds. In this layer, large numbers of servers are linked with high speed networks to provide services to customers. Generally, data centers are built in less populated places, with high power supply availability and low risk of disaster.
- **Infrastructure as a Service (IaaS):** This layer is built on the top of data center layer. It provides the facilities of storage, hardware, servers and networking components. The user pays for the service on per-use basis. The users can save the cost as payment is based on the amount of resources used. Infrastructure can be expanded or removed as per the need. Some of the examples of IaaS are Amazon EC2 (Elastic Cloud Computing) and S3 (Simple storage service).
- **Platform as a Service (PaaS):** It enables an advanced integrated environment for building, testing and deploying custom applications. Examples of PaaS are Google App Engine, Microsoft Azure and Amazon Map Reduce etc.
- **Software as a Service (SaaS):** It enables the distribution of software with specific requirements of applications. The users can access an application and information remotely via Internet and pay only for that they use. Salesforce is an example of this layer. It offers the online Customer Relationship Management (CRM) space. Other examples are online email providers like Google's gmail, Microsoft's hotmail, Google docs and Microsoft's online version of office called BPOS (Business Productivity Online Standard Suite). Microsoft's Live Mesh also allows sharing files and folders across multiple devices simultaneously.

Although the cloud computing architecture can be divided into four layers, some services can be considered as a part of more than one layer. For example, data storage service can be viewed in both IaaS and PaaS. The above classification is well accepted in the industry. A more granular classification is also done on the basis of service provided. These are listed below:

- Storage-as-a-service,
- Database-as-a-service,
- Information-as-a-service,
- Process-as-a-service,
- Application-as-a-service,
- Integration-as-a-service,
- Security-as-a-service,
- Management/Governance-as-a-service,
- Testing-as-a-service.

Mobile Cloud Computing does not separate these functionalities into four layers. Instead, it focuses on the connection between client and cloud, which may differ from common features of cloud computing.

Advantages of MCC

MCC is a promising solution for mobile devices due to many reasons (e.g., mobility, communication, and portability (Forman, G. H. & Zahorjan, J. (1994)). In this section, we illustrate the use of cloud in overcoming the obstacles in mobile computing, thereby pointing out the advantages of MCC.

- **Improved Battery Life:** Battery is the main source of power for mobile devices. Though, several solutions have been proposed to enhance the storage and CPU performance in an intelligent manner (Mayo, R. N. & Ranganathan, P., 2003) in order to reduce the consumed power, but they require the changes in hardware also, thereby increasing the cost. One solution proposed is computation and storage offloading i.e. migrating the large and complex computations from resource-limited devices (i.e., mobile devices) to resourceful machines (i.e., servers in clouds). This technique avoids a long application execution time on mobile devices that consumes large amount of power. Smailagic et. al. (Smailagic, U. & Ettus, M., 2002) demonstrate that remote execution of applications saves energy efficiently.
- **Improved Data Storage Capacity and Processing Power:** Storage capacity is one of the major constraints for mobile devices. MCC facilitates the mobile users to store and access the high amount of data on the cloud through wireless networks. Amazon Simple Storage Service (Amazon S3) (Amazon elastic compute cloud EC2 homepage) is a cloud that supports file storage service. Image Exchange (Vartiainen, E. & Mattila, K.V.V., 2010) is an example which utilizes the large storage space in clouds for mobile users. This service "mobile photo sharing" allows mobile users to upload images to the clouds after capturing them. Cloud facilitates the mobile users to save substantial amount of energy storage space on their mobile devices as all the images are stored and processed on the cloud. MCC reduces the running cost of applications that take long time and large amount of energy when performed on the limited-resource devices. Flickr (flickr homepage) and ShoZu (Shozu homepage) is also the popular mobile photo sharing applications based on MCC. Facebook (Facebook homepage), the most popular social networking application is also an example of cloud sharing images. Cloud computing can efficiently support various tasks for data warehousing, managing and synchronizing multiple documents online.

- **Increased Reliability:** MCC improves the reliability of stored data as applications and data are stored and backed up on a number of computers. Thereby, it reduces the chances of data and application lost on the mobile devices. MCC works as a widespread data security model for both service providers and users. The cloud can protect copyrighted digital contents (e.g., video, clip, and music) from being abused and unauthorized distribution. Also, the cloud can remotely provide the mobile users with security services such as virus scanning, malicious code detection, and authentication (Oberheide, J. & Veeraraghvan, K. & Cooke, E. & Flinn, J. & Jahanian, F., 2008).
- **On-Demand Service Provisioning:** MCC promotes the provisioning of resources on-demand basis. It is the best way for both the service providers and mobile users to run their applications without prior reservation of resources.
- **Scalability:** It is also an important issue in MCC. Applications running on mobile devices need to meet the uncertain user demands due to flexible resource provisioning. Service providers can easily add/expand an application and provide services with or without a trivial constraint on the resource usage.
- **Multi-Tenancy:** Service providers' (i.e. Network operators and data center owners) can share the resources and costs to support a variety of applications and large number of users. MCC facilitates mobile users to upload images easily to the clouds immediately after capturing it, much in the same way as users upload their images on facebook, WhatsApp etc.
- **Integration of Services:** Cloud provides the integration of multiple services from different service providers through the Internet in order to meet the users' demands.

Applications of Mobile Cloud Computing

Mobile applications are gaining exaggeration share in a global mobile market. Mobile cloud applications (Mohan, E.S & Kumar, E. & Suresh, S., 2013) are considered as the next generation of mobile applications, due to connective and elastic computational cloud functionality that permits their processing capabilities on demand. MCC provides the advantages to various mobile applications discussed in this section.

- **Mobile Commerce:** MCC supports mobile commerce (m-commerce) business applications. These applications accomplish operations that require mobility. Some examples of m-commerce applications are mobile transactions and payments, mobile messaging and mobile ticketing etc. The m-commerce applications can be grouped into three categories- finance, shopping and advertising. Banks and financial institutions expedite its users to access their account information and carry out transactions (buying stocks, paying online etc.) with the help of m-commerce. Mobile tickets, vouchers and coupons can be sent to the users via mobile phones. Users can show their vouchers or tickets on their mobile device and avail the services. Mobile advertisements also have bright future. It is reported that a good response is received through mobile market advertisement as compared to traditional advertisement. The m-commerce applications faces various challenges i.e low network bandwidth, high complexity of mobile device configurations, and security (Satyanarayan, M., 1996). To address these issues, m-commerce applications are integrated into cloud computing environment. A 3G E-commerce platform based on cloud computing is proposed (Yang, X. & Pan, T. & Shen, J., 2010). This approach combines the advantages of both 3G network and cloud computing to increase data processing speed and security level (Dai, J. & Zhou, Q., 2010) based on PKI (public key infrastructure).

- **Mobile Learning:** Traditional mobile learning applications have certain limitations such as high cost of devices and network, low network transmission rate and insufficient resources of education. Cloud based mobile learning (m-learning) is introduced to solve these limitations. Cloud can provide large storage capacity and high speed processing ability. Therefore, mobile applications can provide learners significant services i.e. high amount of learning information, fast processing speed and long battery life etc. One of the example that combines m-learning with cloud computing is described by Zhao, W. & Sun, Y. & Dai, L. (2010). It is used to enhance the communication quality between students and teachers. In this application, Smartphone software based on open source JavaME UI framework and Jaber for clients is used. Students can communicate with their teachers at anytime through a website built on Google Apps Engine. A cloud computing based education tool is developed by Ferzli, R. & Khalife, I. (2011) that creates a course about image/video processing. Learners can understand various algorithms used in mobile applications i.e. deblurring, de-noising, image enhancement and face detection etc. using their mobile phones.
- **Mobile Healthcare:** MCC based mobile applications were originated in order to minimize the limitations of traditional medical treatment such as medical report errors (Kopec, D. & Kabir, M.H. & Reinharth, D. & Rothschild, O. & Castiglione, J. A, 2003), security, privacy and limited physical storage capacity. Mobile healthcare (m-healthcare) facilitates mobile users to access patient health records easily and quickly. It also allows hospitals and healthcare organizations different kinds of on-demand services on clouds instead of owning standalone applications on local servers. Varshney, U. (2007) presents different mobile healthcare applications popularly used:
    - Extensive health monitoring services facilitate the monitoring of patients at anytime and anywhere using wireless communications.
    - Intelligent emergency management system can receive calls regarding emergency events (such as road accidents, critical health problem at home etc.) and can manage and coordinate the fleet of emergency vehicles efficiently.
    - Health-aware mobile devices detect pulse-rate, blood pressure, and level of alcohol to alert healthcare emergency system.
    - Pervasive access to healthcare information allows patients or healthcare providers to access the current and past medical information.
    - Pervasive lifestyle incentive management can be used to pay healthcare expenses and manage other related charges automatically.
    - A prototype implementation of m-healthcare information management system i.e @ HealthCloud based on cloud computing and a mobile client running Android operating system (OS) is proposed by Doukas, C. & Pliakas, T. & Maglogiannis, I. (2010).
- **Mobile Gaming:** Mobile gaming (m-gaming) is a potential market generating revenues for service providers. It require large computation resources so it completely offload the game engine to the server in the cloud, and gamers only interact with the screen interface on their devices. It is observed that offloading (multimedia code) can save energy for mobile devices (Li, Z. & Wang, C. & Xu, R., 2001), thereby increasing game playing time on mobile devices.
- **Miscellaneous Applications:** Mobile users are provided with the facility to share photos, audio and video with the emergence of cloud computing. An MCC application MeLog (Li, H. & Hua, X. S. 2010) enables mobile users to share real-time experience of travel, shopping and events over clouds through an automatic blogging. Pendyala, V.S. & Holliday, J. (2010) propose an intelligent mobile search model using semantic in which searching tasks is performed on servers in a cloud. This model

is able to analyze the meaning of a word, a phrase, or a complex multi-phase to produce the results quickly and accurately. Fabbrizio, G. D. & Okken, T. & Wilpon, J. G. (2009) propose a search service via a speech recognition in which mobile users just talk to microphone on their devices rather than typing on keypads or touchscreens. Gu, C. D. & Lu, K. & Wu, J. P. & Fu, Y. L. & Li, J. X. & Xiao, C. S. & Si, M. X. & Liu, Z. B (2011) introduce a photo searching technique based on ontological semantic tags. Mobile users search only recall parameters that are tagged on images before such images are sent to a cloud. The cloud is used to store and process images for resource-limited devices.

Therefore, it can be inferred that MCC is a predominant technology with various applications in the near future.

Issues and Approaches of MCC

MCC has many advantages for mobile users and service providers as discussed in the previous section. But, due to integration of cloud computing with mobile networks, MCC has to face many technical challenges. In this section, we discuss several research issues in MCC related to both mobile communication and cloud computing. We also discuss the available solutions of these problems.

1. **Mobile Communication Issues**
   a. **Low Bandwidth:** MCC inherits all the properties of mobile computing i.e mobility and wireless nature of communication. Typically, mobile networks require longer execution time for an application to run in cloud and it also has network latency issues, making it unsuitable for certain applications. Bandwidth is a scarce resource for wireless networks as compared to traditional wired network. 4G network is a technology (Kumbalavati, S. B., & Mallapur, J. D., 2013) that significantly increases bandwidth capacity for users. It provides data rate up to 1Gbits/s. 4G networks also support other features such as widening mobile coverage area, smothering quicker handoff services etc. Jin, X. & Kwok, Y. K. (2011) propose a solution to share the limited bandwidth among users located in same geographical area and intend to use the same content e.g. audio/video file. In this approach, each user collaborates in sharing and exchanging of video files (i.e. images, sounds and captions) with other users. However, this approach has certain drawbacks. It can be applied in the scenarios where users in specific geographical location are interested in same types of data. It also shows the lack of fairness regarding the distribution policy of each user i.e. it is not clear who would receive how much and which parts of information. Jung, E. & Wang, Y. & Prilepov, I. & Maker, F. & Liu, X. & Akella, V., (2010) solved this problem by developing a distribution policy that determines when and how much portions of available bandwidth are shared among users from which networks (e.g., WiFi and WiMAX). It is based upon the periodic collection of user profiles and creation of decision tables by Markov Decision Process (MDP) algorithm. Satyanarayanan, M. & Bahl, P. & Caceres, R. & Davies, N. (2009) propose Cloudlet concept that is used to improve the latency and bandwidth issue of MCC. Cloudlet is comprised of several multi-core computers with connectivity to remote cloud servers. Cloudlets are situated in common areas such as coffee shops, malls and other public places so that mobile users can connect to cloudlets instead of remote cloud server in order to minimize the latency and bandwidth used. If no cloudlet is available at particular location, mobile device uses the default mode i.e. connects to distant cloud.

b. **Heterogeneity:** MCC is intended to be deployed for heterogeneous environment where different radio access technologies such as GPRS, 3G, WLAN, WiMax are used simultaneously. MCC requires wireless connectivity in highly heterogeneous environment. As different users access the cloud using different network, main issue in MCC is to provide all-time available connectivity, on-demand scalability of wireless connectivity and energy efficiency of mobile devices. Klein, A. & Mannweiler, C. & Schneider, J. & Hans, D. (2010) propose architecture to provide an intelligent network access strategy for mobile users to meet the application requirements.

c. **Availability:** MCC requires an "always-on" connectivity for all users and "on-demand" available wireless connectivity with a scalable link bandwidth. There are many differences between service availability in cloud computing of wired and wireless networks. Service availability is easy to implement in cloud computing with wired networks as compared to MCC. Mobile users may face problems like traffic congestion, network failures and out-of-range. Huerta Canepa, G. & Lee, D. (2010) present a mechanism to discover the nodes in the vicinity of mobile user whose link with cloud disconnects. In this approach, mobile user can connect with cloud in ad-hoc manner by using the connection of neighboring nodes with cloud. The victim node (whose connection has broken with cloud) maintains a list of stable neighboring nodes and connects with cloud though these nodes. This approach does not consider the mobility, capability of devices, and privacy of neighboring nodes. Zhang, L. & Ding, X. & Wan, Z. & Gu, M. & Li, X.Y. (2010) propose a Wi-Fi based multi-hop networking system called MoNet and a distributed content sharing protocol for the situation without any infrastructure. This solution considers the mobility of nodes in the mobile user's vicinity. Each node periodically exchange short control messages with neighboring nodes to inform about its status (i.e., connectivity and setting parameters) and local content updates. Each node maintains a neighboring node table and estimates the role of other nodes based on the disk space, bandwidth, and power supply. Nodes with the shortest hop length path and the highest role level are selected as the intermediate nodes to receive contents. Apart from mobility issue, security aspect is also considered for mobile users when they share information by using account key (to authenticate and encrypt the private content), friend key (to secure channel between two friends), and content key (to protect an access control). The most critical challenge of MCC is to guarantee a wireless connectivity that meets the requirements of MCC with respect to scalability, availability, heterogeneity, energy and cost-efficiency.

2. **Computing Issues**

a. **Computing Offloading:** Offloading is one of the most important concepts used to improve the battery lifetime for the mobile devices and performance of applications. Offloading process requires sending heavy computation to resourceful servers and receiving the results from these servers. Offloading in static environment is not very complex to implement as compared to dynamic environment where resources, mobility and other parameters keep on changing. Kumar, K. & Lu, Y. H. (2010) have presented various cases where offloading does not always prove efficient for solving every type of problem.

b. **Security:** One of the main issues at computing side is security. Protecting user data and applications from unauthorized user is the key challenge in establishing and maintaining mobile user's trust in MCC. Two categories of security in MCC are considered: 1. Mobile user security and 2. Security for data and applications.

i. **Mobile User Security:** Mobile devices such as cellular phone, PDA, and smartphones have security vulnerabilities and hence are exposed to numerous security threats like virus, worm, and Trojan horses. As mobile devices have integrated global positioning system (GPS) device, there are certain privacy issues for mobile users also.

ii. **Mobile App & Data Security:** Using security software such as McAfee, and AVG antivirus programs on mobile devices is the simplest way to detect security threats on the devices. As mobile devices have limited processing and power resources, protecting them from security threats are more difficult as compared to resourceful devices like Personal Computers, laptops etc. It is not feasible to run the virus detection software on mobile devices all the time. Portokalidis, G. & Homburg, P. & Anagnostakis, K. & Bos, H. (2010) present a technique in which security attack detection for a smartphone is performed in the cloud. Here, smartphone records a minimal traces and sends it to security server on cloud rather than running the antivirus program locally on mobile device. This approach improves the efficiency of threat detector and also improves battery lifetime up to 30%.

c. **Privacy:** With the decreasing cost of GPS positioning devices and its variety of applications, mobile users are increasingly using the location based services (LBS). There are certain limitations of LBS such as privacy because mobile users provide private information such as its current location etc. to other users. An adversary can misuse this information. Zhangwei, H. & Mingjun, X. (2010) present a location trusted server (LTS) to address the location privacy issue. LTS server collects the mobile users' requests and cloaks their location information in a certain area called "cloaked region" based on a "k-anonymity" concept as designed by Sweeney, L. (2002). This concept is used to conceal the mobile user's information. The "cloaked region" is sent to LBS, so that they get to know the general information only about the users but cannot identify them.

d. **Context Processing:** Mobile devices gather social information of all contexts and gestures from their surrounding environment. Exponential growth in context and social information creates several challenges such as storing, managing, and processing information on resource constraint smartphones. It is required to design energy efficient, reliable and robust platform for context storage.

3. **Mobile Application Related Issues**

a. **Interoperability:** It's common that there is a mix of mobile devices such as iPhone, Android phones, BlackBerry and others being used by employees in an organization or a group of people sharing a network. In such situations, interoperability issues due to different mobile operating systems and their respective mobile applications can prove to be a major challenge in sending and receiving data across multiple devices connected via Internet.

b. **Cloud Application Flexibility:** It is not necessary that all cloud applications be supported by all mobile cloud infrastructure providers. Different applications require different cloud infrastructure attributes such as computation intensity, network bandwidth and latency, etc.

c. **Mobile Cloud Convergence:** Data distribution is an important factor in integrating cloud computing technology to mobile devices. Mobile cloud convergence provides performance improvement, longer battery life, and a solution to the computation power problem. The fundamental approach of mobile cloud convergence is to partition a problem into sub problems such that the parts that need more computation run on the cloud while remaining parts that are related to the user interface run on the mobile device.

Computation Offloading in MCC

A. Parameters Affecting Computation Offloading

Computation offloading is a complex process and it is affected by different parameters such as user, connection, application model, nature of application, type of mobile device and cloud service. Figure 4 highlights different parameters affecting computation offloading.

- **User:** Several factors such as network data cost, cloud service cost, privacy and total process execution time determine whether a user enables/disables computation offloading. Additionally, it also depends on what actual action the user is performing – e.g. if the user is executing a performance intensive application, he would ideally want to disable computation offloading.
- **Connection:** Each communication technology has its own limitations related to bandwidth and delays. While Wi-Fi provides higher bandwidth and shorter delays, 3G connections have lower bandwidth and higher delays as discussed by Cuervo, E. & Balasubramaniam, A. & Cho, D. K. &Wolman, A. & Saroju, S. & Chandra, R. & Bahl, P. (2010). Most users prefer a Wi-Fi connection over 3G if the former is available. If a Wi-Fi connection is not available, users on 3G/ 4G networks will decide on computation offloading based on available bandwidth and experienced delays.
- **Smartphone:** Most modern-age smartphones have powerful processors, up to 1 GB of memory and ample secondary storage. Such users are less likely to require frequent mobile cloud support as compared to users with feature phones.
- **Application Model:** Khan, AR. & Othman, M. & Madani, S.A & Khan, S.U. (2014) have presented multiple application models which are different in design and objectives. For example, an application model that supports computational offloading would typically be focused on energy efficiency and application performance for devices that lack sufficient resources.
- **Application:** The kind/ nature of application also affect the decision of computation offloading. For example, a resource intensive application which heavily uses GPS, camera, sensors can't execute in the cloud unless it is broken into different components. All local resource independent modules may be moved to the cloud for execution. Similarly, if the data size is too large and application data is unavailable in the cloud, then mobile side computation is encouraged. This scenario involves higher execution time and consumes high energy in terms of communication which may negate the benefits of offloading.
- **Cloud Service:** Computation offloading is also dependent on the type of cloud service provided. A cloud must have runtime support for the offloaded application. The Cloud service must have sufficient resources in order to take advantage of computation offloading. For example, if a cloud service supports the same memory and computation power as a mobile device, then an end user may not be able to achieve any improvements in application performance. Although, it may be a better proposition in terms of energy, but from a performance perspective, it is not appropriate. In fact, application performance may degrade due to extra computations and delay required for offloading.

All these parameters have an important role in the decision of computation offloading. It is the responsibility of application models to consider all above defined parameters and accordingly perform computation offloading.

Figure 4. Parameters affecting computation offloading

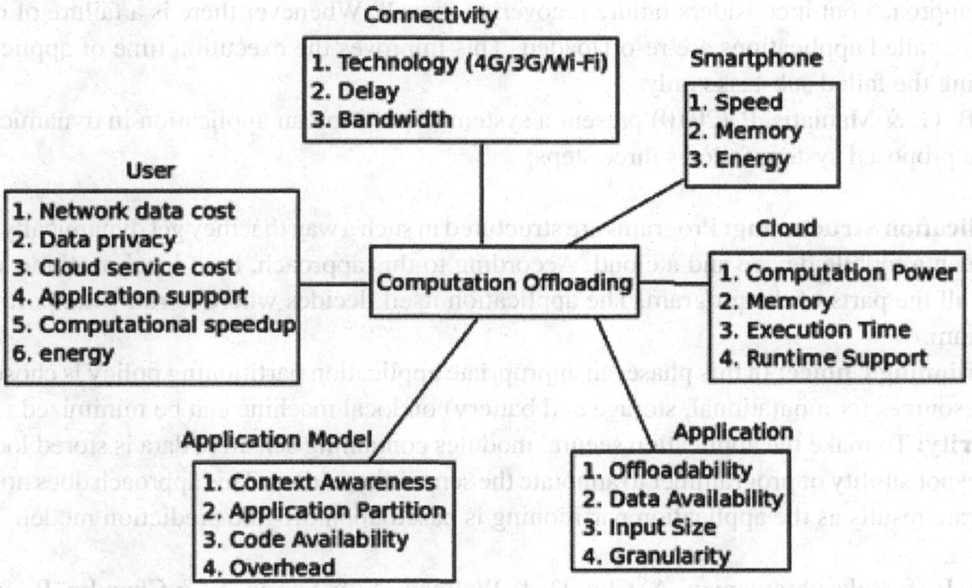

B. Offloading in a Static Environment

Offloading is generally considered an efficient way of saving energy by performing computations and storage in the cloud. However, this does not always lead to the expected gains. Rudenko A. & Reiher, P. & Popek, G. J. & Kuenning, G. H. (1998) have shown that offloading consumes more energy to compile a small piece of code rather processing it locally. Therefore, it is a critical problem for mobile devices to determine whether to offload and which portions of the application's code need to be offloaded to improve the energy efficiency. In addition, different wireless access technologies consume different amount of energy and support different data transfer rates. These factors have to be taken into account while deciding upon the offloading strategy.

Several solutions are proposed to find the optimal decision for partitioning applications before offloading. Wang, C. & Li, Z. (2004) present a polynomial time computation offloading algorithm to find an optimal program division for mobile users. This scheme abstracts the execution of program partitions which run on a device and a server. In this scheme, all physical memory references are mapped into the references of abstract memory locations.

C. Offloading in a Dynamic Environment

A dynamic network environment is characterized by frequent changes in the links and bandwidth between a pair of nodes. Data transmission between nodes may not be reliable and data executed on server may also be lost while returning back to sender due to channel problems.

Ou, S. & Yang, K. & Liotta, A. & Hu, L. (2007) analyze the performance of offloading for wireless environments. They have considered three ways of executing an application to estimate the efficiency of offloading. In the first case, applications are executed locally on the same machine i.e. without offloading. Second case considers the offloading of applications but without failures. Third case is an extension of second approach but it considers failure recoveries as well. Whenever there is a failure of offloaded applications, failed applications are re-offloaded. This improves the execution time of applications by re-offloading the failed sub-tasks only.

Chun, B. G. & Maniatis, P. (2010) present a system to partition an application in dynamic environments. The proposed system follows three steps:

1. **Application Structuring:** Programs are structured in such a way that they get dynamically executed between a mobile device and a cloud. According to this approach, both local machine and cloud have all the parts of the program. The application itself decides where to run what portion of the program.
2. **Partitioning Choice:** In this phase, an appropriate application partitioning policy is chosen so that the resources (computational, storage and battery) on local machine can be minimized.
3. **Security:** To make the application secure, modules containing sensitive data is stored locally. It is the responsibility of programmer to annotate the sensitivity of data. This approach does not produce accurate results as the application partitioning is based upon off-line prediction model.

Cuervo, E. & Balasubramanian, A. Cho, D. & Wolman, A. & Saroiu, S. & Chandra, R. & Bahl, P. (2010) propose architecture to dynamically partition an application at runtime in three phases.

In the first phase, two versions of mobile applications are created- one for execution on local device and other on cloud. As today's smartphones use a different instruction set architecture (ARM) as compared to desktop and servers (which typically use x8) therefore, a module is designed that facilitates the execution of same program on different CPU architectures without access to the program source code.

The second phase classifies the various application modules as "remoteable" or not. Only the remoteable modules of an application are sent to cloud for execution. Other parts of application are run on local machine. For example, a module which implements/uses I/O interface cannot be run on cloud.

In the final step, each module of application is evaluated and the modules are serialized done to determine the communication cost. The authors found that the approach can maximize the energy savings through the fine-grained code offloading while minimizing the changes required to applications.

Open Issues in MCC

In this chapter, we have presented several issues and developments in MCC. This section presents possible research directions in the advancement of MCC.

- **Low Bandwidth:** Limited bandwidth remains a major concern in MCC as the number of mobile and cloud users are increasing exponentially. 4G network and Femtocell are two emerging technologies that may revolutionize bandwidth improvements.
  - **4G Network:** It provides bandwidth up to 100Mbit/s - 128Mbit/s for mobile users as compared to 3G network which supports 14.4Mbit/s. Additionally, it provides other features such as smooth and quicker handoff, wide mobile coverage area etc. Rahman, M. & Mir, F.A.M. (2007) present several issues related to network architecture, access control and quality of service of 4G network.

- **Femtocell:** It is a compact cellular base station used in small area (Boccuzzi, J. & Ruggiero, M., 2011). Concept of femtocells (Hay Systems homepage) is combined with cloud computing in order to implement a scalable, economical and secure network for mobile users. It provides the on demand services to users by adding/removing resources; thereby resulting in economical femtocell network. Femtocells located in homes and offices of mobile users can connect through Internet to cloud in order to connect to network.

- **Quality of Service (QoS):** In MCC, mobile users' access the servers located in a cloud to take the services and resources provided by cloud. But, mobile users suffer from congestion due to limited wireless bandwidth, network disconnection and attenuation caused by mobility of users. QoS reduces significantly when mobile users communicate with cloud. Cloudlet and CloneCloud are two techniques that help in reducing the network latency.
  - **Cloudlets:** It is a cluster of resourceful trusted computers connected to the Internet and provides services to nearby mobile users. When mobile users don't want to offload their requests to cloud (due to high delay, low bandwidth, computation and storage cost etc.), they can take the services of cloudlet. It provides the services to users in less time and cost. If no cloudlet is present in nearby area, default mode is used i.e. services are provided by cloud. However, this approach has some significant issues such as distribution mechanism for processing, storage and communication of information for each cloudlet such that overall cost of the system can be minimized. Apart from these issues, trust and security for cloudlet are very important issues as adversaries can steal mobile user's information by creating a fake cloudlet.
  - **CloneCloud:** Chun, B. G. & Ihm, S. & Maniatis. P. & Naik, M. & Patti, A. (2011) present the concept of CloneCloud that empowered the cloud computing to smart phones. It facilitates the fast execution of smart phone applications by using nearby computers or data centers. The entire data and applications from smart phone are cloned onto the cloud; some operations are executed by clones and sent back to smart phone and integrated there. Multiple clones of same smart phone can be built to make it fast. However, limitation of CloneCloud is that it does not virtualize access to native resources that are not cloned.
- **Cost:** MCC uses the services provided by both mobile service provider (MSP) and cloud service provider (CSP). Both have different policies for service management, customers' management and payment methods. This lead to issue of cost paid by customers i.e. how the price would be set and how the price will be divided among different entities. For example, when a mobile user uses a language translator application; it involves the MSP (for accessing the data through base station), CSP (for running the language translator engine on cloud) and language translator provider (that provides the license of language translator). The price of this application is divided among these three entities in such a way that they get satisfied with the distribution.
- **Interoperability:** It is an important issue when mobile users need to communicate with the cloud. Mobile users and cloud communicate with each other through web interfaces. Web interface have more overhead for mobile devices as it is not specifically designed for them. A standard interface is required that can handle the incompatibility issues among different types of mobile devices. HTML5 WebSockets are expected to provide an interface for different mobile users. However, its development is still in its infancy.
- **Increased Network Performance:** Network performance can be increased by improving the link performance for mobile users and optimizing the bandwidth usage. Cognitive radio (Yucek, T. & Arslan, H., 2009) provides a mechanism for unlicensed users to access the chan-

nel that is originally allocated to licensed users; thereby increase the spectrum utilization. Integration of cognitive radio into MCC solves the problem of spectrum scarcity and reduces the overall cost of the network system. Mobile users in MCC should be capable of detecting the availability of radio resources (with spectrum sensing) without interfering the traditional MCC services.

- **Service Convergence:** With the rapid development in cloud services, it is expected that these services will be differentiated according to the type, availability, cost and quality. A new technique is required that makes use of multiple clouds services in situations where single cloud cannot satisfy mobile user's demands. Sky computing (Keahey. K. & Tsugawa, M. & Matsunaga, A. & Fortes, J., 2009) is the future of cloud computing where services of multiple CSPs are leveraged in order to create large distributed infrastructure. Mobile sky computing is an extension of sky computing that enables users to implement mobile services and applications.

CONCLUSION

According to recent study, more than 250 million businesses will use cloud services via mobile devices by 2015, thereby increasing the revenue of MCC to more than $5.2 billion. This Chapter first highlights the business needs and use cases for a mobile cloud.

We then provide a comparative analysis of various architectural options for MCC solutions. We briefly touch upon how cloud vendors such as Amazon, Google and others are re-defining the paradigm of cloud computing specifically for mobile users by offloading computation to the cloud. We discuss the evolution of cloud computing to support mobile users and how the gap between cloud and mobile users is converging rapidly.

We discuss several factors which are crucial for MCC users but are not that important for non-mobile cloud users.

We illustrate how MCC combines the advantages of both mobile computing and cloud computing. It provides mobile users a seamless, convenient and rich set of services despite the typical resource limitations of mobile devices. MCC provides an infrastructure where data processing and storage can happen outside the mobile device. Therefore, it is not required that mobile devices are equipped with powerful configurations like high speed processor or large storage space as all processing is performed on the cloud.

This chapter provides a detailed assessment of various aspects of MCC including the overall architecture, common applications, pros and cons etc. The most popular MCC applications include mobile commerce, mobile learning and mobile healthcare.

Finally, we briefly touch upon the open research issues related to MCC and the challenges/ opportunities associated with this domain.

REFERENCES

Abolfazli, S., Sanaei, Z., Ahmed, E., Gani, A., & Buyya, R. (2013). Cloud-based augmentation for mobile devices: Motivation, taxonomies, and open challenges. *IEEE Communications Surveys and Tutorials*, (July), 1–32.

Abolfazli, S., Sanaei, Z., Gani, A., Xia, F., & Yang, L. T. (2013). Rich mobile applications: Genesis, taxonomy, and open issues. *Journal of Network and Computer Applications*.

Aepona. (2010). *Mobile cloud computing solution brief.* White Paper. Author.

Amazon Elastic Compute Cloud (EC2). (n.d.). *Microsoft Azure*. Retrieved from http://www.microsoft.com/azure/

Boccuzzi, J., & Ruggiero, M. (2011). *Femtocells: Design and applications*. McGraw-Hill.

Cheng, J., Balan, R. K., & Satyanarayan, M. (2005). *Exploiting rich mobile environments.* Technical Report.

Christensen, J. H. (2009). Using RESTful web-services and cloud computing to create next generation mobile applications. In *Proceedings of the 24th ACM SIGPLAN Conference Companion on Object Oriented Programming Systems Languages and Applications (OOPSLA)* (pp. 451-459). ACM. doi:10.1145/1639950.1639958

Chun, B. G., Ihm, S., Maniatis, P., Naik, M., & Patti, A. (2011). CloneCloud: Elastic execution between mobile device and cloud. In *Proceedings of the 6th Conference on Computer Systems (EuroSys)* (pp. 301-314). Academic Press. doi:10.1145/1966445.1966473

Chun, B. G., & Maniatis, P. (2010). Dynamically partitioning applications between weak devices and clouds. In *Proceedings of the 1st ACM Workshop on Mobile Cloud Computing and Services: Social Networks and Beyond (MCS)*. ACM. doi:10.1145/1810931.1810938

Cuervo, E., Balasubramaniam, A., Cho, D. K., Wolman, A., Saroju, S., Chandra, R., & Bahl, P. (2010). Maui: Making smartphones last longer with code offload. In *Proceedings of 8th International Conference on Mobile Systems, Applications and Services*. ACM.

Cuervo, E., Balasubramanian, A., Cho, D., Wolman, A., Saroiu, S., Chandra, R., & Bahl, P. (2010). MAUI: Making smartphones last longer with code offload. In *Proceedings of the 8th International Conference on Mobile systems, applications and services* (pp. 49-62). Academic Press. doi:10.1145/1814433.1814441

Dai, J., & Zhou, Q. (2010). A PKI-based mechanism for secure and efficient access to outsourced data. In *Proceedings of 2nd International Conference on Networking and Digital Society (ICNDS)*. Academic Press.

Dinh, H.T., Lee, C., Niyato, D., & Wang, W. (2012). A survey of mobile cloud computing: Architecture, applications, and approaches. In *Wireless communications and mobile computing*. Wiley.

Doukas, C., Pliakas, T., & Maglogiannis, I. (2010). Mobile healthcare information management utilizing cloud computing and Android OS. In *Proceedings of Annual International Conference of the IEEE on Engineering in Medicine and Biology Socity (EMBC)* (pp. 1037-1040). IEEE. doi:10.1109/IEMBS.2010.5628061

Fabbrizio, G. D., Okken, T., & Wilpon, J. G. (2009). A speech mashup framework for multimodal mobile devices. In *Proceedings of the 2009 International Conference on Multimodal Interfaces (ICMI-MLMI)* (pp. 71-78). Academic Press. doi:10.1145/1647314.1647329

Facebook. (n.d.). Retrieved from http://www.facebook.com

Fernando, N., Loke, S. W., & Rahayu, W. (2013). Mobile cloud computing: A survey. *Future Generation Computer Systems Journal, Elsevier*, *29*(1), 84–106. doi:10.1016/j.future.2012.05.023

Ferzli, R., & Khalife, I. (2011). Mobile cloud computing educational tool for image/video processing algorithms. In *Proceedings of Digital Signal Processing Workshop and IEEE Signal Processing Education Workshop (DSP/SPE)*. IEEE.

Flickr. (n.d.). Retrieved from http://www.flickr.com/

Forman, G.H. & Zahorjan, J. (1994, April). The challenges of mobile computing. *IEEE Computer Society Magazine*.

Gu, C. D., Lu, K., Wu, J. P., Fu, Y. L., Li, J. X., Xiao, C. S., . . . Liu, Z. B. (2011). The investigation of cloud computing based image mining mechanism in mobie communication WEB on Android. In *Proceedings of the 9th International Conference on Grid and Cooperative Computing (GCC)*. Academic Press.

Hay Systems. (n.d.). Retrieved from http://www.haysystems.com/

Huerta Canepa, G., & Lee, D. (2010). A virtual cloud computing provider for mobile devices. In *Proceedings of 1st ACM Workshop on Mobile Cloud Computing and Services: Social Networks and Beyond (MCS)*. ACM. doi:10.1145/1810931.1810937

Huerta-Canepa, G., & Lee, D. (2010). A virtual cloud computing provider for mobile devices. In *Proceedings of the 1st ACM Workshop on Mobile Cloud Computing and Services: Social Networks and Beyond*. ACM.

Jin, X., & Kwok, Y. K. (2011) Cloud assisted P2P media streaming for bandwidth constrained mobile subscribers. In *Proceedings of the 16th IEEE International Conference on Parallel and Distributed Systems (ICPADS)*. IEEE.

Jung, E., Wang, Y., Prilepov, I., Maker, F., Liu, X., & Akella, V. (2010). User-profile-driven-collaborative bandwidth sharing on mobile phones. In *Proceedings of the 1st ACM Workshop on Mobile Cloud Computing & Services: Social Networks and Beyond (MCS)*. ACM.

Keahey, K., Tsugawa, M., Matsunaga, A., & Fortes, J. (2009). Sky computing. *IEEE Internet Computing Magazine*, *13*(5), 43–51. doi:10.1109/MIC.2009.94

Khan, A.R., Othman, M., Madani, S.A., & Khan, S.U. (2014). A survey of mobile cloud computing application models. *IEEE Communications Surveys & Tutorials, 16*(1), 393-413.

Klein, A., Mannweiler, C., Schneider, J., & Hans, D. (2010). Access schemes for mobile cloud computing. In *Proceedings of the 11th International Conference on Mobile Data Management (MDM)*. Academic Press.

Kopec, D., Kabir, M. H., Reinharth, D., Rothschild, O., & Castiglione, J. A. (2003). Human errors in medical practice: Systematic classification and reduction with automated information systems. *Journal of Medical Systems*, *27*(August), 297–313. doi:10.1023/A:1023796918654 PMID:12846462

Kumar, K., & Lu, Y. H. (2010). Cloud computing for mobile users: Can offloading computation save energy. *Computer Magazine IEEE*, *43*(4), 51–56. doi:10.1109/MC.2010.98

Kumbalavati, S. B., & Mallapur, J. D. (2013). A survey on 4G wireless networks. *International Journal of Cognitive Science, Engineering, and Technology*, *1*(1), 31–36.

Li, H., & Hua, X. S. (2010) Melog: Mobile experience sharing through automatic multimedia blogging. In *Proceedings of the 2010 ACM Multimedia Workshop on Mobile Cloud Media Computing (MCMC)* (pp. 19-24). ACM. doi:10.1145/1877953.1877961

Li, Z., Wang, C., & Xu, R. (2001). Computation offloading to save energy on handheld devices: A partition scheme. In *Proceedings of the 2001 International Conference on Compilers, Architecture and Synthesis for Embedded Systems (CASES)* (pp. 238-246). CASES. doi:10.1145/502251.502257

Liu, F., Shu, P., Jin, H., Ding, L., Yu, J., Niu, D., & Li, B. (2013). Gearing resource-poor mobile devices with powerful clouds: Architecture, challenges and applications. *IEEE Wireless Communications Magazine*, *20*(3), 14–22.

Liu, L., Moulic, R., & Shea, D. (2011). Cloud service portal for mobile device management. In *Proceedings of IEEE 7th International Conference on e-Business Enginering (ICEBE)*. IEEE.

Marinelli, E. (2009). *Hyrax: Cloud computing on mobile devices using MapReduce*. (Master thesis). Carnegie Mellon University, Pittsburgh, PA.

Mayo, R. N., & Ranganathan, P. (2003). Energy consumption in mobile devices: Why future systems need requirements aware energy scale-down. In *Proceedings of the Workshop on Power-Aware Computing Systems*. Academic Press.

Mobile Cloud Computing Forum. (n.d.). Retrieved from http://www.mobilecloudcomputingforum.com/

Mohan, E. S., Kumar, E., & Suresh, S. (2013). Mobile cloud media computing applications: A survey. In *Proceedings of the Fourth International Conference on Signal and Image Processing 2012 (ICSIP 2012)* (pp. 619-628). ICSIP.

Oberheide, J., Veeraraghvan, K., Cooke, E., Flinn, J., & Jahanian, F. (2008). Virtualized in-cloud security services for mobile devices. In *Proceedings of the 1st Workshop on Virtualization in Mobile Computing (MobiVirt)*. Academic Press. doi:10.1145/1622103.1629656

Ou, S., Yang, K., Liotta, A., & Hu, L. (2007). Performance analysis of offloading systems in mobile wireless environments. In *Proceedings of the IEEE International Conference on Communications (ICC)*. IEEE. doi:10.1109/ICC.2007.304

Pendyala, V. S., & Holliday, J. (2010). Performing intelligent mobile searches in the cloud using semantic technologies. In *Proceedings of IEEE International Conference on Granular Computing*. IEEE. doi:10.1109/GrC.2010.16

Perez, S. (2010). *Mobile cloud computing: $9.5 billion by 2014*. Retrieved from http://exoplanet.eu/catalog.php

Portokalidis, G., Homburg, P., Anagnostakis, K., & Bos, H. (2010). Paranoid android: Versatile protection for smartphones. In *Proceedings of the 26th Annual Computer Security Application Conference (ACSAC)* (pp. 347-356). ACSAC.

Rahman, M., & Mir, F. A. M. (2007). Fourth generation (4G) wireless networks- Features, technologies and issues. In *Proceedings of the 6th International Conference on 3G and Beyond*. Academic Press.

Rudenko, A., Reiher, P., Popek, G. J., & Kuenning, G. H. (1998). Saving portable computer battery power through remote process execution. *Journal of ACM SIGMOBILE on Mobile Computing and Communications Review, 2*(1).

Satyanarayan, M. (1996). Fundamental challenges in mobile computing. In *Proceedings of the Fifteenth Annual ACM Symposium on Principles of Distributed Computing (PODC'96)*. ACM. doi:10.1145/248052.248053

Satyanarayanan, M., Bahl, P., Caceres, R., & Davies, N. (2009). The case for VM-based cloudlets in mobile computing. *IEEE Pervasive Computing*, *8*(8), 14–23. doi:10.1109/MPRV.2009.82

Shozu. (n.d.). Retrieved from http://www.shozu.com/portal/index.do

Smailagic, U., & Ettus, M. (2002). System design and power optimization for mobile computers. In *Proceedings of IEEE Computer Society Annual Symposium on VLSI*. IEEE. doi:10.1109/ISVLSI.2002.1016867

Sweeney, L. (2002, February). A model for protecting privacy. *International Journal of Uncertainty Fuzziness and Knowledge-based Systems*.

Varshney, U. (2007). Pervasive healthcare and wireless health monitoring. *Journal on Mobile Networks and Applications,* March, 113-127.

Vartiainen, E., & Mattila, K. V. V. (2010). User experience of mobile photo sharing in the cloud. In *Proceedings of the 9th International Conference on Mobile and Ubiquitous Multimedia (MUM)*. Academic Press. doi:10.1145/1899475.1899479

Wang, C., & Li, Z. (2004). A computation offloading scheme on handheld devices. *Journal of Parallel and Distributed Computing, 64*(6), 740-746.

Yang, X., Pan, T., & Shen, J. (2010). On 3G mobile e-commerce platform based on cloud computing. In *Proceedings of the 3rd IEEE International Conference on Ubi-Media Computing (U-Media)* (pp. 198-201). IEEE.

Yucek, T., & Arslan, H. (2009, March). A survey of spectrum sensing algorithms for cognitive radio applications. *IEEE Communication Surveys and Tutorials*, 116-130.

Zhang, L., Ding, X., Wan, Z., Gu, M., & Li, X. Y. (2010). WiFace: A secure geosocial networking system using Wi-Fi based multi-hop MANET. In *Proceedings of 1st ACM Workshop on Mobile Cloud Computing and Services: Social Networks and Beyond (MCS)*. ACM.

Zhangwei, H., & Mingjun, X. (2010). A distributed spatial cloaking protocol for location privacy. In *Proceeding of the 2nd International Conference on Network Security Wireless Communications and Trusted Computing (NSWCTC)*. NSWCTC. doi:10.1109/NSWCTC.2010.243

Zhao, W., Sun, Y., & Dai, L. (2010). Improving computer basis teaching through mobile communication and cloud computing technology. In *Proceedings of the 3rd International Conference on Advanced Computer Theory and Engineering (ICACTE)* (pp. 452-454). ICACTE.

KEY TERMS AND DEFINITIONS

Cloud App: It is the phrase used to describe a software application that is never installed on a local computer. Instead, it is accessed via the Internet.

Cloud Provider: It is a service provider who offers customers storage or software solutions available via the Internet.

Cloud: It is a network of servers.

Cloudlet: A cloudlet is a new architectural element that emerges from the convergence of mobile computing and cloud computing. It represents the middle tier of a 3-tier hierarchy: mobile device --- cloudlet --- cloud.

Computing: It is the process of utilizing computer technology to complete a task.

Offloading: It is a method to transfer data from a computer or a digital device to another digital device.

Utility: It can be described as the measurement of "useful-ness" that a user obtains from any good. Air, water, food, cloth etc. satisfy people's wants and possess utility.

Chapter 2
The Technical Debt in Cloud Software Engineering:
A Prediction-Based and Quantification Approach

Georgios Skourletopoulos
Scientia Consulting S.A., Greece

Constandinos X. Mavromoustakis
University of Nicosia, Cyprus

Rami Bahsoon
University of Birmingham, UK

George Mastorakis
Technological Educational Institute of Crete, Greece

ABSTRACT

Predicting and quantifying promptly the Technical Debt has turned into an issue of significant importance over recent years. In the cloud marketplace, where cloud services can be leased, the difficulty to identify the Technical Debt effectively can have a significant impact. In this chapter, the probability of introducing the Technical Debt due to budget and cloud service selection decisions is investigated. A cost estimation approach for implementing Software as a Service (SaaS) in the cloud is examined, indicating three scenarios for predicting the incurrence of Technical Debt in the future. The Constructive Cost Model (COCOMO) is used in order to estimate the cost of the implementation and define a range of secureness by adopting a tolerance value for prediction. Furthermore, a Technical Debt quantification approach is researched for leasing a cloud Software as a Service (SaaS) in order to provide insights about the most appropriate cloud service to be selected.

INTRODUCTION

The cloud can be considered as a marketplace (Buyya, Yeo, Venugopal, Broberg, & Brandic, 2009), where the web services of the cloud-based system architectures can be leased (Nallur & Bahsoon, 2012), according to their non-functional requirements (i.e. availability, performance, maintainability, etc.) or their maximum capacity in users. One of the advantages of cloud computing is scalability, where a

DOI: 10.4018/978-1-4666-8225-2.ch002

cloud provider gives the opportunity to easily upscale or downscale the Information Technology (IT) requirements as and when required (Buyya, Ranjan, & Calheiros, 2009; Mousicou, Mavromoustakis, Bourdena, Mastorakis, & Pallis, 2013). Additionally, some of the benefits of using cloud are the reduced cost, rapid development, greater productivity and regular integration (Oza, Münch, Garbajosa, Yague, & Ortega, 2013). In this chapter, the authors motivate the need for predicting and quantifying the Technical Debt on cloud service level in order to gain insights, be more technical debt-aware and make the right decisions within a business context. Seaman et al. (2012) and Snipes et al. (2012) discuss that the Technical Debt data can be used as an effective decision making method, such as for incurring or paying off the Technical Debt instances. Additionally, a cost-benefit analysis is proposed, aiming to elicit and forecast the Technical Debt in order to manage it promptly in the cloud service level and create more precise payback strategies.

In this context, this chapter proposes two novel models for predicting and quantifying the Technical Debt for cloud Software as a Service (SaaS). More specifically, the first model is related to implementing SaaS in the cloud. When implementing SaaS in the cloud, the size of the Technical Debt might be affected due to budget constraints, the levels of experience and productivity of the development team, the introduction of new technologies or any kind of cultural issues. On the contrary, the second model is based on leasing cloud SaaS. In this case, the size of the Technical Debt may be affected due to either the capacity of an offered service or the need to abandon an existing one and/or switch to a more upgraded service. Regarding the latter scenario, a sheer increase in the demand is an inevitable cause of abandoning a service and switching to a more upgraded one, resulting in incurrence of Technical Debt and any positive Technical Debt to be further incurred can be hardly managed.

Following this introductory section, related work approaches are presented in the next section, describing the concept of the Technical Debt from different viewpoints. The subsequent sections elaborate on the need for predicting and quantifying the Technical Debt on cloud service level, including a detailed description of the adopted research approach. Finally, a critical evaluation and conclusion of the chapter is provided, by highlighting directions and fields for future research.

RELATED WORK

The Technical Debt constitutes a metaphor coined by Cunningham (1992), which explains the correlation between the software development and the financial debt. The extra work that is necessary to be held in the future is discussed, aiming to improve some of the non-functional requirements, such as the readability or the complexity (Cunningham, 1992), resulting in additional cost and likely interest payments (Allman, 2012; Curtis, Sappidi, & Szynkarski, 2012; Fowler, 2003; Klinger, Tarr, Wagstrom, & Williams, 2011; Lim, Taksande, & Seaman, 2012). Narrowing in, the term refers to the acceleration of the velocity for releasing software products, which might lead to implications, and forms the tradeoff between short and long-term value (Nord, Ozkaya, Kruchten, & Gonzalez-Rojas, 2012). The rework is the effect when the Technical Debt incurs and can range from a trivial one with few amendments to changes that may affect the whole system. Sterling (2010) mentions that the lifecycle can affect the size of the Technical Debt. For instance, an agile software development process would create less Technical Debt than a waterfall model due to the more flexible structure it has.

In addition, there are several causes that may create a Technical Debt. The most common is business pressures, where the business intends to release a software product sooner than the initial schedule without considering the implications (Brown et al., 2010). Fowler (2003, 2009) states that Technical Debt might incur due to strict deadlines, while Kruchten et al. (2012) indicate that business pressures, lack of experience or nonsystematic verification of the quality are enough in order to generate Technical Debt. The parallel development might be another significant cause, where changes into a codebase from different branches are made in isolation without been merged into a single source base effectively (Levy, 2013). On the other hand, delayed refactoring can be a cause of Technical Debt incurrence. The term indicates that parts of the code need to be refactored in order to be efficient long-term, however the refactoring process is constantly deferred (Buschmann, 2011). This fact results to more code that should be written in the future and, subsequently, to accumulated Technical Debt, which will be cleared out once the refactoring process is completed. Fowler et al. (1999) argue that the refactoring of the bugs process, which aims to improve the initial poor design, can be more beneficial long-term as the interest payments will be decreased in the future, whereas Kerievsky (2005) supports that the more readable the source code is, the more flexible a software can be to extending its features. Leitch and Stroulia (2003) propose a novel method based on predicting the return on investment for a refactoring plan, as the increased adoption of refactoring practices in new agile methodologies and the lack of any prescriptive theory on when to refactor are observed over recent years (Laribee, 2009). Paying interest on various forms of Technical Debt is also met within Google (Morgenthaler, Gridnev, Sauciuc, & Bhansali, 2012). The authors of this work describe the experiences and efforts the software engineers make in order to pay down the debt, as it incurs in dependency specifications, unbuildable targets and unnecessary command line flags. It is also stated that these efforts often create other forms of Technical Debt that need to be managed effectively. Moreover, Oza et al. (2013) mention that the Technical Debt might be a potential risk when using the cloud in distributed software development, concluding that the risks may outweigh the benefits associated with it.

Seaman and Guo (2011) and Sterling (2010) describe the Technical Debt in different domains, such as code, testing, documentation, configuration management or infrastructure debt. In addition, Brown et al. (2010) attempt to define the Technical Debt issue and establish a framework. In this work, the authors argue that the long-term effects of short-term expedients need to be managed effectively in order to successfully deliver complex software-reliant systems. Furthermore, Zazworka et al. (2011) elaborate on the impact the design debt has on the quality of the software products, in terms of god classes. The accumulated debt affects a software product and causes delay in the overall software development process, as rework should be held in order to fix the bugs. Henceforth, god classes are changed more often than non-god classes, ending up to the conclusion that the Technical Debt has a negative impact on software quality, and should therefore be identified during the development process. Another approach is adopted in the work of Theodoropoulos et al. (2011), where a broad definitional framework of the Technical Debt from the stakeholder perspective is proposed, describing how technology gaps affect the quality within the technical environment. Establishing such a framework, would enable the technology stakeholders to build a conceptual model, better aligning their concerns (Conroy, 2012). On the contrary, the work of Wiklund et al. (2012) indicates that the test-driven development methods has become increasingly popular and elaborates on the fact that the development of test automation tools encounter problems due to unpredictable issues. Additionally, a test automation approach linked to the Technical Debt is adopted, performing a case study on a telecommunication subsystem and suggesting improvements in the fields of interaction design and general software design principles.

Nugroho et al. (2011) elaborate on a quantification approach for debts and interest, which can lead to better quality-oriented IT investments, taking into account an empirical assessment method of software quality. The Technical Debt quantification is based on empirical data monitored by the Software Improvement Group (SIG). The approach is applied to a real system, providing insights related to IT investment (i.e. the return on investment in software quality improvement). On the other hand, Letouzey (2012) presents the SQALE method for effectively monitoring, analyzing and estimating the quality and the Technical Debt of the source code. Narrowing in, a Quality and Analysis Model is proposed to estimate the Quality and the Technical Debt of an application source code, providing recommendations and aiming to analyze the structure and the impact of the Technical Debt. Besides, other authors introduce a metric for effectively managing the Technical Debt from an architecture-related and measurement-based viewpoint, in order to optimize the cost of development in the long run (Nord, Ozkaya, Kruchten, & Gonzalez-Rojas, 2012). In addition, a demonstration of this approach is presented, describing its application to an ongoing system development effort. Furthermore, Nallur and Bahsoon (2012) suggest a marketplace, which allows applications to select services in a decentralized manner. In this work, a cloud-based multi-agent system is presented, which uses multiple double auctions to enable applications to self-adapt, based on their Quality of Service (QoS) requirements and budgetary constraints.

Finally, it is worthy to mention that contribution on managing the Technical Debt on cloud-based service selection using real options, can be found in the work of Alzaghoul and Bahsoon (2013a). More specifically, the authors examine the debt of substitution decisions in support for scaling up scenarios; a debt that is necessary to be managed, cleared and transformed to value-added. An option-based approach is taken into consideration in order to inform the selection of candidate web services with varying costs, utilities and system value along with a quantification approach measuring the extent to which the debt is cleared out and provide future options. The same authors introduce an economics-driven approach related to cloud-based architectures (Alzaghoul & Bahsoon, 2013b), where the problem of web service substitution and its Technical Debt valuation is formulated as an option problem. Two types of options are considered (i.e. option to switch between services and option to defer the decision of substitution) and an options analysis approach is used to manage and clear Technical Debt. Elaboration on the evaluation of the Technical Debt in cloud-based architectures using real options is presented in other related work (Alzaghoul & Bahsoon, 2014; Bahsoon & Emmerich, 2003, 2004). Narrowing in, the option to defer the decision of substitution under uncertainty is investigated, exploiting Binomial Options to the formulation. The time-value of the architecture decisions of switching web services and the Technical Debt, which they can imply on the structure, are quantified, while the proposed method builds on Design Structure Matrix (DSM) and introduces time and complexity aware propagation cost metrics to assess the value of deferral decisions relative to changes in the structure.

RESEARCH MOTIVATION

Despite the fact that there are previous related work approaches in the Technical Debt in different domains, only Alzaghoul and Bahsoon (2013a) introduce a new concept of the Technical Debt at service-level. Henceforth, it is deduced that there is a research gap regarding the Technical Debt on cloud service level and the need for predicting and quantifying it, is imperative. More specifically, the work of Alzaghoul and Bahsoon (2013a) discusses that the web service selection decision might incur a Technical Debt that is necessary to be managed. Managing effectively the Technical Debt on the cloud service level by eliciting and visualizing that, could lead to better financial decisions and more precise payback strategies. In this chapter, the authors motivate the need for identifying and estimating the Technical Debt on the cloud service level and two novel models for predicting and quantifying the Technical Debt for cloud SaaS are proposed.

The first model is based on implementing SaaS in the cloud and the total cost is estimated for three different scenarios (optimistic, most likely and pessimistic) according to the ideal value of man-months given from the Constructive Cost Model (COCOMO) (Boehm, 1981) and an applied tolerance value for prediction. In this context, the link between the possible incurrence of the Technical Debt in the future, along with inevitable results emerging from that fact, and budget constraints is explored, in the view of predicting the Technical Debt.

The second model is related to leasing cloud SaaS and the quantification of the Technical Debt is associated with the capacity of an offered cloud service, as well as to what future opportunities can emerge from the selection decision. Towards arriving at a decision, the link between the Technical Debt, which is created by leasing a cloud service, and the evaluation of that service is examined, in the view of promptly managing the Technical Debt.

Therefore, by estimating the total cost for implementing SaaS in the cloud, the authors achieve to:

- Identify the Technical Debt for different scenarios,
- Reduce the uncertainty regarding the optimal budget that should be invested for an Implementation,
- Give an overview of the optimistic and pessimistic scenarios associated with the provided budget,
- Predict the incurrence of Technical Debt and develop a specific strategy for avoiding it,
- Use the data in order to make the right financial decisions.

On the contrary, by quantifying the Technical Debt for leasing cloud SaaS, it is possible to:

- Identify and estimate the Technical Debt,
- Use the Technical Debt data in the financial decision making process,
- Make long-term previsions, according to the linear variation on the demand,
- View the gradual payoff of the Technical Debt,
- Provide insight of the time the Technical Debt will be cleared out,
- Inform about the underutilization or overutilization of a service,
- Predict the incurrence of the Technical Debt and notify potential future actions that should be taken or situations that should be avoided.

RESEARCH APPROACH

Using the COCOMO Model to Predict the Technical Debt

Several classes of cost estimation models and techniques associated with the software development have been adopted over recent years (Boehm, Abts, & Chulani, 2000; Jeffery, Ruhe, & Wieczorek, 2000; Kitchenham & Taylor, 1985; Leung & Fan, 2002; Matson, Barrett, & Mellichamp, 1994; Vinay Kumar, Ravi, Carr, & Raj Kiran, 2008). In this work, the Constructive Cost Model (COCOMO) is exploited in order to predict the Technical Debt on cloud service level, by casting the required applied effort into cost and providing a range of secureness with respect to a tolerance value for prediction. Outside the range of secureness, the risk of entering into a Technical Debt in the future is high. The COCOMO is a software cost estimation model developed by Boehm (1981) and applies to three software development modes (organic, semi-detached and embedded). The model's formulas take the following form (Boehm, 1981):

$$Effort\ Applied\left(E\right) = a_b\left(KLOC\right)^{b_b}\left[man - months\right]$$

$$Development\ Time\left(D\right) = c_b\left(Effort\ Applied\right)^{d_b}\left[months\right]$$

$$People\ Required\left(P\right) = Effort\ Applied\ /\ Development\ Time\left[count\right]$$

where KLOC is the estimated number of delivered source lines of code expressed in thousands. The coefficients a_b, b_b, c_b and d_b for each development mode are presented in Table 1.

Technical Debt Prediction when Implementing SaaS in the Cloud

The total cost for implementing SaaS in the cloud is estimated by casting the applied effort, which is given from the COCOMO model, into cost for three different scenarios (optimistic, most likely and pessimistic). The hypothesis is based on budget constraints. In this context, the difference between the estimated optimal budget, which should be invested, and the actual one that is intended to be invested, is examined; a fact that might have a significant impact to the investment decision and could lead to Technical Debt in the future. It is taken into consideration that each employee has a monthly salary.

The estimated optimal budget to be invested is evaluated according to the following assumptions:

- The implementation process is decomposed in five separate processes (i.e. Development, Configuration, Deployment, Licenses and Infrastructure).
- The COCOMO most likely value is considered the ideal one.
- There is a tolerance value for prediction that reflects -10% of both the most likely total cost and the applied effort for the optimistic scenario and +10% for the pessimistic one.
- Product flexibility of a system is considered the capability to add new features. Henceforth, budget constraints may affect the product's flexibility.

Table 1. Coefficients for different development modes

Software Project	a_b	b_b	c_b	d_b
Organic	2.4	1.05	2.5	0.38
Semi-detached	3.0	1.12	2.5	0.35
Embedded	3.6	1.20	2.5	0.32

For predicting the incurrence of the Technical Debt in the future, the existence of the maximum provided budget within the predetermined range (i.e. optimistic, most likely and pessimistic scenarios) or not is examined. In case that the budget is outside this range, the risk of entering into a Technical Debt in the future lurks with inevitable results, such as the option of abandoning. That fact could result in a new Technical Debt difficult to be managed. On the other hand, in case that the maximum provided budget is within the range of secureness, the risk of entering into a Technical Debt in the future is lower and depends on other factors, such as how experienced and productive the development team is.

The modeling for calculating the total cost for implementing SaaS takes the following form:

$$\begin{aligned}&Total\ Cost\ for\ Implementing\\&= C_{development} + C_{configuration} + C_{deployment} + C_{licences} + C_{infrastructure}\\&= \left(weight_{development} + weight_{configuration} + weight_{deployment} + weight_{licenses} + weight_{infrastructure}\right)\\&*Effort\ applied\ in\ man-months * Average\ monthly\ salary\ per\ employee\\&= Effort\ applied\ in\ man-months * Average\ monthly\ salary\ per\ employee\end{aligned}$$

where $C_{development}$ is the development cost (including the implementation, migration and maintenance cost), represented in monetary units, $C_{configuration}$ is the software configuration cost, represented in monetary units, $C_{deployment}$ is the deployment cost (including the testing cost), represented in monetary units, $C_{licences}$ is the software licenses cost, represented in monetary units, $C_{infrastructure}$ is the infrastructure cost (including the hardware cost), represented in monetary units, $weight_{development}$ is the weighted priority rating for the development process, represented as percentage, $weight_{configuration}$ is the weighted priority rating for the configuration process, represented as percentage, $weight_{deployment}$ is the weighted priority rating for the deployment process, represented as percentage, $weight_{licenses}$ is the weighted priority rating for the licenses process, represented as percentage, and $weight_{infrastructure}$ is the weighted priority rating for the infrastructure process, represented as percentage.

Technical Debt Quantification for Leasing Cloud SaaS

The hypothesis is that the cloud service capacity might have a significant impact on the final selection decision. In this context, the Technical Debt for leasing cloud SaaS is quantified according to the cost that derives from the remaining inactive capacity. More specifically, the link between the investment and the capacity of a cloud service is examined as well as the probability of overutilization, which would lead to accumulated Technical Debt difficult to be managed. The selection decision is made according to the average variation in the demand per year and the way the Technical Debt is gradually paid off. It is taken into account that each active user is charged with a monthly subscription for using a cloud service and there are also charges for servicing a user in the cloud. Both pricing policies may vary during the declared time of return on investment (ROI).

Any candidate cloud service to be leased is evaluated with respect to the following assumptions:

- The years of ROI are considered to be the prevision time for paying off the Technical Debt.
- There is a linear average variation (i.e. increase or decrease) in the demand per year, which affects the variation of the cost for servicing a user in the cloud.
- Market flexibility of a service is considered the adaptability to the market demands, one of which is the increased demand per year.
- The offered web services have comparable functional requirements. The non-functional ones can be either comparable or not, however with different maximum capacities.

For selecting the appropriate cloud service to lease, two possible types of the Technical Debt are encountered:

- Positive Technical Debt, which indicates the underutilization of a service and the probability to satisfy a possible future increase in the demand with respect to the remaining capacity.
- Negative Technical Debt, which demonstrates the overutilization of a service and the need to abandon the existing service and/or switch to a more upgraded one.

The modeling for quantifying the Technical Debt for leasing cloud SaaS takes the following form:

$$TD_i = 12 * \left\{ \left(1 + \frac{\Delta\%}{\lambda}\right)^{i-1} * ppm * \left[U_{max} - \left(1 + \beta\%\right)^{i-1} * U_{curr}\right] - \left(1 + \frac{\delta\%}{\lambda}\right)^{i-1} * C_{u/m} * \left[U_{max} - \left(1 + \beta\%\right)^{i-1} * U_{curr}\right] \right\}$$

$$= 12 * \left[U_{max} - \left(1 + \beta\%\right)^{i-1} * U_{curr}\right] * \left[\left(1 + \frac{\Delta\%}{\lambda}\right)^{i-1} * ppm - \left(1 + \frac{\delta\%}{\lambda}\right)^{i-1} * C_{u/m}\right], with\ i = 1, 2, \dots \lambda.$$

where λ is the expected time of ROI in years, i is the index of the year, U_{max} is the maximum capacity of the service in users, U_{curr} is the current number of users, $\beta\%$ is the expected average variation in the demand per year, represented as percentage, ppm is the price per monthly subscription in monetary units, $\Delta\%$ is the expected average variation in the monthly subscription price for the declared years of ROI, represented as percentage, $C_{u/m}$ is the estimated monthly cost for servicing a user in the cloud in monetary units, $\delta\%$ is the expected average variation in the monthly cost for servicing a user in the cloud for the declared years of ROI, represented as percentage, and TD is the Technical Debt quantification, represented in monetary units.

PERFORMANCE EVALUATION ANALYSIS, EXPERIMENTAL RESULTS, AND DISCUSSION

The goal of this chapter is the development of two novel models that would predict the Technical Debt on cloud service level. From the research viewpoint, the first approach, which is related to the prediction of the Technical Debt when implementing SaaS in the cloud, adopts a comprehensive model, which obtains value considering that a well-established technique, such as the COCOMO model, was incorporated. Regarding the second approach, which is associated with the quantification of the Technical Debt when leasing cloud SaaS, a more complex model was developed. The comprehension of that model depends on the expertise of the user. Henceforth, it is deduced that the simplicity of the models varies from basic to simple; a fact that confirms the quality of modeling, which is based on the level of comprehension of the model formulation. Furthermore, the models are characterized by generality and extensibility. The generality indicates the generic and not complex parameters used, while the extensibility demonstrates how customizable the formulas can be by adding more parameters.

In addition, a quantification tool – the "Technical Debt in Cloud" web application - was developed as a proof of concept. The tool is linked to the research approach, implementing the formulas and aiming to predict and quantify the Technical Debt on the cloud service level in order to be promptly managed. From the development viewpoint, the web application is targeted to be deployed in the Google Cloud Platform supported by the Google App Engine and it was developed in the Java programming language using the Java Servlet technology, the Hibernate framework, the JPA and XML specifications and JavaScript, whereas the database was developed in MySQL. The application can momentarily run on the Java Web Development Server, therefore in case of deployment, the MySQL database should be mirrored in the Google Cloud SQL.

The possible users that might benefit by using the quantification tool are software engineering experts (i.e. software project managers, architects or analysts), who aim to use their own judgments in interpreting and analyzing the results of a special case scenario. The users can become more technical debt-aware as the tool provides insights about the Technical Debt on the cloud service level from every perspective and stakeholder views are greatly valued. The estimations and calculations are crucial in order to deeply understand the progress of different scenarios for a project, identify what aspects can risk the incurrence of accumulated Technical Debt in the future (i.e. budget constraints or the overutilization of a cloud service) and, finally, manage effectively the Technical Debt and avoid undesirable situations long-term.

Technical Debt Prediction when Implementing SaaS in the Cloud: Illustrative Example and Results for Discussion

The need for launching a new software product, building from scratch and deploying it in the cloud, is motivated. The software development mode is considered to be embedded and the product size is expected to come up to twelve thousand (12.000) source lines of code approximately. The above elements are applied to the COCOMO formulas along with the tolerance value for prediction, getting the results as shown in Table 2.

Table 2. Estimations for the optimistic, most likely and pessimistic applied effort scenarios, development time and people required

Estimation Category	Estimation Value
Optimistic Effort Applied	64 man-months
Most likely Effort Applied	71 man-months
Pessimistic Effort Applied	78 man-months
Development Time	9.8 months
People Required	7

It is deduced that 71 man-months of applied effort (most likely), 9.8 months of development time and 7 people approximately are required, in order this product to be successfully released with respect to the results given from the COCOMO model. It is crucial to mention that a tolerance value for prediction is considered, which reflects -10% of the most likely applied effort for the optimistic scenario and +10% for the pessimistic one. Therefore, the required man-months should be in the range from sixty four (64) to seventy eight (78) approximately. Outside that range, it is more likely to enter into a Technical Debt in the future.

Furthermore, the weighted priority ratings for each of the processes are specified as 40, 10, 20, 10, and 20 per cent for the Development, Configuration, Deployment, Licenses and Infrastructure processes respectively and the average monthly salary per employee is 1.500 USA Dollars (USD). The aforementioned parameters are applied to the formula for estimating the total cost when implementing SaaS in the cloud as well as the tolerance value for prediction, getting the corresponding optimistic, most likely and pessimistic cost estimation for each process and the total cost for each scenario as shown in Table 3.

Therefore, the total cost for the implementation in the cloud is expected to come up to 106.500 USD. It is worthy to mention that the adopted tolerance value for prediction in the cost estimations is the same as the one used in the COCOMO results, reflecting -10% of the most likely cost for the optimistic scenario and +10% for the pessimistic one. Hence, the required budget for releasing successfully the product should be in the range from 95.850 to 117.150 USD approximately. Outside that range, it is more likely to enter into a Technical Debt in the future.

According to the above results, different scenarios can be examined. For instance, in case that the maximum provided budget for that implementation is 80.000 USD, the initial plan needs to be rescheduled by decreasing the required man-months to 53 in order to be within the limits of the maximum budget, which means that the development process should be accelerated. As a result, there is a risk of entering into a Technical Debt in the future for that scenario, which will automatically mean rework and additional cost due to the fact that the required man-months were decreased by 18. The 18 man-months effort, which is not applied, constitute the difference between the estimated optimal budget, which should have been invested, and the actual one that is intended to be invested. In addition, the remaining man-months could be used in either testing during the deployment process, documentation during the development process or any other process that would enhance the product's flexibility and would not create the need to abandon the software in the future. Besides, the option of abandoning could create a new possible Technical Debt and any positive Technical Debt to be further incurred can be hardly managed.

Table 3. Optimistic, most likely and pessimistic cost estimation for each process and the total cost for each scenario

Process / Cost (in USD)	Optimistic	Most Likely	Pessimistic
Development	38.340	42.600	46.860
Configuration	9.585	10.650	11.715
Deployment	19.170	21.300	23.430
Licenses	9.585	10.650	11.715
Infrastructure	19.170	21.300	23.430
Total	95.850	106.500	117.150

On the contrary, in case that the maximum provided budget is 99.000 USD, it does not necessarily mean that Technical Debt would incur in the future for that scenario, because the maximum budget belongs within the specified range of secureness. The fact that the required man-months should be decreased to 66, in order to be within the limits of the new maximum budget, might implies that Technical Debt tends to incur in the future, because it does not fulfil the requirements for either the most likely applied effort or the provided budget. However, creating such an "intentional" technical debt (McConnell, 2007) could be proved beneficial, assuming that the development team is very experienced and highly productive. Therefore, less man-months and smaller budget are required compared to the optimal most likely values, under the condition that both belong within the specified range.

Technical Debt Quantification for Leasing Cloud SaaS: Illustrative Example and Results for Discussion

The need for leasing one of the major services of a new professional network is motivated, aiming to avoid accumulated costs that derive from the development process. After searching the cloud marketplace, two different services from the same cloud provider – the Golden and the Silver ones - are examined in order to lease software. The Golden is considered a corporate service with high levels of Quality of Service (QoS), in terms of non-functional requirements (i.e. availability and performance), whereas the Silver is considered a regular one with fewer features in terms of QoS. Another feature that distinguishes the two services is the maximum capacity in users that each one can stand. The Golden service has a maximum capacity of ten thousand users, while the Silver can stand only four thousand users. An overview of the Technical Debt formation over a five-year period is examined for two different scenarios. Narrowing in, the probability of underutilization or overutilization of either the Golden or the Silver service within the examined period, is investigated. Assuming that there could be a linear average raise in the demand per year, the first scenario forecasts 15% of raise in the demand, whereas the second one forecasts 45% of raise. The remaining values that are considered to be essential in order to quantify the Technical Debt over the five-year period are presented thoroughly in Table 4.

Table 4. Values to be applied in the formula related to the technical debt quantification for leasing cloud SaaS

Attributes	Golden Service	Silver Service
Years of ROI	$\lambda = 5$	$\lambda = 5$
Maximum capacity in users	$U_{max} = 10000$	$U_{max} = 4000$
Current number of users	$U_{curr} = 1500$	$U_{curr} = 1500$
Price per monthly subscription (in USD)	$ppm = 10$	$ppm = 10$
Average raise in the monthly subscription price for the declared years of ROI	$\Delta\% = 3\%$	$\Delta\% = 3\%$
Monthly cost for servicing a user in cloud (in USD)	$C_{u/m} = 6$	$C_{u/m} = 6$
Average raise in the monthly cost for servicing a user in the cloud for the declared years of ROI	$\delta\% = 1\%$	$\delta\% = 1\%$

Figure 1. The technical debt quantification comparison over the 5-year period according to a 15% raise in the demand per year

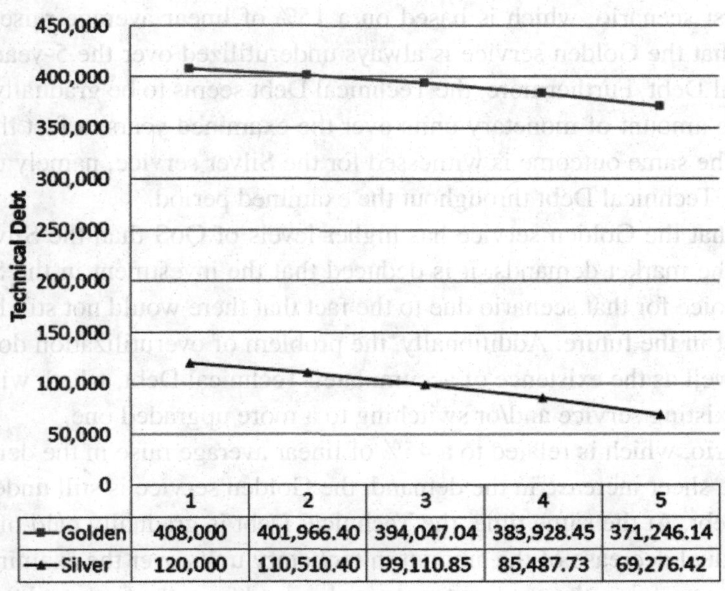

	1	2	3	4	5
Golden	408,000	401,966.40	394,047.04	383,928.45	371,246.14
Silver	120,000	110,510.40	99,110.85	85,487.73	69,276.42

Figure 2. The technical debt quantification comparison over the 5-year period according to a 45% raise in the demand per year

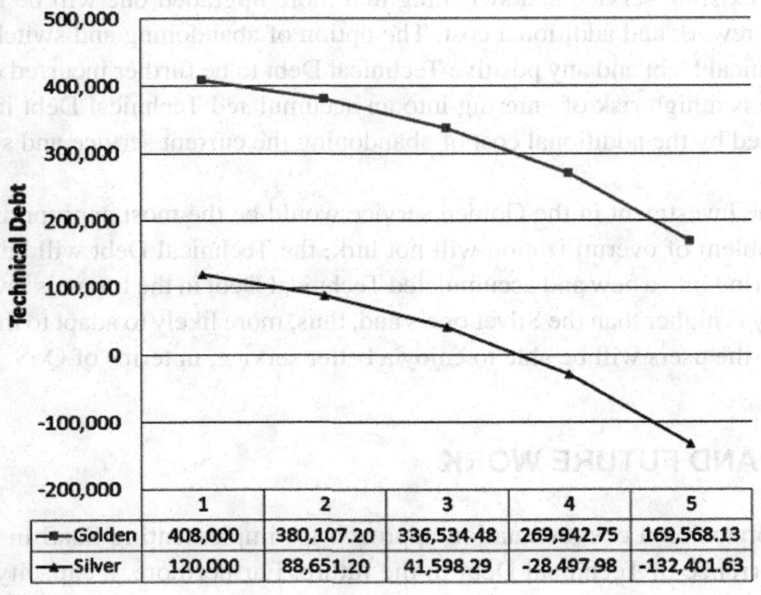

	1	2	3	4	5
Golden	408,000	380,107.20	336,534.48	269,942.75	169,568.13
Silver	120,000	88,651.20	41,598.29	-28,497.98	-132,401.63

The above elements are applied to the formula for quantifying the Technical Debt when leasing cloud SaaS, getting the results and comparisons as shown in Figure 1 and 2 respectively.

Regarding the first scenario, which is based on a 15% of linear average raise in the demand per year, it is observed that the Golden service is always underutilized over the 5-year period, because of the positive Technical Debt. Furthermore, the Technical Debt seems to be gradually paid off according to the decrease in the amount of monetary units over the examined years; a fact that derives from the increased demand. The same outcome is witnessed for the Silver service, namely underutilization and gradual payoff of the Technical Debt throughout the examined period.

Despite the fact that the Golden service has higher levels of QoS than the Silver one and is more flexible to adapt to the market demands, it is deduced that the investment in the Silver service could be proved a better choice for that scenario due to the fact that there would not still be a risk of entering into a Technical Debt in the future. Additionally, the problem of overutilization does not lurk over the examined period as well as the existence of accumulated Technical Debt, which will motivate the need for abandoning the existing service and/or switching to a more upgraded one.

The second scenario, which is related to a 45% of linear average raise in the demand per year, indicates that, despite the sheer increase in the demand, the Golden service is still underutilized due to the positive Technical Debt. At the same time, the Technical Debt is gradually paid off; a fact that can be witnessed by the gradual decrease of the amount in monetary units over the examined period.

Regarding the Silver service, the same outcome is observed from the first until the third year, namely underutilization and gradual payoff of the Technical Debt. Between the third and the fourth year, it is clearly witnessed that the Technical Debt becomes zero at some point, demonstrating that it is totally paid off and this fact constitutes the optimal condition. However, it is noticed that the Technical Debt is negative from the fourth year until the end of the examined period, indicating that the service is overutilized due to the assumption of the linear average raise in the demand per year. As a result, the need of abandoning the existing service and switching to a more upgraded one will be faced in the future; a fact that requires rework and additional cost. The option of abandoning and switching could create a new possible Technical Debt and any positive Technical Debt to be further incurred can be hardly managed. Hence, there is a high risk of entering into an accumulated Technical Debt in the future, which will be overburdened by the additional cost of abandoning the current service and switching to a more upgraded one.

To conclude, the investment in the Golden service would be the most appropriate decision for that scenario as the problem of overutilization will not lurk, the Technical Debt will be gradually paid off and the risk of entering into a new and accumulated Technical Debt in the future is low. Additionally, the service's scalability is higher than the Silver one's and, thus, more likely to adapt to the market demands, not to mention that the users will be able to enjoy a better service, in terms of QoS.

CONCLUSION AND FUTURE WORK

This chapter elaborates on a cost estimation approach for implementing SaaS in the cloud in order to predict the incurrence of Technical Debt in the future. Furthermore, a capacity level approach is researched, aiming to quantify the Technical Debt for leasing cloud SaaS and, therefore, make the appropriate cloud service selection decision. The analysis of the Technical Debt in the cloud service level could enable the software project managers, developers, cloud-based system architects, evaluators of cloud services or analysts, who focus on the evaluation of cloud services for selection, to be more technical debt-aware in order to promptly manage it and avoid unforeseen situations long-term, by eliciting and predicting it.

In the future, scenarios for quantifying the Technical Debt with respect to real options can be further researched, by estimating the values of option valuation techniques (i.e. switch, abandon, etc.). In addition, practices to quantify the Technical Debt associated with the capacity of a cloud service can be examined, once the demand is presented as fluctuations during a predetermined period. Moreover, fields for further investigation include the study of the Technical Debt issue in respect of other resource management frameworks (Dimitriou, Mavromoustakis, Mastorakis, & Pallis, 2013; Mavromoustakis, Dimitriou, Mastorakis, Bourdena, & Pallis, 2014; Mavromoustakis, Andreou et al., 2014; Mavromoustakis et al., 2014; Mavromoustakis, Dimitriou, & Mastorakis, 2012, 2013) as well as the potential adoption and applicability of this approach in cognitive radio network architectures and configurations (Bourdena et al., 2014; Mastorakis, Mavromoustakis, Bourdena, & Pallis, 2013; Mastorakis et al., 2014; Mastorakis, Mavromoustakis, Bourdena, Kormentzas, & Pallis, 2013). Finally, methods to quantify the Technical Debt linked to the mobile cloud computing paradigm and within mobile computing environments can be further examined, based on other published papers (Ciobanu, Comaneci, Dobre, Mavromoustakis, & Mastorakis, 2014; Mavromoustakis, Dimitriou, Mastorakis, & Pallis, 2013; Papanikolaou, Mavromoustakis, Mastorakis, Bourdena, & Dobre, 2014; Saleem, Salim, & Rehmani, 2014).

REFERENCES

Allman, E. (2012). Managing technical debt. *Communications of the ACM*, *55*(5), 50–55. doi:10.1145/2160718.2160733

Alzaghoul, E., & Bahsoon, R. (2013a). CloudMTD: Using real options to manage technical debt in cloud-based service selection. In *Proceedings of 2013 4th International Workshop on Managing Technical Debt (MTD)* (pp. 55–62). San Francisco, CA: IEEE.

Alzaghoul, E., & Bahsoon, R. (2013b). Economics-driven approach for managing technical debt in cloud-based architectures. In *Proceedings of 2013 IEEE/ACM 6th International Conference on Utility and Cloud Computing (UCC)* (pp. 239–242). Dresden: IEEE. doi:10.1109/UCC.2013.49

Alzaghoul, E., & Bahsoon, R. (2014). Evaluating technical debt in cloud-based architectures using real options. In *Proceedings of 2014 23rd Australian Software Engineering Conference (ASWEC)* (pp. 1–10). IEEE. doi:10.1109/ASWEC.2014.27

Bahsoon, R., & Emmerich, W. (2003). ArchOptions: A real options-based model for predicting the stability of software architectures. In *Proceedings of 5th International Workshop on Economic-Driven Software Engineering Research (EDSER-5)* (pp. 38–43). Portland, OR: EDSER.

Bahsoon, R., & Emmerich, W. (2004). Applying ArchOptions to value the payoff of refactoring. In *Proceedings of the Sixth ICSE Workshop on Economics-Driven Software Engineering Research (EDSER-6)* (pp. 66 – 70). Edinburgh, UK: IET. doi:10.1049/ic:20040290

Boehm, B., Abts, C., & Chulani, S. (2000). Software development cost estimation approaches - A survey. *Annals of Software Engineering*, *10*(1-4), 177–205. doi:10.1023/A:1018991717352

Boehm, B. W. (1981). *Software engineering economics*. Englewood Cliffs, NJ: Prentice-Hall.

Bourdena, A., Mavromoustakis, C. X., Kormentzas, G., Pallis, E., Mastorakis, G., & Yassein, M. B. (2014). A resource intensive traffic-aware scheme using energy-aware routing in cognitive radio networks. *Future Generation Computer Systems*, *39*, 16–28. doi:10.1016/j.future.2014.02.013

Brown, N., Cai, Y., Guo, Y., Kazman, R., Kim, M., & Kruchten, P., … Zazworka, N. (2010). Managing technical debt in software-reliant systems. In *Proceedings of the FSE/SDP Workshop on Future of Software Engineering Research* (pp. 47–52). ACM. doi:10.1145/1882362.1882373

Buschmann, F. (2011). To pay or not to pay technical debt. *IEEE Software*, *28*(6), 29–31. doi:10.1109/MS.2011.150

Buyya, R., Ranjan, R., & Calheiros, R. N. (2009). Modeling and simulation of scalable Cloud computing environments and the CloudSim toolkit: Challenges and opportunities. In *Proceedings of International Conference on High Performance Computing & Simulation, 2009 (HPCS'09)* (pp. 1–11). Leipzig: IEEE. doi:10.1109/HPCSIM.2009.5192685

Buyya, R., Yeo, C. S., Venugopal, S., Broberg, J., & Brandic, I. (2009). Cloud computing and emerging IT platforms: Vision, hype, and reality for delivering computing as the 5th utility. *Future Generation Computer Systems*, *25*(6), 599–616. doi:10.1016/j.future.2008.12.001

Ciobanu, N. V., Comaneci, D. G., Dobre, C., Mavromoustakis, C. X., & Mastorakis, G. (2014). OpenMobs: Mobile broadband internet connection sharing. In *Proceedings of 6th International Conference on Mobile Networks and Management (MONAMI 2014)*. Wuerzburg, Germany: MONAMI.

Conroy, P. (2012). Technical debt: Where are the shareholders' interests? *IEEE Software*, *29*(6), 88. doi:10.1109/MS.2012.166

Cunningham, W. (1992). The WyCash portfolio management system. In *OOPSLA '92 addendum to the proceedings on object-oriented programming systems, languages, and applications* (pp. 29–30). Vancouver, Canada: ACM. doi:10.1145/157709.157715

Curtis, B., Sappidi, J., & Szynkarski, A. (2012). Estimating the principal of an application's technical debt. *IEEE Software*, *29*(6), 34–42. doi:10.1109/MS.2012.156

Dimitriou, C. D., Mavromoustakis, C. X., Mastorakis, G., & Pallis, E. (2013, June). On the performance response of delay-bounded energy-aware bandwidth allocation scheme in wireless networks. In *Proceedings of 2013 IEEE International Conference on Communications Workshops (ICC)* (pp. 631–636). Budapest: IEEE. doi:10.1109/ICCW.2013.6649310

Fowler, M. (2003, October 1). *TechnicalDebt*. Retrieved April 12, 2014, from http://www.martinfowler.com/bliki/TechnicalDebt.html

Fowler, M. (2009, October 14). *TechnicalDebtQuadrant*. Retrieved April 12, 2014, from http://www.martinfowler.com/bliki/TechnicalDebtQuadrant.html

Fowler, M., Opdyke, W., & Roberts, D. (1999). *Refactoring: Improving the design of existing code*. Pearson Education India.

Jeffery, R., Ruhe, M., & Wieczorek, I. (2000). A comparative study of two software development cost modeling techniques using multi-organizational and company-specific data. *Information and Software Technology*, *42*(14), 1009–1016. doi:10.1016/S0950-5849(00)00153-1

Kerievsky, J. (2005). *Refactoring to patterns*. Pearson Deutschland GmbH.

Kitchenham, B. A., & Taylor, N. R. (1985). Software project development cost estimation. *Journal of Systems and Software*, *5*(4), 267–278. doi:10.1016/0164-1212(85)90026-3

Klinger, T., Tarr, P., Wagstrom, P., & Williams, C. (2011). An enterprise perspective on technical debt. In *Proceedings of the 2nd Workshop on Managing Technical Debt (MTD '11)* (pp. 35–38). ACM.

Kruchten, P., Nord, R. L., & Ozkaya, I. (2012). Technical debt: From metaphor to theory and practice. *IEEE Software*, *29*(6), 18–21. doi:10.1109/MS.2012.167

Laribee, D. (2009). *Using agile techniques to pay back technical debt*. MSDN Magazine.

Leitch, R., & Stroulia, E. (2003). Understanding the economics of refactoring. In *Proceedings of 5th International Workshop on Economic-Driven Software Engineering Research (EDSER-5)* (pp. 44–49). EDSER.

Letouzey, J.-L. (2012). The sqale method for evaluating technical debt. In *Proceedings of 3rd International Workshop on Managing Technical Debt (ICSE 2012)*. Zurich, Switzerland: ICSE. doi:10.1109/MTD.2012.6225997

Leung, H., & Fan, Z. (2002). Software cost estimation. In Handbook of software engineering. Hong Kong Polytechnic University.

Levy, J. (2013, February 7). *Technical debt and causes of software instability*. Retrieved April 12, 2014, from http://johnlevyconsulting.com/technical-debt-and-causes-of-software-instability/

Lim, E., Taksande, N., & Seaman, C. (2012). A balancing act: What software practitioners have to say about technical debt. *IEEE Software*, *29*(6), 22–27. doi:10.1109/MS.2012.130

Mastorakis, G., Mavromoustakis, C. X., Bourdena, A., Kormentzas, G., & Pallis, E. (2013, September). Maximizing energy conservation in a centralized cognitive radio network architecture. In *Proceedings of 2013 IEEE 18th IEEE International Workshop on Computer-Aided Modeling Analysis and Design of Communication Links and Networks (IEEE CAMAD 2013)* (pp. 175–179). Berlin, Germany: IEEE. doi:10.1109/CAMAD.2013.6708112

Mastorakis, G., Mavromoustakis, C. X., Bourdena, A., & Pallis, E. (2013, June). An energy-efficient routing scheme using Backward Traffic Difference estimation in cognitive radio networks. In *Proceedings of 2013 IEEE 14th International Symposium and Workshops on a World of Wireless, Mobile and Multimedia Networks (WoWMoM)* (pp. 1–6). Madrid: IEEE. doi:10.1109/WoWMoM.2013.6583446

Mastorakis, G., Mavromoustakis, C. X., Bourdena, A., Pallis, E., Sismanidis, G., Stratakis, D., & Papadakis, S. (2014). Energy-efficient routing in cognitive radio networks. In *Resource management in mobile computing environments* (Vol. 3, pp. 323–340). Springer International Publishing. doi:10.1007/978-3-319-06704-9_14

Matson, J. E., Barrett, B. E., & Mellichamp, J. M. (1994). Software development cost estimation using function points. *IEEE Transactions on Software Engineering*, *20*(4), 275–287. doi:10.1109/32.277575

Mavromoustakis, C., Dimitriou, C. D., & Mastorakis, G. (2012, September). Using real-time backward traffic difference estimation for energy conservation in wireless devices. In *Proceedings of AP2PS 2012, The Fourth International Conference on Advances in P2P Systems* (pp. 18–23). Barcelona, Spain: AP2PS.

Mavromoustakis, C., Dimitriou, C. D., & Mastorakis, G. (2013). On the real-time evaluation of two-level BTD scheme for energy conservation in the presence of delay sensitive transmissions and intermittent connectivity in wireless devices. *International Journal on Advances in Networks and Services, 6*(3 and 4), 148–162.

Mavromoustakis, C. X., Andreou, A., Mastorakis, G., Bourdena, A., Batalla, J. M., & Dobre, C. (2014). On the performance evaluation of a novel offloading-based energy conservation mechanism for wireless devices. In *Proceedings of 6th International Conference on Mobile Networks and Management (MONAMI 2014)*. Wuerzburg, Germany: MONAMI.

Mavromoustakis, C. X., Andreou, A., Mastorakis, G., Papadakis, S., Bourdena, A., & Stratakis, D. (2014, August). Energy consumption optimization through pre-scheduled opportunistic offloading in wireless devices. In *Proceedings of EMERGING 2014, The Sixth International Conference on Emerging Network Intelligence* (pp. 22–28). Rome, Italy: Academic Press.

Mavromoustakis, C. X., Dimitriou, C., Mastorakis, G., Bourdena, A., & Pallis, E. (2014). Using traffic diversities for scheduling wireless interfaces for energy harvesting in wireless devices. In *Resource management in mobile computing environments* (Vol. 3, pp. 481–496). Springer International Publishing.

Mavromoustakis, C. X., Dimitriou, C. D., Mastorakis, G., & Pallis, E. (2013, December). Real-time performance evaluation of F-BTD scheme for optimized QoS energy conservation in wireless devices. In *Proceedings of 2013 IEEE Globecom Workshops (GC Wkshps)* (pp. 1151–1156). Atlanta, GA: IEEE; doi:10.1109/GLOCOMW.2013.6825148

McConnell, S. (2007, November 1). *Technical debt*. Retrieved April 12, 2014, from http://www.construx.com/10x_Software_Development/Technical_Debt/

Morgenthaler, J. D., Gridnev, M., Sauciuc, R., & Bhansali, S. (2012). Searching for build debt: Experiences managing technical debt at Google. In *Proceedings of 2012 Third International Workshop on Managing Technical Debt (MTD)* (pp. 1–6). Zurich: IEEE. doi:10.1109/MTD.2012.6225994

Mousicou, P., Mavromoustakis, C. X., Bourdena, A., Mastorakis, G., & Pallis, E. (2013). Performance evaluation of dynamic cloud resource migration based on temporal and capacity-aware policy for efficient resource sharing. In *Proceedings of the 2nd ACM Workshop on High Performance Mobile Opportunistic Systems (HP-MOSys '13)* (pp. 59–66). ACM. doi:10.1145/2507908.2507917

Nallur, V., & Bahsoon, R. (2012). A decentralized self-adaptation mechanism for service-based applications in the cloud. *IEEE Transactions on Software Engineering*, *99*, 1–1.

Nord, R. L., Ozkaya, I., Kruchten, P., & Gonzalez-Rojas, M. (2012). In search of a metric for managing architectural technical debt. In *Proceedings of 2012 Joint Working IEEE/IFIP Conference on Software Architecture (WICSA) and European Conference on Software Architecture (ECSA)* (pp. 91–100). Helsinki: IEEE. doi:10.1109/WICSA-ECSA.212.17

Nugroho, A., Visser, J., & Kuipers, T. (2011). An empirical model of technical debt and interest. In *Proceedings of the 2nd Workshop on Managing Technical Debt* (pp. 1–8). ACM. doi:10.1145/1985362.1985364

Oza, N., Münch, J., Garbajosa, J., Yague, A., & Ortega, E. G. (2013). Identifying potential risks and benefits of using cloud in distributed software development. In *Product-focused software process improvement* (Vol. 7983, pp. 229–239). Springer Berlin Heidelberg. doi:10.1007/978-3-642-39259-7_19

Papanikolaou, K., Mavromoustakis, C. X., Mastorakis, G., Bourdena, A., & Dobre, C. (2014). Energy consumption optimization using social interaction in the mobile cloud. In *Proceedings of 6th International Conference on Mobile Networks and Management (MONAMI 2014)*. Wuerzburg, Germany: MONAMI.

Saleem, Y., Salim, F., & Rehmani, M. H. (2014). Resource management in mobile sink based wireless sensor networks through cloud computing. In *Resource management in mobile computing environments* (Vol. 3, pp. 439–459). Springer International Publishing.

Seaman, C., & Guo, Y. (2011). Measuring and monitoring technical debt. *Advances in Computers*, *82*, 25–46. doi:10.1016/B978-0-12-385512-1.00002-5

Seaman, C., Guo, Y., Izurieta, C., Cai, Y., Zazworka, N., Shull, F., & Vetrò, A. (2012). Using technical debt data in decision making: Potential decision approaches. In *Proceedings of 2012 Third International Workshop on Managing Technical Debt (MTD)* (pp. 45–48). Zurich, Switzerland: IEEE. doi:10.1109/MTD.2012.6225999

Snipes, W., Robinson, B., Guo, Y., & Seaman, C. (2012). Defining the decision factors for managing defects: a technical debt perspective. In *Proceedings of 2012 Third International Workshop on Managing Technical Debt (MTD)* (pp. 54–60). IEEE. doi:10.1109/MTD.2012.6226001

Sterling, C. (2010). *Managing software debt: Building for inevitable change*. Boston: Addison-Wesley Professional.

Theodoropoulos, T., Hofberg, M., & Kern, D. (2011). Technical debt from the stakeholder perspective. In *Proceedings of the 2nd Workshop on Managing Technical Debt (MTD '11)* (pp. 43–46). ACM.

Vinay Kumar, K., Ravi, V., Carr, M., & Raj Kiran, N. (2008). Software development cost estimation using wavelet neural networks. *Journal of Systems and Software*, *81*(11), 1853–1867. doi:10.1016/j.jss.2007.12.793

Wiklund, K., Eldh, S., Sundmark, D., & Lundqvist, K. (2012). Technical debt in test automation. In *Proceedings of 2012 IEEE Fifth International Conference on Software Testing, Verification and Validation (ICST)* (pp. 887–892). Montreal, Canada: IEEE. doi:10.1109/ICST.2012.192

Zazworka, N., Shaw, M. A., Shull, F., & Seaman, C. (2011). Investigating the impact of design debt on software quality. In *Proceedings of the 2nd Workshop on Managing Technical Debt* (pp. 17–23). ACM. doi:10.1145/1985362.1985366

KEY TERMS AND DEFINITIONS

Cloud Service Capacity: The maximum number of users that a service in the cloud can stand.

Cloud Software Engineering: The study and application of software engineering disciplines, such as the design, development and maintenance of software, to cloud computing.

Constructive Cost Model (COCOMO): Constitutes an algorithmic software cost estimation model. It uses a basic regression formula with parameters, which are derived from historical project data and current as well as future project characteristics.

Implementing Software as a Service (SaaS): Refers to the design, development and maintenance tasks that should be completed, aiming to enable a Software as a Service (SaaS) offering in a cloud computing environment.

Leasing Cloud Software as a Service (SaaS): Refers to an online software delivery method that enables a third party to lease a cloud service.

Quantification Tool: A software product that is able to make calculations, estimations and generate graphs.

Technical Debt: The eventual consequences of poor system design, software architecture or software development within a codebase.

Tolerance Value: The permissible limits of variation regarding a measured value.

Chapter 3
Anomaly Detection in Cloud Environments

Angelos K. Marnerides
Liverpool John Moores University, UK

ABSTRACT

Cloud environments compose unique operational characteristics and intrinsic capabilities such as service transparency and elasticity. By virtue of their exclusive properties as being outcomes of their virtualized nature, these environments are prone to a number of security threats either from malicious or legitimate intent. By virtue of the minimal proactive properties attained by off-the-shelf signature-based commercial detection solutions employed in various infrastructures, cloud-specific Intrusion Detection System (IDS) Anomaly Detection (AD)-based methodologies have been proposed in order to enable accurate identification, detection, and clustering of anomalous events that could manifest. Therefore, in this chapter the authors firstly aim to provide an overview in the state of the art related with cloud-based AD mechanisms and pinpoint their basic functionalities. They subsequently provide an insight and report some results derived by a particular methodology that jointly considers cloud-specific properties and relies on the Empirical Mode Decomposition (EMD) algorithm.

INTRODUCTION

Undoubtedly, cloud computing has evolved as a critical asset regarding the adequate deployment of large-scale, always-on services that are nowadays considered as a necessity within a range of important socio-economical ICT environments (e.g. online banking, high frequency trading systems, e-health databases/services). In practice, cloud computing is a paradigm that enables the deployment of dynamic and scalable virtualized resources to the end user through the Internet. Throughout recent years, a plethora of companies such as Google, Microsoft, Amazon and eBay have placed enormous efforts and investments towards the development, maintenance and upgrade of data-centers in order to improve their cloud-based services and further provide the best Quality of Service (QoS) as well as Quality of Experience (QoE) to the end user as indicated by Chengwei et al. (2010). Hence, their thorough analysis and proposition of sufficient frameworks that support the various dimensions (e.g. security, availability, resilience) of the

DOI: 10.4018/978-1-4666-8225-2.ch003

aforementioned domains of QoS and QoE has been prioritized in the agenda of the research community. An extremely core design element towards the healthy operation of virtualized cloud environments is regarded as the provision of mechanisms that may sufficiently confront security challenges that are likely to emerge due to the highly complex and inter-connected persona that persists in such environments.

By virtue of the intra-cloud hardware and software multi-layered nature of several components as well as the direct dependency with the Internet, the cloud composes a number of unique security concerns that need to be efficiently addressed. Apart from the networking aspect in regards to functionality and security, the cloud encompasses many technologies ranging from databases, resource scheduling, transaction management, load balancing up to operating systems and concurrency control. Thus, cloud networks trigger diverse security concerns such as storage security, data security, network security and secure virtualization. Moreover, in contrast with distributed systems as deployed over the Internet in the past where data owners had a full control over their data, their successors which are formulated by cloud environments hold intrinsic beneficial properties such as service transparency and elasticity which at the same time hold a complete control of the original owners' data. Hence, despite the end-user benefits gained by the virtual components that constitute the basis of such systems do also come with a range of threats that exploit the security holes on virtual machines (e.g. rootkit attacks on virtual machines investigated by Christodorescu et al. 2009) as well as with mutated cloud-specific Internet-based attacks that aim to compromise cloud networks (e.g. malware as studied by Gruschka et al. 2010; Marnerides et al. 2013), DDoS attacks on cloud services by Gruschka et al. 2010). According to Chen et al. (2010), blackhat hackers have already identified the potentials of the cloud since the manifestation, maintenance and operation of botnets seems to be much more efficient under a cloud paradigm in comparison with how it was in the past.

Furthermore, due to the aforementioned transparency and shared resource environment offered by the virtualized nature of the cloud, the work in Ristenpart et al. (2009), has demonstrated that hacker techniques have also transformed and evolved. In particular, it was noticed that attackers could easily construct side channels that could allow passive eavesdropping in the intra-cloud network as well as they could create covert channels that in practice send malicious data through the network. These vulnerabilities were achieved by exploiting the Virtual Machine (VM) placing method conducted by the cloud management software by allocating the attacking VM on a physical machine of the underlying datacenter and further by initiating an SSH keystroke timing attack (Song et al. 2001). Hence, the operational architecture and design of the cloud has indirectly aided the construction of new types of attacks that need to be adequately faced.

Hence, there has been a rapid development of cloud-specific security solutions that target to proactively and reactively detect cloud-specific threats either by adjusting the attack signatures of Intrusion Detection/Prevention Systems (i.e. IDS and IPS) or with statistical methods that encompass the notion of anomaly detection. IDS and IPS systems have been the main commercial solution for a number of years in the traditional Internet security domain as well as in current cloud environments and their efficiency has been questioned in several cases (Chengwei et al. 2011; Marnerides et al. 2013). Due to their signature-based concept and their full dependency on monitoring already known threats, such solutions tend to not be in a position at efficiently detecting new types of attacks that may manifest. However, the research community achieved to address this issue by suggesting a number of techniques that go beyond traditional rule and signature-based systems by implementing sophisticated statistical models that perform anomaly detection. Hence, such models have been incorporated in some IDS/IPS formulations (e.g. Snort.AD 2005).

Anomaly detection has been witnessed as a good asset in several disciplines since it has exhibited sufficient prediction, detection and forecasting accuracy in a number of scenarios as pointed in the comprehensive survey by Chandola et al. (2009). The properties embodied within anomaly detection frameworks as used in traditional IP networks (e.g. Lakhina et al. 2004; Zhang et al. 2005) have also led the research community to aim at employing such mechanisms within cloud-specific scenarios. As shown in previous works, it's considered as a good candidate at detecting and adapting in to new types of anomalies that might be caused by either legitimate (e.g. utility anomalies caused by operator errors, hardware/software misconfigurations studied by Chengwei et al. 2010) or malicious intent (e.g. malware analysis by Marnerides et al. 2013). In particular, the studies by Marnerides et al. (2013) and Shirazi et al. (2013) report that techniques derived by anomaly detection methodologies have proven to be much more effective than traditional rule-based approaches. The main reason for the latter statement is related with the fact that the statistical modeling embodied within such models allows the design of robust and holistic normal behavior models that consider a range of operational system and network features in order to be in a position at pinpointing any known and unknown anomalous patterns.

Therefore, in this chapter we initially aim at providing a brief survey on the state of the art in anomaly detection techniques as proposed for virtualized cloud infrastructures[1]. The target behind this survey is to provide a reader with the basic mindset regarding the design and deployment of anomaly detection methodologies in cloud-specific scenarios. Hence, via this comprehensive survey we aim at enlightening the reader on the applicability of anomaly detection techniques for the cloud scenery as well as to pinpoint on how each proposed methodology from the literature was formulated in order to meet cloud-specific requirements. Nonetheless, in order to facilitate an even more robust understanding to the general audience with respect to the usage of anomaly detection in such problems, this chapter is also dedicated at presenting a case study regarding an exemplar anomaly detection technique employed within a controlled experimental cloud test-bed. In particular, the demonstrated anomaly detection approach is mainly concerned with the security domain and particularly for the explicit task of detecting the Kelihos malware that was initially investigated by Garnaeva (2012) under the cloud-specific functionality of VM "live" migration that constitutes the basis on all commercial cloud management software (e.g. VMWare VSphere, 2012). The backbone of this technique is derived by the properties of the *non-parametric* Ensemble Empirical Mode Decomposition (E-EMD) algorithm that is proven to be an effective data-driven method for adequately decomposing highly non-stationary and non-linear signals as it happens with the network and system-wise measurements gathered within a cloud infrastructure.

BACKGROUND ON ANOMALY DETECTION IN CLOUD ENVIRONMENTS

By virtue of the exploding information and the demand of cloud-based online services with respect to processing data with high frequency rates by multiple clusters (i.e. datacenters), anomaly detection in computing and networked environments has gained momentum. The suitability of anomaly detection techniques is not necessarily restricted within the security domain as done by Christodorescu et al. (2009) but also applies for the domains of fault/failure management (Chengwei et al. 2010; 2011; Guan et al. 2013) and network/system resilience (Marnerides et al. 2013; Shirazi et al. 2013; Watson et al. 2013). The main property of an online or offline anomaly detection technique is to establish a threshold of "normal" behavior based on past observations on a given system(s) or network(s) in order to detect any deviations which are considered as anomalous. In general, there are two categories of anomaly detection techniques; i) *parametric,* ii) *non-parametric.* In contrast with parametric techniques, non-parametric approaches do not have *a priori* assumption regarding the distributional behavior of the observed features. Both categories have been employed for a number of problems experienced in cloud environments and they have both shown some promising outputs.

Nevertheless, in order to better structure the various anomaly detection approaches proposed in past and current literature we consider as important to define the notion of the cloud for the purposes of this chapter. Hence, we consider the "cloud" to be the both the application layer services offered to the end-user (e.g. Software as a Service – SaaS) [2] as well as the underlying virtualized layer that is supported by hardware and software that defines the datacenter. Hence, for the remaining of this section we will navigate through a number of anomaly detection techniques that aimed to address security as well as fault management challenges the aforementioned layers.

As already mentioned, regardless of the various and differing cloud computing systems (e.g. Amazon EC2, 2006; Google App Engine, 2008) there have been a number of anomaly detection approaches that mainly aimed to address the various operational and security challenges on the multiple layers that determine the cloud. For instance, the work by Chengwei et al. (2010) placed a strong effort at the online detection of anomalous characteristics on utility clouds using multiple types of metrics from the system components in their investigated cloud (e.g. CPU utilization on server racks, memory utilization, read/write counts on the OS, etc.). In particular their proposed Entropy-based Anomaly Testing (EbAT) system was operating under observations with respect to the Shannon entropy timeseries resulted by the distribution of the measured raw metrics. They have explicitly used the Shannon's entropy formulation (Shannon, 1948) in order to capture the degree of dispersal or concentration of the metric distributions and further aggregate entropy timeseries from each hardware components of the cloud for further processing under wavelets (Cencay et al. 2001). Thus, the explicit anomaly detection aspect was achieved using the online implementation of wavelets as well as with visual inspection of the finalized timeseries (i.e. spike detection). As demonstrated, the EbAT system had promising outcomes with respect to scalability with minimal real-time computational overhead since while the volume of the gathered metrics was growing, their online scheme could scale extremely well with respect to the detection alarm time as well as with the computational complexity invoked.

Within a similar range of objectives with respect to the adequate online detection of anomalous patterns in the cloud, the work by Chengwei et al. (2011) proposed two statistical techniques. The aim behind that study was to demonstrate the effectiveness of the point-threshold-based Tukey algorithm and the windowing-based Relative Entropy approach over captured data from a cloud-based production environment and from a cloud test-bed for multi-tier web applications running on server class machines. In particular, the authors had the objective to illustrate how their two proposed algorithms could overcome the limitations of techniques that implement models with Gaussian assumptions. Moreover, their suggested techniques targeted the improvement of the detection accuracy as well as the system performance in order to aid towards remedies at the onset of an anomalous event caused either from a legitimate or malicious intent. Thus, their approach was directly related and adjusted to operate under scenarios of analyzing continuous measurement streams gathered from various levels of abstraction in the cloud ranging from hardware, system and software up to middleware and upper-layer applications. Throughout the description of their methodology the authors emphasize that both algorithms operate under a non-parametric fashion, thus they do not hold any assumptions regarding the statistical distribution of the observed datasets. Hence, in contrast with some threshold-based techniques that rely on the Gaussian assumption (e.g. the Multivariate Adaptive Statistical Filtering – MASF method) in order to determine a "normal" behavior threshold the examined algorithms were data-driven without complying with any assumptions. As finally exhibited, the Tukey as well as the Relative Entropy approach managed to achieve much higher recall accuracy with a much lower False Positive Rate (FPR)[3] on the detection of various anomalies that were mainly caused by failures or performance degradations manifested in online services.

Inspired by the usage of the wavelet algorithm on detecting anomalous traffic in the Internet as demonstrated by Barford et al. (2001), the work by Guan et al. (2013) provided a novel prototype that enabled an online spatio-temporal anomaly detection scheme in a cloud scenario. Thus, Guan et al. (2013) achieved to initially formulate ad further implement a wavelet-based multi-scale anomaly detection system that relied on measured cloud performance metrics (e.g. CPU utilization, memory) gathered by multiple components (e.g. hardware, software, system) that consisted the examined institution-wide cloud environment. In order to adequately decompose and characterize the various non-stationary measurements as well as to capture the dynamicity of the cloud with respect to its internal (e.g. "live" migration of VMs) and external operations (e.g. service to end-users) there was the need to invoke several time sliding-windowing learning technologies that permitted the construction of meaningful wavelet functions. Hence, there was a coherent statistical description of the normal behavior of numerous metrics that could then be utilized for determining the deviations that could likely be caused by anomalous events. The resulted experimental outcomes were quite promising since the proposed approach reached a 93.3% of sensitivity[4] on detecting anomalous events with only just a 6.1% of the reported events to be false alarms.

Qiang et al. (2013) placed an effort towards the design and development of an autonomic anomaly detection component that could significantly aid at monitoring the health of an entire production cloud. Via tampering the commonly used Principal Component Analysis (PCA) approach the authors composed a strategy that on real-time could adaptively identify the most relevant principal components (MRPCs) for each type of a possible failure in an in-campus 362-node cloud infrastructure. Similarly with the work by Guan et al. (2013) their implementation relied on a total of 518 cloud performance metrics that described several operational aspects such as hardware, system and network performance. Throughout their experimentation the introduced prototype seemed to overcome other well-known algorithms such as Decision Trees, Bayesian Networks and Support Vector Machines (SVMs) since it achieved a rate of 91.4% for sensitivity at detecting various anomalies with an extremely low false positive rate of 3.7%. In order to empower their experimental outcomes, this study also employed the suggested algorithm on emulated datasets gathered from a Google datacenter and achieved similar detection accuracy performance.

Under a different mindset than other pieces of work, the study by Doelitzscher et al. (2013) proposed an anomaly detection methodology that did not solely aimed at characterizing the cloud-specific performance metrics but rather targeted at profiling user behavior within a SaaS cloud. Through carefully designed use case scenarios Doelitzscher et al. (2013) defined the normal behavior of a user's VM(s) based on the events monitored by the cloud management software. Thus, based on the utilization of a VM over the time period it was active they could extrapolate using a neural networks paradigm on whether a VM holds a commonly seen utilization profile or whether it was dysfunctional throughout time due to its persistent re-initiation as seen by the management software. With the development of user-specific normal behavior profiles it was subsequently feasible to create a cloud-wide normal behavior model that in practice generalized the aggregate of user-specific profiles. The implemented scheme was validated under a simulated environment and has shown reasonably good results with extremely low false alarms.

The seminal work by Bhanduri et al. (2011) produced the promising framework of Fault Detection in Cloud Systems (FDCS) that had the objective to detect faulty anomalous characteristics in a cloud setting by using cloud performance metrics under the Ganglia monitoring system (Ganglia, 2000). The FDCS algorithm was implemented in C++ using a Message Passing Interface (MPI) API and it is mainly composed by two phases; the push phase and the pull phase. Both phases synergistically allow the in-network interaction between the physical nodes that consist the clouds' underlying infrastructure (i.e. datacenter) in order to update each other regarding their local health information with respect to the local performance characteristics (e.g. CPU utilization, memory, I/O) after a comparison of the locally produced k-nearest neighbor algorithm (Altman, 1992) as resulted by the locally measured data. With the usage of a distributed version of an outlier ranking function it was feasible for this approach to initially identify locally on whether a given node experienced a fault and further notify the rest of the nodes regarding the occurred failure. Hence, the system could overall pinpoint the global outlier machines within the whole infrastructure. The experimentation conducted in this piece of work considered data from 8 physical machines that run a number of jobs for a period of 3 days and exhibited extremely good results with respect to detection accuracy.

Due to the fact that anomaly detection algorithms are prone to increase the number of flagged anomalies/events while the measured cloud performance metrics grow, Viswanathan et al. (2012) proposed a framework that allows the ranking of the severity of a reported anomaly. In particular, their framework consists of implemented parametric anomaly detection algorithms in conjunction with a ranking technique for specific false positive rates (FPRs) under an *a priori* assumption regarding the underlying distributional behavior of the measured data. With the use of the Z-score statistical metric (Kreyszig, 1979) as applied on two online anomaly detection methods that considered a Gaussian and a Bernoulli approximation respectively, the authors achieved to produce a time window-based anomaly detection and ranking approach that allowed the ranking of each reported anomaly. Through their experimentation that was conduced using synthetic as well as real datasets it was shown that their suggested framework could adequately detect several types of anomalies occurring on multiple cloud abstraction layers (e.g. hardware, system) and could further rank the threats based on the urgency required to act for remediating them. Hence, they managed to construct a system that would act as the main aid to an operator.

Pannu et al. (2012) instrumented an online adaptive anomaly detection (AAD) framework that aimed towards the autonomic detection of failures using execution and runtime cloud performance metrics. The notion of autonomic failure detection had the objective to aid towards the comprehension of emergent cloud-wide phenomena in order to ensure a level of self-management on cloud resources. Nonetheless, the proposed framework relied on an initial feature filtering and extraction process that managed to exclude useless cloud performance metrics, thus helping to increase the detection accuracy. Subsequently, all selected features were inserted within a component where the Support Vector Machine (SVM) algorithm was implemented. Their implemented SVM was based on a specially designed Gaussian kernel function and was in a position to map all the selected performance metrics on a hyper-plane where outliers were spotted as possible anomalous events on real-time. In parallel, the designed kernel function was updated on real-time, thus adapting on newly incoming testing sets. Nevertheless, under a real experimentation over a 362 –node cloud computing environment in a university campus the produced results were extremely promising since they exhibited the efficiency of the proposed scheme that reached over 91% of anomaly detection sensitivity. Moreover, the conclusive alarms flagged by the AAD framework were triggered under a small timeframe of below than 7.5 seconds and the real-time detection process was run on reasonable computational costs.

In the work by Smith et al. (2010) there was the introduction of an autonomic mechanism that was capable to detect anomalous events by the continuous analysis of noisy and multi-dimensional data gathered from compute cloud systems. In contrast with commonly used root-cause analysis tools which are in the majority of cases reliant on simple rules and event signatures, the suggested scheme was operating under a set of techniques that ensured an automatic analysis of real-time monitored data gathered from a range of cloud abstraction layers (e.g. I/O operations, memory read/writes on VMs, memory utilization, network packets). The implemented techniques could adequately transform the raw cloud features into a uniform data format that was subsequently filtered by dedicated feature selection algorithms in order to compose a meaningful dataset for the actual detection phase. In particular, the detection phase was achieved under a Bayesian network-based unsupervised learning scheme that allowed the monitoring of outliers from the normally distributed (i.e. healthy) nodes within a large-scale institutional compute cloud. During the performance evaluation of the proposed scheme it was evidenced that it was feasible to reach high detection accuracy of more than 90%.

Mi et al. (2011) constructed the Magnifier tool that in practice was dealing with the detection of real-time performance problems in large-scale cloud computing systems. By exploiting the traditional hierarchical structure of service components within a given cloud computing system the authors managed to model the user service requests under a hierarchical tree scheme. Given the performance indications by various metrics gathered from the cloud infrastructure, as well as with the usage of pre-defined empirical performance thresholds, the Magnifier tool was comparing the overall system behavior with respect to service component user requests. Thus, it was feasible to identify the most heavily consumed VM service within the examined environment and further localize the experienced anomalous events. The methodology behind the explicit anomaly localization was based on a PCA-based clustering formulation that had as the main objective functions to denote the service response latency and the total processing time for a given service that was running on a VM. The experiments conducted for evaluating the Magnifier tool revealed that in comparison with two other techniques it exhibited high detection accuracy of faults experienced on several cloud services. In addition, the Magnifier tool also demonstrated an extremely good ability at localizing the events and identifying the exact root cause of failure.

Given the wide usage of Googles' MapReduce framework by many cloud providers, the study by Kai et al. (2012) developed an online anomaly detection method explicitly for MapReduce-based cloud environments. MapReduce is a cloud computing framework firstly introduced by Dean and Chemawat (2008) that enables the distributed and parallel operation of applications over large-scale datacenters and is considered as a core software component for several commercial, utility and production cloud deployments. However, the internal scheduling of MapReduce that triggers various parallel processes within different task execution time-lags has an indirect negative impact on the granular detection of anomalous events that are likely to appear within a given datacenters' clusters. Hence, the work by Kai et al. (2012) orchestrated a density-based clustering scheme that based on peer-similarity could identify on real-time the anomalous patterns that could appear on the workload of a computing node within a cluster. In more detail, the suggested technique operates under the assumptions of peer-similarity that: a) in normal conditions the workload posed by the similar tasks is equal; b) in the scenario of an anomalous event, all tasks will indicate different characteristics. Thus, by considering measurements (e.g. disk I/O speed, CPU utilization, memory utilization per process) and with respect to the resource consumption reported by each computing node in a cluster(s) it was feasible to create similarity clusters that denote the normal behavior profile on a given time frame. Hence, any deviating outlier from the composed clusters would correspond to anomalous events. The experimentation conducted in this case was based on simulated attacks and the suggested technique exhibited a high detection accuracy of over 90%.

In parallel, Vallis et al. (2014) in Twitter Inc composed a long-term anomaly detection scheme that aimed to protect the availability and resilience of Twitter's cloud-based web services by predicting possible abnormalities that could likely manifest. With the construction of statistical learning models that were developed based on application (e.g. Tweets per second - TPS) and system metrics (e.g. CPU utilization) gathered from production Twitter cloud data it was feasible to efficiently track and detect anomalous characteristics on long-term timeseries. In particular, Vallie et al. (2014) designed a scheme that employed a generalized Extreme Student Deviate (ESD) test that aided on the decomposition of the examined timeseries. Moreover, by following a piecewise approximation with the usage of Piecewise Median and the Quantile Regression B-Spline methods on the underlying trend on each timeseries this work managed to track the changes on the timeseries trend component. In addition, by accounting for weekly timeseries seasonality this work managed to significantly reduce the number of false positive alarms. The evaluation conducted on the proposed scheme indicated that under a really small computational time it was possible to detect anomalies with high detection accuracy of over 95% with respect to the Recall, Precision and F-measure metrics [5].

Derived by a multi-level, self-organizing network resilience architecture firstly introduced by Shirazi et al. (2013) and subsequently extended by Watson et al. (2013), the technique proposed by Marnerides et al. (2013) targeted the explicit identification and detection of malware as initiated on an HTTP service running on a VM. This seminal offline technique was solely considering operational network traffic as seen on the network interfaces of each VM running on a physical node within an experimental cloud setting. Its algorithmic operation relied on the computation of a matrix that contained meta-statistics based on 13 network raw features (e.g. counts of bytes, packets, flows) that were subsequently used by a covariance analysis approach. In particular, the covariance analysis was in a position to pinpoint the most discriminant feature within the aforementioned matrix that essentially was capable at identifying the initiation and further establishment of the Kelihos malware (Bureau, 2011) over the active HTTP service. It was observed that the most discriminant feature was the energy metric derived by the packet timeseries of each active flow as computed by the Choi-Williams energy Time-Frequency (TF) distribution (Cohen, 1989). As the authors mention, this particular distribution was in a position to adequately capture the non-stationary properties of each unidirectional TCP flow (as also shown in other traffic characterization studies as in Marnerides, Pezaros et al. 2013) and they could further compose a meaningful metric that describe the evolution of transport flows on the TF plane. Hence, this granular view on each flow could effectively aid towards the sufficient construction of normal behavior profiles under the covariance approach. Based on the produced normal behavior profiles it was then feasible to monitor the change of the covariance matrix over time using the Euclidean distance between each computed matrix on every observational time snapshot and identify the malware activities.

The latter mentioned piece of work acted as the triggering point for future studies regarding the deployment of malware detection techniques in the cloud. Hence, in the next section we provide a case study that has the target to thoroughly and coherently present a malware detection scheme based on a non-parametric, data-driven technique that considers both network and system information.

CASE STUDY: MALWARE DETECTION IN THE CLOUD

Given the brief overview of cloud-specific AD techniques covered in the previous section, the aim behind this section is to present a case study on explicitly detecting the anomalous activity initiated by a particular type of malware. As already mentioned, this work was a natural evolution of earlier published work in (Marnerides et al., 2013; Shirazi et al., 2013; Watson et al., 2013) and had the objective to detect the Kelihos malware under the scenario of Virtual Machine(s) (VMs) "live" migration which is a core component within the management functionality of any cloud-based environment. In parallel, a secondary objective behind this experiment was to also answer on whether a VM that is already infected with malware would remain infected when it's migrated to another physical host. The scenario and the controlled experimental setup that we describe in subsequent sections were formulated based on discussions we had with operators from cloud providers in the UK as being part of the activities of the India-UK Advanced Technology Centre (IU-ATC) project (IU-ATC Project, 2008). We following describe the "live" VM migration process as well as the basic properties of the Kelihos malware.

VM "Live" Migration and Kelihos Malware

Due to the heavy concern of cloud operators regarding the security implications of VM "live" migration within an intra-cloud scenario we have considered as necessary to examine the detection of malware under this explicit cloud-specific property. In contrast with "cold" migration where migration occurs for powered-off VMs, live migration allows to move running VMs from one physical host to another. In practice, during this type of migration there is a real-time transfer of Operating System (OS) – related instances alongside all the memory related with all the activities of a given VM between two physical hosts. Live migration is an extremely important functionality contained within any cloud resource management strategy and is mainly executed for resource allocation purposes on real time. Thus, we have explicitly aimed to emulate live migration since the greatest majority of commercial cloud management software (e.g. VMWare VSphere, 2012) utilize this functionality by default.

As already mentioned, the malware sample used in this work is known as "Kelihos" and is regarded as an emerging threat based on investigations conducted by the studies of Bureau (2011) and Garnaeva (2012) and Marnerides et al. (2013). The Kelihos malware (also known as Hlux) is a replacement of the famous Storm worm, which was active in 2007 and replaced by Waledac in 2009.

A study presented by Garnaeva (2012) provided a thorough overview on the functionality of Kelihos and exposed its peer-to-peer network protocol. The authors highlight that the new variant that we use in our experimentation is capable of sophisticated evasion techniques both in system and network components. In practice, this malware monitors network traffic for HTTP and FTP in order to steal sensitive information and propagates through TCP port 80 where data exchange is completely encrypted. Furthermore, the initial infection vector used by Kelihos is through propagation of malicious links embedded in emails where these links are based on domains controlled by the bot master that generally use fast flux techniques.

Data Collection and Experimental Setup

Based on the earlier work of Marnerides et al. (2013) we have managed to build a measurement framework that is actually employed on the hypervisor level of every physical node. In practice, the measurement framework consists of a range of monitoring and post-processing scripts that employ Virtual Machine

Introspection (VMI) using the libVMI library (2011) and the Volatility tool (2011) in order to summarize system-specific features (e.g. process list, count of threads etc.) for every VM that runs on a given physical host. In parallel, we were able to gather network traffic traces from every VMs' network interface with the usage of tcpdump (Tcpdump, 1987). Given both network and system-wise features it was then feasible to construct a joint dataset for each VM. Hence, our dataset can be seen as a joint set of a total of 55 network and system features on the hypervisor level that gives a summarizing measurement view for every VM under a sampling rate of 3 seconds for each measurement.

The experimental setup formulated in this work was achieved within a controlled Local Area Network (LAN) environment in order to have a robust ground truth regarding the normal system and network-wise behavior for all the VMs that composed the test-bed. As shown by Figure 1 the test-bed consists of two physical nodes running multiple VMs with varying resource utilization profiles (Host A and Host B), a management node (Management Host) that regulates the migration process, and some client machines. All physical nodes apart the client machines run Xen v4.1 (Xen, 2003) with the XAPI toolstack and Ubuntu 12.10 Linux as the hypervisor operating system. The VMs used for testing were running Windows XP (SP3) with some regular user activity (e.g. Internet browsing) and the VM that was infected provides HTTP service by virtualizing an HTTP Apache server. Thus, in order to generate some realistic background traffic we have written some custom scripts that enable the client machine(s) within the same LAN to randomly generate HTTP requests to the VM HTTP Apache server.

Overall, this experiment lasted for 20 minutes and we had the Kelihos malware injected on Host A around the 5th minute and the live migration to host B for the VM that run the HTTP server was initiated on the 9th minute. Based on the measurements gathered from all the running VMs of hosts A and B we subsequently constructed the joint system and network matrices for each VM and proceeded with their statistical, signal-oriented decomposition enabled by the Ensemble Empirical Mode Decomposition (E-EMD) algorithm as we describe next.

Methodology: EMD and E-EMD

A basis in the overall anomaly detection methodology is regarded as the robust non-parametric statistical characterization of the gathered measurements that was allowed by the E-EMD algorithm. The E-EMD algorithm is a variant of the EMD algorithm that was firstly proposed as a fundamental building block of the Hilbert-Huang transform (Huang, Attoh-Okine, 2005).

The EMD algorithm is a data-driven technique that allows the decomposition and description of non-linear and non-stationary data. Thus, it can naturally extract meaningful statistical insight regarding the internal properties of a given signal or timeseries that represent the data measurements. The data-driven decomposition instrumented by the EMD algorithm is achieved by considering the local characteristics (i.e. local minima, maxima and envelopes) of a signal on a given time window. The resulted decomposition based on the aforementioned characteristics is formulated with the creation of a small number of modes represented by Intrinsic Mode Functions (IMFs) that yield instantaneous frequency representations with respect to time. A given mode is considered to be a complete IMF if it complies with the following properties:

1. Equality or difference at most by one between the number of extrema and the number of zero crossings.
2. Throughout the whole signal the mean value of the upper and lower envelopes is zero.

Figure 1. The experimental setup for malware detection under VM live migration

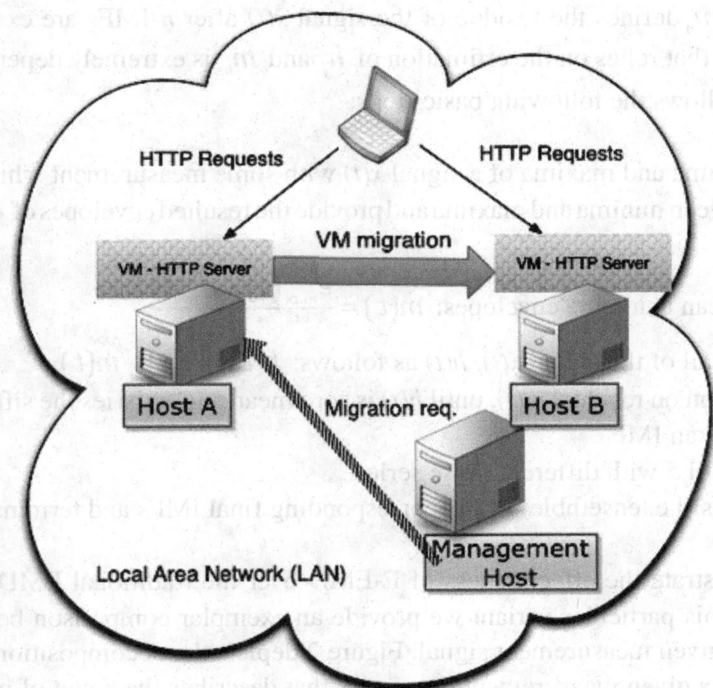

Nevertheless, the original EMD algorithm tends to not be fully capable at decomposing signals or timeseries that hold flat properties (e.g. constant values) for long periods of time. In order to confront the aforementioned constraint, the studies by Torres et al. (2011) and Wu and Huang (2009) proposed a variant of EMD, the Ensemble-EMD that we also use in this work.

The E-EMD formulation behaves as a Noise-Assisted-Data-Analysis (NADA) technique since it considers the measurement noise factor whilst decomposing a given signal. The additive noise aids at composing a uniform reference scale distribution to facilitate the traditional EMD method and achieves to confront the "mode mixing" problem. Hence, the E-EMD initially considers a measurement signal *x(t)* (e.g. the count of memory reads/writes on a VM, the number of captured packets etc.) to be composed as a series of observations in time *t* alongside a measurement random noise for each observation such as the jth "artificial" observation be defined as:

$$x_j(t) = x(t) + w_j(t) \tag{1}$$

As a following step, the E-EMD algorithm decomposes the signal *x(t)* into a sum of IMFs as follows:

$$x(t) = \sum_{j}^{n} h_j + m_n \tag{2}$$

The term h_j denotes a resulted IMF if it complies with the conditions of the EMD algorithm stated earlier and the term m_n defines the residue of the signal $x(t)$ after n IMFs are extracted. Overall, the decomposition of $x(t)$ that relies on the estimation of h_j and m_n is extremely dependent on an iterative sifting process that follows the following basic steps:

1. Identify the minima and maxima of a signal $x(t)$ with some measurement white noise.
2. Interpolate[6] between minima and maxima and provide the resulted envelopes of $e_{\min}(t)$ and $e_{\max}(t)$ respectively.
3. Calculate the mean using the envelopes: $m(t) = \frac{e_{\max}(t) + e_{\min}(t)}{2}$
4. Compute the detail of the signal $x(t)$, $h(t)$ as follows: $h(t) = x(t) - m(t)$
5. Initiate an iteration on residual $m(t)$, until $h(t)$ is zero mean and satisfies the sifting conditions until it's considered as an IMF.
6. Repeat step 1 until 5 with different noise series.
7. Derive the means (i.e. ensemble) of the corresponding final IMFs and terminate the process.

In order to demonstrate the effectiveness of E-EMD over the traditional EMD and further justify our choice on using this particular variant we provide an exemplar comparison between the resulting decompositions on a given measurement signal. Figure 2 depicts the decomposition conducted by both EMD and E-EMD on a given measurement timeseries that describes the count of process handles on a given VM. It is clearly evidenced that the original raw signal depicted on the top plots holds flat properties and as expected the traditional EMD algorithm could not sufficiently narrow down that signal in descriptive IMFs that are terminated to a monotonic function. In particular, the EMD algorithm has

Figure 2. Exemplar decomposition from the traditional EMD (left) and the E-EMD (right) for the count of process handles as measured on a single Virtual Machine (VM)

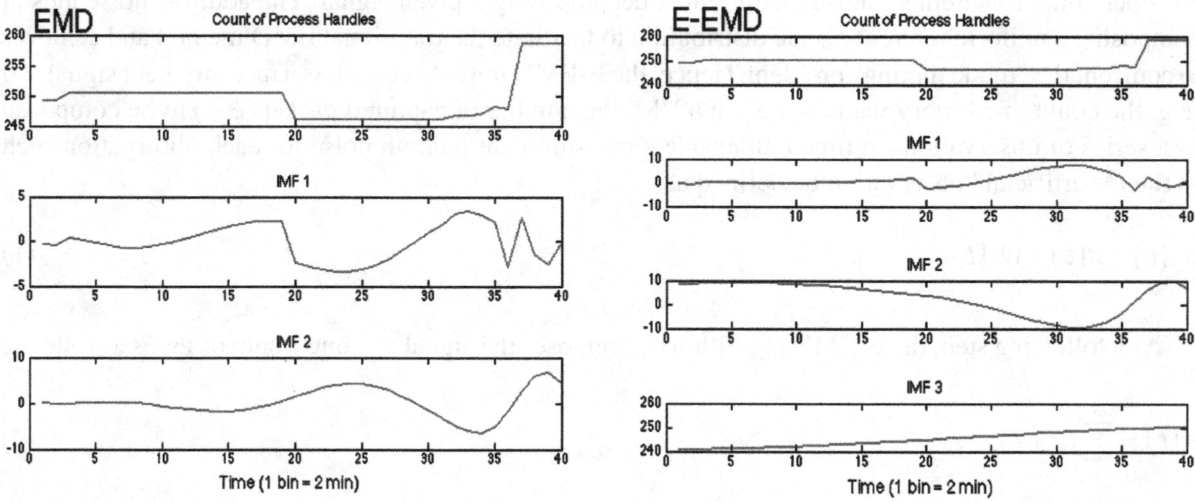

produced two IMFs where the last one (plot on the bottom left of Figure 2) is not fully considered as an absolute monotonic function. Nevertheless, the decomposition resulted by the E-EMD approach exhibited a granular decomposition, hence it produced one more IMF having the last one (plot on the bottom right of Figure 2) is clearly defined as a monotonic function.

Methodology: Anomaly Detection Step

Prior to providing the precise anomaly detection formulation we feel the essence to initially provide some insight regarding the general notation used.

As already mentioned, the presented technique depends on empirical system measurements obtained at the hypervisor level for a number of running Virtual Machines (VMs) as well as the aggregated network traffic as being captured individually on the virtual network interface on each VM. The overall behavior of a hypervisor *H* for the full period of the experiment performed in time *T* is denoted by the sum of all the measurement snapshots captured from each individual VM on a given physical node where the hypervisor *H* runs. Thus, *H* is defined as:

$$H = \sum_{t=1}^{T} VM(t) \tag{3}$$

where a measurements snapshot for a VM in time *t* is represented by:

$$VM(t) = \begin{bmatrix} f_1(\tau) & f_2(\tau) & \cdots & f_n(\tau) \\ \vdots & \vdots & \ddots & \vdots \\ f_1(\tau) & f_2(\tau) & \cdots & f_n(\tau) \end{bmatrix} \tag{4}$$

Given the definition in equation (4), τ is the measurements sampling rate for a feature *f* which in our case was 3 seconds, time *t* is the time taken for a full snapshot and in the presented experiment it was for a period of 2 minutes. The term *n* represents the total number of features where in our case was a total of 55 features. Hence, each column on the matrix of *VM(t)* corresponds to the timeseries of a single system or network feature *f* for a period of 2 minutes.

Due to the controlled experimental cloud test-bed described earlier it was feasible to determine and regulate normal workload activity on each VM before the activation of the Kelihos malware in order to compose a normal behavior model. The normal behavior model serves the purpose at enabling a descriptive statistical threshold that determines normal operation on the hypervisor level. Hence, we initially estimate the corresponding IMFs based on the E-EMD algorithm for each "normal" VM snapshot, and we subsequently compute the correlation matrix between them. Finally, the normal behavior threshold is defined based on the sum of the median correlation matrices. We have particularly used the median correlation matrices rather than the mean correlation matrices in order to gain a centralized average description of E-EMD on every VM snapshot.

Nonetheless, we denote μ to be the mean vector of the resulting snapshot IMFs matrix *Y(t)* for each feature column *f(t)* in a *VM(t)*. Under μ for every *f(t)* we derive a newly composed matrix $X(t) = [\mu_1, \mu_2, \ldots, \mu_n]$, that summarizes the IMF characterization for each VM snapshot. Based on

X(t) we subsequently compute the reference correlation C_{ik} in order to quantify the behaviour of VM_i with VM_k in the snapshot *t* where they both run on the hypervisor *M* under normal operation. Given this quantification we subsequently compute a normal behaviour reference vector as follows:

$$R_{normal}(t) = median\left(C_{ik}\right) \tag{5}$$

Given the composition of the normal behavior profile based on "normal" VM snapshots it is feasible to proceed with the comparison of newly tested VM snapshots in order to determine on whether they pose an anomalous behavior or not. Similarly with the "normal" VM snapshots it is firstly required for every newly tested VM snapshot to get transformed and decomposed by the E-EMD algorithm. The decomposition allowed by the E-EMD algorithm enables the computation of a reference vector $R_{test}(t)$ that provides a statistical description for the tested VM snapshot. With the usage of this newly composed vector as well as with the consideration of the earlier computed $R_{normal}(t)$ we then derive the distance metric *d(t)* that describes the deviation (or not) of the tested VM snapshot against normal behavior as follows:

$$d(t) = \left(\sum_{j=1}^{k} W_{tr} \left| C_j(t) - R_{normal}(t) \right|^{\vartheta} \right)^{\frac{1}{\vartheta}} \tag{6}$$

where *k* is the number of the testing VMs, ϑ is a tuning parameter[7], the term $C_j(t)$ is the correlation matrix of the jth VM snapshot and W_{tr} is a varying weight parameter denoted as:

$$W_{tr} = {R_{test}(t)} \big/ {R_{normal}(t)} \tag{7}$$

The actual detection of malicious activity on a given VM snapshot is achieved under outlier detection allowed by the Median Absolute Deviation (MAD) test as also used by Fontugne et al. (2013). Hence, a VM is anomalous if:

$$d(t) > median\left(R_{normal}(t)\right) + \varphi MAD\left(R_{test}(t)\right) \tag{8}$$

where

$$MAD\left(R_{test}(t)\right) = \beta median\left(\left|R_{test}(t) - median\left(R_{test}(t)\right)\right|\right) \tag{9}$$

The tunable φ parameter at equation 8 seemed to work well when equal to 4 and β is always equal to 1.48.

Results

As already described earlier, the conducted experimentation aimed to address the aspect of VM live migration under the threat of the Kelihos malware. In general, this experiment had the goal to derive some answers with respect to the persistence of the infection after the migration and if it can be adequately detected by the proposed detection scheme. The actual experiment lasted for 20 minutes and it was necessary to construct in an offline mode a ground truth of normal operation from Host A by utilizing data gathered for a period of 10 minutes. As expected we observed that the Kelihos malware was transferred alongside all the other memory of the affected VM from Host A to Host B. Moreover, we have also witnessed the initiation of malicious activity (e.g. new child processes) by Kelihos right after the migration process was terminated and the VM was established on Host B. These observations are also implied by the results obtained by our anomaly detection methodology that are depicted via Figure 3.

In order to initially construct the normal behavior profile and determine the $R_{normal}(t)$ parameter that also affects the normality threshold we have used the data gathered from 5 running VMs on Host A. As evidenced via Figure 3, the introduced E-EMD-based anomaly detection method performed reasonably well on accurately detecting the malware on Host A right after its injection on the 5th minute. However, it seemed to not fully detecting the Kelihos instance on the first 5 minutes after the migration process occurred on Host B. For the first 2 post-migration minutes, the proposed technique achieved to identify that the first observational testing sample of the hypervisor snapshot[8] (i.e. $R_{test}(t)$) had an anomalous activity since it went over the pre-defined threshold. However, the subsequent snapshot was not correctly detected as anomalous regardless of the fact that the Kelihos malware was already injected.

Figure 3. Detection of the Kelihos malware after being injected on a VM HTTP server on Host A where the VM migrates to Host B

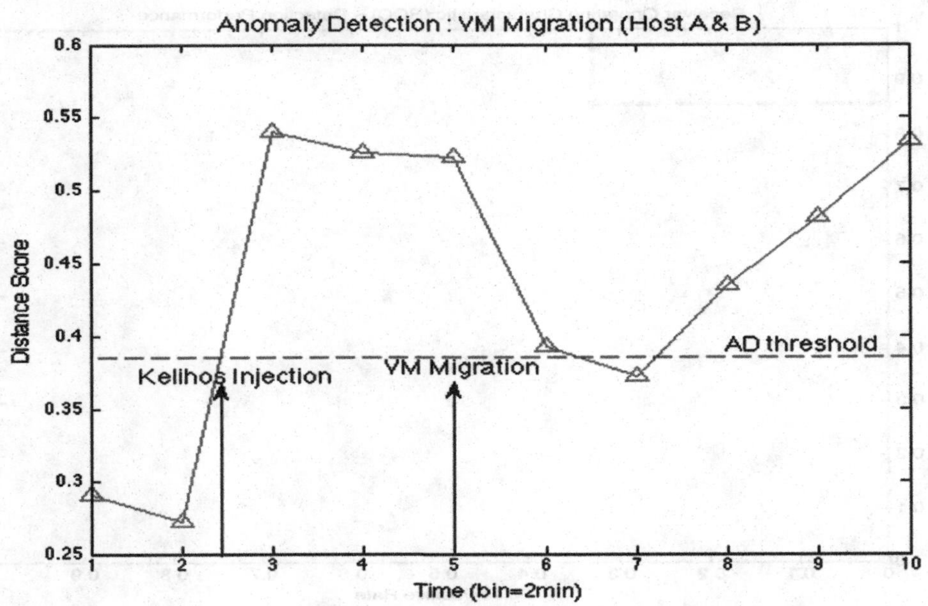

The reason of this inaccuracy relates with the explicit behavior of Kelihos when firstly established on a VM. In particular, the Kelihos malware was rightfully detected on the first hypervisor snapshot (i.e. on the 6th time bin on Figure 3) since the majority of the activity corresponding to system processes triggered were transferred from physical host A to B. Hence, these processes consumed memory that contributed to the amplification of the measured host-specific signals in a point to be tracked by the proposed detection scheme. On the other hand, during the second hypervisor snapshot the system related processes were reduced as they have been ordered by the malware executable in order to not be easily visible. At the same time, until the 14th minute there were not any networking initializations forked by the malware as it happens in the subsequent observational time bins thus the overall decomposition of all the hypervisor snapshots were still relatively close to the anomaly detection threshold. As evidenced by Figure 3, as soon as network-related processes were triggered, both system and network features contributed at amplifying the measurements and resulting to anomalous characteristics in comparison with the pre-defined normal behavior threshold.

A common approach at quantifying the detection performance of a given algorithm is the computation of the Receiver Operating Characteristic (ROC) curve that we also adopt in this work[9]. Hence, we provide Figure 4 that depicts the resulting ROC curve of our proposed detection scheme. Based on the produced ROC curve it is fairly reasonable to state that the detection accuracy rate in the presented technique is quite high. In particular, by considering the number of true positives (TPs) and false negatives (FPs) it is shown that the suggested technique has reached a 90% of overall detection accuracy. The shape of the ROC curve justifies the reported high accuracy rate where all the points hold high values of TPR and zero FPR expect one where an FPR of approximately 0.4 is attained.

Figure 4. Receiver Operating Characteristic (ROC) curve for the proposed detection approach

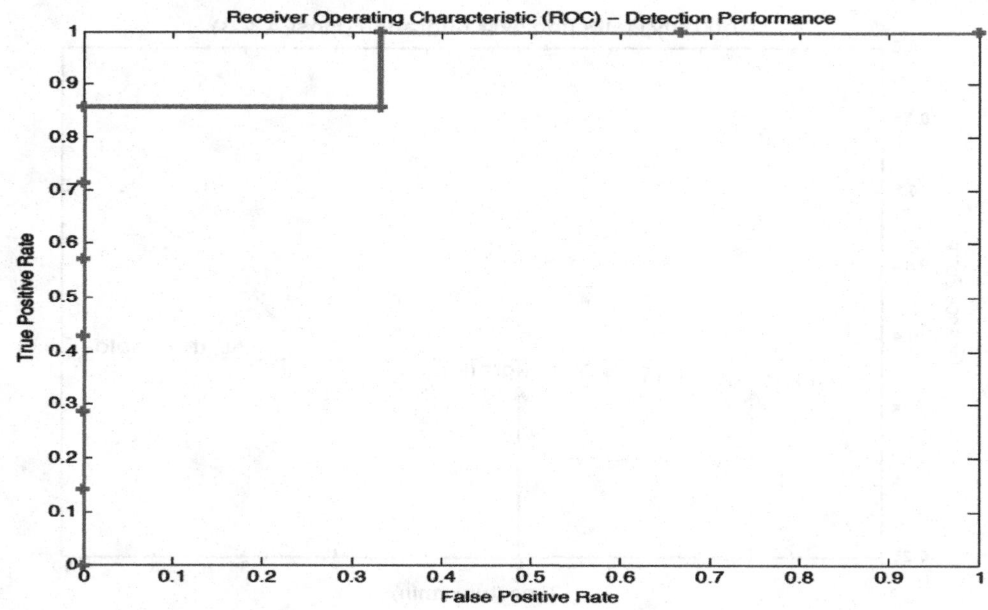

Case Study: Summary and Conclusion

A critical security issue in virtualized cloud environments relates with the adequate identification and detection of malware, thus sophisticated anomaly detection approaches are required to be developed under cloud-specific settings. In this case study we have demonstrated the applicability of an anomaly detection approach that explicitly addresses the detection of malware and relies on the system and network measurements captured from each running VM at the hypervisor level. We have placed a particular focus on the scenario where VM and service migration (in our case with an HTTP server) occurs and regulated an experiment within a controlled cloud test-bed.

Due to the fact that the greatest majority of the monitored network and system features demonstrate highly non-linear and non-stationary properties, the proposed technique initially employs the non-parametric E-EMD algorithm in order to establish a coherent statistical characterization and decomposition of the measurement signals. The resulting outcomes of this experimentation have demonstrated that the proposed exemplar anomaly detection scheme may reach up to 90% of overall accuracy at detecting the Kelihos malware that has been reported to be an evolving threat where a range of attacks may be triggered after its initiation.

Overall, the main objective behind the presentation of this exemplar technique was to provide a practical example to the reader with respect to the design, deployment and evaluation of cloud-specific anomaly detection techniques. However, we feel the essence to clarify that the above described method is surely subject to improvement since the experimentation setup was not covering all the aspects of a real cloud but rather was restricted within specific cloud properties as VM live migration. Furthermore, the proposed technique did not consider any other types of anomalies (e.g. DDoS) or VM services with different workloads (e.g. a VM that runs a transcoding service for IPTV networks) that would surely affect the composition of the normal behavior profile as well as the anomaly detection threshold.

FUTURE RESEARCH DIRECTIONS AND ONGOING PROJECTS IN CLOUD-BASED ANOMALY DETECTION

The rapid growth of dependence by numerous online services in conjunction with the increased complexity forked by cloud deployments has definitely triggered a plethora of challenges with respect to their sufficient maintenance, management and security. As justified by the studies mentioned throughout this chapter, the particular concept of anomaly detection may adequately serve the role of a critical component within any strategy related to the sufficient resource management of a cloud environment. Hence, within the corresponding literature review in this chapter it was clearly evidenced that anomaly detection techniques have been successfully used in a number of resource management tasks that tackled a range of issues ranging from fault/failure management up to security-related problems.

By simply accounting the recent evolution of the Cloud of Things (CoT) (Parwekar et al., 2011) as resulted by the integration of ubiquitous and smart environments that compose the Internet of Things (IoT) (Atzori et al., 2010) it is anticipated to observe amplified operational as well as security concerns. Consequently, the diverse system and network characteristics alongside the intrinsic application-layer requirements posed by each involved heterogeneous environment will directly affect the mindset behind the design of future anomaly detection techniques. It is greatly anticipated that the highly demanding QoS and QoE-related requirements from the exponentially growing number of end-users or automated "smart" devices in such settings would truly place a great obstacle towards the development of real-time anomaly detection techniques due to the multidimensional datasets that need to be monitored, analyzed and further interpreted by a given algorithm. Thus, regardless of the mathematical formulation for a certain technique it would be necessary to systematically re-visit the domain of monitoring and measurements and aim to incorporate anomaly detection methods within native measurement instrumentations. Ultimately such integration will enable efficient and "lightweight" anomaly detection "on the fly" as achieved in Internet-based scenarios in the past as demonstrated by Levy-Leduc and Roueff (2009). Moreover, such formulations would also be in the position at composing situation-awareness given the implicit requirement that their analysis depends on the fusion of multiple and multi-layered metrics gathered by a range of heterogeneous environments.

Nonetheless, a number of the aforementioned topics are seen to be already under investigation by several large-scale European Union (EU) and non-EU research projects. Hence, anomaly detection for multiple aspects in the domain of cloud management (e.g. fault/failure management, security) is placed as a top priority topic in the research agenda of several academic institutions and industrial stakeholders. For instance, the multi-disciplinary EU funded SEcure Cloud computing for CRitical infrastructure IT project (EU SECCRIT, 2012) consists of 10 academic and industrial partners and has the main objective to construct mechanisms that confront the security risks invoked within real cloud deployments. In particular, the SECCRIT project aims at assessing the risks and challenges involved in cloud-based critical ICT environments (e.g. air traffic control systems) in order to identify and further implement anomaly detection components. Consequently, such components would be in a position to ensure a certain level of network and system resilience as well as to determine trustworthy high assurance policies. Moreover, a subset of the activities within the largest multi-disciplinary India-UK research initiative via the India-UK Advanced Technology Center project (IU-ATC, 2008) project targets at the development of anomaly detection techniques in cloud environments. As part of the objectives behind building resilient system and networks mechanisms, scientists involved in this project have already constructed offline and online anomaly detection frameworks (e.g. Marnerides et al. 2013; Shirazi et al., 2013; Watson et al., 2013) that are consistently evaluated over a large-scale experimental cloud test-bed that interconnects all 35 academic and industrial partners. The outcomes of this synergistic research initiative have considered a range of pragmatic scenarios that go beyond the traditional cloud management aspect and they included upper layer intrinsic requirements from areas such as e-agriculture and e-health. In parallel with the aforementioned projects, there is also a large number of other projects (e.g. EU FP7 NEMESYS, 2012, EU FP7 ANIKETOS, 2012) as well as agencies such as the European Network and Information Security Agency (ENISA) that have indicated their strong interest towards the development of anomaly detection techniques in order to target the rise of cyber-attacks (EU ENISA, 2012). Moreover, a strong initiative is also seen in the new strategic goals set by the EU regarding the security and management implications invoked by the evolution of future cloud deployments, thus a large funding scheme has been granted to the new Horizon 2020 research and innovation program (HORIZON2020, 2014).

The domains of critical cloud computing resilience and security have also reached the attraction of several projects funded by the National Science Foundation (NSF, 2010) in the USA. Prestigious institutions and companies are heavily interested towards the design and development of efficient real-time security solutions for large-scale cloud environments. As reported in the strategic plan for the federal cyber-security research and development program by the US National Science and Technology Council (NSTC) a top priority objective is the development of cyber defense mechanisms that may adequately predict and further remediate any threat seen on the national cyber grid in the USA (NSTC, 2011).

Hence, there have been a number of frontier collaborative projects between US academic institutions and industrial partners under the umbrella of a total of 20 US million dollars. Thus, in alignment with the objectives established by the strategic plan of NSTC the collaborative frontier project related with Trustworthy CyberSystems for Health and Wellness (National Science Foundation, 2013) consists of a number of research institutions (e.g. Dartmouth College, John Hopkins University, University of Illinois at Urbana-Champaign) and is particularly investigating techniques that could sufficiently detect anomalous events (e.g. malware) that could manifest in mobile cloud environments that constitute the basis for a number of e-health systems. In parallel, the ongoing activities within another NSF-funded frontier project targets to re-visit the requirements behind the development of secure mechanisms in cloud computing. Hence, a number of institutions including the Stony brook University at New York, the North Carolina State University and Duke University have been allocated with the task at examining and proposing advanced techniques for anomalous incident detection, user and software authentication and secure data transportation. Furthermore, the joint NSF and CISCO-funded NEBULA project (2010) includes a multi-disciplinary team composed by prestigious institutions such as the Massachusetts Institute of Technology (MIT), Cornell University, Stanford University, Princeton University, the University of Texas, Purdue University and the University of California at Berkley in order to address current and future threats in utility cloud environments. In more detail, the consortium addresses the aspects of confidentiality, integrity and availability in such cloud sceneries via a systems approach under their developed NEBULA architecture. An extremely important element within the NEBULA future Internet architecture is considered to be the domain of anomaly detection since it has already proven to be utilized for a number of tasks ranging from cloud resilience, fault tolerance up to cloud resource management.

As shown above, the notion of anomaly detection is widely considered under several cloud-specific scenarios and is used to target issues related with the overall domain of cloud resource management. By virtue of the fact that anomaly detection methodologies depend on generic statistical formulations they hold the advantage at being flexible and adaptive on several problems. Thus, it is highly anticipated that statistical anomaly detection methods would evolve as foundational and possible native solutions in future cloud deployments.

CONCLUSION

Up to a great scale, cloud computing has already grasped and confronted the demanding needs derived by always-on, mission-critical or everyday services offered by a number of systems. IT and unified ICT networked infrastructures opt to outsource their computational tasks on cloud solutions that are proven to be cost effective, extremely optimal on hosting a number of services as well as tremendously efficient at conducting large-scale data processing tasks. Therefore the cloud is considered as a vital element within modern socio-economical ICT environments thus its optimal operation as allowed by adequate management and maintenance mechanisms is paramount. Nevertheless, the increased scalability, transparency and elasticity of services and resources as achieved by the computational and operational properties embodied within the cloud computing paradigm have consequently led to several issues with respect to security, fault diagnosis and the overall domain of cloud management. Hence, in recent years, there has been an emerging trend from both and industry and academia towards the design and development of cloud management schemes that assess the aforementioned issues.

Anomaly detection is a domain derived by data mining and statistics and as already mentioned in earlier sections it has seen a great level of success on several disciplines ranging to health informatics up to image recognition. Thus, it has naturally evolved as an important building block within several cloud management strategies and many formulations have been adjusted for cloud-specific scenarios. In contrast with rule and signature-based fault analysis or intrusion detection schemes, anomaly-based detection mechanisms tend to provide a much more holistic viewpoint with respect to the normal operation of a given network, system or infrastructure in order to become capable at observing deviations from a normal pattern. The intuition behind such schemes is not restricted at already known patterns but they rather center on a statistical baseline that apart from detecting known anomalous it also enables the identification of new types of faults or attacks. Hence, these kind of formulations do not only cover the aspect of cloud security at detecting anomalous patterns caused by malicious intent (e.g. malware, DDoS) but they also address the discovery of events that compose anomalous system of network-wise properties that could have been caused by legitimate events (e.g. Flash Crowds) or human errors (e.g. router, switch, hypervisor misconfiguration).

Therefore, in this chapter we have initially aimed to re-visit several studies that managed to design, deploy and assess the performance of anomaly detection techniques in cloud-specific scenarios. Via a thorough and detailed description of seminal pieces of work, this chapter highlighted the contributions of anomaly detection techniques as applied in all the abstraction layers that consist cloud environments ranging from system, hardware and network-oriented issues up to application-specific problems. Through the designated literature review section, it was feasible to pinpoint the properties derived by *parametric* and *non-parametric* techniques and emphasize on the resulted outcomes produced by each approach. By assessing the conclusive experimental outputs on each of the selected studies we argued in fair of the effectiveness and high detection accuracy performance obtained by each proposed technique and further elaborated on their usefulness on a number of threats or faults that are likely to occur in a cloud scenery. The conducted investigation on each of the introduced experimentations have allowed to empower the argument regarding the applicability of anomaly-based techniques on the adequate identification and detection of not only security-related threats but also on the efficient profiling of anomalies that could directly affect the overall operation and resilience of cloud-based infrastructures.

In order to enlighten the reader on how an anomaly detection technique is instrumented within a cloud scenario, this chapter has also provided a novel anomaly detection scheme that explicitly addressed the detection of the Kelihos malware which is considered to be an emerging threat to cloud environments since it acts as the first point of initiation for several large-scale attacks (e.g. DDoS, phishing, email spam). The proposed offline and non-parametric scheme holds a high dependency on the Noise-Assisted-Data-Analysis (NADA) data-driven Ensemble-Empirical Mode Decomposition (E-EMD) algorithm that enabled the statistical profiling of the aggregated Virtual Machines (VMs) measurements gathered at the hypervisor level of a given physical node. In particular, the presented experimentation was conducted within a controlled experimental testbed and aimed to assess the detection of malware under the scenario of Virtual Machine (VM) "live" migration that is regarded as a core resource management process within any cloud environment. The evaluation of the E-EMD-based malware detection scheme revealed an accuracy of over 95% at detecting the Kelihos malware by using system and network-based features that were captured on the hypervisor level, thus highlighting the efficiency of the introduced technique.

This chapter has also managed to illustrate the importance of anomaly detection schemes in future resource management strategies by discussing on the research agenda from a number of research institutions and organizations. In particular it was briefly emphasized that the design and proposition of new cloud-specific anomaly detection components are currently placed as a top priority within many European Union (EU) and National Science Foundation (NSF) funded research projects. Hence, anomaly detection in the cloud is regarded as a crucial component by many organizations and it is already under investigation for future cloud-based deployments.

Overall, we argue that the content described herein can provide the basic means towards the comprehension of the complexity invoked behind the design and deployment of anomaly detection schemes in cloud environments. Given the thorough background literature review we targeted at a holistic overview of the trends that underpin the development of such schemes and in parallel aimed to describe some core requirements that need to be considered. Moreover, we emphasized upon the intrinsic properties of the cloud and demonstrated how such properties were included within cloud-specific anomaly detection schemes. At the same time, the exemplar E-EMD-based malware detection case study allowed the insightful view with respect to the development, instrumentation and evaluation of an anomaly detection technique. In conjunction with the discussion regarding the importance of anomaly detection as seen by several EU and NSF cloud research projects, this chapter has managed to empower the argument in favor of cloud resource management schemes that should be designed with an underlying dependency on anomaly detection methodologies.

REFERENCES

Altman, N. S. (1992). An introduction to kernel and nearest-neighbor nonparametric regression. *The American Statistician*, *46*(3), 175–185.

Amazon EC2. (2006). Retrieved July 27, 2014, from http://aws.amazon.com/ec2/

Atzori, L., Iera, A., & Morabito, G. (2010). The internet of things: A survey. *Computer Networks*, *54*(15), 2787-2805.

Barford, P., Kline, J., Plonka, D., & Ron, A. (2002), A signal analysis of network traffic anomalies. In *Proceedings of the 2nd ACM SIGCOMM Workshop on Internet Measurment* (IMW '02). ACM. doi:10.1145/637201.637210

Bhaduri, K., Das, K., & Matthews, B. L. (2011). Detecting abnormal machine characteristics in cloud infrastructures. In *Proceedings of Data Mining Workshops (ICDMW)* (pp. 137-144). ICDMW.

Bureau, P. (2011). Same botnet, same guys, new code. In *Proceedings of Virus Bulletin*. VB.

Chandola, V., Banerjee, A., & Kumar, V. (2009, July). Anomaly detection: A survey. *ACM Computing Surveys*, *41*(3), 15. doi:10.1145/1541880.1541882

Chen, Y., Paxson, V., & Katz, R. (2010). What's new about cloud computing security. Technical Report. EECS Department, University of California, Berkeley.

Chengwei, W., Talwar, V., Schwan, K., & Ranganathan, P. (2010), Online detection of utility cloud anomalies using metric distributions. In *Proceedings of Network Operations and Management Symposium (NOMS)* (pp. 96-103). IEEE.

Chengwei, W., Viswanathan, K., Choudur, L., Talwar, V., Satterfield, W., & Schwan, K. (2011). Statistical techniques for online anomaly detection in data centers. In *Proceedings of Integrated Network Management (IM)* (pp. 385-392). Academic Press.

Christodorescu, M., Sailer, R., Schales, D. L., Sgandurra, D., & Zamboni, D. (2009). Cloud security is not (just) virtualization security: A short paper. In *Proceedings of the 2009 ACM Workshop on Cloud Computing Security* (CCSW '09). ACM. doi:10.1145/1655008.1655022

Cohen, L. (1989), Time-frequency distributions-A review, *Proceedings of the IEEE*, 77(7), 941-981. doi:10.1109/5.30749

Dean, J., & Ghemawat, S. (2008, January). MapReduce: Simplified data processing on large clusters. *Communications of the ACM*, *51*(1), 1. doi:10.1145/1327452.1327492

Doelitzscher, F., Knahl, M., Reich, C., & Clarke, N. (2013). Anomaly detection in IaaS clouds. In *Proceedings of Cloud Computing Technology and Science (CloudCom)* (vol. 1, pp. 387-394). Academic Press.

ENISA. (2012). *Report on resilience in critical cloud computing*. Retrieved July 27, 2014, from https://resilience.enisa.europa.eu/cloud-security-and-resilience/publications/critical-cloud-computing

EU FP7 ANIKETOS. (2012). Retrieved July 27, 2014, from http://www.aniketos.eu/

EU FP7 NEMESYS. (2012). Retrieved July 27, 2014, from http://www.nemesys-project.eu//

EU SECCRIT. (2011). Retrieved July 27, 2014, from https://www.seccrit.eu/

Fawcelt, T. (2006). An introduction to ROC analysis. *Pattern Recognition Letters*, *27*(8), 861–874. doi:10.1016/j.patrec.2005.10.010

Fontugne, R., Tremblay, N., Borgnat, P., Flandrin, P., & Esaki, H., (2013). Mining anomalous electricity consumption using ensemble empirical mode decomposition. In *Proceedings of IEEE ICASSP*. IEEE.

Ganglia. (2000). *The Ganglia monitoring system*. Retrieved July 27, 2014, from http://ganglia.sourceforge.net/

Garnaeva, M. (2012). Kelihos/Hlux botnet returns with new techniques. *Securelist*. Retrieved July 27, 2014, from, http://www.securelist.com/en/blog/655/Kelihos_Hlux_botnet_returns_with_new_techniques

Gençay, R., Selçuk, F., & Whitcher, B. (2001). An introduction to wavelets and other filtering methods in finance and economics. Academic Press.

Google App Engine. (2008). Retrieved July 27, 2014, from http://cloud.google.com/products/app-engine/

Gruschka, N., & Jensen, M. (2010). Attack surfaces: A taxonomy for attacks on cloud services. In *Proceedings of Cloud Computing (CLOUD)*. IEEE.

Guan, Q., Fu, S., DeBardeleben, N., & Blanchard, S. (2013). Exploring time and frequency domains for accurate and automated anomaly detection in cloud computing systems. In *Proceedings of Dependable Computing (PRDC)*. IEEE.

HORIZON2020. (2014). The EU framework program for research and innovation. *HORIZON, 2020*. Retrieved from http://ec.europa.eu/programmes/en

Huang, N. E., & Attoh-Okine, N. O. (2005). *The Hilbert-Huang transform in engineering*. CRC Taylor & Francis.

IU-ATC Project. (2008). Retrieved July 27, 2014, from http://www.iu-atc.com

Kai, W., Ying, W., & Bo, Y. (2012), A density-based anomaly detection method for MapReduce. In *Proceedings of Network Computing and Applications (NCA)*. IEEE.

Kreyszig, E. (1979). *Applied mathematics* (4th ed.). Wiley Press.

Lakhina, A., Crovella, M., & Diot, C. (2004, August). Diagnosing network-wide traffic anomalies. *Computer Communication Review*, *34*(4), 219–230. doi:10.1145/1030194.1015492

Lévy-Leduc, C., & Roueff, F. (2009). Detection and localization of change-points in high-dimensional network traffic data. *The Annals of Applied Statistics*, 3. Retrieved July 27, 2014, from http://code.google.com/p/vmitools/wiki/LibVMIIntroduction

Marnerides, A. K., Pezaros, D. P., Kim, H., & Hutchison, D. (2013). Internet traffic classification under energy time-frequency distributions. In *Proceedings of IEEE International Conference on Communications*. Budapest, Hungary: IEEE.

Marnerides, A. K., Watson, M., Shirazi, N., Mauthe, A., & Hutchison, D. (2013). Malware analysis in cloud computing: Network and system characteristics. In Proceedings of IEEE GLOBECOM CCSNA Workshop 2013. IEEE.

Mi, H., Wang, H., Yin, G., Cai, H., Zhou, Q., Sun, T., & Zhou, Y. (2011). Magnifier: Online detection of performance problems in large-scale cloud computing systems. In *Proceedings of Services Computing (SCC)*. IEEE.

NEBULA Project. (2010). *The NEBULA Project*. Retrieved July, 27, 2014, from http://nebula-fia.org/index.html

NSF. (2010). *National science foundation research project awards*. Retrieved July 27, 2014, from http://www.gov/mobile/news/news_summ.jsp?cntn_id=128679&org=NSF&from=news

NSTC. (2011). *Executive Office of the President, trustworthy CyberSpace: Strategic plan for the federal CyberSecurity research and development program*. National Science and Technology Council. Retrieved July 27, 2014, from http://www.whitehouse.gov/sites/default/files/microsites/ostp/fed_cybersecurity_rd_strategic_plan_2011.pdf

Pannu, H. S., Jianguo, L., & Song, F. (2012). AAD: Adaptive anomaly detection system for cloud computing infrastructures. In *Proceedings of Reliable Distributed Systems (SRDS)* (pp. 396-397). IEEE.

Parwekar, P. (2011). From internet of things towards cloud of things. In *Proceedings of Computer and Communication Technology (ICCCT)* (pp. 329-333). ICCCT.

Qiang, G., & Song, F. (2013). Adaptive anomaly identification by exploring metric subspace in cloud computing infrastructures. In *Proceedings of Reliable Distributed Systems (SRDS)* (pp. 205-214). Academic Press.

Ristenpart, T., Tromer, E., Shacham, H., & Savage, S. (2009), Hey, you, get off of my cloud: exploring information leakage in third-party compute clouds. In *Proceedings of the 16th ACM Conference on Computer and Communications Security* (CCS '09). ACM. doi:10.1145/1653662.1653687

Shannon, C. E. (1948). A mathematical theory of communication. *Mobile Computing and Communications Review, 5*(1), 3–55.

Shirazi, N., Watson, M. R., Marnerides, A., K., Mauthe, A., & Hutchison, D. (2013). A multilevel approach towards challenge detection in cloud computing. In *Cyberpatterns*. Academic Press.

Smith, D., Qiang, G., & Song, F. (2010). An anomaly detection framework for autonomic management of compute cloud systems. In *Proceedings of Computer Software and Applications Conference Workshops (COMPSACW)* (pp. 376-381). Academic Press.

Snort AD. (2005). Retrieved July 27, 2014, from http://anomalydetection.info/

Song, D. X., Wagner, D., & Tian, X. (2001). Timing analysis of keystrokes and timing attacks on SSH. In *Proceedings of the 10th conference on USENIX Security Symposium* (SSYM'01) (*Vol. 10*). USENIX Association.

Tcpdump. (1987). Retrieved July, 27, 2014, from http://www.tcpdump.org/

Torres, M.E., Colominas, M.A., Schlotthauer, G., & Flandrin, P. (2011). A complete ensemble empirical mode decomposition with adaptive noise. In *Proceedings of IEEE ICASSP*. IEEE.

Vallis, O., Hochenbaum, J., & Kejariwal, A. (2014). A novel technique for long-term anomaly detection in the cloud. In *Proceedings of the 6th USENIX Workshop on Hot Topics in Cloud Computing*. USENIX HotCloud.

Viswanathan, K., Choudur, L., Talwar, V., Chengwei, W., Macdonald, G., & Satterfield, W. (2012). Ranking anomalies in data centers. In *Proceedings of Network Operations and Management Symposium (NOMS), 2012 IEEE* (pp. 79-87). IEEE. doi:10.1109/NOMS.2012.6211885

VMWare vSphrere. (2012). Retrieved July 27, 2014, from http://www.vmware.com/uk/products/vsphere

Volatility. (2011). Retrieved July 27, 2014, from https://www.volatilesystems.com/default/volatility

Watson, M., Shirazi, N., Marnerides, A. K., Mauthe, A., & Hutchison, D. (2013). Towards a distributed, self-organizing approach to malware detection in cloud computing. In *Proceedings of 7th IFIP International Workshop on Self-Organizing Systems*. IFIP/IFISC IWSOS.

Wu, Z., & Huang, N. E. (2009). Ensemble empirical mode decomposition: A noise-assisted data analysis method. Advances in Adaptive Data Analysis, 1(1), 1-41.

Xen. (2003). *Citrix Systems, Inc*. Retrieved July 27, 2014, from http://www.xen.org/

Zhang, Y., Ge, Z., Greenberg, A., & Roughan, M. (2005), Network anomography. In *Proceedings of the 5th ACM SIGCOMM Conference on Internet Measurement* (IMC '05). USENIX Association.

KEY TERMS AND DEFINITIONS

Anomaly Detection: Detection of anomalous patterns in datasets using statistical techniques.

Cloud Networks: Networks in charge for the delivery of hosted services over the Internet to end-users.

Cloud Resilience: The ability of a cloud network or cloud-based infrastructure to maintain an acceptable level of service in the face of various challenges to its normal operation.

Cloud Security: A sub-domain of cloud resilience in charge of ensuring the secure transmission of data within a network and at the same time responsible for the detection and defense of the cloud environment from any malicious attacks.

Empirical Mode Decomposition: A signal processing technique that allows the decomposition of a given signal into different modes.

Malware Detection: Detection approaches that explicitly aim at detecting malware instances.

Virtual Machine Live Migration: The process where a running Virtual Machine is moved from one physical host to another.

ENDNOTES

1. By virtue of the large number of mathematical principles invoked in every reported work we do not provide the formulations employed in each study but rather direct an interested reader to the corresponding bibliography.
2. Several vendors may also mention SaaS under the acronyms of Platform as a Service (PaaS) or Infrastructure as a Service (IaaS) according to their products. However, for the purposes of this chapter we will only refer to SaaS as the definition for all the services offered by a given cloud to the end-user.
3. Recall accuracy is denoted as the rate of the number of successful detections over the number of total anomalies. The FPR is defined as the ratio of the number of false alarms over the total number of alarms.
4. Sensitivity or True Positive Rate (TPR) is defined as the rate of True Positives (TPs) over the sum of True Positives (TPs) with False Negatives (FNs).
5. The precision metric is defined as the ratio of True Positives (TP) over the sum of True Positives (TPs) with False Positives (FPs). The F-measure metric is also known as the F1 score and is defined as the harmonic mean of precision and sensitivity. For detailed formulations we refer any interested reader to Fawcelt (2006).
6. The analysis described in this chapter was carried out by using the cubic spline interpolation approach.
7. In our case the ϑ parameter worked well when equal to 2.
8. We remind the reader, that the hypervisor snapshot is denoted by the sum of measurements gathered by all the running VMs on a given physical node.
9. A ROC curve is a plot that demonstrates the evolvement of the detections' true-positive rate (TPR) against false-positive rate (FPR) where points towards the bottom left correspond to high thresholds (or low sensitivity) and those on the top right to low thresholds (or high sensitivity). The best performance is indicated by curves that reside on the top left, as these imply that sensitivity may be decreased and eliminate more False Positives (FPs) without degrading the TPR (Fawcelt, 2006).

Section 2
Mobile Cloud Resource Management

This section examines the various types of resource management techniques that are available for the mobile clouds, such as resource offloading, mobile cloud infrastructure and mobile device power control, control theory, data mining, machine learning, radio spectrum management, and mobile cloud computing economic-oriented mechanisms. It also elaborates on issues related to the social-oriented context of the mobile cloud computing environments to support optimal energy conservation of the mobile devices. Finally, it elaborates on traffic analysis and measurement issues in emerging mobile computing systems.

Chapter 4
Mobile Cloud Resource Management

Konstantinos Katzis
European University Cyprus, Cyprus

ABSTRACT

Providing mobile cloud services requires seamless integration between various platforms to offer mobile users optimum performance. To achieve this, many fundamental problems such as bandwidth availability and reliability, resource scarceness, and finite energy must be addressed before rolling out such services. This chapter aims to explore technological challenges for mobile cloud computing in the area of resource management focusing on both parts of the infrastructure: mobile devices and cloud networks. Starting with introducing mobile cloud computing, it then stresses the importance of resource management in the operation of mobile cloud services presenting various types of resources available for cloud computing. Furthermore, it examines the various types of resource management techniques available for mobile clouds. Finally, future directions in the field of resource management for mobile cloud computing environment are presented.

INTRODUCTION

Mobile devices such as tablets, phablets, smartphones etc. are increasingly becoming an essential part of our daily life as the most effective and convenient tool regarding communication, work, general knowledge access, maps, diary, health monitor, etc. The explosion in numbers of such devices increased mobile broadband coverage and as a result the need for always-on collaborative services. Microsoft CEO Satya Nadella stated in his keynote speech at Worldwide Partner Conference 2014 in Washington DC on the 16th of July 2014 that there is a "tremendous opportunity" with mobile and cloud solutions and that Microsoft is focused on defining the "next-generation of productivity" (Nadella, 2014). He also stated that there are going to be more than 3 billion people with connected devices on top of 200 billion sensors all of which will generate tons and tons of zettabytes of data and they are going to consume and reason over the large data. It is true that there has been significant advances in cloud computing and mobile technologies both changing our lives, the way we do business and the way we communicate and this is

DOI: 10.4018/978-1-4666-8225-2.ch004

primarily because of the rapid scalability of cloud services, the ubiquitous network access, on-demand self-service etc. Mobile users experience on a daily basis various mobile cloud services, which either run on their devices and / or remote servers with both data storage and data processing happening outside their mobile device. However, this experience is highly dependent on how cloud-resources are managed.

A cloud-computing infrastructure as described by Pallis (2010), is a complex system that is constantly evolving, consisted of numerous devices (infrastructure, platforms and software) with a great deal of requirements, aiming towards the evolution and convergence of several independent computing trends such as internet delivery, distributed computing, storage, content outsourcing, security etc. Cloud computing is based on a large number of shared resources that are subject to spatial and temporal based varying resource requests. The nature of resource requests varies thus making resource management a complex task. Resource management can play a decisive role in optimizing the performance of such a complex system by efficiently and fairly managing performance, functionality and cost. Inefficient resource management can result in negatively affecting the performance and cost while it may also impair system functionality. Due to its complexity and inhomogeneity in the type of services it offers, cloud resource management requires complex policies and decisions to fulfil a multi-objective optimization. This is extremely challenging because of the vast scale of the system, which makes it impossible to have accurate global state information that are not subjected to unpredictable interactions. According to Marinescu (2013), the main strategies for cloud resource management are associated with the three types of cloud delivery models. These are: Infrastructure as a Service (IaaS), Platform as a Service (PaaS) and Software as a Service (SaaS). In all cases, the cloud services providers are faced with large, fluctuating loads that sometimes are unable to serve.

Cloud Computing envisages that future computer applications and services are constructed, delivered and managed in a much different way than what we are used to so far. Cloud Computing aims to move computing and data away from the common desktop and portable computers to allow the use of smaller, more portable and less power demanding devices. According to Dikaiakos et al. (2009), there are two different architectural models being identified. The first one is designed to scale out by providing additional computing instances for supplying SaaS and PaaS services and the second is designed to provide data and compute-intensive applications via scaling capacity. Setting the physical layout of a cloud infrastructure can vary significantly since there isn't a specific recipe to be followed. More specifically, a cloud can be restricted to single organization or a group as a private cloud or it can be available to the general public as a public cloud or something in-between as a hybrid cloud. In essence, any type of cloud is comprised of three basic elements. The processing, network and storage element each of which defines the level of quality of service required by the customers. This is presented by Dikaiakos et al. (2009) and illustrated in Figure 1 as a cloud architecture consisted of 3 layers. Starting from bottom up first comes the infrastructure, which involves storage and computing capabilities. Second comes the platform layer that provides the means for developing, testing, deploying, hosting and maintaining applications in an integrated environment that is the cloud. The application layer is the last one, which aims to offer a complete application as a service.

Performance in cloud computing is subject to how well the hardware and software are integrated and managed. Current trends show that computer architecture is shifting towards multiple core processors to address the increasing levels of parallelism whereas software is constantly redesigned by academia and industry for parallel and data-intensive computing. A generalized version of cloud computing architecture is illustrated in Figure 2 where a "cloud" of computing and data centers are interconnected to form a virtual single seamless platform. This platform is consisted of numerous computers employ-

Figure 1. Basic example of cloud computing architecture

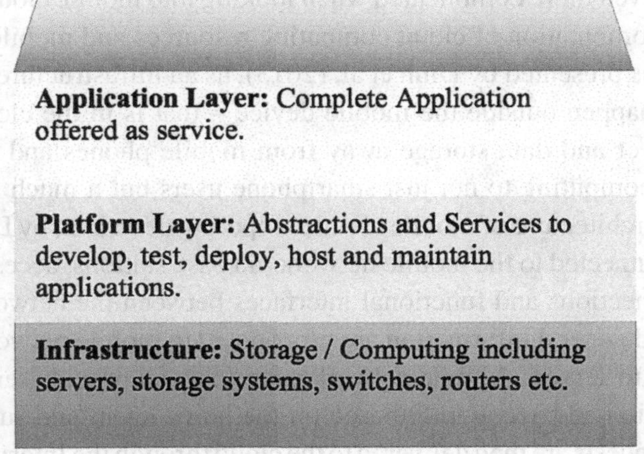

ing multi-core processing capabilities along with multiple data-centers all dispersed around different geographical areas. A user can make use of these resources based on the service level agreement signed with the provider. The service level agreement (SLA) specifies the bandwidth, computing power and memory required to maintain a certain level of quality of service. The challenging part here is the process of managing all resources in order to fulfill the minimum requirements stated in the service level agreement achieving maximum revenue for the provider. This can be achieved by employing novel, power-efficient resource schemes.

Application Layer: Complete Application offered as service.
Platform Layer: Abstractions and Services to develop, test, deploy, host and maintain applications.
Infrastructure: Storage / Computing including servers, storage systems, switches, routers etc.

Significant advances have been recorded by the High Performance Computing and Grid Computing communities presented in (Foster & Kesselman, 1997), (Foster & Kesselman, 1998), (D. Gannon, 2002) and (Berman, Fox, & Hey, 2003) towards the establishment of resource provisioning standards. Nevertheless, this process still remains somewhat open for a user with complex resource requirements.

Figure 2. A cloud of processing centers and data centers

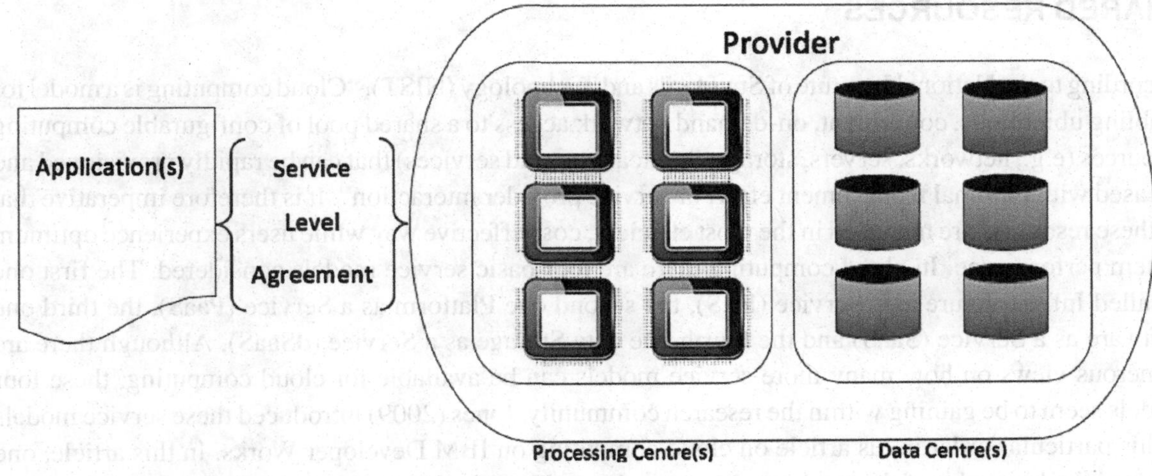

Further to the complex resource management techniques required for delivering clouds services based on SLAs, things become even more complicated when looking into mobile cloud services. Mobile cloud computing is in effect a combination of cloud computing resources and mobile network infrastructure. Mobile cloud computing is presented by Dinh et al. (2013), as an infrastructure where both data storage and the data processing happen outside the mobile device – that is in the cloud. Mobile applications move the computing power and data storage away from mobile phones and into the cloud, bringing applications and mobile computing to not just smartphone users but a much broader range of mobile subscribers. The general architecture of mobile cloud computing described by Dinh et al. (2013) dictates that mobile devices are connected to the mobile network via base stations, access points or satellites that establish and control connections and functional interfaces between the networks and mobile devices. Mobile users' requests and general information are propagated to mobile network services through central processors connected to servers. Mobile network operators can provide services to mobile users as authentication, authorization and accounting based on the home agent and subscribers' data stored in databases. Subscribers' requests are then delivered to the cloud through the Internet for further processing. Cloud controllers process the requests to provide mobile users with the corresponding cloud services.

Providing mobile cloud services can be a difficult task as it comes with many problems such as resource scarceness, finite energy and low connectivity as outlined by Satyanarayanan (1996) preventing users from executing many useful programs. Tim O'Reilly, the founder of O'Reilly media, a publisher of technology books who devised the term "Web 2.0", stated that 'the future belongs to services that respond in real time to information provided either by their users or by nonhuman sensors' (The Economist, 2008). Real time applications demand high levels of responsiveness and as a result intensive computing resources from mobile devices. Such applications can be image processing for video games, speech synthesis, natural language processing, augmented reality, wearable computing etc. All these applications demand high computational capacities and power thus limiting developers when implementing applications for mobile phones. Considering the trends in mobile phone architecture and battery, it is unlikely that these problems will be solved in the near future. This is a barrier that needs to be addressed in order to realize the full potential of mobile computing and this can be achieved through efficient mobile cloud computing resource management.

SHARED RESOURCES

According to the National Institute of Standards and Technology (NIST), "Cloud computing is a model for enabling ubiquitous, convenient, on-demand network access to a shared pool of configurable computing resources (e.g., networks, servers, storage, applications, and services) that can be rapidly provisioned and released with minimal management effort or service provider interaction". It is therefore imperative that all these resources are managed in the most efficient, cost-effective way while users experience optimum system performance. In cloud computing there are four basic service models considered. The first one is called Infrastructure as a Service (IaaS), the second one Platform as a Service (PaaS), the third one Software as a Service (SaaS) and the fourth one data Storage as a Service (dSaaS). Although there are numerous views on how many more service models can be available for cloud computing, these four models seem to be gaining within the research community. Jones (2009) introduced these service models in this particular order in his article on cloud computing on IBM Developer Works. In this article, one can find the hierarchy of the models with examples as illustrated in Table 1.

Table 1. A hierarch of cloud offering (Jones, 2009)

Abbreviation	Service Models	Examples
SaaS	Software-as-a-Service	Google Apps, Microsoft "Software+Services"
PaaS	Platform-as-a-Service	IBM IT Factory, Google AppEngine, Force. com
IaaS	Infrastructure-as-a-Service	Amazon EC2, IBM Blue Cloud, Sun Grid
dSaaS	Data-Storage-as-a-Service	Nirvanix SDN, Amazon S3, Cleversafe dsNet

In this subsection, the first three models are described (SaaS, PaaS and IaaS) in order to give the reader some basic insight on the architecture of the cloud computing service models. Based on these descriptions, the rest of the chapter will then analyze the resource management mechanisms that are currently used in mobile cloud networks in order to achieve the required levels of user experience and overall optimum system performance.

Infrastructure as a Service (IaaS)

Infrastructure as a Service (IaaS) type of systems are described in (Nurmi et al., 2009) as systems that give users the ability to run and control entire virtual machine instances deployed across a variety of physical resources. Furthermore, (P. Mell & T. Grance, 2011) describe IaaS as a model that provides the consumer with the capability to provision processing, storage, networks, and other fundamental computing resources. The consumer in this case is able to deploy and run arbitrary software, which can include operating systems and applications. Although he/she is not in a position to manage or control the underlying cloud infrastructure, control is given over operating systems, storage, and deployed applications; and possibly limited control of select networking components.

Among all types of cloud services, it is IaaS that essentially represents cloud computing (Harris, 2012). In EUCALYPTUS project (Nurmi et al., 2009), computational and storage infrastructure commonly available to academic research groups has been employed to provide a platform that is modular and open to experimental instrumentation and study. This is in order to address major unanswered questions such as what is the right distributed architecture for a cloud computing system and what resource characteristics must virtual machine instance schedulers consider to make most efficient use of the resources? Furthermore, how can anyone construct virtual machine instance networks that are well-performing, and secure? In the case of (Nurmi et al., 2009), the underlying virtualized resources are managed through the cloud controller, a collection of web services. The function of the cloud controller proposed is focused on resource services, data services and interface services. In the case of resource services, users are able to manipulate properties of the virtual machines and networks while monitoring both system components and virtual resources. In the case of data services, the function here is to manage persistent user and system data. For interface services, user-visible interfaces are devised to handle authentication and protocol translation, and expose system management tools provided. There are numerous examples of IaaS cloud computing systems that provide an interface which enables dynamically provision of entire virtual machines such as Amazon EC2, Enomaly, and others that can be found in (Amazon Web Service, 2014), (Enomaly, 2014), (Keahey, Foster, Freeman, Zhang, 2005), (Chase, Irwin, Grit, Moor & Sprenkle, 2003) and (McNett, Gupta, Vahdat & Voelker, 2007).

Flexible customizability of IaaS clouds has made them an attractive solution to the problem of dynamically extending resources of a static site to adjust to changes in demand. This advantage has also become a great challenge for researchers in managing all available resources as well as expanding them in an efficient and practical way. Marshall, Healy and Freeman (2010) have looked into this matter and proposed elastically extending sites that efficiently adapt services within a site, such as batch schedulers, storage archives, or web services to leverage elastically provisioned IaaS cloud resources in response to changes in demand. Such services are carefully selected by considering various technical, logistical, and economic differences between cloud providers. Their implementation seamlessly and securely extends Torque clusters with Nimbus-based clouds and Amazon EC2 on demand by introducing three policies: on demand, steady stream, and bursts to respond intelligently to changes in demand by acquiring or terminating cloud resources.

Given the numerous and diverse examples of IaaS Cloud computing that are currently available, there is a major challenge to evaluate their performance in a fair way. This is primarily due to the nature of cloud infrastructures and services offered with different terminologies, definitions, and goals (Prodan & Ostermann, 2009). To overcome this problem, a novel taxonomy is proposed by Li (2014) to help profile and clarify the nature of IaaS services performance evaluation. Based on this, a three-layer conceptual model has been built to generalize the existing performance evaluation practices. The paper collected and arranged elements of IaaS services performance evaluation into a novel taxonomy, which is constructed based on performance feature and experiment. The Performance Feature dimension looks into the existing IaaS service features to be evaluated. These are transaction speed, availability, latency, reliability, data throughput, scalability, variability, storage, memory (cache), computation and communication. The Experiment dimension covers the potential scenes for setting up evaluation experiments. These range based on the different types of Cloud Services and their Provider(s) as well as the nature of the experiments such as repeating an experiment for a period of time or for a number of times, testing sequential or concurrent work or trying out different providers with the same amount of workload.

Platform as a Service (PaaS)

PaaS is another type of Cloud computing services where users create applications using any tools available from the cloud platform. According to (Mell & Grance, 2011), the user has the power to deploy onto the cloud infrastructure user-created or acquired applications created using programming languages, libraries, services, and tools supported by the provider. Traditionally typical complex issues such as distributed resource management are not an issue anymore when writing programs on a PaaS platform since the user does not manage or control the underlying cloud resources including network, servers, operating systems, or storage. Control is mainly allocated to the user over the deployed applications and possibly configuration settings for the application-hosting environment. From the user's point of view, resources can be divided into computing units and storage capability. Nevertheless, the platform somehow must organize its distributed resources and provide a relatively stable selection of resources for the users. This can be achieved through resource aggregation.

Resource aggregation is one of the central parts of a PaaS platform and one of its important requirements is scalability. Employing scalability gives the system the flexibility to increase its total throughput under an increased load when resources are added. The resource aggregation service must be able to identify and aggregate any available resources and deliver them to the users. One way of achieving resource aggregation is through virtualization (Neiger et al., 2005). In a virtualized system, there is a layer between physical machine and operating system, which its purpose is to manage accesses to the underlying physical host platform's resources. A virtual machine can be regarded as a single unit for a user. However, virtualization is not always the best solution as it focuses on sharing a physical powerful machine, but it is not capable of aggregating less powerful available resources into a single powerful machine. In order to run distributed programs over many virtual machines, an additional layer must be introduced to manage resources between virtual machines and applications. This introduces more complexity for programmers.

Another method for providing resource aggregation service is by developing a working unit according to specific applications. It is implemented in process/thread level, and provides basic services such as a communication interface, dynamic-monitor, process-scheduler etc. This working unit executes the program that has been designed for. Typical examples include Google App Engine (Zahariev, 2009), Hadoop (White, 2009), Dryad (Isard, Budium, Yu, Birell & Fetterly, 2007), etc. The disadvantage of a working unit, is that it is usually implemented in a specific system and so it does not consist a general approach. Another way of providing resource aggregation is through a scalable multi-user resource aggregation service of an Erlang/OTP PaaS platform (Zhan, Kang, Liu & Cao, 2013). Here, a logical structure in which, a set of distributed autonomous virtual computing nodes are provided for every user and can be changed at runtime. These sets of nodes are isolated from each other so as to avoid the possible conflict between different users. On top of these nodes, a manager is introduced and it is responsible for controlling tasks and monitor system runtime information such as providing a consistent view about system resources for users.

Software as a Service (SaaS)

According to Mell and Grance (2011), SaaS can be considered as a model that enables consumers to use the provider's applications running on a cloud infrastructure. Accessibility is provided from various client devices through either a thin client interface, such as a web browser, or a program interface. In SaaS, consumer does not manage or control the underlying cloud infrastructure including network, servers, operating systems, storage, or even individual application capabilities. SaaS can help organizations avoid capital expenditure and run their business without worrying about support services such as IT infrastructure management, software maintenance etc. Nevertheless, an organization who has heavily invested on SaaS services can be "hostage" of the provider since its productivity depends entirely on web-based applications. Currently there are several vendors offering SaaS based products and organizations must plan wisely on what sort of features and services to choose from. This means that prioritization of requirements is required which involves deciding the weights of parameters. Godse and Mulik (2009) propose a widely accepted expert driven analytical hierarchy process approach to deal addressing this problem. The proposed selection process involves calculation of weights of selection parameters and scores for products. These weights and scores are more rational than subjective opinions usually based on judgment.

RESOURCE MANAGEMENT TECHNIQUES

Cloud computing aims to revolutionize the way IT industry operates by making software even more attractive as a service and redefine how IT hardware is designed and purchased. In order to do this, the new type of infrastructure must be capable of managing its resources in order to address issues such as over-provisioning for a service whose popularity does not meet their predictions, thus wasting costly resources, or under-provisioning for one that becomes wildly popular, thus missing potential customers and revenue (Armbrust et al., 2010). So, one of the most important tasks of the cloud services is resource allocation and management. Resource allocation may vary depending on the type of cloud computing service it is designed for and of course the technology / platform that it is running on. Nevertheless, resource allocation must be able to automatically adapt to dynamic workload changes in a shared virtualized infrastructure to achieve optimum user experience and optimum application performance.

Some of the common tasks presented here regarding resource allocation for mobile cloud computing services are: Resource offloading, Power control, Data Mining mechanisms, Machine Learning, Radio Spectrum Management including spectrum sharing - bandwidth reliability and availability and Resource Management Economics.

Resource Offloading

As mobile devices have limited resources such as battery life, network bandwidth, storage capacity and processor performance, they are sometimes incompetent executing certain tasks. For example, mobile phones are battery powered and environmental sensors have small physical sizes with slow processors and small amounts of storage. All these devices use wireless networks and their bandwidths are significantly lower than wired networks. Offloading is a solution to augment these mobile system's capabilities by migrating computation to the cloud infrastructure (Kumar, Liu, Lu & Bhargava, 2013). A solution which is different from traditional techniques used in multicore systems and grid computing, where a process may be migrated for load balancing. In a mobile cloud computing environment, computation offloading implies that programs are migrated to servers outside of the users' immediate computing environment.

Resource offloading in cloud computing allows employing different techniques to achieve optimum performance for mobile cloud computing services (Dinh, Lee, Niyato & Wang, 2013). The first one is Dynamic provision of resources on a fine-grained, self-service, contract-service basis and it is a flexible way for service providers and mobile users to run their applications without advanced reservation of resources. The second one is scalability where the deployment of mobile applications can be performed and scaled to meet the unpredictable user demands due to flexible resource provisioning. The third one is multi-tenancy where service providers (e.g. network operator and data center owner) can share the resources and costs to support a variety of applications and large number of users. Despite which technique someone employs, resource offloading involves computation offloading and data offloading. Computation offloading techniques may save energy and improve performance on mobile systems. However, this depends on various parameters such as the network bandwidth availability and the amounts of data exchanged through the networks. Many algorithms have been proposed to optimise offloading decisions and this was based on analysing parameters including bandwidth, processing speeds, memory availability, server loads, and the amounts of data exchanged between servers and mobile systems. Techniques developed based on the parameters listed above, include predicting parametric variations in application behavior and execution environment.

One of the critical issues in mobile cloud computing devices is the execution failure due to the lack of processing resources. Mousicou et al. (2013) in their paper proposed employing offloading process through a resource/task migration mechanism to perform cooperative migration of resources thus enabling efficient resource manipulation without any intermittent execution of the claimed tasks by the mobile devices. This significantly reduced crash failures that lead all serves to become unavailable within a rack. The scheme proposed introduces a modular resource migration scheme for failure-aware resource allocation, where according to the estimated performance of the resource sharing process, resources were migrated to another cloud rack. The methodology employed hosted the rack utility maximisation scheme, which considered the availability of resources and the rack utilization degree. Results indicated that during the resource migration process, the proposed scheme offered high successful execution delivery rates.

Since offloading migrates computation to a more resourceful computer, it involves making a decision regarding whether and what computation to migrate. Literature indicates that current research deals with two types of parameters when taking such a decision. The first is based on performance improvement and the second on energy saving. For the first case, offloading becomes an attractive solution for meeting response time requirements on mobile systems as applications become increasingly large and complex. For example an autonomous vehicle would need to recognize an object in time to avoid colliding with it. If the onboard processor is slow, then the computation may be offloaded (Nimmagadda, Kumar, Lu & Lee, 2010). Another application is context aware computing where multiple streams of data from different sources such as maps, accelerometers, temperature sensors, GPS, etc. need to be analyzed together in order to obtain real time information about a user's context. In these cases, mobile systems can offload these tasks to the remote servers with faster computing speed capabilities. For the second case, energy consumption and energy saving is recognized as one of the most critical issues of mobile devices. Anyone who is using a smartphone on a regular basis will know that their battery does not last much longer than 24h. The reason for this is because there are many applications that are too computation-intensive to be performed on a mobile system. Kumar & Y-H Lu (2010) looked at IEEExplore and identified four research categories looking at saving energy and extending battery lifetime. The first one is adopting new techniques for the new generation of semiconductor technology in which transistors are smaller than previously and come in greater numbers. The second category is looking into avoiding wasting energy by entering a whole system or parts of it in standby or sleep modes. The third category investigates the processor's speed that a program is executed and the fourth category looks into performing computation somewhere else, thus the mobile system's battery lifetime can be extended.

Offloading is not always the right option for mobile cloud computing. Nimmagadda et al. (2010) stated in their paper that computational offloading is subject to the difference between the time required for the mobile system to run the program locally and the time required for the mobile system to offload the program to a server plus the time required by the server to run it. If the total time required to offload and run the program on a remote server is less than the case where the code runs locally, then offloading can improve performance. However this is not always the right decision to make if the time required to run the application on the server is far less than the time required for offloading it (bandwidth depended). Mobile devices rely on bandwidth availability to achieve the minimum time required for their offloading and as this is explained later in this chapter, this can be addressed through better management of radio resources. Devices connected to the cloud through wire might not experience this problem at this extend as they enjoy much faster Internet connectivity.

Another driving factor for resource offloading is the limited and expensive storage capacity of mobile devices. Data-offloading enables mobile users to store/ access the large data on the cloud through wireless networks. One example of such a case is Amazon Simple Storage Service (Amazon S3) which supports file storage service. Another example is Flickr and ShoZu that store, process and share images uploaded by users. Further to image related services, another example is Microsoft Office 365 which applications run on a server. Current issues with data offloading from mobile devices can be identified as the costs associate with using mobile data services through mobile network operators (currently 3G, 4G), the technical challenges associated when using free wireless services such as a WiFi access point whilst being on the move and of course the major problem of bandwidth availability. Regarding the costs associated with using wireless mobile networks, the price increases dramatically with the exchange of large amounts of data between the mobile device and the cloud. The concept of unlimited data offered when 3G networks where initially introduced is now over. It is no longer economically feasible for operators to offer unlimited 3G or 4G data plans since the number of smartphone devices increased exponentially over the last 7 years. More specifically, AT&T reported that mobile data consumption increased by a staggering 8000% between 2007 and 2010. This coincides with the release of the first iPhone device and later Google Nexus device, which revolutionized the way people use their mobile phones to communicate. There are different data plans with mobile network operators varying from 1GB to few GBs per month at a substantial price. For example, currently 3 (Three) in UK offers 1GB/month for 3G data services at £7.50/month or 10GB/month at £15 and EE offers 1GB 4G data services at £10/month or 3GB/month at £15. In Cyprus MTN offers a 2GB data plan for €34. The contracts selected here are the cheapest ones available without a smartphone included in the price and for the case of MTN Cyprus, the offer includes unlimited phone calls and text messages in the country. Regarding data offloading for moving smartphones through a Wi-Fi access point is a challenging task due to the limitation of Wi-Fi antennas deployed on existing smartphones and the short contact duration (Ding et al., 2013). Authors in this work show that the number of open-accessible Wi-Fi access points is very limited for smartphones in metropolitan areas, which this significantly affects the offloading opportunities for previous schemes that use only open access points. To address this issues, they propose an energy-aware algorithm for energy-constrained devices to assist the offloading decision by enabling smartphones to select the most energy efficient WiFi access point for offloading. The experimental evaluation of this work indicated that an 80% energy saving can be achieved. In terms of bandwidth availability and data offloading, providers will improve current price rates when there is enough bandwidth to be distributed among the users. The concept of bandwidth availability and sharing as it is explained later in this chapter can be addressed through better management of radio resources.

Cloud Infrastructure and Mobile Devices Power Control

As Cloud computing infrastructure grows, data centers also continue to increase in terms of computing and data handling capacities to meet the growing business requirements. It is therefore imperative that high-density servers are used due to space considerations. One of the main concerns of high-density servers is their power and cooling requirements that must be addressed within the limited space inside the server chassis. Traditionally, servers have been designed with the worst-case operating conditions in mind (open-loop design). That is overprovisioning the power and cooling delivery systems to support few real extreme cases of excessive workload. Overprovisioning adds cost to the system both in manufacturing and maintaining especially if this is a large scale network of servers. To address this over-simplistic non-optimum design approach, server designers have considered adopting a "better than worse case" approach (Colwell, 2004). Servers in this case dynamically adjust their level of performance (processing speed) based on the available operating margin that they are constantly monitoring achieving optimum performance based on the power and thermal system constraints. An example of such technology has been introduced by Intel and it is called Thermal Design Power (Intel, 2006). Similar technique is proposed by Lefurgy et al. (2007) where authors introduced a feedback controller that uses precise system-level power measurements to periodically select highest performance state that keeps the server within the desired power constraint. The feedback controller sets the server to operate at full speed when the server runs below the upper limits of the power supply capacity and it sets the server to lower operating speed when the server power requirements become greater than the power supply capacity. Lefurgy et al. (2007) show how closed-loop control can provide higher performance when compared to open-loop under certain conditions. The experiments were conducted on an IBM BladeCenter HS20 server and results obtained demonstrated an 82% higher application performance of the closed-loop control when compared to open-loop and up to 17% higher performance compared to used ad-hoc technique. The BladeCenter chassis used by Lefurgy et al. (2007) employed two power domains and was configured with four 2000W power supplies. Each power domain was redundantly connected to two of the power supplies so that in the event of a single supply failure, the domain would continue operating with the remaining power supply. This sort of design allows the vendors to use smaller and cost effective power supplies while still allowing the servers to optimally handle the typical operating conditions as well as the extreme ones with minor performance degradation. Behind the power control mechanism stands feedback control theory. As Hellestein et al. (2004) show in their work, feedback control theory is an effective way in improving performance computing systems. Further to this idea, Skadron et al. (2002) use control theory to manage microprocessor temperature dynamically. A similar approach has also been taken by Wu et al. (2005) who manage power using dynamic voltage scaling by controlling the synchronizing queues in multi-clock-domain processors. In the following section, control theory is presented looking into different aspects of mobile cloud computing.

In terms of mobile computing, power management refers to a somewhat different aspect of the mobile cloud computing system architecture making it even more important for the viability of mobile cloud services. In order to achieve mobility, communication and portability, it is imperative that the crucial issue of extending battery lifetime is addressed. Several solutions have been proposed to address this issue for mobile computing devices (tablets, phablets, smartphones, etc.). For example Kakerow (2003), Paulson (2003), Davis (1993) and Mayo and Ranganathan (2003) proposed to enhance CPU performance, manage the disk and screen in an intelligent manner to reduce power consumption. However, these solutions sometimes require changes in the software operation of mobile devices, or they require a new hardware that results in an increase of cost and may not be feasible for all mobile devices. An alternative way that improves power consumption independent of the mobile itself is employing the computation offloading technique. As described before, computation-offloading technique requires that large computations and complex processing be migrated from resource-limited devices (mobile devices) to resourceful machines (cloud infrastructure). Saving processing power from mobile devices means significantly reducing power consumption.

The effectiveness of computation offloading has been evaluated by Smailagic and Ettus (2002) and Rudenko et al. (1998). Their results demonstrate that the remote application execution can significantly save energy. Rudenko et al. (1998) evaluate large-scale numerical computations showing that there can be up to 45% reduction for large matrix calculation. Another example is presented by Kremer (2001).

Authors here present an offloading, compiler optimization for image processing that can reduce energy consumption by 41%. In addition using memory arithmetic unit and interface (MAUI) to migrate mobile game components to servers in the cloud can save up to 27% of energy consumption for computer games (Cuervo et al., 2010). Additionally to computation offloading, in a multi node wireless network environment, Mavromoustakis and Mastorakis (2012) examined a new scheme for sharing resources using opportunistic networking paradigm. This scheme enables energy conservation by allowing real-time traffic-based dissimilar sleep/wake schedules to wireless devices. The scheme considers the resource sharing process which, according to the duration of the traffic through the associated channel, it impacts the sleep-time duration of the node. Results from this work showed the scheme's efficiency for enabling energy conservation and provide a schematic way for minimizing the energy consumption in real-time, in contrast to the delay variations between packets. This work was extended by Mavromoustakis et al. (2014) who introduced a resource intensive traffic-aware scheme, incorporated into an energy-efficient routing protocol that enabled maximum energy conservation and efficient data flow coordination, among secondary cognitive radio communicating nodes with heterogeneous spectrum availability in cognitive radio networks. Simulation results presented validate the efficiency of the proposed traffic-aware scheme for minimizing energy consumption and routing delays. In addition resources exchange between secondary communication nodes were maximized.

Control Theory

Control theory has an important role to play in the development of new cloud computing systems, especially complex software systems. In recent years, there has been an increasing interest from the research community in the use of formal methods from control theory in the design of commercial software including email servers, web servers, databases, computing clusters, and networks. Cloud computing allows users to use resources based on their needs for storage and computational capabilities. Currently most of the services on demand are available based on resource capacity (Nathuji, 2010). This does not guarantee optimum application performance, which is still a difficult task for service providers given the complexity involved in the management of virtual machines. Variable conditions such as the time-varying nature of the demands and the direct dependency of shared resources and applications complicate the negotiation of service level agreements to guarantee a Quality of service (QoS) (Zhu et al., 2009) (Heo, Zhu, Padala & Wang, 2009). Control theory is employed in Cloud Computing to provide a systematic approach to designing feedback loops in order to avoid wild oscillations and achieve system stability as well as system optimization. Feedback loops can fulfill their primary objectives such as target response times for service level management, and settle quickly to their steady state values. This has been presented in the previous subsection where feedback loops have been used to form a closed-loop type of power control.

Another example of using control theory in cloud computing is presented by Luna and Abdallah (2011) in their work "Control in Computing Systems: Part I". In this paper, authors illustrate how model estimation, optimization, and control approaches developed by control theorists are highly applicable in the fast moving area of data center control. More specifically they discuss how control can be used at the data center level. Multiple computers working together and sharing resources are assumed in order to carry out computations while focusing on workload management and power and performance. Workload management is becoming more and more crucial for cloud computing services since data centers have become predominant in enterprise computing. Commercial users are willing to use services from companies with well established facilities and long experience in data center administration such as Amazon, HP, Microsoft, SalesForce, and Google for on-demand computing services (Hilley, 2009). Researchers from RESERVOIR FP7 (Reservoir-FP7, 2008) have been working on different aspects to improve cloud computing infrastructure aiming to encourage solutions related to the automatic allocation and deployment of resources depending on fluctuation on demands. Luna and Abdallah (2011) presented two approaches employing control theory related to workload management addressing the problem of guaranteeing Quality of Service (QoS) in data centers. The first one was "Fluid Approximations and Optimal Control" and the second one "Model Estimation and Optimal Control". Fluid Approximations and Optimal Control has been first discussed by Malrait (2010). In his paper, Malrait has stated and solved an optimization problem which is finding the configuration that maximizes the availability of the multi-tier server system for a given performance constraint. Malrait (2010) also presents the design of a simple dynamic model for server systems. Based on this, an optimal admission control has been derived when the system is exposed on high loads. The control mechanism guarantees the best availability of the system for a given performance constraint. Nevertheless, simulation results indicate that the proposed optimal configuration meets the QoS objectives under high loads but for light loads admission it becomes inefficient. These results indicate that open-loop control strategies for such systems might be inefficient due to the time-varying nature of their environment. The optimal results that these open loop control strategies may provide can be useful to evaluate other control strategies. For "Model Estimation and Optimal Control", Padala et al. (2009), presented in their paper AutoControl, a resource control system that automatically adapts to dynamic changes in a shared virtualized infrastructure to achieve application service level objectives. AutoControl combines an online model estimator and a novel multi-input, multi-output resource controller. The model estimator records the complex relationship between application performance and resource allocation. The multi-input, multi-output controller allocates the right amount of resources to achieve application service level objectives. AutoControl has been evaluated using a test-bed consisting of Xen virtual machines and various single-tier and multi-tier applications and benchmarks. Experimental results showed that AutoControl can detect processor and disk bottlenecks across multiple nodes and can re-adjust resource allocation to achieve end-to-end application-level service level objectives. In addition, it has been shown that AutoControl can cope with shifting resource bottlenecks and provide a level of service differentiation according to the priority of individual applications.

For power and performance, Luna and Abdallah (2011) explore a technique proposed by (Fu, Lu & Wang, 2010), to optimize power consumption in data centers by using Linear Quadratic Control. As stated by Fu et al. (2010), thermal management is critical for clusters because of the increasing power consumption of modern processors, their compact architecture and their constantly growing numbers. Thermal balancing through dynamic load distribution among server, mitigates hot spots in a cluster.

Data Mining in Cloud Networks

It has been estimated that the amount of data stored in the world's databases doubles every 20 months. With Cloud computing services becoming more common this is going to get only worse. As the flood of data increases, data mining becomes a necessity. Data mining is a practical technology employed to analyze and extract patterns from raw data. The patterns can transform the original data into knowledge and beneficial information. Implementing programmes that search for regularities or patterns through databases make accurate predictions on future data provided that strong patterns are identified. Intelligently analyzed data is a valuable resource that can be used to provide new insights and, in commercial settings, to competitive advantages (Witten & Frank, 2005). In the last 15 years, there have been significant activities in standardizing data mining for example the 1999 European Cross Industry Standard Process for Data Mining (CRISP-DM 1.0) and the 2004 Java Data Mining standard (JDM 1.0). In addition to standardization, there are freely available open-source software systems related to dada mining such as the R Project, Weka, KNIME, RapidMiner etc.

In mobile cloud environment, data mining techniques are required to be energy efficient due to the limited power that mobile phones have. This can possibly be addressed either by offloading computational tasks associated with data mining or in a distributed manner where mobile devices cooperate peer to peer to perform data mining tasks, tackling the problem of energy capacity shortage. This is achieved by distributing the energy consumption among the available devices. Comito et al. (2013) proposed an energy-aware scheduling strategy that assigns data mining tasks over a network of mobile devices optimizing the energy usage that aims to prolong network lifetime by balancing the energy load among the devices.

One research-challenging task presented by Tengjiao Wang et al. (2009) is mining user's moving records continuously. Knowing the moving patterns for different customer groups, it is possible for a service provider to dynamically manage resources to improve service quality such as adjusting the angles of antennas or reallocate bandwidth. Similarly, Li Zheng et al. (2011) presented in the application of data mining techniques in addressing disaster information management challenges on mobile devices. More specifically, they proposed techniques for creating a collaborative solution on a mobile platform using advanced data mining and information retrieval techniques for disaster preparedness and recovery that helps impacted communities better understand the current disaster situation and how the community is recovering. Data-mining techniques can be further exploited for mining spectrum usage data. SiXing Yin et al. (2012) examine the first and second order statistics of data collected in the 20MHz to 3GHz spectrum band and at four locations concurrently in Guangdong province of China. Results indicated that the channel vacancy durations follow an exponential-like distribution, but are not independently distributed over time, and that significant spectral and spatial correlations are found between channels of the same service. Authors exploit spectrum correlation to develop a 2-dimensional frequent pattern mining algorithm. Results show that this algorithm can accurately predict channel availability based on past observations.

Machine Learning

Service Level Agreements (SLAs) between providers and customers specify a set of requirements that can guarantee a satisfactory level of Quality of Service (QoS). SLAs can be an important parameter for any customer to outsource their work to the cloud. Efficient resource management ensures that the cloud providers adequately accomplish their obligations towards the SLA while maximizing the utilization of underlying infrastructure. Such a resource management scheme would require to automatically allocate to each service request, the minimal resources possible that can achieve the desired levels of QoS according to the SLA. This leaves the surplus resources free to deploy more virtual machines or to allocate them to customers that have set high levels of QoS for their services in their SLA.

As part of the efficient distribution of resources within the Cloud, Cloud computing services require pervasive and aggressive use of statistical machine learning as a diagnostic and predictive tool to allow dynamic scaling, automatic reaction to performance and correctness problems, and automatically managing many other aspects of these systems. Scaling quickly up and down in response to load variations is important in order to save money, but without violating service level agreements (SLA). Machine Learning contains massive advantageous methods to make classification and prediction.

Machine Learning is primarily concerned with the design and development of algorithms, which are using empirical data, such as from sensor data or databases to recognize complex patterns and make intelligent decisions based on that data. Machine learning comes hand in hand with data-mining when this involves databases or mobile user behavior.

There are two main types of Machine Learning algorithms. These are "supervised learning" and "unsupervised learning". Supervised learning maps inputs to the expected outcomes by deducing a function from training data. The output of the function can be a regression, a predicted continuous value or a classification, a predicted class label from a discrete set for the input object. The supervised learner will then use any valid input object from a number of training examples in order to predict the value of the function. Regression analysis, neural network, k-nearest neighbor algorithm, support vector machines, Bayesian statistics and decision tree are the most widely used classifiers. When using an unsupervised machine-learning algorithm, the algorithm determines how the inputs are formed like clustering where a learner is given unlabeled examples. Unsupervised learning incorporates many other techniques that seek to summarize and explain key features of the data. Some forms of unsupervised learning is clustering, self-organizing map. Fang (2010) in his master thesis has looked into some important machine learning techniques. In this work, Fang presented three different machine-learning methodologies to make classifications and predictions from source datasets. These are linear regression, decision tree and model tree and Bayesian networks. These methodologies can be used by distributed decision systems. The experimental evaluation platform demonstrated, offered detailed performance estimation and evaluation of referred methods.

Machine learning can also be applied in enforcing system-level performance objectives on chip multiprocessors (CMPs). Bitirgen et al. (2008) in their work propose a framework that manages multiple shared CMP resources in a coordinated fashion to enforce higher-level performance objectives by formulating global resource allocation as a machine-learning problem. At runtime, the proposed resource management scheme monitors the execution of each application, and learns a predictive model of system performance as a function of allocation decisions. By mapping each application's performance response to different resource distributions, it is possible to predict the impact of allocation decisions at runtime with little runtime overhead on the system-level performance. This work concludes that a coordinated approach to managing multiple interacting resources is vital for delivering high-performance in multiprogrammed workloads. This can only be achieved by employing efficient search mechanisms. Authors here implemented their search algorithm on specific sub-regions of the global allocation space. Each sub-region restricts resource allocation optimization to a subset of the applications, and systematically gives the other applications their fair share. Results from this work show that it is possible to build a single mechanism that consistently delivers high performance under various important performance metrics.

Radio Spectrum Management

Bandwidth availability is one of the big issues in mobile cloud computing since the radio spectrum for wireless networks is a limited resource. The extensive allocation of the radio spectrum and the high demand for greater data-rates drives research community towards finding ways to improve spectrum utilization and increase system capacity. Some examples of radio resource allocation techniques are presented by Katzela and Naghshineh (1996) and radio resource allocation techniques employing cell overlap by Katzis et al. (2004, February) and Katzis et al. (2004, September). A first general look at the problem suggests that spectrum shortage is not allowing new technologies to rise and greater bandwidth to be allocated. However, a study contacted by QinetiQ for Ofcom showed that most of radio spectrum is being underutilized by the current spectrum technologies (QinetiQ Ltd, 2007). To address this problem, a new radio technology has been proposed initially by Joseph Mitola called Cognitive Radio (CR). Mitola, (2000), Mitola and Maguire (1999) and Akyldiz (2008) showed that CR can be employed to enhance the utilization of radio spectrum by searching for available frequency spectrum holes (unoccupied radio spectrum) on a temporal and spatial basis.

Regulatory bodies have spent years driving the research community into investigating new methods for improving current spectrum management techniques. CR evolved from software-defined radio and provides users with intelligent and dynamic mechanisms of spectrum sensing, spectrum management, and dynamic spectrum access to share the spectrum. CR has the ability to sense temporal and spatial variations in the radio environment, allowing it to find in real-time, portions of spectrum holes. To make use of these holes, CR is dynamically adjusting operating frequency, bandwidth and other physical layer parameters (Haykin, 2005), (Thomas, DaSilva & McKenzie, 2005). The challenge in CR is to efficiently utilize spectrum opportunities without upsetting primary users (PUs) – licensed users where their frequencies might be used by the secondary users (SUs) – unlicensed users. SUs may need to decide the number of PU channels to access in the available spectrum pool based on their bandwidth requirements. Although someone can state that SUs might take advantage of this opportunity and exploit more available spectrum for higher throughput, several factors may affect the optimal bandwidth selection of a SU. Using a large number of PU channels, increases the probability that the PU is likely to reclaim a part of the band more quickly and the SU will have to switch to a different set of channels thus increasing signaling. Xu et al. (2008) present in their paper an optimal bandwidth allocation for secondary users by considering the following tradeoff: SU increases its instantaneous throughput by accessing larger bands. Nevertheless, due to random switching activities of the PUs, there is an increasing channel switching overhead for SUs which creates higher liability for larger bandwidths. Authors here presented how to find the optimal bandwidth allocation in both single SU and multiple SU cases, accounting for the effects of channel switching overhead. For the case where SU are forced to keep switching channels, Southwell et al. (2012) model the scenario of switching channels as a game which is equivalent to a network congestion game in the literature after proper and non-trivial transformations. Based on this, authors present their design of a protocol, which users can apply to find Nash equilibria in a distributed manner. Further to channel selection of CR enabled secondary users, Katzis et al. (2013) introduced a type of opportunistic networks that exploit spectrum availability in a distributed ad-hoc manner where nodes kept track of their traffic history and fed all relevant information into a routing algorithm. This paper showed that by employing cooperative sensing for monitoring the radio environment, it is possible to improve the system performance. This is achieved by using the statistical information prior establishing the route between the source and the destination. One of the challenges claimed in this work was memory and processing requirements. These can be addressed through a mobile cloud type of network. Furthermore, Ko et al. (2011) presented in their paper a Cognitive Radio Cloud Network operating in TV white spaces (TVWS). The network proposed employs cooperative spectrum sensing (SS) and resource scheduling in TVWS. Both of these can be efficiently implemented making use of scalability and the vast storage and computing capacity of the cloud. Based on the sensing reports collected on the Cognitive Radio Cloud from distributed secondary users, the authors study and implement a sparse Bayesian learning algorithm for cooperative spectrum sensing in TVWS using Microsoft's Windows Azure Cloud Platform. A database for the estimated locations and spectrum power profiles of the primary users is established on cognitive radio cloud network. Moreover to enhance the performance of the sparse Bayesian learning based spectrum sensing on Cognitive Radio Cloud Network, a hierarchical parallelization method was also implemented with Microsoft's .Net 4.0. Another example where CR and cloud computing are coupled together to optimize mobile cloud computing performance is presented by Reddy and Ellis (2013). Authors here propose a new type of CR network called cognitive radio networks with cloud (CRNC). The motivation behind this work is to ease the burden of CR mobile devices to detect unused spectrum while employing complex computational algorithms affecting dramatically their battery levels. Their proposed model eliminates the current problems in transmission of information and helps in the real-time process.

Several projects have been carried out around the globe working towards cognitive radio enabled wireless networks. Some have been dedicated towards developing cognitive radio platforms and some others focusing into developing efficient algorithms. Cognitive Radio Oriented Wireless Networks (CROWN) is one of them, funded under FET-Open scheme within FP7. The main purpose of the CROWN project was to understand the technical issues of Cognitive Radios, through a proof of concept demonstrator. Another major project was Cognitive Radio Experimentation World (CREW) which aimed at establishing an open federated test platform that in fact it is still facilitating experimentally-driven research on advanced spectrum sensing, cognitive radio and cognitive networking strategies in view of horizontal and vertical spectrum sharing in licensed and unlicensed bands. The CREW platform consists of 5 individual wireless testbeds representing 5 diverse wireless technologies such as heterogeneous Industrial Scientific and Medical (ISM) bands, heterogeneous licensed, cellular, wireless sensor, heterogeneous outdoor. These technologies are augmented with state-of-the-art cognitive sensing platforms. Further to these, there is Beyond next generation mobile broadband (BuNGee) project that has been funded through FP7 as well and its aim was to increase overall mobile network infrastructure capacity density and user throughput to well beyond what current next-generation technologies such as LTE, WiMAX are promising. The project targeted the following breakthroughs: unprecedented joint design of access and backhaul over licensed and license exempt spectrum, beyond next-generation networked and distributed multiple input multiple output and interference techniques, protocol suite facilitating autonomous ultra-high capacity deployment. To evaluate the effectiveness of these approaches, a high capacity radio cell prototype was built targeting over 1Gbps/km^2 (BuNGee, 2010).

The concept of CR can be applied in future generation architectures such as mobile cloud computing that will allow a seamless delivery of wireless services and optimum bandwidth utilization. CR have the potential to create robust, self-organizing wireless networks capable of providing substantially more bandwidth than the current 4G networks, thus allowing resource offloading in mobile cloud networks to be carried out much faster, cheaper and in a more reliable way. Numerous researchers across the globe are working on different aspects of CR wireless networks such as energy detection and spectrum sensing, opportunistic access, routing algorithms specifically designed to incorporate CR capabilities, coexistence and cooperation with existing legacy wireless systems in order to enable the coordination of the network elements with the operators infrastructure and many other topics (Di Benedetto & Bader, 2014). CR can play a significant part in mobile cloud computing technology since it has the potential to alleviate performance of current mobile devices. This can be achieved by significantly increasing their operational bandwidth, thus achieve faster offloading of tasks or data towards the cloud while allowing users to choose their price tag for this service.

Market Oriented: Economic Mechanisms

One of the critical questions one might ask regarding cloud computing economics is whether an organization should use cloud computing or stick on its own resources. The answer is not simple as this depends on a number of factors stated by Velte et al. (2010) which are: cost/benefit ratio, speed of delivery, sensitivity of date, organization's corporate, used capacity, and IT structure. Furthermore, how can anyone significantly improve all these factors for the benefit of providers and clients, since cloud computing is based on a number of technologies such as distributed storage system, cloud programming models, virtualization, service flow and workflow, service oriented architecture and Web 2.0 (Velte, Velte, & Elsenpeter, 2010). In addition to the cloud infrastructure, a company will also be required to heavily invest on the mobile cloud infrastructure. This involves the mobile devices as well as the wireless services required for the operation of the mobile cloud network.

Searching through literature on economics for cloud computing and mobile cloud computing, an interesting article came up written by Alford and Morton (2010) entitled "The Economics of Cloud Computing", which states that the budget submitted to the Congress in 2010, highlighted opportunities for the federal government to achieve significant long-term cost savings through the adoption of cloud computing technologies. The proposed budget made three key points: (1) up-front investment should be made in cloud computing, (2) long-term savings are expected, and (3) the savings are expected to be significantly greater than the investment costs. It is clear that one can benefit from using cloud computing such as large organizations or governments. Authors here, used Booz-Allen detailed cost model that created a life-cycle cost (LCC) estimates to arrive at a first-order estimate of each of the three key points in the budget. According to authors, the government's budget expectations can be met, but the overall degree of economic benefit depends on several factors which some of them are addressed in their paper. More specifically, the potential aggregate costs and savings across the federal government were determined by modeling three high level scenarios. These scenarios represented potential migration paths, using each agency's current budget for data centers. These are public cloud adopters, hybrid cloud adopters and finally the private cloud adopters in which agency's mission and data sensitivity will drive its decisions on which scenario to follow. Furthermore, it is shown that costs are mostly depended by data centers associated with moving IT infrastructure to the cloud. The cloud computing cost and economic model used by Alford and Morton (2010) focuses on the costs involved in a cloud migration. Such costs involve server hardware and software, associated contractor labor during the transition phase related to the engineering and planning of the migration, hardware and software maintenance, IT operations labor, and IT power/cooling costs. A sensitivity analysis conducted showed that several variables in the proposed cost model determine major drivers for cloud economics. The two most influential factors are (1) the reduction in hardware by employing smaller number of virtualized servers in cloud, replace physical servers in the status quo data center and (2) the length of the cloud migration schedule.

As the author state there, there can be several factors that cause agencies to realize lower economic benefits than what is presented in the paper, including the underestimation of any of the costs associated with the investment. One factor that was targeted was the server utilization rates (both in the current environment and the new cloud environment) since supporting multiple agencies of varying sizes could lead into servers being significantly underutilized. Initial analysis conducted indicated that an average utilization rate of 12% of the available CPU capacity in the status quo environment and 60% in the virtualized cloud scenario. The difference in server utilization seen here translates into a large reduction in the number of servers required in a cloud environment to process the same workload as in the status quo environment. In cases where agencies had relatively high server utilization rates, the potential savings where expected lower than in a virtualized cloud environment. However the two major trends (i.e., the number of servers to be migrated and the migration schedule) must be given a set of cost data and server utilization rates which should apply to all cloud migration initiatives.

Migration towards cloud computing services is vital for the success of clouds. So far it has been seen that organizations need to consider a vast number of parameters to make the migration worthwhile. No one can deny that the most obvious prohibiting factor for migrating to a cloud, apart from companies entrusting various providers with their valuable data, is the pricing of cloud services. Literature is enriched with various research papers on pricing of cloud services. For example, Mihailescu and Teo (2010) present a dynamic pricing mechanism for the allocation of shared resources and evaluate its performance. The economic properties of this pricing scheme is formally proved using the mechanism design framework. Teng and Magoules (2010) propose a new resource pricing and allocation policy in cloud computing in which clients can predict future resource prices. This is modeled based on game theory to solve the multi-user equilibrium allocation problem. Furthermore, Yeo et al. (2010) proposed an autonomic metered pricing for a utility computing service as currently cloud providers charge users using a simple pricing scheme, fixed prices based on resources required. Instead they proposed pricing should be differentiated based on the value of computing services provided to different types of users.

Another important aspect of the pricing of cloud computing is how much will the mobile part of a cloud cost to operate? Looking at future Mobile Cloud Computing Cognitive Networks which are designed based on the concept of dynamic spectrum sharing where cognitive radio users can opportunistically share the radio spectrum, pricing for service is not a simple task. As described by Niyato and Hossain (2008), in case of vertical spectrum sharing, a spectrum owner (or primary user/service) can share (or sell) its licensed spectrum with (to) other users (i.e., secondary users/services). This way one can trade spectrum for money thus allowing better utilization of radio spectrum. The objective of spectrum trading is to maximize the revenue of the spectrum owner, and at the same time enhance the satisfaction of the cognitive radio users. Authors here identify three basic models of spectrum sharing in CR networks. The first one is public commons model, which the radio spectrum is open to anyone for access with equal rights and it operates on the free Industrial, Scientific and Medical (ISM) bands. The second one is the exclusive usage model where the radio spectrum can be exclusively licensed to a particular user while allowing dynamic allocation and spectrum trading by the spectrum owner. The third one is the private commons model where different users in CR network (both primary, secondary, tertiary and quaternary users) can have different priorities to share the spectrum.

Price plays an important role in spectrum trading since it indicates the value of spectrum to both the seller and buyer. Niyato and Hossain (2008) in their paper present spectrum trading as the process of exchanging spectrum, which can be performed based on the exchange of different resources such as frequency band, time slot with money. The exchange takes place between the spectrum seller (owner, primary user) and spectrum buyer, which is (buyer, secondary user). Spectrum trading can be direct or via a broker. Prior to trading, the cognitive radio users are required to perform spectrum exploration and spectrum exploitation. With spectrum exploration users are required to discover and maintain the levels of usage of spectrum, and identify potentially available holes in spectrum. During exploration, a cognitive radio transceiver is required to measure and observe the transmissions in the surrounding environment. In the spectrum exploitation the cognitive radio transceiver makes a decision on whether and how to exploit the spectrum opportunities. Now upon identification of the available spectrum, the buyer and seller need to apply a spectrum-sharing model. Such models vary with some of them requiring explicit permission from the spectrum owner or cooperation from the primary user for allowing spectrum access. It might also be arbitrary. Like any market, sellers can be single, or multiple meaning that there will be monopoly or oligopoly when trading spectrum. In case of one owner, the process of trading can be seller or buyer driven. For the case of seller driven, the seller sets the price and broadcasts the information on available spectrum and for the case of buyer driven the buyer determines the spectrum demand and proceeds to buy the spectrum. In the case where there are multiple sellers, buyer can choose the best offer to maximize its satisfaction in both performance and price. There is also an additional market structure for spectrum trading where the spectrum seller is not permanent and all users have the right to access the spectrum. In case where a particular user requires more spectrum, the other users affected will need to be compensated.

CONCLUSION

This chapter presented the concept of mobile cloud computing architecture emphasizing on areas related to resource management. The content of this chapter has presented resource management from the point of view of the cloud as well as from the point of view of mobile devices. The first section in this chapter presented the three cloud delivery models, IaaS, PaaS and SaaS presenting their general characteristics. It has then presented tasks regarding resource allocation for mobile cloud computing services such as: Resource offloading, Power control, Data mining mechanisms, Machine Learning, Radio Spectrum Management including spectrum sharing - bandwidth reliability and availability and Resource Management Economics.

The section on resource management starts with presenting resource offloading and states that resource offloading in cloud computing allows employing different techniques such as dynamic provision, scalability and multi-tenancy to achieve optimum performance for mobile cloud computing services. Resource offloading mainly refers to computing and data offloading with this being an extremely important task in mobile devices particularly for saving energy. The chapter then goes through power control and stresses the importance of employing an intelligent mechanism for managing power and optimizing the system performance in terms of computing power in order to save energy especially for mobile devices. Furthermore, control theory is presented as it has been directly linked with many aspects of the operation of mobile cloud computing system since it provides a systematic approach to designing feedback loops in order to avoid wild oscillations and achieve system stability as well as system optimization. It is shown that control theory is particularly useful for successfully managing computing power and performance thus providing an alternative control to thermal balancing between servers. In addition to control theory, this chapter goes through what is well known as data mining and presents how this practical technology is employed to analyze and extract patterns from the data in order to make accurate prediction on future data and improve the user's experience and hence the QoS. For mobile cloud computing devices data mining is crucial for achieving more accurate results analyzing spectrum usage data in a shorter time. Machine learning is also presented here, as this is another research area that is highly related to resource management. Using machine learning, it is possible to device a statistical machine which can be used as a diagnostic and predictive tool to allow dynamic scaling, automatic reaction to performance and correctness of problems, and automatically managing many other aspects of these systems. Following, the concept of radio spectrum management is presented stressing the need for better spectrum utilization, better capacity and longer range. All these mechanisms that improve resource distribution and optimization are directly connected to the economic mechanisms of Cloud computing. The final section of this chapter is looking into examples from literature describing cases of pricing cloud computing services.

Concluding, resource management is important for delivering optimal cloud computing services. It is a constantly evolving multi-level and multi-disciplinary research area involving computer science and engineering techniques as well as mathematics, statistics and economics. Optimization of resources such as Communication Channels (Bandwidth / Reliability), wireless systems coexistence and convergence, cloud database, resource availability, power control and consumption requires careful planning and extensive modeling. There is not a perfect design for all types of services and all types of clients but there is always an opportunity to device a system enriched with cognitive capabilities to perform its best under time varying loads. Migration towards cloud computing services is vital for the success of clouds in order to increase research and development activities within the academia and industry. So far it has been presented that organizations need to consider a vast number of parameters to make the migration worthwhile. No one can deny that the most obvious prohibiting factor for migrating to a cloud, apart from companies entrusting various providers with their valuable data, is the pricing of cloud services. Resource availability and management can ensure that mobile cloud services are optimized thus achieving the lowest possible cost at the best possible performance.

REFERENCES

Abdelzaher, T., Diao, Y., Hellerstein, J. L., Lu, C., & Zhu, X. (2008). *Introduction to control theory and its application to computing systems* (pp. 185–215). Annapolis, MD: Academic Press. doi:10.1007/978-0-387-79361-0_7

Akyildiz, I. F., Lee, W.-Y., Vuran, M. C., & Mohanty, S. (2008). A survey on spectrum management in cognitive radio networks. *IEEE Communications Magazine, 46*(4), 40-48.

Alford, T., & Morton, G. (2010). *The economics of cloud computing, addressing the benefits of infrastructure in the cloud.* Booz Allen Hamilton. Retrieved July 3, 2014 from http://www.boozallen.com/media/file/Economics-of-Cloud-Computing.pdf

Amazon Web Services. (n.d.). *Home page.* Retrieved July 10, 2014, from http://aws.amazon.com/

Armbrust, M., Fox, A., Griffith, R., Joseph, A. D., Katz, R., Konwinski, A., & Zaharia, M. et al. (2010, April). A view of cloud computing. *Communications of the ACM, 53*(4), 50–58. doi:10.1145/1721654.1721672

Berman, F., Fox, G., & Hey, T. (2003). *Grid computing: Making the global infrastructure a reality.* Wiley and Sons. doi:10.1002/0470867167

Bitirgen, R., Ipek, E., & Martinez, J. F. (2008). Coordinated management of multiple interacting resources in chip multiprocessors: A machine learning approach. In *Proceedings of the 41st annual IEEE/ACM International Symposium on Microarchitecture (MICRO 41).* IEEE Computer Society. doi:10.1109/MICRO.2008.4771801

BuNGee. (2010). *BuNGee: Beyond next generation mobile broadband.* Retrieved July 10, 2014, from http://cordis.europa.eu/fp7/ict/future-networks/projectsummaries/bungee.pdf

Chase, J., Irwin, D., Grit, L., Moore, J., & Sprenkle, S. (2003). Dynamic virtual clusters in a grid site manager. In *Proceedings of High Performance Distributed Computing*. IEEE. doi:10.1109/HPDC.2003.1210019

Colwell, B. (2004). We may need a new box. *Computer, 37*(3), 40-41.

Comito, C., Falcone, D., Talia, D., & Trunfio, P. (2013). Scheduling data mining applications in mobile computing environments. ERCIM News, (93) April 2013. Retrieved July 10, 2014, from http://library.certh.gr/libfiles/E-JOURS/FULL-TXT/ERCIMN-93-APR-2013-PP-60.pdf#page=15'.

Cuervo, E., Balasubramanian, A., Cho, D., Wolman, A., Saroiu, S., Chandra, R., & Bahl, P. (2010) MAUI: Making smartphones last longer with code offload. In *Proceedings of the 8th International Conference on Mobile Systems, Applications, and Services* (pp. 49-62). Academic Press. doi:10.1145/1814433.1814441

Davis, J. W. (1993). Power benchmark strategy for systems employing power management. In *Proceedings of Electronics and the Environment.* IEEE. doi:10.1109/ISEE.1993.302825

Di Benedetto, M.-G., & Bader, F. (Eds.). (2014). *Cognitive radio and networking for heterogeneous wireless networks*. Springer.

Dikaiakos, M. D., Katsaros, D., Mehra, P., Pallis, G., & Vakali, A. (2009). Cloud computing: Distributed internet computing for IT and scientific research. *IEEE Internet Computing, 13*(5), 10-13

Ding, A. Y., Han, B., Xiao, Y., Hui, P., Srinivasan, A., Kojo, M., & Tarkoma, S. (2013). Enabling energy-aware collaborative mobile data offloading for smartphones. In *Proceedings of Sensor, Mesh and Ad Hoc Communications and Networks* (SECON). IEEE.

Dinh, H. T., Lee, C., Niyato, D., & Wang, P. (2013). A survey of mobile cloud computing: Architecture, applications, and approaches. *Wirel. Commun. Mob. Comput., 13*(18), 1587–1611. doi:10.1002/wcm.1203

Enomaly, Enomalism Elastic Computing Infrastructure. (n.d.). Retrieved July 10, 2014, from http://www.enomaly.com

Fang, Z. (2010). *Resource management on cloud systems with machine learning*. (Master Thesis). Barcelona School of Informatics, Technical University of Catalonia.

Foster, I., & Kesselman, C. (1997). Globus: A metacomputing infrastructure toolkit. *International Journal of Supercomputer Applications.* Retrieved July 10, 2014, from http://www.globus.org/ftppub/globus/papers/globus.pdf

Foster, I., & Kesselman, C. (Eds.). (1998). *The grid – Blueprint for a new computing infrastructure*. Morgan Kaufmann.

Fu, Y., Lu, C., & Wang, H. (2009). Control-theoretic thermal balancing for clusters. In *Proceedings of International Workshop on Feedback Control Implementation and Design in Computing Systems and Networks* (FeBID'09). Academic Press.

Fu, Y., Lu, C., & Wang, H. (2010). Robust control-theoretic thermal balancing for server clusters. In *Proceedings of IEEE International Parallel and Distributed Processing Symposium* (IPDPS'10). IEEE. doi:10.1109/IPDPS.2010.5470480

Gannon, D., Bramley, R., Fox, G., Smallen, S., Rossi, A., Ananthakrishnan, R., & Govindaraju, N. et al. (2002). Programming the grid: Distributed software components, p2p and grid web services for scientific applications. *Cluster Computing*, *5*(3), 325–336. doi:10.1023/A:1015633507128

Godse, M., & Mulik, S. An approach for selecting software-as-a-service (SaaS) product. In *Proceedings of the IEEE International Conference on Cloud Computing (CLOUD '09)* (pp. 155–158). IEEE. doi:10.1109/CLOUD.2009.74

Harris, D. (2012). What Google compute engine means for cloud computing. In *GigaOM - Tech news, analysis and trends*. Academic Press.

Haykin, S. (2005). Cognitive radio: Brain-empowered wireless communications. *IEEE Journal on Selected Areas in Communications*, *23*(2), 201–220.

Hellerstein, J., Diao, Y., Parekh, S., & Tilbury, D. M. (2004). *Feedback control of computing systems*. John Wiley & Sons. doi:10.1002/047166880X

Hellerstein, J. L., Singhal, S., & Wang, Q. (2009). Research challenges in control engineering of computing systems. *IEEE Transactions on Network and Management*, *6*(4), 206–211.

Heo, J., Zhu, X., Padala, P., & Wang, Z. (2009). Memory overbooking and dynamic control of xen virtual machines in consolidated environments. In *Proceedings of the IFIP/IEEE Symposium on Integrated Management* (IM'09) (pp. 630–637). IEEE.

Hilley, D. (2009). *Cloud computing: A taxonomy of platform and infrastructure-level offerings*. Georgia Institute of Technology. Retrieved from http://gigaom.com/cloud/what-google-compute-engine-means-for-cloud-computing/

Intel. (2006, June). *Dual-core Intel Xeon processor 5100 series thermal/mechanical design guide*. Retrieved June 20, 2014 from http://www.intel.com/content/dam/www/public/us/en/documents/design-guides/xeon-5100-thermal-guide.pdf

Isard, M., Budiu, M., Yu, Y., Birrell, A., & Fetterly, D. (2007). Dryad: Distributed data-parallel programs from sequentia building blocks. In *Proceedings of EuroSys 2007*. Academic Press.

Jones, M. T. (2009). *Cloud computing with Linux*. Retrieved July 10, 2014, from http://www.ibm.com/developerworks/linux/library/l-cloud-computing/index.html

Kakerow, R. (2003). Low power design methodologies for mobile communication. In *Proceedings of IEEE International Conference on Computer Design: VLSI in Computers and Processors*. IEEE. doi:10.1109/ICCD.2002.1106739

Katzela, I., & Naghshineh, M. (1996). Channel assignment schemes for cellular mobile telecommunication systems: A comprehensive survey. *IEEE Personal Communications, 3*(3), 10-31.

Katzis, K., Papanikolaou, K., & Iakovou, M. (2013). Reinforcement learning in hierarchical cognitive radio wireless networks. In *Proceedings of the 2nd ACM Workshop on High Performance Mobile Opportunistic Systems (HP-MOSys '13)*. ACM. doi:10.1145/2507908.2507910

Katzis, K., Pearce, D. A. J., & Grace, D. (2004, February). Fixed channel allocation techniques exploiting cell overlap for high altitude platforms. In *Proceedings of the Fifth European Wireless Conference Mobile and Wireless Systems beyond 3G*. Barcelona, Spain: Academic Press.

Katzis, K., Pearce, D. A. J., & Grace, D. (2004, September). Fairness in channel allocation in a high altitude platform communication system exploiting cellular overlap. In *Proceedings of Wireless Personal Multimedia Communications Conference* (WPMC). Abano Terme, Italy: Academic Press.

Keahey, K., Foster, I., Freeman, T., & Zhang, X. (2005). Virtual workspaces: Achieving quality of service and quality of life in the grid. *Sci. Program.*, *13*(4), 265–275.

Ko, C.-H., Huang, D. H., & Wu, S-H. (2011). Cooperative spectrum sensing in TV white spaces: When cognitive radio meets cloud. In *Proceedings of Computer Communications Workshops* (INFOCOM WKSHPS). IEEE.

Kremer, U., Hicks, J., & Rehg, J. (2001). A compilation framework for power and energy management on mobile computers. In *Proceedings of the 14th International Conference on Languages and Compliers for Parallel Computing* (pp. 115 – 131). Academic Press.

Kumar, K., & Lu, Y-H. (2010). Cloud computing for mobile users: Can offloading computation save energy?. *Computer, 43*(4), 51-56.

Kumar, K., Liu, J., Lu, Y.-H., & Bhargava, B. (2013, February). A survey of computation offloading for mobile systems. *Mobile Networks and Applications*, *18*(1), 129–140. doi:10.1007/s11036-012-0368-0

Lefurgy, C., Wang, X., & Ware, M. (2007). Server-level power control. In *Proceedings of Autonomic Computing*. Academic Press.

Li, Z., O'Brien, L., Zhang, H., & Cai, R. (2014). On the conceptualization of performance evaluation of IaaS services. *IEEE Transactions on Services Computing*, (99).

Low, Y., Bickson, D., Gonzalez, J., Guestrin, C., Kyrola, A., & Hellerstein, J. M. (2012). Distributed GraphLab: A framework for machine learning and data mining in the cloud. *Proc. VLDB Endow., 5*(8), 716-727. doi:10.14778/2212351.2212354

Luna, J. M., & Abdallah, C. T. (2011). Control in computing systems: Part I. In *Proceedings of Computer-Aided Control System Design* (CACSD). IEEE. doi:10.1109/CACSD.2011.6044541

Malrait, L. (2010, August). QoS-oriented control of server systems. *SIGOPS Oper. Syst. Rev.*, *44*(3), 59–64. doi:10.1145/1842733.1842744

Marinescu, D. (2013, October). Cloud computing: Manage your resources. *TechNet Magazine*. Retrieved June 20, 2014 from http://technet.microsoft.com/en-us/magazine/dn456533.aspx

Marshall, P., Keahey, K., & Freeman, T. (2010). Elastic site: Using clouds to elastically extend site resources. In *Proceedings of Cluster, Cloud and Grid Computing* (CCGrid). IEEE. doi:10.1109/CCGRID.2010.80

Mavromoustakis, C. X. (2011, February). Synchronized cooperative schedules for collaborative resource availability using population-based algorithm. *Simulation Practice and Theory Journal, Elsevier*, *19*(2), 762–776. doi:10.1016/j.simpat.2010.10.005

Mavromoustakis, C. X., & Mastorakis, G. (2012). Using real-time backward traffic difference estimation for energy conservation in wireless devices. In *Proceedings of the Fourth International Conference on Advances in P2P Systems*. Academic Press.

Mavromoustakis, C. X., Mastorakis, G., Bourdena, A., & Pallis, E. (2014). Energy efficient resource sharing using a trafficoriented routing scheme for cognitive radio networks. *IET Networks, 3*(1), 54-63.

Mayo, R. N., & Ranganathan, P. (2003). Energy consumption in mobile devices: Why future systems need requirements aware energy scale-down. In *Proceedings of the Third international conference on Power - Aware Computer Systems* (PACS'03). Springer-Verlag.

McNett, M., Gupta, D., Vahdat, A., & Voelker, G. M. (2007). Usher: An extensible framework for managing clusters of virtual machines. In *Proceedings of the 21st Large Installation System Administration Conference* (LISA). Academic Press.

Mell, P., & Grance, T. (2011). *NIST definition of cloud computing*. National Institute of Standards and Technology, Special Publication 800-145.

Mihailescu, M., & Teo, Y. M. (2010). On economic and computational-efficient resource pricing in large distributed systems. In *Proceedings of the 2010 10th IEEE/ACM International Conference on Cluster, Cloud and Grid Computing*. IEEE.

Mitola, J. (2000). *Cognitive radio an integrated agent architecture for software defined radio*. (PhD Thesis). KTH Royal Institute of Technology, Stockholm, Sweden.

Mitola, J. & Maguire, G. (1999). Cognitive radio: Making software radios more personal. *IEEE Personal Communications, 6*(4), 13-18.

Mousicou, P., Mavromoustakis, C. X., Bourdena, A., Mastorakis, G., & Pallis, E. (2013). Performance evaluation of dynamic cloud resource migration based on temporal and capacity-aware policy for efficient resource sharing. In *Proceedings of the 2nd ACM Workshop on High Performance Mobile Opportunistic Systems (HP-MOSys '13)*. ACM. DOI= doi:10.1145/2507908.2507917

Nadella, S. (2014). *Keynote speech at Worldwide Partner Conference 2014 in Washington DC, 16/7/2014*. Retrieved July 20, 2014, from https://wpc.tri-digital.com/videoConnect.aspx?guid=9afb907f-f214-43d5-aa79-ec7872d45b99

Nathuji, R., Kansal, A., & Ghaffarkhah, A. (2010). Q-clouds: Managing performance interference effects for qos-aware clouds. In *Proceedings of the ACM European Society in Systems Conference 2010*. Paris, France: ACM. doi:10.1145/1755913.1755938

Neiger, G., Rodgers, D., Santoni, A.L., Martins, F.C.M., Anderson, A.V., Bennett, S.M., … Smith, L. (2005). Intel virtualization technology. *Computer, 38*(5), 48-56.

Nimmagadda, Y., Kumar, K., Lu, Y.-H., & Lee, C. S. G. (2010). Realtime moving object recognition and tracking using computation offloading. In Proceedings of IEEE International Conference on Intelligent Robots and Systems (pp. 2449–2455). IEEE.

Niyato, D., & Hossain, E. (2008). Spectrum trading in cognitive radio networks: A market-equilibrium-based approach. *IEEE Wireless Communications, 15*(6), 71-80.

Nurmi, D., Wolski, R., Grzegorczyk, C., Obertelli, G., Soman, S., Youseff, L., & Zagorodnov, D. (2009). The eucalyptus open-source cloud-computing system. In *Proceedings of Cluster Computing and the Grid, CCGRID '09*. IEEE. doi:10.1109/CCGRID.2009.93

Padala, P., Hou, K-Y., Shin, K. G., Zhu, X., Uysal, M., Wang, Z., … Merchant, A. (2009). Automated control of multiple virtualized resources. In *Proceedings of the 4th ACM European Conference on Computer Systems* (EuroSys '09). ACM. doi:10.1145/1519065.1519068

Pallis, G., (2010). Cloud computing: The new frontier of internet computing. *IEEE Internet Computing, 14*(5), 70-73.

Paulson, L. D. (2003). Low-power chips for high-powered handhelds. *IEEE Computer Society Magazine, 36*(1), 21–23. doi:10.1109/MC.2003.1160049

Prodan, R., & Ostermann, S. (2010). A survey and taxonomy of infrastructure as a service and web hosting cloud providers. In *Proc. 10th IEEE/ACM Int. Conf. Grid Computing (Grid 2009)* (pp. 17–25). IEEE.

Qineti. (2002). Cognitive radio technology: A Study for Ofcom. In *Proceedings of Symposium on Electronics and the Environment*. Author.

Reddy, Y. B., & Ellis, S. (2013). Modeling cognitive radio networks for efficient data transfer using cloud link. In *Proceedings of Information Technology: New Generations* (ITNG). Academic Press. doi:10.1109/ITNG.2013.87

Reservoir-FP7. (2008). *Resources and services virtualization without barriers*. Retrieved June 20, 2014 from http://62.149.240.97/uploads/Publications/ReservoirWhitepaper_for_OGF23_-_V3.pdf

Rudenko, A., Reiher, P., Popek, G. J., & Kuenning, G. H. (1998). Saving portable computer battery power through remote process execution. *Journal of ACM SIGMOBILE on Mobile Computing and Communications Review, 2*(1).

Satyanarayanan, M. (1996). Fundamental challenges in mobile computing. In *Proceedings of the Fifteenth Annual ACM Symposium on Principles of Distributed Computing, PODC'96*. ACM. doi:10.1145/248052.248053

Skadron, K., Abdelzaher, T., & Stan, M. R. (2002). Control-theoretic techniques and thermal-RC modeling for accurate and localized dynamic thermal management. In *Proceedings of the Eighth International Symp. on High-Performance Computer Architecture*. Academic Press.

Smailagic, A., & Ettus, M. (2002). System design and power optimization for mobile computers. In *Proceedings of IEEE Computer Society Annual Symposium on VLSI*. IEEE. doi:10.1109/ISVLSI.2002.1016867

Southwell, R., Huang, J., & Liu, X. (2012). Spectrum mobility games. In *Proceedings of INFOCOM*. IEEE. doi:10.1109/INFCOM.2012.6195776

Teng, F., & Magoules, F. (2010). Resource pricing and equilibrium allocation policy in cloud computing. In *Proceedings of the 2010 10th IEEE International Conference on Computer and Information Technology*. Washington, DC: IEEE.

The Economist. (2008, October 23). *On the periphery*. Retrieved June 20, 2014 from http://www.economist.com/node/12411896

Thomas, R. W., DaSilva, L. A., & McKenzie, A. B. (2005). Cognitive networks. In *Proceedings of New Frontiers in Dynamic Spectrum Access Networks*. IEEE.

Velte, A. T., Velte, T. J., & Elsenpeter, R. (2010). *Cloud computing: A practical approach*. New York: McGraw-Hill.

Wang, T., Yang, B., Gao, J., Yang, D., Tang, S., Wu, H., & Pei, J. et al. (2009). MobileMiner: A real world case study of data mining in mobile communication. In *Proceedings of the 2009 ACM SIGMOD International Conference on Management of data (SIGMOD '09)*. ACM. doi:10.1145/1559845.1559988

White, T. (2009, June 5). *Hadoop: The definitive guide*. O'Reilly Media, Yahoo! Press.

Witten, I. H., & Frank, E. (2005). Data mining practical machine learning tools and techniques (2nd ed.). Morgan Kaufmann.

Wu, Q., Juang, P., Martonosi, M., Peh, L-S., & Clark, D.W. (2005). Formal control techniques for power performance management. *IEEE Micro, 25*(5), 52-62.

Xu, D., Jung, E., & Liu, X. (2008). Optimal bandwidth selection in multi-channel cognitive radio networks: How much is too much? In *Proceedings of New Frontiers in Dynamic Spectrum Access Networks*. IEEE.

Yeo, C. S., Venugopal, S., Chu, X., & Buyya, R. (2010). *Autonomic metered pricing for a utility computing service*. Amsterdam, The Netherlands: Future Generation Computer Systems.

Yin, Chen, & Zhang, Liu, & Li. (2012). Mining spectrum usage data: A large-scale spectrum measurement study. *IEEE Transactions on Mobile Computing*, *11*(6), 1033–1046.

Zahariev, A. (2009). Google app engine. In *Proceedings of TKK T-110.5190 Seminar on Internetworking*. Helsinki University of Technology. Retrieved June 20, 2014 from http://www.cse.hut.fi/en/publications/B/5/papers/1Zahariev_final.pdf

Zhan, H., Kang, L., Liu, L., & Cao, D. (2013). Scalable resource aggregation service of an ErlangOTP PaaS platform. In *Proceedings of Service Oriented System Engineering* (SOSE). IEEE.

Zheng, L., Shen, C., Tang, L., Li, T., Luis, S., & Chen, S.-C. (2011). Applying data mining techniques to address disaster information management challenges on mobile devices. In *Proceedings of the 17th ACM SIGKDD International Conference on Knowledge Discovery and Data Mining (KDD '11)*. ACM. doi:10.1145/2020408.2020457

Zhu, X., Uysal, M., Wang, Z., Singhal, S., Merchant, A., Padala, P., & Shin, K. (2009). What does control theory bring to system research? *Operating Systems Review*, *43*(1), 62–69. doi:10.1145/1496909.1496922

KEY TERMS AND DEFINITIONS

Cloud-Computing Infrastructure: A complex system dynamically evolving consisted of numerous devices/platforms featuring hardware and software components running on different sets of requirements. It aims to combine a large number of shared resources to deliver seamless cloud services.

Cognitive Radios: New type of radio systems that provide cognitive radio users (also referred as secondary users) with intelligent and dynamic mechanisms of spectrum sensing, spectrum management and dynamic spectrum access to share the radio spectrum on a spatial-temporal basis between them or with existing primary users.

IaaS: Infrastructure-as-a-service refers to cloud systems that allow users to run and control entire virtual machine instances deployed across a variety of physical resources.

PaaS: Platform-as-a-service refers to cloud systems that allow users to create applications using available tools from the cloud platform such as programming languages, libraries, services and tools supported by the provider.

Radio Spectrum Management: It is the process of efficiently managing radio spectrum between mobile devices aiming at improving spectrum utilization and increasing system capacity.

Resource Offloading: It is the process where devices such as mobile devices with limited capabilities (memory, processing power, power, etc.) migrate some of the tasks they are assigned to perform to the cloud infrastructure.

SaaS: Software-as-a-service refers to cloud systems where consumers use applications available from their provider running on a cloud infrastructure without being able to manage or control the underlying cloud infrastructure.

Service Level Agreements: Are a set of requirements that can guarantee a satisfactory level of Quality of Service (QoS) and can be an important parameter for customers to outsource their work to the cloud.

Shared Resources: Networks, servers, storage, applications and services can be identified as shared resources managed under a cloud-computing infrastructure regime.

Chapter 5
A Social-Oriented Mobile Cloud Scheme for Optimal Energy Conservation

Constandinos X. Mavromoustakis
University of Nicosia, Cyprus

George Mastorakis
Technological Educational Institute of Crete – Agios Nikolaos, Greece

Athina Bourdena
University of Nicosia, Cyprus

Evangelos Pallis
Technological Educational Institute of Crete – Heraklion, Greece

Dimitrios Stratakis
Technological Educational Institute of Crete – Heraklion, Greece

Emmanouil Perakakis
Technological Educational Institute of Crete – Agios Nikolaos, Greece

Ioannis Kopanakis
Technological Educational Institute of Crete – Agios Nikolaos, Greece

Stelios Papadakis
Technological Educational Institute of Crete – Agios Nikolaos, Greece

Zaharias D. Zaharis
Aristotle University of Thessaloniki, Greece

Christos Skeberis
Aristotle University of Thessaloniki, Greece

Thomas D. Xenos
Aristotle University of Thessaloniki, Greece

ABSTRACT

This chapter elaborates on energy usage optimization issues by exploiting a resource offloading process based on a social-oriented mobile cloud scheme. The adoption of the proposed scheme enables for increasing the reliability in services provision to the mobile users by guaranteeing sufficient resources for the mobile application execution. More specifically, this chapter describes the process to improve the energy consumption of the mobile devices through the exploitation of a social-oriented model and a cooperative partial process offloading scheme. This research approach exploits social centrality, as the connectivity model for the resource offloading, among the interconnected mobile devices to increase the energy usage efficiency, the mobile nodes availability, as well as the process of execution reliability. The proposed scheme is thoroughly evaluated to define the validity and the efficiency for the energy conservation increase of future mobile computing devices.

DOI: 10.4018/978-1-4666-8225-2.ch005

INTRODUCTION

Social networking experiences a great increase in the current mobile networks, becoming part of the users' daily routines, while it creates a communications overlay that can be exploited by several services and applications (Hu, Mostashari, Xie, 2010). The mobile users connect to the social media platforms via small devices (e.g. smart phones, tablets) that require increased resources (e.g. memory, processing resources etc.) availability. In addition, the emerging mobile networks will exhibit unique properties, depending on the behavior of the mobile users, their mobility and their local concentration. The prediction of their behavior is a complicated task, while the relation with social-oriented issues could be a solution, towards successfully managing the resources under an efficient approach. Furthermore, the sharing of the resources by the mobile devices is even more demanding, since the applications require sharing to happen in a seamless way, with the minimum possible delays and the maximum possible Quality of Experience (QoE) (Mavromoustakis, 2010). This is a demanding target due to the fact that the wireless networks cannot reliably commit to share the resources, towards creating a consistent communication between the users, since there is no way to guarantee resource allocation. In addition, the mobility factor plays an important role, since it imposes further limitations, as the network topology continuously generates fluctuation in the resource usage and their availability. Furthermore, the dependency on the device capabilities limits particular solutions to be adopted, lacking generality in its applicability. In this framework and by taking into account all such issues, this chapter elaborates on a social interactivity method to model and perform resource sharing in wireless networking platforms.

Since social networking platforms are exploited, by a vast majority of 87% of the mobile users to communicate each other and exchange messages, they form an underlying web, towards interconnecting the mobile devices and enabling for a reliable resource sharing process (Tang, Musolesi, Mascolo, Latora, & Nicosia, 2010). By exploiting the social-oriented connectivity, as well as the interactivity patterns, it is possible to support adaptability to the device capabilities and their operating environment, enabling for devices adaption to frequent changes in location and context. In addition, one of the ever spare resources of the mobile devices is the energy (Mavromoustakis, Dimitriou & Mastorakis, 2012) that they consume (Dimitriou, Mavromoustakis, Mastorakis & Pallis, 2013). As the energy is stored in batteries (Bourdena, et al., 2014), it forms the only source for the mobile device operation and as new and more power demanding applications are developed (Mastorakis, Bourdena, Mavromoustakis, Pallis & Kormentzas, 2013), an energy usage optimization scheme is required (Mastorakis, Mavromoustakis, Bourdena & Pallis, 2013), approached by both hardware and software solutions. In this context, this chapter elaborates on a social-oriented model for optimizing the energy consumption by the mobile devices in an opportunistic approach (Mavromoustakis, et al., 2014). The proposed social interaction model is based on the social centrality principle, enabling users to share resources when a contact limit is satisfied. The energy intense processing, as well as other actions are disseminated, by exploiting the proposed model to enable mobile nodes running low on energy resources, alleviating their demands and extending their life. More specifically, the centrality principle, as well as the "ageing" timing rule are applied, to produce a more effective usage of the available energy (Mastorakis, et al., 2014). Therefore, opportunistic energy conservation takes place, towards supporting efficient energy management to other mobile nodes (Mavromoustakis, Mastorakis, Bourdena, Pallis, Kormentzas & Dimitriou, 2014) and guaranteeing end-to-end availability for the longest time possible, in a wireless mobile environment. In this context and by taking into account this introduction, this chapter elaborates on a social interaction model to achieve optimal resources exploitation, forming the key novelty of the proposed framework. This framework evaluates the energy state of each mobile node, by taking into account the type, energy demands, as well as the energy usage (Mavromoustakis, Dimitriou, Mastorakis, Bourdena & Pallis, 2014), determining if the node is able to receive or provide energy to the entire network. By exploiting the proposed framework, the ability to adaptively perform tasks for another node increases, depending on the node current energy state, as well as on its "friendship" degree. In addition, the proposed framework strengthens or relaxes the energy usage (Mastorakis, Panagiotakis, Kapetanakis, Dagalakis, Mavromoustakis, Bourdena & Pallis, 2014) and the task allocation scheme, according to the social contacts and the user's interaction parameters. In this direction, next section elaborates on a background on related research issues. Then, a section has been devoted to present the proposed social-oriented scheme for opportunistic and the socially-aware energy sharing, as well as the process off-loading. In addition, a section is exploited to present the performance evaluation of the proposed scheme through the experimental evaluation, while the final section concludes this chapter, by highlighting future potential directions for further research and experimentation.

BACKGROUND

Social networking paradigm (Papanikolaou, Mavromoustakis, Mastorakis, Bourdena & Dobre, 2014) is exploited through the current wireless networks infrastructures and protocols to form users' connections and data sharing (Mavromoustakis Andreou, Mastorakis, Bourdena, Batalla & Dobre, 2014). Its appeal and huge popularity primarily came from the fact that the social activity was enhanced in the online environment with the use of multimedia services, giving users instant access to information. Another aspect of the online environment was the ability of the social network users to share their location with others, instantly advertising their present coordinates either using applications, such as FourSquare or having automatic tracking, by exploiting the mobile devices GPS capabilities. The use of the user mobility in opportunistic networks will help to realize the next generation of applications based on the adaptive behavior of the devices for resource exchange. The problem of the energy usage optimization (Mavromoustakis, Dimitriou, Mastorakis & Pallis, 2013) that considers energy as a finite resource (Mavromoustakis, Mastorakis, Bourdena & Pallis, 2014), which needs to be shared among users, providing most processing power whilst maintaining group connectivity, will greatly benefit via the use of the social centrality model. Opportunistic networks (Mastorakis, Mavromoustakis, Bourdena, Pallis & Sismanidis, 2013) will greatly benefit from the capability of the mobile devices to gather information from any hosted application, in order to better utilize network resources (Mavromoustakis, et al., 2014). The task allocation and load balancing can be strictly or voluntarily associated with the social communication. Research approaches such as the one in (Sachs et al., 2004) propose architectures that rely on the local information derived by the devices and their local views, in optimizing load balancing and energy management, as well as even some self-behaving properties, like self-organization. In (Sachs et al., 2004) resource manipulation optimization is offered, but this occurs without considering social parameters, such as friendship, contact rate or the temporal parameters (i.e. users' location). In contrast, the contribution of this chapter is to combine the energy management scheme with the proposed social parameters and model for each node, in order to optimize the energy management and load sharing process. In the game theoretic approach (Cuervo et al., 2010), the energy usage optimization problem is translated to a contention game, where the nodes compete to access the energy resources, reaching to the Nash equilibrium. This is a method that improves on the random and individualized approach. In (Cuervo et al., 2010) the proposed system supports fine grained offload to minimize energy savings with minimal burden on the programmer. The model decides at runtime, which methods should be remotely executed driven by an optimization engine that achieves the best energy savings possible under the mobile devices current connectivity constraints. In (Ren & van der Schaar, 2013) the energy offloading is viewed as potentially energy saving but the overheads of privacy, security and reliability need to be added as well. The integration of social connectivity into the process is an unexplored area. Social connectivity takes into consideration users associations, location profiles and social interactions as a basis for creating an index for users' resources over time for subsequent resource offloading.

In this work, a social-oriented methodology is used for minimizing the energy consumption for highly demanding applications with high memory/processing requirements. The social-oriented model with the associated friendships as the basis for social mobility, utilizes the introduced social-centrality, for selecting and offloading energy hungry partitionable tasks (parts of executable applications and processes) under the availability optimization objective. In addition, this work considers the motion coefficients for each user (using normalized [0..1] parameter) and encompasses these characteristics into the proposed energy utilization scheme for enabling maximum temporal node availability without reducing the processing capabilities of the system as a whole. The proposed scheme uses both the pre-scheduled opportunistic offloading (Khamayseh, BaniYassein, AbdAlghani & Mavromoustakis, 2013) and the social interactions that take place among the collaborative users and their associated strength of friendship. The scheme improves on predicting user mobility under the end-to-end availability. In order to assess the effectiveness of the proposed scheme, exhaustive simulations take place considering the offered energy by the social-collaborative network within the mobility context. The results of these lead to thorough measurements of the energy consumption optimization for mobile nodes/users.

On the other hand, cloud computing paradigm (Skourletopoulos, Bahsoon, Mavromoustakis, Mastorakis & Pallis, 2014) that refers to both the datacentres software and hardware infrastructures, is essential for enterprises and organizations. When a cloud based system is available for the general public in a pay-as-you-go way, it is referred as Public, while a cloud that is constructed for the sake of enterprises or organizations and cannot be accessed by the general public, is referred as Private. Enterprises usually exploit cloud facilities, in order to reduce their infrastructure and administration costs, through improved resource utilization, achieving scalability, speeding-up the deployment procedure, facilitating collaboration and encouraging innovation. Cloud computing uses network connection, in order to provide Software as a Service (SaaS), Platforms as a Service (PaaS) and Infrastructures as a Service (IaaS) (Frey & Hasselbring, 2010). From hardware perspective, three important issues can be highlighted in cloud computing. Firstly, the sensation that the computing resources provided are boundless and available on demand. Secondly, the fact that it lacks of an up-front commitment by the user. Finally, the ability that the computing resources can be used and released as needed (Fox et al., 2009). A critical issue for a cloud is to be able to know its current and future ability to serve customers. To achieve that, the user makes a request for resources, including start and end date which is evaluated by the administrator of the cloud. In this way, it is assured that resources, which are already fully committed, will not be provided. Enterprises and organizations that consider IT migration to the cloud have to evaluate the benefits and the risks of cloud migration. Cloud computing facilitates collaboration of groups and liberates innovators from concerning about digital assets. An important issue is the investigation of the potential decrease of infrastructure costs (software licenses, equipment, staff costs etc.). Enterprises and organizations do not have to build and maintain private computing infrastructures, but just lease resources in a "pay-as-use" model. That is, only the services that are used must be paid. The sensation of endless availability of demanded resources is provided. The provisioning of resources is flexible and analogous to requirements, which differ from time to time. On the other hand, there are justifiable concerns about confidentiality and privacy of data (Sultan, 2010). Firstly, it must be ensured that access of data will be done only by authorized users. Secondly, the fact that service providers have access to all the data (email, health records etc.) introduces possible undesirable consequences. For example, it is possible sensitive personal data to be revealed or used for unauthorized purposes, either accidentally or deliberately. The law system should clarify issues concerning privacy and protection of data migrated into the cloud. Reliability concerns are also raised, as there are several examples that providers failed to serve their customers (McAfee, 2011). It must be guaranteed that the user obtains the facilities, which are included in the service engaged by the provider. Several decision tools are available in order to ease enterprises to choose for migration (Khajeh-Hosseini, Sommerville, Bogaerts & Teregowda, 2011).

Moreover, as the mobile devices (e.g. smartphones, tablets) are carried by users almost all day long, they needed to be small, light and have long life batteries. These demands cause a decrease of computing power comparative to static devices. Reduction of weight and size, increase of battery life, ergonomic improvement and achievement of heat dissipation conflict with processor speed, memory size and disk capacity (Khan, Othman, Madani & Khan, 2013). Although contemporary mobile devices have considerable computational power, there are several applications (e.g. those relevant to multimedia processing, decision making, collaborative processing etc.), which demand energy and processing capabilities that portable devices cannot offer (Gkatzikis, Koutsopoulos, 2013). Mobility also requires wireless communication. Network access must be obtained from any place, at any time and under various environmental conditions. In addition, sophisticated applications of modern smartphones require fast broadband services. Mobile devices are not able to execute several tasks due to processing and energy capability limitations. When a mobile device is overloaded, a dynamic transfer of tasks to another machine might be necessary. During this procedure the minimization of the interruption for the users is a critical demand. Several approaches have been proposed for efficient computation loading from mobile devices to remote cloud resources or closely located computing resources known as cloudlets. Mobile Cloud Computing (MCC) provides the ability the tasks to be offloaded to remote cloud servers (Mavromoustakis, Bourdena, Mastorakis, Pallis & Kormentzas, 2015). Since a task is placed for execution in the cloud, a new VM is created and assigned to a physical server. According to the solution of virtualization, on a single physical machine several VMs can be executed. Each VM is self-contained and runs its own operating system. It also provides resources such as CPU, memory and input/output devices (Mishra, Das, Kulkarni & Sahoo, 2012). A VM is accompanied with data of changeable volume. For example, video compression causes decreasing of data. On the other hand, scientific calculations might increase their data volume. It is obvious that the load of a server in the cloud is continuously changing due to several factors such as the mobility of devices, the changeable nature of data volume of a virtual machine, the generation and termination of VMs. In order to balance the load of the system and minimize the execution time, a task might migrate to a new server. Migration implies that the task must stop its execution at the current server and the VM's state (memory pages) has to be retransferred to a new server. There, a new virtual machine will start. Live migration can be accomplished through several techniques such as suspend-and-copy, pre-copy and post-copy, depending on the way the transfer of the memory pages is accomplished. However, before the migration is carried out, important decisions must be taken about which VM is to be migrated, when and where. A cloud provider wishes to improve its competitive profile and, therefore, faces the challenge of selecting the best migration strategy in order to improve the quality of services that a client experiences.

The procedure of migration induces delay. The challenge is the minimization of the execution time of a task, as well as the time needed for data to be transferred to the user. Several approaches have been introduced for the purpose of estimating the performance of a VM migration (Akoush, Sohan, Rice, Moore & Hopper, 2010). Virtual machine migration mechanisms have been proposed in order to facilitate cloud providers to control a server's load. Due to centralized approaches, the cloud provider has to determine the best migration strategy for the whole cloud. According to distributed approaches, the migration policy must be estimated by each server or task. Virtualization can accomplish full utilization of servers. Thus, it obviates resource wastefulness. Several tasks are executed using the same hardware platform. The interaction of the tasks is prevented, as each one is placed in an individual virtual machine and has access only to its own data. Nevertheless, latency and execution time may be decreased because of the contention of the virtual machines for the same physical resources. As computational power is highly requested, data centers consume huge quantities of electrical power. The consumption of power is strongly connected to the number of active servers and the load of each server. Virtualization allows several virtual machines to run on the same physical server. In this way, less physical devices are in use while the utilization of the active ones is highly increased. The concentration of tasks into fewer servers would decrease the power demands but, on the other hand, might also load some servers heavily causing reduction of the Quality of Service. The challenge is to reduce energy consumption without downgrading the services provided to the client.

Green computing is an area of highly increasing interest, which aims the minimization of energy consumption and at the same time to preserve optimal utilization of computational resources (Younge, Von Laszewski, Wang, Lopez-Alarcon & Carithers, 2010). Efforts have been made to reduce the dependence of datacenters on the electrical grid and exploit the facilities that provide renewable energy sources (Beloglazov & Buyya, 2010). An educational Institution, which occupies itself with the development of provided services has to focus on the development in technology and renew its software and hardware infrastructure from time to time. In this way, students will be attracted to participate in courses and teachers will be able to follow evolution in their field of interest rather than being occupied with software licenses and updates. Nevertheless, the applications' installation and maintenance, drives to huge outlays that are unbearable during the economic crisis that the world experiences. In many countries, even in Africa, cloud computing has been adopted in education (Ercan, 2010), in order to reduce the expenses derived from upgrading IT systems. Of course, the necessity of software and hardware equipment still remains. In fact, all that is required is an access device, even an inexpensive one, an Internet connection and a common web browser. Several cloud computing solutions for education (Alabbadi, 2011) have been proposed (Al Noor, Mustafa, Chowdhury, Hossain & Jaigirdar, 2010). The advantages that the solution of cloud computing introduces to educational Institution are considerable. Computers in educational Institutions have usually short storage capability, unlike the cloud which allows users to upload big amount of data of any type. This data can be accessed, regardless the location of the user and the device that is used, as long as an Internet connection and a typical web browser are available. The back-up privilege is provided and prevents users from losing data, when for example a computer crashes. Portable data storage devices are no longer necessary for users to have access to their data whenever or wherever they like. The collaboration facility is also remarkable. It simplifies the cooperation of students in groups by exchanging and sharing files, without having to purchase, install and update office applications or other tools needed to materialize their projects. Assignments can be uploaded by teachers, who are no longer obliged to print and copy documents for their students. Every document relevant to a lesson, such as notes or assignments can be uploaded to the cloud. Teachers will focus on their core business of teaching and will not be concerned about technical matters regarding the software and hardware equipment of the educational unit.

In addition, cloud computing refers to the provision of software and data services to users, who have an Internet connection and a common web browser. The adoption of this technology by Institutions or organizations introduces remarkable benefits, as well as risks. Many countries, even in Africa, enjoy cloud computing in education. It is claimed that it would facilitate the educational procedure and eliminate the expenses derived from maintaining proprietary IT systems. Cloud computing has been discussed from many as the long-held dream of Information Technology as a utility. Although there exists a general positive aspect of this new technology, there are some new fields of study that arise by the new. Traditional data centers are more or less transforming by using virtualization techniques to cloud services providers, offering subscription based access to their clients. The change from classic IT infrastructures with static resources to a dynamic cloud of on demand resources raises new challenges for the researchers. Furthermore, at present, there is an increase in the number of users and enterprises that choose to step away from the classic data center services and move towards cloud computing to store and access their data. Providers like Amazon, Google, Salesforce, IBM, Microsoft and Sun Microsystems have already begun to establish new data centers around the globe for hosting cloud computing applications, in order to provide redundant and reliable services to their users (Buyya, et al., 2009). Although cloud computing is already offered as a service in various models by the providers, it has to be noticed that it is still an emerging technology and there is still a lot of research to be done before anyone can conclude that cloud computing is here to stay. Now days, cloud computing tries to deal with a number of problems that range from privacy and security to resource allocation management. As cloud computing systems become more and more complex (in size), challenges like resource allocation and failure management also get more challenging in order to have efficient cloud computing systems. Resource allocation (Mavromoustakis, Pallis & Mastorakis, 2014) is a major concern in cloud computing due to the fact that a cloud is a virtual entity that does not have any dedicated physical components but instead borrows resources from an underlying data center(s); inadequate usage of the aforementioned resources has an great impact on both the cloud provider and the end user. There are several different approaches that researchers use in order to address resource provisioning in cloud computing systems. Each approach takes into account different resource allocation strategies, different algorithms and different models. According to the literature there are two main categories in dealing with failure aware cloud computing systems. Each of these two categories takes a totally different approach to the problem. On one hand, methodologies exist that try to foresee a compute node failure (either in hardware or in software) and enable the system to take proactive measures, while on the other hand there are methodologies that act reactively, by keeping "screenshots" of the nodes process, in order to be able to restart the job in case of a failure.

One of the most common strategies for resource allocation is the use of policies (Sagar, et al., 2013) that enable a cloud provider to provision resources based on demand. Authors in (Javadi, et al., 2012) provide a three step resource allocation policy that is both cost and failure aware. The first step, called Adaptive Brokering Strategy, is to create a routing strategy for resource requests that can take into account the associated cost and the response time of each resource provider. By the end of the first step, the system has computed the routing probabilities for the incoming resource requests; in the next step the proposed system must dispatch these requests to the routing queues. This step is called Dispatch Sequences and its work is to dispatch the incoming requests to the resource providers with two different methods. One takes into account the previous resource requests (Adaptive with Deterministic Sequence) while the other one is random (Adaptive with Random Sequence). The last step of the procedure, called Scheduling Algorithms, performs the scheduling request by the use of three different scheduling algorithms (conservative, aggressive and selective backfilling) to the provider's VM. In addition, in this stage the system can provide a fault-tolerant environment for serving requests, by using a reactive technique called checkpointing (Bouguerra, et al., 2010). This specific approach by the authors can work for both public and private clouds. A different approach and solution to the problem of failure aware resource allocation is presented in (Pannu, et al., 2012). In this work, the authors argue that the techniques used for fault recovery should not rely on a checkpoint mechanism, which adds a significant overhead on large scale systems, but on failure prediction and proactive technologies. Their method on attacking the same problem involves a Virtual Machine (VM) technology strategy. VM is a virtual system that hosts its own guest operating system, where user jobs are running. Their work for a reconfigurable distributed virtual machine (RDVM) uses a daemon called DVM, which resides on a compute node and is responsible for the communication of VM information with the other parts of the system that are the VM Coordinator, the Failure Predictor and the VM Load Manager. The VM Load Manager job is to analyze performance data that the DVM daemon sends and to construct VM workload reports. Failure Predictor uses the same performance data in conjunction with failure events that occurred in the past, in order to be able to predict imminent failures. Both workload reports and failure predictions are subsequently sent to the VM Coordinator of the system, who is responsible in issuing any needed reconfiguration decisions based on the data. In addition, the Coordinator is responsible for creating new RDVM instances on compute nodes, in order to serve tasks required by the users. In special environments like cloud systems the physical location of the underlying infrastructure has to be taken into account. The work from (Chester, et al., 2011) refers to the exact situation. They express the idea that cloud computing providers, in order to maximize resource utilization and operation efficiency tend to use racks to accommodate the physical resources and as a result expose them to co-locations issues. So, in the event of a network switch failure or power shortage, a whole rack can fail, resulting to failure of multiple servers. The authors in their work try to address this issue, by designing failure aware dynamic resource allocation (DRA) policies. By default, DRAs are not failure aware and due to that fact the providers already use them. The authors propose as a solution, a failure aware allocator module, which works in sync with the DRAs already in place, in order to overcome the problem. In this work, they introduce a new metric called Capacity Loss, which is used to grasp the change, in terms of capacity that the failing rack caused to an application. The desired objective is to minimize Capacity Loss and ideally have a value of 0. Nevertheless, DRAs do not have information about the locality of its server, thus the authors have developed a component called Allocator, which is rack-aware and has the ability to translate DRAs decisions and Capacity Loss metric, to racks, in which the configuration transforms must occur.

MOBILE CLOUD COMPUTING SCHEME FOR EFFICIENT ENERGY CONSUMPTION

Wireless devices have many resource constraints in terms of availability of resources and temporal task/object sharing, whereas performance and reliability characteristics are significantly affected by the connectivity and mobility constraints of each device. The implications of mobility cannot be determined over time as the network topology is dynamically changing. In our work, the mobility model used is based on the probabilistic Fraction Brownian Motion (FBM) where nodal motion is done according to certain probabilities in accordance with location and time. Assume that we need to support a mobile node that is low on energy reserves and requires an energy heavy application to run. This implies that in a non-static, multi-hop environment, there is a need to model the motion of the participating nodes in the end-to-end path such that the requesting nodes can move through the network and conserve its resources. We also assume a clustered-mobility configuration scenario presented in (Mavromoustakis, 2010), where each node has its own likelihood for the motion it follows. To predict whether a node will remain within the cluster, we aggregate these probabilities. This also shows the probabilities for the other nodes remaining in the cluster. The mobility scenario used in this work is modelled and hosted in a scheme that enables the utilization of social feedback into the model. Unlike the predetermined relay path in (Khamayseh, BaniYassein, AbdAlghani & Mavromoustakis, 2013) and the known location/region, the mobility scenario used in this work is a memoryless FBM (Camp, Boleng, Davies, 2002), with no stationary correlation among users' movements. FBM can be derived probabilistically from the random walk mobility model and can be expressed as a stochastic process that models the random continuous motion. The mobile node moves from its current location with a randomly selected speed, in a randomly selected direction in real time as users interact. However, in real life the real time mobility that the users exhibit, can be expressed as an ordinary walk, where the users spot-out some environmental stimuli and are attracted to them. Their decisions may be relayed to their respective social communication. In the proposed scenario, the walking speed and direction are set for the mobile users and are both chosen from predefined ranges, $[V_{\min}, V_{\max}]$ and $[0, 2\pi)$, respectively (Lawler, 1995). The new speed and directions are maintained for an arbitrary length of time randomly chosen from $(0, t_{\max}]$. The node makes a memoryless decision for new speed and direction when the chosen time period elapses. The movements can be described as a Fractional Random Walk on a weighted graph [1], with the total likelihood P_{ij}^{L} in L^{n}.

We model the movement of each device using a graph theoretical model, in which a device can move randomly according to a topological graph $G = (V, E)$,that comprises of pair of sets $V\ (or\ V(G))$ and $E\ (or\ E(G))$ called edges. The edges join different pairs of vertices. This walk considers a connected graph with n nodes labeled $\{1, 2, 3, ..., n\}$ in a cluster L^{n} with weight $w_{ij} \geq 0$ on the edge (i, j). If edge (i, j) does not exist, we set $w_{ij} = 0$. We assume that the graph is undirected so that $w_{ij} = w_{ji}$. A node walks from a location to another location in the graph in the following random walk manner. Given that node i *is in reference*, the next location j is chosen from among the neighbors of i with probability:

$$p_{ij}^{L} = \frac{w_{ij}}{\sum_{k} w_{ik}} \tag{1}$$

where in (1) above the p_{ij} is proportional to the weight of the edge (i, j), then the sum of the weights of all edges in the cluster L is:

$$w_{ij}^{L} = \sum_{i,j:j>1} w_{ij} \tag{2}$$

Then the stationary distribution according to [1] is given by

$$\pi_{i}^{L} = \frac{w_{i}^{L}}{2w} \tag{3}$$

where, it can be seen that the preceding distribution satisfies the relationship $\pi P = \pi$ when the movement is performed for a node/device i to location j (stationary distribution of the Markov chain as each movement of the users usually has a selected predetermined path (i.e. corridor etc.)) associated as follows:

$$\sum_i \pi_i P_{ij} = \sum_i \left\{ \frac{w_i}{2w} \times \frac{w_{ij}}{w_i} \right\} = \sum_i \left\{ \frac{1}{2w} w_{ij} \right\} = \frac{1}{2w} \sum_i \left\{ w_{ij} \right\} = \frac{w_j}{2w} = \pi_j \tag{4}$$

Equation 4 above denotes that the stationary probability of state of i is proportional to the weight of the edges emanating from node i. By using the motion notation we can express the track of requests as a function of the location (i.e. movements and updates $P_{i,j}{}^{L}$ as: $R_i(I_{ij}, P_{ij}{}^{L})$ *where* R_i is the request from node i, I_{ij} is the interaction coefficient measured in Equation 2. We use the representation of the interactions by utilizing notations of weighted graphs (Equation 1).

Different types of links or involvements are expressed in different ways in social connectivity modeling. Consequently, several types of centralities are defined in the directed or undirected graphs (Hu, Mostashari, Xie, 2010). Users may have or not a certain type of association with any other user in the global network and this is modelled with the concept of the social network. Nodes carry weights that represent the degree of associativity with other nodes. These weights are associated with each edge linking two nodes and are used to model the interaction strength between nodes (Scott & Carrington, 2011). This models the degree of friendship that each node has with the other nodes in the network. The weights are assigned and used to measure the degree of the strength of the association of the connecting parts. Consequently the degree of social interaction between two devices can be expressed as a value in the range of $[0,1]$. A degree of 0 signifies that the two nodes/devices are not socially connected and therefore no social interaction exists between them. As social interaction increases so does the weight reaching 1 indicating very strong social interaction. The strength of the social interaction and the energy state of each node will form the basis for offloading processes to other nodes in the network. In this work, we propose such a model for efficient energy management prolonging node lifetime based on the social association scheme.

We propose that the strength of social interaction will also affect the offloading process, which as the next sections show will affect the energy conservation mechanism. The social interaction can be represented by the 5x5 symmetric matrix (Equation 2 matrix is based on the social population in the network), the names of nodes correspond to both rows and columns and are based on the interaction and connectivity. The latter matrix, forms the Interaction Matrix which represents the social relationships between nodes. The generic element i, j represents the interaction between two individual elements i and j, the diagonal elements represent the relationship an individual has with itself and are set to 1. In (5), the I_{ij} represents all the links associated to a weight before applying the threshold values which will indicate the stronger association between two nodes.

$$I_{ij} = \begin{bmatrix} 1 & 0.766 & 0.113 & 0.827 & 0 \\ 0.132 & 1 & 0.199 & 1 & 0.321 \\ 0 & 0.231 & 1 & 0.542 & 0.635 \\ 0.213 & 0 & 0 & 1 & 0.854 \\ 0 & 0 & 0.925 & 0.092 & 1 \end{bmatrix} \tag{5}$$

Figure 1. Roundtrip "friendship" of a node i via other peers, and the "reach-back" notation to the node via the intermediate peers

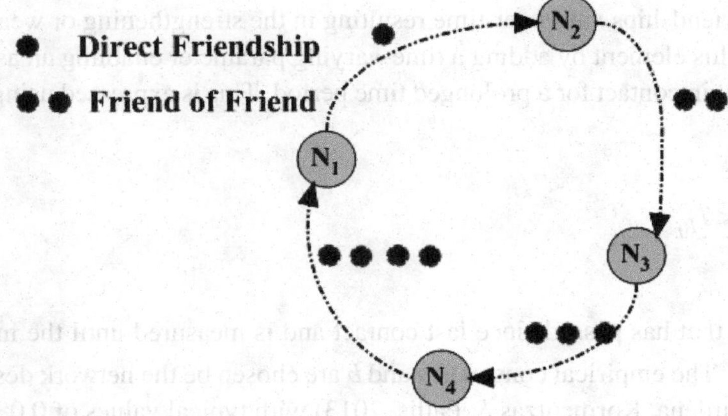

Social-Oriented Data Exploitation for Efficient Resource Offloading

The elements of the Matrix I_{ij} (5) represent the measure of the social relationship "friendship" between the users. This is determined by the amount of direct or indirect social interaction among the different users belonging to the network as follows:

$$f_{i\to j}^{d} = norm\left[c(t)\cdot P(t)\right]^{0..1}\ \forall i,j \quad (6)$$

where $f_{i\to j}^{d}$ is the defined as the direct friendship evaluation from node i to node j. $P(k_t)$ is the probability $P(k)$ of a node being connected to k other nodes at time t in the network decays as a power law, given by: $P(k)=k^{-\gamma}$ where for the value of the power γ is estimated as follows $2<\gamma<3$ as explored in various real networks (Mavromoustakis, Dimitriou & Mastorakis, 2013). This results in a large number of nodes having a small node degree and therefore very few neighbors, but a very small number of nodes having a large node degree and therefore becoming hubs in the system. $c(t)$ consists of the duration of the communication among "friends", and is determined as a function of the communication frequency and the number of roundtrip "friendships". The roundtrip "friendships" are determined by the "hop-friendships" of the node i to a node k, as Figure 1 presents. These are the "friends-of-friends" where according to the node i any "friend-of-friend" can reach –on a roundtrip basis- the node i again.

Then, the c (t) of any of the "friendship" peers can be evaluated as the: $c(t)=\frac{1}{N}f_{i\to j}^{d}$, where N is the number of peers away from i for reaching a friendship within $f_{i\to k}^{d}$ for a specified time slot *t*. Each element in the I_{ij} is re-estimated and varies through time according to the enhancement of the relation of the individuals as follows:

$$I_{ij}=\frac{I_{ij}+\Delta I}{1+\Delta I} \quad (7)$$

where I_{ij} is the association between two individuals that is strengthened or weakened (if less than $\nabla I_{ij} = I_{ij(\tau)} - I_{ij(\tau-1)}$) and ∇I represents the difference from the previous I_{ij} association between i, j. As associations and friendships vary over-time resulting in the strengthening or weakening of different links we incorporate this element by adding a time-varying parameter enabling an association to fade if two individuals are not in contact for a prolonged time period. This is expressed using the flowing equation:

$$\Delta I_{ij} = \frac{a}{t_{age}} + b, \forall t_{age} < T_{R_L} \tag{8}$$

where t_{age} is the time that has passed since last contact and is measured until the individuals abandon the clustered plane L. The empirical constants a and b are chosen be the network designer (Mastorakis, Mavromoustakis, Bourdena, Kormentzas & Pallis, 2013) with typical values of 0.08 and 0.005 respectively. The proposed model encompasses the impact of the mobility on the interaction elements I_{ij} as the derived matrix consisting of the elements of w_{ij}^{L} and I_{ij} as follows:

$$M_{ij} = I_{ij} \cdot p_{ij}^{L} \tag{9}$$

where the element w_{ij} derived from the p_{ij}^{L} matrix of the plane area L, is the likelihood of an individual to move from i to a certain direction to j, as Figure 1 shows.

Mobile Cloud Offloading by Exploiting Social Centrality

The determination of the importance of each node in a wireless mobile network is a very important task. This importance is based on the node's position, connectivity and interactivity patterns, as well as on motion thought time. A large number of connections and interactions signify an important and social central node. The term of centrality that has been introduced in (Hu, Mostashari & Xie, 2010) combines user behavior of each individual device with respect to its placement and behavior with the other devices within the cluster (Mavromoustakis, 2010). From a group of nodes a subset of the individuals is sampled and used to produce a subgraph, consisting only of those individuals and the links among them. The subgraph produced is used for performing the centrality approximation with the centrality scores of the sample being used as approximations. In social networks the high connectivity degree nodes serve as bridges in order to provide connectivity to lower degree nodes. A node's degree can be measured, by $D_c(aj) = \sum_{i=1}^{n} d(ai, aj)$, where $d(ai, aj) = \begin{cases} 1 \forall ai, aj \in D \\ 0 \forall ai, aj \notin D \end{cases}$, D denotes the direct connectivity. As the maximum number of connected nodes for any graph is *n-1,* the formula to calculate the centrality of the node by using the proportion of the number of adjacent nodes to the maximum number (n-1) is as follows:

$$D'_c(aj) = \frac{\sum_{i=1}^{n} d(ai, aj)}{n-1} \tag{10}$$

Centrality is used to indicate the relative importance of a node in a network of nodes (Mavromoustakis & Dimitriou, 2012) and its relative contribution to the communication process as derived by the duration and distance covered with the frequency and parameterized in the context of avoiding network communication partitioning. Adding to this, social centrality measures the social closeness of two or more nodes. With social centrality we measure the number of times a node is chosen to host the "best-effort" parameters, process offloading in our case, for time t in L. A node with high social betweenness centrality βai will have to strongly interact with the other nodes belonging to social cluster L, measured as:

$$\beta_{ai} = \frac{\sum_{1}^{j} P_{aj \to ak}}{\sum_{1}^{k} P_{ij} \forall P \in ai} \tag{11}$$

with $P_{aj \to ak}$ representing the number of paths in the cluster via which the requested memory/capacity resources can be served between nodes aj and ak and P_{ij} represents the number of paths in the social cluster that include $ai, \forall P \in ai$. Based on the latter, we introduce the social-oriented stability parameter $\sigma_{c(t)}$ for a specified time t, as:

$$\sigma_C(t) = \left[\frac{R_{ij|t} \cdot (1 - norm(\beta_{ai})) \cdot N_{C(i \to j|t)}}{\inf(C_r) \cdot R_{C(t)}} \right] m_{ij}(t) \tag{12}$$

where R_{ij} is the normalized communication ping delays between i and j nodes at time t, β_{ai} is the normalized $[0..1]$ social betweenness centrality showing the strong ability to interact with other nodes in the cluster L, $N_{c(i \to j|t)}$ is the successfully offloaded capacity/memory units over the total allowed capacity, C_r *is* the multi-hop channel's available capacity, $m_{ij}(t)$ is the interaction measures derived from Equation 8 at the time interval t and $R_{c(t)}$ is the end-to-end delay in the cluster's pathway. The social-oriented stability parameter $\sigma_C(t)$ indicates the capability and transmitability of the node i to offload a certain process according to the ranked criteria of each process in L for time t.

Energy consumption is important for wireless nodes as non-optimized energy usage can lead to uncertainty in availability and reliability for each node and consequently the whole of the network. In this work, we use the social centrality aspect of the network as the substrate for efficient energy conservation. As the social centrality degree differs per node, processes are offloaded so as to minimize the total energy consumption and provide a total higher node availability for the most popular nodes, thus maintaining network connectivity. The system will decide when and where to offload processes, according the current energy state of each device. The degree of social centrality allows the node to offload resources according to the social model and the estimation of the each node's energy consumption as in Equation 14. So ultimately, in order to achieve energy conservation, resources may be offloaded to the cloud or any other peer-neighboring device (so that the device that needs to run the executable resource will potentially conserve energy). Thus, the measurable energy consumption can be evaluated according to the:

$$E_{r(a_j)} = E_C\left(a_j\right) \cdot \frac{C}{S_{a_j}} \tag{13}$$

where C is the parameter indicating the number of instructions that can be processed within T_t, S_{a_j} represents the processing time at the server-device and $E_c(a_j)$, represents the relative energy consumption which is expressed as:

$$E_C\left(r_i\right) = \frac{Cost_{C(r_i)}}{S_{C(r_i)}} \cdot W_C \tag{14}$$

where S_c is the server instruction processing speed for the computation resources, $Cost_c$ the resources instruction processing cost for the computation resources and W_c signifies the energy consumption of the device in mW.

Each mobile device should satisfy an energy threshold level and a specified centrality degree in the system in order to proceed with process execution offloading. By using N devices within *2-hops vicinity coverage* which is evaluated based on the measurements regarding the maximum signal strength and data rate model (Ciobanu, Marin, Dobre, Cristea & Mavromoustakis, 2014)) the following should be satisfied:

$$\frac{Cost_{c(r_i)}}{S_{c(r_i)}} \cdot W_c\Big|^{r_i} > \frac{Cost_{c(r_i)}}{S_{c(r_i)}} \cdot W_c\Big|^{1,2..N} \tag{15}$$

$$W_{r_i} > W_c \forall f_{i \to j}^{d} \ devices \tag{16}$$

The energy consumption of each device should satisfy the (15)-(16) for each of the resources (executable processes) running onto the device MN_{m-1} hosting the r_i resource. The $r_1, r_2, r_3, .. r_i$ parameters represent the resources that can be offloaded to run onto another device based on the resources' availability as in (Mousicou, Mavromoustakis, Bourdena, Mastorakis & Pallis, 2013). In this respect, the r_i with the maximum energy consumption is running in a partitionable manner to minimize the energy consumed by other peer-devices. These actions are shown in the steps of the proposed algorithm in Table 1.

The resource allocation will take place, towards responding to the performance requirements as in (Mavromoustakis, 2010) and (Mousicou, Mavromoustakis, Bourdena, Mastorakis & Pallis, 2013). A significant measure in the system is the availability of memory and the processing power of the mobile

Table 1. Centrality-based offloading scheme

Inputs: MN_m, Location, resources $r_{1,}r_2,r_3,..r_i \forall MN_m$ with certain mobility direction w_{ij}^L for all Cloud devices that have association of $f_{i\to j}^d$ and satisfy $c(t) = \frac{1}{N} f_{i\to j}^d$

find from $r_{1,}r_2,r_3,..r_i$ the r_i that can be offloaded to run onto another device

for all MN_{m-1} do{

Estimate $\sigma_C(t) = \left[\frac{R_{ij|t} \cdot (1 - norm(\beta_{ai})) \cdot N_{C(i\to j|t)}}{\inf(C_r) \cdot R_{C(t)}} \right] m_{ij}(t)$

if ($\sigma_C(t)$ is valid and above a threshold){

search for MN_{m-1} device that satisfies

$\frac{Cost_{c(r_i)}}{S_{c(r_i)}} \cdot W_c\Big|^{r_i} > \frac{Cost_{c(r_i)}}{S_{c(r_i)}} \cdot W_c\Big|^{1,2..N}, W_{r_i} > W_c \forall 1,2,3,...N$

offload (r_i, $MN_{k(i)}$) //to $MN_{k(i)}$ to execute resource *(i)* onto *k* node

end **if**

end **for**

end **for**

cloud devices, as well as the server-based terminals. The processing power metric is designed and used to measure the processing losses for the terminals that the r_i will be offloaded, as in (17), where a_j is an application and T_k^j is the number of terminals in forming the cloud (mobile and static) rack that are hosting application a_j and $T_{aj}(r)$ is the number of mobile terminals hosting process of the application across all different cloud-terminals (racks).

$$C_{a_j} = \frac{T_k^j}{\sum_k T_{a_j}(r)} \forall \min(E_c(r_i)) \in f_{i\to j}^d \tag{17}$$

Equation 17 shows that if there is minimal loss in the capacity utilization i.e. $C_{aj\cong 1}$ then the sequence of racks $T_{aj}(r)$ are optimally utilized. The latter is shown through the conducted simulation experiments in the next section. The dynamic resource migration algorithm is shown in Table I with the basic steps for obtaining an efficient execution for a partitionable resource that cannot be handled by the mobile device in reference and therefore the offloading policy is used to ensure execution continuation. The entire scheme is shown in Table I, with all the primary steps for offloading the resources onto either MN_{m-1} neighbouring nodes (or –as called- server nodes (as in (Mousicou, Mavromoustakis, Bourdena, Mastorakis & Pallis, 2013))) based on the delay and temporal criteria of the collaborating nodes.

PERFORMANCE EVALUATION ANALYSIS, EXPERIMENTAL RESULTS AND DISCUSSION

Performance evaluation results encompass comparisons with other existing schemes for offered reliability degree, in contrast to the energy conservation efficiency. The mobility model used in this work is based on the probabilistic Fraction Brownian Motion (FBM) adopted in (Mousicou, Mavromoustakis, Bourdena, Mastorakis & Pallis, 2013), where nodes are moving, according to certain probabilities, location and time. The simulated scenario uses 80 nodes that are randomly initialized with social parameter and through the transient state during simulation the system estimates the social betweenness centrality in regards to the ability to interact with other nodes in *L,* and successfully offload memory or processing intense processes to be partially executed onto socially-collaborating peers based on the criteria depicted in Table 1 pseudo-code. "Friendship" degree with the completed requested offloads is shown in Figure 2 for three different schemes. It is important to mark out that by using the social interactions the number of completed offloading processes are greater and outperforms the applied scheme with no social interactions at all. In Figure 3 the Complementary Cumulative Distribution Function (CCDF or tail distribution) with the degree of "friendship" is shown within the respective values of ageing factor (Equation 8).

Figure 4 shows the execution time during simulation for mobile nodes with different mobility patterns and it is evaluated for GSM/GPRS, Wi-Fi/WLAN and for communication within a certain Wi-Fi/WLAN to another Wi-Fi/WLAN remotely hosted. The latter scenario -from a Wi-Fi/WLAN to another Wi-Fi/WLAN- shows to exhibit significant reduction, in terms of the execution time duration, whereas it hosts the minimum execution time through the FBM with distance broadcast mobility pattern. Figure

Figure 2. Friendship degree with the completed requested offloads

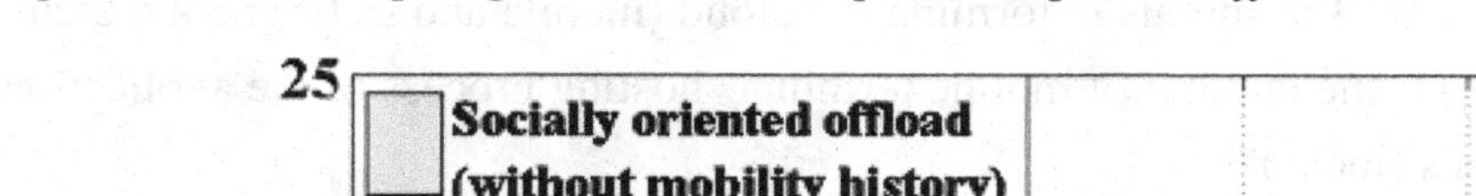

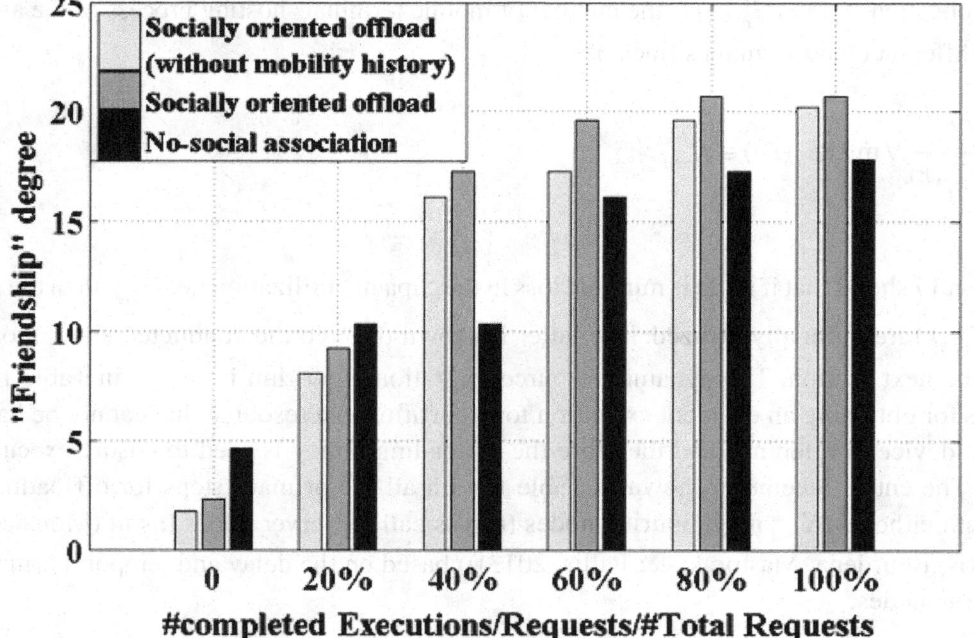

Figure 3. CCDF with the degree of friendship

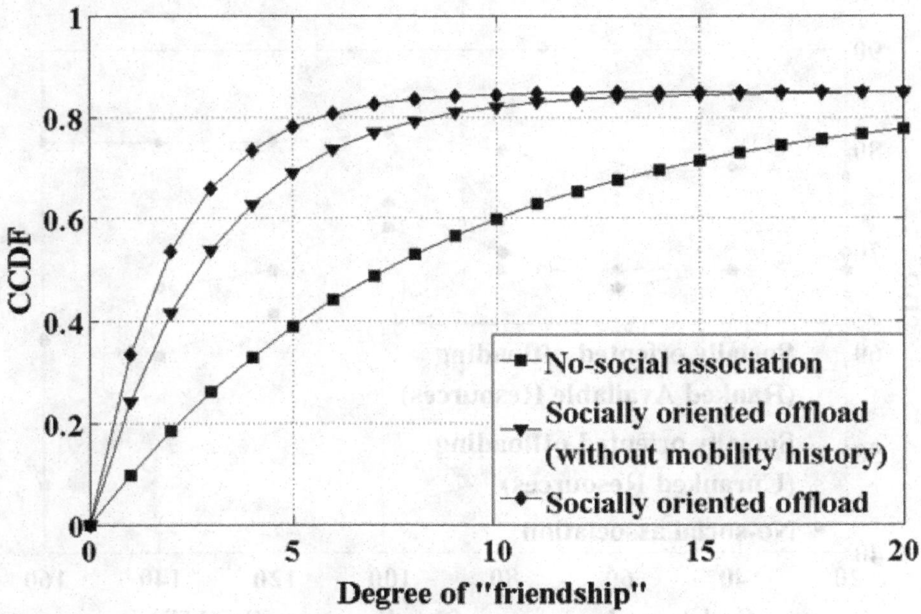

Figure 4. Execution time through simulation

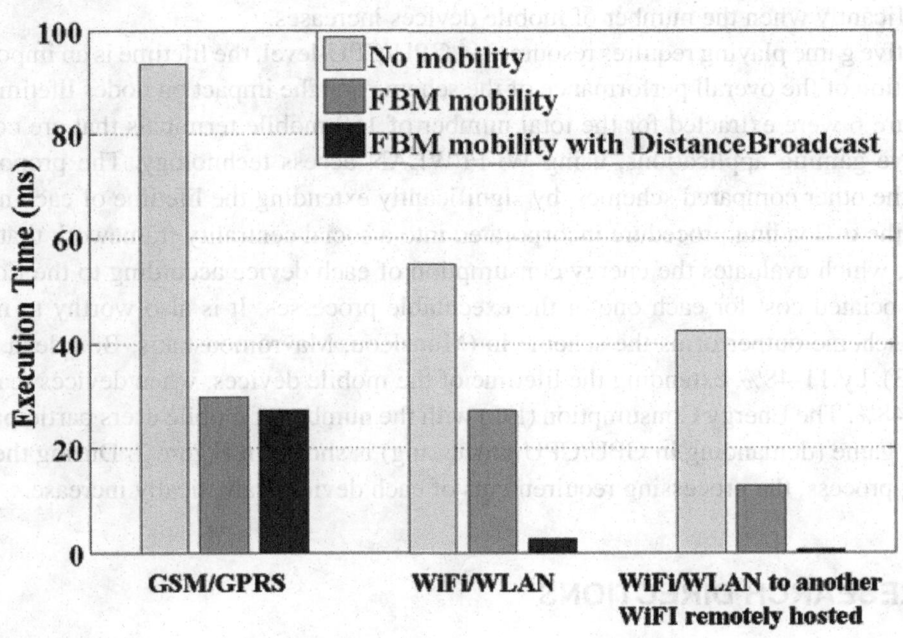

Figure 5. Successful delivery rate with the End-to-End resource offloading capacity based on the "friendship" model

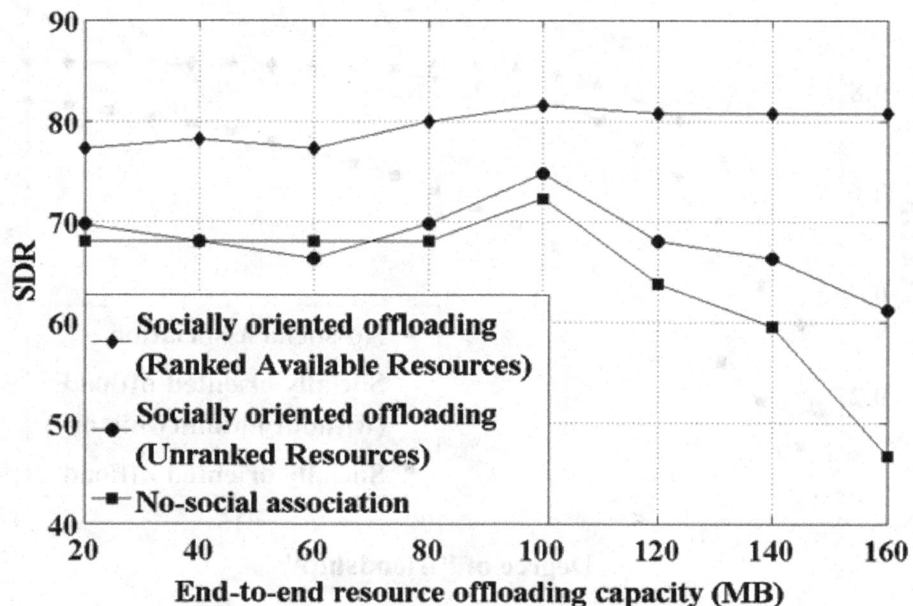

5 shows the Successful Delivery Rate (SDR) with the End-to-End resource offloading capacity based on the "friendship" model, whereas Figure 6 shows that the proposed scheme extends the average node's lifetime significantly when the number of mobile devices increases.

As interactive game playing requires resources in GPU/CPU-level, the lifetime is an important metric for the evaluation of the overall performance of the scheme and the impact on nodes lifetime. Measurements in Figure 6 were extracted for the total number of 150 mobile terminals that are configured to host interactive gaming applications, using Wi-Fi/WLAN access technology. The proposed scheme outperforms the other compared schemes, by significantly extending the lifetime of each node. This is as a result of the offloading procedure incorporated into a social centrality framework that takes place on each node, which evaluates the energy consumption of each device according to the Equations 15-17 for the associated cost for each one of the executable processes. It is also worthy to mention that the proposed scheme outperforms the scheme in (Mousicou, Mavromoustakis, Bourdena, Mastorakis & Pallis, 2013), by 11-48%, extending the lifetime of the mobile devices, when devices reach 150 by a maximum of 48%. The Energy Consumption (EC) with the number of mobile users participating during an interactive game (demanding in GPU/CPU processing) is shown in Figure 7. During the interactive game-playing process, the processing requirements of each device dramatically increase.

FUTURE RESEARCH DIRECTIONS

Future directions in our on-going research encompass the improvement of an opportunistically formed mobile cloud, which will allow delay-sensitive resources to be offloaded, using the mobile peer-to-peer (MP2P) technology.

Figure 6. Average node's lifetime extensibility with the number of mobile devices for three different schemes in the evaluated area (evaluated for the most energy draining resources)

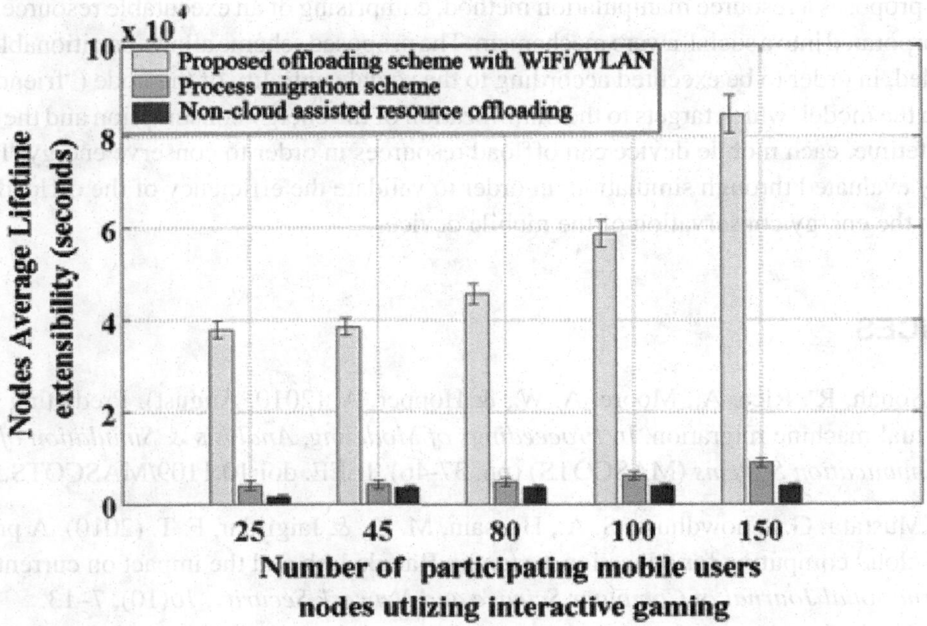

Figure 7. Energy Consumption (EC) with the number of mobile users participating during an interactive game

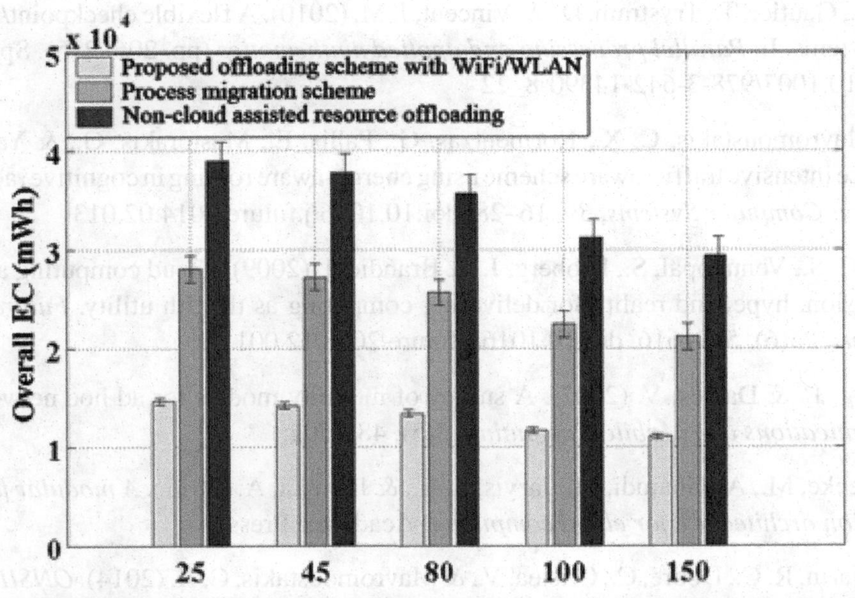

CONCLUSION

This chapter proposes a resource manipulation method, comprising of an executable resource offloading scheme, incorporated into a social-aware mechanism. The proposed scheme allows partitionable resources to be offloaded, in order to be executed according to the social centrality of the node ("friendship" list). According to the model, which targets to the minimization of the energy consumption and the maximization of the lifetime, each mobile device can offload resources in order to conserve energy. The scheme is thoroughly evaluated through simulation, in order to validate the efficiency of the offloading policy, in contrast to the energy conservation of the mobile devices.

REFERENCES

Akoush, S., Sohan, R., Rice, A., Moore, A. W., & Hopper, A. (2010, August). Predicting the performance of virtual machine migration. In *Proceedings of Modeling, Analysis & Simulation of Computer and Telecommunication Systems* (MASCOTS) (pp. 37-46). IEEE. doi:10.1109/MASCOTS.2010.13

Al Noor, S., Mustafa, G., Chowdhury, S. A., Hossain, M. Z., & Jaigirdar, F. T. (2010). A proposed architecture of cloud computing for education system in Bangladesh and the impact on current education system. *International Journal of Computer Science and Network Security*, *10*(10), 7–13.

Alabbadi, M. M. (2011, September). Cloud computing for education and learning: Education and learning as a service (ELaaS). In *Proceedings of Interactive Collaborative Learning* (ICL) (pp. 589-594). IEEE.

Beloglazov, A., & Buyya, R. (2010, May). Energy efficient resource management in virtualized cloud data centers. In *Proceedings of the 2010 10th IEEE/ACM International Conference on Cluster, Cloud and Grid Computing* (pp. 826-831). IEEE Computer Society. doi:10.1109/CCGRID.2010.46

Bouguerra, M. S., Gautier, T., Trystram, D., & Vincent, J. M. (2010). A flexible checkpoint/restart model in distributed systems. In *Parallel processing and applied mathematics* (pp. 206–215). Springer Berlin Heidelberg. doi:10.1007/978-3-642-14390-8_22

Bourdena, A., Mavromoustakis, C. X., Kormentzas, G., Pallis, E., Mastorakis, G., & Yassein, M. B. (2014). A resource intensive traffic-aware scheme using energy-aware routing in cognitive radio networks. *Future Generation Computer Systems*, *39*, 16–28. doi:10.1016/j.future.2014.02.013

Buyya, R., Yeo, C. S., Venugopal, S., Broberg, J., & Brandic, I. (2009). Cloud computing and emerging IT platforms: Vision, hype, and reality for delivering computing as the 5th utility. *Future Generation Computer Systems*, *25*(6), 599–616. doi:10.1016/j.future.2008.12.001

Camp, T., Boleng, J., & Davies, V. (2002). A survey of mobility models for ad hoc network research. *Wireless Communications and Mobile Computing, 2*(5), 483-502.

Chester, A. P., Leeke, M., Al-Ghamdi, M., Jarvis, S. A., & Jhumka, A. (2011). *A modular failure-aware resource allocation architecture for cloud computing*. Academic Press.

Ciobanu, R. I., Marin, R. C., Dobre, C., Cristea, V., & Mavromoustakis, C. X. (2014). *ONSIDE: Socially-aware and interest-based dissemination in opportunistic networks*. Academic Press.

Cuervo, E., Balasubramanian, A., Cho, D. K., Wolman, A., Saroiu, S., Chandra, R., & Bahl, P. (2010, June). MAUI: Making smartphones last longer with code offload. In *Proceedings of the 8th International Conference on Mobile Systems, Applications, and Services* (pp. 49-62). ACM. doi:10.1145/1814433.1814441

Dimitriou, C. D., Mavromoustakis, C. X., Mastorakis, G., & Pallis, E. (2013, June). On the performance response of delay-bounded energy-aware bandwidth allocation scheme in wireless networks. In *Proceedings of Communications Workshops (ICC)* (pp. 631-636). IEEE. doi:10.1109/ICCW.2013.6649310

Ercan, T. (2010). Effective use of cloud computing in educational institutions. *Procedia: Social and Behavioral Sciences*, *2*(2), 938–942. doi:10.1016/j.sbspro.2010.03.130

Fox, A., Griffith, R., Joseph, A., Katz, R., Konwinski, A., Lee, G., . . . Stoica, I. (2009). Above the clouds: A Berkeley view of cloud computing. Dept. Electrical Eng. and Comput. Sciences, University of California, Berkeley, Rep. UCB/EECS, 28, 13.

Frey, S., & Hasselbring, W. (2010, November). Model-based migration of legacy software systems to scalable and resource-efficient cloud-based applications: The cloudmig approach. In *Proceedings of CLOUD COMPUTING 2010, The First International Conference on Cloud Computing, GRIDs, and Virtualization* (pp. 155-158). Academic Press.

Gkatzikis, L., & Koutsopoulos, I. (2013). Migrate or not? Exploiting dynamic task migration in mobile cloud computing systems. IEEE Wireless Communications, 20(3).

Hu, F., Mostashari, A., & Xie, J. (Eds.). (2010). *Socio-technical networks: Science and engineering design*. CRC Press.

Javadi, B., Thulasiraman, P., & Buyya, R. (2012, June). Cloud resource provisioning to extend the capacity of local resources in the presence of failures. In *Proceedings of High Performance Computing and Communication & 2012 IEEE 9th International Conference on Embedded Software and Systems* (HPCC-ICESS) (pp. 311-319). IEEE. doi:10.1109/HPCC.2012.49

Khajeh-Hosseini, A., Sommerville, I., Bogaerts, J., & Teregowda, P. (2011, July). Decision support tools for cloud migration in the enterprise. In *Proceedings of Cloud Computing* (CLOUD) (pp. 541-548). IEEE.

Khamayseh, Y. M., BaniYassein, M., AbdAlghani, M., & Mavromoustakis, C. X. (2013). Network size estimation in VANETs. *Network Protocols and Algorithms*, *5*(3), 136–152. doi:10.5296/npa.v5i3.3838

Khan, A., Othman, M., Madani, S., & Khan, S. (2013). *A survey of mobile cloud computing application models*. IEEE Communication Surveys and Tutorials.

Lawler, G. F. (1995). *Introduction to stochastic processes*. CRC Press.

Mastorakis, G., Bourdena, A., Mavromoustakis, C. X., Pallis, E., & Kormentzas, G. (2013, July). An energy-efficient routing protocol for ad-hoc cognitive radio networks. In *Future network and mobile summit (FutureNetworkSummit), 2013* (pp. 1–10). IEEE.

Mastorakis, G., Mavromoustakis, C. X., Bourdena, A., Kormentzas, G., & Pallis, E. (2013, September). Maximizing energy conservation in a centralized cognitive radio network architecture. In *Proceedings of Computer Aided Modeling and Design of Communication Links and Networks (CAMAD)* (pp. 175-179). IEEE. doi:10.1109/CAMAD.2013.6708112

Mastorakis, G., Mavromoustakis, C. X., Bourdena, A., & Pallis, E. (2013, June). An energy-efficient routing scheme using backward traffic difference estimation in cognitive radio networks. In *Proceedings of World of Wireless, Mobile and Multimedia Networks (WoWMoM)* (pp. 1-6). IEEE. doi:10.1109/WoWMoM.2013.6583446

Mastorakis, G., Mavromoustakis, C. X., Bourdena, A., Pallis, E., & Sismanidis, G. (2013, November). Optimizing radio resource management in energy-efficient cognitive radio networks. In *Proceedings of the 2nd ACM Workshop on High Performance Mobile Opportunistic Systems* (pp. 75-82). ACM. doi:10.1145/2507908.2507920

Mastorakis, G., Mavromoustakis, C. X., Bourdena, A., Pallis, E., Sismanidis, G., Stratakis, D., & Papadakis, S. (2014). Energy-efficient routing in cognitive radio networks. In *Resource management in mobile computing environments* (pp. 323–340). Springer International Publishing. doi:10.1007/978-3-319-06704-9_14

Mastorakis, G., Panagiotakis, S., Kapetanakis, K., Dagalakis, G., Mavromoustakis, C. X., Bourdena, A., & Pallis, E. (2014). Energy and resource consumption evaluation of mobile cognitive radio devices. In *Resource management in mobile computing environments* (pp. 359–388). Springer International Publishing. doi:10.1007/978-3-319-06704-9_16

Mavromoustakis, C., Andreou, A., Mastorakis, G., Papadakis, S., Bourdena, A., & Stratakis, D. (2014, August). Energy consumption optimization through pre-scheduled opportunistic offloading in wireless devices. In *Proceedings of EMERGING 2014, The Sixth International Conference on Emerging Network Intelligence* (pp. 22-28). Academic Press.

Mavromoustakis, C., Dimitriou, C. D., & Mastorakis, G. (2012, September). Using real-time backward traffic difference estimation for energy conservation in wireless devices. In *Proceedings of AP2PS 2012, The Fourth International Conference on Advances in P2P Systems* (pp. 18-23). Academic Press.

Mavromoustakis, C., Dimitriou, C. D., & Mastorakis, G. (2013). On the real-time evaluation of two-level BTD scheme for energy conservation in the presence of delay sensitive transmissions and intermittent connectivity in wireless devices. *International Journal on Advances in Networks and Services, 6*(3 and 4), 148-162.

Mavromoustakis, C. X. (2010, March). Collaborative optimistic replication for efficient delay-sensitive MP2P streaming using community oriented neighboring feedback. In *Proceedings of Pervasive Computing and Communications Workshops (PERCOM Workshops)* (pp. 105-110). IEEE. doi:10.1109/PERCOMW.2010.5470611

Mavromoustakis, C. X., Andreou, A., Mastorakis, G., Bourdena, A., Batalla, J. M., & Dobre, C. (2014). On the performance evaluation of a novel offloading-based energy conservation mechanism for wireless devices. In *Proceedings of 6th International Conference on Mobile Networks and Management* (MONAMI 2014). Academic Press.

Mavromoustakis, C. X., Bourdena, A., Mastorakis, G., Pallis, E., & Kormentzas, G. (2015). An energy-aware scheme for efficient spectrum utilization in a 5G mobile cognitive radio network architecture. *Telecommunication Systems Journal.*

Mavromoustakis, C. X., Dimitriou, C., Mastorakis, G., Bourdena, A., & Pallis, E. (2014). Using traffic diversities for scheduling wireless interfaces for energy harvesting in wireless devices. In *Resource management in mobile computing environments* (pp. 481–496). Springer International Publishing.

Mavromoustakis, C. X., & Dimitriou, C. D. (2012, May). Using social interactions for opportunistic resource sharing using mobility-enabled contact-oriented replication. In *Proceedings of International Conference on Collaboration Technologies and Systems (CTS 2012). In Cooperation with ACM/IEEE, Internet of Things, Machine to Machine and Smart Services Applications (IoT 2012)* (pp. 21-25). ACM.

Mavromoustakis, C. X., Dimitriou, C. D., Mastorakis, G., & Pallis, E. (2013, December). Real-time performance evaluation of F-BTD scheme for optimized QoS energy conservation in wireless devices. In Proceedings of Globecom Workshops (GC Wkshps) (pp. 1151-1156). IEEE. doi:10.1109/GLOCOMW.2013.6825148

Mavromoustakis, C. X., Mastorakis, G., Bourdena, A., & Pallis, E. (2014). *Energy efficient resource sharing using a traffic-oriented routing scheme for cognitive radio networks*. IET Networks.

Mavromoustakis, C. X., Mastorakis, G., Bourdena, A., Pallis, E., Kormentzas, G., & Rodrigues, J. (2014, December). Context-oriented opportunistic cloud offload processing for energy conservation in wireless devices. In Proceedings of Globecom Workshops (GC Wkshps). IEEE.

Mavromoustakis, C. X., Mastorakis, G., Bourdena, A., Pallis, E., Kormentzas, G., & Dimitriou, C. D. (2014, December). Joint energy and delay-aware scheme for 5G mobile cognitive radio networks. In Proceedings of IEEE Globecom. IEEE.

Mavromoustakis, C. X., Pallis, E., & Mastorakis, G. (2014). *Resource management in mobile computing environments: Modeling and optimization in science and technologies*. Springer. doi:10.1007/978-3-319-06704-9

McAfee, A. (2011). What every CEO needs to know about the cloud. *Harvard Business Review*, *89*(11), 124–132. PMID:21370809

Mishra, M., Das, A., Kulkarni, P., & Sahoo, A. (2012). Dynamic resource management using virtual machine migrations. *Communications Magazine, IEEE*, *50*(9), 34–40. doi:10.1109/MCOM.2012.6295709

Mousicou, P., Mavromoustakis, C. X., Bourdena, A., Mastorakis, G., & Pallis, E. (2013, November). Performance evaluation of dynamic cloud resource migration based on temporal and capacity-aware policy for efficient resource sharing. In *Proceedings of the 2nd ACM Workshop on High Performance Mobile Opportunistic Systems* (pp. 59-66). ACM. doi:10.1145/2507908.2507917

Pannu, H. S., Liu, J., Guan, Q., & Fu, S. (2012, December). AFD: Adaptive failure detection system for cloud computing infrastructures. In *Proceedings of Performance Computing and Communications Conference* (IPCCC) (pp. 71-80). IEEE.

Papanikolaou, K., Mavromoustakis, C. X., Mastorakis, G., Bourdena, A., & Dobre, C. Energy consumption optimization using social interaction in the mobile cloud. In *Proceedings of 6th International Conference on Mobile Networks and Management* (MONAMI 2014). Academic Press. doi:10.1007/978-3-319-16292-8_31

Ren, S., & van der Schaar, M. (2013). Efficient resource provisioning and rate selection for stream mining in a community cloud. *IEEE Transactions on Multimedia*, *15*(4), 723–734. doi:10.1109/TMM.2013.2240673

Sachs, D. G., Yuan, W., Hughes, C. J., Harris, A. F., III, Adve, S. V., Jones, D. L., . . . Nahrstedt, K. (2004). *GRACE: A hierarchical adaptation framework for saving energy*. University of Illinois Technical Report UIUCDCS-R-2004-2409.

Sagar, M. S., Singh, B., & Ahmad, W. (2013). Study on cloud computing resource allocation strategies. *International Journal (Toronto, Ont.)*, *3*, 107–114.

Scott, J., & Carrington, P. J. (Eds.). (2011). *The SAGE handbook of social network analysis*. SAGE Publications.

Skourletopoulos, G., Bahsoon, R., Mavromoustakis, C. X., Mastorakis, G., & Pallis, E. (2014, December). Predicting and quantifying the technical debt in cloud software engineering. In *Proceedings of Computer Aided Modeling and Design of Communication Links and Networks (CAMAD)*. IEEE. doi:10.1109/CAMAD.2014.7033201

Sultan, N. (2010). Cloud computing for education: A new dawn? *International Journal of Information Management*, *30*(2), 109–116. doi:10.1016/j.ijinfomgt.2009.09.004

Tang, J., Musolesi, M., Mascolo, C., Latora, V., & Nicosia, V. (2010, April). Analysing information flows and key mediators through temporal centrality metrics. In *Proceedings of the 3rd Workshop on Social Network Systems* (p. 3). ACM. doi:10.1145/1852658.1852661

Younge, A. J., Von Laszewski, G., Wang, L., Lopez-Alarcon, S., & Carithers, W. (2010, August). Efficient resource management for cloud computing environments. In *Proceedings of Green Computing Conference* (pp. 357-364). IEEE. doi:10.1109/GREENCOMP.2010.5598294

KEY TERMS AND DEFINITIONS

Energy Conservation: It refers to reducing energy consumption through using less of an energy service.

Mobile Cloud Computing: It is the combination of cloud computing, mobile computing and wireless networks to bring rich computational resources to mobile users, network operators, as well as cloud computing providers.

Mobile Computing: It is the human–computer interaction, by which a computer is expected to be transported during normal usage.

Network Performance: It refers to measures of service quality of a telecommunications product as seen by the customer.

Social Centrality: In graph theory and network analysis, centrality refers to indicators, which identify the most important vertices within a graph. Applications include identifying the most influential person(s) in a social network, key infrastructure nodes in the Internet or urban networks, and super spreaders of disease.

Social Media: It is the social interaction among people, in which they create, share or exchange information and ideas in virtual communities and networks.

Social Networking Service: It is a platform to build social networks or social relations among people who share interests, activities, backgrounds or real-life connections. A social network service consists of a representation of each user (often a profile), his or her social links, and a variety of additional services.

Chapter 6 Traffic Analyses and Measurements: Technological Dependability

Rossitza Goleva
Technical University of Sofia, Bulgaria

Desislava Dimitrova
ETH Zurich, Switzerland

Dimitar Atamian
Technical University of Sofia, Bulgaria

Lubina Grigorova
Vivacom JSCO, Bulgaria

Seferin Mirtchev
Technical University of Sofia, Bulgaria

Rosen Rangelov
Lufthansa Technik-Sofia, Bulgaria

Aneliya Ivanova
Technical University of Sofia, Bulgaria

ABSTRACT

Resource management schemes in current data centers, including cloud environments, are not well equipped to handle the dynamic variation in traffic caused by the large diversity of traffic sources, source mobility patterns, and underlying network characteristics. Part of the problem is lacking knowledge on the traffic source behaviour and its proper representation for development and operation. Inaccurate, static traffic models lead to incorrect estimation of traffic characteristics, making resource allocation, migration, and release schemes inefficient, and limit scalability. The end result is unsatisfied customers (due to service degradation) and operators (due to costly inefficient infrastructure use). The authors argue that developing appropriate methods and tools for traffic predictability requires carefully conducted and analysed traffic experiments. This chapter presents their measurements and statistical analyses on various traffic sources for two network settings, namely local Area Network (LAN) and 3G mobile network. LAN traffic is organised in DiffServ categories supported by MPLS to ensure Quality of Service (QoS) provisioning. 3G measurements are taken from a live network upon entering the IP domain. Passive monitoring was used to collect the measurements in order to be non-obtrusive for the networks. The analyses indicate that the gamma distribution has general applicability to represent various traffic sources by proper setting of the parameters. The findings allow the construction of traffic models and simulation tools to be used in the development and evaluation of flexible resource management schemes that meet the real-time needs of the users.

DOI: 10.4018/978-1-4666-8225-2.ch006

INTRODUCTION

Information and communication services experience most vigorous advances in modern networks. The adoption of new technological paradigms such as cloud computing, opportunistic communication, delay tolerant networking, ubiquitous sensors networks and machine-to-machine communication only stressed the importance of ubiquitous connectivity and information availability at any place, time and quality. At the same time, users demand forever increasing diversity of services in a technology transparent manner. Often, these are services with high quality demands, i.e., according to Cisco (Cisco, 2013) and Ericsson (Ericsson, 2013) video and multicast services will dominate the mobile network traffic by 2020. The combined effects of the above phenomena on the network is a fluctuating demand for network capacity (bandwidth) caused by the large variety of applications and services and their corresponding needs to move data in the network, quickly and at high frequency.

Several factors contribute to the varied nature of current network traffic. On the one hand, novel services are no longer symmetric. Most services are implemented between devices without the direct influence of the end-user. For example, sensor networks offer high variety of applications ranging from body area monitoring to video surveillance with quadcopters. On the other hand, applications running on top of different technologies generate distinct traffic patterns – transactions (read, write and search) in the Fibre Channel Protocol (FCP) are rather different from transactions among sensors in Body Area Networks (BANs) or smart phones' broadband applications. Video and voice traffic additionally cause variations in the traffic pattern, depending on the applied codecs for video and voice over IP, which codecs are able to adjust the packet length and rate to match the channel conditions. Similarly, TCP sessions adapt window size also depending on the end-to-end channel status.

Another factor with strong influence on traffic patterns is the network itself. As traffic flows pass network devices they become object of traffic policing and traffic shaping algorithms or simply stay in a queue. For some services, queues at the far-end are intentionally introduced to deal with delay jitter equalization. In other cases after waiting in a congested node, the traffic pattern is different due to the congested node's behaviour. Therefore, there is a need for end-to-end traffic performance management and of distributed Quality of Service (QoS) algorithms that could be dynamic and react depending on the technology and the current circumstances (Rolla, & Curado, 2013).

As result of service diversification and network policing, current data traffic is characterized by a large diversity of traffic patterns. Current traffic tends to be bursty with video and voice traffic flooding. Traditional approached towards traffic prediction fail to reflect the rapidly changing traffic characteristics. Traffic engineering approaches developed by Erlang and Engset are not directly applicable in this new service environment (Schwerdel, Reuther, Zinner, Müller, & Tran-Gia, 2014). Hence, the need for appropriate network traffic modelling occurs. Proper traffic modelling cannot be done in the lack of proper traffic measurements and analyses in the forward and backward directions as well as at the access, edge and core parts of the networks. Such measurements and the following statistical analyses of the flows' behaviour are the starting point for on-the-fly resource configuration and dynamic management mechanisms (Mousicou, Mavromoustakis, Bourdena, Mastorakis, Pallis, 2013).

The aim of this chapter is to make traffic measurements and analyses at up-to-date traffic sources in IP and 3G networks and to find a distribution function that is flexible enough to map to different flows' pattern by tuning the function's parameters. The conducted research covers experimental analysis in two phases. During the first phase, measurements are performed in the lab, whereas the second phase is related to measurements in a UMTS network. The measured data are evaluated by three different statistical tools, i.e. Easyfit, Crystal Ball and Wolfram Mathematica. The output from evaluation are main statistical parameters of the flows and best fitting probability density functions of the inter-arrival times and packet sizes. Attention is paid to the traffic shaping effect. There are also experiments conducted with and without outliers detection in the forward and backward communication directions. Finally, we also present an experiment for mapping the inter-arrival time distribution function to gamma distribution with two and three parameters (Gao, Liu, Chen, Wu, El-khatib, & Edwards, 2009). Future work plans and conclusion are discussed in last section.

BACKGROUND

The problem of both end-to-end and per-node traffic changes in packet switched technologies is still not well studied. It is, however, of high importance for the end user's service satisfaction, i.e., Quality of Service (QoS) and Quality of Experience (QoE) (Freire, & Pereira, 2008). Inappropriate management of the traffic behaviour can lead to inefficient use of resources, causing underutilization for the operator and degraded service quality for the end user (Svoboda, 2008; Mousicou, Mavromoustakis, Bourdena, Mastorakis, & Pallis, 2013). Therefore, much effort has been dedicated to study and appropriately model the traffic behaviour. Most works focus on a specific traffic situation and a more generally applicable modelling is not yet at hand.

Many papers address the problem of traffic modelling in the scope of a specific technology (Bulakci, Bou Saleh, Redana, Raaf, & Hämäläinen, 2013; Goleva & Mirtchev, 2010). Others analyse specific protocols and services (Buhagiar, & Debono, 2009; Halas, Javorcek, & Kováč, 2012) or the impact of specific information coding to the QoS (Voznak, Rozhon, & Rezac, 2012). Classification, based on the service type, is motivated by its importance on performance management as in (Svoboda, 2008), which makes an attempt to map probability density functions of the inter-arrival times and packet sizes to the experienced QoS. Analysis in the scope of machine-to-machine communication is made in (Shafiq, Ji, Liu, Pang, & Wang, 2012). Power management are another factor with strong impact on traffic modelling. Distributed environments such as cloud computing are additional challenge. There are several attempts to find a flexible, unified approach to represent the distributed nature of traffic management in cloud computing by failure detection (Lavinia, Dobre, Pop, & Cristea, 2011). Some of the papers also take into account user behaviour (Marin, Dobre, & Xhafa, 2014). In mobile environments, such as wireless sensor networks, energy efficiency is essential (Mastorakis, Mavromoustakis, Bourdena, & Pallis, 2013). Nodes can transmit at different power levels and rates, depending on fading or interference, in order to maximise the node lifetime (Mavromoustakis, & Zerfiridis, 2010).

Statistical approaches to study the traffic behaviour are equally divers. There are analyses of the traffic in different environments that map the mean and the variance of the traffic to QoS network configuration parameters (Baltoglou, Karapistoli, & Chatzimisios, 2012). Some authors make attempts to understand traffic dynamics (Paul, Subramanian, Buddhikot, & Das, 2011; Mavromoustakis & Karatza, 2008). Best-fitting statistical models of the traffic patterns could be seen in many works. In (Samanta, Bhattacharjee, & Sanyal, 2010) mapping between cellular wireless traffic inter-arrival times and gamma distribution function is shown. A very interesting approach, taking into consideration resource sharing, is presented in (Bulakci, Bou Saleh, Redana, Raaf, & Hämäläinen, 2013). Traffic is also related to the configuration management in (Wang, Chuang, Tseng, & Shen, 2013) especially in sensor networks where telegrams' exchange is irregular.

Different analytical approaches to traffic management and concerning the network topology have been evaluated last two decades (Brazio, Tran-Gia, Akar, Beben, Burakowski, Fiedler, Karasan, Menth, Olivier, Tutschku, & Wittevrongel, 2006). Single server interface have been analyzed in (Mirtchev & Goleva, 2009a; Mirtchev & Goleva, 2008). Multi server case could be seen in (Mirtchev & Goleva, 2012). Advanced, more complicated approaches for distributed QoS management are given in (Schmeink, 2011; Eslami, Elliott, Krzymień & Al-Shalash, 2013; Harsini & Lahouti, 2012), which considers the end-to-end queuing effect. Dynamic traffic changes reflect directly of the resource management and energy consumed (Charalambous, Mavromoustakis, &Yassein, 2012). Elactic traffic analyses and influence on traffic loss is analysed in (Moscholios, Vasilakis, Vardakas, & Logothetis, 2011).

In this chapter, we argue about the capability of the gamma distribution to represent the packet inter-arrival times of different flow patterns. Our argumentation is based on measurements and analyses and points to gamma distribution's features and applications. The gamma distribution is a compound type of distribution. This means that its parameter has a distribution on its own. This feature allows modelling of the range of processes after proper parameterization (Mirtchev, Goleva, & Alexiev, 2010; Eng Hwee Ong & Khan, 2009; Sun & Williamson, 2008). It also could be approximated at different time scales.

TECHNOLOGICAL DEPENDABILITY OF THE TRAFFIC

Statistical Analyses of Traffic Sources

All measurements in this chapter are comprised of voice and video over IP real-time and ftp data traffic sources. The QoS requirements for such distinct traffic types are different and are usually managed separately by the network (Voznak, Rozhon, & Rezac, 2012; Schmeink, 2011; Harsini & Lahouti, 2012). The non-elastic traffic nature of video and voice over IP requires higher priority in comparison to data transmissions. In addition, TCP is capable to adjust the flow of segments and window size in congested channels. Video codecs are capable to adapt packet payload and rate. The measurements performed aim to obtain precise pattern of the different flows that will allow dynamic traffic generation for QoS analyses and resource allocation.

The output of the measurements analysis are probability density functions of the inter-arrival times and packet sizes accompanied by mean, mean standard deviations, variance, skewness and kurtosis. The obtained parameters are a base for configuration management (Mirtchev & Goleva, 2009a; Schmeink, 2011; Mirtchev & Goleva, 2009b; Mirtchev & Goleva, 2008).

The technology dependability is taken into account by setting up two different experimental phases. The first phase has been carried out in a local area network. The second phase has been conducted in the access-core part of a mobile network. Network measurements were performed using conventional Wireshark traffic analyser. Collected traces are exported to three different statistical tools such as Crystal Ball, Easyfit and Wolfram Mathematica. The tools produce the best fitting PDF, statistical parameters and use the last evaluation for PDF generation as well. The aim is to determine a simplified but accurate procedure for traffic mapping that could fit to any traffic pattern, irrespectively of technology, Open System Interconnection (OSI) layers, type of interface or end-user (end-device) behaviour. The traffic generation function could be applied in test scenarios, typically out of the norm such as disasters, excessive environmental conditions, weather fluctuations, network congestion, server attacks, traffic anomaly simulation and detection.

A single generic distribution function that is adaptable to most of the traffic patterns is needed. This is particularly important in the context of changing traffic over an end-to-end session. The PDF plots show that the traffic is changing its nature after any interface even without additional policing and shaping. In works like (Mirtchev & Goleva, 2008; Mirtchev & Goleva, 2012; Mirtchev, Goleva, & Alexiev, 2010; Mirtchev, Mavromoustakis, Goleva, Kassev, & Mastorakis, 2014) there is already demonstration of the applicability of the Pareto and Polya distribution in discrete and continuous time queuing systems. Also in (Goleva, Atamian, Mirtchev, Dimitrova, & Grigorova, 2012; Goleva, Atamian, Mirtchev, Dimitrova, & Grigorova, 2013) there is a mapping between gamma distribution function and traffic behaviour.

The gamma distribution has been already applied in modelling of many life events and especially for modelling of waiting times. It is a continuous distribution function and thus it is appropriate for modelling of inter-arrival time and servicing time distributions in network queues. The two or three parameter gamma function explains well location, scale and shape of the traffic flows' pattern. After obtaining the PDF function, the different traffic patterns could be generated by simple change of the distribution function parameters. Application of the gamma distribution function that match to almost any type of traffic is valuable for any distributed mobile QoS and resource management environment (Schmeink, 2011; Eslami, Elliott, Krzymień, & Al-Shalash, 2012; Harsini & Lahouti, 2012).

There are differences between the best fitting PDF and the statistical parameters obtained by the Oracle's Crystal Ball, Easy Fit Professional and Wolfram Mathematica. The tools apply Anderson-Darling, Kolmogorov-Smirnov and Chi-Square algorithms to determine the best fir. The difference in results is due to the implementation of the approximation function by each tool and is usually negligible. The evaluated characteristics are important because:

- PDF shows the nature of the traffic flows. It is crucial in further traffic generation because the flows should be simulated correctly.
- Mean value μ is essential for traffic generation and preliminary traffic calculations

$$\mu = \frac{\sum X}{N}, \tag{1}$$

where X is observed value, **n** is a total number of observations.

- Standard deviation σ (Variance σ^2) is important for statistical accuracy calculation and further performance analysis

$$\sigma = \sqrt{\frac{\sum_{i=1}^{n}(X_i - \bar{X})^2}{n}}. \tag{2}$$

- Skewness S_k demonstrates the symmetry of the statistical data and its tendency. Changes in skewness could overflow interfaces. It could be positive or negative

$$S_k = \frac{\mu_3}{\sigma^3}, \tag{3}$$

where μ_3 is a third central moment calculated by:

$$\mu_3 = \frac{\sum_{i=1}^{n}(X_i - \bar{X})^3}{n}. \tag{4}$$

- Kurtosis E_x is a typical scaling parameter of the flow and shows the sharpness of the function. It also shows how many observations contribute significantly to the form of the PDF and whether the distribution has a long or short tail:

$$S_k = \frac{\mu_4}{\sigma^4}, \tag{5}$$

where μ_4 is the fourth central moment calculated by:

$$\mu_4 = \frac{\sum_{i=1}^{n}(X_i - \bar{X})^4}{n}. \tag{6}$$

First Experimental Phase Setup

The first part of the measurements was performed in the lab where it was possible to change the configuration of the equipment and to experiment with different IP flows (Figure 1). The model consists of seven Juniper routers. It also includes a L2 EX4000 node of the same producer. This allows experiments of different network features over a corporate or core network set-up. The configuration supports many different traffic servicing disciplines and algorithms that support Class of Service (CoS) and QoS.

The experiment set-up for the local lab network is illustrated in Figure 2. The traffic is generated by VoIP software phones under Windows and via Asterisk VoIP server. The codec applied is GSM 6.10. Multimedia Windows Net Meeting with H.263 codec for video and H.723.1 for voice is started. FTP service runs over Windows Information Services and is a standard Windows FTP client. IP cameras support TCP/HTTP and UDP/RTP for video flows. The experiment is performed with UDP/RTP transport. During the trials, two end-users speak over Net Meeting and exchange files using FTP.

The connection between hosts 192.168.50.2 and 192.168.10.2 transmits H.263, G.723 and FTP traffic. Hosts 192.168.50.4 and 192.168.10.4 exchange H.263, G.723 flows. Hosts 192.168.10.2 and 192.168.50.200 as well as 192.168.10.4 and 192.168.50.200 exchange GSM flows. Hosts 192.168.10.2,

Figure 1. Laboratory experiments set-up with seven Juniper routers

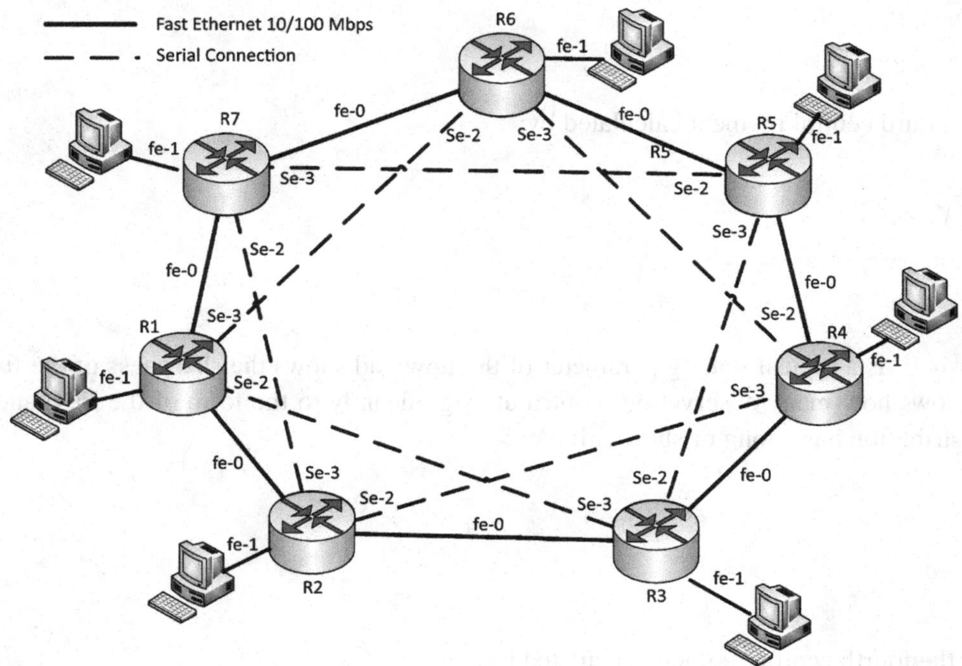

192.168.10.4, 192.168.50.2 and 192.168.50.4 are laptops of the model HP ProBook 8440p running Windows XP Professional, Intel PRO/ Wireless 802.11 a/b/g/n. The routers are J2320 from Juniper and support additionally intrusion detection, anti-virus, web filtering and DOS attack detection. The switches are not shown on the figure and are Juniper EX4000. Switches connect hosts via UTP cables and routers via optical cables. Connections between routers are duplicated. Load balancing is not applied. Host 192.168.50.200 is an HP server used for the Asterisk (HP DL180G5 E5420).

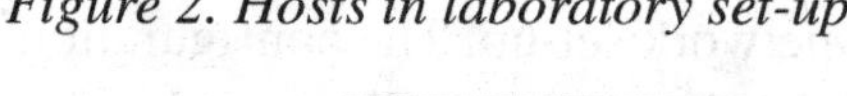

Figure 2. Hosts in laboratory set-up

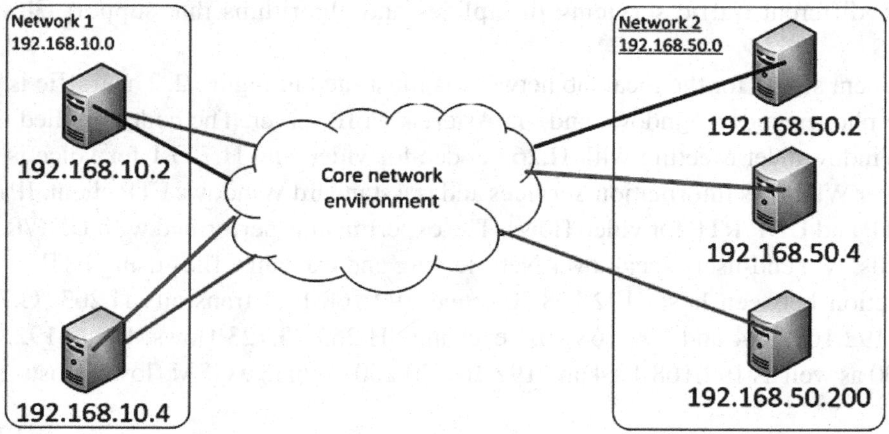

VoIP calls are generated from XLite SIP and Microsoft Net Meeting 3.1 H.323. The server is Elastix. FTP sessions are started from standard client and server in Windows Information Services. Virtual networks are configured over the existing topology.

VoIP calls are generated from XLite SIP and Microsoft Net Meeting 3.1 H.323. The server is Elastix. FTP sessions are started from standard client and server in Windows Information Services. Virtual networks are configured over the existing topology.

Network monitoring and analyses are done in passive way. It consists of generation of a traffic copy on mirror port and its capturing by a traffic monitoring tool. The data captured could be analyzed and used in different ways. It is possible to apply sniffers like Wireshark or use other network resource analyzers. The results are used for better network configuration and are especially interesting for network service providers and system administrators. The experiment covers all communication requirements for small office or home network.

Passive monitoring is typically applied when there are performance problems in the networks. The main difference from active monitoring is that it does not generate additional traffic and does not invoke additional procedures in the network. Passive monitoring is used mostly for post-event traffic analyses. It does not support dynamic configuration procedures and adapt the performance of the network nodes in real time. Passive monitoring is used here to investigate the nature of the Internet traffic in access, edge and core network. It is usually a starting point for active monitoring. Traffic generators apply data obtained from passive monitoring.

The experiments start with Net Meeting running. The connection works on H.263 and G.723.1 flows and UDP/RTP/H.323 protocols for voice. GSM flows are generated by X-lite using UDP/RTP/GSM protocols. FTP service is the last to start. Duration of the experiments is about 2-3 minutes. The traffic is analyzed by Wireshark as real-time protocol traffic. Streams are separated in forward and backward directions. It is obvious that the number of packets in both directions is different due to the specific features of the codecs.

The traffic asymmetry in both directions is demonstrated. Special attention is paid to the statistical parameters of the traffic as inter-arrival times, jitter, skew, capacity, packet status. Many additional parameters are also calculated including maximum delay, maximum and mean jitter, maximum skewness, number of packets transmitted, losses, reordered packets and session duration.

All results including traces and statistical data are exported in CSV format to Excel, the Oracle Crystal Ball and the EasyFit Professional tools. Both statistical tools apply well known approximations and propose the best-fitting probability density function of the data. In addition to the PDF, the statistical tools also calculate statistical data. Data applied to the best-fitting PDF and comparison to the other probability density functions is also generated for further analyses.

Experiments at First Phase

Within the proposed network, the QoS is managed per hop over the aggregated traffic using DiffServ, MPLS (Multi-Protocol Label Switching) tunnels with and without priorities. This allows to measure and experiment different type of priority algorithms, perform precise traffic classification, traffic control and policing, traffic shaping both end-to-end and per-hop. The proposed configuration allows exploring the traffic at any kind of nodes with input, intermediate and output queueing with priorities. The model could also fit to small business and home networks with real-time and non-real-time traffic.

The experiments conducted at first phase are configured with and without priorities. All traffic channels are limited to 1 Mbps aiming to reach overflow status under specific traffic conditions. On next tables and figures:

- IP 1500 or IP 1,5 k means that the Maximum Burst Size (MBS) is bounded to 1500 bytes and there are no priorities in the channel.
- IP 3000 or IP 3 k means that the MBS is bounded to 3000 bytes and there are no priorities in the channel.
- IP 6000 or IP 6 k means that the MBS is bounded to 6000 bytes and there are no priorities in the channel. MBS limit of 10000 bytes is also experimented.
- DSCP (DiffServ Code Point) means that there is a priority of the video over IP traffic. The priority applied is EF (Expedited Forwarding) and the packets are served in a separate queues.
- MPLS means that real-time traffic like high priority video over IP sources goes through static MPLS tunnel.
- MPLS EXP (experimental) means that within the MPLS tunnel the experimental bits in MPLS header are set to 4 (100 binary) that corresponds to the Assured Forwarding (AF) 31 QoS in DiffServ.

The data from the experiment with ftp session (line 1, black) and two RTP flows (lines 2 and 3 in red and green) is shown on Figure 3. The MBS is bounded on 1500 bytes and the overall capacity of the line is 1 Mbps. There are no priorities applied. All flows compete for the same channel in a best effort manner. The flows with ports 49586 and 49582 are H.263 video UDP/RTP segments. The VoIP calls are between 192.168.50.200, 192.168.10.2 and 192.168.10.4 with GSM 06.10 codec and UDP/RTP segments. The session 92.168.50.2 is TCP ftp.

Because the bandwidth is limited, ftp and respectively TCP successfully occupied more than 80% of the available capacity. In this case, the adoption is performed well at IP and TCP layer. TCP traffic dominates due to the lack of priority for the real-time traffic. The packet sizes have multimodal distribution as shown on Figure 4. Further optimization of the TCP performance parameters is possible but it is not presented here (Buhagiar & Debono, 2009).

The multimodal distribution is due to the traffic in both directions, i.e. packets in size of 320-639 bytes for data and acknowledgements in size of 40-79 bytes. UDP/RTP traffic from GSM codec generates packets with completely different sizes. It is because the Linier Predictive Coding (LPC) manipulation of the codec sends irregular amount of information at different time slots and therefore the size of the packets generated are different (Figure 5).

Details about further simulation of the multimodal distribution of the servicing time could be seen in (Mirtchev & Goleva, 2010). In (Mirtchev, Mavromoustakis, Goleva, Kassev, & Mastorakis, 2014; Chakchai So-In, 2006) it is proven that when the traffic is self-similar the servicing time has no significant influence on the traffic characteristics in comparison to the influence of inter-arrival times distribution.

The behaviour of the traffic sources is different during the experiment when there are priorities. The line capacity is kept at 1 Mbps, MBS is again 1500 bytes but video traffic is prioritized (lines 2 and 3 on the Figure 6). DiffServ expedited forwarding service is applied for the priority traffic. DiffServ service allows video packets to be transmitted first and to suppress tcp traffic. The picture is opposite to the one shown on Figure 3.

Figure 3. Pure IP network with 1 Mbps capacity and 1500 bytes MBS

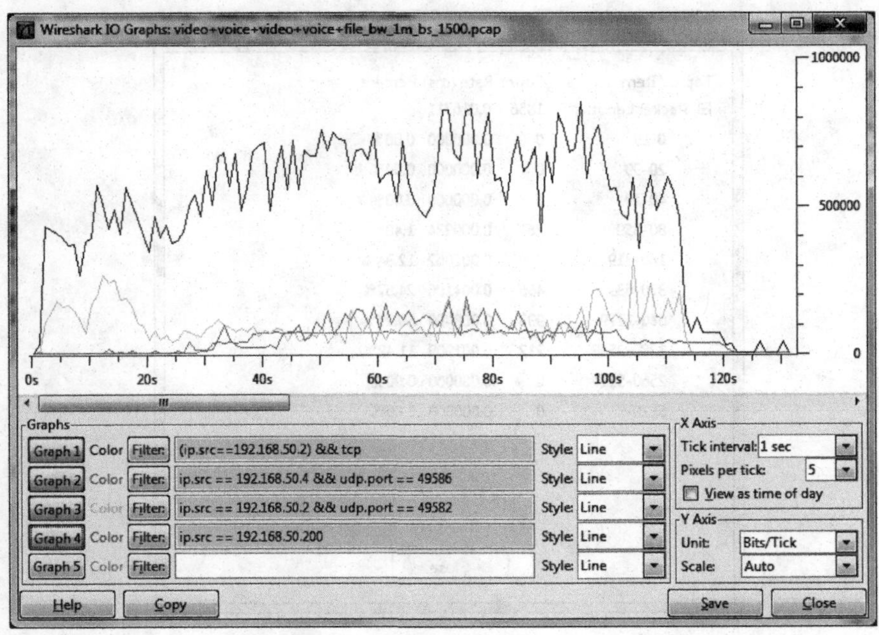

Figure 4. Packet size distribution of ftp session

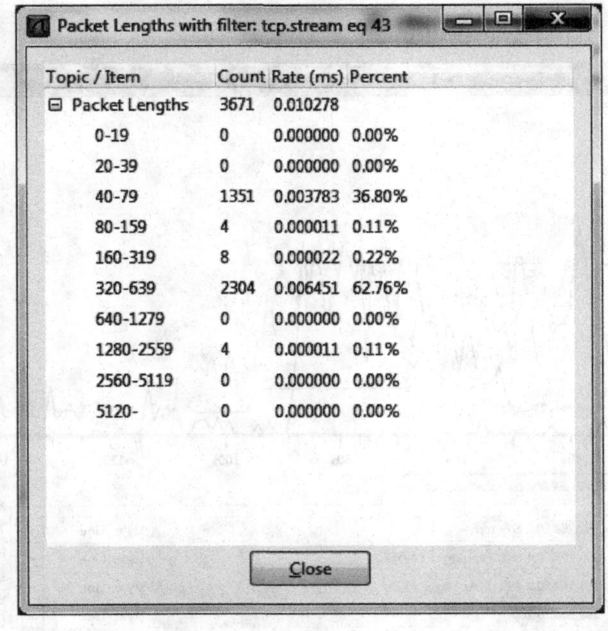

Packet Lengths with filter: tcp.stream eq 43

Topic / Item	Count	Rate (ms)	Percent
⊟ Packet Lengths	3671	0.010278	
0-19	0	0.000000	0.00%
20-39	0	0.000000	0.00%
40-79	1351	0.003783	36.80%
80-159	4	0.000011	0.11%
160-319	8	0.000022	0.22%
320-639	2304	0.006451	62.76%
640-1279	0	0.000000	0.00%
1280-2559	4	0.000011	0.11%
2560-5119	0	0.000000	0.00%
5120-	0	0.000000	0.00%

Close

Figure 5. Packet size distribution of VoIP GSM codec session

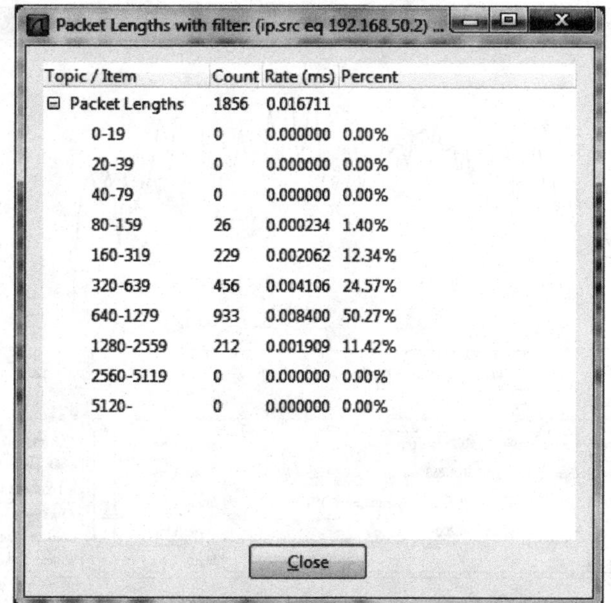

Packet Lengths with filter: (ip.src eq 192.168.50.2) ...

Topic / Item	Count	Rate (ms)	Percent
⊟ Packet Lengths	1856	0.016711	
0-19	0	0.000000	0.00%
20-39	0	0.000000	0.00%
40-79	0	0.000000	0.00%
80-159	26	0.000234	1.40%
160-319	229	0.002062	12.34%
320-639	456	0.004106	24.57%
640-1279	933	0.008400	50.27%
1280-2559	212	0.001909	11.42%
2560-5119	0	0.000000	0.00%
5120-	0	0.000000	0.00%

Close

Figure 6. Served traffic in 1 Mbps line, MBS=1500 bytes and DiffServ expedited forwarding priority for video traffic

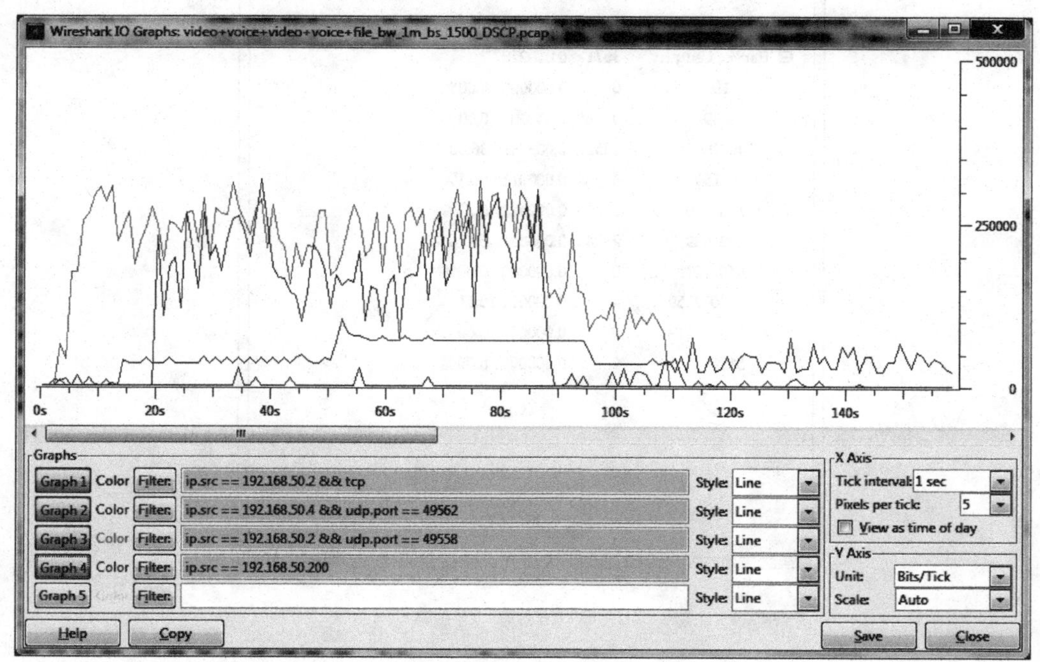

Figure 7. Served traffic in 1 Mbps line, MBS=1500 bytes and MPLS static tunnel for VoIP and video over IP traffic

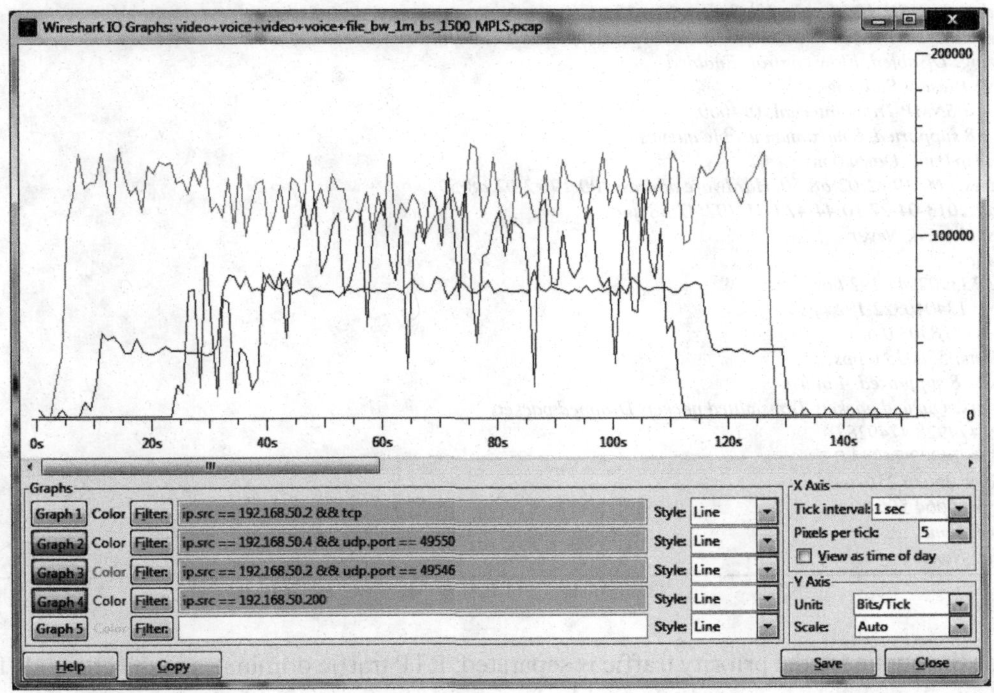

Figure 8. Real-time video and voice traffic over static MPLS tunnel with EXP 100 is served before TCP ftp flow

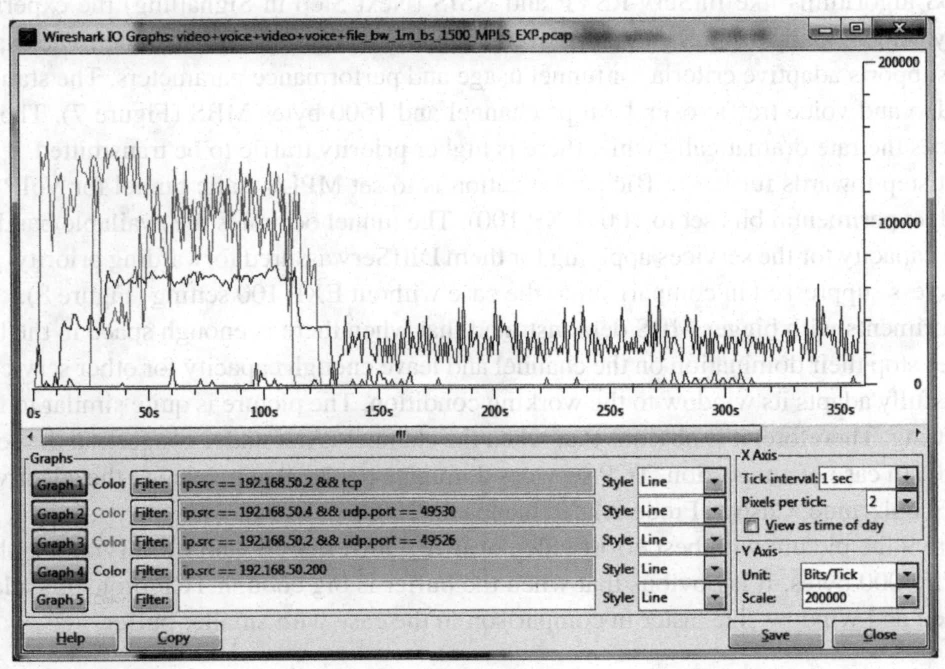

Table 1. Egress queues distribution at router interface

Physical interface: fe-0/0/0, Enabled, Physical link is Up *Interface index: 137, SNMP ifIndex: 25, Generation: 138* *Link-level type: Ethernet, MTU: 1518, Speed: 100mbps, Loopback: Disabled,* *Source filtering: Disabled, Flow control: Enabled* *Device flags : Present Running* *Interface flags: SNMP-Traps Internal: 0x4000* *CoS queues : 8 supported, 8 maximum usable queues* *Hold-times : Up 0 ms, Down 0 ms* *Current address: 00:19:e2:02:a8:50, Hardware address: 00:19:e2:02:a8:50* *Last flapped : 2013-04-27 10:44:47 UTC (07:47:38 ago)* *Statistics last cleared: Never* *Traffic statistics:* *Input bytes: 133902941 192 bps* *Output bytes: 134040322 192 bps* *Input packets: 578303 0 pps* *Output packets: 578033 0 pps* *Egress queues: 8 supported, 4 in use* *Queue counters: Queued packets Transmitted packets Dropped packets* *0 best-effort 474928 474928 0* *1 expedited-fo 74333 74333 0* *2 assured-forw 25676 25676 0* *3 network-cont 5064 5064 0* *Active alarms: None* *Active defects: None*

Because the queue for the priority traffic is separated, RTP traffic dominates in the channel. The FTP service adapts its transmission rate to the residual part of the capacity. Table 1 presents the queue length seen at one of the router output interfaces. Configuration supports up to 8 queues. Four of them are configured and supported best effort, expedited forwarding, assured forwarding, network control disciplines.

Because DiffServ works on aggregated traffic and could not make precise reservation in contrast to other QoS algorithms like IntServ-RSVP and NSIS (Next Step in Signalling) the experiments are expanded by MPLS. It allows QoS guarantee over statically configured MPLS tunnel. The experimental equipment supports adaptive criteria for tunnel usage and performance parameters. The static tunnel is used for video and voice traffic over 1 Mbps channel and 1500 bytes MBS (Figure 7). The FTP-TCP traffic reduces the rate dramatically while there is higher priority traffic to be transmitted.

The next step towards further traffic prioritization is to set MPLS static tunnel for VoIP and video sources with experimental bits set to 100 (EXP 100). The tunnel occupies the available bandwidth and reserves the capacity for the services applying for them DiffServ assured forwarding priority. As a result ftp traffic is less suppressed in comparison to the case without EXP 100 setting (Figure 8).

The experiments with bigger MBS demonstrated that when there is enough space in the buffers the TCP services stop their domination on the channel and leave enough capacity for other services as well. TCP successfully adapts its window to the working condition. The picture is quite similar to MPLS and EXP 100 setting. Therefore, it is obvious that when the channel is not under congestion the services behave properly. In case of congestion, TCP services dominate on the channel due to the adaptive window algorithm (Schulzrinne, Casner, Frederick, & Jacobson, 2003).

On Figure 9 the picture with best effort video over IP, GSM over IP and ftp service are shown with buffer size of 6000 bytes. It is obvious that when the buffer is big enough TCP protocols adapts transmission speed and window size faster in comparison to the case with smaller buffer.

Figure 9. Best effort IP services over 1 Mbps channel and MBS=6000

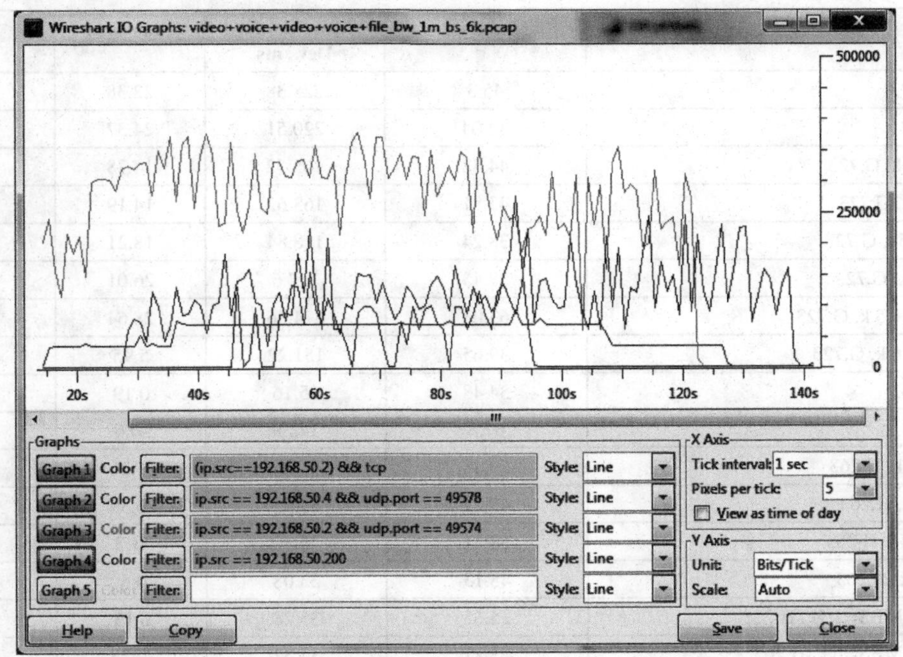

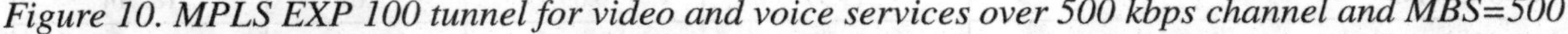

Figure 10. MPLS EXP 100 tunnel for video and voice services over 500 kbps channel and MBS=500

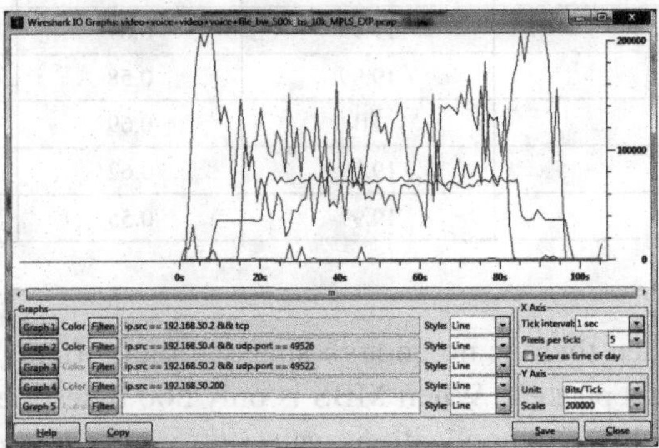

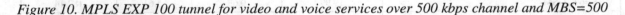

In case the application layer requires and could afford big buffers the traffic is self-regulated similarly to the case with priorities. The GSM codec has stable parameters. The buffer size above 6000 k allows even better transmission performance (Juniper, 2013). In combination with MPLS EXP 100 configuration, the traffic in the channel is well balanced with priorities. The same MPLS EXP priority works in the same way also in small buffers with MBS equal to few packets (Figure 10). The last option seems to be fully adjusted QoS-aware scenario.

The statistical data related to the inter-arrival time of the flows is presented on Tables 2-4. As seen from the data the main concern is real-time video traffic that overloads the channels in case of small burst size. In this situation, MPLS tunnel with EXP 100 helps in traffic regulation and fair capacity manage-

Table 2. Measured statistical parameters of inter-arrival times in access network for host 192.168.10.2

Streams	Mean, ms	Mean Standard Dev., ms	Skewness	Kurtosis
MBS=1.5k, G.723	45.3	228.38	22.38	594.36
MBS=6 k, G.723	42.04	220.51	24.37	659.29
DSCP, MBS=1.5k, G.723	44.88	165.52	14.78	270.17
DSCP, MBS=6 k, G.723	43.81	163.62	14.19	225
MPLS, MBS=1.5k, G.723	38.24	118.84	18.21	374.66
MPLS, MBS=6 k, G.723	38.43	127.6	26.01	851.05
MPLS EXP 100, 1.5 k, G.723	63.08	574.56	28.64	945.5
MPLS EXP 100, 6 k, G.723	39.65	151.22	5.95	399.28
MBS=1.5k, H.263	34.48	35.16	0.19	1.36
MBS=6 k, H.263	67.8	14.59	-0.6	10.05
DSCP, MBS=1.5k, H.263	59.48	26.06	-1.26	4.23
DSCP, MBS=6 k, H.263	45.22	33.95	-0.36	1.63
MPLS, MBS=1.5k, H.263	58.51	26.82	-1.2	3.88
MPLS, MBS=6 k, H.263	48.13	33.08	-0.52	1.86
MPLS EXP 100, MBS=1.5k, H.263	35.65	35.28	0.13	1.36
MPLS EXP 100, MBS=6 k, H.263	43.77	34.32	-0.28	1.55
MBS=1.5k, GSM	19.99	0.67	-5.85	178.92
MBS=6 k, GSM	19.99	0.63	-5.61	182.14
DSCP, MBS=1.5k, GSM	19.99	0.65	-6.11	192.78
DSCP, MBS=6 k, GSM	19.99	0.67	-5.61	182.1
MPLS, MBS=1.5k, GSM	19.99	0.58	-6.36	236.04
MPLS, MBS=6 k, GSM	20	0.69	0.17	329.13
MPLS EXP 100, MBS=1.5k, GSM	19.99	0.62	-6.47	221.97
MPLS EXP 100, MBS=6 k, GSM	19.99	0.55	-9.94	363.24

ment. It is especially valid when there is no enough space in the buffers. For example, when MBS is 1,5 k there is place for only few packets. When MBS is only 500 bytes there is a place for 1-2 packets in the queue and packets from different applications wait end-to-end (Figure 10). Than, losses are going to be high and time-constrains could be kept quite easily (Mirtchev, Mavromoustakis, Goleva, Kassev, & Mastorakis, 2014). The shaping effect is paid by additional delay and burstiness of the traffic, i.e. the variance is becoming higher. When the buffers are big enough and have high value of mean burst size like 6 k or more, there is enough waiting capacity at the interface and the shaping effect is supported by the queue. The influence of the MPLS over overall performance characteristics is not visible. Ftp service is behaving differently. The parameters of the host 192.168.10.2 and 192.168.10.4 are different thanks to the traffic interference in the channel.

The best fitting probability density functions of the inter-arrival times are shown on next figures. The approximation is done using Easyfit statistical tool. It is obvious that the distribution function is changing depending on the technology, policy, type of interface, traffic management. On Figure 11 there is a PDF of inter-arrival time measured at 192.168.10.2 host when MBS = 1,500 k and codec is H.263. The

Table 3. Measured statistical parameters of inter-arrival times in access network for host 192.168.10.4

Streams	Mean, ms	Mean Standard Dev., ms	Skewness	Kurtosis
MBS=1.5k, G.723	42.94	193.96	20.95	497.45
MBS=6 k, G.723			23.07	631.39
DSCP, MBS=1.5k, G.723	42.1	135.26	12.62	174.51
DSCP, MBS=6 k, G.723			16.37	304.47
MPLS, MBS=1.5k, G.723	39.9	134.82	17.35	342.98
MPLS, MBS=6 k, G.723			15.37	277.21
MPLS EXP 100, MBS=1.5k, G.723	60.41	342.13	14.81	248.58
MPLS EXP 100, MBS=6 k, G.723			30.02	987.94
MBS=1.5k, H.263	67.73	14.82	-0.7	10.7
MBS=6 k, H.263	68.83	12.11	1.3	6.24
DSCP, MBS=1.5k, H.263	68.43	13.66	0.8	12.89
DSCP, MBS=6 k, H.263	60.69	24.83	-1.34	4.79
MPLS, MBS=1.5k, H.263	68.61	12.55	0.77	7.89
MPLS, MBS=6 k, H.263	64.7	20.27	-1.5	7.38
MPLS EXP 100, MBS=1.5k, H.263	66.65	16.74	-1.27	9.63
MPLS EXP 100, MBS=6 k, H.263	64.58	20.37	-1.5	7.33
MBS=1.5k, GSM	19.99	0.67	-8.24	248.05
MBS=6 k, GSM	19.99	0.68	-7.22	216.24
DSCP, MBS=1.5k, GSM	19.99	0.76	-8.36	225.82
DSCP, MBS=6 k, GSM	19.99	0.66	-8.6	264.53
MPLS, MBS=1.5k, GSM	19.99	0.57	-10.44	372.5
MPLS, MBS=6 k, GSM	19.99	0.63	-11.01	355.01
MPLS EXP 100, MBS=1.5k, GSM	19.99	0.61	8.33	274.76
MPLS EXP 100, MBS=6 k, GSM	19.99	0.65	-9.25	289.12

servicing discipline is best effort. The best fitting probability density function for the inter-arrival times is Pearson 5. Results on Figure 12 are from the same experiment with DSCP marks. The best fitting PDF is Cauchy distribution. MPLS application PDF best fitting to Cauchy distribution could be seen on Figure 13. Figure 14 presents the results from the experiment with MPLS EXP 100 best fitting to Weibull distribution. On all figures below the measured data is plotted as bars whereas the approximated PDF function is plotted as a line.

Depending on the traffic policy at the interface, the PDF is changing. The PDF of H.263 video flow is Pierson V in the case of best effort traffic (Lane, Scott, Hebl, Guerra, Osherson, & Zimmer, 2008). The distribution function depends on the skewness and the kurtosis of the flows. After applying DiffSerf QoS management for real-time flows, the PDF function changes to Cauchy distribution (Hazewinkel, 2001). Similar picture is obtained for the case with MPLS tunnels for real-time video and voice traffic. Pearson V distribution depends highly on skewness and kurtosis of flows. Cauchy distribution depends on the median and the mode of packet flow. After application of the EXP 100 setting the PDF function of H. 263 flow

Table 4. Measured statistical parameters of inter-arrival times in access network for host 192.168.10.2 and ftp service

Streams	Mean, ms	Mean Standard Dev., ms	Skewness	Kurtosis
MBS=1.5k, FTP	0.07	0.22	3.63	21.28
MBS=6 k, FTP	0.01	0.07	8.45	76.83
DSCP, MBS=1.5k, FTP	0.07	0.19	2.56	7.86
DSCP, MBS=6 k, FTP	0.04	0.14	3.75	15.79
MPLS, MBS=1.5k, FTP	0.1	0.22	2.33	7.49
MPLS, MBS=6 k, FTP	0.02	0.11	5.95	38.15
MPLS EXP 100, MBS=1.5k, FTP	0.1	0.22	2.09	6
MPLS EXP 100, MBS=6 k, FTP	0.04	0.15	4.05	18.49

Figure 11. Inter-arrival time PDF of H.263 flow at 192.168.10.2 interface, best effort, Pierson 5 distribution

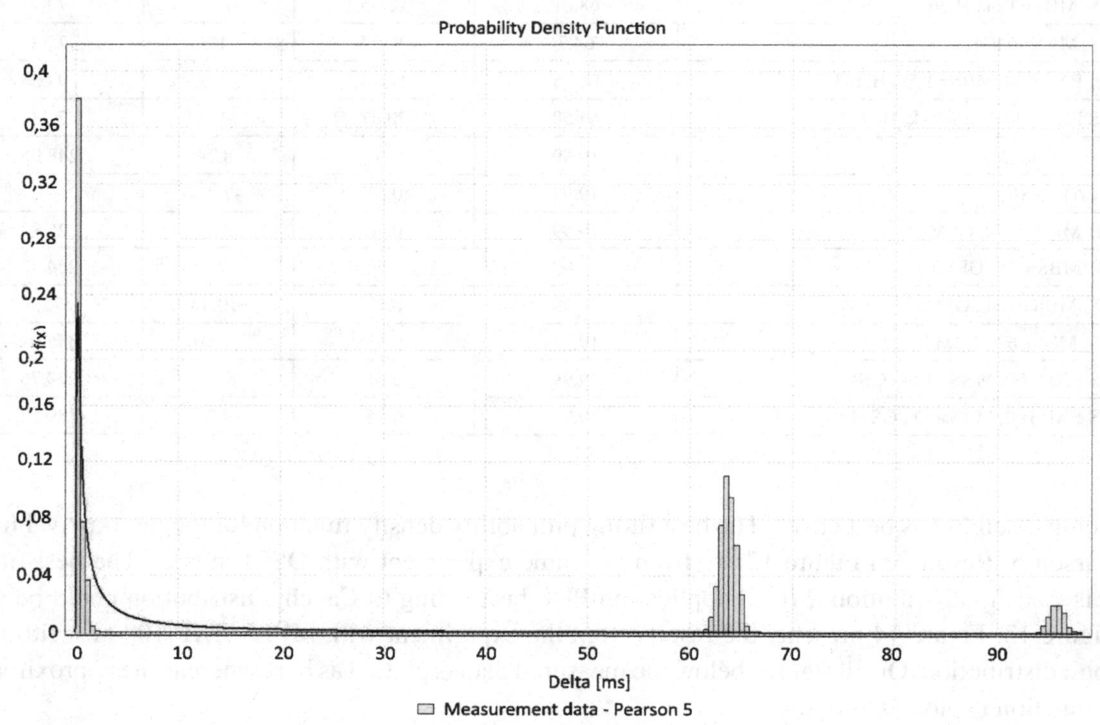

changes to Weibull distribution. Weibull distribution function is also changing depending on the variance, skewness and kurtosis of the flow. In all cases, the traffic shaping effect is obvious. Although the inter-arrival times are concentrated into three areas between 0 and 4 ms, between 60 and 70 ms and between 95-100 ms depending on the codec the nature of the traffic is changing all the time along end-to-end connection. Possible rough approximation of flow's PDF in such cases could be deterministic one. There is also a possible approximation with gamma distribution (Goleva, Atamian, Mirtchev, Dimitrova, & Grigorova, 2013).

Figure 12. Inter-arrival time PDF of H.263 flow at 192.168.10.2 interface, DSCP, Cauchy distribution

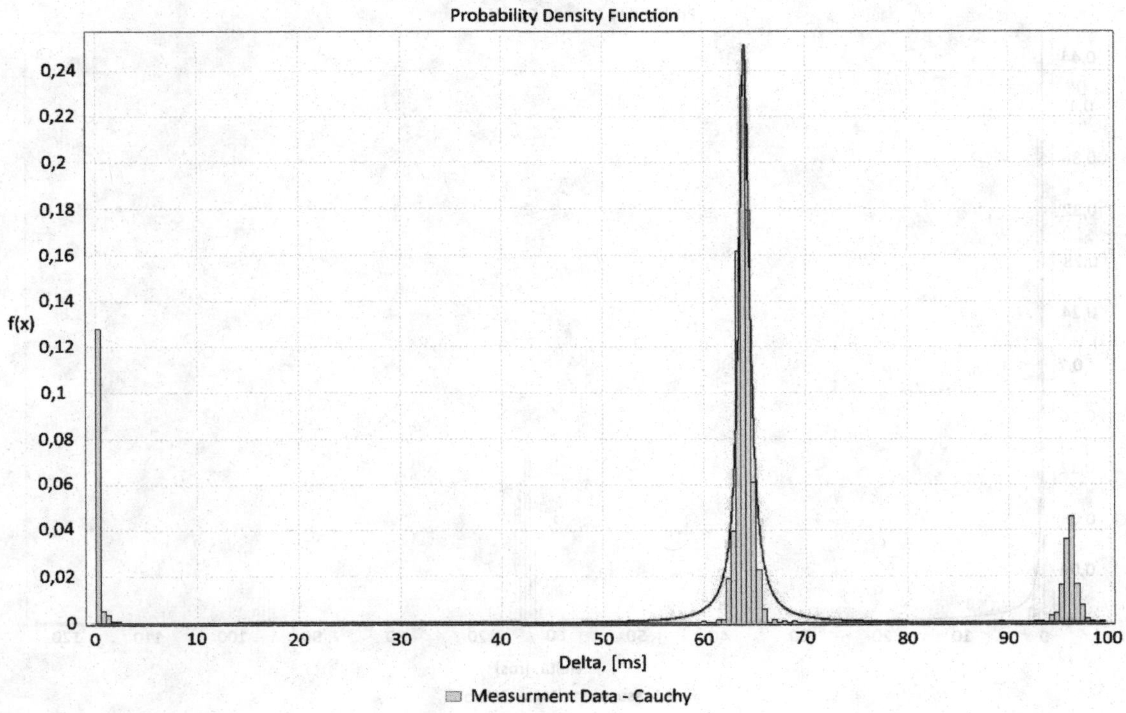

Figure 13. Inter-arrival time PDF of H.263 flow at 192.168.10.2 interface, MPLS, Cauchy distribution

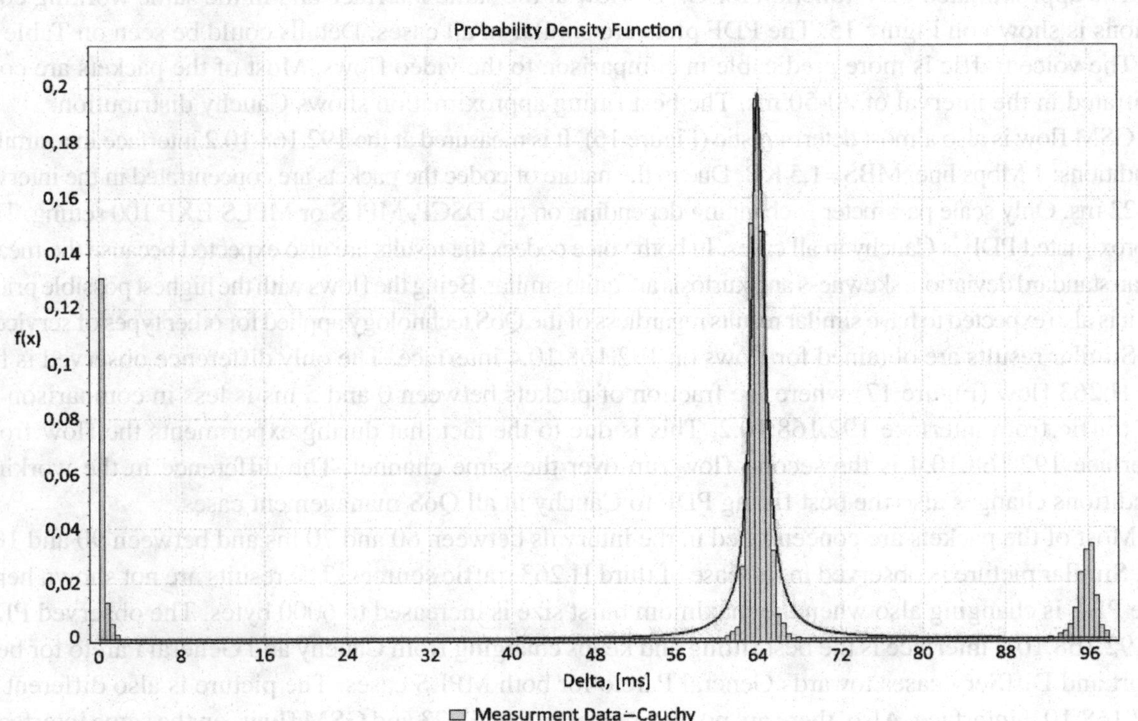

Figure 14. Inter-arrival time pdf of H.263 flow at 192.168.10.2 interface, MPLS 100, Weibull distribution

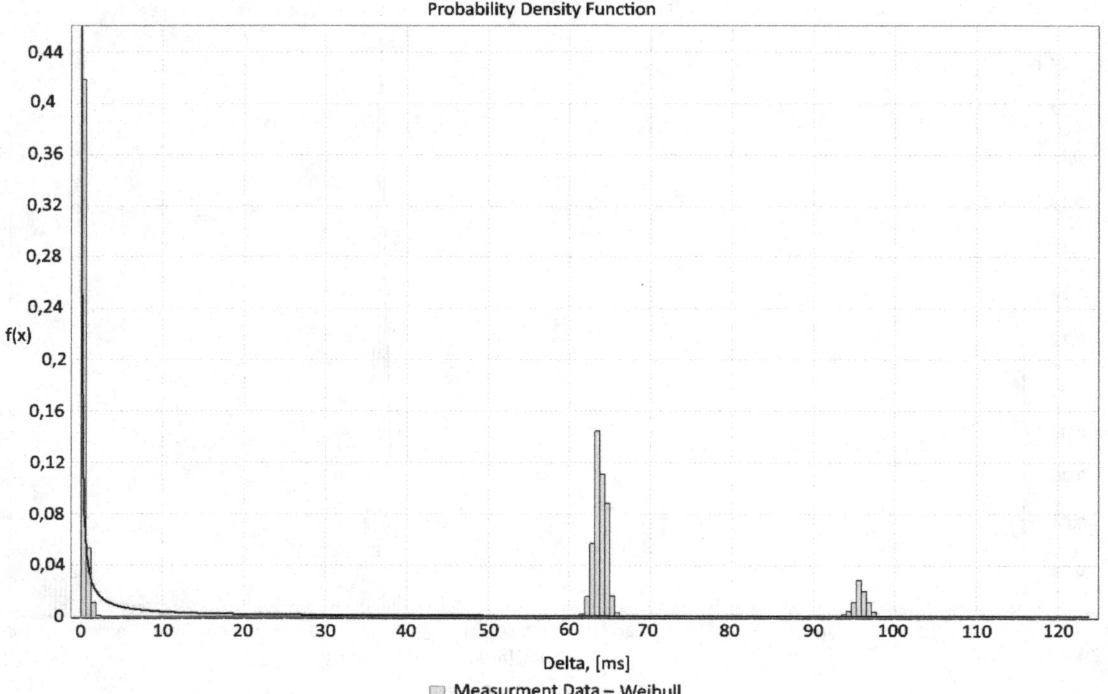

The approximated PDF function for G.723 flow at the same interface and in the same working conditions is shown on Figure 15. The PDF plots are similar in all cases. Details could be seen on Table 2.

The voice traffic is more predicable in comparison to the video flows. Most of the packets are concentrated in the interval of 30-50 ms. The best fitting approximation shows Cauchy distribution.

GSM flow is also almost deterministic (Figure 16). It is measured at the 192.168.10.2 interface in a similar conditions: 1 Mbps line; MBS=1,5 KB. Due to the nature of codec the packets are concentrated in the interval 18-22 ms. Only scale parameter is changing depending on the DSCP, MPLS or MPLS EXP 100 setting. The approximated PDF is Cauchy in all cases. In both voice codecs the results are also expected because the mean, mean standard deviation, skewness and kurtosis are quite similar. Being the flows with the highest possible priority, it is also expected to have similar results regardless of the QoS technology applied for other types of services.

Similar results are obtained for flows on 192.168.10.4 interface. The only difference observed is for the H.263 flow (Figure 17) where the fraction of packets between 0 and 5 ms is less in comparison to the traffic from interface 192.168.10.2. This is due to the fact that during experiments the flow from interface 192.168.10.4 is the second flow run over the same channel. The difference in the working conditions changes also the best fitting PDF to Cauchy in all QoS management cases.

Most of the packets are concentrated in the intervals between 60 and 70 ms and between 90 and 100 ms. Similar picture is observed in the case of third H.263 traffic sources. The results are not shown here. The PDF is changing also when the maximum burst size is increased to 6000 bytes. The observed PDF at 192.168.10.2 interface is the best fitting and keeps changing from Cauchy and General Pareto for best effort and DiffServ cases towards General Pareto for both MPLS cases. The picture is also different at 192.168.10.4 interface. Also, there are no differences in the G.723 and GSM flows on the same interface.

Figure 15. Inter-arrival times PDF of G.723 flow at 192.168.10.2 interface with Cauchy distribution in all cases

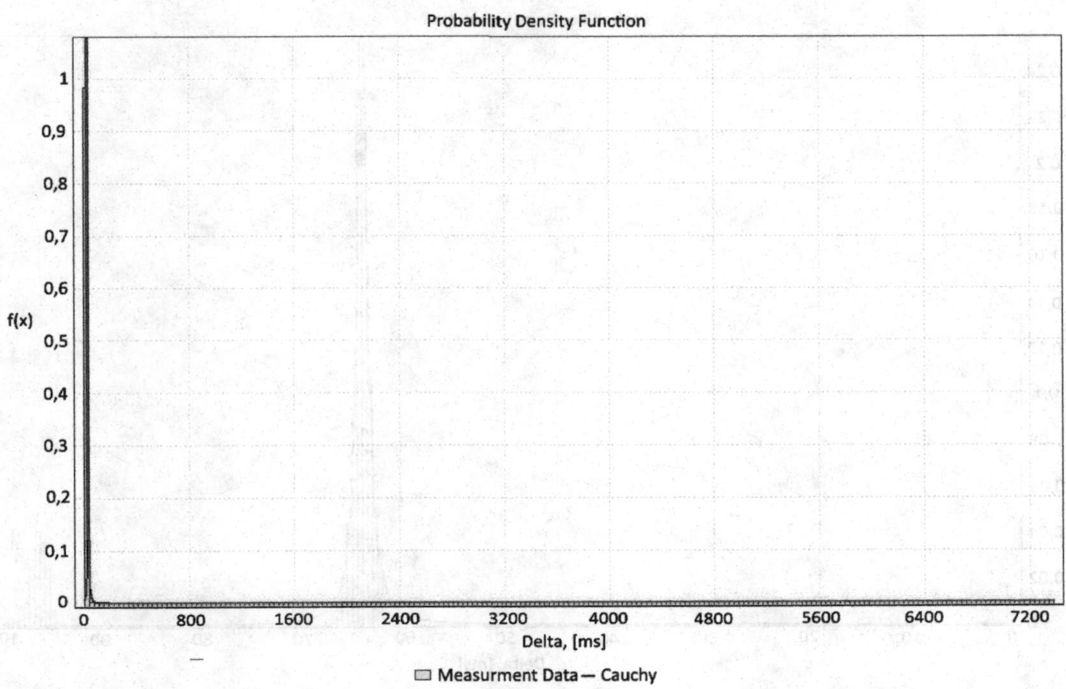

Figure 16. Inter-arrival time PDF of GSM flow at 192.168.10.2 interface with Cauchy distribution in all cases

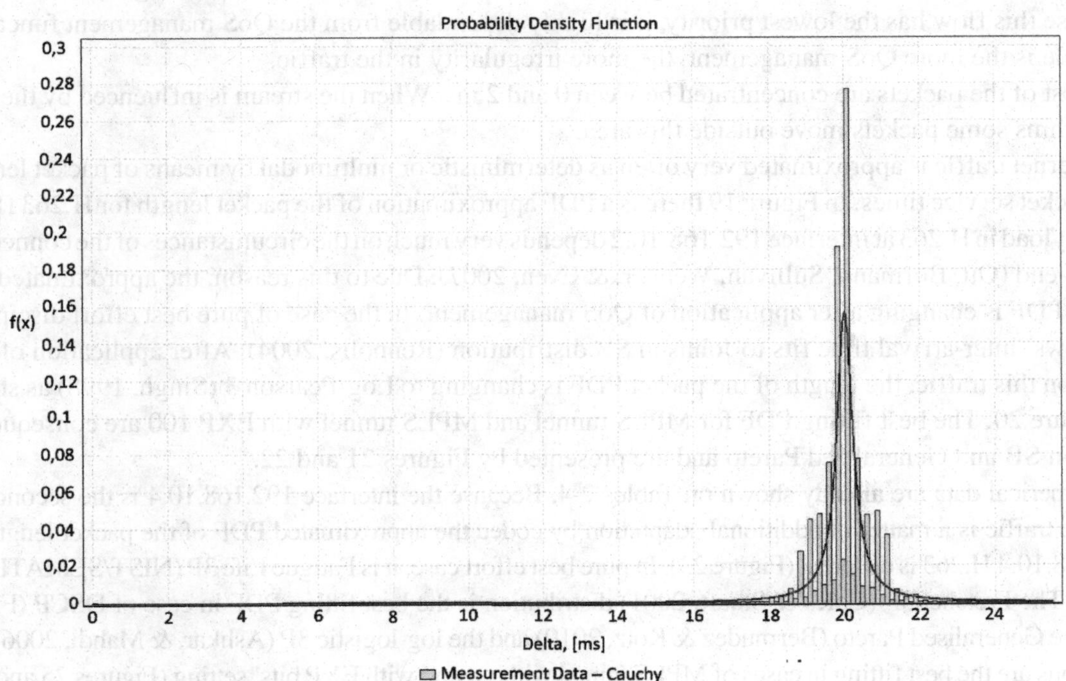

Figure 17. Inter-arrival time PDF of H.263 flow at 192.168.10.4 interface with Cauchy distribution in all cases

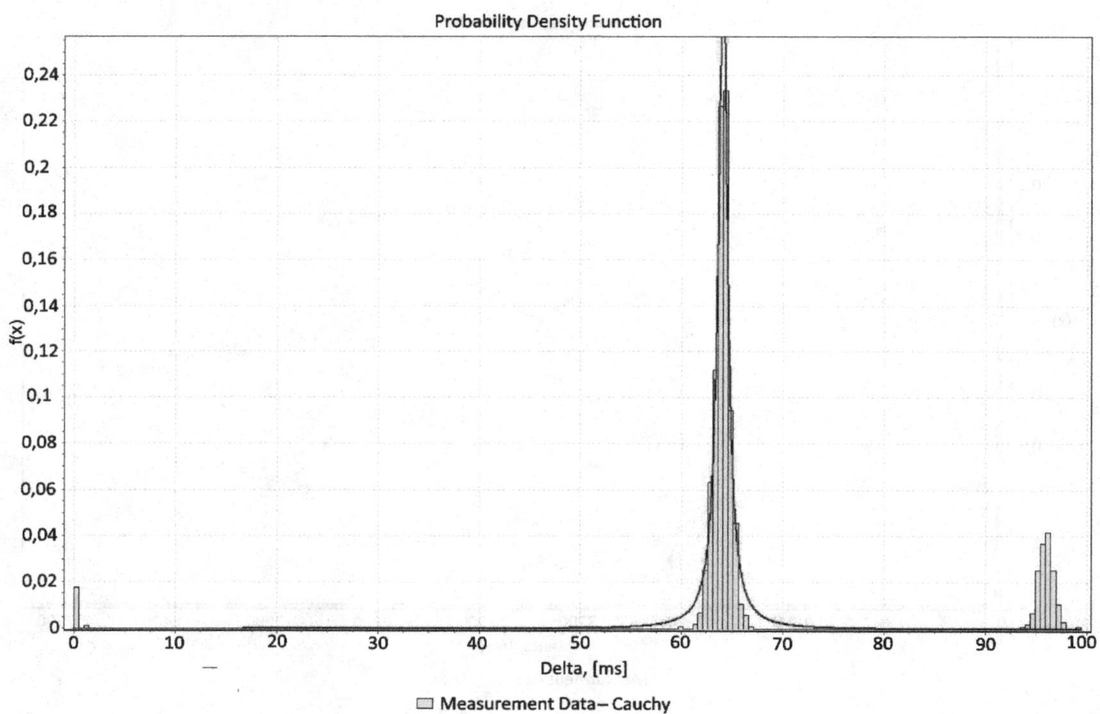

A little bit different is the picture with ftp flows shown on Figure 18. The best fitting PDF is Cauchy. Because this flow has the lowest priority, it is highly dependable from the QoS management functions. The rule is the more QoS management, the more irregularity in the traffic.

Most of the packets are concentrated between 0 and 2 ms. When the stream is influenced by the QoS algorithms some packets move outside this area.

Internet traffic is approximated very often as deterministic or multimodal by means of packet lengths and packet service times. In Figure 19 there is a PDF approximation of the packet length for H.263 flows. The payload in H.263 at interface 192.168.10.2 depends very much on the circumstances of the connection end-to-end (Ott, Bormann, Sullivan, Wenger, & Even, 2007). Due to this reason, the approximated best fitting PDF is changing after application of QoS management. In the case of pure best effort discipline, the flows' inter-arrival time fits to Johnson SB distribution (Rennolls, 2004). After application of DiffServ on this traffic, the length of the packet PDF is changing to Log-Pearson 3 (Singh, 1998) as shown on Figure 20. The best fitting PDF for MPLS tunnel and MPLS tunnel with EXP 100 are consequently Johnson SB and Generalised Pareto and are presented by Figures 21 and 22.

Numerical data are already shown on Tables 2-4. Because the interface 192.168.10.4 is the second one and the traffic is a matter of additional adaptation by codec the approximated PDF of the packet length for 192.168.10.4 H.263 is different (Figure 23). In pure best effort case, it is Fatigue Life 3P (NIST/SEMATECH, 2012). The Fretchet 3P (Coles & Stuart, 2001) distribution is the best fitting PDF in case of DSCP (Figure 24). The Generalised Pareto (Bermudez & Kotz, 2010) and the log-logistic 3P (Ashkar, & Mahdi, 2006) distributions are the best fitting in cases of MPLS tunnel without and with EXP bits' setting (Figures 25 and 26).

Figure 18. Inter-arrival time PDF of ftp flow with Cauchy distribution in all cases

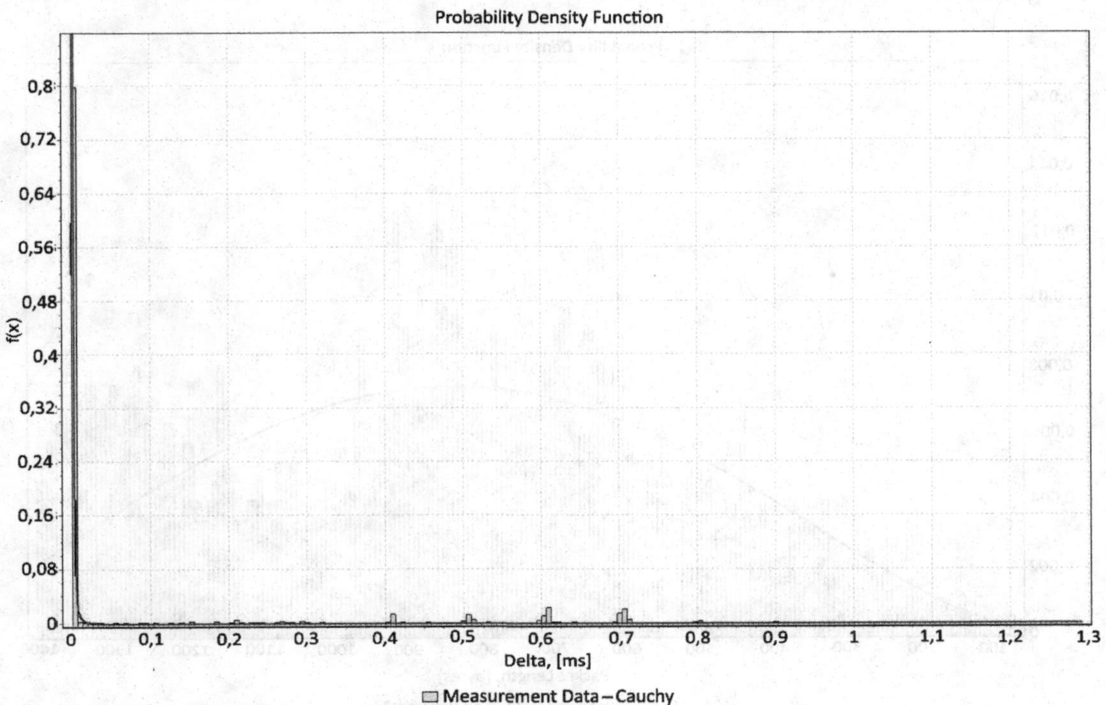

Figure 19. Packet length PDF of H.263 traffic source 192.168.10.2 with MBS=1,5 KB and 1 Mbps, best effort, Johnson SB distribution

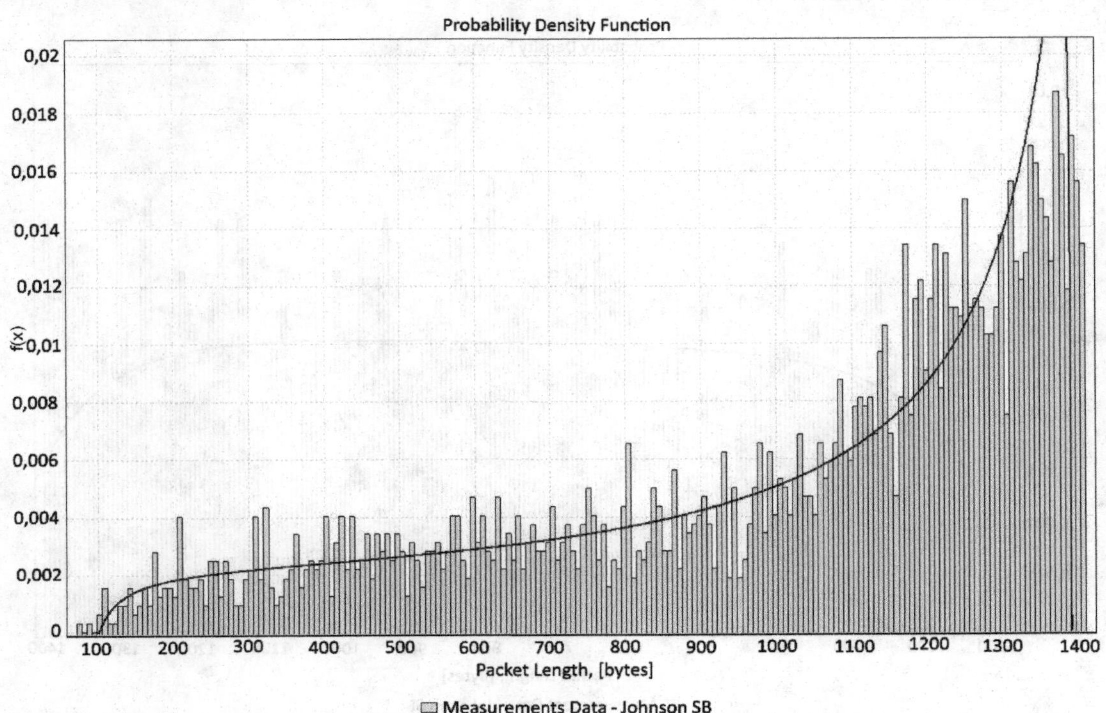

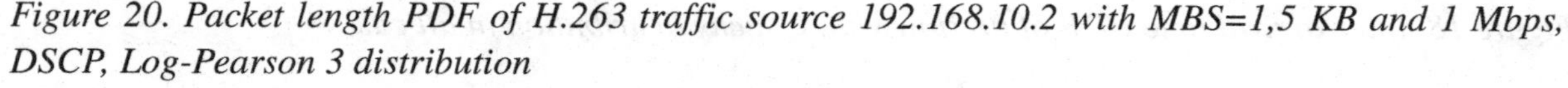

Figure 20. Packet length PDF of H.263 traffic source 192.168.10.2 with MBS=1,5 KB and 1 Mbps, DSCP, Log-Pearson 3 distribution

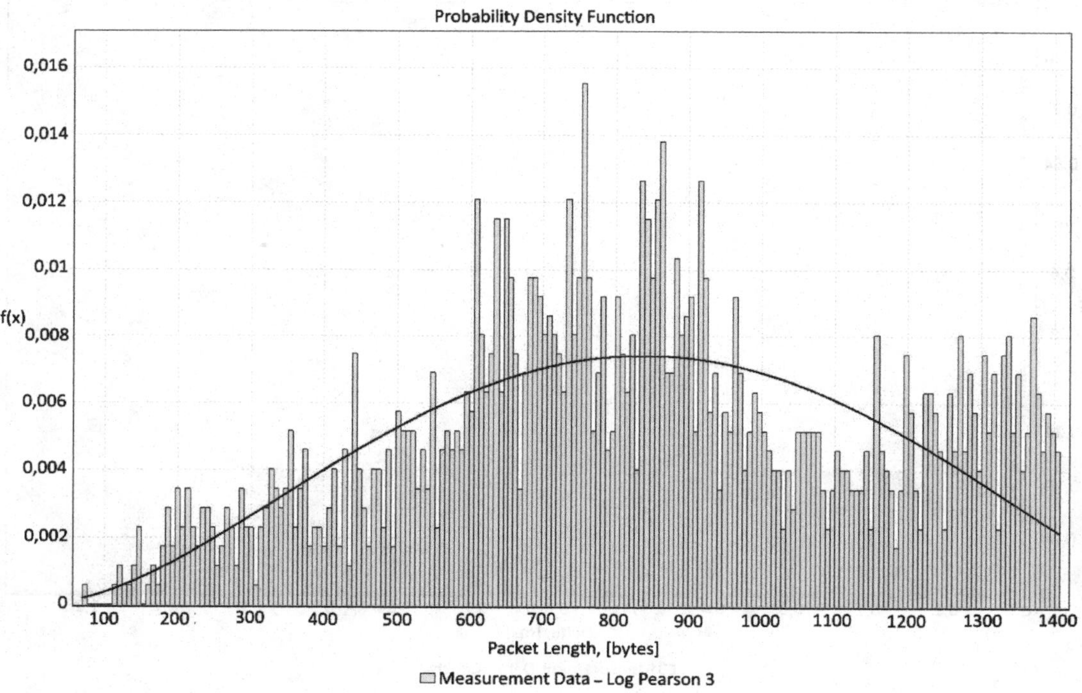

Figure 21. Packet length PDF of H.263 traffic source 192.168.10.2 with MBS=1,5 KB and 1 Mbps, MPLS, Johnson SB distribution

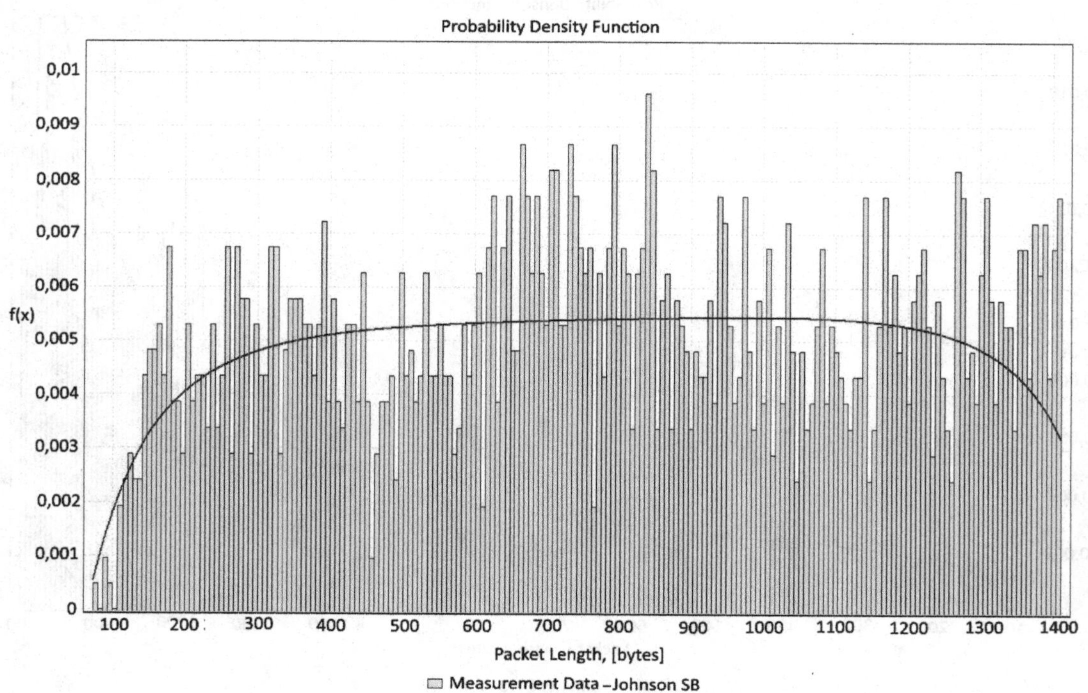

Figure 22. Packet length PDF of H.263 traffic source 192.168.10.2 with MBS=1,5 KB and 1 Mbps, MPLS 100, Gen Pareto distribution

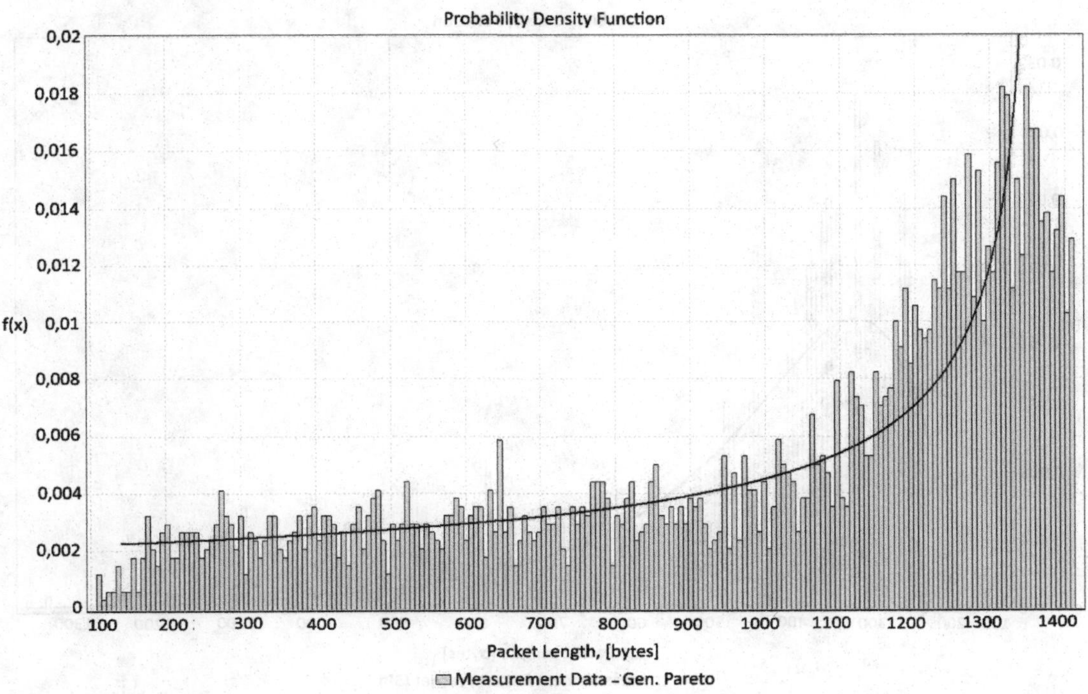

Figure 23. Packet length PDF of H.263 traffic source 192.168.10.4 with MBS=1,5 KB and 1 Mbps, best effort, Fatique Life (3P) distribution

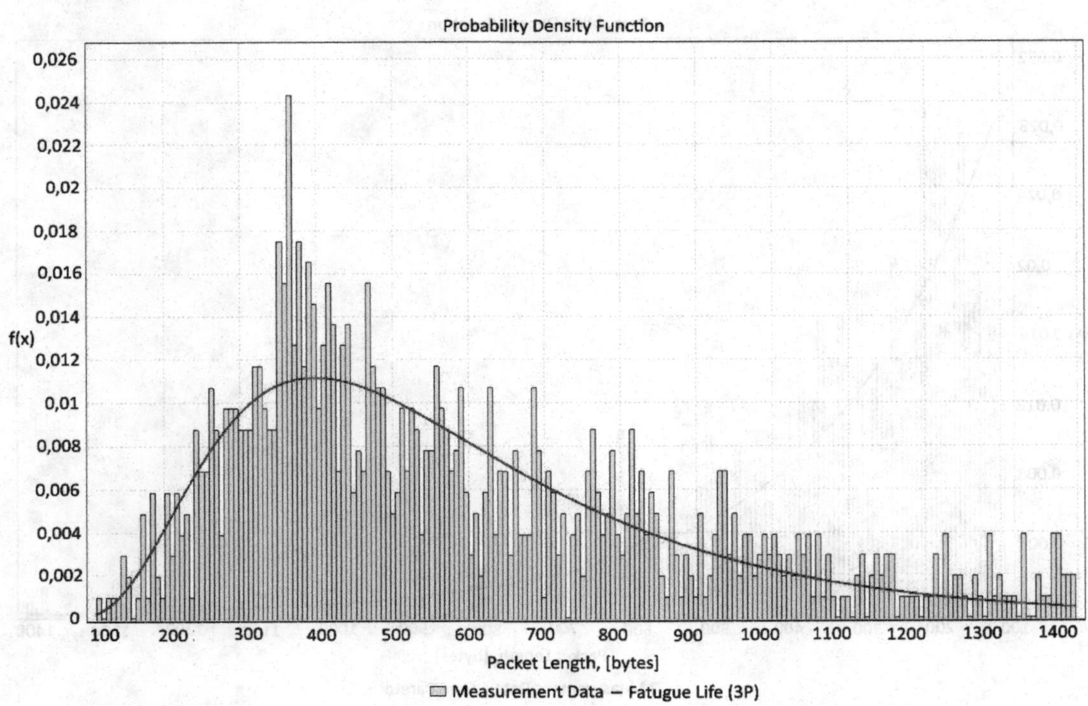

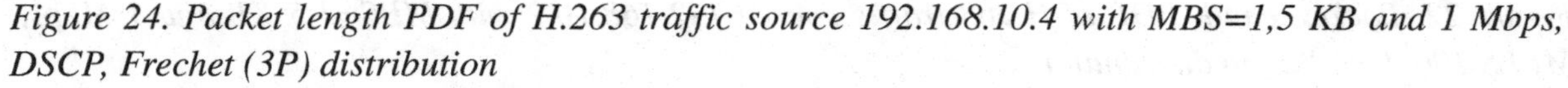

Figure 24. Packet length PDF of H.263 traffic source 192.168.10.4 with MBS=1,5 KB and 1 Mbps, DSCP, Frechet (3P) distribution

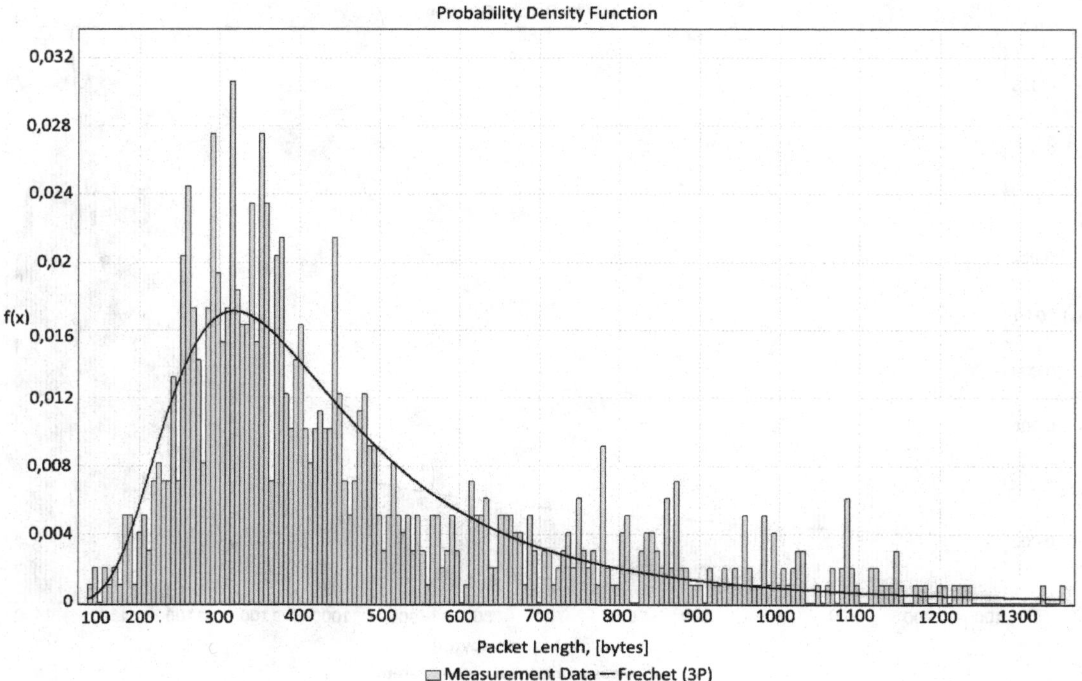

Figure 25. Packet length PDF of H.263 traffic source 192.168.10.4 with MBS=1,5 KB and 1 Mbps, MPLS, Gen Pareto distribution

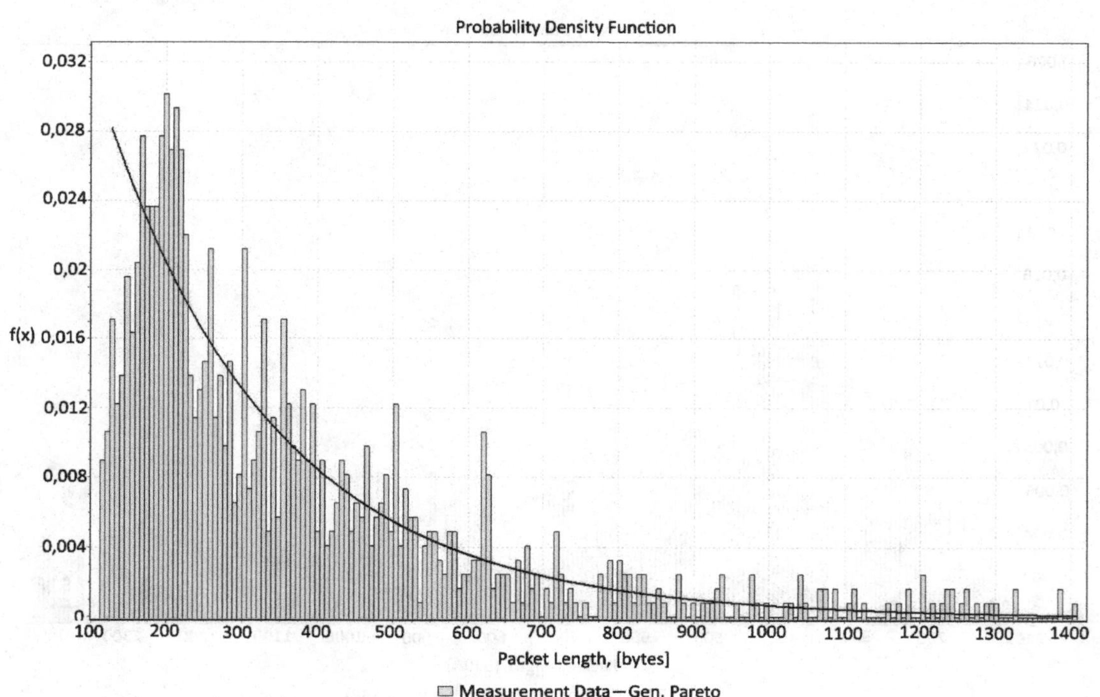

Figure 26. Packet length PDF of H.263 traffic source 192.168.10.4 with MBS=1,5 KB and 1 Mbps, MPLS 100, Log-Logistic (3P) distribution

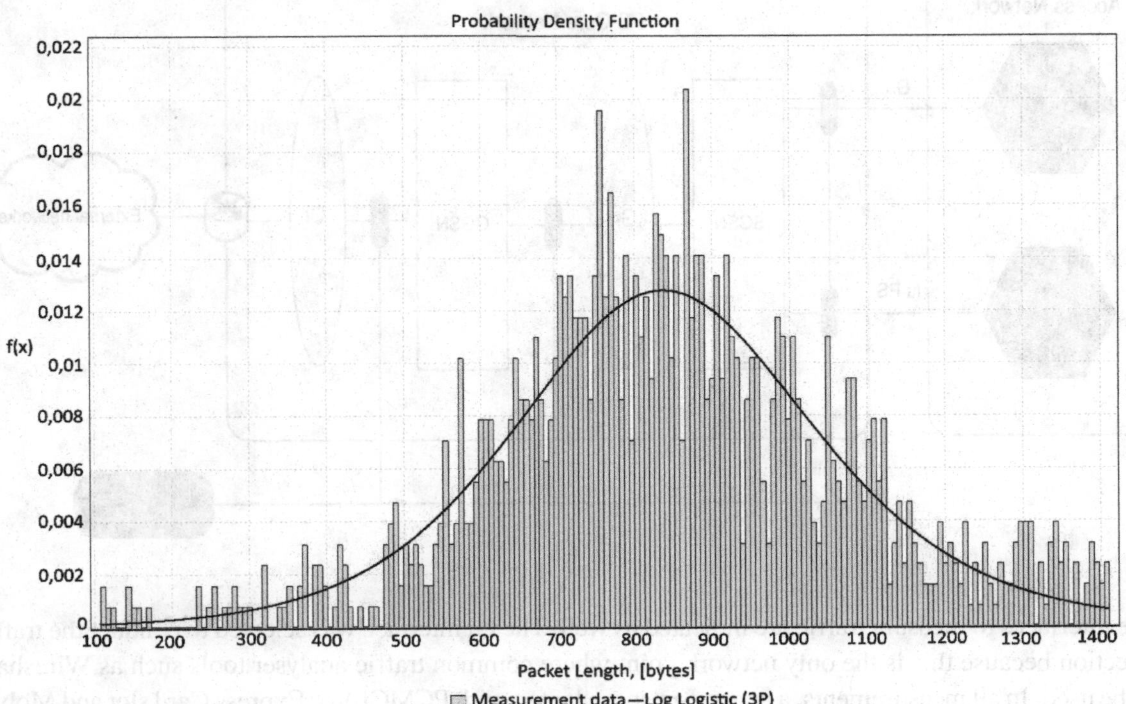

Similar data is obtained for the cases with MBS=6 k at both interfaces. The H.263 codec adapts the packet length to the available bandwidth and therefore changes the PDF function in many of the cases between Fatigue Life 3P, Johnson SB, Beta, Pearson 6 (4P), Generalized Pareto (Sharma, & Singh, 2010; Hazewinkel, 2001).

For comparison the packet length distribution of the ftp flow generated by 192.168.10.2 host has a clear deterministic nature. Due to the approximation, the algorithms applied by Easyfit tool, the best-fit distribution functions in all cases of applied priorities are exotic. The priorities consider always the other traffic than ftp. In addition, the hosts are not capable to adapt dynamically the payload of the packets like in the case of H.263 codec. So, even obtaining distributions like log-logistic for best effort and DiffServ servicing disciplines, Burr 4P for MPLS tunnel and Weibull 3P for MPLS EXP 100 tunnel one should consider the traffic deterministic (Cousineau, 2009; Al-Hussaini, 1991).

Network Set-Up at Second Phase

The second phase of the experiments is performed in a functional 3G network. Hence, the traffic is observed in a realistic network configuration. Attention is paid to both the forward and backward communication directions. All measurements are collected in a passive way at the Gi interface of the network (Svoboda, 2008; Shafiq, Ji, Liu, Pang, & Wang, 2012). Figure 27 illustrates the interfaces and the connecting network nodes of a GSM/UMTS network. In the figure, SGSN stands for Serving GPRS Support Node and GGSN for GPRS Gateway Support Node (Goleva, Atamian, Mirtchev, Dimitrova, & Grigorova, 2013). Other pos-

Figure 27. Traffic measurements points in 3G network

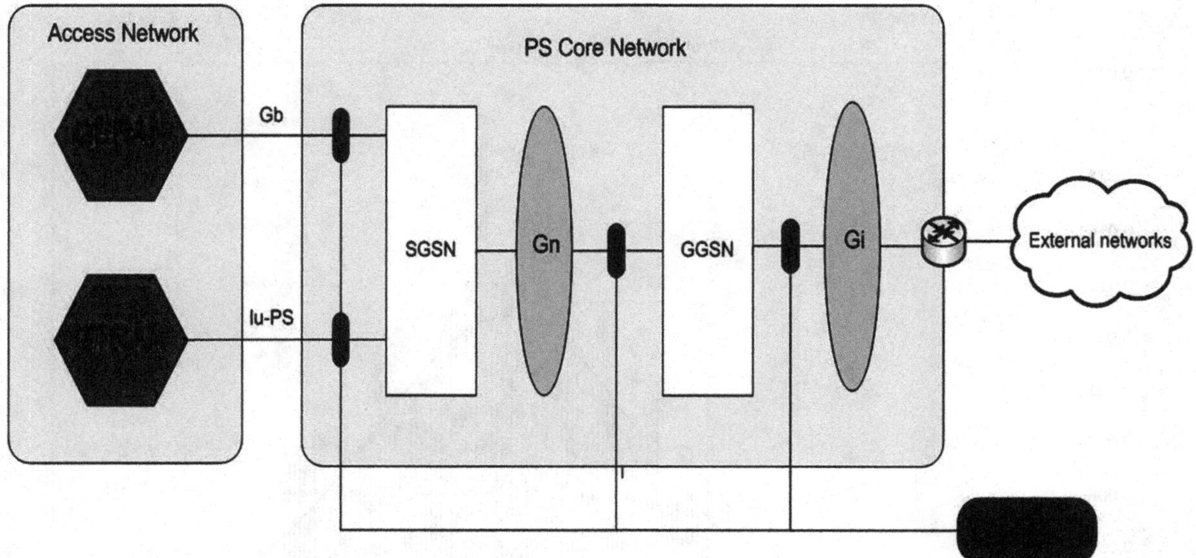

sible interfaces to measure traffic are indicated as well. The Gi interface was selected to conduct the traffic collection because this is the only network point where common traffic analyser tools such as Wireshark can be used. In all measurements, a general-purpose laptop with PCMCIA or Express Card slot and Mobile Connect Card is used. Nine test scenarios with duration of one minute were conducted.

The measurements were conducted at packet level. Packets from signalling, session layer, and application layer are removed as outliers during the last steps of the presented analysis. In the case of voice traffic the G.711, G.729A, and GSM codecs and UDP/RTP/SIP protocol were used. Video sources generate packets according to H.263, H.263+ and H.264 (low and high end) codecs (Svoboda, 2008). For both traffic types (voice and video) measurements in both forward and backward directions were collected, which allows us to observe the shaping effect in both directions. Traces were captured by the Wireshark tool and the data is exported to the Wolfram Mathematica and Crystal Ball tools for statistical analysis.

Traffic Analyses during the Second Phase

The measurements are focusing on analysis of the PDF of the inter-arrival times and accompanying statistical parameters with and without outliers. The general rule of 3σ is applied for outliers, where σ is the standard deviation of the inter-arrival times. Usually these packets are from signalling, session layer, and application layer. The overall number of removed packets is less than 1%. Working with outliers is not often considered in the statistics. However, there is an approximation performed with outliers because these packets form the long tails observed in the distributions of many services.

In the cases with outliers, the best fitting mapping is determined by the Crystal Ball tool. Subsequently, after outliers' removal the best fitting is performed to a gamma distribution by the Crystal Ball tool (blue line on all graphs) and by Wolfram Mathematica (red line). In all cases, the distribution parameters corresponding to the analyzed traffic are evaluated and to used in simulation. The distribution parameters are given for each scenario in an accompanying table.

Figure 28. Measured and evaluated exponential PDF of the packet inter-arrival times of VoIP call (GSM codec) with outliers forward by Crystal Ball

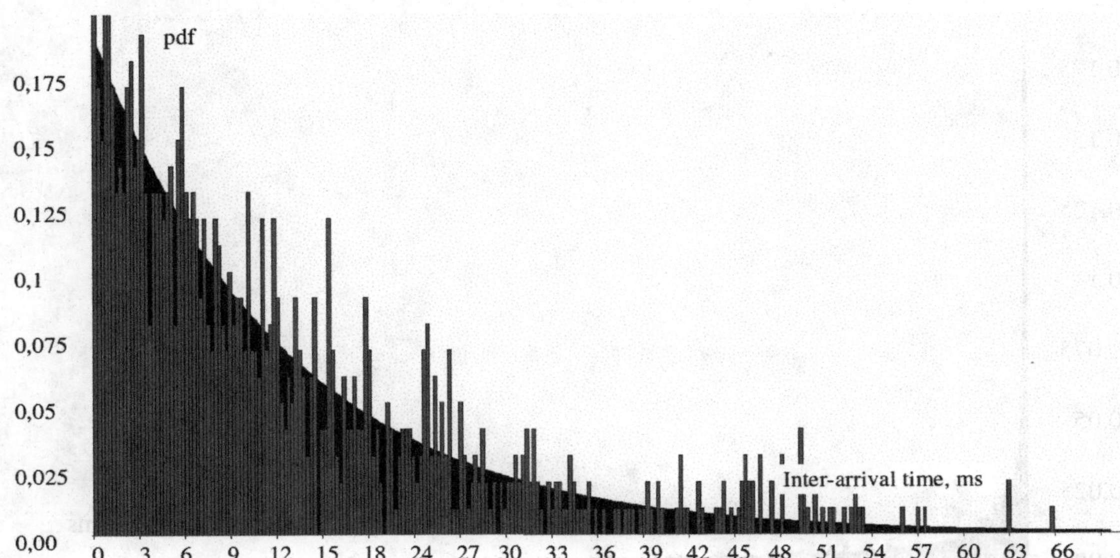

An important observation is that the distribution functions in a backward direction are different from the PDFs in forward direction even in cases when the traffic is symmetric by nature. The difference is due to influences by end-to-end queuing delay, priorities and shaping effect within the nodes on the session path. Pure distribution parameters with and without outliers allow the easy and predictable traffic simulation in a realistic network model. Such feedback is essential for performance measurements in opportunistic networks and dynamic resource management.

The first three scenarios (test 1 to 3) focus purely on VoIP traffic. The type of codec shows significant effect on the distribution of the packet inter-arrival times. A VoIP call is generated from a laptop with GSM 06.10 codec during test 1. The PDF of the packet inter-arrival times 'with outliers' is plotted on Figures 28 and 29. According to the Kolmogorov-Smirnov algorithm, the traffic is exponentially distributed in the forward direction and gamma distributed in the backward drection. The results after removing the outliers are plotted on Figures 30 and 31. As it is observed the gamma distribution is appropriate for both directions of communication. The distribution parameters as mean value, variance, mean standard deviation, skewness, and kurtosis for both cases are given in Tables 5 and 6. They are used to simulate traffic patterns. The difference between PDFs forward and backward is related with end-to-end shaping effect and resource management.

A VoIP call with codec G.711 A-Law, which generates more than two times bigger packets compared to the GSM codec, is run in test scenario 2. In the case 'with outliers' (Figures 32 and 33) the best fitting mapping of measured data indicates gamma and log-normal distributions for the forward and backward direction respectively. The approximations applied are Kolmogorov-Smirnov and Anderson-Darling tests. The difference between the two directions is significant. Figures 34 and 35 show the fitting of the gamma distribution to the measured data after outliers' removal. The distribution parameters are given in Tables 5 and 6. It is important to note that the VoIP service with small packets (i.e., GSM codec) tends to speed up the end-to-end traffic. On the contrary, when the packets are bigger, as in the case of a G.711 codec, the packet delay can vary significantly end-to-end.

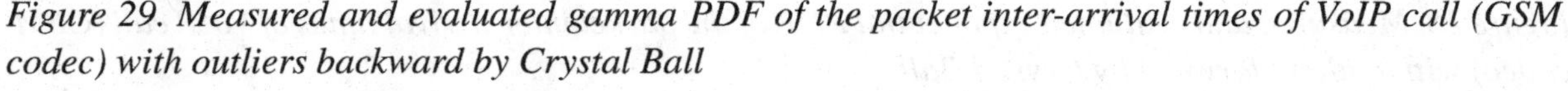

Figure 29. Measured and evaluated gamma PDF of the packet inter-arrival times of VoIP call (GSM codec) with outliers backward by Crystal Ball

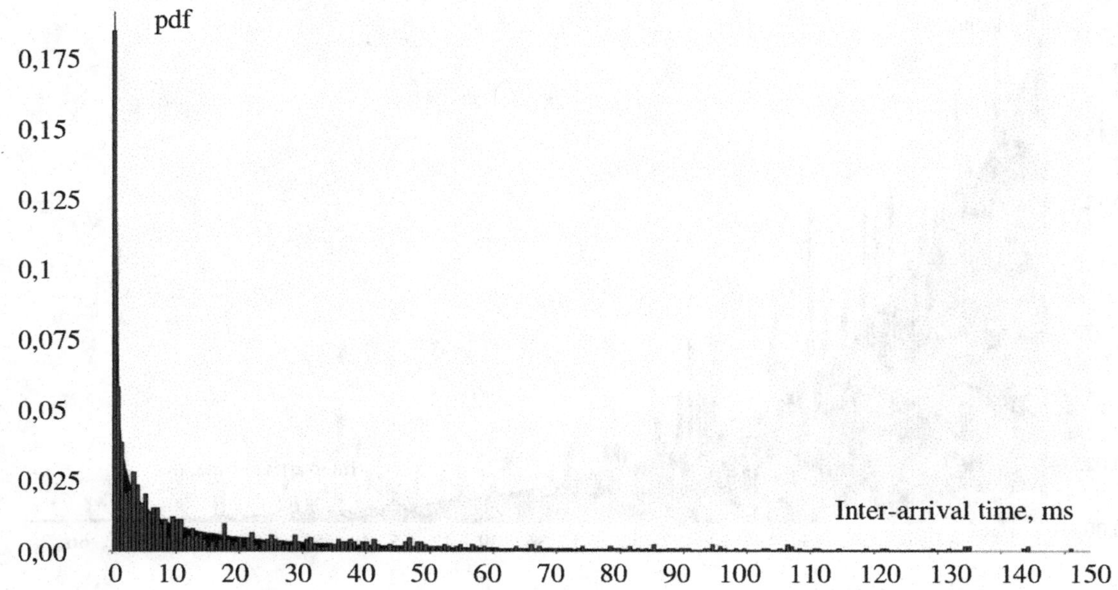

Table 5. Measured statistical parameters of inter-arrival times in 3G network with VoIP codecs

Test 1, VoIP, GSM Codec	Mean, ms	Variance, ms	Mean Standard Dev., ms	Skewness	Kurtosis
Calling user, data with outliers	20	33	5.76	-0.49	
Called user, data with outliers	20	0.81	0.904	1.07	
Calling user, data without outliers	10.16	55.262	7.434	0.457	-0.48
Called user, data without outliers	10.22	36.876	6.072	0.193	0.038
Test 2, VoIP, A-law Codec	**Mean, ms**	**Variance, ms**	**Mean Standard Dev., ms**	**Skewness**	**Kurtosis**
Calling user, data with outliers	20	0.774	0.88	0.88	
Called user, data with outliers	20	7.87	2.8	39.9	
Calling user, data without outliers	10.23	52.482	7.244	0.026	-1.041
Called user, data without outliers	10.25	37.364	6.113	0.140	-1.183
Test 3, VoIP, G.729 Codec	**Mean, ms**	**Variance, ms**	**Mean Standard Dev., ms**	**Skewness**	**Kurtosis**
Calling user, data with outliers	19.56	19.23	4.385	-0.654	
Called user, data with outliers	18.56	12.77	3.57	-1.85	
Calling user, data without outliers	9.714	41.848	6.469	0.446	-0.610
Called user, data without outliers	9.724	50.534	7.109	0.100	-1.054

Table 6. Measured and evaluated PDFs for VoIP codecs

Test 1, VoIP, GSM Codec	Evaluated PDF by Crystal Ball	Evaluated PDF by Wolfram Mathematica
Calling user, data with outliers	Exponential	
Called user, data with outliers	Gamma	
Calling user, data without outliers	Gamma. Location=0. Shape=0.49 Scale=20.39	Gamma. Location=0. Shape=0.55 Scale=18.17
Called user, data without outliers	Gamma. Location=-33.60 Shape=52.65 Scale=0.83	Gamma. Location=-33.60 Shape=0.596 Scale=16.81
Test 2, VoIP, A-Law Codec	**Evaluated PDF by Crystal Ball**	**Evaluated PDF by Wolfram Mathematica**
Calling user, data with outliers	Gamma	
Called user, data with outliers	Log-normal	
Calling user, data without outliers	Gamma. Location=-47.53 Shape=64.41 Scale=0.89	Gamma. Location=0 Shape=0.35 Scale=28.35
Called user, data without outliers	Gamma. Location=1.25 Shape=2.85 Scale=3.95	Gamma. Location=0 Shape=1.66 Scale=6.03
Test 3, VoIP, G.729 Codec	**Evaluated PDF by Crystal Ball**	**Evaluated PDF by Wolfram Mathematica**
Calling user, data with outliers	Log-normal	
Called user, data with outliers	Gamma	
Calling user, data without outliers	Gamma. Location=-0.9 Shape=2.18 Scale=4.79	Gamma. Location=0 Shape=1.06 Scale=8.98
Called user, data without outliers	Gamma. Location=0 Shape=0.39 Scale=24.16	Gamma. Location=0 Shape=0.35 Scale=27.22

Figure 30. Measured and evaluated gamma PDF of the packet inter-arrival times of VoIP call (GSM codec) without outliers forward by Wolfram Mathematica

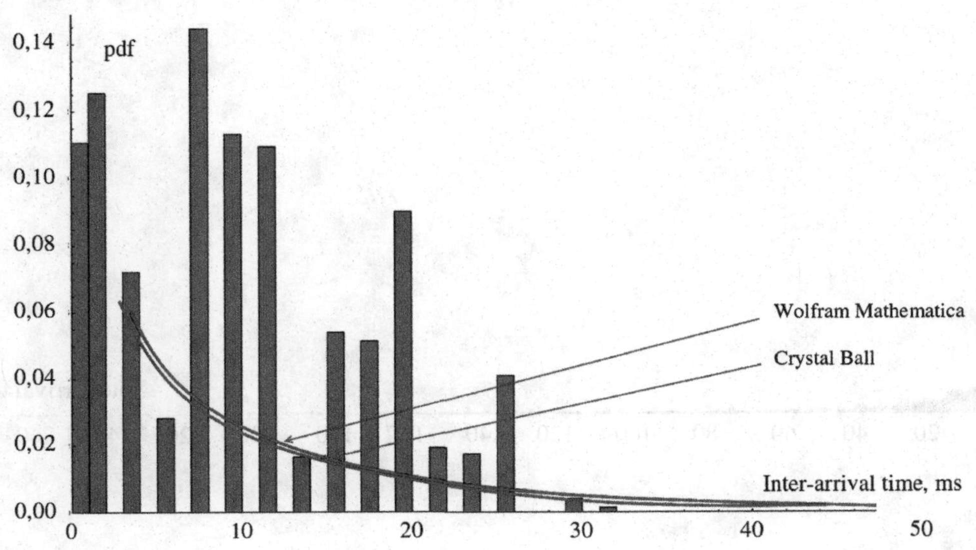

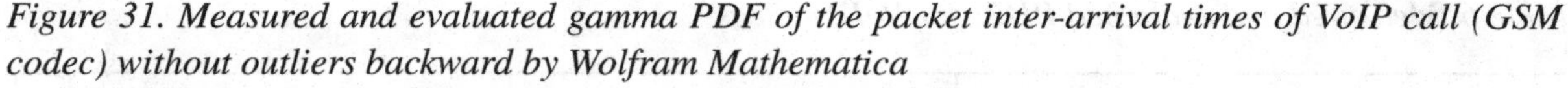

Figure 31. Measured and evaluated gamma PDF of the packet inter-arrival times of VoIP call (GSM codec) without outliers backward by Wolfram Mathematica

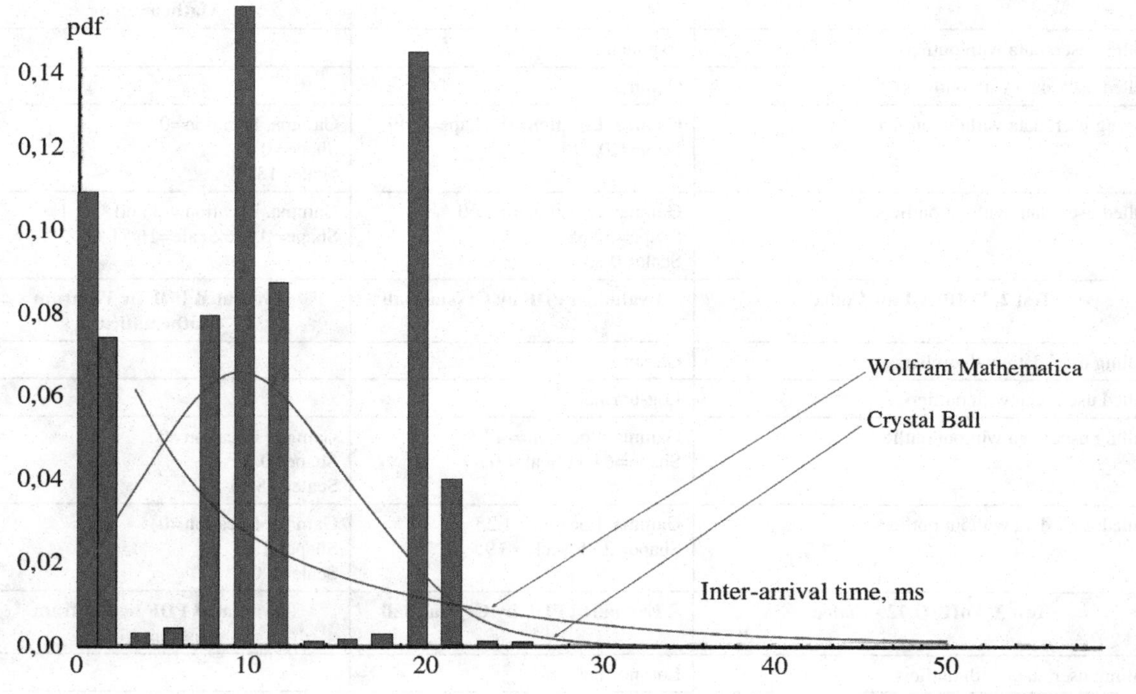

Figure 32. Measured and evaluated gamma PDF of the packet inter-arrival times of VoIP call (A-law) with outliers forward by Crystal Ball

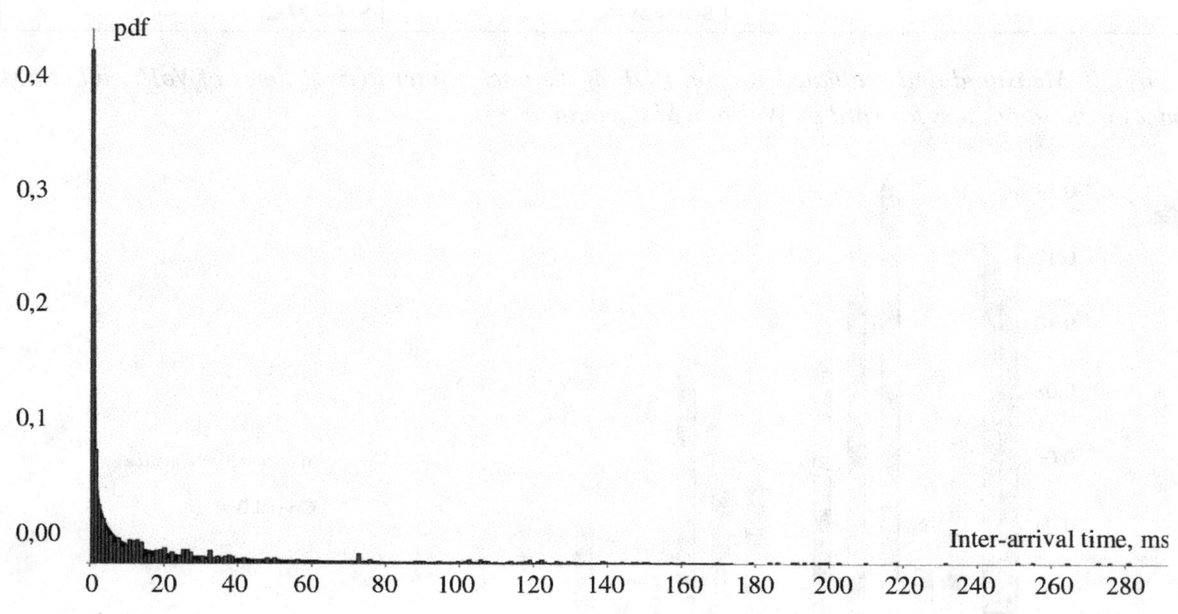

Figure 33. Measured and evaluated lognormal PDF of the packet inter-arrival times of VoIP call (A-Law) with outliers backward by Crystal Ball

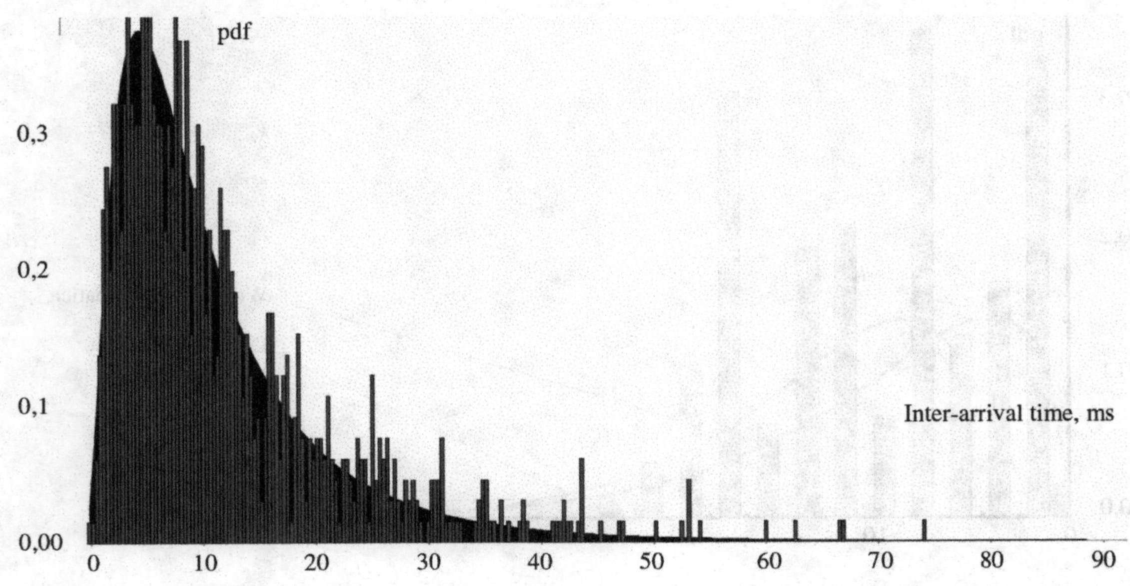

Figure 34. Measured and evaluated gamma PDF of the packet inter-arrival times of VoIP call (A-Law) without outliers forward by Wolfram Mathematica

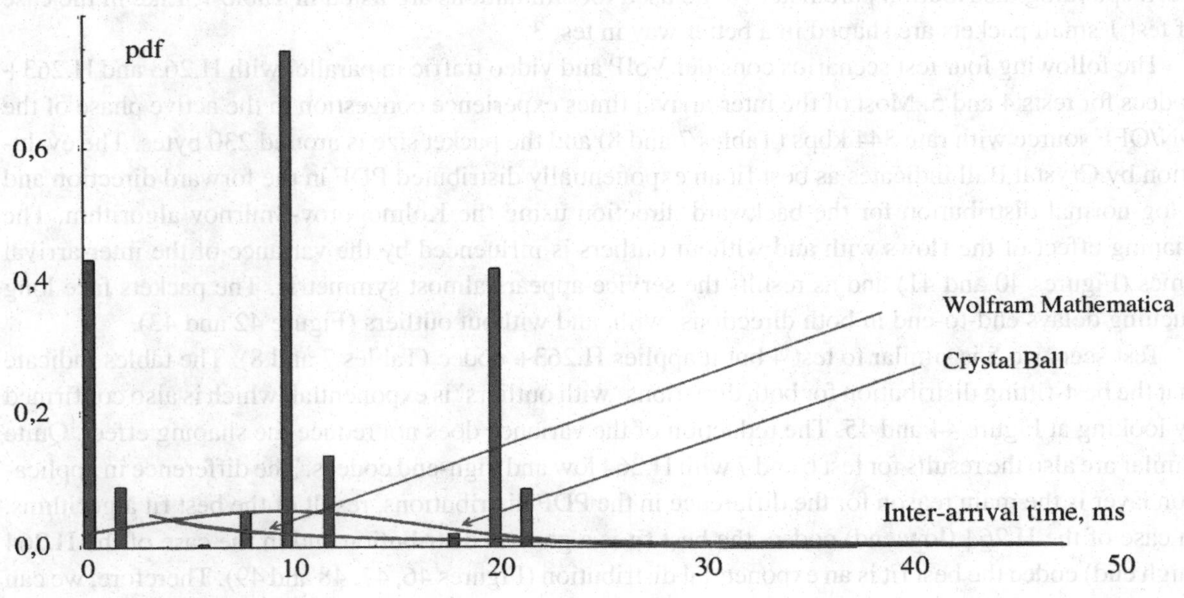

Figure 35. Measured and evaluated gamma PDF of the packet inter-arrival times of VoIP call (A-Law) without outliers backward by Wolfram Mathematica

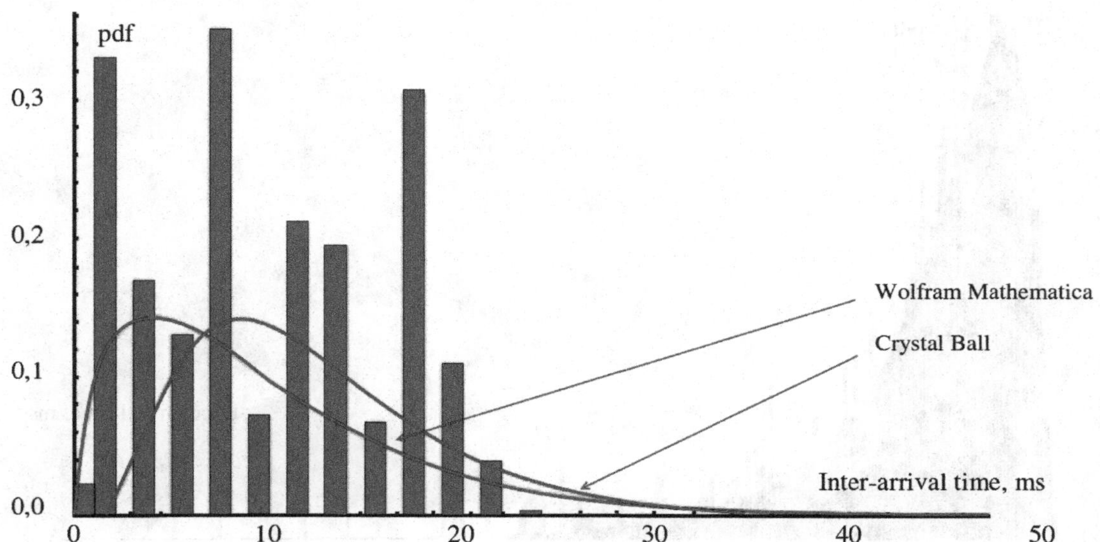

A VoIP call with G.729 codec that can be considered as an ON/OFF traffic source is measured in test 3. As shown in Figures 36 and 37 the best fitting functions are log-normal forward and gamma distribution backward by applying Kolmogorov-Smirnov and Anderson-Darling algorithms 'with outliers'. Again the fitting for the 'without outliers' case can be seen in the accompanying Figures 38 and 39. Corresponding distribution parameters to be used for simulations are listed in Table 7. Like in the case of test 1 small packets are shaped in a better way in test 3.

The following four test scenarios consider VoIP and video traffic in parallel with H.263 and H.263+ codecs for tests 4 and 5. Most of the inter-arrival times experience congestion in the active phase of the ON/OFF source with rate 344 kbps (Tables 7 and 8) and the packet size is around 230 bytes. The evaluation by Crystal Ball indicates as best fit an exponentially distributed PDF in the forward direction and a log-normal distribution for the backward direction using the Kolmogorov-Smirnov algorithm. The shaping effect of the flows with and without outliers is influenced by the variance of the inter-arrival times (Figures 40 and 41) and as results the service appears almost symmetric. The packets face long queuing delays end-to-end in both directions, with, and without outliers (Figure 42 and 43).

Test scenario 5 is similar to test 4 but it applies H.263+ codec (Tables 7 and 8). The tables indicate that the best-fitting distribution for both directions 'with outliers' is exponential, which is also confirmed by looking at Figure 44 and 45. The reduction of the variance does not reduce the shaping effect. Quite similar are also the results for test 6 and 7 with H.264 low and high-end codecs. The difference in application layer is the main reason for the difference in the PDF distributions, result of the best fit algorithms. In case of the H.264 (low end) codec, the best fit is a gamma distribution and in the case of the H.264 (high end) codec the best fit is an exponential distribution (Figures 46, 47, 48 and 49). Therefore, we can conclude that even small changes in the codecs can influence significantly the flows (Tables 7 and 8).

Figure 36. Measured and evaluated log-normal PDF of the packet inter-arrival times of VoIP call (G.729) with outliers forward by Crystal Ball

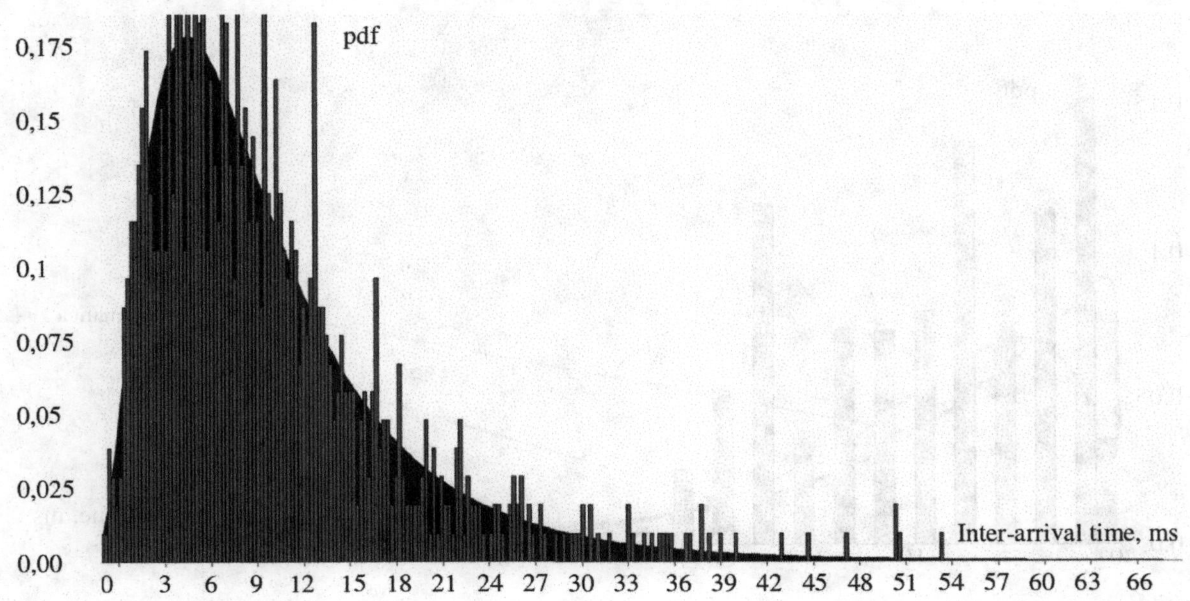

Figure 37. Measured and evaluated gamma PDF of the packet inter-arrival times of VoIP call (G.729) with outliers backward by Crystal Ball

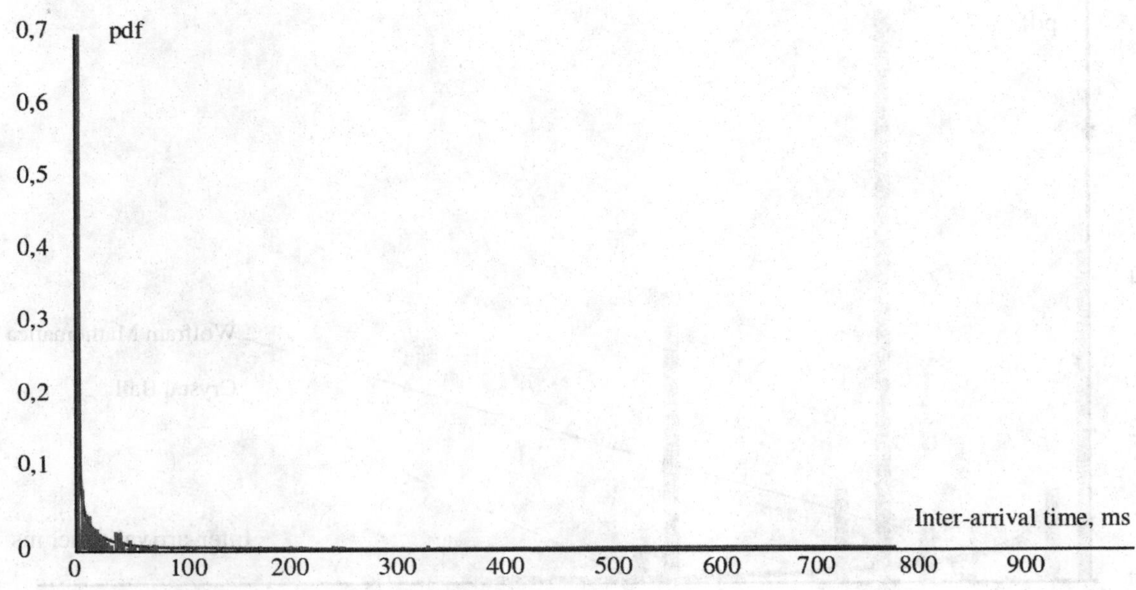

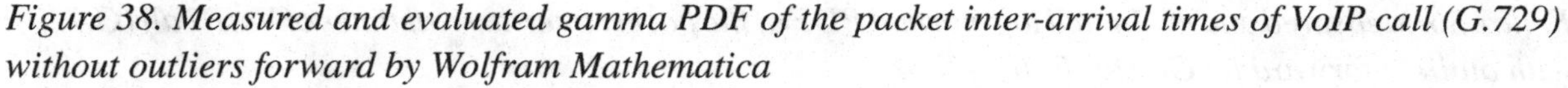

Figure 38. Measured and evaluated gamma PDF of the packet inter-arrival times of VoIP call (G.729) without outliers forward by Wolfram Mathematica

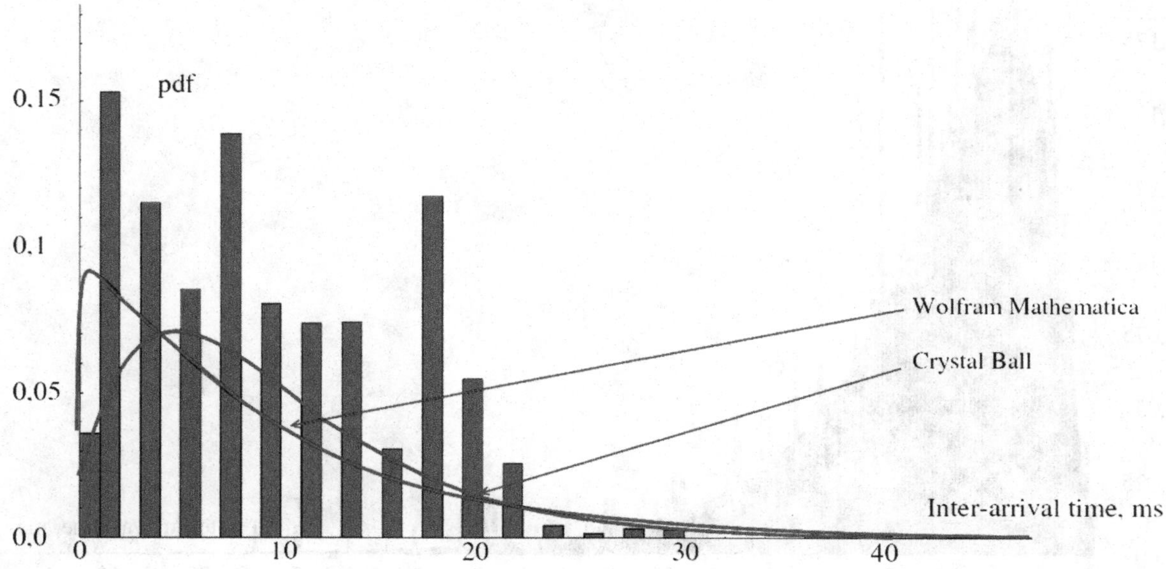

Figure 39. Measured and evaluated gamma PDF of the packet inter-arrival times of VoIP call (G.729) without outliers backward by Wolfram Mathematica

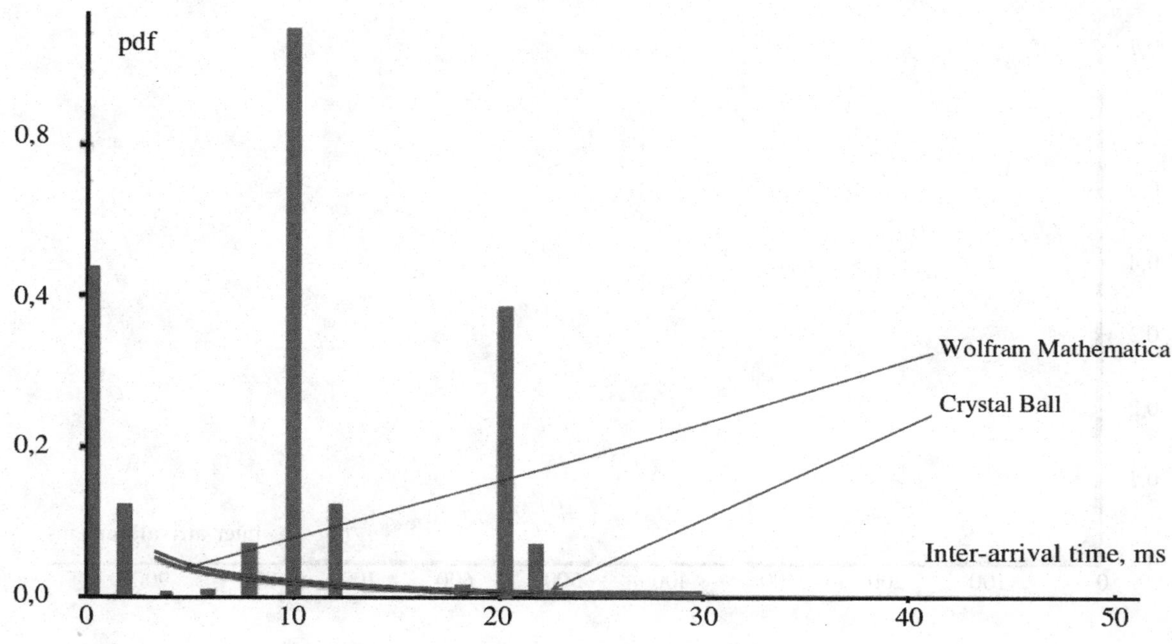

Table 7. Measured statistical parameters of inter-arrival times in 3G network for video over IP codecs

Test 4, Voice and Video Over IP, H.263 Codec	Mean, ms	Variance, ms	Mean Standard Dev., ms	Skewness	Kurtosis
Calling user, data with outliers	36.61	955.42	30.91	14.22	
Called user, data with outliers	41.35	306.44	17.51	1.41	
Calling user, data without outliers	6.756	33.709	5.806	1.246	2.954
Called user, data without outliers	6.802	28.068	5.298	0.828	-0.282
Test 5, Voice and Video H.263+ Codec	**Mean, ms**	**Variance, ms**	**Mean Standard Dev., ms**	**Skewness**	**Kurtosis**
Calling user, data with outliers	39.47	1156.5	34	14.78	
Called user, data with outliers	41.43	308.25	17.56	1.4	
Calling user, data without outliers	6.86	35.410	5.951	1.233	2.450
Called user, data without outliers	6.91	35.952	5.996	0.815	0.229
Test 6, Voice and Video, H.264 (Low End) Codec	**Mean, ms**	**Variance, ms**	**Mean Standard Dev., ms**	**Skewness**	**Kurtosis**
Calling user, data with outliers	23.75	2027	45	6.57	
Called user, data with outliers	23.86	1899	43.59	4.22	
Calling user, data without outliers	5.662	65.457	8.091	2.682	8.529
Called user, data without outliers	5.517	67.529	8.218	2.320	6.230
Test 7, Voice and Video, H.264 (High End) Codec	**Mean, ms**	**Variance, ms**	**Mean Standard Dev., ms**	**Skewness**	**Kurtosis**
Calling user, data with outliers	35.3	1152	33.95	13.25	
Called user, data with outliers	35.83	366	19.14	0.43	
Calling user, data without outliers	6.559	38.863	6.234	1.327	2.182
Called user, data without outliers	6.602	29.201	5.404	0.971	0.228

Figure 40. Measured and evaluated exponential PDF of the packet inter-arrival times of H.263 with outliers forward by Crystal Ball

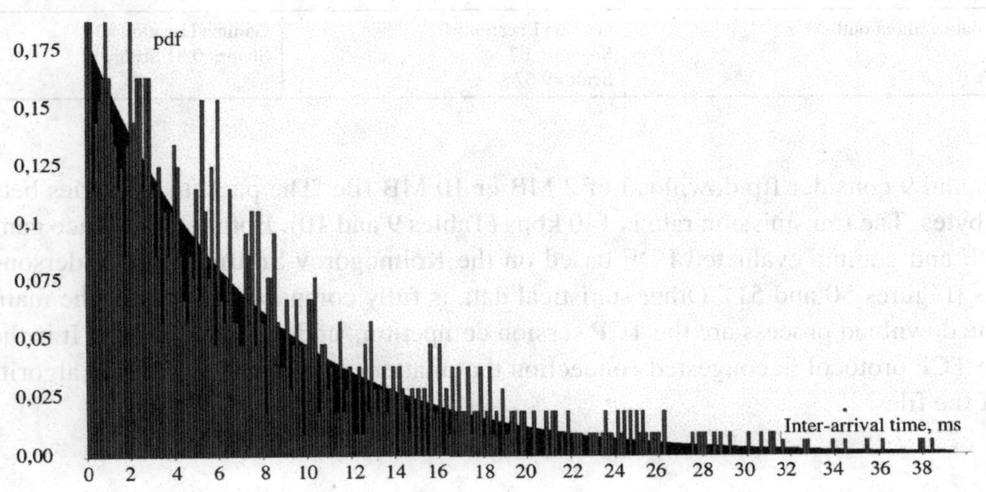

Table 8. Evaluated PDFs of inter-arrival times in 3G network for video over IP codecs

Test 4, Voice and Video Over IP, H.263 Codec	Evaluated PDF by Crystal Ball	Evaluated PDF by Wolfram Mathematica
Calling user, data with outliers	Exponential	
Called user, data with outliers	Log-normal	
Calling user, data without outliers	Gamma Shape=0.67 Scale=9.88	Gamma Location=0 Shape=0.82. Scale=8.047
Called user, data without outliers	Gamma Location=-0.13 Shape=1.39 Scale=4.86	Gamma Location=0 Shape=0.99. Scale=6.713
Test 5, Voice and Video H.263+ Codec	**Evaluated PDF by Crystal Ball**	**Evaluated PDF by Wolfram Mathematica**
Calling user, data with outliers	Exponen-tial	
Called user, data with outliers	Exponen-tial	
Calling user, data without outliers	Gamma Shape=0.5 Scale=13.46	Gamma Location=0 Shape=0.53 Scale=12.83
Called user, data without outliers	Gamma Location=0 Shape=0.66 Scale=10.13	Gamma Location=0 Shape=0.6018 Scale=11.215
Test 6, Voice and Video, H.264 (Low End) Codec	**Evaluated PDF by Crystal Ball**	**Evaluated PDF by Wolfram Mathematica**
Calling user, data with outliers	Gamma	
Called user, data with outliers	Gamma	
Calling user, data without outliers	Gamma Shape=0.33 Scale=17.14	Gamma Location=0 Shape=0.28 Scale=19.76
Called user, data without outliers	Gamma Location=0. Shape=0.47 Scale=11.79	Gamma Location=0 Shape=0.4 Scale=13.65
Test 7, Voice and Video, H.264 (High End) Codec	**Evaluated PDF by Crystal Ball**	**Evaluated PDF by Wolfram Mathematica**
Calling user, data with outliers	Exponen-tial	
Called user, data with outliers	Exponen-tial	
Calling user, data without outliers	Gamma Shape=0.48 Scale=13.29	Gamma Location=0 Shape=0.614 Scale=10.47
Called user, data without outliers	Gamma Location=0 Shape=0.67 Scale=9.67	Gamma Location=0 Shape=0.81 Scale=8

Tests 8 and 9 consider ftp download of 2 MB or 10 MB file. The packet size varies between 80 and 1500 bytes. The transmission rate is 140 kbps (Tables 9 and 10). Both tests produce gamma best fitting PDF and gamma evaluated PDF based on the Kolmogorov-Smirnov and Anderson-Darling algorithms (Figures 50 and 51). Other statistical data is fully comparable as well. The main factors shaping the download process are the TCP session competitors and the window size. It is the behaviour of the TCP protocol in congested connection that matters more the transmission algorithm than the size of the files.

Figure 41. Measured and evaluated lognormal PDF of the packet inter-arrival times of H.263 with outliers backward by Crystal Ball

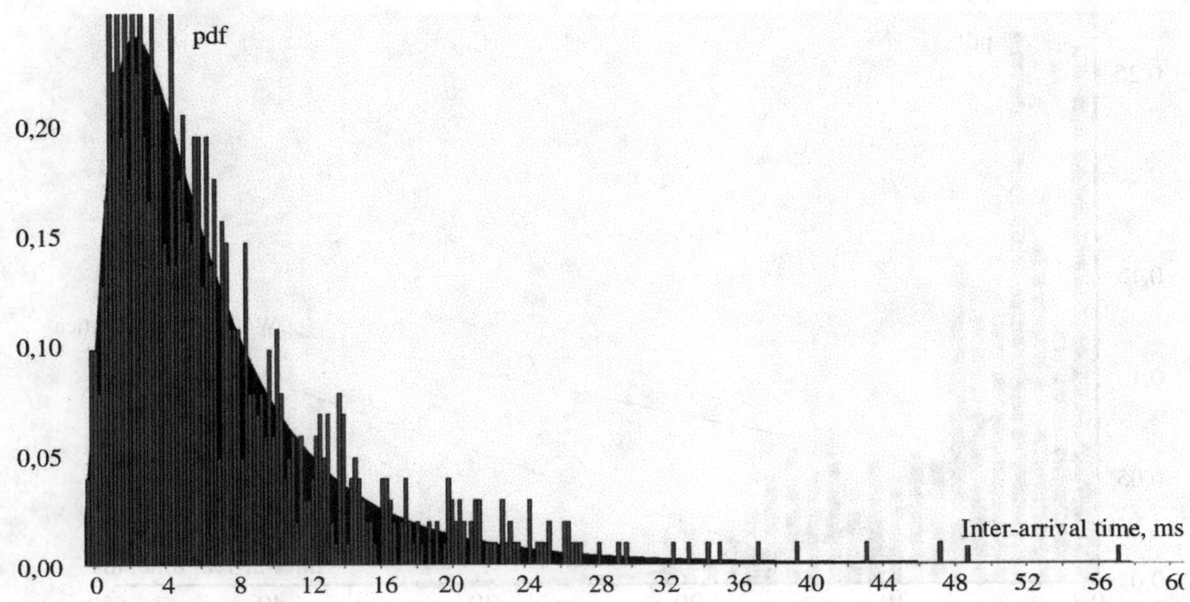

Figure 42. Measured and evaluated gamma PDF of the packet inter-arrival times of H.263 without outliers forward by Wolfram Mathematica

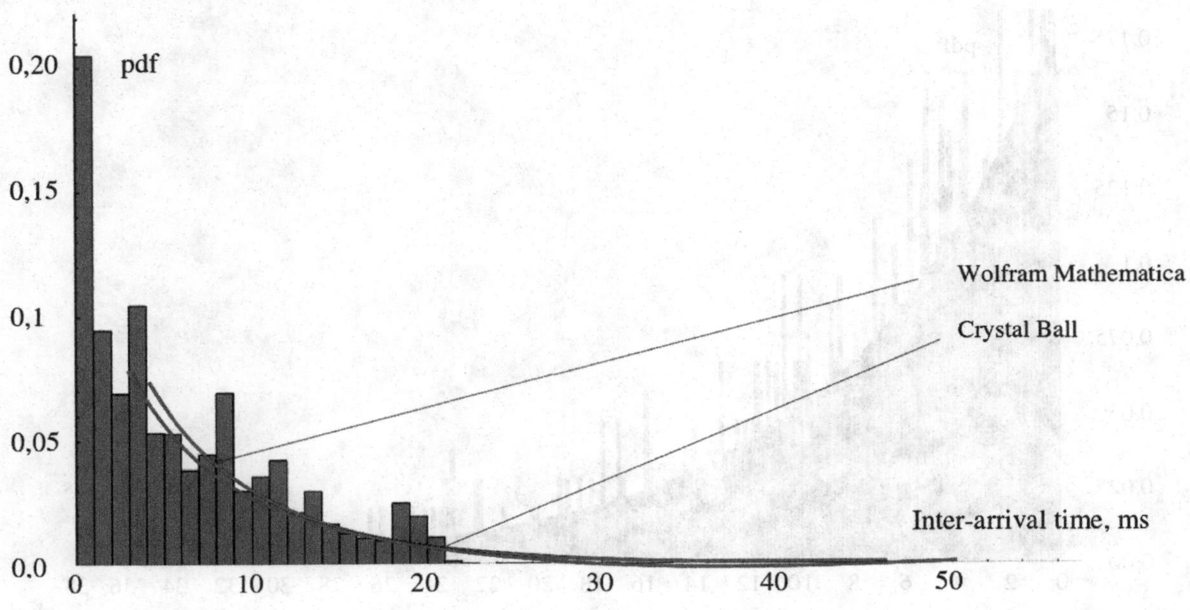

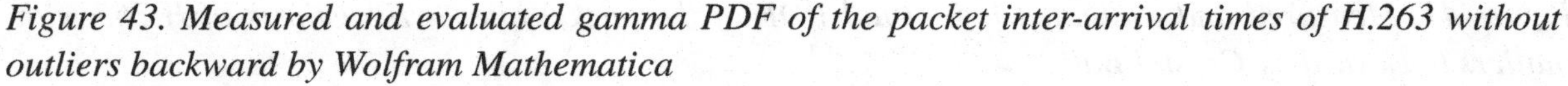

Figure 43. Measured and evaluated gamma PDF of the packet inter-arrival times of H.263 without outliers backward by Wolfram Mathematica

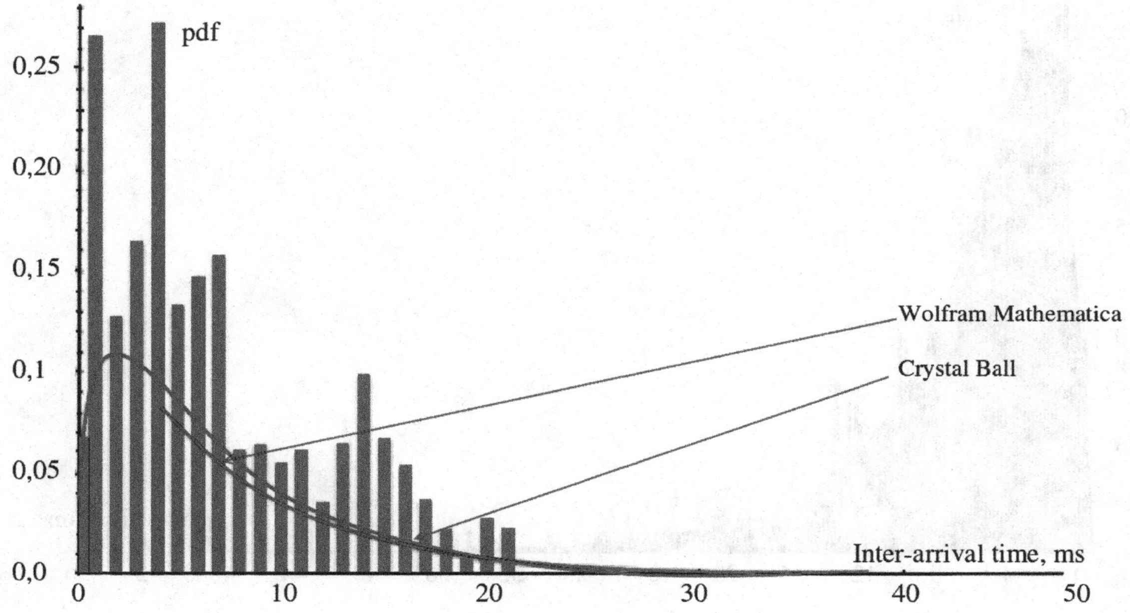

Figure 44. Measured and evaluated exponential PDF of the packet inter-arrival times of H.263+ with outliers forward and backward by Crystal Ball

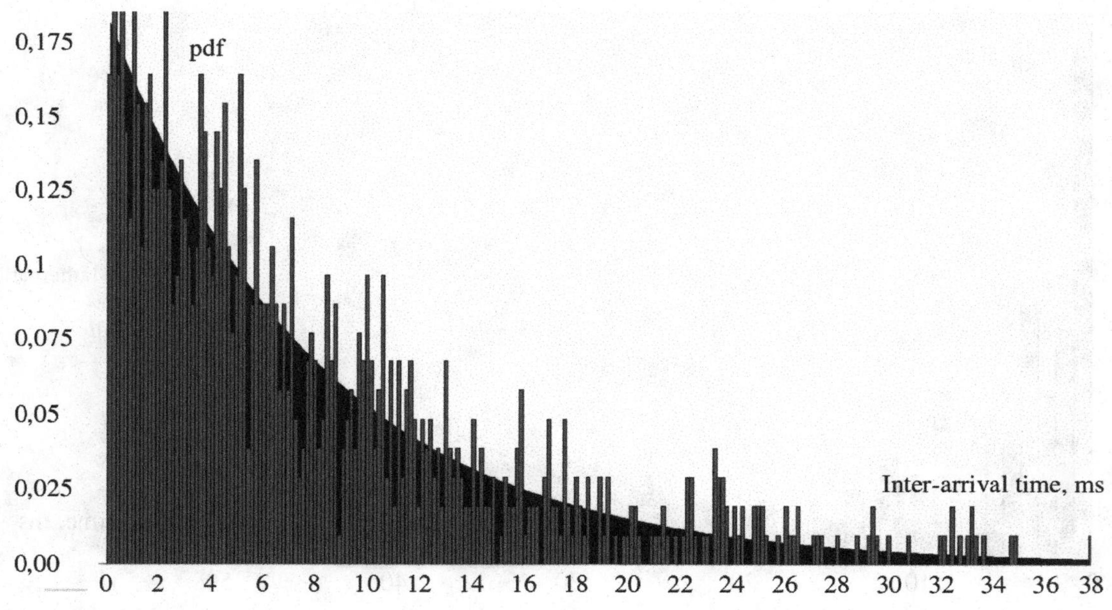

Figure 45. Measured and evaluated gamma PDF of the packet inter-arrival times of H.263+ without outliers forward and backward by Wolfram Mathematica

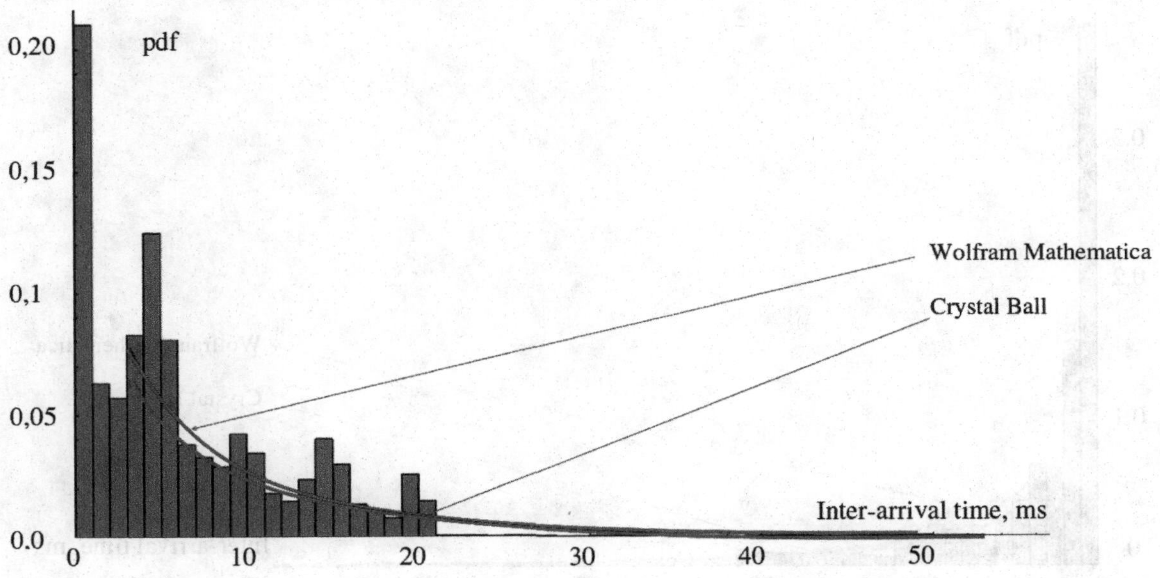

Figure 46. Measured and evaluated gamma PDF of the packet inter-arrival times of H.264 (low end) with outliers forward and backward by Crystal Ball

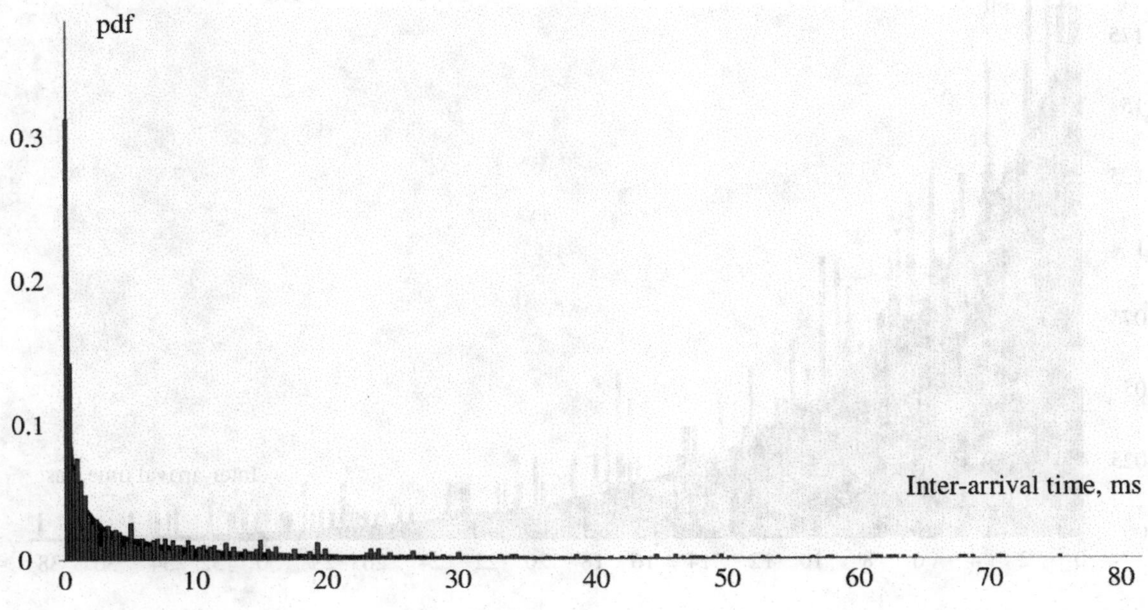

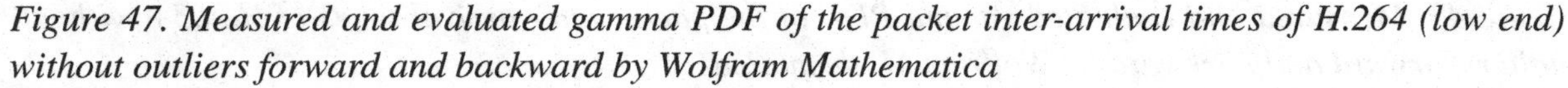

Figure 47. Measured and evaluated gamma PDF of the packet inter-arrival times of H.264 (low end) without outliers forward and backward by Wolfram Mathematica

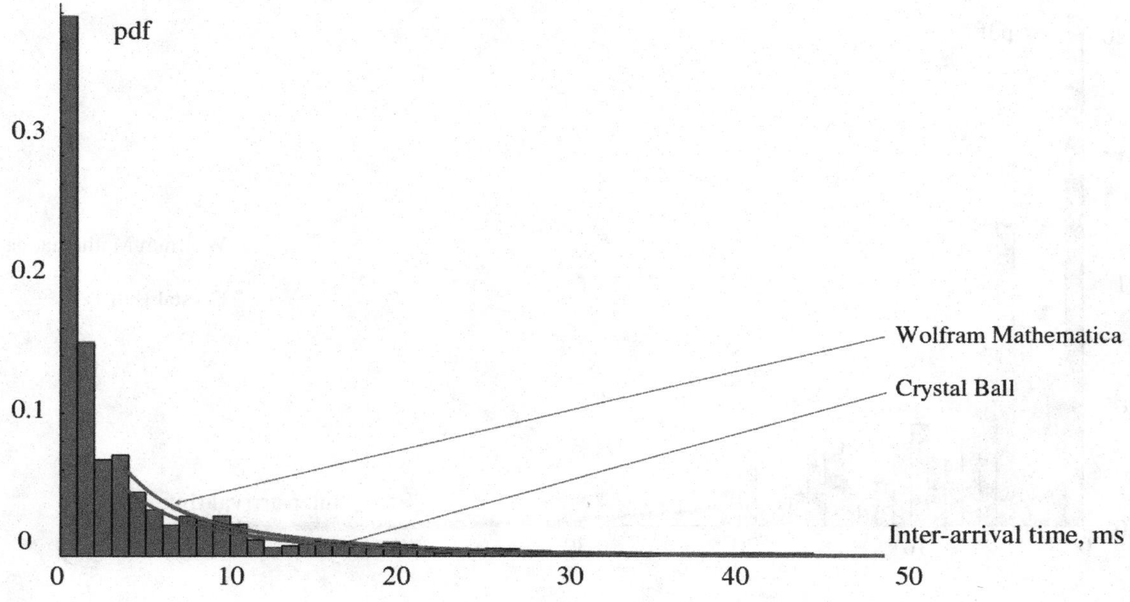

Figure 48. Measured and evaluated exponential PDF of the packet inter-arrival times of H.264 (high end) with outliers forward and backward by Crystal Ball

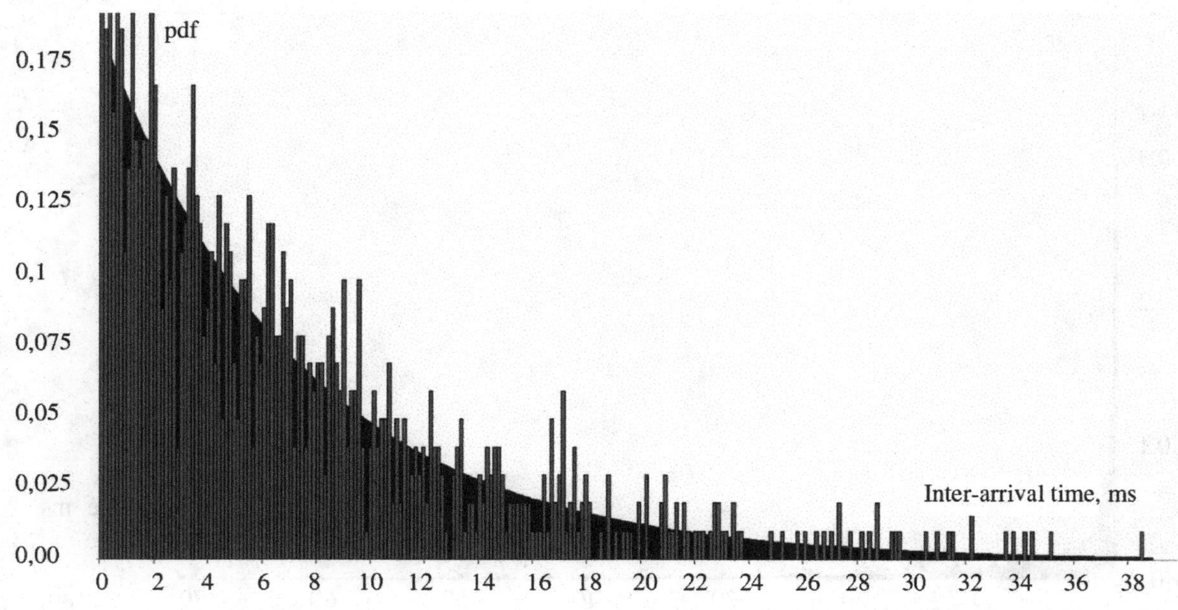

Figure 49. Measured and evaluated gamma PDF of the packet inter-arrival times of H.264 (high end) without outliers forward and backward by Wolfram Mathematica

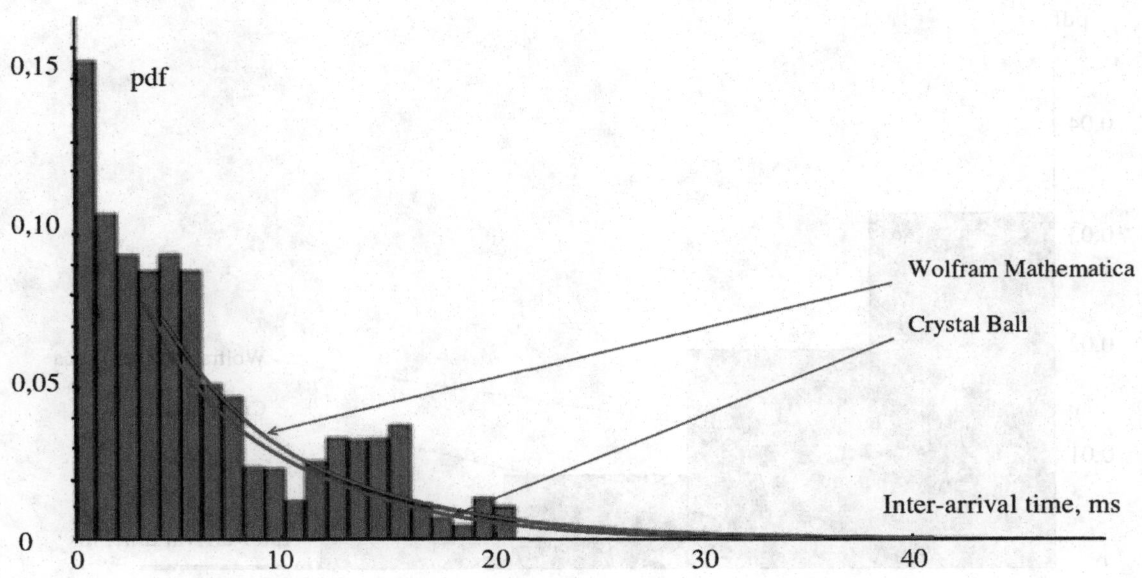

Figure 50. Measured and evaluated gamma PDF of the packet inter-arrival times of ftp with outliers forward and backward by Crystal Ball

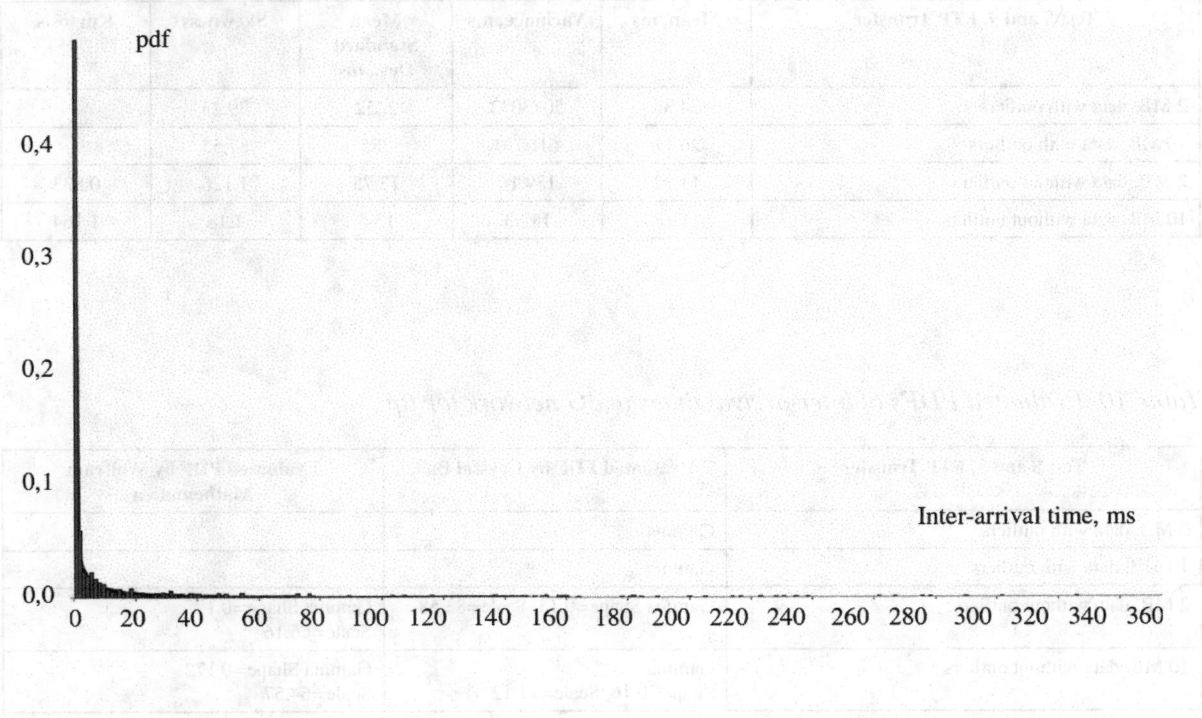

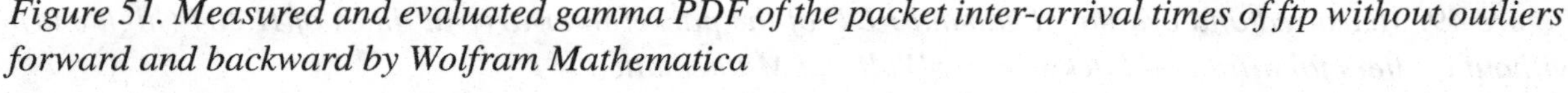
Figure 51. Measured and evaluated gamma PDF of the packet inter-arrival times of ftp without outliers forward and backward by Wolfram Mathematica

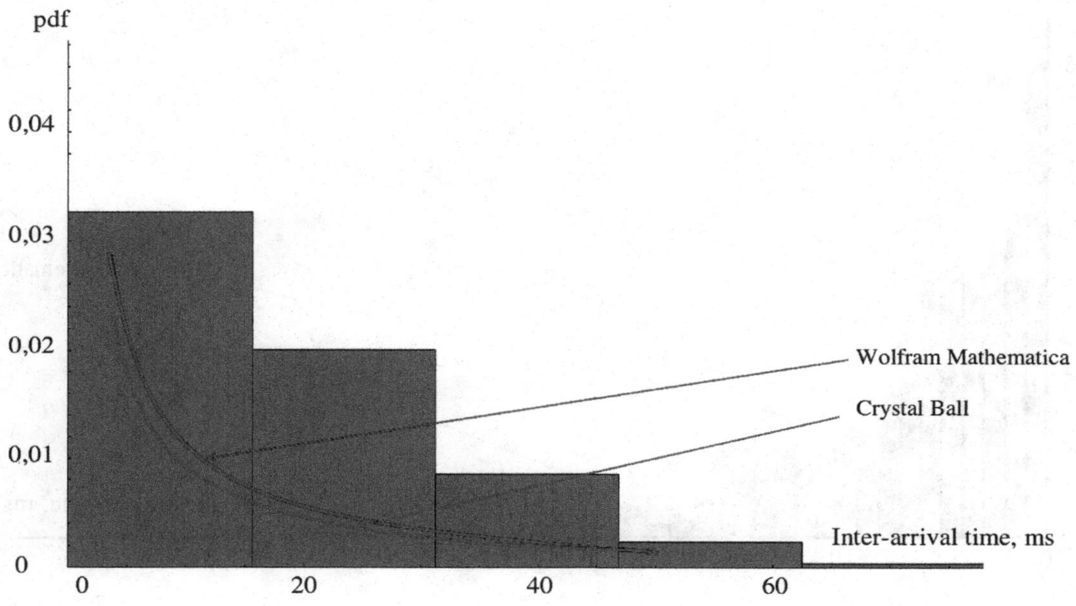

Table 9. Measured statistical parameters in 3G network for ftp transfer

Test 8 and 9, FTP Transfer	Mean, ms	Variance, ms	Mean Standard Dev., ms	Skewness	Kurtosis
2 MB, data with outliers	74.88	5073032	2252	39.23	
10 MB, data with outliers	26.11	616670	785	87.55	
2 MB, data without outliers	11.32	189.16	13.75	1.126	0.833
10 MB, data without outliers	11.18	182.3	13.5	1.18	1.164

Table 10. Evaluated PDFs of inter-arrival times in 3G network for ftp

Test 8 and 9, FTP Transfer	Evaluated PDF by Crystal Ball	Evaluated PDF by Wolfram Mathematica
2 MB, data with outliers	Gamma	
10 MB, data with outliers	Gamma	
2 MB, data without outliers	Gamma Shape=0.13. Scale=83.58	Gamma Shape=0.17 Scale=66.16
10 MB, data without outliers	Gamma Shape=0.16. Scale=71.12	Gamma Shape=0.172 Scale=64.57

FUTURE RESEARCH DIRECTIONS

After proving the vitality of the proposed modelling of traffic with a gamma distribution, the work can continue towards the development of better traffic pattern profiling. Technology dependability of the traffic offers endless opportunities for further analyses, especially in case there is a need for optimization of the presented results. Pdf statistical parameters acquisition and traffic profile mapping is an interesting topic. The results of such work can prove of sufficient accuracy to create representative traffic generators with incorporated traffic profiles. Representative traffic generator is among the critical factors to allow the simulation of end-to-end sessions and the evaluation of distributed QoS, QoE and resource management. In a mobile cloud computing the session routing and resource availability are so dynamic that there is a need for flexible approximated solutions in almost real-time. Possible connection between gamma and Polya distributions could allow further analyses at session layer and investigation of long-range dependent stochastic processes. Batch arrivals and renewal process are very challenging area of future research. Moreover, scalability of the proposed modelling solution requires it to adapt to different traffic collection points in the network. An artificial intelligence approach to real-time traffic monitoring, dynamic resource management and distributed traffic shaping in opportunistic networks and cloud computing could be essential in further research.

CONCLUSION

This chapter presents measurements and analyses of the technological dependability of traffic flows in a local area network as well as in a mobile network. Whereas a local area network is considered access part of the cloud, a mobile network could be seen as the access and edge part of the cloud. It is shown by means of statistical analysis that the same codecs applied in different network domains behave differently and produce distinct traffic patterns. This important feature proves the necessity of the end-to-end distributed QoS and resource management in near-real-time scale.

The traffic shaping measurements in the local area network with and without priorities demonstrate the behaviour and dependability of the services in an access network. It is vital when the number of interfaces, the bandwidth, and the number of traffic sources are limited. On the contrary in a mobile (3G) network the variety of codecs, protocols and traffic sources could produce sporadic or smooth flooding traffic patterns.

After measurements analyses the PDF and application of best fit distribution algorithms, the gamma distribution functions were produced. We present a clear mapping to a gamma distribution of the PDFs of the inter-arrival times and packet sizes. Symmetric and non-symmetric traffic types are equally considered. Furthermore, we propose and demonstrate the use of the gamma distribution as composite generic approach for representing various traffic sources in opportunistic networks. A generic approach will allow dynamic and distributed resource management per node, per interface, per session, per domain, end-to-end, and per peer based on the current traffic. The analyzed distribution parameters can be applied for distributed resource management. It can be done by mapping of the gamma distribution parameters and configuration parameters pet hop and end-to-end. Attention is be paid to the peakedness analyses of the traffic inter-arrival times, intended and unintended shaping effect evaluation. Evaluation of the distribution of loss at packet, session or application layer as well as cross-layer analysis may lead to better Quality of Experience planning.

ACKNOWLEDGMENT

Our thanks to ICT COST Action IC1303: Algorithms, Architectures and Platforms for Enhanced Living Environments (AAPELE), Smartcom JSCO, Bulgaria, Mobiltel JSCO, Bulgaria, Comicon company, Bulgaria.

REFERENCES

Al-Hussaini, E. K. (1991). A characterization of the Burr type XII distribution. *Applied Mathematics Letters, 4*(1), 59-61.

Ashkar, F., & Mahdi, S. (2006). Fitting the log-logistic distribution by generalized moments. *Journal of Hydrology, 328*(3–4), 694-703.

Baltoglou, G., Karapistoli, E., & Chatzimisios, P. (2012). IPTV QoS and QoE measurements in wired and wireless networks. In *Proceedings of the Global Communications Conference (GLOBECOM)* (pp. 1757-1762). IEEE. doi:10.1109/GLOCOM.2012.6503369

Bermudez, P. Z., & Kotz, S. (2010). Parameter estimation of the generalized Pareto distribution—Part I. *Journal of Statistical Planning and Inference, 140*(6), 1353-1373.

Brazio, B., Tran-Gia, P., Akar, N., Beben, A., Burakowski, W., Fiedler, M., . . . Wittevrongel, S. (Eds.). (2006). Analysis and design of advanced multiservice networks supporting mobility, multimedia, and internetworking: COST action 279 final report. Springer. doi:10.1007/0-387-28173-8

Buhagiar, J. K., & Debono, C. J. (2009). Exploiting adaptive window techniques to reduce TCP congestion in mobile peer networks. In *Proceedings of the 2009 IEEE conference on Wireless Communications & Networking Conference* (WCNC'09) (pp. 1962-1967). IEEE Press. doi:10.1109/WCNC.2009.4917718

Bulakci, O., Bou Saleh, A., Redana, S., Raaf, B., & Hämäläinen, J. (2013). Resource sharing in LTE-Advanced relay networks: Uplink system performance analysis. *Transactions on Emerging Telecommunications Technologies, 24*(1), 32–48. doi:10.1002/ett.2569

Chakchai, S-I. (2006). *Survey of network traffic monitoring and analysis tools*. Retrieved from https://www.researchgate.net/publication/241752391_A_Survey_of_Network_Traffic_Monitoring_and_Analysis_Tools

Charalambous, M. C., Mavromoustakis, C. X., & Yassein, M. B. (2012). A resource intensive traffic-aware scheme for cluster-based energy conservation in wireless devices. In *Proceedings of High Perf. Comp. and Comm. & 2012 IEEE 9th Int. Conf. on Embedded Software and Systems (HPCC-ICESS)*, pp. 879-884, doi:10.1109/HPCC.2012.125

Cisco. (2013). *Cisco visual networking index: Global mobile data traffic forecast update, 2012-2017*. Cisco.

Coles, S. (2001). *An introduction to statistical modeling of extreme values*. Springer-Verlag. doi:10.1007/978-1-4471-3675-0

Cousineau, D. (2009). Fitting the three-parameter weibull distribution: review and evaluation of existing and new methods. *IEEE Transactions on Dielectrics and Electrical Insulation, 16*(1), 281-288. doi: 10.1109/TDEI.2009.4784578

Ericsson White Paper. (2013). *LTE broadcast: A revenue enabler in the mobile media era*. Ericsson.

Eslami, M., Elliott, R.C., Krzymień W.A., & Al-Shalash, N. (2013). Location-assisted clustering and scheduling for coordinated homogeneous and heterogeneous cellular networks. *Transactions on Emerging Telecommunications Technologies*, *24*(1), 84–101.

Freire, M., & Pereira, M. (2008). *Encyclopedia of Internet technologies and applications*. IGI Global. doi:10.4018/978-1-59140-993-9

Gao, P., Liu, T., Chen, Y., Wu, X., El-khatib, Y., & Edwards, C. (2009). The measurement and modeling of a P2P streaming video service. In Proceedings of Networks for Grid Applications (LNICS). Berlin: Springer.

Goleva, R., Atamian, D., Mirtchev, S., Dimitrova, D., & Grigorova, L. (2012). Traffic sources measurement and analysis in UMTS. In *Proceedings of the 1st ACM Workshop on High Performance Mobile Opportunistic Systems HP-MOSys '12* (pp. 29-32). ACM. doi:10.1145/2386980.2386987

Goleva, R., Atamian, D., Mirtchev, S., Dimitrova, D., & Grigorova, L. (2013). Traffic shaping measurements and analyses in 3G network. In *Proceedings of the 2nd ACM Workshop on High Performance Mobile Opportunistic Systems HP-MOSys '13*. ACM. http://doi.acm.org/10.1145/2507908.2507916

Goleva, R., & Mirtchev, S. (2010). Traffic modeling in disruption-tolerant networks. In *Proceedings of Annual Seminar of the PTT College, Modeling and Control of Information Processes*. Academic Press.

Halas, M., Javorcek, L., & Kováč, A. (2012). Impact of SRTP protocol on VoIP call quality. In *Proceedings of Workshop of the 12th International Conference KTTO 2012*. Malenovice, Czech Republic: KTTO.

Harsini, J. S., & Lahouti, F. (2012). Effective capacity optimization for multiuser diversity systems with adaptive transmission. *Transactions on Emerging Telecommunications Technologies*, *23*(6), 567–584. doi:10.1002/ett.2511

Hazewinkel, M. (Ed.). (2001). *Encyclopaedia of mathematics*. Kluwer.

Lane, M. D., Scott, D., Hebl, M., Guerra, R., Osherson, D., & Zimmer, H. (2008). *Introduction to statistics*. Retrieved from http://onlinestatbook.com/Online_Statistics_Education.PDF

Lavinia, A., Dobre, C., Pop, F., & Cristea, V. (2011). A failure detection system for large scale distributed systems. *International Journal of Distributed Systems and Technologies*, *2*(3), 64–87. doi:10.4018/jdst.2011070105

Marin, R. C., Dobre, C., & Xhafa, F. (2014). A methodology for assessing the predictable behaviour of mobile users in wireless networks. *Concurrency and Computation: Practice and Experience*, *26*(5), 1215-1230.

Mastorakis, G., Mavromoustakis, C. X., Bourdena, A., & Pallis, E. (2013). An energy-efficient routing scheme using backward traffic difference estimation in cognitive radio networks. In *Proceedings of the 2013 IEEE 14th International Symposium on A World of Wireless, Mobile and Multimedia Networks (WoWMoM)*. IEEE. doi:10.1109/WoWMoM.2013.6583446

Mavromoustakis, C. X., & Karatza, H. D. (2008). End-to-end layered asynchronous scheduling scheme for energy aware QoS provision in asymmetrical wireless devices. In *Proceedings of the 2008 12th Enterprise Distributed Object Computing Conference Workshops* (EDOCW '08). IEEE Computer Society. doi:10.1109/EDOCW.2008.31

Mavromoustakis, C. X., & Zerfiridis, K. G. (2010). On the diversity properties of wireless mobility with the user-centered temporal capacity awareness for EC in wireless devices. In *Proceedings of the Sixth IEEE International Conference on Wireless and Mobile Communications* (pp. 367-372). IEEE.

Mirtchev, S., & Goleva, R. (2008). Evaluation of Pareto/D/1/k queue by simulation. Information Technologies & Knowledge, 2, 45-52.

Mirtchev, S., & Goleva, R. (2009a). Discrete time single server queueing model with a multimodal packet size distribution. In *Annual proceedings of institute of matemathics* (pp. 83–101). Bulgarian Academy of Science.

Mirtchev, S., & Goleva, R. (2009b). *A discrete time queuing model with a constant packet size*. Bulgaria: Tarnovo.

Mirtchev, S., & Goleva, R. (2012). New constant service time Polya/D/n traffic model with peaked input stream. *Simulation Modelling Practice and Theory*, *34*, 200-207.

Mirtchev, S., Goleva, R., & Alexiev, V. (2010). Evaluation of single server queueing system with Polya arrival process and constant service time. In *Proceedings of the International Conference on Information Technologies*. InfoTech.

Mirtchev, S., Mavromoustakis, C. X., Goleva, R., Kassev, K., & Mastorakis, G. (2014). Generic IP network traffic management from measurement through analyses to simulation. In *Resource management in mobile computing environments*. Springer International Publishing.

Moscholios, I. D., Vasilakis, V. G., Vardakas, J. S., & Logothetis, M. D. (2011). Retry loss models supporting elastic traffic. *Advances in Electronics and Telecommunications*, *2*(3), 2011.

Mousicou, P., Mavromoustakis, C. X., Bourdena, A., Mastorakis, G., & Pallis, E. (2013). Performance evaluation of dynamic cloud resource migration based on temporal and capacity-aware policy for efficient resource sharing. In *Proceedings of the 2nd ACM Workshop on High Performance Mobile Opportunistic Systems* (HP-MOSys '13). ACM. http://doi.acm.org/10.1145/2507908.2507917

Ong, E. H., & Khan, J. Y. (2009). A unified QoS-inspired load optimization framework for multiple access points based wireless LANs. In *Proceedings of Wireless Communications and Networking Conference*. IEEE. doi:10.1109/WCNC.2009.4917550

Ott, J., Bormann, C., Sullivan, G., Wenger, S., & Even, R. (Eds.). (2007). *Request for comments: 4629. RTP Payload Format for ITU-T Rec. H.263 Video*. IETF.

Paul, U., Subramanian, A. P., Buddhikot, M. M., & Das, S. R. (2011). Understanding traffic dynamics in cellular data networks. In *Proceedings of INFOCOM* (pp. 882-890). IEEE. doi:10.1109/INFCOM.2011.5935313

Rennolls, K. (2004). *Visualization and re-parameterization of Johnson's SB distribution*. Taiwan: Informatics, Modelling and Statistics.

Rolla, V., & Curado, M. (2013). A reinforcement learning-based routing for delay tolerant networks. *Engineering Applications of Artificial Intelligence*, *26*(10).

Samanta, R. J., Bhattacharjee, P., & Sanyal, G. (2010). Modeling cellular wireless networks under gamma inter-arrival and general service time distributions. *World Academy of Science, Engineering, & Technology*, *44*, 417.

Schmeink, A. (2011). On fair rate adaption in interference-limited systems. *European Transactions on Telecommunications*, *22*(5), 200–210.

Schulzrinne, H., Casner, S., Frederick, R., & Jacobson, V. (2003). *RTP: A transport protocol for real-time applications*. Request for Comments: 3550. Retrieved from http://tools.ietf.org/rfcmarkup?rfc=3550

Schwerdel, D., Reuther, B., Zinner, T., Müller, P., & Tran-Gia, P. (2014). Future internet research and experimentation: The g-lab approach. *Computer Networks, 61*(14), 102-117.

Shafiq, M. Z., Ji, L., Liu, A. X., Pang, J., & Wang, J. (2012). A first look at cellular machine-to-machine traffic: large scale measurement and characterization. In *Proceedings of the 12th ACM SIGMETRICS/PERFORMANCE Joint International Conference on Measurement and Modeling of Computer Systems* (SIGMETRICS '12). ACM. doi:10.1145/2254756.2254767

Sharma, M. A., & Singh, J. B. (2010). Use of probability distribution in rainfall analysis. *New York Science Journal, 3*(9).

Singh, V. P. (1998). Log-pearson type III distribution. Entropy-Based Parameter Estimation in Hydrology, 30, 252-274.

Sun, H., & Williamson, C. (2008). Downlink performance for mixed web/VoIP traffic in 1xEVDO revision a networks. In *Proceedings of Communications*. IEEE.

Svoboda, P. (2008). *Measurement and modelling of internet traffic over 2.5 and 3G cellular core networks*. (Ph.D. dissertation). Vienna University of Technology, Vienna, Austria.

Voznak, M., Rozhon, J., & Rezac, F. (2012). Relation between computational power and time scale for breaking authentication in SIP protocol. In *Proceedings of the 12th International Conference KTTO 2012*. Malenovice, Czech Republic: Academic Press.

Wang, Y.C., Chuang, C.H., Tseng, Y.C., & Shen, C.C. (2013). A lightweight, self-adaptive lock gate designation, scheme for data collection in long-thin wireless sensor networks. *Wireless Communications and Mobile Computing*, *13*(1), 47-62.

ADDITIONAL READING

Aceto, G., Botta, A., Pescape, A., & D'Arienzo, M. (2012). Unified architecture for network measurement: The case of available bandwidth. *Journal of Network and Computer Applications*, *35*(5), 1402–1414. doi:10.1016/j.jnca.2011.10.010

Adami, D., Garroppo, R. G., & Giordano, S. (2009). Performance Evaluation of MoIP Applications over Satellite: An Experimental Study. *Proceedings of the IEEE, ICC*, 2009.

Ameigeiras, P., Ramos-Munoz, J. J., Navarro-Ortiz, J., & Lopez-Soler, J. M. (2012). Analysis and modelling of YouTube traffic. *Trans Emerging Tel Tech*, *23*(4), 360–377. doi:10.1002/ett.2546

Avallone, S., Stasi, G. D., & Kassler, A. (2013, July). A Traffic-Aware Channel and Rate Reassignment Algorithm for Wireless Mesh Networks. *Mobile Computing. IEEE Transactions on*, *12*(7), 1335–1348. doi:10.1109/TMC.2012.107

Barbuzzi, A., Boggia, G., & Alfredo Grieco, L. (2010). DeSRTO: an effective algorithm for SRTO detection in TCP connections. *Proc. of Traffic Monitoring and Analysis Workshop, TMA, Zurich, Switzerland*, Apr.,http://telematics.poliba.it/publications/2010/TMA10/desrto.PDF

Barcelo-Arroyo, F., Martin-Escalona, I., & Manente, C. (2010). A field study on the fusion of terrestrial and satellite location methods in urban cellular networks. *Eur. Trans. Telecomm*, *21*(7), 632–639. doi:10.1002/ett.1433

Bergfeldt, E., Ekelin, S., & Karlsson, J. M. (2011). Real-time bandwidth measurements over mobile connections. *Eur. Trans. Telecomm*, *22*(6), 255–267. doi:10.1002/ett.1474

Brogle, M., Milic, D., & Braun, T. (2007). QoS enabled multicast for structured P2P networks. In Proceedings of the *Consumer Comm. and Netw. Conf. CCNC 2007*, pp. 991-995, doi:10.1109/CCNC.2007.200

Casas, P., Belzarena, P., & Vaton, S. (2008). End-2-End Evaluation of IP Multimedia Services, a User Perceived Quality of Service Approach. *International Teletraffic Congress*, pp. 13-25.

Castro, M. C., Villanueva, E., Ruiz, I., Sargento, S., & Kassler, A. J. (2008). Performance Evaluation of Structured P2P over Wireless Multi-hop Networks. In Proceedings of the *Sensor Technologies and Applications, 2008. SENSORCOMM '08. Second International Conference on*, pp.796-801, 25-31 Aug., doi:10.1109/SENSORCOMM.2008.15

Cosma, R., Cabellos-Aparicio, A., Domenech-Benlloch, J., Gimenez-Guzman, J., Martinez-Bauset, J., Cristian, M., . . . Quemada, J. (2008). Measurement-based analysis of the performance of several wireless technologies. In Proceedings of the *Local and Metropolitan Area Networks, 2008. LANMAN 2008.* 16th IEEE Workshop on, pp. 19-24, 3-6 Sept., doi:10.1109/LANMAN.2008.4675838

Goleva, R., Mirtchev, S., Atamian, D., Dimitrova, D., & Asenov, O. (2012). Experimental Analysis of QoS Provisioning for Video Traffic in Heterogeneous Networks. In Proceedings of the *Joint ERCIM eMobility and MobiSense Workshop*, in conjunction with Wired/Wireless Internet Communications 2012, Santorini, Greece, June, pp. 62-69, ISBN 978-3-9522719-3-3.

Inaltekin, H., Mung Chiang, Poor, H.V., & Wicker, S.B. (2009). On unbounded path-loss models: effects of singularity on wireless network performance. *Selected Areas in Communications, IEEE Journal on*, 27(7), 1078-1092, September, doi: .10.1109/JSAC.2009.090906

Jordan, S. (2009). Four Questions that Determine Whether Traffic Management is Reasonable. In Proceedings of the *2009 IFIP/IEEE International Symposium on Integrated Network Management (IM 2009)*, pp. 137-141. doi:10.1109/INM.2009.5188801

Juniper (2013). *Traffic Policer*. http://www.juniper.net/techpubs/en_US/junos12.3/topics/reference/configuration-statement/burst-size-limit-edit-firewall-policer.html

Kanda, Y., Fukuda, K., & Sugawara, T. (2010). Evaluation of anomaly detection based on sketch and PCA. In Proceedings of the *Global Telecommunications Conference (GLOBECOM 2010)*, 2010 IEEE, pp. 1-5, 6-10 Dec., doi:10.1109/GLOCOM.2010.5683878

Karlsson, J., Kassler, A., & Brunstrom, A. (2009). Impact of packet aggregation on TCP performance in Wireless Mesh Networks. In Proceedings of the *World of Wireless, Mobile and Multimedia Networks & Workshops, 2009. WoWMoM 2009. IEEE International Symposium on a*, pp.1-7, 15-19 June, doi:10.1109/WOWMOM.2009.5282435

Kdouh, H., Farhat, H., Zaharia, G., Brousseau, C., Grunfelder, G., & Zein, G. E. (2012). Performance analysis of a hierarchical shipboard Wireless Sensor Network. In Proceedings of the *Personal Indoor and Mobile Radio Communications (PIMRC), 2012 IEEE 23rd International Symposium on*, pp. 765-770, 9-12 Sept. 2012, doi:10.1109/PIMRC.2012.6362886

Koutelakis, G. V., Anastassopoulos, G. K., & Lymberopoulos, D. K. (2012). Application of multiprotocol medical imaging communications and an extended DICOM WADO service in a teleradiology architecture. *International Journal of Telemedicine and Applications*, *2012*, 1–11. doi:10.1155/2012/271758 PMID:22489237

Mahmood, A., Yigitler, H., & Jantti, R. (2013). Stochastic packet collision modeling in coexisting wireless networks for link quality evaluation. In Proceedings of the *Communications (ICC), 2013 IEEE International Conference on*, pp.1915-1920, 9-13 June, doi:10.1109/ICC.2013.6654802

Marchese, M., & Mongelli, M. (2008). Protocol Structure Overview of QoS Mapping over Satellite Networks. In *Proceedings of IEEE ICC 2008*, pp. 1956-1961. doi:10.1109/ICC.2008.375

Mavromoustakis, C. X., Pallis, E., & Mastorakis, G. (Eds.). (2014). Resource Management in Mobile Computing Environments, volume 3, 2014, series: Modelling and Optimization in Science and Technologies, ISBN: 978-3-319-06703-2 (Print) 978-3-319-06704-9 (Online),Springer International Publishing.

NIST/SEMATECH. (2012). e-Handbook of Statistical Methods. http://www.itl.nist.gov/div898/handbook/

Peng, C., Tao, L., Yanming, C., Xingyao, W., El-khatib, Y., & Edwards, C. (2009), Primet, V., Pascale, Kudoh, Tomohiro, & Mambretti, Joe (Ed). The Measurement and Modeling of a P2P Streaming Video Service. Networks for Grid Applications, Vol. 2, Lecture Notes of the Institute for Computer Sciences, Social Informatics and Telecommunications Engineering, 978-3-642-02079-7, , Springer Berlin Heidelberg. doi:10.1007/978-3-642-02080-3_3

Pouzols, F. M., Lopez, D. R., & Barros, A. B. (2011). Mining and Control of Network Traffic by Computational Intelligence. ISBN 978-3-642-18083-5 e-ISBN 978-3-642-18084-2, DOI , Studies in Computational Intelligence ISSN 1860-949X, Library of Congress Control Number: 2011921008, c 2011 Springer-Verlag Berlin Heidelberg10.1007/978-3-642-18084-2

Prokkola, J., Hanski, M., Jurvansuu, M., & Immonen, M. (2007). Measuring WCDMA and HSDPA Delay Characteristics with QoSMeT. In Proceedings from ICC, pp. 492-498. doi:10.1109/ICC.2007.87

Ralsanen, V. (2003). *Implementing Service Quality in IP Networks*. John Wiley & Sons Ltd. doi:10.1002/047086379X

Ralsanen, V. (2006). Service Modelling: Principles and Applications. ISBN: 978-0-470-01807-1.

Ramprashad, S. A., Anjue Li, D., Kozat, U. C., & P'epin, C. (2008). An Analysis of Joint Aggregation, Bursting, Routing, and Rate Adaptation for Increasing VoIP Capacity in Multi-Hop 802.11 Networks. *IEEE Transactions on Wireless Communications*, *7*(8), 3128–3140. doi:10.1109/TWC.2008.070207

Ray, S., Starobinski, D., & Carruthers, J. B. (2005). Performance of wireless networks with hidden nodes: a queuing-theoretic analysis. *Computer Communications,* 28(10), June 2005, 1179-1192, DOI=.10.1016/j.comcom.2004.07.024

Ricciato, F. (2006). Traffic Monitoring and Analyses for the Optimization of a 3G Network. *IEEE Wireless Communications*, December, 42-49.

Ricciato, F., Svoboda, P., Motz, J., Fleischer, M., Sedlak, M., Karner, M., & Rupp, M. et al. (2006). Traffic monitoring and analysis in 3G networks: Lessons learned from the METAWIN project. *Elektrotechnik & Informationstechnik*, *123*(7/8), 288–296. doi:10.1007/s00502-006-0362-y

Salvador, P., Nogueira, A., Mendes, J., & Petiz, I. (2014). Statistical characterization of P2P-TV services and users. Telecommun. Syst. 55, 3 (March 2014), pp. 363-376. DOI=.10.1007/s11235-013-9793-z

Serral-Gracia, R., Cerqueira, E., Curado, M., Yannuzzi, M., Monteiro, E., & Masip-Bruin, X. (2010). An overview of quality of experience measurement challenges for video applications in IP networks, *Book Sect., 2010*, 978-3-642-13314-5.

Shrestha, P. L., & Hempel, M., Yi Qian, Sharif, H., Punwani, J., & Stewart, M. (2013). Performance modeling of a multi-tier multi-hop hybrid sensor network protocol. *Wireless Communications and Networking Conference (WCNC), 2013 IEEE*, pp. 2345-2350, 7-10 April 2013, doi:10.1109/WCNC.2013.6554927

Thorpe, L., Speranza, F., Rahrer, T., Renaud, R., & Meier, R. (2008). Preparing High-Quality Subjective Datasets For the Evaluation of Objective Video Quality Metrics, In *Proceedings of the International Teletraffic Congress*, pp. 25-33.

Urgaonkar, R., & Neely, M. J. (2011). Network Capacity Region and Minimum Energy Function for a Delay-Tolerant Mobile Ad Hoc Network. In Proceedings of the *Networking, IEEE/ACM Transactions on*, 19(4), 1137-1150, Aug., doi:10.1109/TNET.2010.2103367

Vassileva, N., & Barcelo-Arroyo, F. (2008). Survey of routing protocols for maximizing the lifetime of ad hoc wireless networks, *Int. J. of Soft. Eng. and Its Appl.*, 2(3).

Vassileva, N., & Koucheryavy, Y. (2013a). Effect of AMC on fixed-rate traffic with hard delay constraints in mobile broadband systems. *Wirel. Commun. Mob. Comput., 2013*. doi:10.1002/wcm.2374

Vassileva, N., & Koucheryavy, Y. (2013b). Fair cut-off prioritisation scheme for voice calls in mobile broadband systems. *Trans Emerging Tel. Tech, 2013*. doi:10.1002/ett.2642

Wang, H., Prasad, D., Teyeb, O., & Schwefel, H. P. (2005). *Performance Enhancements of UMTS networks using end-to-end QoS provisioning*. Alborg, Denmark: Aalborg University.

KEY TERMS AND DEFINITIONS

Cloud Computing: A technology that allows transparent storage capacity in space and time.

Gamma Distribution: A continuous time probability distribution function that could change its shape, scale and location.

Gamma to Polya Distribution Mapping: A technology that will map inter-arrival and service times with number of packets, sessions in the packet network.

Polya Process: A process similar to the Poisson process applied in packet networks.

Probability Density Function of the Traffic: A plot of the probability density function that could show the trends in the traffic source behavior.

Quality of Experience Analyses: A subjective estimation technology for service satisfaction at application layer.

Quality of Service Analyses: A technology that allows estimation of the end-user satisfaction from the used service.

Resource Management: A technology of resource reservation, allocation and release in order to reach better utilization.

Traffic Measurement: A technology that allow to capture network traffic for further analyses.

Traffic Shaping: A technology of changing the traffic pattern aiming better Quality of Service.

Traffic Statistical Analyses: A technology that applies math for traffic analyses in order to prove the statistical value of the results.

Section 3

Content-Aware Streaming in Mobile Cloud

This section provides some novel applications that have been made possible by the rapid emergence of cloud computing resources and elaborates on content-aware streaming issues in mobile cloud computing environments. More specifically, it presents novel adaptation methods of cloud resources and media streaming techniques in mobile cloud networks for efficient media delivery. It then elaborates on context-awareness issues in opportunistic mobile cloud computing environments and context-aware adaptive streaming based on the latest video coding standard H.265 in the context of Internet-centric mobile cloud networking.

Chapter 7
Adaptation of Cloud Resources and Media Streaming in Mobile Cloud Networks for Media Delivery

Jordi Mongay Batalla
National Institute of Telecommunications, Poland & Warsaw University of Technology, Poland

ABSTRACT

Multimedia content delivery is one of the use cases of Mobile Cloud Networks. Cloud Networks are then called Media Clouds. Since mobile devices are becoming increasingly important receptors of Multimedia content, Mobile Cloud Computing is undertaking an important role for delivering Multimedia content from the Cloud through the Internet towards the Mobile users. On the other hand, high requirements of Multimedia content streaming establish the necessity of crossp-layer mechanisms for avoiding or decreasing the effects of, for example, mobile network congestion or cloud congestion. This chapter introduces an exemplary solution, at the application layer, which takes into account the state of the network for efficient Media streaming in Mobile Cloud networks (Media Mobile Cloud). Concretely, the presented solution proposes a novel adaptation algorithm that adapts not only Media bitrate in the case when there is a congestion in Mobile last mille, but also adapts Media content source when the Cloud suffers from congestion.

1. INTRODUCTION

Given the tremendous evolution of multimedia-related technologies over the Internet, the demand for an efficient, unified, secure and seamless media distribution solution has never been greater.

Today media content (TV, video, music) distribution generates a significant part of the global Internet traffic and the amount of this traffic is expected to double in 2015, compared to 2012 (Consumer Internet Traffic, 2012-2017), reaching more than 30 PB/month out of an overall traffic of 50 PB/month.

DOI: 10.4018/978-1-4666-8225-2.ch007

Cloud Computing has emerged as a new paradigm for hosting and delivering services over the Internet. Having been mainly exploited as resources infrastructures for computing costly applications, now cloud solutions have been extended and may be exploited as media distribution systems, acting as a virtualized complete serving infrastructure to a large number of end users. To achieve high network performance, the today's clouds are based on Data Centres infrastructures located all around the globe. In this way, a Service Provider can leverage geo-diversity to achieve Media Delivery to the final users. The challenging issue still remains the quality of the delivery coming up to the user's expectations, without escalating the cost. This is the idea behind the so-called Media Cloud[1], which refers to the use of Cloud Computing resources for delivering Media content to the end users.

Mobile Cloud Networks (MCN) are a great opportunity for Media delivery integrating mobile users (Bourdena, Pallis, Kormentzas, & Mastorakis, 2013) and media content servers but, at the same time, it presents a number of challenges due to the limit of resources in the mobile access networks as well as to the congestion of the cloud (Dinh, Lee, Niyato, & Wang, n.d.)

In fact, most of the recognised problems of MCN (Mongay & Krawiec, 2014; Mousicou, Mavromoustakis, Bourdena, Mastorakis, & Pallis, 2013) affect directly Media delivery and should be addressed to for offering integrated solutions of Media Mobile Clouds. The issues specified below have been already approached within the ongoing FP7 MONICA[2] project (MONICA project):

- Limited processing power in mobile devices, which makes difficult the implementation of complex mechanisms.
- Limited bandwidth in wireless connection.
- Variability of wireless connections. For example, the bandwidth changes in short-time scale due to the nature of the wireless, which causes variable quality of transmission.
- Network disconnection situations, which may bring problems of transmission stability.

The first three have serious repercussions for the quality of Media delivery. Therefore, additional mechanisms at different layers should be introduced for safeguarding the quality of the Media experience. MONICA assumes that Mobile networks should be adapted to accommodate the services offered by the cloud (among others, Multimedia delivery service) and Clouds should evolve to recognize and remove the limitations of Mobile networks.

MONICA project proposes to solve some of these issues at the network layer. So, the project focuses primarily on identifying constraints of mobile devices and improving their efficiency. Along this line, the scenario of application migration is considered and the proposed solution lies in the increase of bandwidth resources (reservation) for maintaining the Quality of Experience by the reduction of jitter and delay.

The general idea of improving the quality of the services in MCN environments consists in the orchestration of atomic services that consider Mobile End User requirements together with the limitations of wired networks and the access to the cloud. Moreover, these services should take into account the cloud itself, i.e., the limitations of hardware and geographical distribution. In other words, the services in MCN tend to extend the Cloud concept by considering end-to-end scenario (Mongay & Krawiec, 2014) and not only data centres infrastructures. Such was the approach of FP7 Mobile Cloud Networking[3] project (Mobile Cloud Networking project) started to implement novel mobile network architecture and technologies. They to support on-demand network provisioning based on guaranteed resources contracted with multiple heterogeneous domains by different Service Level Agreements. The agreements consider wireless, mobile core and data centres. A second scope is to provide orchestration of services that will use the contracted resources. These services integrate computing and storage resources (in addition to network resources) in data centres.

Therefore, Mobile Cloud Computing extends Cloud Computing framework and proposes new services for mobile devices instead of developing existing services only. It introduces the concept of end-to-end Mobile Cloud service orchestration (integrating Authentication, Authorization and Accounting, Service Level Agreement, Charging for Anything-as-a-Service XaaS-based services, etc.) and integrates different network infrastructures (e.g., IP Multimedia Subsystem- IMS and Content Delivery Network- CDN) as services of the MCN (IMSaaS, CDNaaS).

At last, MobileCloud[4] (Mobile Cloud project) is an FP7 Marie Curie project, which aims to optimize cloud computing resources for end-to-end Mobile applications by taking into account the restrictions of Mobile devices (as, for example, lifetime of the battery, processing capacity and storage), Mobile access networks (related to bandwidth capacity and heterogeneity of underlying technologies) as well as limitations of cloud infrastructures (management of virtualized resources accessed by multiple end users' applications).

So, the list of main limitations of Mobile Cloud Networks that affect Media delivery is as follows:

- **Low Bandwidth in the Access Networks:** Even when 4G technology increased the bandwidth in mobile devices, the continuous raise of demand for mobile applications, even today, challenge access networks. And so Fomtocell was designed for small cellular areas in order to divide the spectrum among fewer users (Mehta, Ajmera, Jondhale, & Sanghvi, 2013).
- **Excessive Latency in Access Networks:** Due to physical media delay, are caused by limited connectivity with cell tower, and to the latency of the protocol of access to the physical media (Qureshi, Ahmas, Rafique, & Shuja-ul-islam, 2011).
- **Non-Optimal Management of Access Network Resources:** The management of resources should be effective in order to decrease the latency in access networks as well as to manage correctly the accessible bandwidth (Fernando, Loke, & Rahayu, 2012).
- **Service Atomicity:** Multimedia distribution comprises a number of atomic services (content delivery, advertising, content publication, etc.) which should be attuned in order to offer a high-quality service to the end users (Mehta et al., 2013).
- **Resource Limitations of Mobile Devices:** Specifically, power and storage capacity. In the case of video applications, an added resource limitation in mobile devices is the poor display (in comparison to laptops or TV) (Qureshi et al., 2011).
- **Cloud Intermittency:** Constant internet connectivity should be ensured in cloud computing together with adequate computing resources to ensure Media delivery from the content source to the mobile end user (Qureshi et al., 2011).

On the other hand, the noteworthy challenges of Media delivery related to Mobile Cloud Networks taken up in recent years are:

- **User-Centric Principle:** In multimedia distribution, changes the connectivity paradigm from server-client connectivity towards anywhere-user connectivity (Huang, 2011).
- **User Context Awareness:** The applications can utilize the sensing capabilities from each mobile device to learn the context of a given application (Huang, 2011).

- **Personalized Media Services:** Mobile device serves as a personal information assistant to help mobile users to learn their activities and behaviors (Huang, 2011).
- **Caching Capability:** Crucial for new business models as p2p-based users' cloud distribution (Andreou, Mavromoustakis, Mastorakis, Bourdena & Pallis, 2014; Mavromoustakis, 2010).
- **Improved Quality of Service/Experience:** Is expected by users proportionally to the quality of mobile device and mobile contract (Mehta et al., 2013; Bęben, Mongay, Wiśniewski & Xilouris, 2014).

As a conclusion, both, the limitations of Mobile Cloud Networks (outlined by the research investigations) and challenges standing before Media delivery in the Future Internet, should be addressed to in future scenarios for the content delivery in Mobile Cloud networks. Media transmission in MCN environment requires a number of new cross-layer mechanisms which would involve several actors for improving the quality of the Media event experience.

In this chapter, we will deal with one of the mechanisms: adaptation, and propose a number of steps increasing its efficiency in Mobile Cloud Networks. Specifically, we will analyze the potential adaptation actions performed at the client's terminal during media delivery and we will focus on the definition of the dual adaptation capabilities. By dual adaptation we understand the possibility of adapting the media bitrate of the transmission (as it is done in the current adaptive protocols) and the media content source resources in Mobile cloud networks. Dual adaptation enhances the capacity of the end application to react to the changes of the network and/or content source.

The importance of adaptation in the current multimedia content streaming is emphasized by most of the content service providers as the unique way to control the countless variations that can occur inside the Mobile network, e.g., the competition in home- and access- networks or the traffic handling between Internet Service Providers (ISP). In a recent interview, Senior Engineer for Netflix has recognized that the best thing that the company can do in order to improve the Quality of Experience of the Users is,, to try to adapt" (Netflix Eds., 2011).

Adaptation is a strong added-value having impact on the whole system and allowing all the actors to have advanced capabilities towards Media content. Adaptation allows, among others, for efficient network and content source resource utilization, device-independent universal media access and optimized Quality of Experience (QoE). In the case of mobile clients, the adaptation actions have decisive influence on the QoE of media delivery services due to the limited bandwidth in the last mile connection. In the case of cloud networks, it is also necessary to consider the variability of the service conditions at the cloud introduced by changing conditions of servers and access to the servers. Current adaptation algorithms cover merely the first cause of instability (user context) but not the variations on the server side.

2. BACKGROUND

Continuously increasing multimedia traffic demands in IP together with the introduction of new models (as Mobile Cloud Networks) create an urgent need to dynamically adapt data format and transfer parameters to the characteristics of the network and end devices. We can define adaptation as all modifications at any layer appointed to improve the quality of media on the consumer side in the event of deterioration of transfer conditions.

Taking into consideration the element adapted, we can classify adaptation as Media adaptation, access network adaptation, content source adaptation, etc. By the term Media adaptation we mean the transformation of Media content to adapt to device and network capabilities. The supremacy of Multimedia communication in the Internet has encouraged many studies in Media adaptation, which is currently one of the main research innovation areas in Media streaming applications (Sodagar, 2011, pp.62-67; Wenger, Wang, Schierl, & Eleftheriadis, 2011). The access network adaptation refers to the selection of access network depending on the claimed service (e.g., to Media content). Generally, access network adaptation refers to mobile networks where capability and cost are evenly balanced. Content source adaptation refers to the selection of content server depending on consumer device, consumer location or network state. In the case of cloud networks, this adaptation may decrease the cloud overload.

Considering the necessary information to perform adaptation we can differentiate context awareness, content awareness and network awareness. Context awareness may be the information about the consumer device or the consumer access network. Content awareness refers to the information of what kind of Media content is transferred by the network. At last, network awareness is all possible information about the network, especially, the current state of the network.

Finally, depending on where the adaptation is performed, we could divide it into: Edge, At-source and In-network adaptation. Edge adaptation is performed at the Edge of the network (normally the access networks) and it may be the Edge on the consumer side or on the server side. At-source adaptation is performed in the Media content source (or sending user in case of user-to-user communication). In-network adaptation may occur anywhere within the network.

In Mobile Cloud Networks we propose to integrate Media adaptation, which is the most accepted adaptation technique, together with at-source content source adaptation. It is expected that such a combination (Media and content source adaptations) will enhance the behavior in Mobile Cloud Networks since Media adaptation will be able to deal with Cloud overload.

Last years have brought many novel tools providing Media bitrate adaptation. There are basically three adaptive streaming techniques (De Cicco, Mascolo, & Palmisano, 2011; Psannis & Ishibashi, 2008): (1) transcoding-based technique which assumes that the adaptation algorithm (the algorithm deciding about the characteristics of the Media content to be transmitted) influences directly the transcoding process; (2) scalable encoding approach that presents a scalable video codec controlled by the adaptation algorithm allowing for the change of parameters of the scalable video for transmission. H264/MPEG-4 AVC belong to this group; and (3) stream-switching technique that assumes the encoding of the video content at increasing bitrates. Then, the adaptation algorithm decides which of the encoded video files (called representations) should be transmitted. Dynamic Adaptive Streaming over HTTP (DASH) is one of the stream-switching streaming protocols. Others are Akamai HD Video Streaming (AHDVS), Adobe Dynamic Streaming and Apple HTTP Adaptive Live Streaming.

In the last two years DASH (ISO/IEC 23009-1:2012E, 2012) standard has appeared and captured the market of Media streaming thanks to its openness, simplicity and flexibility.

A brief survey of the Internet literature suffices to understand that there is a countless number of papers dedicated to the aforementioned adaptive protocols. At the beginning, the research was devoted to the ways of understanding of the possible models of adaptation logic. These studies were based on the so-called "inverse engineering" that employs learning the behavior of engineering methods by observing it in some concrete scenarios and then transferring the conclusions drawn into another scenario. Although the inverse engineering is not as powerful as the analysis or the simulations, it remains the unique tool when the analysed implementation is close source as was the case of the first implementation of adaptive streaming over HTTP. In fact, it until now it prevails in most of the implementations.

The conclusions of the papers devoted to the adaptation logic of different adaptive streaming protocols show that most of the engineering decisions on the implementation of adaptation logic were based on heuristics. For example, (Akhshabi, Begen, & Dovrolis, 2011) compared the rate adaptation of the biggest service providers that offer stream-switching codec and concluded that they are too aggressive or too conservative depending on the tested scenario. Also (Akhshabi, Anantakrishnan, Dovrolis, & Begen, 2012) analyzes SmoothStreaming for interpreting this implementation that uses the periodic strategy for downloading chunks instead of the continuous consecutive download. In all the papers studying the existent implementations the authors agree that adaptive streaming does work but its optimization is not so easy .

Some papers analyzed the internal behavior (e.g., bitrate switching behavior) of the adaptive streaming tool, by modeling and simulating, in response to bandwidth variation (De Cicco et al., 2011; Akhshabi et al., 2012; Harmonic mean; De Cicco & Mascolo, n.d.; Rao, Lim, Barakat, Legout, Towsley, & Dabbous, 2011). For example, (Akhshabi et al., 2012) dealt with the fundamental conflict between maintaining stable video rate and stable buffer size, that arises out of the unavoidable network bandwidth variations. From the end user's point of view, video rate fluctuations are much more disturbing than buffer size oscillations. Some more general conclusions were drawn as, e.g., the idea that adaptation algorithm should be based on the bitrate estimation of TCP streaming. Further research on this topic resulted in many systems as the one proposed in (Seo & Zimmermann, 2012) where the bitrate is measured only in a number of chunks m and not from the beginning of the streaming. The number m could change according to the state of the network. Likewise, the conclusion of (Dobrian et al., 2011) is that the player should use the throughput (observed for each chunk) and the chunk size in order to estimate the available network bandwidth and the suitable bitrate for the next chunk. A good policy could be to maintain an adequate video playback buffer to minimize rebuffering. (Dovrolis, Jain, & Prasad, n.d.) proposed to monitor the path using network bandwidth measurement tools like pathload (in order to monitor TCP connection). History-based and machine-learning-based TCP throughput prediction were presented in (He, Dovrolis, & Ammar, 2005) and (Mirza, Sommers, Barford, & Zhu, 2007). They used measurement parameters as, e.g., packet loss rate, packet delay, file size or actual TCP throughput.

Many other mechanisms have been proposed for improving the adaptation logic. One of the most persistent approaches consists in taking out the adaptation logic from the end user player. A good strategy seems to be the development of a logically centralized video controller that can have a global view of network conditions to assign bitrates to each user (Liu et al., 2012). In-source (Sodagar, 2011) and in-network (Akhshabi et al., 2012; Houdaille & Gouache, 2012; Rejaie & Kangasharju, 2011) centralized solutions have been also analyzed. Centralized solutions could be the approach to Cloud networks where the Media transmission is controlled inside the cloud. The authors of (Sodagar, 2011) proposed a feedback control mechanism to control the sending buffer size on the server side. Anyway, a client-side solution is fundamentally necessary for two reasons. First, the client is in the best position to detect and respond to the dynamics. Second, the recent work makes us aware of the need for cross-CDN optimizations, which implies the need for keeping minimal state in the network or servers (Liu et al., 2012; Liu, Wang, Yang, Tian & Wang, 2012).

Other improvements that have been brought about to the adaptation logic are: TCP changes to avoid bursts (Ghobadi, Cheng, Jain & Mathis, 2012); the use of multiple connections or multipath solutions which could improve throughput and reduce the bandwidth variability (Gouache, Bichot, Bsila, & Howson, 2012; Havey, Chertov, & Almeroth, 2012; Kuschnig, Kofler, & Hellwagner, 2011; Liu, Bouazizi, & Gabbouj, 2011); or advanced approaches for better bandwidth prediction and stability techniques (Akhshabi, 2012; Liu, Bouazizi, & Gabbouj, 2011; Miller, Quacchio, Gennari, & Wolisz, 2012).

Nowadays, the high-level analysis of the adaptive streaming drives to the design of robust adaptive video algorithm when multiple players compete at bottleneck links (De Cicco, 2011; Akhshabi, 2012; Houdaille & Gouache,2012; Esteban, Benno, Beck, Guo, Hilt, & Rimac, 2012), which is the case of Mobile Cloud Networks. Added parameters have been proposed in order to compare the adaptation algorithms in the presence of multiple players, for example, fairness, efficiency, and stability when two players share a bottleneck link (Akhshabi, 2012; Houdaille & Gouache,2012; Jiang, Sekar & Zhang, 2012). These studies have identified some problems of the adaptive streaming mechanism when other players use the same environment. The most significant is the biased feedback loop effect that may provoke high instability (Huang, Handigol, Heller, McKeown, & Johari, 2012). Another problem is the unfairness of bandwidth repartition, i.e., the players selecting higher bitrate are able to observe higher bandwidths (Jiang, Sekar & Zhang, 2012).

In the parallel studies, a number of papers were addressed to the impact of Media adaptation on Quality of Experience (QoE). The behavior of the users was thoroughly investigated in many studies and it seems that the users become distrustful in front of frequent switches (Cranley, Perry, & Murphy, 2006), sudden changes in bitrate (Akhshabi, 2012; Mok, Chan, Luo & Chang R, 2011), and buffering (Dobrian, 2011), which can adversely impact user engagement. (Mok et al., 2011) suggests that the gradual change of quality levels is preferable. Finally, how to measure the QoE has been tackled by, among others, (Balachandran, Sekar, Akella, Stoica, & Zhang, 2012) and (Song et al., 2011); but still today the theme remains an open issue.

Next Section presents a new approach to DASH protocol that consists of integrating bitrate adaptation and content source switching. The proposed algorithm is able to switch the content server, from which the Media content is being streamed, in the case when the server suffers overload.

3. DUAL ADAPTATION MECHANISM IN MOBILE CLOUD NETWORKS

The main idea is to extend the adaptation capabilities by creating a feedback between the areas of Cloud and Mobile user's device. Current adaptive streaming mechanisms consider only Media bitrate adaptation. This chapter presents dual adaptation, which consists in grouping together Media bitrate adaptation with content source adaptation. The added adaptation feature processes the information gathered by the end user's device to dynamically (during the transmission) select the content source (and Media bitrate) from which the content is streamed. Whenever the Mobile terminal device receives the information (real time information) that the connection is transmitting with poor quality, it may trigger a handover of the connection to Content source suggested by the Cloud provider. The end user's terminal should be aware of its previous decisions to avoid an avalanche effect, especially in case of rearranging multiple connections. Once this new adaptation feature is introduced, the end user gains in Quality of Experience of the received media content and the Cloud provider is able to ensure better service, thus gaining clients.

The proposed dual adaptation mechanism is independent of the streaming protocol, however, the presented solution has been deployed for DASH protocol.

The dual adaptation assumes the collaboration between the Cloud provider and the End user. The Cloud provider shares several addresses of sources where the requested content is stored. Moreover, the Cloud provider can disclose information about the current or average state of the physical and/or virtual machines where the content sources are located. This additional information is more sensitive for the Cloud provider and, therefore, it is optional in our solution.

Table 1. Verification test results: alert sent to the service manager

Step Description	To detect whether the Seamless Handover module (at the DASH client) is able to detect and report faults in the transmission. The reporting of such faults is passed to the adaptation logic module for introducing seamless handover in future segment requests.
Focus	Communication between Seamless Handover @ DASH client and Service Manager.
Precondition (Optional)	Monitoring tool controlling the bandwidth.
Involved Components	DASH Client and Service Manager.
Test Performed	We have enforced a bandwidth bottleneck into the output link of the CP server 1. Afterwards we examined the Seamless Handover module logs and messages arrived to the Service Manager module.
Results Observed	PASS: Within a time period less or equal to T_0 (100 ms), the DASH client communicates to the Seamless Handover module and this sends a *SH_QoS_alert* to the Service Manager. The Service Manager receives a valid *SH_QoS_alert* with the address of the End User terminal and CP server 1.

These data are provided in the Media Presentation Description (MPD) file as presented in Box 1. The current standard of MPEG-DASH (ISO/IEC 23009-1:2012E, 2012) considers Multi-BaseURL (i.e., more than one URL address) but it does not introduce server parameters. Because of this, we extend functionalities of current MPEG-DASH implementation and, at the same time, we ensure interworking with current MPEG-DASH clients by maintaining the standard conformance (see Box 1). Legacy MPEG-DASH applications simply ignore extra parameters of the BaseURL tag.

The server information included in the file depends on the Cloud provider that offers the service (Media Cloud provider). The Media cloud provider generates the MPD file and is responsible for updating this information, for this dynamic MPD (ISO/IEC 23009-1:2012, 2012) can be used. The client uses the parameters describing the state of the content servers for selecting the best server to download the content from. Let v_{is} (i=1..m, s=1..S) be the value of the i-parameter of the s-content server provided in the MPD file. Then the decision algorithm for content server selection is as indicated in (1), following the idea presented by Mongay Batalla, Beben & Chen (2012). This approach introduces a reduction of the importance in the selection decision for the variables for which the space of feasible solutions has low variance. In other words, when all the feasible solutions have a similar value for a given decision variable i, then choosing any of them does not have influence in the state of the system after the decision (all of them loads the system in a similar way for variable i). Therefore, this variable should be ignored (less weight) in the decision algorithm.

$$\max_s \{\min_i \frac{\max_s(v_{is}) - v_{is}}{\sqrt{\frac{\sum_{s=1}^{S}(v_{is} - \sum_{j=1}^{S}\frac{v_{ij}}{S})^2}{S}}}\}, \quad i = 1..m, s = 1..S \tag{1}$$

Box 1. Extension of MPD file

```
<?xml version="1.0"?>
<MPD
...
  <BaseURL capacity="975.2" bandwidth="9876"> http://cdn.server1.com/</BaseURL>
  <BaseURL capacity="930.1" bandwidth="8243"> http://cdn.server2.com/</BaseURL>
```

The MPEG-DASH client (situated into the Mobile device of the end user) monitors the rate of the stream for each segment of the content (also called chunk) which corresponds to 2-15 seconds of video. At the end of the chunk, the MPEG-DASH client runs the dual adaptation process and decides whether the current representation is appropriate and whether the current content source may serve the next segment with the adequate quality of transmission. Once again, the decision algorithm for selecting the new content source (for next segment) is as presented in (1). If there is no information about the state of content servers in the MPD file, then the new server is selected randomly (or, simply, the next one in the BaseURL list of the MPD).

During the transmission of the consecutive chunks, the user's application can automatically change the rate of the content stream (as it is actually performed in the adaptive streaming) and also can automatically switch the content server from where the content is streamed. Often, there exists an overload problem on the server side; in this case, by changing the rate of the chunk, the problem is only partially solved. In this situation, the second adaptation (content source) could maintain the quality of the transmission without reducing bitrate. This is the characteristic feature of dual adaptation.

The client application implements the algorithm for adaptation decisions basing on the monitoring measurements (download bitrate). We propose a novel algorithm that aims at maintaining stable length of the playback buffer. Hence, the client application is able to react more effectively to the changes of the transmission's bitrate. The playback buffer is responsible for absorbing the asynchrony between the video download and the video playback. By stabilizing the playback buffer, we avoid a number of glitches that could occur during the playback. This is the principle of all the adaptation methods. This algorithm finds the value of the video playback rate that (hopefully) will maintain the same playback buffer occupancy.

The proposed algorithm considers the same measurements of current solutions but it requires the storage of some extra data in the MPED-DASH client as, e.g., the Media rate of the downloaded segments from the beginning of the transmission, and the timestamps of the moment when each segment finishes the download. We decided not to monitor the playback buffers because of performance efficiency reduction since monitoring the playback buffer requires many CPU resources that are not accessible in Mobile devices.

The algorithm decides if the Media bitrate (representation) of the next chunk to be downloaded should change (from the present chunk) and when a handover of content source should be done. The algorithm is presented in two steps: at the beginning the algorithm directed to maintain stable buffer length is described and analyzed and, afterwards, some variations are presented for introducing dual adaptation capabilities.

Table 2. Verification test results: Handover_request created by the measurement system at the DASH client and passed to the adaptation logic module at the DASH client

Step Description	Seamless Handover actions between CP Server 1 and CP Server 2.
Focus	Content delivery from the servers controlled by DASH client on the base of MPD file.
Precondition (Optional)	Content servers with content stored. Service Manager with correct MPD file (two URLs).
Involved Components	DASH client, CP Server 1, CP Server 2.
Test Performed	We have introduced bandwidth bottleneck at the output port of CP server 1. Afterwards we examine live DASH client module logs to determine if the source content server is switched after *Handover_request* is received from the measurement module in the DASH client.
Results Observed	PASS: After receiving the *Handover_request* message (in adaptation logic), the next segment is requested from CP server 2. Let us remark that the *Handover_request* message is generated by the measurement module inside of the DASH client.

3.1. Algorithm for Maintaining Stable Buffer Length

The following definitions will be used for defining the algorithm (see Box 2).

Let us consider the following assumptions:

The first chunk (segment) is completely downloaded before the video playback starts
The first chunk is downloaded with the minimum rate, i.e., $V_1 {}^{*}= V^1$

Then the value of $q(t)$ for the first chunk is:

$$q(t) = \int_0^t b(\tau)d\tau \tag{2}$$

And the size of the playback buffer when the first chunk is completely downloaded is defined by:

$$q(t_1) = \int_0^{t_1} b(\tau)d\tau = V_1 {}^{*}\cdot\Omega \tag{3}$$

For the second chunk, the formulas that define the size of the playback buffer are described in (4). Note that there are two possibilities: the first one presents the case when the chunk 2 is being downloaded during the playback of chunk 1; the second possibility is when the chunk 1 playback is finished during the download of chunk 2 and the same chunk 2 starts playback. Let us notice that these two cases can be described following the timeline: the first case is when $t\text{-}t_1 \leq \Omega$ and the second case is when $\Omega < t\text{-}t_1$.

Box 2.

> Let $v^{(r)}=\{v^1, v^2,\ldots, v^r\}$ be the r possible representations of given content, i.e., the r possible video playback rates, where $v^i< v^j$ if and only if $i<j$, $i,j=1..r$
> Let V_i^*, $i=1..s$ be the playback rate estimated for the segment i. V_i^* values are the output of the algorithm
> Let define $\lfloor V \rceil = V^i \in V^{(r)}$ if and only if $V\geq V^i$ and $V<V^{i+1}$
> Let define $\lceil V \rfloor = V^i \in V^{(r)}$ if and only if $V\leq V^i$ and $V>V^{i-1}$
> Ω is the duration (assumed to be constant) of each segment
> $b(t)$ is the video download bitrate. It depends on the network state and is dynamic in time
> t_i is the download time of segment i, $i=1..s$, i.e., the so-called Segment Download Time (SDT)
> $q(t)$ is the number of bits buffered in the playback buffer

$$q(t)=\begin{cases} V_1^*\cdot\Omega - V_1^*(t-t_1)+\int_{t_1}^{t} b(\tau)d\tau; & 0\leq t-t_1\leq\Omega \\ \max\{\int_{t_1}^{t} b(\tau)d\tau - V_2^*(t-t_1-\Omega);0\}; & \Omega<t-t_1 \end{cases} \tag{4}$$

The size of the buffer when the second chunk is downloaded $q(t_2)$ also depends on the relation between download and playback rates, as shown in (5).

$$q(t_2)=\begin{cases} V_1^*(\Omega-t_2+t_1)+V_2^*\cdot\Omega; & 0\leq t_2-t_1\leq\Omega \\ \max\{V_2^*(2\Omega-t_2+t_1);0\}; & \Omega<t_2-t_1 \end{cases} \tag{5}$$

The playback buffer size during the download of chunk 3 is presented in Equation (6) and the values at t_3 are presented in (7).

$$q(t)=\begin{cases} (V_1^*+V_2^*)\cdot\Omega - V_1^*(t-t_1)+\int_{t_2}^{t} b(\tau)d\tau; & 0\leq t-t_1\leq\Omega \\ V_2^*\cdot\Omega - V_2^*(t-t_1-\Omega)+\int_{t_2}^{t} b(\tau)d\tau; & \Omega\leq t-t_1\leq 2\Omega \\ \max\{\int_{t_2}^{t} b(\tau)d\tau - V_3^*(t-t_1-2\Omega);0\}; & 2\Omega<t-t_1 \end{cases} \tag{6}$$

$$q(t_3)=\begin{cases} (V_1^*+V_2^*+V_3^*)\cdot\Omega - V_1^*(t_3-t_1); & 0\leq t_3-t_1\leq\Omega \\ (V_2^*+V_3^*)\cdot\Omega - V_2^*(t_3-t_1-\Omega); & \Omega\leq t_3-t_1\leq 2\Omega \\ \max\{V_3^*(3\Omega-t_3+t_1);0\}; & 2\Omega<t_3-t_1 \end{cases} \tag{7}$$

The general formula for segment i is described in (8), whereas the values of $q(t_i)$ are shown in (9).

$$q(t)=\begin{cases}\sum_{j=1}^{i-1} V_j*\cdot\Omega-V_1*(t-t_1)+\int_{t_{i-1}}^{t} b(\tau)d\tau; & 0\le t-t_1\le\Omega\\ \sum_{j=2}^{i-1} V_j*\cdot\Omega-V_2*(t-t_1-\Omega)+\int_{t_{i-1}}^{t} b(\tau)d\tau; & \Omega\le t-t_1\le 2\Omega\\ \vdots & \\ \sum_{j=k}^{i-1} V_j*\cdot\Omega-V_k*(t-t_1-(k-1)\cdot\Omega)+\int_{t_{i-1}}^{t} b(\tau)d\tau; & (k-1)\cdot\Omega\le t-t_1\le k\cdot\Omega\\ \vdots & \\ \max\{\int_{t_{i-1}}^{t} b(\tau)d\tau-V_i*(t-t_1-(i-1)\cdot\Omega);0\}; & (i-1)\cdot\Omega<t-t_1\end{cases} \tag{8}$$

$$q(t_i)=\begin{cases}\sum_{j=1}^{i} V_j*\cdot\Omega-V_1*(t_i-t_1); & 0\le t_i-t_1\le\Omega\\ \sum_{j=2}^{i} V_j*\cdot\Omega-V_2*(t_i-t_1-\Omega); & \Omega\le t_i-t_1\le 2\Omega\\ \vdots & \\ \sum_{j=k}^{i} V_j*\cdot\Omega-V_k*(t_i-t_1-(k-1)\cdot\Omega); & (k-1)\cdot\Omega\le t_i-t_1\le k\cdot\Omega\\ \vdots & \\ \max\{V_i*(i\cdot\Omega-t_i+t_1);0\}; & (i-1)\cdot\Omega<t_i-t_1\end{cases} \tag{9}$$

Our algorithm centers on achieving the same values of the playback buffer size at the end of the download of the consecutive segments, this is $q(t_i)= q(t_{i+1})$. In order to avoid glitches in the playback, we should avoid states when the buffer is very short, it means that we should avoid the case when (i-1) $\Omega<t_i-t_1$. Therefore, we assume that we are working in the other work points (i.e., $(k-1)\Omega\le t_i-t_1\le k\Omega$) and afterwards we check if this is the real work point of the system.

Taking into account this assumption, the general formula of the algorithm is defined by:

$$\begin{aligned}&\sum_{j=k}^{i} V_j*\cdot\Omega-V_k*(t_i-t_1-(k-1)\cdot\Omega)=\sum_{j=k'}^{i+1} V_j*\cdot\Omega-V_{k'}*(t_{i+1}-t_1-(k'-1)\cdot\Omega)\\ &\textit{where}\quad (k-1)\cdot\Omega\le t_i-t_1\le k\cdot\Omega;\qquad k\in\{1,2,..,i-1\}\\ &\textit{and}\quad (k'-1)\cdot\Omega\le t_{i+1}-t_1\le k'\cdot\Omega;\qquad k'\in\{1,2,..,i\}\end{aligned} \tag{10}$$

We assume that the download rate during the download of the chunks *i* and *i+1* is the same. So, we assume the Equation (11):

$$\frac{\int_{t_{i-1}}^{t_i} b(\tau)d\tau}{t_i - t_{i-1}} = \frac{\int_{t_i}^{t_{i+1}} b(\tau)d\tau}{t_{i+1} - t_i} \tag{11}$$

In this case:

$$t_{i+1} - t_i = \frac{V_{i+1}*}{V_i*}(t_i - t_{i-1}) \tag{12}$$

And considering then the Equation (12), we can calculate the value of $V_{i+1}*$ from the Equation (10) as follows:

$$V_{i+1}* = \frac{1}{\Omega - \frac{V_{k'}*}{V_i*}(t_i - t_{i-1})}\left[\sum_{j=k}^{k'-1} V_j * \cdot \Omega - V_k * (t_i - t_1 - (k-1)\cdot\Omega) + V_{k'} * (t_i - t_1 - (k'-1)\cdot\Omega)\right]$$

$$\textit{where} \quad (k-1)\cdot\Omega \le t_i - t_1 \le k\cdot\Omega; \qquad k \in \{1,2,..,i-1\} \tag{13}$$

$$\textit{and} \quad (k'-1)\cdot\Omega \le \frac{V_{i+1}*}{V_i*}(t_i - t_{i-1}) + t_i - t_1 \le k'\cdot\Omega; \qquad k' \in \{1,2,..,i\}$$

Table 3. Verification test results: seamless Handover_3

Step Description	To detect if the dual adaptation logic runs properly for different network states.
Focus	The dual adaptation algorithm should provide handover of content server when the bottleneck is at the server side whereas it should provide rate adaptation action in the case of bottleneck at the user side.
Precondition (Optional)	Monitoring tool working and Arrangement module running properly.
Involved Components	DASH client, Content Servers.
Test Performed	We have enforced bandwidth bottleneck into the output link of the CP server 1 and observed the actions (handover and/or bitrate adaptation) taken by the DASH client adaptation logic. We have enforced bandwidth bottleneck into the input link of the DASH client and observed the actions (handover and/or bitrate adaptation) taken by the DASH client adaptation logic.
Results Observed	PASS: When the *Handover_request* arrives, it is requested a re-order of available content servers by using the information stored in the MPD file (static information). The next segment is requested from the best CP server following the ordered list from the MPD (but not the current server).

In the next lines, we present the algorithm for calculating V_{i+1}* by considering all the cases of k and k'. Please, note that $k'>k$ for all the cases, since $t_{i+1}>t_i$ and $k,k' \in N$ (see Box 3).

This algorithm was implemented as a plugin of VideoLan Client (VLC) media player. In fact, we have modified the code of libdash version 1.x, which can function as a VLC plugin or can be used for the easy development of streaming playback applications. The library exposes multimedia content to the application through a file-like call interface and performs all actions required to obtain the stream: first it downloads an appropriate MPD file from the MPD server (provided by Cloud provider), then it gets the subsequent chunks from the chosen server and adapts the streaming as necessary.

Libdash is a multithreaded library that consists of numerous submodules responsible for different tasks. The most important from the algorithm's point of view is the adaptation-logic submodule, which is responsible for adaptation. This submodule was modified and the adaptation algorithm has been implemented as specified above.

Box 3.

1) $V_{i+1}=V_i^*$; incr=0

2) Calculate such k that $(k-1)\cdot\Omega \le t_i - t_1 \le k\cdot\Omega$

3) Calculate such k' that $(k'-1)\cdot\Omega \le \frac{V_{i+1}}{V_i*}(t_i - t_{i-1}) + t_i - t_1 \le k'\cdot\Omega$

4) If $k==k'$, then
incr=1;
if $V_{i+1}==V^t$ *then* (*$V^t=\max\{V^{(r)}\}$ is the representation with highest playback rate*)
$V_{i+1}*=V_{i+1}'=V_{i+1}$; end
else $V_{i+1}=\lceil V_{i+1}\rceil$; go to 3) (*note that this case means that during the download of (i+1)-segment, the segment that is playing does not finish its playback, so the download is faster than the playback. Therefore, at first the algorithm tries to increase the playback rate (V_{1+1}) and in the successive steps it will reduce V_{1+1} if needed*)

5) else calculate such V_{i+1}' as follows:

$$V_{i+1}' = \frac{1}{\Omega - \frac{V_{k'}*}{V_i*}(t_i - t_{i-1})}\left[\sum_{j=k}^{k'-1} V_j*\cdot\Omega - V_k*(t_i - t_1 - (k-1)\cdot\Omega) + V_{k'}*(t_i - t_1 - (k'-1)\cdot\Omega)\right]$$

6) if $\lfloor V_{i+1}'\rfloor < V_{i+1}$ then
if $V_{i+1}==V^l$ *then* (*$V^l=\min\{V^{(r)}\}$ is the representation with the lowest playback rate*)
$V_{i+1}*=V_{i+1}$; end
else $V_{i+1}=\lfloor V_{i+1}\rfloor$
if incr==1 then
$V_{i+1}*=V_{i+1}$; end (* conservative approach, when the playback rate is between two possible representations, the algorithm chooses the lower one)
else go to 3)

7) else if $\lfloor V_{i+1}'\rfloor = V_{i+1}$ then
$V_{i+1}*=V_{i+1}$; end

8) else if $\lfloor V_{i+1}'\rfloor > V_{i+1}$ then
$V_{i+1}=\lceil V_{i+1}\rceil$; incr=1; go to 3)

We compare our algorithm with the original libdash 1.x solution. Libdash 1.x algorithm assumes that the first segment is downloaded with the minimum Media bitrate $V^{(1)}$ and the following segments are downloaded according to the actual bitrate of the transmission. That is, the client application monitors the average of the Media bitrate and selects (at the beginning of each segment download) the Media bitrate of the segment following the Equation (14):

$$V_{i+1}^* = \left\lfloor \frac{\sum_{j=1}^{i} V_i^* \times \Omega}{t_i} \right\rfloor \qquad (14)$$

Libdash 1.x original algorithm considers the re-buffering state. This state is described as follows: whenever, the size of the buffer at the end of downloading of any segment is less than 20% of the buffer size, then the algorithm selects the minimum Media bitrate representation $V^{(1)}$. This representation will be selected in all the consecutive segments until the moment when the buffer size (measured at the end of any segment downloading) is greater than 80% of the buffer size. This characteristic is not considered in the following comparative analysis.

We analyze the representation selected by both algorithms for given download bitrate. Namely, we assume constant and constantly increasing sinusoidal functions of download bitrate $b(\tau)$. Note that the function of the download bitrate $b(\tau)$ depends on the network conditions so we assume very specific functions. The segments are 2 seconds long and four possible representations are considered: 2.5, 5.0, 7.5 and 10.0 Mbps. As Figure 1 shows, the two algorithms take different decisions for the same network states, as it has been expected. The algorithm we have proposed follows more closely the download bitrate (see Figure 1(b)), where the decisions of the proposed algorithm reach the download bitrate more quickly. Instead, Figure 1(c) shows that the libdash 1.x algorithm is more stable since it does not embrace the rapid changes of the download bitrate. Such a behavior is due to the fact that our algorithm considers the download bitrate of the last segment, whereas libdash 1.x copes with the average of the download bitrate from the beginning of the streaming.

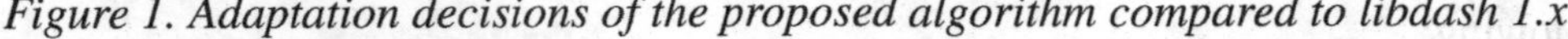

Figure 1. Adaptation decisions of the proposed algorithm compared to libdash 1.x

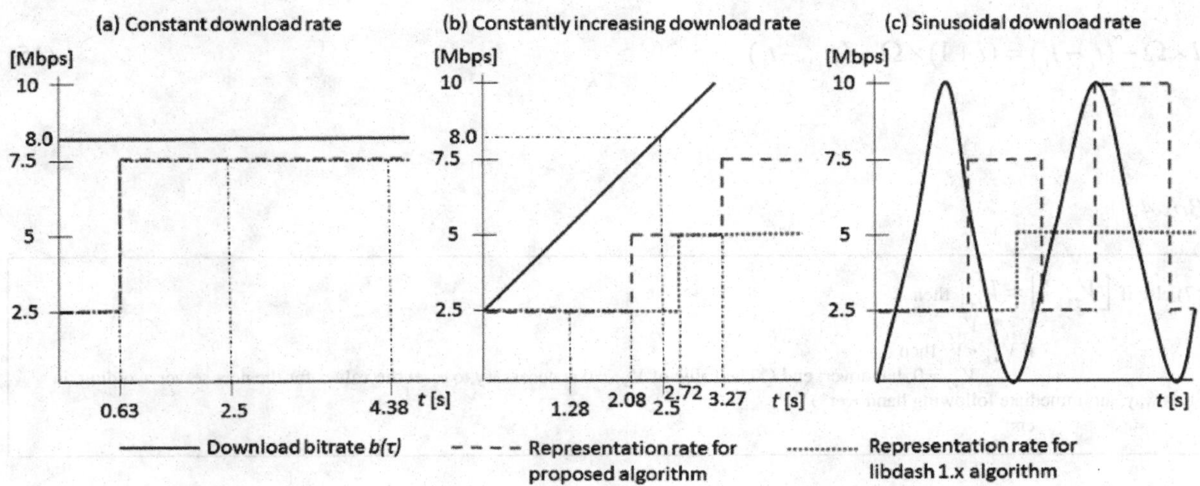

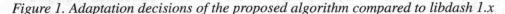

3.2. Dual Adaptation Decision Algorithm

We introduce a modification in the algorithm presented above in order to integrate dual adaptation (Media adaptation and Content source handover) capabilities in the client application.

The aim is to see whether the download bitrate is decreasing slowly. By the term *slowly* we mean that even if it is not necessary to select for the download of the next segment a lower representation than the current one (last downloaded segment), the download bitrate for the last downloaded segment will be lower than for the previous one. In other words, in the case when the algorithm decides not to change the representation, then it checks whether the download rate is minor than in the previously downloaded segment and, if the answer is positive, the algorithm selects a new server for streaming next segments. Let us remark that a slow decrease of download bitrate means that the server is getting more loaded, whereas a fast decrease of download bitrate (when the representation must be reduced) indicates that the mobile access network has suffered a sudden reduction of available bandwidth, e.g., because of a new TCP connection. In this case, it is not worth changing the content source in the cloud since the overload appears within the mobile access.

In order to introduce the handover of the content source in the case of slow decrease of download bitrate, we should change Step 7 in the above algorithm into the following (see Box 4).

Note that the handover means that next segment must be requested from another Content Server, whose URL is in the MPD file. The decision algorithm for selecting the best Content Server was presented in Equation (1).

The algorithm for Content source handover performs a handover when the calculated V_{i+1}' is lower than V_i' and $V_{i+1}^* = V_i^*$. So, Media adaptation and the Content source handover can run only within different segment boundaries.

In the case of unpredictable and very variable network conditions (as mobile access networks conditions), the video rate fluctuations worsen the QoE on user side more than the buffer size oscillations, as discussed previously by Mok in (Mok, Luo, & Chang, 2012). Our tests confirmed this, so we decided to use a more conservative algorithm for unpredictable scenarios in order to gain stability of the dual adaptation algorithm.

This algorithm requires that at the end of each segment download we select a representation that ensures the same buffer size in seconds of playback video. So, the formula to be verified at the end of each chunk is the following:

$$i \times \Omega - (t_i - t_1) = (i+1) \times \Omega - (t_{i+1} - t_1) \quad (15)$$

Box 4.

7) else if $\lfloor V_{i+1}' \rfloor = V_{i+1}$ then
$V_{i+1}^* = V_{i+1}'$;
if $V_{i+1}' < V_i'$ then
$V_{i+1}' = 0$; handover; end (*The value of $V_{i+1}' = 0$ is necessary to reset the values for the new server avoiding, in this way, an immediate following handover*)
end

Assuming (as above) that the download rate of segment $i+1$ will be the same as for segment i, we have:

$$\frac{1}{t_i - t_{i-1}} \int_{t_{i-1}}^{t_i} b(\tau)d\tau = \frac{1}{t_{i+1} - t_i} \int_{t_i}^{t_{i+1}} b(\tau)d\tau \qquad (16)$$

From Equations (15) and (16) we can obtain the decision for the adaptation as shown in (17):

$$V_{i+1}^* = \left\lfloor \frac{V_i^* \times \Omega}{t_i - t_{i-1}} \right\rfloor \qquad (17)$$

This is the decision algorithm for Media bitrate adaptation in the scenarios with variable network conditions. The dual adaptation is the combination of Equation (17) with the Content source adaptation algorithm shown above (Step 7).

4. TEST RESULTS

The methodology for testing the DASH Client with implemented advanced algorithm and seamless handover (of content server) capabilities can be split into two phases: Verification, where the module is tested in artificial scenarios to verify their correctness, and Validation, which aims to confirm that the developed product fulfills requirements and behaves correctly in real-world scenarios. Additionally, performance tests are conducted to assess efficiency of developed algorithms.

- Verification phase includes creating and performing unit tests of the methods inside developed modules, but also more general artificial tests such as verifying that, when the Service Manager receives request for an MPD, it responds with a valid document in a format intended for local MPDs, or checking whether the module answers to the web service requests as intended.
- In Validation phase, the end-to-end streaming is performed using a topology as the one shown in Figure 2. In this scenario, the VLC media player is used on the client side to request content from the ALICANTE system and it is expected that the system will successfully discover content and provide the media stream in correct format to the user. The test also aims to verify adaptation and seamless handover mechanisms. Also, overall performance of the novel adaptation algorithm is assessed based on results extracted from this test.

The components of the system that take part in this test are the following: two CP (Content Provider) Servers hosting content in AVC-DASH format using 2-second segments (CP Server 1 will host content A and B, while CP Server 2 will host only content B), the Service Manager and the terminal of the end user including new modules for handover integration. In this test we assume that the network layer of the system works and we do not focus on measurements in this area. Communication between Service Manager and End User Terminal is implemented by means of RESTful web services which enable message exchange over the Internet. RESTful web services provide a lightweight communication protocol with minor overhead which is crucial when dealing with a potentially high number of end users in the network.

Figure 2. Physical test topology for verification and validation tests

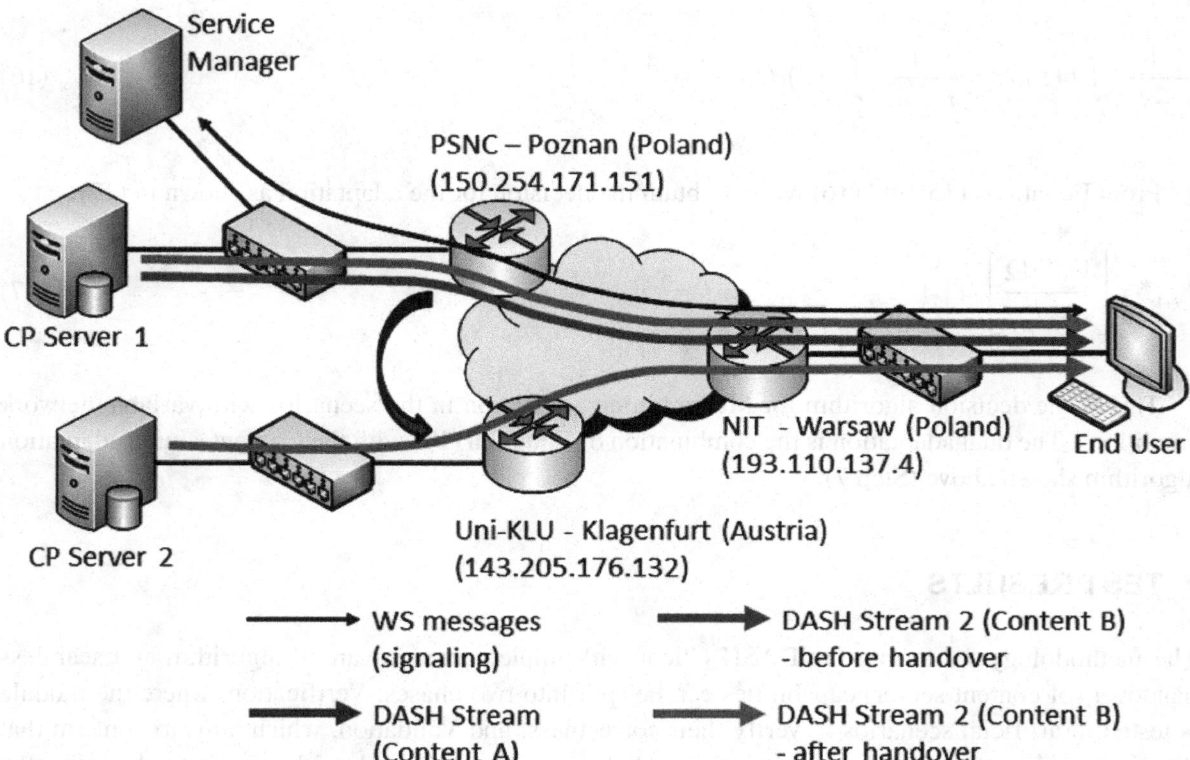

The test starts from the End-User requesting Content A from the system by opening a URL in the VLC player. The request will reach the Service Manager which is expected to perform content discovery, retrieve Server MPD, and initialize Data Plane modules to support streaming session, generate local MPD and send it to the DASH client in response. Then, the DASH client should follow to request chunks of the stream and we expect the video to start playing. At this point it will be clear that the system is working and correctly performs its basic functionalities.

We proceed to verify that the adaptation and Seamless Handover of Content Provider server work as intended. To achieve this, a bottleneck is simulated in the CP Server 1. First, we test adaptation algorithm without possibility of Handover (since Content A is hosted only on Content Provider- CP Server 1). We expect the adaptation to follow changes in available bandwidth and the playback to continue smoothly in the client application. After that, we force the same bottlenecks while the user watches Content B (which is available on both CP Servers). This allows checking whether the system performs handover when it is expected and also verifies that the handover is as seamless as intended (in the sense that no freezes are observed at the client side).

For the Verification tests, the results are limited to indication whether the test passes or not and optionally additional debugging information in the case of failure. However, during the Validation tests many other different measurements are performed with two goals in mind: to verify that communication in the Control Plane of the system meets the specification and to assess performance of the system with emphasis on adaptation and content server handover. To achieve this we may: observe reception of media in the End User application (VLC level), save output and log files of the modules and collect traffic statistics from selected network interfaces using tcpdump tool. Useful information may be extracted from this data using traffic analyzer (e.g. Wireshark), auxiliary tools to process text files and a spreadsheet to visualize results.

4.1. Verification Tests

These tests are directed to check whether signaling communication between all the entities involved within the test bed are running properly. We test the Service Manager, which is the central element for managing the service lifecycle. The Service Manager is the responsible of the content provisioning and content delivery and, inside of these operations, there is the MPD building functionality. The MPD takes information about the possibility of performing handover, as discussed above.

Testing the Service Manager may include two types of tests:

- **Functional Tests:** The goal of these tests is to check whether all required functions of the Service Manager are working according to the specifications.
- **System Tests:** The goal of these tests is to check if the Service Manager works correctly when it is part of the proposed ecosystem.

For conducting the functional tests we setup a test bed environment which includes the Service Manager and client application which implements queries for all the web methods exposed by the Service Manager web service. The tests start by running the Service Manager client application and publishing content and service to the Service Manager. Then we validate that the publish contents and services are registered in the Service Manager database. The second phase is to test the discovery methods of the Service Manager: we execute content discovery query using the Service Manager client application and wait to see whether the Service Manager finds matching content. The next phase is to test the get end point functionality. We issue a get end point request to the Service Manager, the response is evaluated against the data we have published in the first phase. The last phase of the functional tests test the unregister functionality. We issue unregister content request from the Service Manager client application and evaluate that the content is removed from the database.

For conducting the system tests we setup a test bed environment which includes the Service Manager and End-User Terminal (EUT). The test starts by lunching the EUT, then the End-User publishes content to the Service Manager. We expect that the DASH client is sending a publish content query to the Service Manager with the information related to the content published by the End-User. We evaluate the success of this step by checking the Service Manager database to see if the content exists. In the next step the End-User enters a query for content to the EUT. The DASH client sends content discovery request to the Service Manager and this responses with lists of relevant content based on the input query. The DASH client presents on the EUT the list of contents. We evaluate that the relevant contents where returned in response to the discovery request. In the next step the End-User selects one of the contents presented in the EUT. The DASH client sends *get end point* request to the Service Manager, in return the Service Manager returns the content end point information (which includes actual URI, MPD, classification information). At last, we check that the proper information has returned from the Service Manager database. All the aforementioned tests have been passed correctly so we may conclude that the control plane works properly.

The other verification tests are directed to see whether the seamless handover of content servers works as expected. This is, it performs correctly a content server switching and such a process is not observed during the playout of the video in the VLC application. The results of these verification tests are presented in Table 1, Table 2, and Table 3. As we can see, all the tests are passed positively so we can perform the validation tests in order to check the functioning of the system with the new proposed adaptation algorithm.

4.2. Validation Tests

To validate the adaptation algorithm, we have carried out tests in which we have compared the presented algorithm with the adaptation mechanisms already present in the current DASH Client implementations. Specifically, we have set together the dual adaptation algorithm with the libdash 1.x library which is described in (Müller & Timmerer, 2011). We have used two machines: the Content Server and the Client (installed in Mobile device). The former was running apache2 http server software and hosting first two minutes of the Big Buck Bunny video in 2-second segments. The latter was running the VLC media player, which received video stream from our modified libdash-based client application that communicated with the server. Moreover, the network bottlenecks were enforced by using token bucket filter through the tc command on the outgoing link of the server.

The first tests are to contribute to the understanding of the behavior of Media bitrate adaptation in both algorithms. To this aim, three scenarios are tested: in the first scenario a single constant bottleneck of 3.6 Mbps is introduced (Figure 3A). In the second scenario, the bottleneck is equal to 2.6 Mbps at the beginning, after 30 seconds is increased to 4.2 Mbps until the end of transmission (Figure 3B). In the third scenario, the bottleneck is equal to 2.6 Mbps at the beginning, after 30 seconds was increased to 4.2 Mbps and then after another 30 seconds returned to 2.6 Mbps (Figure 3C).

Figure 3 presents the results of the tests. Bottlenecks for each test are marked on the result charts as a black, dotted line. The blue broken line corresponds to the adaptation algorithm proposed above whereas the red continuous line represents the libdash 1.x adaptation algorithm. The horizontal axis of the charts shows the time in seconds in which segments are downloaded. The coding bitrate of the representation to which the currently downloaded segment belongs is shown on the vertical axis and expressed in bits per second. Each data point marks the beginning and the end of the segment.

The first thing that can be noticed is that libdash 1.x adaptation is much more conservative and is very reluctant to change the bitrate after downloading a few segments. It is especially visible in the scenarios where the bottleneck changes. Not only does it delay the temporary increase in bandwidth in the scenario shown in Figure 3B but, as shown in Figure 3C, it also stays with the lowest representation even after the bottleneck has admitted more bandwidth than is needed even for the best representation. On the contrary, our adaptation algorithm frequently switches representations in a seemingly chaotic way, which may be especially surprising in the scenario of Figure 3A where the bottleneck is constant. However, it is important to note that the charts show the average bitrates of representations. Moreover, the sizes of individual segments -and thus the actual bitrates - can vary significantly within one representation. For example, in our test video, within the best representation which had reported average bitrate of 4.2 Mbps, the smallest segment had the size as little as 313KB, whereas the highest weight was 2.2MB, which corresponds to the bitrates of the segments equal to 1.2 Mbps and 8.6 Mbps, respectively. As the adaptation algorithm tries to maintain the downloading time of each segment as close to its duration as possible, it is more influenced by these actual bitrates of segments than by reported average bitrate of the representation. We consider it beneficial, as it allows for more precise adaptation than relying on a single, average value only.

Figure 3. Bitrates of selected representations for each downloaded segment for: A- constant 3.6 Mbps bottleneck, B- bottleneck increased after 30 seconds, C- bottleneck increased after 30 seconds and reduced after 30 seconds

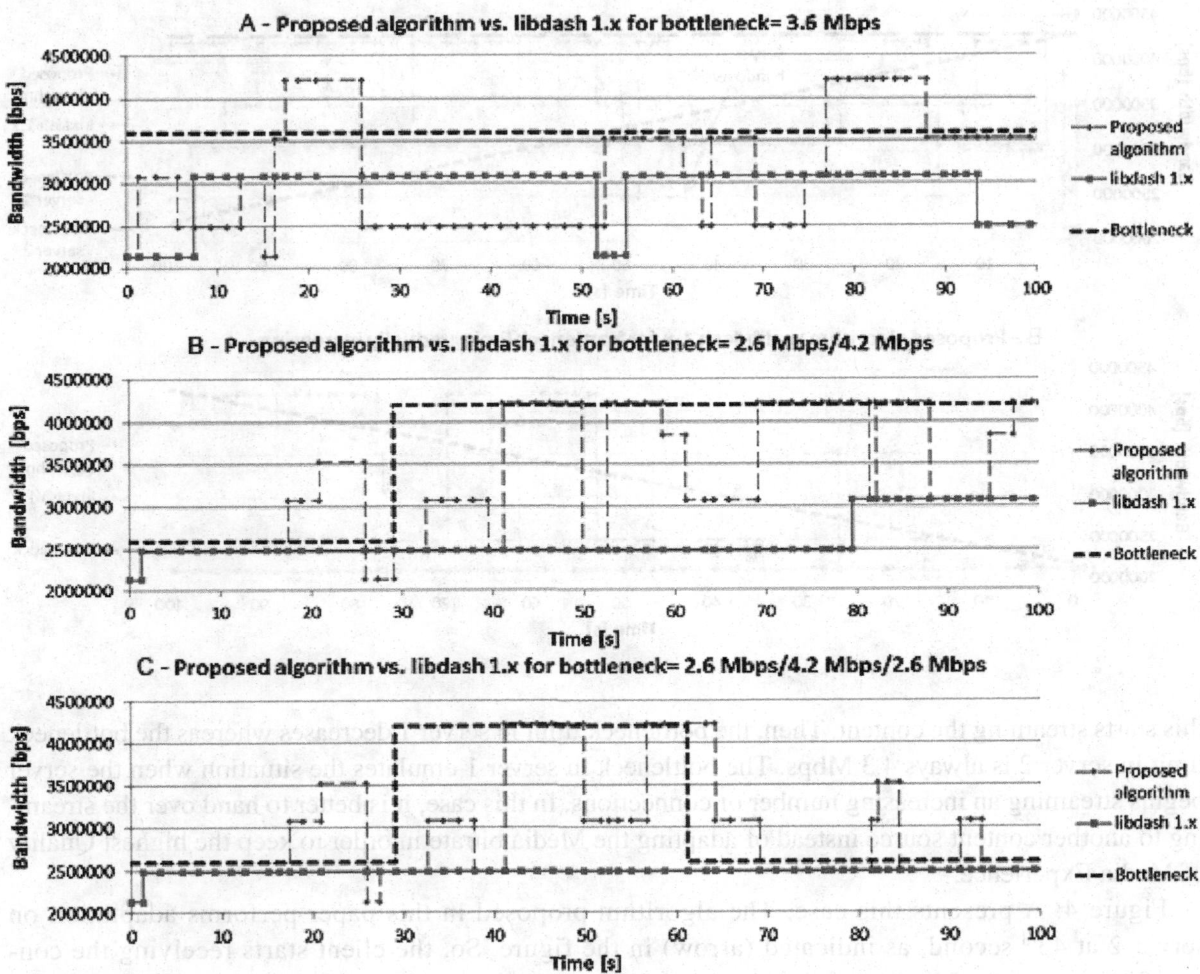

Having in mind the above relation, it is easy to spot fragments of the content where the actual segment bitrate is lower than the reported representation bitrate. One such fragment can be found between 15th and 25th second. In all charts (Figure 3 and Figure 4) it is visible as a 4-5 segment long spike where the selected representation has higher bitrate than the bottleneck. What is more, the height of the spike clearly depends on the currently imposed bottleneck and is higher in Figure 3A than in Figure 3B, which further supports the argument. In future we plan to investigate the discrepancy between the actual segment bitrate and the reported bitrate of the representation.

In the following tests, we check the content source adaptation feature of the algorithm. In these test scenarios, we put two content sources, both storing the requested content. At the beginning both servers have a bottleneck limit equal to 4.3 Mbps. The client receives an MPD file with the URLs of the two servers, so it may ask for content from each server. The client requires the first segment on server 1 and

Figure 4. Bitrates of selected representations for each downloaded segment for: A- bottleneck limit gradually decreasing, B- bottleneck limit gradually increasing

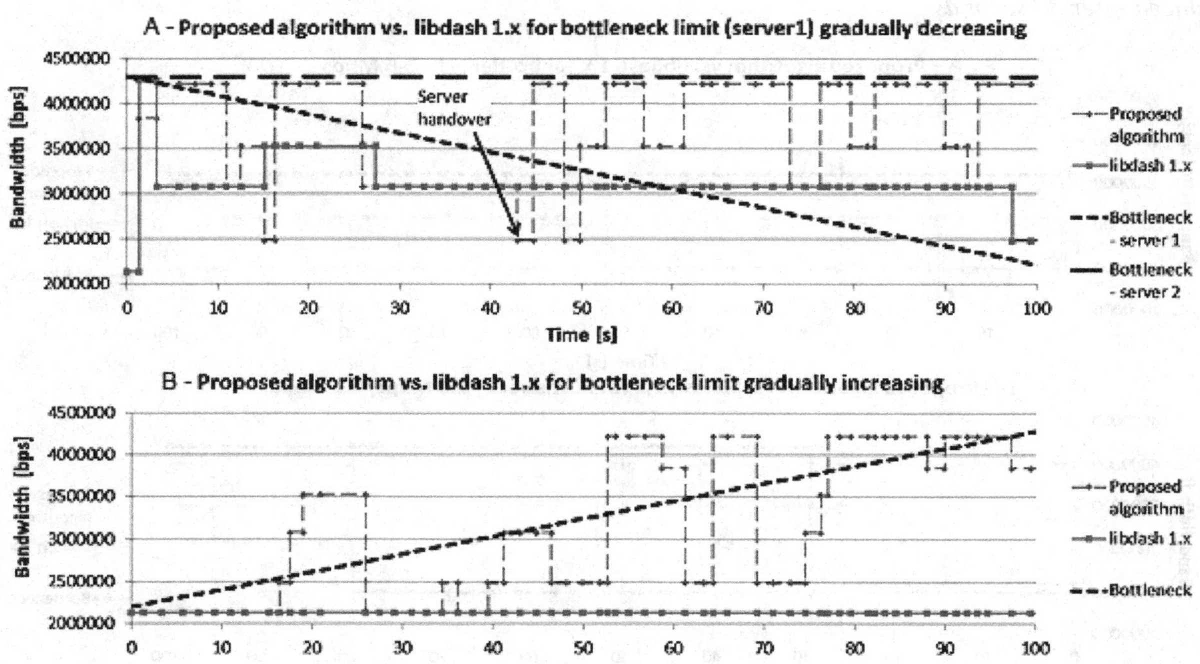

this starts streaming the content. Then, the bottleneck limit in server 1 decreases whereas the bottleneck limit in server 2 is always 4.3 Mbps. The bottleneck in server 1 emulates the situation when the server begins streaming an increasing number of connections. In this case, it is better to hand over the streaming to another content source instead of adapting the Media bitrate in order to keep the highest Quality of Media Experience.

Figure 4. A presents this case. The algorithm proposed in this paper performs adaptation on server 2 at 43rd second, as indicated (arrow) in the figure. So, the client starts receiving the content from server 2 of better quality than the client with libdash 1.x (libdash 1.x does not perform server handover). Another conclusion of the tests is that the conservative approach of libdash 1.x can lead to potential problems with playback smoothness, as indicated in Figure 4A – the selected representation bitrate did not change for a long time even though it exceeded bottleneck value for over 30 seconds (15 segments).

Figure 4. B illustrates the bottleneck limit gradual increase. The user receives increasingly better stream, so the algorithm tries to adapt by increasing the Media bitrate. In this case, content source adaptation has no sense since the server is getting less loaded.

The results show that the proposed algorithm reacts faster to download changes than libdash 1.x, but, on the other hand, the actions of the proposed algorithm are less stable. In fact, both algorithms run as proportional-integral-derivative (PID) controllers and try to adjust the streaming rate to the download rate. The algorithm proposed in libdash 1.x, basing uniquely on the average of signal, has a very strong integral component. Hence it is very stable but reacts too slowly in response to the changes in the signal.

The presented algorithm has a non-zero derivative component since it compares the current situation of the buffer length with the final situation of the previous chunk download. The derivative component introduces instability. The characteristics of the network should define which algorithm is more appropriate.

On the other hand, the results also pointed to the gain in Quality of Experience (higher representations) of the content source adaptation compared to Media bitrate adaptation for the scenarios where the server becomes overloaded.

5. FUTURE RESEARCH DIRECTIONS

The future research will be directed to test the proposed algorithm in the active Mobile Cloud Networks and to propose additional mechanisms that can reduce the instability when the download rate is similar to the representation bitrate. In fact, in this situation the algorithm often tends to change the representation, which may decrease the quality of the video playback.

To conduct the tests, we will install the client into the DELTA Consortium test bed. DELTA test bed considers the use of a commercial cloud network in Cyprus where the final solution of the algorithm will be tested on a large user population.

6. CONCLUSION

The main focus of this chapter was the role of Mobile Cloud Computing in Multimedia content delivery. We claim that an urgent challenge for Mobile Cloud Networks is video streaming, and we call for new solutions that would ensure the desired quality of Multimedia event. To achieve this standard we must, additionally, meet the requirements that have been specified by the latest research in media delivery for Future Internet and that concern reaching high quality content distribution, i.e. among others: user context awareness, content awareness and preparation of content delivery based on user profile (e.g., personalized advertisements).

Dealing with the issue of adapting content transmission in the delivery phase, we propose an algorithm for adapting Media bitrate and for switching the content source when it becomes overloaded. Such a dual adaptation is to do away with a variable availability of the bandwidth of Mobile connections and with the fact that cloud services may be affected by a sudden increase of users' requests, which limits the capacity of a single server for content streaming. It turns out that the proposed algorithm reacts faster to the changes of streaming but introduces greater instability in the selection of the representation, so an additional mechanism should be proposed for limiting the variability of representations during the playback, which decreases QoE (Cranley, Perry, & Murphy, 2006).

As far as the content source handover is concerned, the results show that the adaptation algorithm fulfills the expectations when the available bandwidth decreases not abruptly (which indicates a gradual loading of content source). This is the most innovative feature of the proposed algorithm. In the case of Media bitrate adaptation, the proposed algorithm has quicker reaction time than other algorithms existing in the market (libdash 1.x), but is more instable.

ACKNOWLEDGMENT

This work was undertaken in collaboration with the EUROSTARS DELTA Project (for Cloud computing research) and with the CHIST-ERA DISEDAN Project (for DASH clients investigation into the Mobile access network). I want to thank the colleagues for their support and fruitful discussions.

REFERENCES

Akhshabi, S., Anantakrishnan, L., Dovrolis, C., & Begen, A. C. (2012). What happens when HTTP adaptive streaming players compete for bandwidth? In *Proc. NOSSDA*. Academic Press.

Akhshabi, S., Begen, A. C., & Dovrolis, C. (2011). An experimental evaluation of rate-adaptation algorithms in adaptive streaming over http. In *Proceedings of ACM MMSys*. ACM.

Andreou, A., Mavromoustakis, C. X., Mastorakis, G., Bourdena, A., & Pallis, E. (2014). Adaptive heuristic-based P2P network connectivity and configuration for resource availability. In Resource management in mobile computing environments (pp. 221-240). Springer International Publishing. doi:10.1007/978-3-319-06704-9_10

Balachandran, A., Sekar, V., Akella, A., Stoica, S., & Zhang, H. (2012). *A quest for an internet video quality-of-experience metric.* Academic Press.

Bęben, A., Mongay Batalla, J., Wiśniewski, P., & Xilouris, G. (2014). A scalable and flexible packet forwarding method for future internet networks. In *Proc. IEEE Globecom*. IEEE. doi:10.1109/GLOCOM.2014.7037099

Bourdena, A., Pallis, E., Kormentzas, G., & Mastorakis, G. (2013). Radio resource management algorithms for efficient QoS provisioning over cognitive radio networks. In *Proc. IEEE International Conference on Communications*. Cisco VNI Publisher. Retrieved from http://www.cisco.com/web/solutions/sp/vni/vni_forecast_highlights/index.html

Cranley, N., Perry, P., & Murphy, L. (2006). User perception of adapting video quality. *International Journal of Human-Computer Studies*, *64*(8), 637–647. doi:10.1016/j.ijhcs.2005.12.002

De Cicco, L. & Mascolo, S. (n.d.). *An experimental investigation of the Akamai adaptive video streaming*. HCI in Work and Learning, Life and Leisure.

De Cicco, L., Mascolo, S., & Palmisano, V. (2011). Feedback control for adaptive live video streaming. In Proceedings of MMSys'11. San Jose, CA: Academic Press. doi:10.1145/1943552.1943573

Dinh, H. T., Lee, C., Niyato, D., & Wang, P. (n.d.). A survey of mobile cloud computing: Architecture, applications, and approaches. *Wireless Communications and Mobile Computing*.

Dobrian, F., Sekar, V., Awan, A., Stoica, I., Joseph, D. A., Ganjam, A., . . . Zhang, H. (2011). Understanding the impact of video quality on user engagement. In Proceeedings of SIGCOMM. ACM. doi:10.1145/2018436.2018478

Dovrolis, C., Jain, M., & Prasad, R. (n.d.). *Measurement tools for the capacity and load of internet paths*. Retrieved from http://www.cc.gatech.edu/fac/Constantinos.Dovrolis/bw-est/

Esteban, J., Benno, S., Beck, A., Guo, Y., Hilt, V., & Rimac, I. (2012). Interactions between HTTP adaptive streaming and TCP. In *Proc. NOSSDAV*. Academic Press.

Fernando, N., Loke, S., & Rahayu, W. (2012, June). Mobile cloud computing: A survey. Elsevier.

Ghobadi, M., Cheng, Y., Jain, A., & Mathis, M. (2012). Trickle: Rate limiting YouTube video streaming. In *Proc. USENIX ATC*. Academic Press.

Gouache, S., Bichot, G., Bsila, A., & Howson, C. (2012). Distributed and adaptive HTTP streaming. In *Proc. ICME Harmonic Mean*. Retrieved from http://en.wikipedia.org/wiki/Harmonic_mean

Havey, D., Chertov, R., & Almeroth, K. (2012). Receiver driven rate adaptation for wireless multimedia applications. In Proc. MMSys. Academic Press. doi:10.1145/2155555.2155582

He, Q., Dovrolis, C., & Ammar, M. (2005). On the predictability of large transfer TCP throughput. In *Proc. ACM SIGCOMM*. ACM. doi:10.1145/1080091.1080110

Houdaille, R., & Gouache, S. (2012). Shaping http adaptive streams for a better user experience. In Proc. MMSys. Academic Press. doi:10.1145/2155555.2155557

Huang, D. (2011) Mobile cloud computing. IEEE COMSOC MMTC E-Letter, 1(4).

Huang, T.-Y., Handigol, N., Heller, B., McKeown, N., & Johari, R. (2012). Confused, timid, and unstable: Picking a video streaming rate is hard. In *Proc. IMC. IMC.* doi:10.1145/2398776.2398800

ISO/IEC 23009-1:2012E. (2012, April). *DASH — Part 1: Media presentation description and segment formats: Dynamic adaptive streaming over HTTP.* ISO.

Jiang, J., Sekar, V., & Zhang, H. (2012, December). Improving fairness, efficiency, and stability in HTTP-based adaptive video streaming with FESTIN. In *Proc. CoNEXT'12. Academic Press.* doi:10.1145/2413176.2413189

Kuschnig, R., Kofler, I., & Hellwagner, H. (2011). Evaluation of http-based request-response streams for internet video streaming. *Multimedia Systems*, 245–256.

Liu, C., Bouazizi, I., & Gabbouj, M. (2011a). Parallel adaptive HTTP media streaming. In *Proc. ICCCN*. ICCCN.

Liu, C., Bouazizi, I., & Gabbouj, M. (2011b). Rate adaptation for adaptive http streaming. In *Proc. ACM MMSys*. ACM.

Liu, H., Wang, Y., Yang, Y. R., Tian, A., & Wang, H. (2012). Optimizing cost and performance for content multihoming. In *Proc. SIGCOMM*. ACM. doi:10.1145/2342356.2342432

Liu, X., Dobrian, F., Milner, H., Jiang, J., Sekar, V., Stoica, I., & Zhang, H. (2012). A case for a coordinated internet video control plane. In *Proc. SIGCOMM*. ACM. doi:10.1145/2342356.2342431

Mavromoustakis, C. X. (2010). Collaborative optimistic replication for efficient delay-sensitive MP2P streaming using community oriented neighboring feedback. In *Proceedings of 8th IEEE International Conference on Pervasive Computing and Communications Workshops* (PERCOM Workshops). IEEE.

Mavromoustakis, C. X., Pallis, E., & Mastorakis, G. (2014). *Resource management in mobile computing environments* (vol. 3). Springer International. Retrieved from http://www.fp7-mobilecloud.eu/

Mehta, M., Ajmera, I., Jondhale, R., & Sanghvi, J. (2013, October). Mobile cloud computing. *International Journal of Electronics and Communication Engineering & Technology.*

Miller, K., Quacchio, E., Gennari, G., & Wolisz, A. (2012). Adaptation algorithm for adaptive streaming over HTTP. In *Proc. Packet Video Workshop*. Academic Press. doi:10.1109/PV.2012.6229732

Mirza, M., Sommers, J., Barford, P., & Zhu, X. (2007). A machine learning approach to TCP throughput prediction. In *Proc. ACM SIGMETRICS Mobile Cloud Networking Project*. ACM. Retrieved from http://www.mobile-cloud-networking.eu/site/

Mok, E. C. R., Luo, X., & Chang, R. (2012). Qdash: A qoe-aware dash system. In *Proceedings of ACM Multimedia Systems*. ACM.

Mok, R. K. P., Chan, E. W. W., Luo, X., & Chang, R. K. C. (2011). Inferring the QoE of HTTP video streaming from user-viewing activities. In Proceedings of SIGCOMM W-MUST. ACM.

Mongay Batalla, J., Beben, A., & Chen, Y. (2012, October). *Optimization of decision process in network and server-aware algorithms*. IEEE.

Mongay Batalla, J., & Krawiec, P. (2014). Conception of ID layer performance at the network level for Internet of Things. *Springer Journal Personal and Ubiquitous Computing, 18*(2). Retrieved from http://www.fp7-monica.eu/

Mousicou, P., Mavromoustakis, C. X., Bourdena, A., Mastorakis, G., & Pallis, E. (2013) Performance evaluation of dynamic cloud resource migration based on temporal and capacity-aware policy for efficient resource sharing. In *Proc. 2nd ACM Workshop on High Performance Mobile Opportunistic Systems*. ACM. doi:10.1145/2507908.2507917

Müller, C., & Timmerer, C. (2011, November). A VLC media player plugin enabling dynamic adaptive streaming over HTTP. In *Proc. ACM Multimedia*. ACM. doi:10.1145/2072298.2072429

Netflix Eds. (2011, December). *Netflix sees cost savings in MPEG DASH adoption*. Retrieved from http://www.streamingmedia.com/Articles/ReadArticle.aspx?ArticleID=79409

Psannis, K., & Ishibashi, Y. (2008). Enhanced H.264/AVC stream switching over varying bandwidth networks. *IEICE ELEX Journal*, *5*(19), 827–832. doi:10.1587/elex.5.827

Qureshi, S., Ahmas, T., Rafique, K., & Shuja-ul-islam. (2011). *Mobile cloud computing as future for mobile applications- Implementation methods and challenging issues*. Paper presented at IEEE CCIS2011.

Rao, A., Lim, Y.-S., Barakat, C., Legout, A., Towsley, D., & Dabbous, W. (2011). Network characteristics of video streaming traffic. In Proc. CoNext. Academic Press.

Rejaie, R., & Kangasharju, J. (2011). Mocha: A quality adaptive multimedia proxy cache for internet streaming. In *Proc. NOSSDAV*. Academic Press.

Seo, W. C. B., & Zimmermann, R. (2012). Efficient video uploading from mobile devices in support of http streaming. In *Proc. ACM MMSys*. ACM.

Sodagar, I. (2011, April). The mpeg-dash standard for multimedia streaming over the internet. *Multi-Media, IEEE, 18*(4), 62–67. doi:10.1109/MMUL.2011.71

Song, H. H., Ge, Z., Mahimkar, A., Wang, J., Yates, J., Zhang, Y., . . . Chen, M. (2011). Q-score: Proactive service quality assessment in a large IPTV system. In *Proc. IMC*. Academic Press. doi:10.1145/2068816.2068836

Wenger, S., Wang, Y.-K., Schierl, T., & Eleftheriadis, A. (2011, May). *RTP payload format for scalable video coding*. IETF RFC 6190.

KEY TERMS AND DEFINITIONS

Cloud Resources Management: Framework and technologies for managing the resources of the Cloud networks as, e.g., output bandwidth and CPU load.

Content Server Adaptation: Action of switching the content source for adapting to the network conditions during Multimedia transmission.

Dynamic Adaptive Streaming over HTTP: Standard universally accepted for adaptive transmission of Multimedia content over http connections. Briefly known as DASH.

Media Bitrate Adaptation: Action of changing the bitrate of the Multimedia transmission for adapting to the network conditions. This action is performed by selecting another representation of the content.

Media Cloud: System capable of storing Media content within the cloud (unknown source) for streaming to the clients.

Mobile Access Resources Management: Framework and technologies for managing the resources of the access to the Mobile (wireless) network. In special, the resources are the bandwidth of the access.

Mobile Cloud Computing: Communication that combines source Cloud networks with mobile end users in wireless networks.

Multimedia Streaming: Transmission of Multimedia content towards the network from the Content source until the end user.

ENDNOTES

1 Note that the term "media cloud" also corresponds to an open-source content analysis tool that aims to map news media coverage of current events (e.g., http://civic.mit.edu/media-cloud). Anyway, we use the term media cloud as defined in "A Roadmap for Advanced Cloud Technologies under H2020" document, i.e., a distribution platform of multimedia and video content.

2 Research issues addressed in MONICA project are the following.

Firstly, there is the issue of how to adapt the current mobile wireless networks to accommodate the specific features imposed by mobile cloud applications and their supporting cloud platforms. For instance, more bandwidth is needed during application migration at a delay as low as possible to satisfy application user's quality of experience. This involves in cloud application identification, communications between cloud applications and network algorithms, adaptation or even re-design of network protocols and algorithms.

On the other hand, cloud computing architecture, platforms and services also need to evolve, by taking into consideration the specific features of mobile networks that are different from these of fixed IP networks, to better serve cloud applications operating over mobile wireless networks. Therefore, the project deals with research and development into the mobile IaaS framework, which provides fundamental, infrastructure-level support to Mobile Cloud Computing (MCC). Moreover it is assumed research into the SaaS, that is particularly attractive to mobile applications, because can free resource-constrained mobile devices from having many applications installed and executed on them.

At last, the MONICA project aims to create an MCC environment over a heterogeneous wireless network infrastructure and to provide integrated cloud services across different types of networks. For wireless network technologies, there are not only 3G (such as UMTS/WCDMA), 3.5G (HSDPA), and LTE (Long-term Evolution) but also IEEE 802 wireless network technologies such as WiFi (IEEE 802.11g/n), WiMAX (IEEE 802.16), and medium independent handover (MIH) standard (IEEE 802.21) for heterogeneous networks» (Description of Work of MONICA project)

3 Mobile Cloud Networking (MCN) is a European FP7 Large-scale Integrated Project, which aims at investigating, implementing and evaluating the technological foundations for novel mobile network architecture and technologies. Additionally, MCN aims at extending cloud computing to support on-demand and elastic provisioning of novel mobile services and providing service orchestration with guaranteed end-to-end Service Level Agreements across multiple heterogeneous technological domains – wireless, mobile core and data centers. The top objectives of the Mobile Cloud Networking project are to: 1. Extend the Concept of Cloud Computing beyond data centers towards the Mobile End-User. 2. One Service (atomic): Mobile Network + Computing + Storage. 3. The Mobile Network Architecture for Exploiting and Supporting Cloud Computing. 4. Deliver and Exploit the Concept of an End-to-End Mobile Cloud for Novel Applications» (Description of Work of Mobile Cloud Networking project).

4 MobileCloud is an FP7 Marie Curie IRSES project, where eight leading universities and research institutions in Europe and China jointly investigate innovative methodologies and approaches to optimize mobile cloud computing resources in the emerging cloud computing era. Issues addressed in the project are the next: 1. Portable devices are restricted by their battery lifetime, computational and storage capacity, which prevents them from performing complicated tasks and deploying content-rich or computation-intensive applications. 2. Portable devices are operated on heterogeneous wireless networks, which cause the unevenness of network bandwidth capacity and communication quality; 3. The mobile cloud computing platform needs to manage virtualized resources accessed by a large number of mobile devices in a flexible way, and leverage the workload of mobile applications by providing remote processing and storage support (Description of Work of MobileCloud project).

Chapter 8
Context-Awareness in Opportunistic Mobile Cloud Computing

Radu-Corneliu Marin
University Politehnica of Bucharest, Romania

Vlad Barosan
University Politehnica of Bucharest, Romania

Radu-Ioan Ciobanu
University Politehnica of Bucharest, Romania

Mihail Costea
University Politehnica of Bucharest, Romania

Radu Pasea
University Politehnica of Bucharest, Romania

Ciprian Dobre
University Politehnica of Bucharest, Romania

ABSTRACT

Smartphones have shaped the mobile computing community. Unfortunately, their power consumption overreaches the limits of current battery technology. Most solutions for energy efficiency turn towards offloading code from the mobile device into the cloud. Although mobile cloud computing inherits all the Cloud Computing advantages, it does not treat user mobility, the lack of connectivity, or the high cost of mobile network traffic. In this chapter, the authors introduce mobile-to-mobile contextual offloading, a novel collaboration concept for handheld devices that takes advantage of an adaptive contextual search algorithm for scheduling mobile code execution over smartphone communities, based on predicting the availability and mobility of nearby devices. They present the HYCCUPS framework, which implements the contextual offloading model in an on-the-fly opportunistic hybrid computing cloud. The authors emulate HYCCUPS based on real user traces and prove that it maximizes power saving, minimizes overall execution time, and preserves user experience.

INTRODUCTION

Nowadays, the ubiquity of mobile devices is no longer a futuristic figment, but has actually become a present day reality. Spanning from wireless sensors to intelligent handhelds, mobile devices are gradually interweaving themselves into the surrounding environment, thus starting to resemble what Mark Weiser called "technologies that disappear" (Weiser, 1991). The advent of smartphones has brought forth cut-

DOI: 10.4018/978-1-4666-8225-2.ch008

ting edge technologies in mobile computing that are rivaling those normally found in traditional desktop systems - dual-core or even quad-core platforms with extensive memory and storage capacities. These impressive features are augmented by high-end sensors, such as accelerometers, digital magnetometers and many more. But probably the most attractive feature of all is given by the high speed and large bandwidth wireless radios embedded in said devices, such as WiFi, 3G, and, as of currently, 4G networks. Furthermore, mobile software has also seen a shift in perspective as the need for rich applications to be deployed on a plethora of device platforms is growing in urgency.

The continuous development and improvement of smartphone platforms have yielded a most important issue which seems to have eluded mobile Original Equipment Manufacturers (OEMs) and software engineers alike, namely extreme energy consumption. Such a concern could have been ignored or even gone unnoticed if it hadn't overlapped with another pressing matter: battery manufacturers are struggling with the physical limit of current technologies (Schlachter, 2012). These two concurrent factors are endangering the reputation of both mobile hardware and software providers, as customer dissatisfaction is increasing with each passing day. It seems that the excelling computing power and the myriad feature sets of smartphones are being dragged down by low battery life (which eventually leads to the low availability of the mobile device).

Energy efficiency has been addressed by the mobile computing community either in hardware, by bounding resource consumption, or in software, by energy-aware scheduling and allocation of said resources to applications. This involves complicated techniques that focus on individual hardware components: the CPU (Liang, Lai, and Chiou, 2010; Liang and Lai, 2010), the display (Anand, Thirugnanam, Sebastian, Kannan, Ananda, Chan, and Balan, 2010; Ye, Dobson, & McKeever, 2012) or network transfers (Agarwal, Chitnis, Dey, Jain, Navda, Padmanabhan, Ramjee, Schulma, & Spring, 2010; Balasubramanian, Balasubramanian, & Venkataramani, 2009; Schulman, Navda, Ramjee, Spring, Deshpande, Grunewald, Jain, & Padmanabhan, 2010). Although such techniques provide undeniable power reduction, their applicability proves to be limited as smartphone requirements grow even larger, increasing at *exponential* rates. A more recent approach to deal with mobile energy efficiency is represented by the mobile cloud computing (MCC) paradigm, according to which power-hungry tasks are offloaded from mobile devices to be executed in the cloud. Thus, handhelds only require thin clients for cloud-enhanced applications. The advantages of MCC are invaluable to mobile application development as they include: extending the battery lifetime by moving computation away from mobile devices, better usage of data storage capacity and of available processing power, and improving the reliability and availability of mobile applications. Furthermore, MCC also inherits the benefits of cloud computing (CC) as well: dynamic provisioning, scalability and the *pay-as-you-go* model. However, the advantages of mobile clouds must be weighed by the shortcomings of such solutions. First of all, most MCC applications rely heavily on the availability and steadfastness of large bandwidth mobile networks (3G/4G); unfortunately, due to the inherent mobility of users, there is no guarantee that such communication media is always available and, in its absence, mobile cloud applications are unreliable or, in worst-case scenarios, are rendered useless or even faulty. Furthermore, mobile networks tend to be more expensive both financially and energetically, given that 3G is more power hungry that WiFi (Cuervo et al, 2010). Energy efficiency has yet to be taken into serious consideration by most MCC solutions and, ironically, in attempting to reduce power consumption, mobile cloud applications end up exhausting battery life through network transfers towards clouds instead of choosing local computation. An additional concern in MCC is the lack of privacy when storing data on public clouds as recent advancements prove it is best to make use of private or hybrid solutions for storing data more securely than previously attempted (Robison, 2010).

Last, but not least, MCC implies that mobile application developers must understand, learn and make use of cloud computing, which can in turn entail financial burdens that were not present until now (Kemp, Palmer, Kielmann, & Bal, 2012).

In an attempt to solve the above-mentioned issues, we propose a hybrid solution where mobile devices are both clients and resources in an ad-hoc opportunistic mobile cloud. By putting together their combined resources, handhelds are able to reduce their global energy needs by intelligently collaborating over opportunistic networks (ONs). Our solution is not intended as a replacement for MCC, but instead it attempts to complement mobile clouds in order to fill the aforementioned missing gaps. We introduce the concept of *mobile-to-mobile contextual offloading*, in which handhelds make use of a contextual search algorithm to schedule the remote execution of tasks in trusted smartphone communities based on predicting the availability and mobility of nearby devices. We present the Hybrid Contextual Cloud for Ubiquitous Platforms comprised of Smartphones (HYCCUPS), a framework that implements the above contextual offloading model. HYCCUPS is focused on energy efficiency and, as such, it aims at bringing cloud resources closer to the mobile devices in order to reduce network transfers. Moreover, it makes use of opportunistic communication channels as they are less power consuming in comparison to mobile networks. By doing so, it also solves the connectivity problems of MCC applications in the lack of support for the latter. Opportunistic networking also addresses the problem of privacy, as data will only be shared within a trusted community, namely the hybrid cloud. Furthermore, the burden on mobile application developers is eased, as offloading is hidden from them behind inter-process communication constructs and, of course, because the offloaded tasks are executed on other mobile devices using the same (local) implementation. The novelty of the solution is two-fold: (1) we introduce a novel mobile smart collaborative cloud model formed between collocated mobile devices capable of working together and sharing their resources in order to the reach a global optimization goal (energy efficiency) and (2) we prove the validity of our cloud concept, by proposing and evaluating concrete resource management and scheduling algorithms in realistic scenarios, based on the use of contextual data, showing the capability of our solution to lead to a significant reduction in energy consumption.

Preliminary versions of our work were published in Marin and Dobre (2013). This chapter presents more extensive work, by providing the rationale behind the offloading model and behind HYCCUPS' proposed architecture and design, together with advanced evaluation results. Furthermore, it describes several extensions over the previously presented proposal, and it also provides insights on the challenges we were faced with while carrying out contextual tracing experiments, with an emphasis on the social aspects of collecting data from users.

BACKGROUND

Mobile energy efficiency is an urgent challenge that the mobile computing community is currently facing. There are two current trends that are targeted at solving the aforementioned issue: throttling resources in order to reduce power consumption, and offloading tasks in order to take advantage of more powerful computing infrastructures (e.g. clouds). Although the former techniques have rendered interesting results, we consider them to be limited, as they ultimately lead to a decreased user experience. On the other hand, mobile cloud computing is a more feasible solution, as it takes full advantage of current wireless technologies and of existing cloud computing infrastructures in order to enhance the mobile user experience, by paving the way for the development of rich context-aware applications.

The main idea behind mobile cloud computing is to offload the execution of power-hungry tasks and to move the data pertaining to said computation from mobile devices onto clouds, with respect to the intrinsic mobility of mobile users and human behavioral patterns. Hoang, Lee, Niyato, and Wang (2012) point out the main advantages of using MCC: extending the battery lifetime by moving computation away from mobile devices, better usage of data storage capacity and of available processing power, and improving the reliability and availability of mobile applications. Furthermore, MCC inherits the benefits of cloud computing as well: dynamic provisioning, scalability, multitenancy, and ease of integration. These features of MCC enable mobile application developers to create a consistent user experience, regardless of the multifarious devices on the market, thus offering fairness and equality to all users (Kemp et al., 2012). The remainder of this section tackles the background work, as well as other solutions related or similar to HYCCUPS. Not only do we describe solutions that offload execution from smartphones onto traditional computing clouds, but also solutions that imply mobile devices as being explicit resources in the cloud.

In the *mobile-to-cloud offloading* model introduced by MCC, most challenges arise from partitioning the mobile application code into tasks that can be executed remotely and tasks that are bound to the device, based on the dependencies of each task. As such, MCC solutions can be categorized by partitioning technique into *static* and *dynamic*, and by offloading semantics into *explicit* and *implicit*. The following proposed solutions directly impact the burden of the application developers when integrating with the cloud, as each solution must be weighed in terms of the problem that needs to be solved. For example, *implicit* solutions might be preferred, as they imply less understanding of cloud computing. However, they are more likely to lead to programming errors, as developers do not fully understand how device dependencies should be handled when offloading a task (e.g. failing to send the device context along with the task). There is no perfect answer for application partitioning, although, as will be further seen, composing the above techniques usually leads to better solutions.

Zhang, Schiffman, Gibbs, Kunjithapathamm, and Jeong (2009) highlight the need for creating a secure elastic application model which should support partitioning into multiple autonomous components, called *weblets*. They propose a secure elastic runtime which presents authentication between remote and local components, authorization based on weblet access privileges in order to access sensitive data, and the existence and identification of a trusting computing base for deployment of the elastic application. Furthermore, Zhang, Kunjithapatham, Jeong, and Gibbs (2011) extend the previous work by adding a contextual component responsible for the decision of offloading onto the cloud based on device status (CPU load, battery level), performance measures of the application for quality of experience and, of course, user preferences. By doing so, the application model supports multiple running modes: power-saving mode, high speed mode, low cost mode or offline mode.

As opposed to using explicit language constructs for remote code (Zhang et al., 2009; Zhang et al., 2011), Cuervo et al. (2010) use meta-programming and reflection to identify remotable methods in applications running on their system, called MAUI. The basic idea behind MAUI is to enable a programming environment in which developers partition application methods statically, by annotating which methods can be offloaded for remote execution. Furthermore, each method of an application is instrumented as to determine the cost of offloading it. The MAUI runtime then decides which tasks should be remotely executed, driven by an optimization engine which is aimed at achieving the best possible energy efficiency through the analysis of three factors: the device's energy consumption characteristics, the application's runtime characteristics, and the network characteristics. Moreover, they rule in favor of bringing cloud resources closer to mobile devices, as they prove that minimizing latency not only fixes the overwhelming energy consumption of networking, but also addresses the mobility of users. Chun, Ihm, Maniatis, Naik, and Patti (2011) also use static partitioning and dynamic optimization for offloading, but take such systems one step further by migrating the entire thread of execution into a virtual machine clone running on the cloud. This approach proposes maintaining a clone of the entire virtual machine from the mobile device onto the cloud, by constantly synchronizing the state of the device with its cloud counterpart, thus guaranteeing that an offload will execute correctly in terms of device context. Such an approach eases the mobile application developer's effort of assuring that all of an offloaded task's state and dependencies are correctly sent to the cloud. Moreover, given that the cloud will execute the same implementation (as if it were running locally), cloud computing knowledge is no longer a requirement, thus reducing the development life cycle of cloud-enhanced mobile applications. However, maintaining such a strict synchronization between the mobile device and the cloud incurs considerable mobile network traffic, which leads to high operational costs.

As opposed to the previous research, Chun and Maniatis (2010) rule in favor of dynamically partitioning mobile applications as to provide better user experience. The decision to execute remote computation is taken at runtime based on predictions obtained after offline analysis in the sense of optimizing what is actually needed: battery usage, CPU load, and operational cost.

However, the benefits of using such solutions must be weighed with the security threats of cloud computing. The main concern of MCC is the lack of privacy in storing data on clouds as it faces multiple impediments: judicial, legislative and societal (Robison, 2010). Bisong and Rahman (2011) advise developers in MCC not to store any data on public clouds, but to turn their attention towards internal or hybrid clouds. In this sense, Marinelli (2009) proposes the use of smartphones as the resources in the cloud, instead of as its mere clients. He introduces Hyrax, a platform derived from Hadoop which offers cloud computing for Android devices, allowing client applications to access data and offload execution on heterogeneous networks composed of smartphones. Interestingly enough, Hyrax offers such features in a distributed and transparent manner towards the developer. Although Hyrax is not primarily oriented at reducing energy consumption, but at fully tapping into distributed multimedia and sensor data without large network transfers, it represents a valuable endeavor due to its general architecture, in which smartphones are the main resources offered by the cloud, while mobility is treated as a problem of fault tolerance.

Moreover, Huerta-Canepa, and Lee (2010) introduce a framework that allows creating ad-hoc cloud computing providers based on devices in the nearby vicinity which are focused on reaching a common goal, in order to treat disconnections from the cloud in a more elegant fashion. As such, they rule in favor of enforcing existing cloud APIs over communities of mobile devices as to allow seamless integration with cloud infrastructures, while preserving the same interface for the collocated virtual computing providers. On the other hand, Kemp et al. (2012) take advantage of the existing Android partitioning of the user interface (through Activities) from the background computational code (through Services) and inject remote execution of methods by bypassing the compilation process and rewriting the interface between the aforementioned components transparently to both the developer and the user. By doing so, they ease the design and implementation of MCC applications, as mobile application developers do not require any cloud computing knowledge, such as integrating with offloading APIs.

Murray, Yoneki, Crowcroft, and Hand (2010) take one further step towards opportunistic computing by introducing crowd computing. It combines mobile devices and social interactions, in order to take advantage of the substantial aggregate bandwidth and processing power from users in opportunistic networks, with the goal of achieving large-scale distributed computing. By deploying a task farming computing model similar to that of Marinelli (2009) onto real-world traces, they place an upper-bound on the performance of opportunistically executing computationally-intensive tasks and obtain a 40% level of useful parallelism.

Unlike the previous solutions, HYCCUPS proposes the creation of a hybrid computing cloud in which the main resources are smartphones, and focuses on reducing the overall consumed power of the interconnected devices. The main differentiating factor of HYCCUPS from other platforms is that the decision of whether to run a task remotely or locally is taken by a contextual search method based on a real-life trace model. Moreover, the context takes into consideration both the mobility and availability of a node to offload a task, and it also does not neglect the overall quality of experience of the users which are part of the cloud. Furthermore, similar to Kemp et al. (2012), we rule in favor of injecting the offloading code transparently to the developer, by hiding it behind inter-process communication constructs. By so doing, we preserve the mobile application development process, as the developer is unaware of the underlying mechanisms and is only left with the possibility of giving hints about code that may be offloaded. Such a development model encourages the decoupling of components and the modularity of mobile applications.

CONTEXT SENSING

In any mobile contextual search solutions, context is of paramount importance in imposing two necessary characteristics of fault tolerant and highly available mobile applications: proactiveness and adaptability (Hong, Suh, and Kim, 2009). If the former relates to reacting correctly to external stimuli, the latter refers to adjusting the behavior of the application upon context changes. Sensing and collecting contextual information thus becomes a cornerstone of situation-aware systems, as it is needed both internally (for adapting to environmental changes at runtime), but also externally (for offline processing and analysis).

In the past few years, there has been a growing interest for real-life user contextual data in the field of human dynamics, starting with the work of Barabasi (2005), which disproved the use of synthetic mobility models, and further introduced a queuing model that explained the heavy bursts and long tails in the distributions of events in human activities. More recently, Song, Blum, and Barabasi (2010) demonstrate once again the predictability of human behavior and mobility, by analyzing various user traces obtained from mobile carriers.

As for smartphones, collecting contextual data has proven to be an invaluable source for improving and even enhancing user experience. OEMs are deploying context tracing applications able to adapt to contextual changes, in order to reduce energy consumption and improve mobile data traffic. One of the most interesting approaches to sensing context is the *infamous* case of Carrier IQ (Holly, 2014), where OEMs and mobile telephony carriers were deploying a context tracing application software, IQ Agent, with the purpose of gathering, storing and forwarding diagnostic measurements on their behalf. The traced data included: battery levels, the state of the network, firmware, performance metrics for applications and web browsing, voice and data connectivity between smartphones and cell towers, and many more. This information was collected by an application running in the background, and each customer of Carrier IQ would decide which criteria was to be stored and forwarded to their servers for offline analysis. However, as opposed to performance metrics, it was discovered that Carrier IQ software was also tracking privacy infringing information, which led to a series of lawsuits in both civil and criminal court (Peralta, 2011).

In our case, collecting contextual data from real-world mobile users has multiple purposes:

1. Validating the feasibility of a solution such as *mobile-to-mobile contextual offloading* by proving the predictability of users interacting over wireless networks, as well as showing that the users naturally tend to form well-structured and durable communities over opportunistic networks.
2. Creating predictive models for availability and mobility to be used in contextual search algorithms.
3. Simulating our contextual search algorithm based on user-collected tracing data, in order to correctly measure the performance of our offloading model in real-life situations.

As such, in Marin, Dobre, and Xhafa (2012) we presented implementation details for an Android application which collects contextual data from smartphones, namely the *HYCCUPS Tracer*. The application is designed to run in the background and trace multiple features (see below), which can further be classified by the temporality of acquisition into static or dynamic, or by the semantic interpretation into availability or mobility features. Moreover, static properties are determined at application start-up and are comprised of the device's traits, while dynamic features are momentary values acquired on-demand. In terms of semantic interpretation, availability features represent values pertaining to the overall computing system state, while mobility features describe the interaction of the device with the outside world. The features collected by the HYCCUPS Tracer are as follows:

- **Minimum and Maximum Frequency:** Static properties describing the bounds for Dynamic Voltage/Frequency Scaling (DVFS);
- **Current Frequency:** Momentary value of the frequency according to DVFS;
- **CPU Load:** The current CPU load computed from */proc/stat*;
- **Total Memory:** Static property of the device describing the total amount of memory;
- **Available Memory:** Momentary value which represents the amount of free memory on the device (bear in mind that, in Android, free memory is wasted memory);
- **Out of Memory:** Asynchronous event notifying that the available memory has reached the minimal threshold and, in consequence, the Out Of Memory (OOM) Killer will engage in stopping applications;
- **Memory Threshold:** The minimal memory threshold that, when reached, triggers the OOM events;
- **Sensor Availability:** Static properties which convey the presence of certain sensors (e.g. accelerometer, proximity);
- **Accelerometer:** The accelerometer modulus is a mobility feature which characterizes fine grain movement (if available);
- **Proximity:** Proximity sensor readings (if available);
- **Battery State:** The current charging level (expressed in %) and also the current charge state;
- **Application Activity:** Availability events representing user actions that trigger opening/closing application activities;
- **Bluetooth Interactions:** Momentary beacons received from nearby paired or discoverable devices;
- **WiFi Interactions:** Interactions over WiFi modeled using the Alljoyn framework. AllJoyn is an open-source peer-to-peer software development framework, developed by Qualcomm Connected Experiences, Inc., which offers the means to create ad-hoc, proximity-based, opportunistic inter-

device communication. The true impact of AllJoyn is expressed through the ease of development of peer-to-peer networking applications provided by: common APIs for transparency over multiple operating systems, automatic management of connectivity, networking and security and, last but not least, optimization for embedded devices;

- **WiFi Scan Results:** Periodic wireless access point scan results.

The tracing process is executed both periodically (with predefined time intervals for different monitored parameters), and asynchronously (the process is triggered with the occurrence of events such as WiFi interactions or user events).

The HYCCUPS Tracer was used to carry out a tracing experiment in the Faculty of Automatic Control and Computer Science of the University Politehnica of Bucharest, Romania, which lasted for 65 days (March-May 2012) (Marin et al., 2012). A total of 66 students and faculty members volunteered and were selected to participate, in order to have a wide range of study years and specializations covered.

One of the main challenges we faced during the experiment was the lack of conscientiousness of the volunteer participants; we obtained an average usage rate of the tracing application of about 20-30%. Interestingly enough, other such studies (Barabasi, 2005; Song et al., 2010) also suffered from similar problems, although they were analyzing contextual data collected directly from mobile carriers (similar to Carrier IQ); they obtained an information factor about 20%, most likely caused by devices being turned off or outside of the service of the targeted cell towers. Based on the work from Barabasi (2005) and Marin et al. (2012), in Marin, Dobre, and Xhafa (2014) we proposed a methodology for assessing the predictability of human interactions, to be used when analyzing tracing data. The methodology operates with a low information factor, by focusing on the nodes with higher degrees of conscientiousness, and by computing predictability using a modified version of a compression algorithm which is able to work with incomplete data. Based on this methodology, we proved that not only do users adhere to stable and durable social communities based on wireless interactions, but we also showed an undeniable predictability of users interacting amongst themselves, as well as with wireless access points. Although the proposed methodology can aid researchers in studying patterns in human behavior, it does not solve the lack of conscientiousness, but merely bypasses it.

In order to delve deeper into this problem, we conducted a survey amongst the volunteers which have participated in the experiment, so as to discover the underlying issues regarding the lack of conscientiousness. We uncovered that there are two types of issues that led to the poor utilization of the tracing application: technical aspects and social aspects. While the former are only linked to an increased power consumption induced by the tracing application itself, the latter are more complex. Similar to the case of Carrier IQ, the volunteers in our tracing experiment were reluctant to participate due to the following issues:

1. *Invasion of privacy.* Users are less likely to share contextual data that can be easily tracked back to them. Although the tracing application does not collect any personal data, participants were wary about uploading tracing data containing their synergic patterns. Moreover, some users suspected that the tracing application was collecting additional privacy-infringing information as well.
2. *Lack of interest (or even lack of understanding) regarding the purpose of collecting contextual data.* Unfortunately, users have limited knowledge about the possibilities/advantages of context-aware applications. Also, due to the fact that there is a limited set of situation-aware applications available on the market, mobile users have not had direct access to software that takes full advantage of the surrounding environment to augment their mobile experience.

In order to increase the degree of conscientiousness for future tracing experiments, we have redesigned the HYCCUPS Tracer so as to attempt to solve the above-mentioned issues. While tackling the reported increased power consumption caused by the tracing application, we have uncovered a design flaw that was forcing the CPUs to remain online instead of entering sleep states. Not only was this issue incurring additional overhead, it was also biasing the collected CPU tracing data. Furthermore, after analyzing the behavior of each implemented context collector, we noticed that the Bluetooth interactions tracing was the most power hungry task in the application. Fortunately, Marin et al. (2012) proved that WiFi opportunistic interactions are much more feasible than those over Bluetooth, as the latter tend to isolate micro-communities due to lower range, which eventually leads to far less synergy between nodes. As such, we were able to trim down this feature, leading to a much lower power consumption of the entire tracing infrastructure.

In terms of privacy, we have employed multiple measures to guarantee the transparency and anonymity of the tracing procedure. First of all, we have enforced a Model-View-Controller (MVC) architectural pattern for context collectors. By doing so, we are forcing the implementation of each context tracer to display the collected context to the user. Therefore, the suspicions that our application is secretly gathering privacy-infringing data should be reduced. Furthermore, we will be making the source code of the application available to all participants in future experiments, to further prove the soundness and transparency of our solution. Additionally, we are applying anonymization techniques, by computing and storing only the hash sums of all potential privacy-infringing information, such as wireless access points SSIDs and BSSIDs. This measure should solve the issue of contextual data being traced back to the originating device or user. Last, but not least, each user will be given secure access to her uploaded data for offline browsing.

While the first two issues have rather intuitive solutions, the last social aspect, namely the lack of interest or understanding about the purpose of contextual tracing, is more challenging, due to the fact that it is not related to the actual tracing application, but rather to how users perceive it. As such, we believe that a potential solution for growing user interest in context-aware applications is to provide incentive examples which demonstrate the importance and novelty of tracing and using context to enhance and augment the mobile user experience. Therefore, we rule in favor of developing such applications and deploying them in future tracing experiments alongside the HYCCUPS Tracer, in hope of increasing the conscientiousness of participants. The first step taken in this sense is to modify and extend the functionality of the tracing infrastructure so that it offers the collected contextual data to any application requesting access to it. By doing so, we are enabling mobile application developers to make use of the HYCCUPS Tracer as a means for sensing and sharing context.

Furthermore, we devised Chatty, an Android application for exchanging messages in opportunistic networks. It is implemented over the WiFi interactions collector, taking advantage of contacts between mobile nodes to carry messages from sources to destinations. Chatty allows two types of communication: point-to-point (where a node *A* wants to send a message to a node *B*) and dissemination (where a node *A* marks a message with certain tags, and sends it to all the nodes that are interested in receiving data marked with at least one of those tags).

Although Chatty is used for communication in opportunistic networks, where no Internet connection is assumed, the user is required to connect with her Facebook account when installing the application. This is done for two reasons, the first one being that the application needs a list of contacts for point-to-point communication. Thus, we decided to use the list of Facebook friends that have installed the Chatty application. Moreover, we consider a user's ID in the network to be the same as her Facebook ID, for the sake of simplicity. Secondly, the opportunistic communication module benefits from social network information when taking routing and disseminating decisions, in order to optimize its behavior in terms of hit rate, delivery latency and congestion. Once a user logs for the first time, there's no further need for Internet access, since the communication is done opportunistically. Aside from only offering chatting capabilities, Chatty also allows a user to see when one of her contacts is in opportunistic communication range, or (if not) when a contact was last seen in range. As an example, this can be useful in a crowded room, if a user is searching for a friend.

We envision Chatty as a helpful tool in an academic environment, to be used for communication between students, teachers, the faculty offices, etc. For instance, it can be used by professors or assistants to disseminate information about classes, or by the faculty offices to disseminate various announcements. In order to do the latter, a message is sent with a tag such as "faculty announcement", and all students that have this tag marked as an interest receive the message opportunistically, after a contact with a node that is a carrier for that message. Communication can also be performed between students located in opposite corners of the campus, through contacts with other mobile device owners that have installed Chatty. We consider a faculty campus as a suitable deployment environment for Chatty, since it is a small environment, with a high density, therefore the number of contacts is high.

We have conducted a tracing experiment on a smaller scale in a controlled academic environment by deploying the enhanced HYCCUPS Tracer along with the Chatty incentive application and we have observed a higher degree of conscientiousness after only a few weeks of tracing, with a usage rate of about 40-50%. Therefore, we are planning on developing a more complex set of incentive applications similar to Chatty, as to further carry out larger scale tracing experiments in the hope of collecting contextual data with a higher degree of information.

MOBILE-TO-MOBILE CONTEXTUAL OFFLOADING

In order to promote energy efficiency, we propose a novel mobile collaboration solution based on a contextual search algorithm which schedules remote execution of tasks in an opportunistic community by predicting the availability and mobility of nearby devices, namely *mobile-to-mobile contextual offloading*.

Contextual search is a technique used in pervasive systems to augment a query with context data from users in order to obtain content optimized for a specific situation (Kraft, Maghoul, and Chang, 2005; Minkov, Cohen, and Ng, 2006; Challam, Gauch, and Chandramouli, 2007). In order to perform contextual search, multiple phases are required:

1. **Sensing Contextual Data:** Gathering or tracing raw context data from sensors in the environment;
2. **Aggregating and Recording Traced Data:** Aggregating raw context data into higher level context and persistently storing it;
3. **Conducting the Context-Enhanced Search:** Augmenting queries by means of the contextual records.

While sensing context has been thoroughly treated in the previous section, we are making use of the collected tracing data in the experiment conducted in Marin et al. (2012). Out of the myriad traced features, only the following are considered interesting for recording: CPU load, CPU fre-

Table 1. Record types and sampling intervals for features of interest

Feature	Record Type	Sampling Interval (Min)
CPU Load	Averaging	1
CPU Frequency	Averaging	1
Available Memory	Averaging	1
Battery Level	Averaging	5
Battery Charging?	Probability	10
Peers Connected?	Probability	10
User active?	Probability	10

quency, available memory, interactions with peers over WiFi, battery level, battery charging state and application activity events. The tracing data is aggregated into the trained availability records; each record behaves similar to a circular buffer, as it contains aggregated contextual data for each day of the week with a given sampling rate. We consider a week to be sufficient, as human behavioral patterns in academic and office environments are subject to repeatability within this interval. When storing a feature value, it is aggregated with the previous tracing data at the closest sampling point smaller than the timestamp of the event. Based on the aggregation method, there are two types of records:

1. **Averaging Records:** The data stored in these records is a continuous real value and it is aggregating by using the average;
2. **Probability Records:** These records contain boolean events and the aggregation method is the probability that the event is true.

Based on the features of interest, Table 1 depicts the types of records used and the sampling intervals.

The sampling intervals were chosen by inspecting the inter-event times for each feature from the HYCCUPS tracing experiment in the previous section, and also by taking into consideration the mobile development aspect. Given that *mobile-to-mobile contextual offloading* will be deployed onto handhelds, the size of the records is important. Therefore, in the cases of CPU load and frequency, we made a compromise between informedness and spatial restraints. The reader should be advised that, although the CPU features will be less reliable, they will still offer valuable quantitative information.

As long as the contextual search is running on a device, the records are continuously updated so that the offloading algorithm is able to adapt to environmental changes (e.g. user changes her patterns or battery health degrades). However, these averaged momentary values have no meaning on their own, they simply represent an instance in a user's history. In order to make good use of these values, we need to extract temporal patterns over intervals of execution so that the system can predict future values for them.

In order to predict the values for features on any given interval of time, the offloading model uses univariate linear regression to determine a hypothesis h of the form $h(x) = \Theta_1 + \Theta_2 \times x$, which is able to approximate values for features for any given timeframe. So basically, the predictor for the average of a feature of over the interval $[currentTime, currentTime + \Delta t]$ is of the following form: $predictFeature(\Delta t)$ and it computes this future value by following the steps below:

1. Construct the statistical analyzed interval: $[currentTime - \Delta t, currentTime + 2\Delta t]$; we triple the predicted interval as to provide sufficient information for the actual prediction.
2. Extract the n samples from the feature's record in the statistical analyzed interval. The records are considered to be circular (the weeks wrap around).
3. Construct the X matrix, where x_i is the i-th sampling point in the analyzed interval:
4. $X = \begin{bmatrix} 1 & x_1 \\ 1 & x_2 \\ \cdots & \cdots \\ 1 & x_n \end{bmatrix}$
5. Construct the y column vector, where y_i is the i-th feature value:
6. $y = \begin{bmatrix} y_1 \\ y_2 \\ \cdots \\ y_n \end{bmatrix}$
7. Compute the Θ column vector, by solving the following equation: $X \times \Theta = y$. The Θ column vector contains the parameters of our heuristic h which is able to predict values of a feature and is computed using the normal function:
8. $\Theta = (X^T \times X)^{-1} \times X^T \times y$
9. Compute the average of the feature in the prediction interval:
10. $h(\frac{currentTime + \Delta t}{2})$

Given that such an offloading model is constantly adapting to environmental changes, it is only natural to believe that predictors may output erroneous values. In this sense, the prediction output is weighed against degree of informedness and to their own accuracy:

$$predictFeature(\Delta t) = w \times h\left(\frac{currentTime + \Delta t}{2}\right) + (1 - w) \times momentary\_value$$

where w is the feedback weight, computed as:

$$w = \frac{informedness}{2} + \frac{accuracy}{2}$$

The degree of informedness expresses the number of samples that have been recorded in the statistical analysis interval:

$$informedness = \frac{no\_filled\_samples}{no\_total\_samples}$$

In order to measure the effectiveness of the predictor, our offloading model uses balanced accuracy:

$$accuracy = \frac{1}{2} \times \frac{positives}{positives + false\_positives} + \frac{1}{2} \times \frac{negatives}{negatives + false\_negatives}$$

The heart of the *mobile-to-mobile contextual offloading* model is the contextual search algorithm based on the above feature prediction model, which is responsible for deciding whether to offload a task on a nearby device or to execute it locally. To be able to schedule tasks in opportunistic networks, the contextual search is split into two phases:

1. **Workload Profiling:** Ascertaining the amount of resources needed to actually run a task.
2. **Offloading Decision:** Determining if a task is better run locally or on a different device.

Given that any task can run on multiple devices, each of them having specific traits, workload profiling needs to first determine which resources are required by the task (and to what extent), compute a workload score which uniquely describes the computational requirements of the task and, last but not least, normalize the workload score to be able to compare executional needs of a task for multifarious mobile platforms. In this sense, we introduce the computational potential (or simply potential), which is defined as follows: the computing potential is the time required by the processor to run a workload, considering current and predicted values for CPU load and CPU frequency in the nearby future.

In essence, the potential is a measure of the CPU time required by a task on a specific device. At a first glance, this measure may seem inequitable, as devices with better performing CPUs might seem disadvantaged, but (as we shall see further on in this section) time turns out to be a good invariant in our problem. Let us take on an example: two devices - a low end device (A) and a high end device (B) with a 5 times faster CPU - are currently interacting; device (A) shortly becomes overwhelmed by the tasks it is executing, so it offloads 5 tasks with $potential_A = 1s$ to (B), which evaluates each at $potential_B = 0.2s$ so, instead of (A) executing them in 5s, (B) runs all of them in 1s; not much later, the user of device (B) becomes active and launches a task which (B) evaluates to $potential_B = 1s$, and offloads it to (A), which evaluates it to $potential_A = 5s$. Now both devices have cleared their debt and were able to run more efficiently (while the remote device was executing the offloaded task, the local device was able to execute other tasks). The reader should bear to mind that the workload of a task is usually directly proportional to the computational possibilities of the device that it's running on (because users tend to use applications that are suited for their device). As such, tasks from low end devices such as (A) are usually much smaller than tasks running on high end devices such as (B).

Furthermore, in order to reduce the number of leechers in the system, a cost model was put in place. Each time a node offloads a task for another, it remembers the debt it is owed by that node as the sum of negative potentials; also, the node which is requesting the offload stores the debt it owes the other node as the sum of positive potentials. When a node responds to an offload request, it will advertise that it's potential is: $potential = true\_potential - debt\_for\_requestor$. This ensures altruism, as it discourages nodes to take advantage of other nodes, and it encourages nodes with debt to offload in order to reduce their debt.

Having said that, it is high time we moved on to computing the potential of a task on a device. The following steps are required to determine the potential, given the number of CPU cycles estimated for a task through workload profiling:

1. Determine the maximum acceptable time (MAT) to run a task (the time needed to run a task at lowest frequency with 50% CPU load):
2. $MAT = num\_cycles \times \frac{1}{0.5 \times min\_frequency}$
3. Determine the potential of a task (the predicted time to run a task in current conditions):
4. $potential = num\_cycles \times \frac{1}{predicutCPULoad(MAT) \times predictCPUFreq(MAT)}$

Although it's not the absolute maximum time of running a task on a device, the maximum acceptable time represents the absolute maximum time that we would allow an offloaded task to run on a device, and it should be considered as the lower acceptable limit for offloading a task. It's more of a quantitative approach to determine the interval of time that a task should be executed in. As such, we compute the actual potential by predicting the CPU performance over the MAT interval. Therefore, the maximum acceptable time is computed only to determine the interval of prediction for the potential.

Based on a task's estimated potential, the offloading model is now able to correctly schedule a task in an opportunistic network. When a task is generated by an application, it passes through the workload profiler, which determines its computing potential. This potential will further augment the contextual search algorithm that actually decides whether to execute the task locally or offload it. Given that the task is executed in an opportunistic network, the decision is distributed. Therefore, there are actually two types of decisions that need to be taken:

1. **Local Decision:** The current device decides whether it is best to execute the task locally (e.g. the device is charging) or whether it should be offloaded.
2. **Remote Decision:** A remote node receives the offloading task request and it needs to determine if it can handle the execution of the remote task.

The Local Decision

Before offloading a task onto nearby devices, a node first decides, through contextual search, if the task actually needs to be offloaded and executed remotely, or if is better run locally. Figure 1 depicts the decision tree for local resolution of tasks. Each decision node in the tree is actually a feature predictor, as previously described in this section.

If the offloading model decides to remotely execute the task, it sends a task offload request to all connected peers, and waits for their potentials to run the task. After gathering all of the results, it adds the local potential to the list as well, and chooses the best candidate that will use minimal potential to execute the task. The reader should bear in mind that the task can still be run locally if the local node has the smallest potential. It should be noted that, under certain conditions (e.g. when the local device is charging), the offloading model is bypassed and the task is directly executed locally.

Figure 1. Local decision for offloading

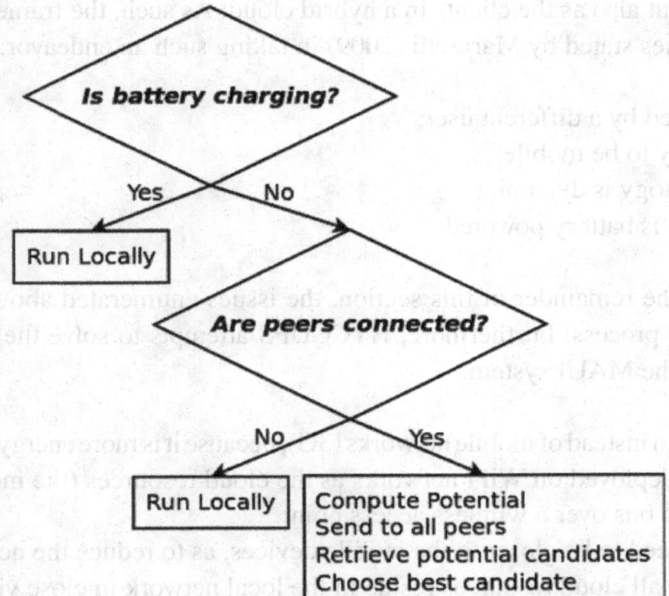

The Remote Decision

When a node receives an offload request, the offloading model needs to decide whether it will accept to run the task, or if it will reject it because it is unable to spare the resources. The contextual search in the remote decision is illustrated in Figure 2. Similar to the local decision, each node in the decision tree is a feature predictor, as previously described in this section.

It is fairly obvious that the remote decision is much more intricate than the local one, because each node wants to maximize the number of offloaded tasks, while minimizing the offloading it's actually doing. However, the cost model presented above is refereeing this process so that no node will be taken advantage of by others.

Also, similar to the local decision, under certain conditions (e.g. when a node is charging), it will attempt to act altruistically and it will advertise only a tenth of its actual potential to execute the task. The main reason behind this is to encourage other nodes to offload to it while it is still charging.

HYCCUPS

The Conceptual Framework

HYCCUPS is a ubiquitous computing conceptual framework which proposes to offer smartphone devices the opportunity to collaborate over high-speed wireless networks in a distributed and transparent manner, in order to reduce the overall power consumption by implementing the *mobile-to-mobile con-*

textual offloading model. The cornerstone of the solution stems from the use of smartphones as both the computing resources, but also as the clients in a hybrid cloud. As such, the framework was designed to fully cover the four issues stated by Marinelli (2009) in taking such an endeavor:

1. Each node is owned by a different user;
2. Each node is likely to be mobile;
3. The network topology is dynamic;
4. Each mobile node is battery powered.

As will be seen in the remainder of this section, the issues enumerated above influence the entire design and deployment process. Furthermore, HYCCUPS attempts to solve the issues pointed out by Cuervo et al (2010) in the MAUI system:

1. WiFi should be used instead of mobile networks (3G), because it is more energy-efficient: HYCCUPS is designed to be deployed on WiFi networks as the cloud resources (the mobile devices) are discovered by using a bus over a wireless access point.
2. Cloud resources need to be closer to the mobile devices, as to reduce the network transfers: when using HYCCUPS, all cloud resources reside in the local network in close vicinity of each other.

In the HYCCUPS framework, partitioning of remotable code is done statically at task level by injecting the offloading code in language constructs specific to the smartphone platform on top of which it is deployed. Although this process is transparent to the developer, it is still her responsibility to give hints

Figure 2. Remote decision for offloading

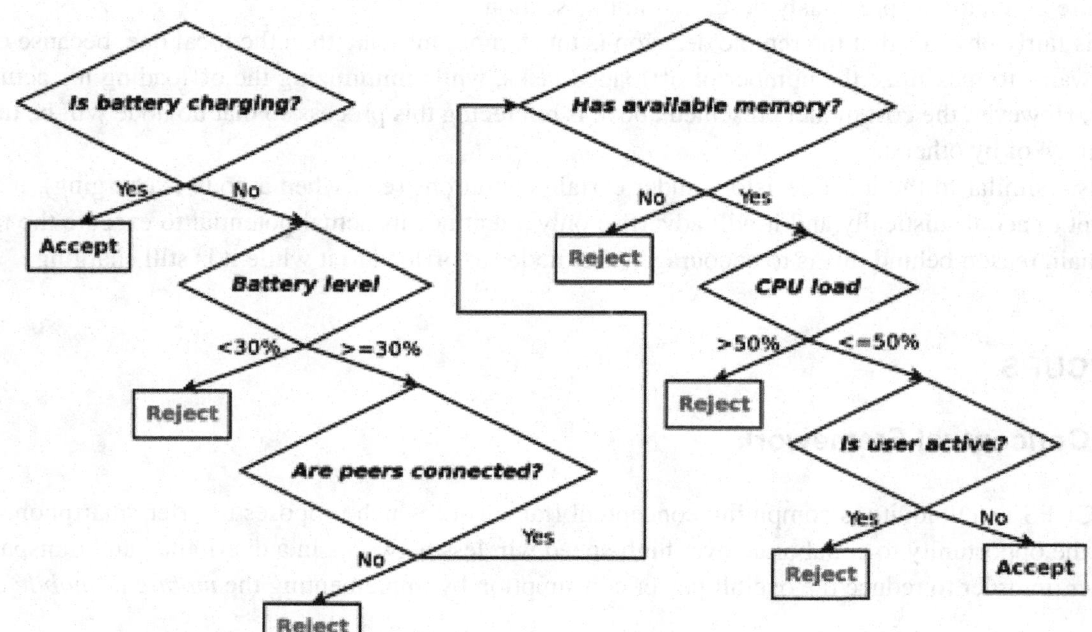

about which tasks can be remotely executed. We prefer to inject this implementation behind message sending subsystems, which allow communication between components of the same or even of different processes and applications. As such, we enforce modularity in the mobile application development process. Moreover, we create a certain type of symmetry, as the developer must write both the user interface, as well as the task executor module. As such, when the task is executed either remotely or locally, it is treated in the same manner by the same module implementation.

Considering that a mobile cloud is, by definition, always in perpetual motion, and that its components are usually owned by multiple users, a node's availability of processing a submitted workload is uncertain. As such, HYCCUPS uses a contextual search method to determine if a workload should run remotely or locally, and acts as a medium of offloading the current task to the best candidate in the mobile cloud, as to reduce the power consumption while preserving the quality of experience. Also considering the heterogeneity of a cloud, a node needs to be able to update its trained data by means of a feedback process, in order for it to evolve as to guarantee better availability resolution.

The main purpose of the HYCCUPS framework is to provide a middleware layer on top of which developers will be able to seamlessly design, build and deploy applications which will take advantage of the full potential of contextual execution offloading. The overall architecture of HYCCUPS is illustrated in Figure 3. The right hand side of Figure 3 represents the hybrid cloud deployment over a WiFi network. There are three types of cloud terminals:

1. **Mobile Terminal (MT):** A smartphone terminal, not plugged in. Its main characteristic is mobility. Not always available for executing workloads.
2. **Fixed Mobile Terminal (FMT):** A plugged-in smartphone terminal. Acts as a Fixed Terminal, but may rapidly return to a mobility state (MT).
3. **Fixed Terminal (FT):** A wearable computer. Will always be available for executing workloads. This is an optional component, as it raises compatibility issues: the developer has to explicitly redesign the mobile application code so it can be deployed on other platforms.

Figure 3. HYCCUPS architecture

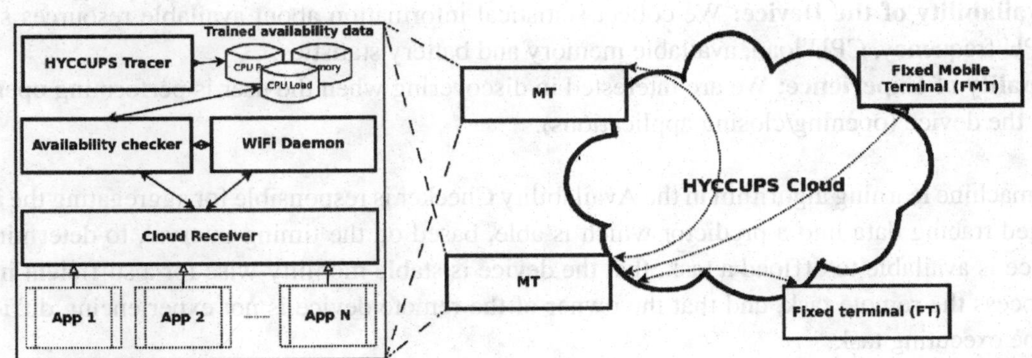

The left hand side of Figure 3 illustrates the anatomy of an MT (because FT and FMT do not impose any issues, the reader should expect them to act as regular cloud computing resources). The main components of an MT are:

1. **HYCCUPS Tracer:** As described in Section 3, this component is an application designed to collect contextual data from smartphones.
2. **Trained Availability Data Records:** Persistent datastores that aggregate the contextual information gathered by the HYCCUPS Tracer, also as described in Section 3.
3. **WiFi Daemon:** The component in charge of creating and maintaining the WiFi bus, and also responsible for resource discovery. This component is the actual glue holding the entire cloud together.
4. **Availability Checker:** This component is the cornerstone of HYCCUPS' foundation, because it is responsible for conducting the contextual search that determines if a task should be offloaded and/or if an incoming remotable task should be executed locally.
5. **Cloud Receiver:** The component responsible for resolving the execution runtime of incoming/outgoing remote tasks. If the decision of offloading is done by the Availability Checker, the actual enforcing of that decision is done by the Cloud receiver.

We rule in favor of tracing models, since we find that they better map onto real life situations than synthetic models, as Barabasi (2005) proves that the distributions of inter-event times in human activity are far from being normal, presenting bursts and heavy tails. It is for this reason that we use custom tracing applications to be able to acquire all needed mobility, availability and quality of experience tracing data. Moreover, the tracing interval can be set to reflect the particular needs of the mobile cloud users. For example, in academic and office environments the usual timing unit is an hour and is quite stable, whereas in a shopping mall users are quite mobile and the tracing interval should be far less (in the order of minutes).

We take the following features into consideration as tracing data:

- **Mobility:** We are more interested in wireless mobility than geographical tracking; as such, we aim at tracing patterns of users interacting over WiFi;
- **Availability of the Device:** We collect statistical information about available resources such as CPU frequency, CPU load, available memory and battery statistics;
- **Quality of Experience:** We are interested in discovering when the user is performing operations on the device (opening/closing applications).

The machine learning algorithm in the Availability Checker is responsible for aggregating the abovementioned tracing data into a predictor which is able, based on the timing interval, to determine that the device is available to offload a task, that the device is stable mobility-wise for a sufficient interval as to process the remote task, and that the owner of the remote device is not experiencing difficulties due to the executing task.

The basic behavior of an MT is to attempt to offload execution onto the cloud and respond to other workloads submitted into the cloud. There are two typical scenarios:

1. An application submits a workload onto the cloud. Based on the Availability Checkers' offloading decision, the Cloud Receiver passes the task either to the WiFi daemon, or to the local application. Needless to say, because of the middleware layer, the user will never know if the submitted workload was offloaded or if it actually executed locally. The mobile cloud does not impose that all execution be done on other devices, it only attempts to schedule it to run on the device that will maximize both energy efficiency and user experience.
2. The Cloud Receiver receives a task from the cloud, it assesses that it can execute the workload (via the Availability Checker) and accepts or declines accordingly. If more than one device accepts a workload, the availability will be the tie-breaker (FT and FMT will always have highest availability).

Giving Android the HYCCUPS

The main reason which convinced us to choose the Android platform is its openness. Not only does it provide stable and easy to use APIs and tools, but it also provides the source code for the internal implementation of the framework itself, thus offering insights for us in implementing and integrating HYCCUPS in Android.

Before we can go any further, we feel obliged to present some basic notions for developing applications in Android. The Android software stack is constructed based on the following building blocks:

- **Activity:** Represents a user interaction component. It's usually defined as a focused action that a user may perform. An Activity is responsible for creating a window where user interaction elements are inserted and which supports interaction events.
- **Service:** Represents a background worker. Its main responsibilities include: performing of longer computation operations without user interaction, or supplying functionality for other components or even other applications.
- **Content Provider:** Manages access to structured sets of data, usually SQLite databases. Similarly to Services, Content Providers may be spanned over multiple applications.
- **Broadcast Receiver:** Base component used for asynchronous events which are actually manifested by means of Intents. Broadcast Receivers are registered into the Android system on behalf of applications, and are used to filter and react only when receiving certain types of Intents.
- **Intent:** Represents the glue between Android components. Represented as structured messages, Intents are used to implement an inter-component communication (ICC), a process much similar to UNIX inter-process communication (IPC).

Considering that HYCCUPS will have to extend the Android API in order to offer a transparent middleware layer, we have taken much interest in the Intent ICC process. As Intents are mostly used to broadcast messages throughout the system as to asynchronously notify components of actions that need to be offloaded towards them, it seems to be the most likely candidate for our extensions. In order for our extensions to be clearly understood, we are obliged to provide a description of Intents and their behavior.

Basically, an Intent is a structured message which may contain the following data:

- **Action:** The general action to be performed;
- **Data:** An URI expressing the general data on which the action will be performed;
- **Category:** Gives additional data about the action to be performed;
- **Type:** Specifies an explicit MIME type for the data;
- **Component:** Explicit name of a component which will treat this intent;
- **Extras:** Supplementary data attached to an intent.

For the ICC process to be complete, the system must be able to identify the receiver for a specific intent, process denominated as *Intent Resolution*. According to Meier (2010), intent resolution is comprised of the following steps:

1. The system aggregates all intent filters that were registered;
2. Intent filters which do not match the action or category are dropped;
    a. Actions match if both are alike or no action was provided;
    b. All categories defined in an intent must have a correspondent in the filter;
3. The intent data URI is compared to the filter's data scheme; any difference in scheme, host/authority, MIME type, automatically removes the intent filter;
4. If more components are resolved to an intent, a list of comprising candidates is offered in return.

As can be seen, the Intent ICC design principle encourages decoupling and extensibility of components and applications. Furthermore, it proves to be the component which HYCCUPS needs to extend, in order for a task to cross the bounds of the device itself and into the cloud. A significant issue regarding the Android extension is formulated now as to reflect our design considerations: in order for HYCCUPS to be able to run on (mostly) all versions of Android, we cannot modify the software stack itself. In consequence, we use the Intent ICC mechanism to cover the internals of HYCCUPS and to offer a transparent middleware layer for developers of applications.

The following components represent the Android extension of Intents and Broadcast Receivers used to support HYCCUPS:

1. **Cloud Intent:** An Intent container which adds an extra action and extra component (the extra fields in the Cloud Intent are used instead of the original ones). The main action of the Intent is CLOUD INTENT and the extra action is used in the Intent Resolution mechanism in the cloud to substitute for the main one. The main component of the Intent will be set to Cloud Receiver, and the extra component is provided as to substitute for the main one used by HYCCUPS. At this point, we separate Cloud Intents into two categories: Selfish Goal Intents and Common Goal Intents. This separation stems from the duality of HYCCUPS: it can be either used for tapping into distributed mobile data disregarding energy consumption, or it can be used to achieve energy efficiency by collaboration.
2. **Cloud Receiver:** A Broadcast Receiver registered into the system and waiting for CLOUD INTENT actions. This component is responsible for reacting to cloud intents, internal (from the device) or external (from the cloud). This component will further interact with the HYCCUPS framework to offload execution into the cloud.

In order for the mobile cloud to react seamlessly and coherently, an efficient Android peer-to-peer communication solution is needed to fulfill all responsibilities of communication in the cloud. In this respect, we have selected AllJoyn as our communication framework.

AllJoyn is an open source software framework which offers a peer-to-peer communication environment for heterogeneous distributed systems across different device classes with emphasis on mobility, security and dynamism, by implementing the D-Bus protocol. It provides an abstraction layer allowing it to run on multiple operating systems such as Linux distributions (Ubuntu included) and most versions of Microsoft Windows (Windows 7 included). Such a feature will allow us to register wearable computers into the mobile cloud as Fixed Terminals, in order to provide powerful offloading of mobile execution onto them as illustrated in Figure 3.

AllJoyn's main goal is to provide a software bus that offers distributed advertising and discovery services in a secure mobile environment. In addition, the system supplies a Java-like location-transparent RMI. In the AllJoyn world, the most significant abstraction is the software bus, which connects and glues together all the clients and services, and implicitly all of the wearable devices. Being a peer-to-peer system, all peers connect to the aforementioned bus by means of bus attachments. The bus attachment is another software abstraction that exists in the peer space and actually represents the link to the inter-process communication that connects clients and services alike to the AllJoyn daemon. At the time of connection, each bus attachment is assigned a unique name by the system and, if advertising is needed, the aforesaid bus attachment may request a unique well-known name, by means of which it can make itself public to the rest of the distributed system. Well-known names are human-readable names which reside in a reversed-domain, like a self-managed namespace. The sheer existence of a bus attachment of a specific name directly implies the existence of at least one instance of a bus object implementing the interface specified by said name. Bus objects are organized in a hierarchy in which the bus attachment is root, similar to a UNIX file system. An AllJoyn interface consists of bus methods, bus properties and bus signals. Bus methods are traditional RMI method implementations, properties are actual fields accessed by remote setters and getters, and signals are similar to methods, except that they do not expect any results (they are more akin to broadcasting). Services implement interfaces through bus objects and advertise their possibilities by means of well-known names. Clients are expected to use proxy bus objects for ease of interaction with the service, by means of simple interfaces.

In order for AllJoyn to work on Android, it is sufficient to install the AllJoyn Daemon: the glue that holds the entire distributed system together and which runs in the background, without user focus, waiting for events and reacting to them accordingly. The Daemon's implementation provides an operating system abstraction layer, which represents a wrapper over the native binaries, and upon which the entire transport system is built. The OS abstraction layer actually provides the necessary abstractions for implementing the platform-neutral feature, so that the daemon may be run on Linux, Windows and Android alike. Moreover, the security issues of HYCCUPS are covered by AllJoyn through using authentication with x509 certificates.

EXPERIMENTAL RESULTS

Evaluating such a complex system as HYCCUPS proved to be more difficult than anticipated. The issue did not arise due to the arduousness of implementing and deploying the actual framework for a specific smartphone platform (as the previous Section showed that a port to Android is straightforward), but because of the lack of applications implemented for our framework. In order to thoroughly test it, we need to create a vast number of Android applications that take advantage of the HYCCUPS cloud and which pose interest to the users.

As was noticed in the tracing experiment in Marin at al. (2012), the greatest pitfall of such endeavors is the lack of conscientiousness of participants. In order to attempt such an experiment, both volunteers and application developers alike need to be convinced of the benefits that HYCCUPS offers. Without the support of both aforementioned parties, such an endeavor will be in vain.

To overcome said issues, we have developed the HYCCUPS Emulator, which provides valuable insight into the inner-workings and performances of the entire framework. It makes use of the traced contextual data described in the tracing experiment from Marin et al. (2012), which was proven to be sufficient for our needs, by means of the methodology and guidelines provided in Marin et al. (2013).

The HYCCUPS Emulator is implemented in Java, as to ease the porting of the algorithm from Android (which also uses Java, but also proprietary APIs). The traced data was stored in a MySQL database, and the connection to the emulator was made through the *Connector/J Java Database Connectivity* (JDBC) driver. The emulator also makes use of the *Efficient Java Matrix Library* (EJML) for implementing linear regression (by using the normal function as previously explained).

The emulator is built based on the following assumptions:

1. All devices use the same reference for time: due to the fact that the devices involved in the tracing dataset did not use a network clock, we must assume that they all are synchronized to the same time reference.
2. All environmental events are synchronous and sequentially executed for all users. As such, each event for any device acts as a barrier for all users. By so doing, we are able to implement deterministic heuristics for generating repeatable workloads.
3. All devices have only a single core: the tracing data did not include anything about the number of available cores or about the number of online cores.
4. There is no network transfer delay: all of the workloads generated are purely computational. The emulator does not assume that workloads are sending data as well, instead it presumes that the data is already present on the device. Therefore, all workloads are expressed in CPU cycles.
5. The bandwidth of the network is considered to be unlimited.

Workloads are generated in a deterministic manner so as to be repetitive, using a heuristic that takes into account the following features: the user of the device is active, or the device is connected to the AllJoyn bus. The main difficulty with working with the tracing dataset is the lack of conscientiousness of the volunteers. Because of this, there are not many nodes actively involved in offloading, as only three devices out of all 65 participants seem to be collaborating in an energetic manner. This will impact the results, as will be seen in the remainder of this Section.

We have attempted to cover multiple types of workloads while analyzing the HYCCUPS framework. We have generated three scenarios using a total of 726 tasks over 2 months of emulator execution, which are sent in a pseudo-random fashion to all active users in the system, with the following computational requirements:

1. **100Mcycle Tasks:** Small tasks which are easily executed by any node. Such tasks can be associated to computing a move in a game of chess.
2. **1Gcycle Tasks:** Regular-sized tasks which should be executed by most devices. This scenario could be associated with computing the value of π.
3. **10Gcycle Tasks:** Large tasks which should be a burden for all devices. These tasks could relate to the analysis of satellite images (given that the images are already downloaded).

Figures 4, 5, and 6 show the total debt accumulated by all users on a daily basis for all three scenarios. As can be seen in all three cases, the cost model gives better performance, as it seems that altruism serves the community better than leeching off of other nodes. Furthermore, Table 2 shows that, even though working without a cost model can actually offload more, the overall benefit of using such a model is much greater, as it actually saves more computing time. As can be seen, HYCCUPS manages to save valuable computing, which is actually proportional to the size of the task. The reader should be advised that, although at a first glance the amount of saved time does not seem to be large, only three devices were actively offloading tasks. This should generally change the perspective over the results. Also, since more than a quarter of the tasks were executed remotely on devices that were charging, the actual computing power save increases. Moreover, out of the 57(55) offloaded tasks, none of them failed to complete, which proves that the adaptive and predictive models used in collaboration with the contextual search algorithm are working properly and correctly.

Last, but not least, charts in Figures 7, 8, and 9, illustrate the total execution time as tasks are sequentially run. Moreover, they compare the HYCCUPS execution model with the current traditional Android model. As can be observed, the HYCCUPS framework speeds up mobile applications by means of offloading onto remote idle nodes. However, these figures do not contain the execution for all of the

Figure 4. Total accumulated debt, for 100 MCycle tasks

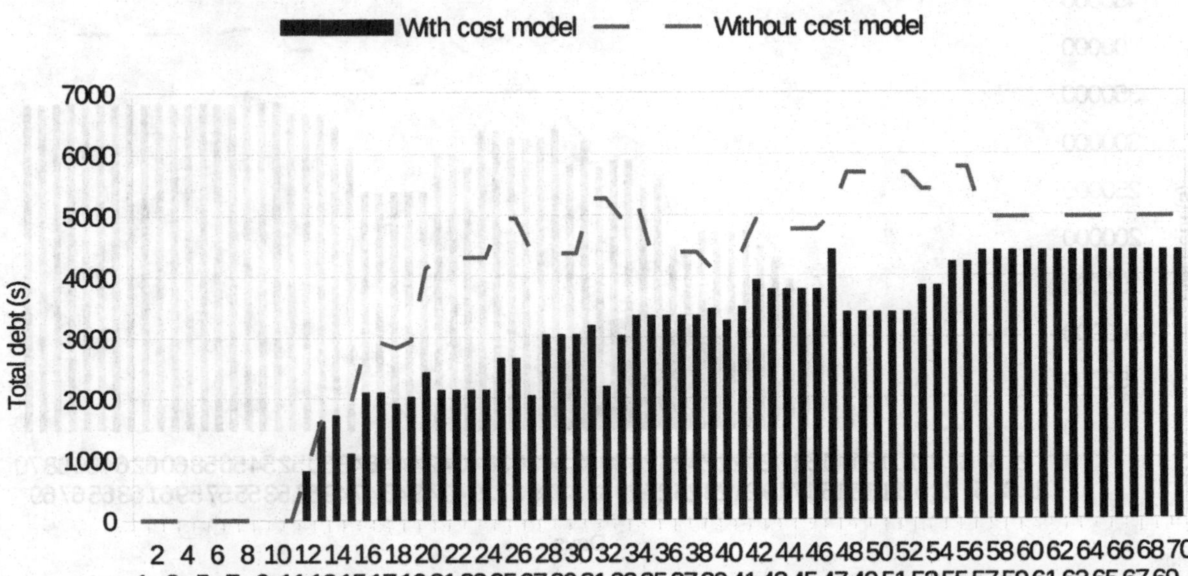

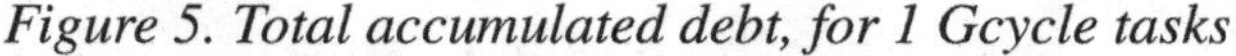

Figure 5. Total accumulated debt, for 1 Gcycle tasks

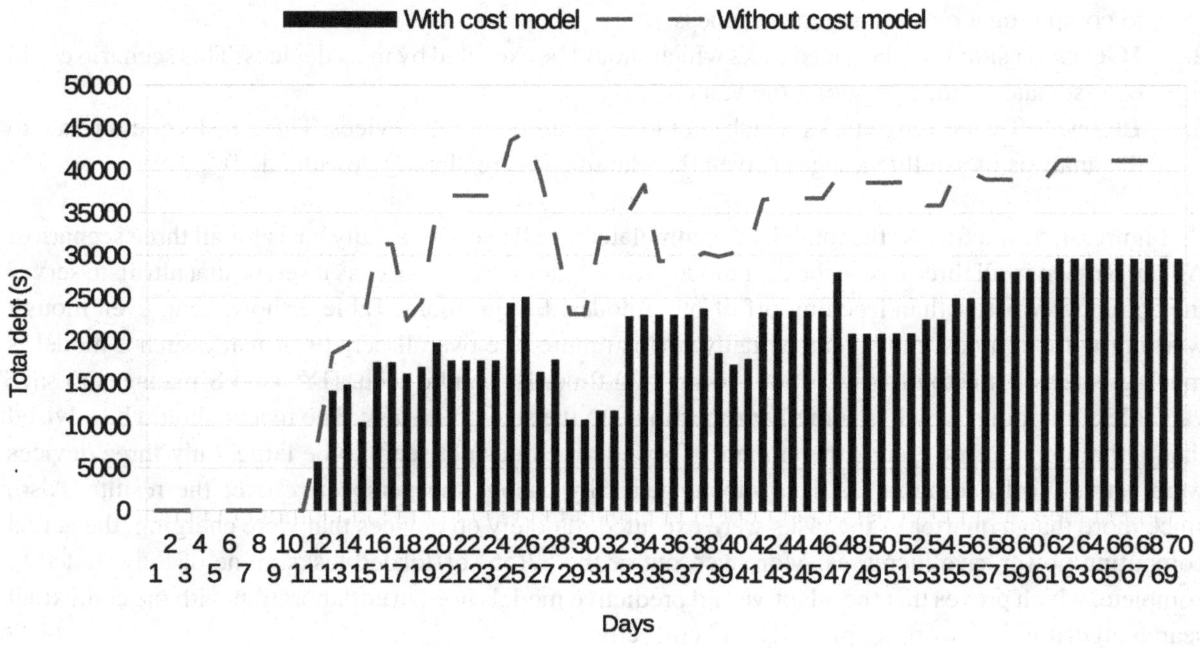

Figure 6. Total accumulated debt, for 10 GCycle tasks

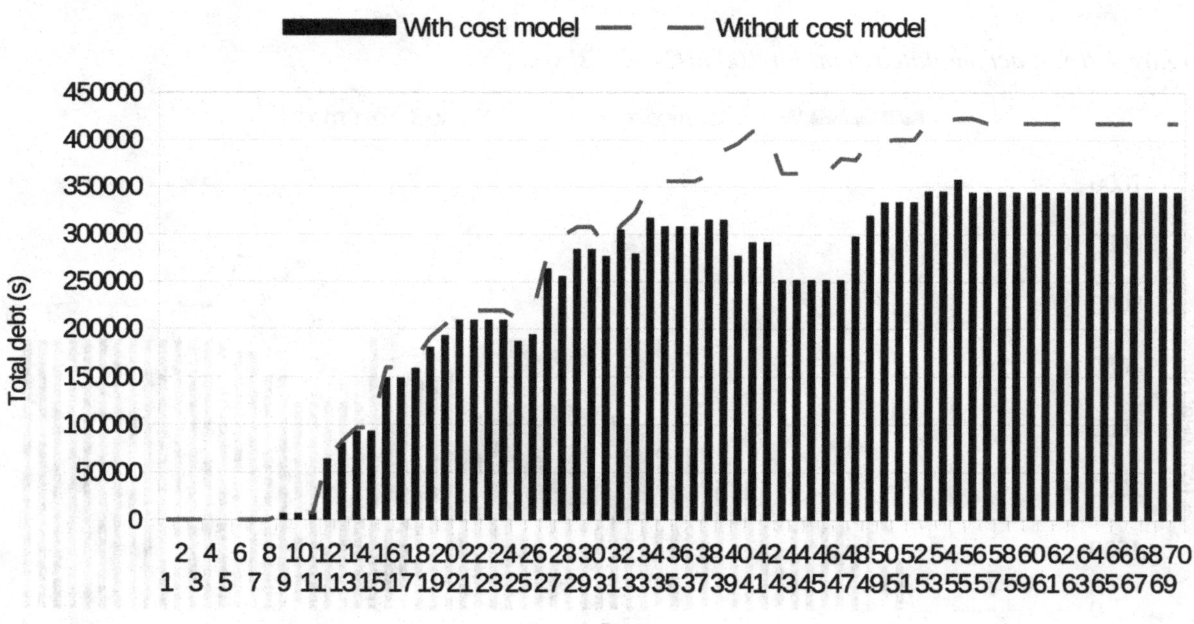

Figure 7. Total accumulated execution time for offladed tasks, for 100 MCycle tasks

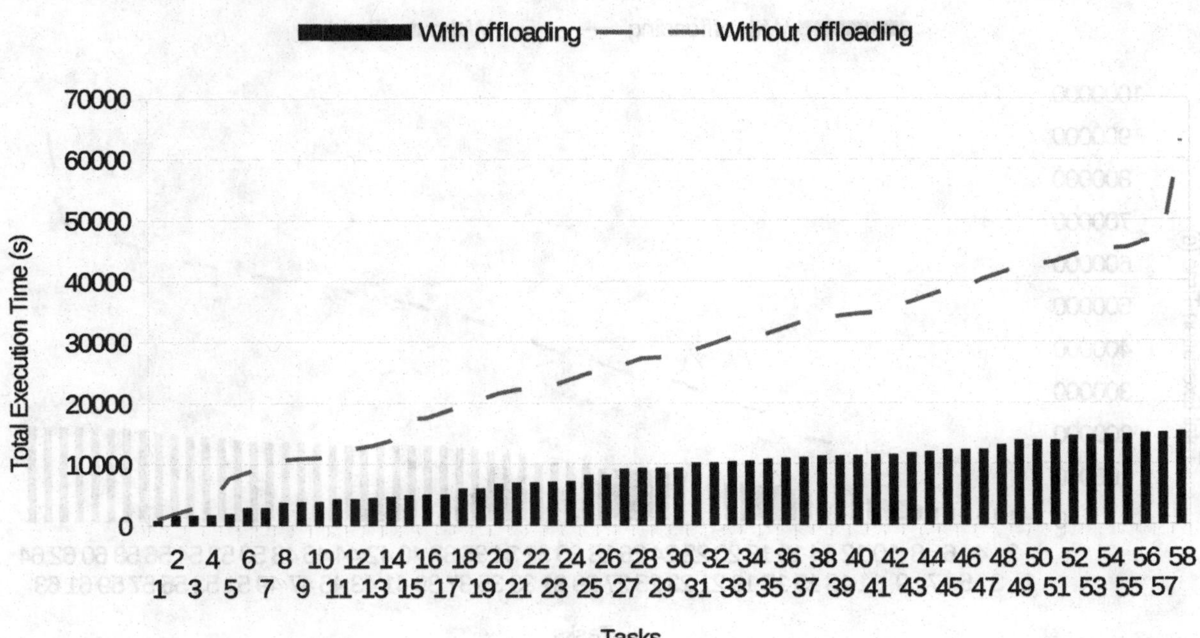

Figure 8. Total accumulated execution time for offloaded tasks, for 1 GCycle tasks

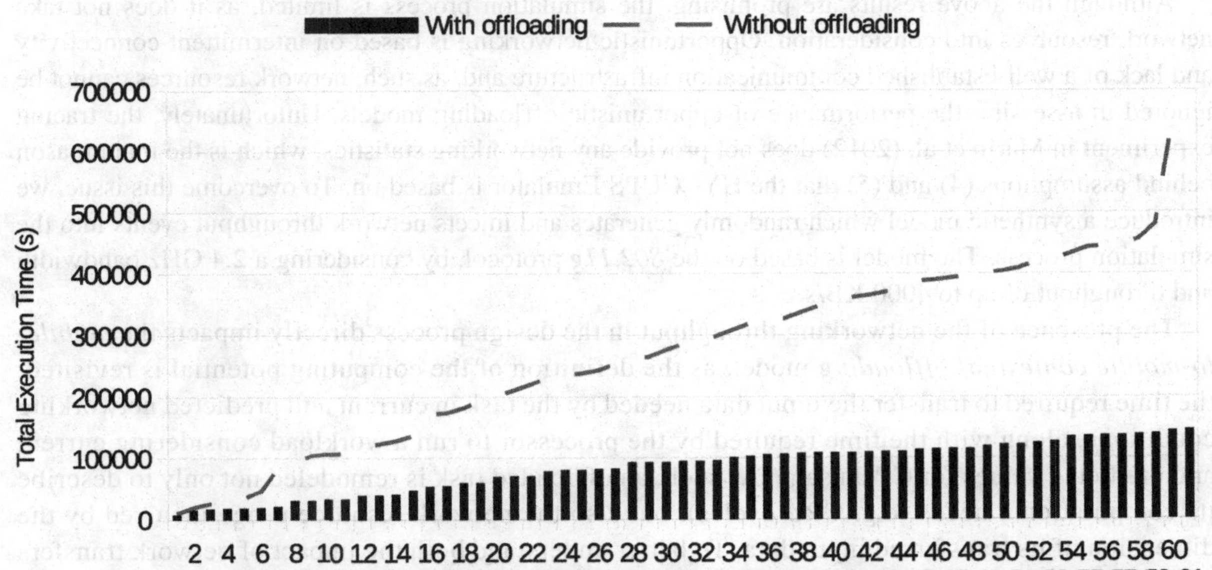

Figure 9. Total accummulated execution time for offloaded tasks, for 10 GCycle tasks

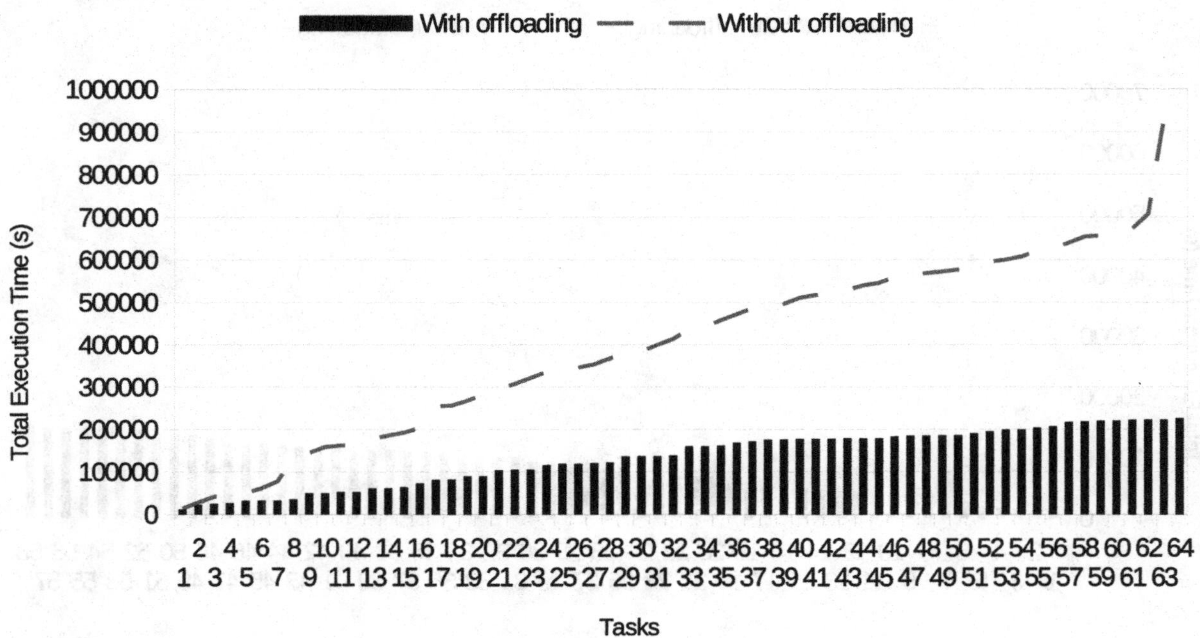

726 tasks, but only for the 57(55) offloaded tasks. We are not interested in the tasks that are always run locally, as HYCCUPS can only optimize workloads that actually have the possibility to be offloaded (although the predictors might have missed some offloading opportunities).

Although the above results are promising, the simulation process is limited, as it does not take network resources into consideration. Opportunistic networking is based on intermittent connectivity and lack of a well-established communication infrastructure and, as such, network resources cannot be ignored in assessing the performance of opportunistic offloading models. Unfortunately, the tracing experiment in Marin et al. (2012) does not provide any networking statistics, which is the main reason behind assumptions (4) and (5) that the HYCCUPS Emulator is based on. To overcome this issue, we introduce a synthetic model which randomly generates and injects network throughput events into the simulation process. The model is based on the *802.11g* protocol, by considering a 2.4 GHz bandwidth and throughput of up to 4000 KB/s.

The presence of the networking throughput in the design process directly impacts the *mobile-to-mobile contextual offloading* model, as the definition of the computing potential is revisited: the time required to transfer the input data needed by the task in current and predicted networking conditions, along with the time required by the processor to run a workload considering current and predicted values for CPU usage. As such, an offloaded task is remodeled not only to describe its computational needs (e.g. CPU cycles), but also the network resource usage incurred by the dimension of its transferred input data. To better understand both the impact of network transfers on offloading, and also of the relationship between task input size and offloading success rate, we have performed parameter sweeps on the simulation of the HYCCUPS framework, by varying the input size and network throughput, respectively the input data size and the computational needs of tasks.

Table 2. Offloading statistics for all three scenarios

Scenario	Cost Model?	Total Offloaded	Failed Offloads	FMT Offloads	Total Saved Time (s)
100 Mcycle	Y	57	0	16	48000
100 Mcycle	N	57	0	16	45000
1 Gcycle	Y	57	0	15	472000
1 Gcycle	N	57	0	16	448000
10 Gcycle	Y	55	0	15	4723000
10 Gcycle	N	57	0	16	4481000

The contextual offloading model is heavily impacted by network transfers, as Figures 10 and 11 show that the number of successfully offloaded tasks is halved (from 40 down to 20 offloads) when the input size reaches its maximum value. As expected, the best case scenario is when the tasks are heavily computational and do not require any network transfers. On the other hand, as the input data size increases linearly, the number of offloaded tasks decreases at quadratic rates. Interestingly enough, the number of offloaded tasks levels out when the task's computational needs are higher than 40 Mcycles and input data size is higher than 4MB. This proves that the contextual offloading model is still able to provide undeniable energy efficiency in situations closer to real-life. Moreover, Figure 10 illustrates

Figure 10. Total saved time, for varying CPU cycles and input data size

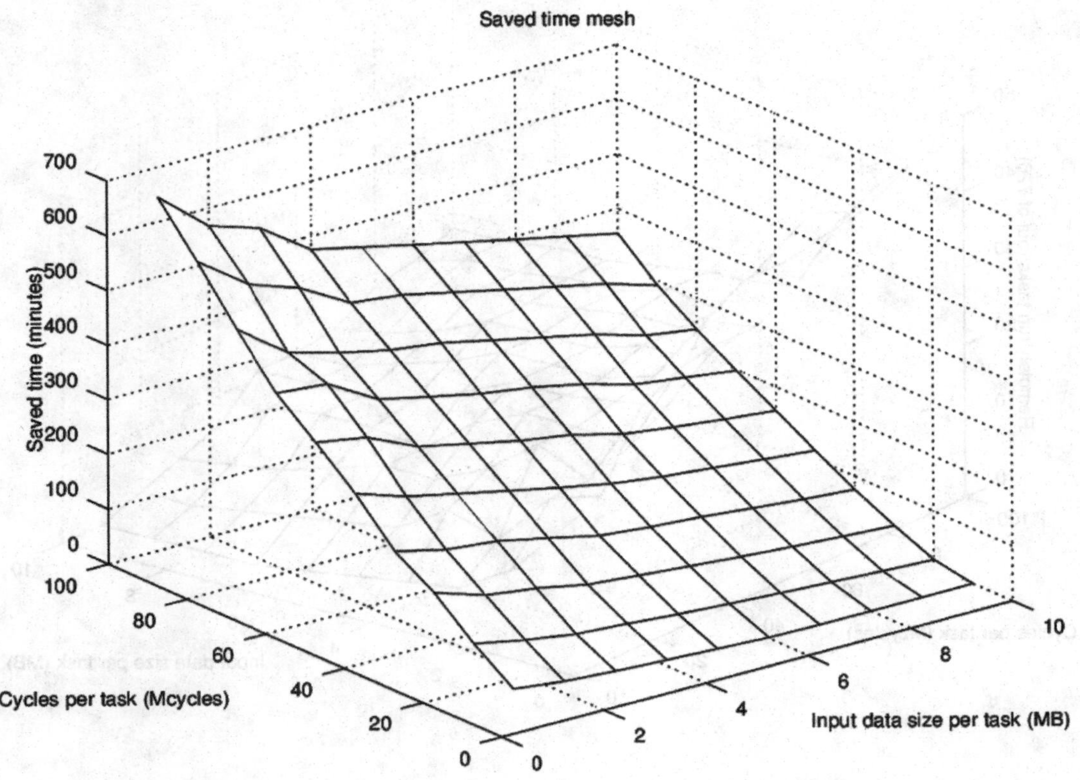

the influence of network transfers on the total time saved through contextual offloading; as expected, the saved time increases linearly, proportional to computational needs. However, when increasing the input data size of tasks, the overall speedup of applications decreases linearly, but with a fairly smaller slope. This is further evidence of the increased performance of the offloading model, which, in the case of highly computational tasks that require large transfers, it is able to provide impressive application speedup, by saving up to about 400 min out of the almost 700 min saved in the base case that involves no network transfers.

As previously stated, the actual communication infrastructure is highly important in opportunistic networking. By also varying the throughput of the underlying communication channels, Figure 13 illustrates how the offloading model is able to handle real-world conditions. As also observed in Figures 10 and 11, the number of successfully offloaded tasks sensibly decreases when the wireless networks are experiencing increasing traffic, but it still manages to level out when the throughput is higher than 2 MB/s and input data size is higher than 4MB. As opposed to task size, the network load has less influence when the throughput has acceptable rates (higher than 2MB/s), as it decreases with a more acceptable downward slope. However, when the data input size of tasks is very high, the actual time saved through offloading experiences a harsh drop, this being the worst-case scenario for offloading, as all tasks will end up being run locally.

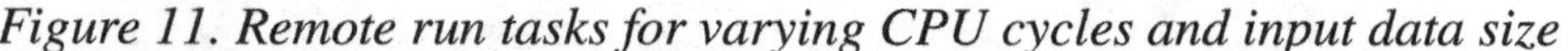

Figure 11. Remote run tasks for varying CPU cycles and input data size

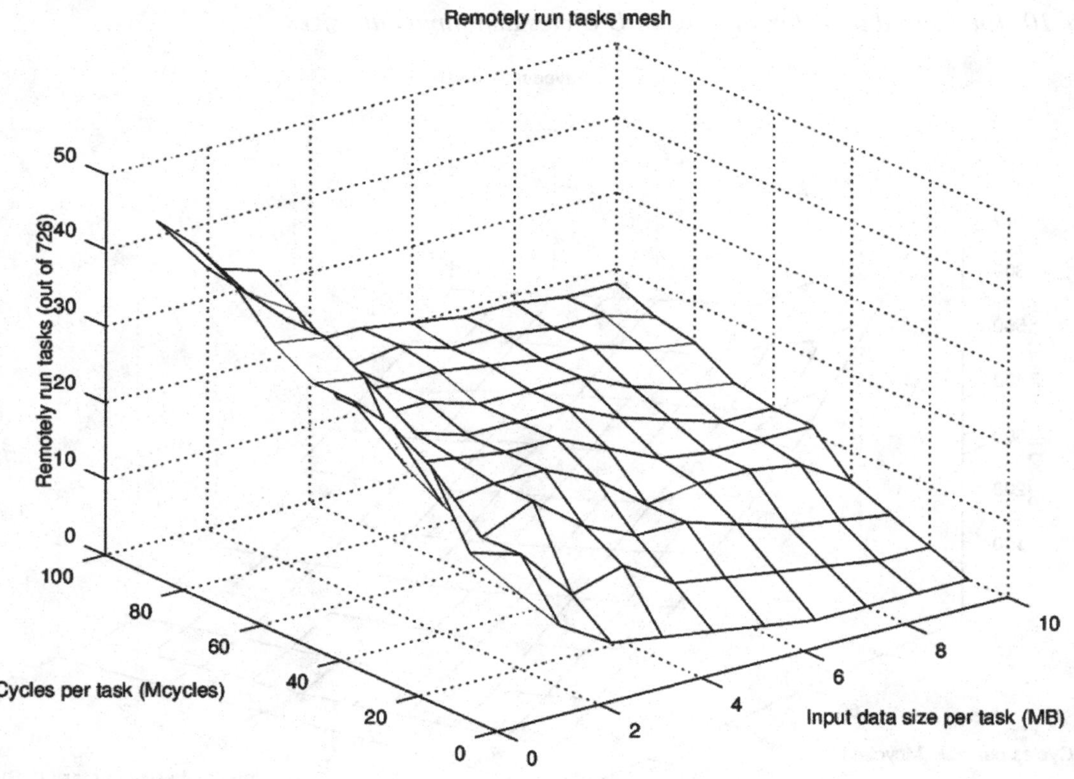

Figure 12. Total saved time for varying throughput input data size

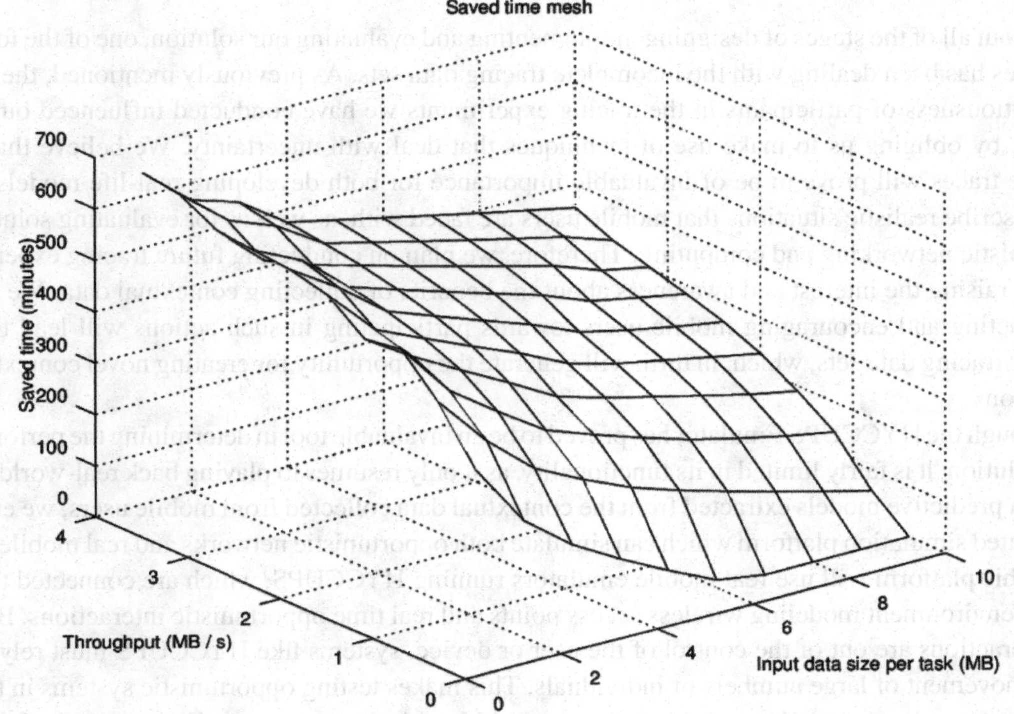

Figure 13. Remote run tasks for varying throughput and input data size

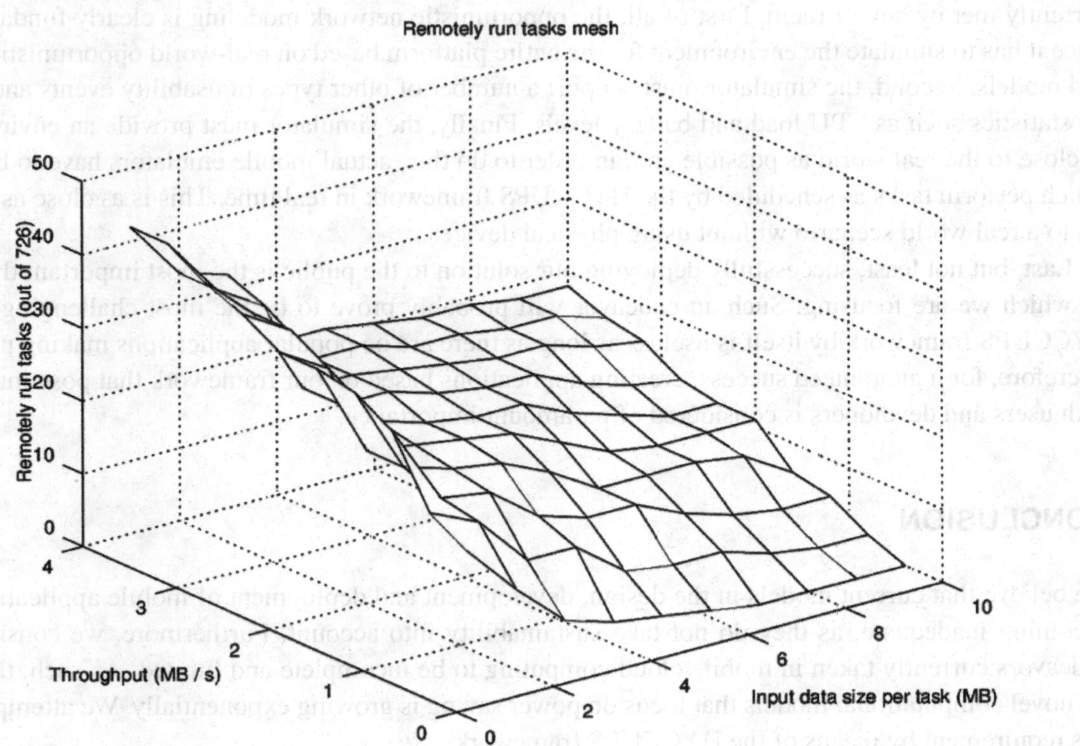

FUTURE WORK

Throughout all of the stages of designing, implementing and evaluating our solution, one of the foremost challenges has been dealing with the incomplete tracing data sets. As previously mentioned, the lack of conscientiousness of participants in the tracing experiments we have conducted influenced our entire research, by obliging us to make use of techniques that deal with uncertainty. We believe that more complete traces will prove to be of invaluable importance for both developing real-life models which better describe realistic situations that mobile users are faced with, as well as for evaluating solutions in opportunistic networking and computing. Therefore, we plan on conducting future tracing experiments aimed at raising the interest and awareness about the benefits of collecting contextual data. We believe that attracting and encouraging mobile users towards participating in such actions will lead to more complete tracing data sets, which, in turn, will generate the opportunity for creating novel context-aware applications.

Although the HYCCUPS Emulator has proved to be an invaluable tool in determining the performance of our solution, it is fairly limited in its functionality, as it only resumes to playing back real-world traces. Based on predictive models extracted from the contextual data collected from mobile users, we envision a distributed simulation platform which can simulate both opportunistic networks and real mobile device usage. This platform will use real mobile emulators running HYCCUPS, which are connected through a virtual environment modeling wireless access points and real time opportunistic interactions. Because such interactions are out of the control of the user or device, systems like HYCCUPS must rely on the natural movement of large numbers of individuals. This makes testing opportunistic systems in the real world not feasible, so simulators have to be used. Although some opportunistic network simulators have been developed, in order to validate HYCCUPS, there are a number of requirements which are not currently met by any of them. First of all, the opportunistic network modeling is clearly fundamental, since it has to simulate the environment for the entire platform based on real-world opportunistic traces and models. Second, the simulator must support a number of other types of usability events and monitor statistics such as CPU load and battery levels. Finally, the simulator must provide an environment as close to the real world as possible and, in order to do this, actual mobile emulators have to be used, which perform tasks as scheduled by the HYCCUPS framework in real time. This is as close as we can get to a real world scenario without using physical devices.

Last, but not least, successfully deploying our solution to the public is the most important direction on which we are focusing. Such an endeavor will probably prove to be the most challenging, as the HYCCUPS framework by itself is useless as long as there are no popular applications making use of it. Therefore, for a guaranteed success, creating applications based on our framework that pose interest to both users and developers is considered of paramount importance.

CONCLUSION

We believe that current models in the design, development and deployment of mobile applications are becoming inadequate, as they do not take sustainability into account. Furthermore, we consider the endeavors currently taken in mobile cloud computing to be incomplete and limited. As such, the need for novel computational models that focus on power saving is growing exponentially. We attempt to fill this requirement by means of the HYCCUPS framework.

HYCCUPS introduces intelligent collaboration, a new computational model which offers feasible synergy between interacting peers in opportunistic networks by correlating mobility with availability information by means of a contextual search algorithm. Moreover, the algorithm is adaptive to environmental changes so as to improve battery health, maximize power save, minimize overall execution time of mobile applications and, last, but not least, to preserve or even enhance user experience.

We design a simple deployment model hidden behind language constructs specific to the smartphone platform on top of which it is distributed. By so doing, we encourage researchers and application developers to design and implement applications to make use of HYCCUPS. Moreover, such a deployment model does not require any additional training for the developers, as they will be using the same APIs in creating applications. We also enforce modularity into the development process, as programmers will have to implement both the GUI components, as well as the task executors. This component symmetry will also make the code easier to understand, as it is presented in the current traditional method of designing applications.

In conclusion, we believe that the HYCCUPS framework will render better results, considering both sustainability and efficiency, as it is based upon a novel intelligent *mobile-to-mobile contextual offloading* model, and will offer on-the-fly cloud capabilities to sets of interconnected smartphones. Moreover, it will allow seamless development of Android applications that can take advantage of such a contextual community.

ACKNOWLEDGMENT

The research presented in this chapter is supported by national project MobiWay, PN-II-PT-PC-CA-2013-4-0321. The work is aligned with COST Action IC1303, "Algorithms, Architectures and Platforms for Enhanced Living Environments (AAPELE)", and COST Action IC1406, "High-Performance Modelling and Simulation for Big Data Applications (cHiPSet)".

REFERENCES

Agarwal, B., Chitnis, P., Dey, A., Jain, K., Navda, V., Padmanabhan, V. N., . . . Spring, N. (2010). Stratus: Energy-efficient mobile communication using cloud support. In S. Kalyanaraman, V. N. Padmanabhan, K. K. Ramakrishnan, R. Shorey & G. M. Voelker (eds.), SIGCOMM (pp. 477-478). ACM. doi:10.1145/1851182.1851272

Anand, B., Thirugnanam, K., Sebastian, J., Kannan, P. G., Ananda, A. L., Chan, M. C., & Balan, R. K. (2010), Adaptive display power management for mobile games. In *Proceedings of the 9th International Conference on Mobile Systems, Applications, and Services, MobiSys '11* (pp. 57-70). New York, NY: ACM.

Balasubramanian, N., Balasubramanian, A., & Venkataramani, A. (2009). Energy consumption in mobile phones: A measurement study and implications for network applications. In FeldmannA.MathyL. (Eds.), *Internet measurement conference* (pp. 280-293). ACM. doi:10.1145/1644893.1644927

Barabasi, A.-L. (2005). The origin of bursts and heavy tails in human dynamics. *Nature*, *435*(7039), 207–211. doi:10.1038/nature03459 PMID:15889093

Bisong, A., & Rahman, S. M. (2011). An overview of the security concerns in enterprise cloud computing. *CoRR*, abs/1101.5613

Challam, V., Gauch, S., & Chandramouli, A. (2007). Contextual search using ontology-based user profiles. In D. Evans, S. Furui, & C. Soulé-Dupuy (Eds.), RIAO: CID. Academic Press.

Chun, B.-G., Ihm, S., Maniatis, P., Naik, M., & Patti, A. (2011). CloneCloud: Elastic execution between mobile device and cloud. In C. M. Kirsch & G. Heiser (Eds.), EuroSys (pp. 301-314). ACM. doi:10.1145/1966445.1966473

Chun, B.-G., & Maniatis, P. (2010), Dynamically partitioning applications between weak devices and clouds. In *Proceedings of the 1st ACM Workshop on Mobile Cloud Computing & Services: Social Networks and Beyond, MCS '10* (pp. 7:1-7:5). New York: ACM. doi:10.1145/1810931.1810938

Cuervo, E., Balasubramanian, A., Cho, D., Wolman, A., Saroiu, S., Chandra, R., & Bahl, P. (2010). MAUI: Making smartphones last longer with code offload. In S. Banerjee, S. Keshav, & A. Wolman (Eds.), MobiSys (pp. 49-62). ACM.

Hoang, D. T., Lee, C., Niyato, D., & Wang, P. (2013). A survey of mobile cloud computing: Architecture, applications, and approaches. *Wireless Communications and Mobile Computing*, *13*(18), 1587–1611. doi:10.1002/wcm.1203

Holly, R. (2011). *How much of your phone is yours?*. Retrieved May 2014 from http://www.geek.com/mobile/how-much-of-your-phone-is-yours-1440611/

Hong, J., Suh, E., & Kim, S.-J. (2009). Context-aware systems: A literature review and classification. *Expert Systems with Applications*, *36*(4), 8509–8522. doi:10.1016/j.eswa.2008.10.071

Huerta-Canepa, G., & Lee, D. (2010). A virtual cloud computing provider for mobile devices. In *Proceedings of the 1st ACM Workshop on Mobile Cloud Computing & Services: Social Networks and Beyond* (MCS '10). ACM. http://doi.acm.org/10.1145/1810931.1810937

Kemp, R., Palmer, N., Kielmann, T., & Bal, H. (2012). Cuckoo: A computation offloading framework for smartphones mobile computing, applications, and services. In Proceedings of Social Informatics and Telecommunications Engineering (LNICS), (vol. 76, pp. 59–79). Springer.

Kraft, R., Maghoul, F., & Chang, C.-C. (2005). Y!Q: Contextual search at the point of inspiration. In O. Herzog, H.-J. Schek, N. Fuhr, A. Chowdhury, & W. Teiken (Eds.), CIKM (pp. 816-823). ACM.

Liang, W.-Y., & Lai, P.-T. (2010). Design and implementation of a critical speed-based DVFS mechanism for the Android operating system. In *Proceedings of Embedded and Multimedia Computing* (EMC). Academic Press.

Liang, W.-Y., Lai, P.-T., & Chiou, C. (2010). An energy conservation DVFS algorithm for the Android operating system. *Journal of Convergence*, *1*(1), 93–100.

Marin, R.-C., & Dobre, C. (2013). Reaching for the clouds: Contextually enhancing smartphones for energy efficiency. In C. X. Mavromoustakis, T. Dagiuklas, & L. Shu (Eds.), *HP-MOSys* (pp. 31–38). ACM. doi:10.1145/2507908.2507912

Marin, R.-C., Dobre, C., & Xhafa, F. (2012). Exploring predictability in mobile interaction. In Proceedings of EIDWT (pp. 133-139). EIDWT.

Marin, R.-C., Dobre, C., & Xhafa, F. (2014). A methodology for assessing the predictable behaviour of mobile users in wireless networks. *Concurrency and Computation*, *26*(5), 1215–1230. doi:10.1002/cpe.3064

Marinelli, E. E. (2009). *Hyrax: Cloud computing on mobile devices using MapReduce*. (Unpublished Masters dissertation). School of Computer Science, Carnegie Mellon University, Pittsburgh, PA.

Meier, R. (2010). Professional Android 2 application development. Academic Press.

Minkov, E., Cohen, W. W., & Ng, A. Y. (2006). Contextual search and name disambiguation in email using graphs. In E. N. Efthimiadis, S. T. Dumais, D. Hawking, & K. Järvelin (Eds.), SIGIR (pp. 27-34). ACM. doi:10.1145/1148170.1148179

Murray, D. G., Yoneki, E., Crowcroft, J., & Hand, S. (2010). The case for crowd computing. In L. P. Cox & A. Wolman (Eds.), MobiHeld (pp. 39-44). ACM.

Peralta, A. (2011). *Samsung, HTC And Carrier IQ face suit over logging software*. Retrieved December 2011 from http://www.npr.org/blogs/thetwo-way/2011/12/02/143051586/samsung-htc-and-carrier-iq-face-suit-over-logging-software

Robison, W. J. (2010). Free at what cost? Cloud computing privacy under the Stored Communications Act. *The Georgetown Law Journal*, *98*(4). Retrieved from http://papers.ssrn.com/sol3/Delivery.cfm/SSRN_ID1596975_code1461162.pdf?abstractid=1596975&mirid=2

Schlachter, F. (2012). Has the battery bubble burst? *APSNews*, *8*(21), 8. Retrieved October 2012 from http://www.aps.org/publications/apsnews/

Schulman, A., Navda, V., Ramjee, R., Spring, N., Deshpande, P., Grunewald, C., . . . Padmanabhan, V. N. (2010). Bartendr: A practical approach to energy-aware cellular data scheduling. In N. H. Vaidya, S. Banerjee & D. Katabi (Eds.), MOBICOM (pp. 85-96). ACM. doi:10.1145/1859995.1860006

Song, C., Qu, Z., Blumm, N., & Barabási, A.-L. (2010). Limits of predictability in human mobility. *Science*, *327*(5968), 1018–1021. doi:10.1126/science.1177170 PMID:20167789

Weiser, M. (1991). The computer for the 21st century. *Scientific American*, *265*(3), 66–75. doi:10.1038/scientificamerican0991-94 PMID:1754874

Zhang, X., Kunjithapatham, A., Jeong, S., & Gibbs, S. (2011). Towards an elastic application model for augmenting the computing capabilities of mobile devices with cloud computing. *MONET*, *16*, 270–284.

Zhang, X., Schiffman, J., Gibbs, S., Kunjithapatham, A., & Jeong, S. (2009). Securing elastic applications on mobile devices for cloud computing. In R. Sion & D. Song (Eds.), CCSW (pp. 127-134). ACM. doi:10.1145/1655008.1655026

KEY TERMS AND DEFINITIONS

AllJoyn: Is an open source software framework which offers a peer-to-peer communication environment for heterogeneous distributed systems across different device classes with emphasis on mobility, security and dynamism, by implementing the D-Bus protocol. It provides an abstraction layer allowing it to run on multiple operating systems such as Linux distributions (Ubuntu included) and most versions of Microsoft Windows (Windows 7 included).

Cloud Intent: Is an Intent container which adds an extra action and extra component (the extra fields in the Cloud Intent are used instead of the original ones). The extra action is used in the Intent Resolution mechanism in the cloud to substitute for the main one.

Cloud Receiver: Is a Broadcast Receiver registered into the system and waiting for Cloud Intent actions. This component is responsible for reacting to cloud intents, internal (from the device) or external (from the cloud). This component further interacts with the HYCCUPS framework to offload execution into the cloud.

Context-Awareness: Is a property of mobile devices that is defined complementarily to location awareness. Whereas location may determine how certain processes in a device operate, context may be applied more flexibly with mobile users, especially with users of smart phones. Context awareness originated as a term from ubiquitous computing or as so-called pervasive computing which sought to deal with linking changes in the environment with computer systems, which are otherwise static.

Energy Efficiency: Is the goal to reduce the amount of energy required to provide products and services. There are many motivations to improve energy efficiency. Reducing energy use reduces energy costs and may result in a financial cost saving to consumers if the energy savings offset any additional costs of implementing an energy efficient technology. Reducing energy use is also seen as a solution to the problem of reducing carbon dioxide emissions.

Fixed Mobile Terminal (FMT): Is a plugged-in smartphone terminal. Acts as a Fixed Terminal, but may rapidly return to a mobility state (MT).

Fixed Terminal (FT): Is a wearable computer, and will always be available for executing workloads. This is an optional component, as it raises compatibility issues: the developer has to explicitly redesign the mobile application code so it can be deployed on other platforms.

Mobile Cloud Computing (MCC): Is the combination of cloud computing, mobile computing and wireless networks to bring rich computational resources to mobile users, network operators, as well as cloud computing providers. The ultimate goal of MCC is to enable execution of rich mobile applications on a plethora of mobile devices, with a rich user experience. MCC provides business opportunities for mobile network operators as well as cloud providers.

Mobile Terminal (MT): Is a smartphone terminal, not plugged in. Its main characteristic is mobility. Not always available for executing workloads.

Mobile-to-Mobile Contextual Offloading: Is a concept in which handhelds make use of a contextual search algorithm to schedule the remote execution of tasks in trusted smartphone communities based on predicting the availability and mobility of nearby devices.

Opportunistic Mobile Networks: Consist of human-carried mobile devices that communicate with each other in a store-carry-and-forward fashion, without any infrastructure. Compared to the classical networks, they present distinct challenges. In opportunistic networks, disconnections and highly variable delays caused by human mobility are the norm rather than an exception. The solution consists of dynamically building routes, as each node acts according to the store-carry-and-forward paradigm. Thus, contacts between nodes are viewed as opportunities to move data closer to the destination. Such networks are therefore formed between nodes spread across the environment, without any knowledge of a network topology. The routes between nodes are dynamically created, and nodes can be opportunistically used as a next hop for bringing each message closer to the destination. Nodes may store a message, carry it around, and forward it when they encounter the destination or a node that is more likely to reach the destination.

Chapter 9
H.265 Video Streaming in Mobile Cloud Networks

Qi Wang
University of the West of Scotland, UK

Chunbo Luo
University of the West of Scotland, UK

James Nightingale
University of the West of Scotland, UK

Zeeshan Pervez
University of the West of Scotland, UK

Jose M. Alcaraz-Calero
University of the West of Scotland, UK

Xinheng Wang
University of the West of Scotland, UK

Christos Grecos
University of the West of Scotland, UK

ABSTRACT

Mobile video applications have started to dominate the global mobile data traffic in recent years, and both opportunities and challenges have arisen when the emerging mobile cloud paradigm is introduced to support the resource-demanding video processing and networking services. This chapter offers in-depth discussions for content- and context-aware, adaptive, robust, secure, and real-time video applications in mobile cloud networks. The chapter describes and analyses the essential building blocks including the state-of-the-art technologies and standards on video encoding, adaptive streaming, mobile cloud computing, and resource management, and the associated security issues. The focus is context-aware adaptive streaming based on the latest video coding standard H.265 in the context of Internet-centric mobile cloud networking. Built upon selected building blocks underpinned by promising approaches and emerging standards, an integrated architecture is proposed towards achieving next-generation smart video streaming for mobile cloud users, with future research directions in this field identified.

INTRODUCTION

Mobile video has become the dominant consumer of mobile network bandwidth in recent years. According to Cisco (2014), mobile video traffic exceeded 50% for the first time in history in 2012. It is predicted that mobile video will account for 69% of the total mobile data traffic by 2018, increasing 14 folds from 2013. Such remarkable growth in mobile video will pose tremendous challenges to mobile

DOI: 10.4018/978-1-4666-8225-2.ch009

network operators, video service providers as well as end mobile users, who are equipped with mobile devices such as smartphones or tablets. These mobile devices are typically resource constrained in terms of storage, computation and processing capacity, energy (battery) and network bandwidth.

Meanwhile, the Mobile Cloud Computing and Networking (MCCN) model has emerged as a promising paradigm towards resolving the increasing conflict between the resource-demanding mobile video applications and the resource-limited mobile networks and devices. Such an integration between mobile devices and applications, and mobile cloud computing and networks has been widely recognised and indeed appears inevitable. According to Gartner (2013), Mobile Device Diversity and Management, Mobile Apps and Applications, and five cloud-related technologies are listed among the top ten technological trends for 2014. Although no universal definition exists for various mobile clouds, a mobile cloud is typically a mobile extension to an existing infrastructure-based cloud, which features a huge wealth of computing powers, storage and other resources. Mobile video processing tasks can thus be offloaded from the mobile device to the mobile cloud for faster processing, higher storage capacity and reduced battery consumption, among other potential benefits. By exploring MCCN, mobile application developers are enabled to develop applications that can harness the power of virtualised resources for processing huge volume of data and provisioning a richer app usage experience.

However, there are a number of open research issues to be addressed. In particular, there is typically a communication resource bottleneck between the cloud and the mobile cloud users. Fortunately, the latest advances in video compression standards can help substantially reduce the bandwidth requirement for transmitting or storing the videos. The ITU-T H.265 standard (ITU-T, 2013), also known as High Efficiency Video Coding (HEVC) and MPEG-H Part 2, was standardised in 2013 and is the next-generation video coding scheme. (It is noted that H.265 and HEVC are used inter-changeably in this chapter.) H.265 is capable of doubling the compression efficiency and thus halving the bandwidth demands without losing the visual quality, compared with the current H.264 Advanced Video Coding (H.264/AVC) standard (ITU-T, 2012). Such a remarkable bandwidth saving in H.265 coded videos particularly appeals to mobile communications, where bandwidth and storage is often constrained. On the other hand, the high compression efficiency in H.265 is achieved at the cost of high computation complexity. This in turn entails the exploitation of cloud computing technologies. Nevertheless, it is challenging to achieve real-time video processing in a mobile cloud environment.

Moreover, adaptive video transmission schemes, such as the MPEG Dynamic Adaptive Streaming over HTTP (DASH) standard (ISO/IEC, 2014a), are able to adapt to the context such as the variations in network conditions especially bandwidth and the end user's preference or device capability. Content awareness of the video stream being delivered can be leveraged to significantly improve the performance of the adaptation. For instance, it can be explored to prioritise the video packets in terms of their importance in affecting the end user's perceived visual quality. Consequently, the video application server or other Media-Aware Network Element (MANE) along the end-to-end route can selectively drop the least important packets first in response to the reduced bandwidth. When delivered over error- and/or loss-prone networks such as the concerned Internet Protocol (IP) based mobile clouds, end-to-end robust transmission and processing should be addressed including error correction, error/loss concealment and other protection or recovery schemes. In light of the growing prominence of the new H.265 standard, more research into H.265 codec-specific, content- and context-aware video applications is highly demanded.

In addition, more intelligent cloud resource management including resource monitoring, allocation and so on is desired to cope with the enormous workloads generated by computation-intensive video processing tasks. End-to-end security concerns associated with video processing, storage, distribution and access using MCCN should also be dealt with. Finally, an integrated architecture is still missing towards achieving advanced H.265-encoded video streaming in MCCN.

This chapter highlights the key challenges and promising solutions for H.265-based mobile cloud video streaming in the above context. The reminder of the chapter is structured as follows. The Background section introduces MCCN, and networked video applications in cloud environments. The subsequent sections present the state of the art in areas related to H.265 video streaming. It is started with H.265 video coding, especially cloud-assisted processing. Next, various adaptive H.265 streaming approaches based on DASH, SHVC (the scalable extension to HEVC) and MMT (MPEG Media Transport) are highlighted. Resource and security management for H.265 cloud applications are then discussed. Based on the critical analysis of the above related areas, a novel framework is proposed that seamlessly integrates the essential building blocks, built upon the most promising standards and approaches, towards realising next-generation video applications in MCCN environments.

BACKGROUND

Mobile Cloud Computing and Networking (MCCN)

Mobile Cloud Computing and Networking (MCCN) have recently emerged with the convergence of mobile networking and cloud computing, driven by the requirements of ubiquitous access to mobile Internet services including cloud services. There are various MCCN models and platforms, as discussed by Fernando et al. (2013) and Liu et al. (2013). The most common MCCN paradigm is formed by extending Internet-resident infrastructure-based cloud services to mobile network users, and can be referred to as Internet-centric MCCN. In Internet-centric MCCN, the cloud infrastructure and services are located in the Internet, and the cloud services are delivered to the mobile cloud users via the Internet, e.g., an Internet-based Content Distribution Network (CDN), and one (or more) radio access network (RAN). To facilitate localised cloud access, a scaled-down version of a cloud, often referred to as a cloudlet, can be deployed in the local area wireless network or a RAN. This kind of paradigm can be called cloudlet MCCN. Another type of MCCN is based on ad hoc network-based cloud, where a number of mobile nodes employ cloud computing technologies to share their computation and/or storage capability to provide peer-to-peer infrastructure-less, sometimes opportunistic, cloud services to each other. As shown in Figure 1, this chapter focuses on video streaming in the context of Internet-centric MCCN, which is the most widely recognised MCCN paradigm. It is noted that a core mobile network that has a packet-switched domain will be required to be located between the RAN and the Internet when the RAN needs the core mobile network to function, as commonly found in cellular systems such as the Third Generation (3G) e.g., WCDMA (Wideband Code Division Multiple Access), the Fourth Generation (4G) e.g., the LTE (Long Term Evolution) Advanced and beyond. When WiFi is the RAN, it directly provides Internet access. For brevity, the potential core mobile network is not shown in Figure 1.

Numerous MCCN projects and studies are pre-existing or on-going. Highlighted here are two notable international projects that further couple the cloud domain and the mobile network by pushing the principles of cloud computing to the RAN level for elastic, on-demand and cost-effective services.

Figure 1. Internet-centric MCCN system

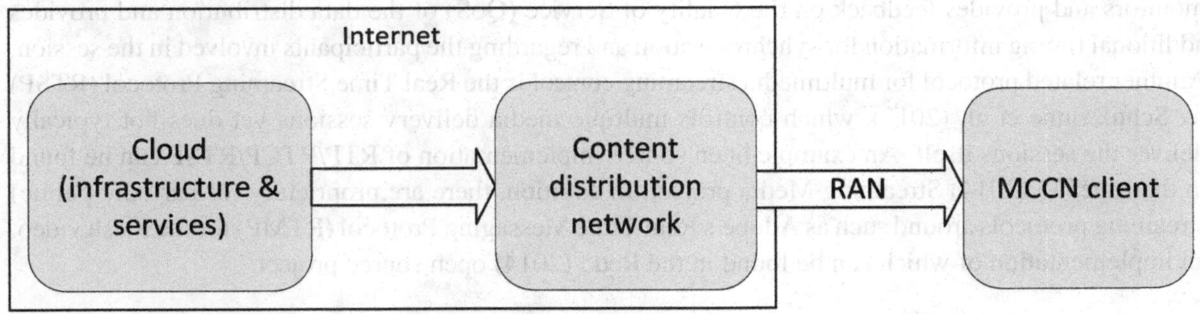

The EU MCN (Mobile Cloud Network) project (MCN, 2014) focuses on designing an Internet-centric MCCN architecture that is compliant with 3GPP (The Third Generation Partnership Project). MCN has been investigating various related issues to apply cloud computing and virtualisation technologies to telecommunication (cellular) networks such as the virtualisation of RANs and the LTE core network, cloud service migration and continuity in cloud-based LTE networks, end-to-end mobile-aware service deployment and a follow-me cloud concept (content follows the movement of the user), and so on. Sharing a similar vision in virtualising the RAN, the WNC (Wireless Network Cloud) project by Zhu et al. (2011) attempts to offer all the necessary transmission and processing resources for a RAN to operate in a cloud mode by exploring cloud computing and virtualisation in general-purpose, low-cost IT platforms. A prototype has been created featuring a software radio defined virtual WiMAX (Worldwide Interoperability for Microwave Access) base station implemented on a commodity server. Whilst those studies mainly emphasise advancing the MCCN infrastructure, this chapter focuses on video applications especially streaming in MCCN environments.

Video Coding Standards and Streaming Protocols

Video coding standards have been evolving rapidly in the last two decades. Among various standards from different standardisation bodies, the MPEG-x/H.26x series are of particular interest. These standards are jointly developed by the International Telecommunication Union - Telecommunication Standardization Sector (ITU-T) and the International Organization for Standards/International Electrotechnical Commission (ISO/IEC). The most well-known ones are MPEG-2/H.262 and MPEG-4/H.264 standards. The latter, in particular H.264/AVC, is the current-generation video coding standard that dominates today's MPEG video applications. JM (2014) and x264 (2014) are example open source H.264 implementations. H.265 (or HEVC) is the latest video compressing standard, defined in 2013.

Video streaming applications including Video on Demand (VoD), IPTV, live Internet streaming, video conferencing, online gaming and so on have gained tremendous popularity in recent years. Regarding the underlying video streaming protocols, the Internet Engineering Task Force (IETF) has defined several related standards. The Real-Time Transport Protocol (RTP) by Schulzrinne et al. (2003) is the primary end-to-end multimedia streaming standard for IP networks and typically operates over the UDP transport-layer protocol. RTP offers timing information for playback synchronisation via timestamps, detection of packet loss or out-of-order delivery via sequence numbers, and application-level framing via profiles and payload formats (including the H.26x family). Whilst RTP packetises (at the application level) and delivers the actual media data such as video, the companion RTP Control Protocol (RTCP) monitors and provides feedback on the Quality of Service (QoS) of the data distribution and provides additional timing information for synchronisation and regarding the participants involved in the session. Another related protocol for multimedia streaming control is the Real Time Streaming Protocol (RTSP) by Schulzrinne et al. (2013), which controls multiple media delivery sessions yet does not typically deliver the sessions itself. An example open source implementation of RTP/RTCP/RTSP can be found in the Live555 (2014) Streaming Media project. In addition, there are proprietary (or partially public) streaming protocols around such as Adobe's Real-Time Messaging Protocol (RTMP) for the Flash video, an implementation of which can be found in the Red5 (2014) open source project.

Cloud-Assisted Video Processing and Streaming

Despite the great promise by (mobile) cloud computing and networking, deploying cloud video applications and systems poses various challenges. Video applications such as video streaming (either live or on-demand) are delay-sensitive and demand high bandwidth to deliver. However, achieving high QoS in terms of low latency/delay and high throughput is not straightforward considering the time-consuming video coding and processing operations even assisted by a cloud and the best effort transmission nature of Internet.

Firstly, to speed up the video processing, parallelised/distributed computation in a cloud platform needs to be explored. Hadoop MapReduce (Dean & Ghemawat, 2008) is a powerful and popular approach for this purpose and has been employed for different cloud-assisted video processing tasks such as encoding by Pereira et al. (2010) and transcoding by Lao et al. (2012). Essentially, the input video is split into multiple independent video segments, which are then mapped (allocated) to different processing units to be processed in parallel as sub-tasks. The results from each processing unit are reduced (aggregated) into a single output video stream. A tricky part is to ensure that the video segments can be independently processed, and this is typically achieved through a GOP (Group of Pictures) based splitting. Lin et al. (2013) further considered adaptive task segmentation and sub-task load balancing to reduce the total time to complete the whole video transcoding task, which optimises this approach towards more timely processing support.

Secondly, to minimise network delivery delay once the video is processed, delay-aware transmission schemes should be applied to help low-latency cloud media streaming applications. For instance, Space4time (Zeng, Veeravalli, & Wei, 2014) is a latency-sensitive content distribution and request routing scheme, which balances storage and network capacity for reduced delay performance. Meanwhile, delay performance may be jointly considered with bandwidth consumption to optimise content distribution through Traffic-Latency-Minimisation (Guan & Choi, 2014). Moreover, caching at the streamer is a useful mechanism for faster video release, and caching policies should be carefully designed to minimise both the initial waiting time for an end user's video demand request and the total disruption time during the stream. The cloud-based QoS-aware streaming architecture presented by Sebestyen et al. (2013) offers a solution employing on-demand dynamic resources allocation and caching capabilities. In addition, architectural enhancements to the Internet-centric MCCN can be introduced. For instance, distributed localised cloudlets that are closer to the cloud video application user can be deployed to complement the services provided by a cloud located in the remote Internet. Aligned with this idea, Islam and Grégoire (2012) presented the Edge Cloud architecture and demonstrated a prototype that transcodes audio/video stream.

Thirdly, context awareness can facilitate adaptive video streaming that improves the QoS and user's perceived Quality of Experience (QoE). For instance, Chang, Lai and Huang (2012) considered various context factors including mobile device resources, multimedia codec characteristics and the current network environment in their design of an adaptive streamer for mobile devices. Improved QoS was achieved in terms of timely streaming, decreased content storage and reduced power consumption of mobile devices.

Finally, streaming performance under user mobility in the MCCN environment needs to be addressed, and thus a corresponding streaming service migration (mobility/handover) scheme should be incorporated by a mobile cloud streaming system. To this end, among a number of researchers, Sardis et al. (2013) proposed a QoS-aware service populating model, where services run on a home public cloud can be migrated to other public clouds in different geographical locations depending on service demands and network status.

Whilst H.265 defined in 2013 has emerged as the latest video coding standard, it is noted that the vast majority of MPEG-based cloud video applications and systems employ H.264 or its precursor MPEG-2, and so far very few have explored H.265, which will be focused on from the next section.

H.265 HIGH EFFICIENCY VIDEO CODING

The new H.265 video compression standard offers benefits in terms of reduced bandwidth consumption and the ability to handle larger spatial resolutions such as the new 4k and 8k Ultra-High Definition (UHD) (Nakasu, 2012) formats. However, these benefits are achieved at the expense of substantially increased computational complexity compared with its predecessors. Encoding times for the new standard can be up to 11 times greater than for H.264/AVC, as discussed by Bossen et al. (2012), and Hu and Yang (2014). The decoding complexity of H.265 is not significantly greater than that of H.264 though, as presented by Bossen et al. (2012), and Viitanen et al. (2012). Software decoding of 3840×2160 (2160p) video can be performed in real-time (Fraunhofer-HHI, 2014a). Therefore, the biggest practical obstacle to adoption of the new standard is the complexity of the encoding process. This need for greater computational resources may prompt content providers to consider cloud-based encoding and transcoding systems, where on-demand resource allocation is available. In the consumer domain, the latest mobile devices are already capable of capturing UHD content but may not have the computational or battery resources to encode with H.265 in real time. Cloud-based H.265 encoding offers a potential solution to resource limitations in both mobile (MCCN) environments and large-scale commercial production scenarios. Efforts to reduce the encoding time of H.265 have focused on two main areas: complexity reduction and parallelisation.

Complexity of H.265

The coding layer of H.265 is based on the same hybrid coding approach employed in H.264/AVC. The main features include inter-picture motion-compensated prediction and intra-picture prediction, closed-loop filtering, 2D transformation of spatial residual difference signals, and adaptive entropy coding. Figure 2 shows a simplified block diagram of the H.265 encoder.

Figure 2. A simplified block diagram showing the main operations of the H.265 encoder

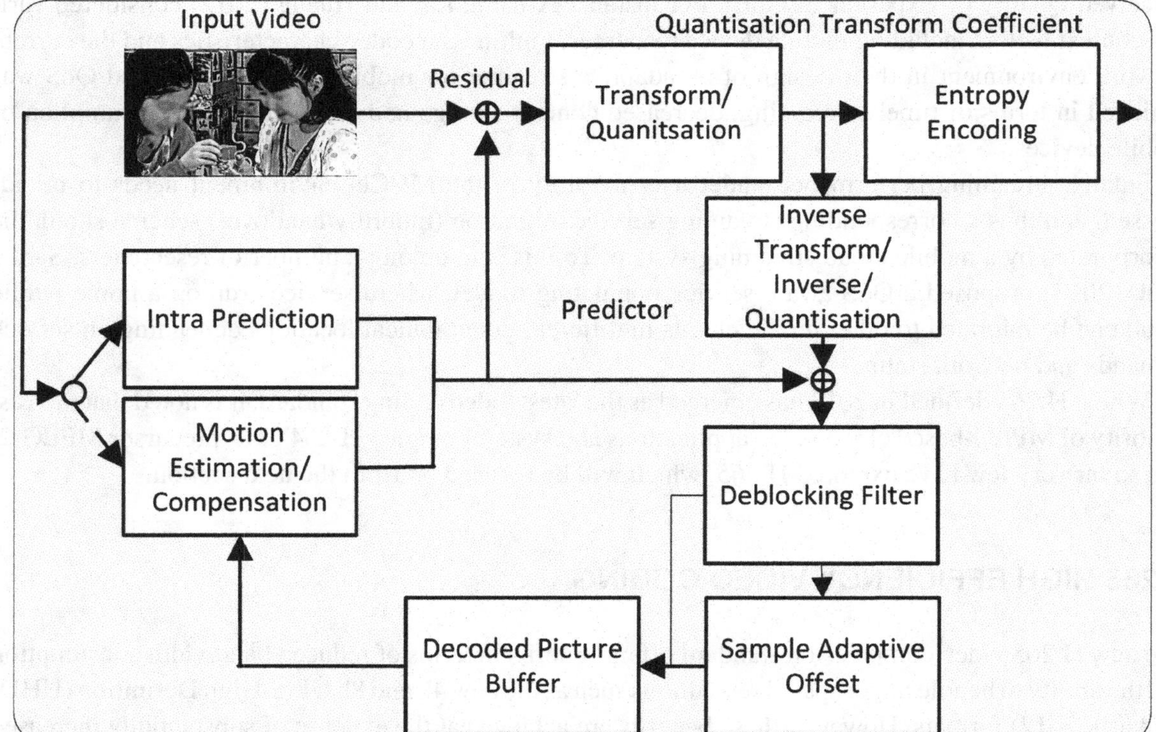

The biggest change from previous standards is a new, larger coding block structure with more flexible sub-partitioning. Variable-block-sized Coding Units (CUs) sub-partition a picture into rectangular regions. CUs replace the macroblocks used in H.264. Each CU is the root of a quadtree-based coding structure, containing variable-block-sized Prediction Units (PUs) and Transform Units (TUs). At each level of the quadtree structure, the Rate-Distortion (RD) costs of either encoding as a single block or as four equal sub-divisions are compared, and the lower cost option is chosen as the candidate. This recursive search is computationally intensive and significantly increases encoding time compared with previous standards. An example of H.265 picture partitioning is shown in Figure 3, with CUs denoted by blue lines and PU shapes by green lines.

Fast Encoding Methods for H.265

Complexity reduction proposals for H.265 limit the number of operations needed to determine CU, PU and TU sizes, usually by reducing the search domain. A rough mode decision algorithm included in the standard reduces the number of angular prediction modes that need to be tested using RD optimization. A lightweight method of encoding of images (Liang, Peng, & Xu, 2013) using Intra prediction leveraged the observation that some features of H.265 add complexity to Intra encoding but deliver only marginal improvements in efficiency. By limiting the maximum coding unit size to 16x16, having a maximum quadtree depth of two and skipping the residual quadtree search at the transform stage, encoding times were cut by 82%.

Figure 3. An example of picture partitioning in H.265

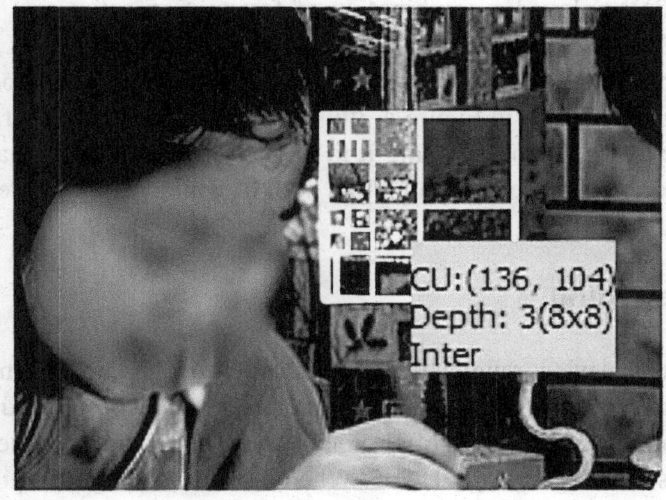

Reducing Inter prediction complexity was addressed by Correa et al. (2011), who firstly proposed a dynamic CU selection scheme giving encoding time reductions of up to 60% and a subsequent enhanced method, which took account of spatial and temporal aspects of the video to further improve the RD performance of their initial scheme. Other approaches to complexity reduction for Inter prediction have included the fast pyramid motion divergence method by Xiong et al. (2014), where CU size was selected based on the similarity of the current CU to its nearest neighbours. A confidence interval based fast motion estimation method (Hu & Yang, 2013) aimed to reduce encoding times by up to 70%. Each of these approaches was based on the HM reference software (HM, 2014) for HEVC. Alternative H.265 software encoders include the open source x265 project (MultiCoreWare, 2014) and proprietary encoders such as a real-time full HD encoder developed by Fraunhofer-HHI (2014b). Texas Instruments (Hazari, Karandikar, & Sanghvi, 2014) have developed an experimental System on Chip (SoC) architecture for H.265 encoding of 4k resolution video on handheld devices. However, encoding in the mobile domain will continue to present challenges that may be best addressed by offloading resource-intensive tasks to cloud-based platforms.

HEVC Transcoding

A great deal of the existing video content amassed by content providers is in either MPEG-2 or H.264/AVC (MPEG-4) formats. If H.265 is to be widely adopted, this existing content needs to be available in the new format. Most of the proposed methods of transcoding from MPEG-2 or H.264/AVC to H.265 have adopted a common approach that reduces the need for a full decode and re-encode cycle. Motion-related information is extracted from the encoded domain of an incoming stream and used to predict CU splitting or PU mode decisions in the H.265 encoder. The MPEG-2 to HEVC scheme by Shanableh et al. (2013) and the H.264 to HEVC scheme by Peixot et al. (2014) both initially performed full decoding and re-encoding of early frames in the video to train their algorithm. Subsequently, mappings between the motion characteristics of the input and output codecs were predicted for the rest of the frames in the sequence. This approach may have limitations for sequences with scene cuts.

To H.264 transcode streams, Jiang and Chen (2013) employed a motion vector clustering approach, while Shen et al. (2013) employed a combination of fast motion estimation and prediction mode determination derived from motion vectors in the H.264 input stream. Fang et al. (2014) also took a similar approach of mapping H.264 motion vectors, residuals and prediction modes to those of H.265. A basic transcoder diagram, shown in Figure 4, illustrates the principle of extracting motion-related information from the existing video and using it to predict H.265 encoding parameters such as CU depth selection and prediction mode determination, both of which result in a reduced search domain and quicker encoding.

Cloud-Based Transcoding

Since media is consumed on devices ranging from smartphones to high-end TVs, media files uploaded to a VoD service may be transcoded into a format more suitable for client device and transmission network capabilities. Existing commercial services offer cloud-based transcoding between MPEG-2, MPEG-4 or other popular formats, although not yet H.265. When fast transcoding is required, incoming videos are spilt across a number of workflows that are each allocated to a different node or cluster within the cloud environment, as shown in Figure 5.

Figure 4. Block diagram of a typical H.264 or MPEG-2 to H.265 transcoder

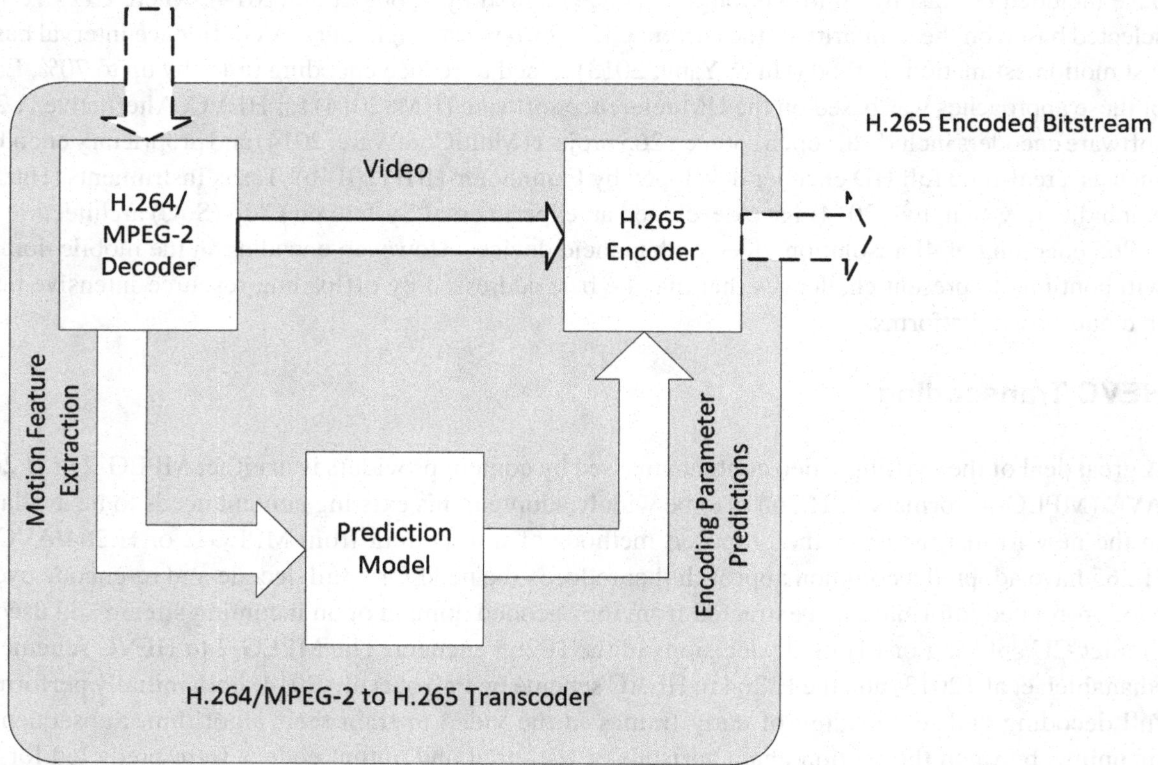

Figure 5. Fast parallel transcoding of a single video in the cloud

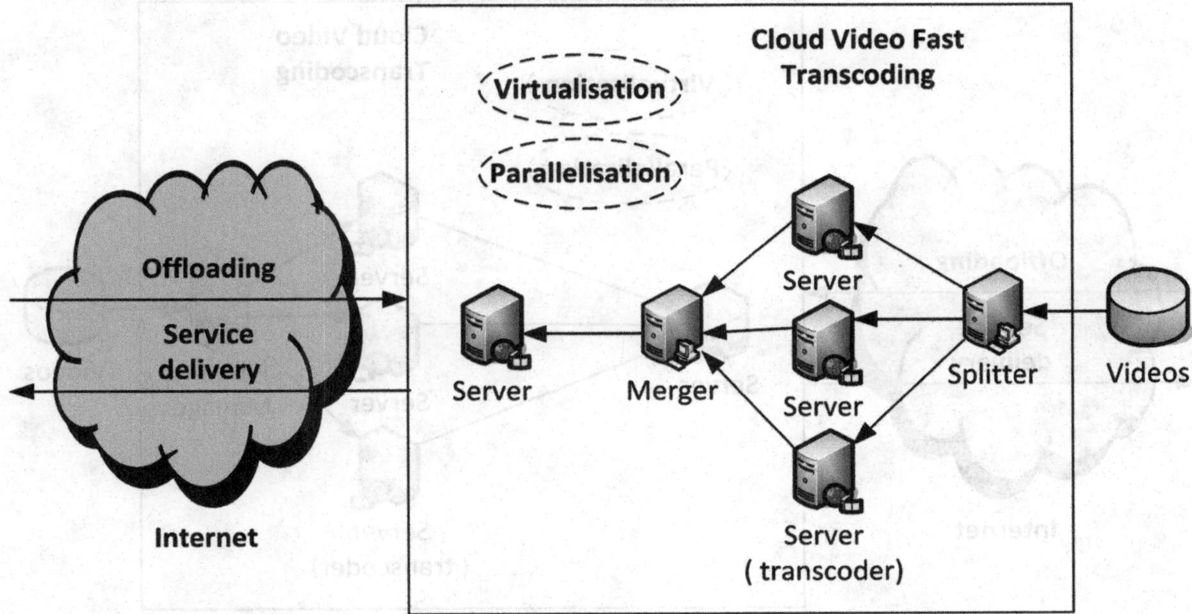

Either spatial or temporal splitting approaches may be employed. If transcoding is chosen on the basis of cost or resource availability with no time constraint, each video sequence may be allocated a single node with multiple sequences concurrently being decoded (Figure 6).

Managing resource allocation and work queues can be challenging. Jokhio et al. (2013) used a temporal splitting approach in a scheme to predict resource allocation needs for transcoding in the cloud. Barlas (2012) conducted extensive studies of cluster-based parallel video transcoding and recommended strategies, including two-pass encoding for efficient deployment of variable bitrate video encoding. In the CloudMov proposal by Wu et al. (2013), both Infrastructure as a Service (IaaS) and Platform as a Service (PaaS) were employed in a scheme for cloud-based transcoding of television content for delivery to mobile client devices, taking into account the state of the transmission channel available to each mobile client.

Cloud-Assisted HEVC Processing and HEVC Parallelization

Using H.265 to encode video, especially at UHD resolutions, requires substantial computing resources. The standard defines parallel processing tools including Tiles, Wavefront Parallel Processing (WPP) etc., which can be used to deliver fast implementations of multi-threaded encoders for multi-core processors and GPUs or parallel encoders that make use of the resources available in the cloud. In addition to the Tiles and WPP implementations included in the HM reference software (JCT-VC, 2013), Khan et al. (2014) have made available the ces265 lightweight, open source parallel encoder based on H.265 Tiles.

Offloading the complex computation of H.265 encoding to cloud-based resources is an attractive proposition with many potential use cases. Li et al. (2011) proposed a cloud-assisted method of selecting reference pictures, which aimed to maintain coding efficiency while minimising the size of decoder

Figure 6. Transcoding of multiple videos concurrently using pipeline management

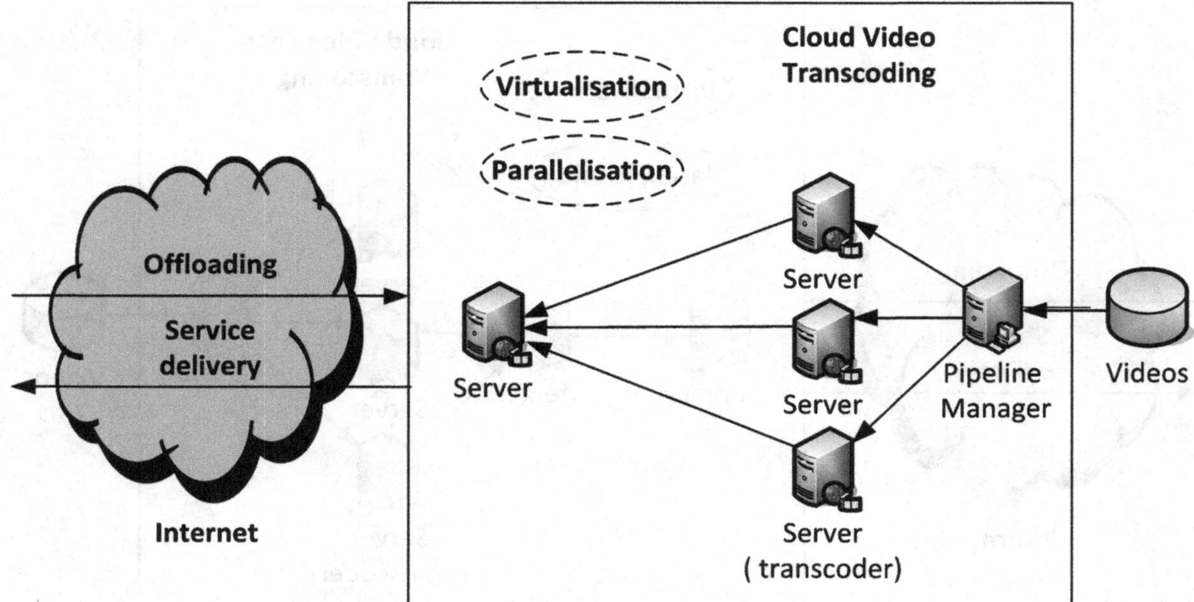

buffers. A two-tier system utilised multiple nodes to concurrently calculate the RD cost of using different reference frames with the results passed to a controlling node, which chooses the optimum reference frame. Although parallel processing tools are available for H.265, there are still challenges in implementing them efficiently on cloud platforms. Yan et al. (2014) have identified the issue of dependencies between neighbouring CUs of the same frame, which reduce the effectiveness of parallelisation strategies. They mitigated this problem by identifying which CUs are dependent on others. CUs were then appropriately organised on the parallel work queues (in their case threads for a multicore processor) to reduce the number of processes that need to wait for another to finish. Similarly, Choi and Jang (2012) considered dependencies between adjacent CUs and suggested strategies to select the appropriate scan order and detect when parallel PU skip/merge operations could be performed in H.265 Tiles-based parallel encoding. Both of these proposals and that of Zhao et al. (2013) investigated the less complex case of Intra encoding of H.265 in parallel, with schemes primarily aimed at multicore architectures rather than the distributed architectures of cloud platforms. Therefore, further research in this area is still highly demanded.

H.265 ADAPTIVE STREAMING IN MOBILE CLOUD

HEVC Streaming Overview

In light of the superior efficiency in video storage and transmission by utilising H.265 coding, H.265-based video streaming is a promising approach for future multimedia applications. There are various standard-based frameworks that can be explored to deploy an H.265 mobile cloud streaming system.

Figure 7 shows the high-level protocol stack of H.265 streaming systems. Streaming applications based on H.265 (or its extensions such as SHVC) can operate over MPEG DASH (ISO/IEC, 2014a) or the emerging MPEG Media Transport (MMT) standard (ISO/IEC, 2014b), with the video data in both cases typically encapsulated in the ISO Base Media File Format (BMFF). DASH in turn runs over HTTP/TCP, whilst MMT supports existing application-level transport protocols such as HTTP and RTP, as well as the new MMT Protocol (MMTP). Alternatively, H.265 streaming applications can directly operate over RTP, under which UDP is typically employed. The bottom layer of this stack is IP networks, where IP-based mobile cloud networks are of particular interest.

Very few HEVC streaming proposals are pre-existing and most of them employed RTP directly for HEVC streaming. One of the earliest contributions to this field is the HEVStream framework proposed in (Nightingale, Wang, & Grecos, 2012), who designed and implemented a practical end-to-end infrastructure-mode wireless testbed for streaming and evaluating HEVC-encoded video content over lossy IP networks. It is noted that packet loss/error has a noticeable negative impact on the quality of the received H.265 video, and should be addressed to support mobile cloud users, who would experience packet loss and errors due to mobility and being wireless. When compared with H.264/AVC, the impairment visibility is more evident in H.265 due to the increased temporal prediction between pictures and thus prolonged propagation of the visual artefacts through pictures, as reported by Wallendael et al. (2012). In addition, the performance of HEVC in error-prone mobile networks was further studied by Pinol et al. (2013), who applied HEVC streaming in a vehicular network simulator. In the simulation, road-side units broadcast the same H.265 video in a synchronised fashion. To mitigate the propagation of visual impairment caused by packet loss, an intra refresh scheme was introduced. This mechanism was shown

Figure 7. H.265 streaming systems

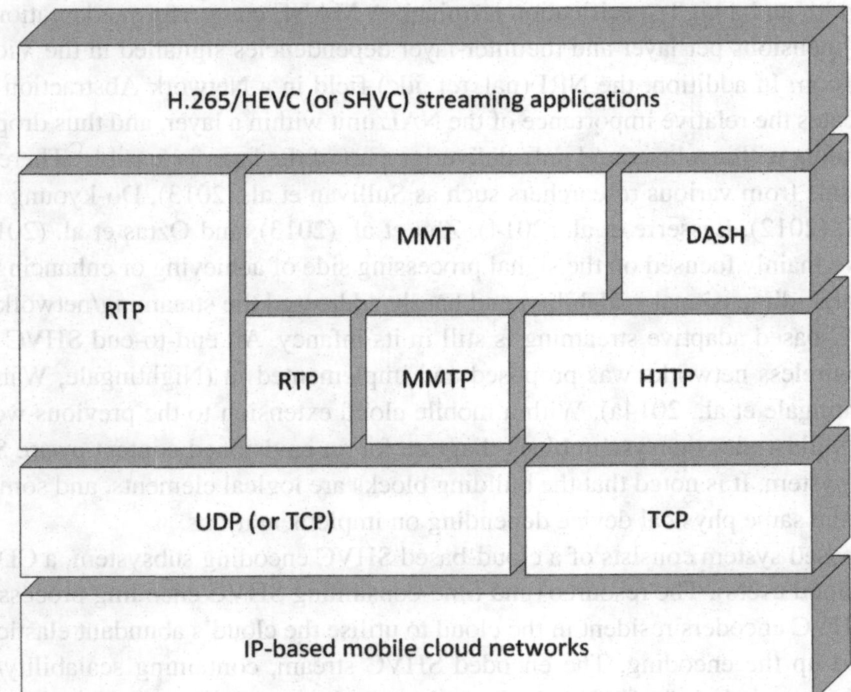

to improve the error resilience of the streaming, yet not sufficiently when the packet loss deteriorated, e.g., due to increased background traffic that competed to occupy the communication channel. These findings indicate that further adaptive streaming schemes with enhanced error-resilience capabilities would be needed for acceptable quality in such disadvantaged networking conditions. In addition, both studies (Nightingale et al., 2012; Pinol et al., 2013) employed HEVC over RTP directly for the streaming. In the following, highlighted are more advanced streaming approaches based on SHVC, DASH and MMT respectively, integrated with cloud-assisted processing, H.265 media/codec awareness and context awareness.

SHVC-Based Streaming

SHVC, the scalable extension to HEVC, is an emerging standard being developed by JCT-VT, and the draft text can be found in the Test Model document edited by Chen et al. (2013). SHVC aims to achieve scalability-based HEVC video adaptation to network resources, terminal capabilities and/or other context concerns. In SHVC, videos are encoded into different, prioritised temporal, spatial and quality (SNR) layers and the prioritisation is determined by the importance of a corresponding layer in terms of its impact on the visual quality of the video. For each of the three dimensions, temporal (already available in HEVC), spatial and quality, the corresponding base layer is the most important layer and thus has the highest priority, whilst the enhancement layers have lower and lower priorities with the increase of the distance from the base layer. To adapt to the context such as the time-varying network bandwidth and/or different mobile user terminals' screen resolution, either all or part of the layers will be selected and then delivered by a MANE in the CDN to the end user. For instance, the base layer only may be delivered over a heavily loaded network and to a legacy terminal; or, the base layer plus the first enhancement layer and part of the second enhancement layer may best match a different scenario featured with higher available bandwidth and a high-specification terminal. A MANE can perform adaptations by utilising the scalability dimensions per layer and the inter-layer dependencies signalled in the Video Parameter Set (VPS) extension. In addition, the NRI (nal_ref_idc) field in a Network Abstraction Layer (NAL) unit header indicates the relative importance of the NAL unit within a layer, and thus dropping the least important NAL units within a layer and only delivering part of the layer is feasible. There are a number of related proposals from various researchers such as Sullivan et al. (2013), Do-kyoung and Budagavi (2013), Shi et al. (2012), Lasserre et al. (2014), Zhu et al. (2013), and Oztas et al. (2014). However, these studies have mainly focused on the signal processing side of achieving or enhancing SHVC's one or more of the three-dimensional scalability, and hardly addressed the streaming/networking side.

In fact, SHVC-based adaptive streaming is still in its infancy. An end-to-end SHVC streaming architecture over wireless networks was proposed and implemented in (Nightingale, Wang, & Grecos, 2013) and (Nightingale et al., 2014a). With a mobile cloud extension to the previous work taken into account, Figure 8 illustrates the system block diagram for an envisioned context-aware SHVC mobile cloud streaming system. It is noted that the building blocks are logical elements, and some of them can be collocated in the same physical device depending on implementations.

This SHVC-based system consists of a cloud-based SHVC encoding subsystem, a CDN and SHVC clients (mobile cloud users). The resource- and time-consuming SHVC encoding process is performed by a cluster of SHVC encoders resident in the cloud to utilise the cloud's abundant elastic computation capacity to speed up the encoding. The encoded SHVC stream, containing scalability/prioritisation information, is then copied to the CDN, which can be a traditional CDN or a cloud-based one located

Figure 8. Context-aware SHVC mobile cloud streaming system

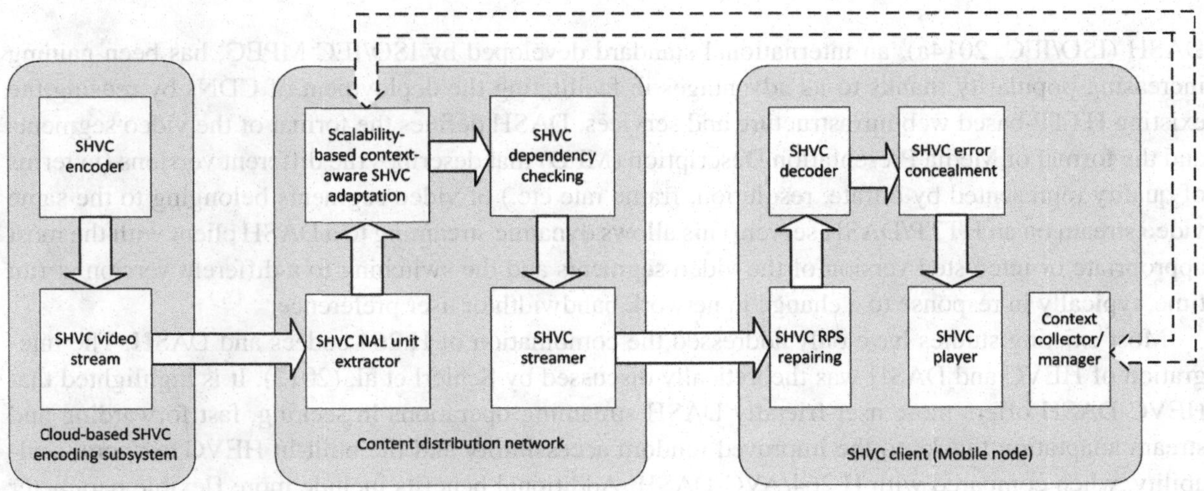

within the same or a different cloud to explore the storage capacity of the cloud. The CDN is equipped with MANEs, which perform scalability-based adaptations based on the mobile cloud user's current context, fed from a context collector and manager agent, which is desirably resident at the mobile node. Typical context parameters may include available network bandwidth, the mobile terminal's capability such as preferred resolution (e.g., HD or SD) and frame rate for playback, energy/power (battery level), cost, and other user preferences. Typically such context awareness is established and dynamically updated between the client and the MANE throughout the streaming session's lifetime, as shown by the dotted arrows in Figure 2. Accordingly, SHVC NAL units are either selected or dropped according to their individual prioritisation information, which includes but is not limited to the information carried in the header of the SHVC NAL units extracted from the received video stream. The streaming itself can employ RTP directly, or alternatively utilise DASH or MMT.

Before the actual streaming, an additional dependency checking step is introduced to ensure that none of the remaining NAL units is dependent on a NAL unit that has been dropped in the previous step for decoding. For instance, no higher enhancement layer NAL units should be scheduled to be streamed unless all its lower enhancement layers and the base layer of the same picture have been selected and scheduled. In addition, for each quality and spatial layer, the SHVC Reference Picture Set (RPS) inter-dependency constraint should be taken into account. At the SHVC client, before the received stream is decoded, RPS repairing should be in place to deal with missing reference pictures due to transmission loss/errors. Replacement reference pictures are re-created, e.g., by copying the nearest counterparts. The decoder can then work properly to decompress the SHVC video. Error concealment schemes to handle the artefacts are further applied to enhance the perceived quality of the pictures.

It is worth noting that the content-importance-aware based SHVC prioritisation can be further explored to support other schemes in robust video transmission such as Unequal Error Protection (UEP) or Layer-Aware FEC (LA-FEC), which would further increase the error resilience of the streaming system. An example of employing LA-FEC for H.264/SVC was studied by Hellge et al. (2011), yet this approach in principle can be applied to SHVC in a similar fashion.

DASH-Based Streaming

DASH (ISO/IEC, 2014a), an international standard developed by ISO/IEC MPEG, has been gaining increasing popularity thanks to its advantages in facilitating the deployment of CDNs by reusing the existing HTTP-based web infrastructure and services. DASH defines the format of the video segments and the format of Media Presentation Description (MPD) that describes the different versions (in terms of quality represented by bitrate, resolution, frame rate etc.) of video segments belonging to the same video stream on an HTTP/DASH server. This allows dynamic streaming to a DASH client with the most appropriate or interested version of the video segments and the switching to a different version at run time, typically in response to a change in network bandwidth or user preference.

Most existing studies have only addressed the combination of H.264 codecs and DASH. The integration of HEVC and DASH was theoretically discussed by Schierl et al. (2012). It is highlighted that HEVC-DASH offers more user-friendly DASH streaming operations in seeking, fast forwarding and stream adaptation thanks to the improved random accessibility and the built-in HEVC temporal scalability, when compared with H.264/AVC-DASH. Additional benefits include more flexible parameter generation and the obviously higher video compression efficiency. Furthermore, the performance of H.265-DASH in loss-prone IP networks was empirically evaluated in (Irondi, Wang, & Grecos, 2014).

The following presents a context-aware H.265-DASH streaming system for mobile cloud users, and the building blocks are shown in Figure 9. The system comprises an H.265-DASH encoding subsystem, a CDN, and the DASH clients (mobile nodes). The H.265-DASH encoding is carried out by context-aware H.265 encoders in a cloud. This subsystem creates context-aware H.265-encoded video segments and context-aware MPD files that contain extensions to the standard MPD files with context information included. Both are then copied to a CDN. Upon a request from a DASH client, these video segments are streamed by a DASH streamer to the client via HTTP. The MPD files can be delivered via HTTP or other means. The client employs standard HTTP client as well as DASH segment and MPD parsers. Similar to SHVC streaming, schemes to deal with packet loss and errors after delivery are required for proper decoding and playing back the video. In addition, packetisation and depacketisation are also needed before the video packets are delivered and after they are received, respectively. For simplicity, these functions are not shown in Figure 9.

Figure 9. Context-aware H.265-DASH mobile cloud streaming system

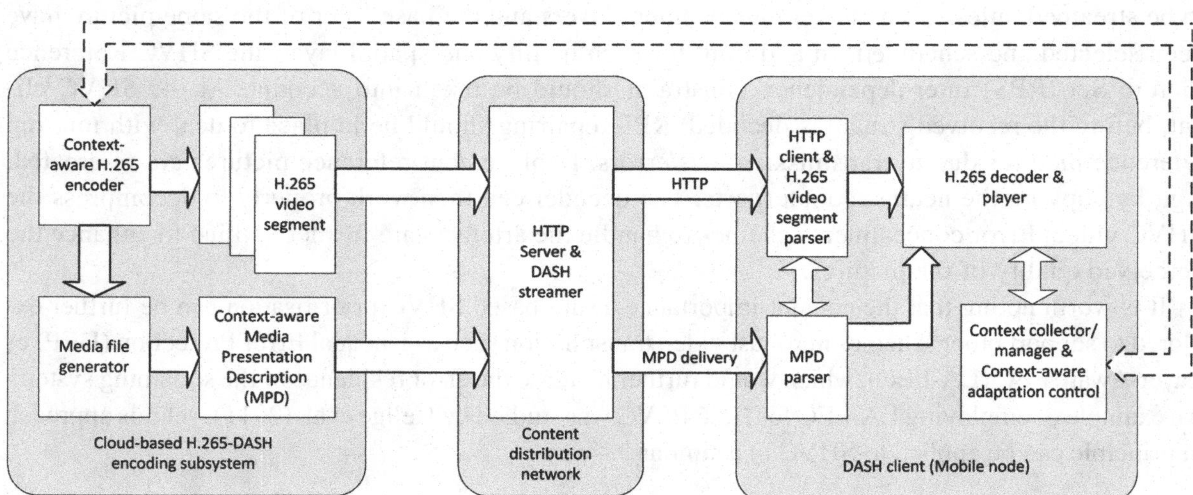

The customisable context collector/manager and the corresponding context-aware adaptation control module is responsible for monitoring and managing the concerned context parameters, and performing the desired adaptations by demanding the switching to video segments that are more suitable for the current context. Again, the context can be represented by one or more contextual parameters including but not limited to available network bandwidth. An agreement of specific context awareness in terms of pre-defined context parameters can be pre-established or dynamically negotiated between the client and the encoding server, and such interactions are logically indicated with the dotted arrows in Figure 9. In simplified scenarios, e.g., where a single context parameter is interested and an agreement is pre-established, such interactions may not be explicitly required.

It is noted that very little existing work have addressed context-aware H.265/HEVC-DASH streaming. In one of the notable early studies, He et al. (2013) proposed a power-aware HEVC-DASH streaming system, where the power consumption in the mobile client is concerned and the aim is to maximise the video quality given the available battery whilst ensuring full-length playback of the video. The resultant adaptation is to change to video segments with lower decoding complexity (and thus lower battery consumption) when it is predicted that the current battery level is not sufficient to complete the full video playback. Further research in addressing more complex context and its adaptation can be foreseen in future work.

MMT-Based Streaming

MPEG Media Transport (MMT) is an emerging standard, defined in MPEG-H Part 1 (ISO/IEC, 2014b). The development of this new standard and DASH are motived by improving the current MPEG-2 Transport Stream (MPEG-TS) standard (ISO/IEC, 2007) for real-time multimedia streaming. Whilst DASH offers an immediate solution to adaptive streaming using the legacy HTTP setting, MMT is expected to address emerging and future Internet delivery environments such as content-centric networks as discussed by Lim et al. (2013). MMT specifies a codec-agnostic encapsulation format called Media Processing Unit (MPU) format. MPUs are created through an MMT packaging process, after which the MPUs can be either packetised into MMT packets for streaming or stored in MMT files. MMT packets and MMT files can be converted to each other easily. Furthermore, MMT defines a new delivery protocol called MMT Protocol (MMTP), and signalling messages for the consumption and transport of multimedia data over heterogeneous packet-switched networks with a focus on IP networks. In the following, MMTP is focused on.

The design of MMTP has particularly taken into account the characteristics of packet-switched networks including IP networks to achieve efficient, robust and QoS-aware media delivery. Firstly, multiplexing and in-order delivery are enabled to facilitate single packet flow transmission and help efficient synchronisation of different multimedia data. Secondly, the delivery timing model is independent of presentation time so as to adapt to a wide range of network jitter; the built-in jitter calculation (using the Timestamp field in the MMTP header) and removal functions (using a de-jitter buffer) yield a constant delay for applications. Thirdly, MMTP provides a built-in application-level Forward Error Correction (FEC) mechanism for reliable delivery in loss-prone IP networks including mobile cloud networks. In particular, an LA-FEC scheme can be applied to SHVC. In addition, the signalling process for ARQ (Automatic Repeat reQuest) error correction is also defined. Fourthly, congestion control by the streamer is required but not specified by MMTP, which operates over UDP.

Lastly but most interestingly, QoS indication is provided through three QoS classifier parameters whose values are stored in the delay_sensitivity field, the reliability_flag field, and the transmission_priority field respectively in the header of an MMTP packet. A mapping between the QoS classifier and the underlying QoS management scheme can then be established. For instance, the delay_sensitivity value can be mapped to the DiffServ (Differentiated Services) DSCP (DiffServ Code Point) code based on a predefined mapping policy so that delay-sensitive applications like the concerned real-time video streaming can be protected against delay-tolerant or best effort applications. More importantly with regard to adaptive streaming, the transmission_priority field can be utilised to indicate the loss priority of the current MMTP packet. One scheme to achieve this is to map the NRI field's value in the NAL unit header to this field, and the NRI value can be set according to the different importance levels of different NAL units. An example of the latter operation was provided by Wang et al. (2011) for H.264, yet it can be extended for H.265 or SHVC. In addition, MMTP further defines a Cross-Layer Interface (CLI) to enable inter-layer information exchange between the application layer and the underlying Internet and network access layers. This facility can assist context awareness and QoS management. Thanks to the above additional functionality for QoS support, enhanced robustness and multiplexing etc., MMTP is able to provide superior application-level transport support compared with current protocols such as RTP.

Figure 10 summarises and integrates the key MMT concepts into an MMT-based mobile cloud system for context-aware adaptive video streaming encoded in H.265 (and its extensions such as SHVC). In this proposed system, the priority information mapped from H.265 or SHVC semantics and carried in MMTP packets is explored for adaptive streaming, driven by the dynamic context requirements input by the mobile cloud video client. The context awareness interactions can utilise the MMTP signalling messages. In addition, the priority information is further utilised to assist congestion control, which discards packets with low priority under congested network conditions.

Figure 10. Context-aware H.265-MMT mobile cloud streaming system

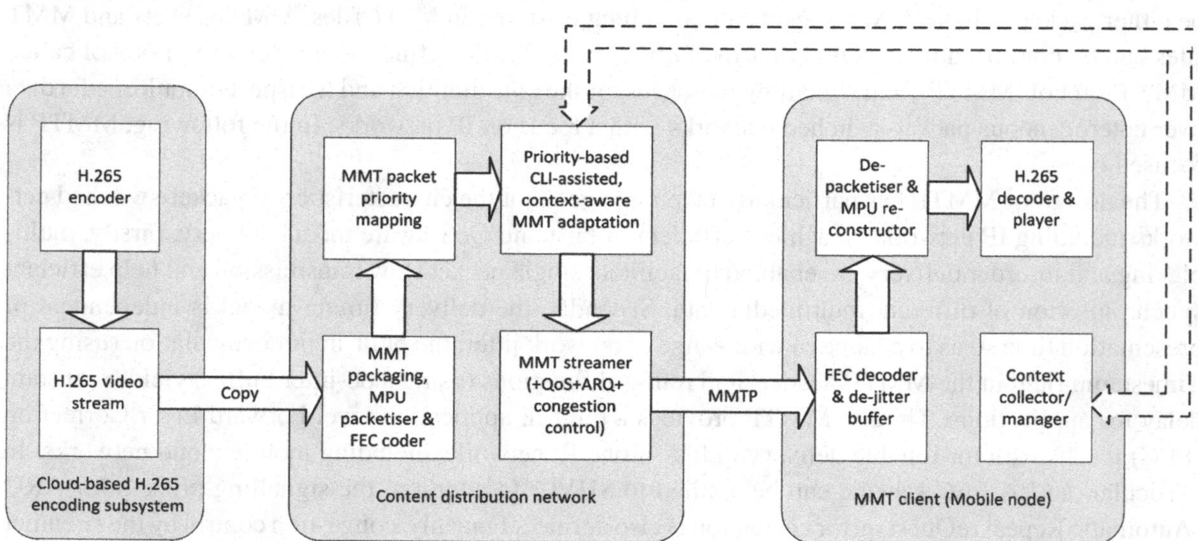

RESOURCE MANAGEMENT IN MOBILE CLOUD

The usage of cloud computing infrastructures for the provisioning of video applications such as the concerned streaming services to mobile users requires an efficient resource management of both the cloud infrastructures and the mobile devices in an MCCN environment. The QoS requirements associated with video applications such as high bandwidth, low delay, low packet loss rate, etc. pose great challenges to the management plane of mobile cloud infrastructure. The following subsections describe different aspects related to the resource management of MCCN infrastructures with a particular focus on video applications.

Cloud Resource Management

To better explain the resource management issues in a cloud, Figure 11 illustrates an overview of the main components and essential services available in a cloud computing infrastructure (OpenStack, 2014). Mobile users of the cloud use the Web UI (User Interface) to interact with the cloud infrastructure. The API (Application Programming Interface) service enables programmatic interaction with the cloud computing infrastructure. The Authentication service authenticates the users and controls the actions allowed for them. The Scheduler service is in charge of allocating the virtual resources in the physical machines of the cloud infrastructure. The VM Images service manages the images of different operating systems available, and these images are used in the Virtual Machines (VM) rented by the cloud consumer. The Storage service manages the storage devices used by the consumer. The Billing service controls the usage and billing of the resources. The Networking service controls the configuration of networking associated to the VMs. The Certificate service controls the cryptographic information used into the VMs. The previous services compose the Cloud Controller, which can be seen in the upper part of Figure 11. There is also a set of computers employed to allocate the computational resources rented to the cloud consumers. These machines usually have a virtualization layer to enable the management of VMs, virtual partitions, etc. These machines have also installed a Computing service to connect the machines to the communication middleware. This connection allows the reception of messages from the Cloud Controller to perform actions in the virtualization layer. These machines can be seen in the centre of Figure 11. When a mobile application requires more computational power, this application creates VMs composing the virtual infrastructures created by each consumer, as can be seen in the lower part of Figure 11.

Some of the main aspects related to the management of mobile cloud computing infrastructures were highlighted by Manvi et al. (2013). Firstly, multi-tenancy enables the simultaneous usage of the same cloud infrastructure by different organizations. Multi-tenancy requires dealing with an efficient management of cloud resources in order to enforce the isolation and security boundaries of resources between organizations. This management is usually achieved by mean of the usage of a Virtualization Layer that enables the abstraction of every hardware component available in the cloud infrastructure so that organizations can re-group such hardware components for their convenience, seeing them as virtual hardware resources. The Virtualization Layer also enforces the security boundaries between such virtual resources controlling the visibility and usage of such resources. Secondly, for the management of resource allocation, the Scheduler service enables the efficient allocation of virtual resources to handle the dynamic workload fluctuations and the provisioning of QoS guaranties to the end users. This scheduler performs different actions using the Virtualization Layer such as resource mapping, resource provision-

Figure 11. Architectural overview of a cloud computing infrastructure

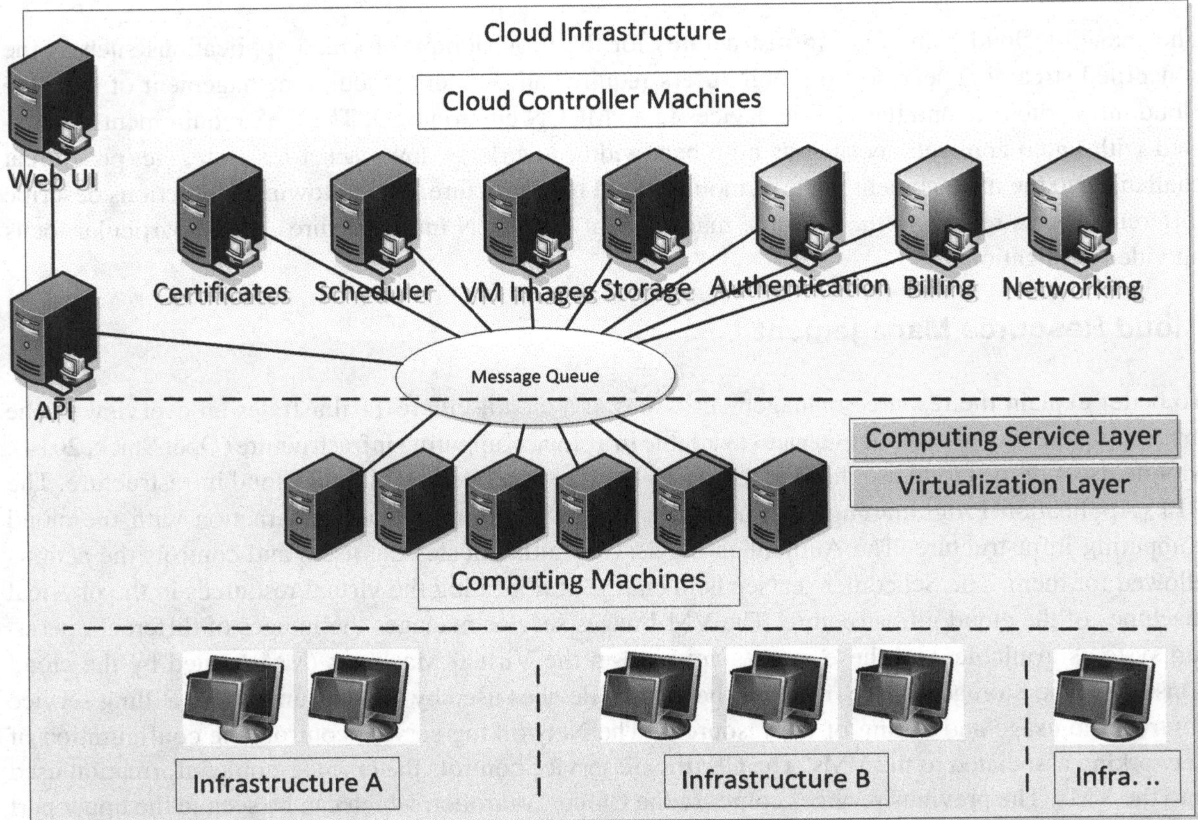

ing, resource allocation and resource adaption to maximise the performance of the cloud infrastructure. Thirdly, for network infrastructure management, the Networking service enables management of virtual switches and routers to connect all the virtual resources managed in the infrastructure. This service is also in charge of isolating the networking traffic between different users by means of an effective dynamic configuration of firewalls. Lastly, for data management, the Storage service enables the management of large-scale distributed file systems to provide flexibility in the creation of virtual volumes and disks.

Cloud Resource Monitoring

The usage of a mobile cloud computing infrastructure for video applications requires the top performance available in the infrastructure and thus it is imperative to deploy an exhaustive monitoring of the status of the different hardware and software services available in the cloud infrastructure to use such information as the foundation over which performing a smart resource management of the cloud infrastructure for optimum performance in video applications.

Alcaraz and Gutierrez (2014) provided a novel monitoring architecture that enables the integration of a traditional large-scale monitoring solution with the cloud infrastructure to retrieve a complete overview of the cloud infrastructure. This was accomplished by employing an adaptive distributed monitoring architecture (Nagios, 2014) and the OpenStack cloud computing infrastructure (OpenStack, 2014). The central point of this architecture resides in the creation of a new service inserted in the Cloud Controller (Figure 11) called MonPaaS (2014). This service is in charge of inspecting all the messages shared between all the services available in the Cloud Controller. MonPaaS intercepts and processes the information available in these messages, and performs a dynamic update of the monitoring architecture in real time. The result is a monitoring architecture that is able to be adapted to constant changes in the virtual and physical topologies of the mobile cloud infrastructure and able to retrieve hundreds of metrics about hardware, computers, networks, services, protocols, applications, operating system, QoS and so on. Figure 12 shows a screenshot of the Nagios monitoring software enhanced with MonPaaS.

Cloud Resource Management for Video Applications

The metrics gathered by the monitoring architecture for cloud computing infrastructures can be utilised for performing a smart management of the cloud resources for optimising video applications.

For instance, Alasaad et al. (2014) proposed the usage of cloud computing infrastructures to provide the elastic infrastructure to media content providers (VoD providers) to obtain streaming resources that match the demand. However, most of the existing cloud providers use a non-linear time-discount tariffs. They proposed an algorithm for deciding the right amount of resources reserved in the cloud, and their

Figure 12. Screenshot of Nagios monitoring Software integrated in a cloud computing infrastructure using MonPaaS

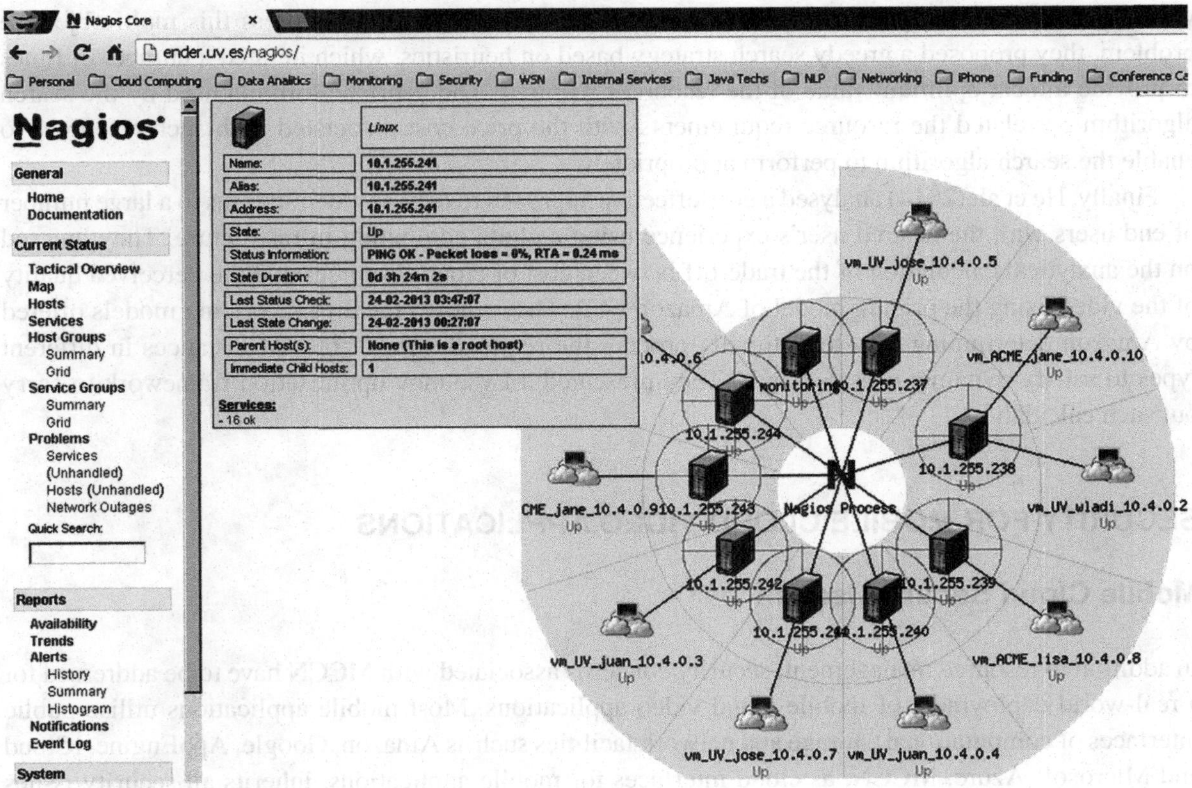

reservation time to reduce such financial cost. The algorithm took into account the information provided by the monitoring architecture of the cloud infrastructure, which was used to infer the actual demand of resources with probabilistic confidence. Thus, for any window size in seconds, the minimum amount of required reserved virtual resources during such time can be calculated. These virtual resources were used to deploy infrastructures like those shown in Figure 5 and Figure 6.

A different approach was suggested by Aggarwal et al. (2013), who were concerned with significantly reducing the costs associated with the renting of virtual machines in a cloud infrastructure for providing real-time IPTV services. They considered two alternatives for optimising VoD requests in cloud infrastructures. One is a Postponement strategy, which assumed that each chunk for VoD had a deadline, seconds after the request for that chunk. This strategy enabled users to play the content up to seconds after the request. The other is an Advancement strategy, which assumed that all chunks would be requested and thus the deadline for each chunk was different. For example, the first chunk has deadline of zero, the second chunk has deadline of one and so on. Using these strategies, they analytically estimated the resource requirements for serving the arriving requests, which had a delay constraint. This analytical model was then applied to better estimate the number of virtual resources required for the virtual infrastructure of the VoD. The proposed techniques for reducing server loads are also suitable for MCCN architectures.

Another interesting work on resource management for video applications was presented by Hu et al. (2014). They defined a video service that needs to serve numerous streams to users residing on various locations. To meet the QoS constraints, the video service needs a CDN built on resources leased from a number of cloud infrastructures located across the Internet. To address this problem, the work focused on the calculation of the optimum number of resources rented from the cloud infrastructures, each one with a particular price, performance, bandwidth, latency and so on. To address this multi-objective problem, they proposed a greedy search strategy based on heuristics, which iterated a number of times to provide a local optimum value of the resources required. The heuristic formula used by the search algorithm correlated the resource requirements with the price cost associated with such resources to enable the search algorithm to perform appropriately.

Finally, He et al. (2014) analysed a cost-effective approach to deliver video streams to a large number of end users with the desired user's experience using a cloud computing infrastructure. They focused on the analytical calculation of the trade-off between cost of cloud resources and the perceived quality of the video using the pricing model of Amazon EC2. They studied the diverse pricing models offered by Amazon determining how to optimally procure the required number of VM instances in different types to satisfy dynamic user demands. They presented a Lyapunov optimisation framework to carry out such calculation.

SECURITY FOR MOBILE CLOUD VIDEO APPLICATIONS

Mobile Cloud Security Issues

In addition to resource management, security concerns associated with MCCN have to be addressed for a real-world deployment of mobile cloud video applications. Most mobile applications utilise public interfaces of computational, storage and network facilities such as Amazon, Google, AppEngine, iCloud and Microsoft Azure. MCCN, as cloud interfaces for mobile applications, inherits all security issues that are related to processing and provisioning personal data in public cloud networks, which are an untrusted domain. However, typical security and privacy solutions of public cloud computing may not be applicable to a mobile cloud since the resource-constrained mobile devices would struggle to perform the resource-intensive cryptographic operations and key exchange protocols, which require frequent network access etc. Therefore, to ensure amiable computational, storage and network requirements of security and privacy solutions for MCCN, there is a need of lightweight security and privacy framework that can harness the power of public cloud computing with the consideration of limited resource and bandwidth consumption. In addition, the adoption of MCCN among mobile application developers and end users (app users) is greatly influenced by the transparency of a Cloud Service Provider (CSP). The ability of evaluate and audit security and privacy procedures of a CSP can assist end users in making decisions to allow mobile apps to utilise a mobile cloud to access private and personal information.

The following investigation presents typical existing security and privacy frameworks that attempt to ensure that private and personal data (e.g., video, text file, images etc.) cannot be compromised by the CSP or malicious cloud users in MCCN environments. Firstly, data integrity is a challenging problem to solve, considering limited control over cloud infrastructure, lack of trust on CSP and power consumption constraints. Itani et al. (2010) proposed an energy-efficient mobile cloud storage framework with integrity verification capabilities for mobile users' data. The proposed framework was based on incremental cryptography and trusted computing. Trusted coprocessor was installed and configured on a remote cloud infrastructure with a trusted third party responsible for that. The coprocessor was explored to generate cryptographic keys to ensure confidentiality of the data in an untrusted domain of CSP. Integrity of the data was verified by computing message authentication codes using trusted coprocessor and later verifying those codes on mobile devices, once CSP transmitted the data. The proposed framework also incorporated data updates by enabling mobile users with block insertion and deletion operations. Similar to integrity checks update operations could also be verified.

Secondly, secure data sharing schemes over a cloud are essential for media distribution and redistribution. To this end, a Secure Data Service Mechanism in Mobile Cloud Computing (SDSM) was proposed by Jia et al. (2011). SDSM was based on proxy re-encryption: a ciphertext transformation algorithm, which transformed ciphertext into different form without needing to decrypt it. By employing proxy re-encryption, the proposal ensured that all computation-intensive tasks were delegated to a CSP without compromising confidentiality and privacy of the outsourced data. In SDSM, the data sharer, the data owner and the CSP were considered as the involved entities. A data owner was responsible for encrypting the data, generating the transformation and user keys by using the master key. Transformation keys for individual authorised users were transmitted to the CSP along with the encrypted data. User keys were shared with data sharers only. By utilising proxy re-encryption, SDSM ensured that outsourced data need to be encrypted once and utilising transformation keys CSP could transform the encrypted data from one state to another, according to the data sharer's request.

Thirdly, Authentication, Authorisation and Accounting (AAA) are challenging issues in MCCN. Hsueh et al. (2011) proposed a secure data storage framework, which emphasised on user authentication ensuring that only legitimate users had valid credentials and access privileges to outsource and share data. In their system, mobile user, CPS, certificate authority and telecommunication module were considered as the involved entities. The framework utilised certificate authority to issue user identity information (i.e., digital certificates), while the telecommunication module was responsible for generating password for individual mobile user based on mobile user's certificate. The password generated by the telecommunication module was used by the user to access secure cloud storage i.e., outsourcing and accessing encrypted data. The proposed framework relied on the assumption that communication between the mobile user, the certificate authority and the telecommunication module was secured with asymmetric encryption and session keys to prevent replay attack.

The fourth security issue of MCCN is provable data possession in an untrusted domain, addressing how to ensure that CSP is working honestly and not discarding an outsourced data based on data access patterns of mobile users. For example, a CSP service can learn over a period of time that a certain video clip is never watched for its full length of time, and can decide to discard the unwatched frames. Urge to discard the unwatched frames might be driven by shortage of storage capacity within public cloud infrastructure. By doing this for a fairly large number of video clips CSP could significantly increase its storage capacity; however, this could have serious consequences on mobile cloud users. Yang et al. (2011) proposed a data possession framework based on Merkel Hash Tree (MHT), which is a binary tree that stored hash values of individual data blocks of the outsourced data, as leaf nodes. The root node of the MHT could only be re-constructed if leaf nodes (hash values) had correct values. The framework utilised trusted third party to compute MHT for the outsourced data, and verification of the root node.

Finally, myriad frameworks and protocols have been proposed to ensure data confidentiality, integrity and possession checks. However, another privacy concern that is related to outsourcing private and confidential information to an untrusted domain is indirect privacy infringement. MCCN providers can deduce information about the outsourced data by learning access patterns of mobile users, even if outsourced data is in encrypted form. For example, if encrypted outsourced data is accessed by users having expertise in a specific domain (e.g., medicine, insurance etc.), it can be deduced that there is a possibility that the outsourced data contain information related to that particular domain. This could have devastating consequence on mobile user's privacy as well. Considering the privacy implications of MCCN there is a need of lightweight framework that can ensure end-to-end privacy and can obliviously process the data within the untrusted domain. Additional detailed discussions on other aspects of MCCN security such as secure VM management were presented by Khan et al. (2013).

Mobile Media Cloud Security

There are additional security concerns related to the end-to-end generation and distribution of media contents over a large number of users using (mobile) cloud computing infrastructure. One can argue that conventional security and privacy measures for cloud infrastructure were not designed to cater heterogeneous networks and devices having different processing and storage capabilities. For instance, Khan et al. (2013) proposed security and privacy improvements in cloud computing infrastructure considering different consumers and bandwidth requirements. A solution for securing scalable video by using cloud infrastructure was presented, which dealt with various threat models for video distribution. The proposed solution emphasised on authentication of the broadcaster, and generation and storage of encryption key to secure video contents. Multiple encryption keys were generated using suitable time intervals and secure cryptographic one-way hash functions. Nevertheless, the concerned scalable video is in a generic format and thus the proposed scheme was not optimised for the current scalable video coding standard H.264/SVC or the more desired emerging standard H.265/SHVC.

Towards this direction, Wallendael et al. (2013) proposed an HEVC-compliant encryption and watermarking system to secure video distribution. An end-to-end commutative security approach was advocated to allow encryption, watermarking and encoding/transcoding operations to commute flexibly. Consequently, both watermarking and transcoding were applicable to the compressed and encrypted video, and did not affect each other, thereby facilitating the flexible manipulation of the video throughout the distribution chain. A practical solution was devised and empirically shown to achieve a good trade-off between the concerned operations to minimise overhead and visual impairment. Also notably, Shahid and Puech (2014) presented one of the first schemes that were specifically designed to protect the content of HEVC videos. Selective encryption of HEVC-CABAC (Context Adaptive Binary Arithmetic Coding) binstrings was performed, and an algorithm was proposed to ensure that the resultant encrypted bitstream was format compliant and maintained the same bitrate. The proposed technique is appealing to mobile users as it demands little processing power. However, both proposals were not contextualised in the MCCN environments, and thus did not take advantage of cloud processing.

To explore the processing capabilities of a cloud, Diaz-Sanchez et al. (2012) described a cloud-based distributed video encoding and encryption system for H.264/SVC. The system employs MapReduce (Dean & Ghemawat, 2008) and contains an input splitter (splitting the input raw video into independent slices), an H.264/SVC encoder (encoding, encrypting, and encapsulating the slices into the MPEG-TS format), a merger (joining the MPEG-TS pieces into a single stream), a wrapper (generating and multiplexing the different MPEG-TS Program Specific Information tables and messages for the key distribution protocol) and the output protected video. It is noted that this architecture can be adapted to and further optimised for H.265 and its extensions especially SHVC by exploring the built-in parallelisation tools available in H.265.

Another important security issue of mobile media distribution is the trust and integrity of the outsourced media contents. Broadcasting large media files on varied resolution possess more stringent security requirements as mobile devices consuming media contents have limited computational capabilities and have energy-consumption constraints. Wang et al. (2014) proposed a lightweight secure content distribution framework that dealt with integrity of the media data and authentication of mobile users. To restrain CSP from compromising security of the data, a multi-cloud media distribution framework was proposed to ensure that if a single CSP was compromised it was infeasible for an attacker to derive the whole information. In addition, a watermarking solution could be employed to authenticate users outsourcing data to the media cloud. When consuming outsourced media, watermarking solution was exploited to ensure that media content was not compromised and outsourced by a legitimate user. Figure 13 summarises the main security issues involved in an end-to-end system for mobile cloud video streaming applications.

Figure 13. Overview of mobile video cloud security

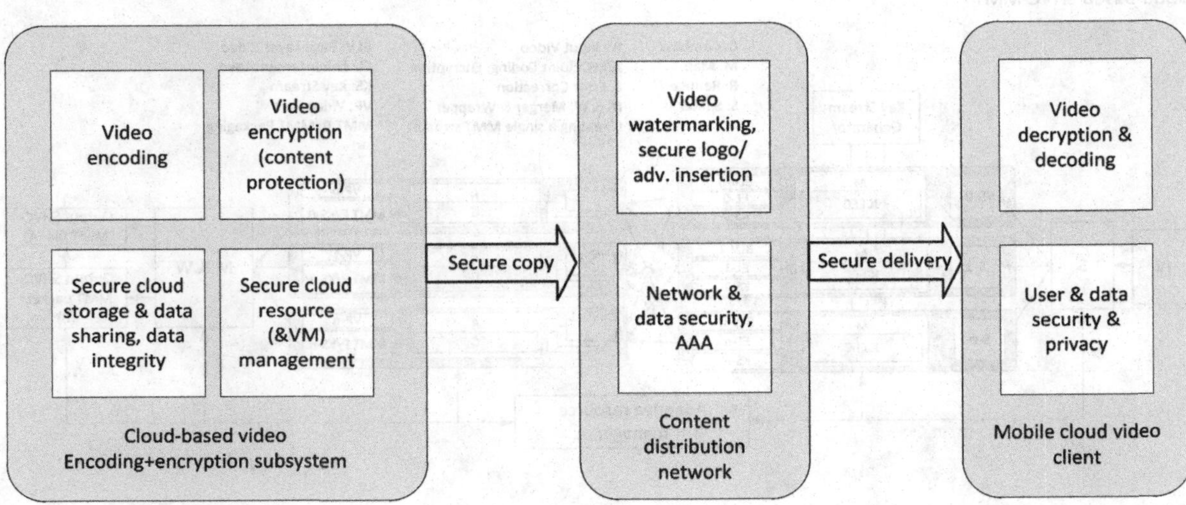

PROPOSED INTEGRATED ARCHITECTURE

Based on the critical literature review on the related building blocks, a preliminary integrated architecture is envisioned and outlined towards realising next-generation mobile cloud video streaming, which would be featured with content-, context- and resource-aware, QoE-oriented, secure, robust and real-time H.265 video streaming in mobile cloud networks. Highlighted in Figure 14 is the conceptual framework of the architecture's core part, a cloud-assisted SHVC processing subsystem. The proposed integrated architecture has a set of desirable features as follows.

MMT-Compliant H.265/SHVC Processing with Security and Robustness by Design

Among the streaming framework choices, the MMT approach is preferred owning to its forward-looking design with emerging Internet applications taken into account. Either H.265/HEVC or its scalable extension SHVC can be supported and explored in an MMT-based streaming system. When H.265 is employed, the built-in parallelisation tools in HEVC should be utilised to achieve parallelised processing in the cloud. When SHVC is applied especially for scalability-based adaptive streaming, additional preparation of the input video may be required depending on the implementation. For instance, the SHVC reference encoder described by Chen et al. (2013) requires one input file for each layer representation. These are normally obtained by capturing the original at the highest resolution (spatial) and then using down-sampling tools to produce the lower layer input files. For quality scalability, rather than two different input files (for two layers) the same input file is used for each layer with a different Quantisation Parameter (QP) setting. For temporal scalability on its own only one input file is needed as the HEVC encoder handles temporal scalability through its RPS management classes.

Figure 14 outlines the procedure to perform cloud-based H.265/SHVC processing to create MMT-compliant packages. Towards accomplishing security and robustness in video streaming by design and increase the cloud processing efficiency, it is proposed that a joint distributed and parallelised video

Figure 14. Cloud-based SHVC-MMT with integrated encoding, encryption and error correction

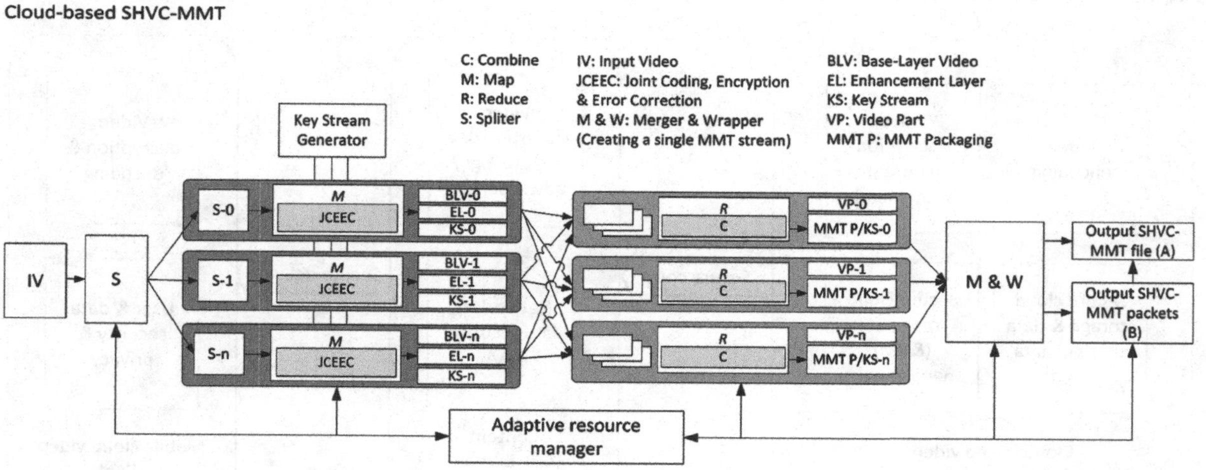

Cloud-based SHVC-MMT

Encoding, Encryption and Error correction (EEE) e.g., FEC be devised. Little existing work has considered the integration of the EEE processing especially in a cloud environment. The Hadoop MapReduce model (Dean and Ghemawat, 2008) can be explored for a rapid prototyping and practical realisation. Accordingly, the combined H.264/SVC coding and encryption scheme by Diaz-Sanchez et al. (2012) can be adapted and extended to support H.265/SHVC integrated EEE processing. The Splitter splits the input H.265/SHVC video into independent segments, which are then mapped to go through joint EEE processing in a distributed/parallelised fashion to speed up this time-consuming task. The results of the subtasks are then reduced (combined), and a single MMT-compliant stream is finally created after merging and wrapping in the format of either an SHVC-MMT file for storage (A) or a series of continuous SHVC-MMT packets to be streamed (B) after network-level packetisation.

Media- and EEE-Aware Resource Management

Also shown in Figure 14 is an adaptive cloud resource manager, which is responsible for global resource calculation, reservation, dynamic allocation and real-time monitoring in the cloud for the EEE operations. The arrows indicate interactions between the resource manager and the rest of the system. The design of this resource manager should firstly consider the efficient resource allocation to video segments that are commonly differently sized after a parallelisation technique is applied. Further design considerations should address the potentially different parallelisation tools and different encryption and/or error correction methods employed for the input H.265/SHVC videos. Moreover, different codecs including H.265, H.264 and others may also need to be deployed and supported in a hybrid system. Additionally, cost-effective resource management for streaming is required to meet the QoS requirements of the application. Therefore, an adaptive resource manager is desired, which is able to perform dynamic resource management in response to the varying EEE processing requirements. The MonPaaS service proposed by Alcaraz and Gutierrez (2014) could be extended towards realising an adaptive media- and EEE-aware resource management in response to the varying resource and QoS requirements of H.265-based processing and streaming.

QoE-Driven Adaptation with Context and Content Awareness

In addition to QoS, the users' perceived quality QoE is emphasised in driving the adaptive streaming. Context parameters will be collected by the mobile cloud streaming client, and be input to the media streaming adaptation control unit or a MANE on the network side, e.g., a context-aware streamer at the CDN. The concerned context parameters can include H.265/SHVC encoder/decoder parameters, video content metrics, network performance metrics, and user profiles and context-sensitive preferences and so on. It is proposed to further explore content awareness beyond codec setting, NAL unit header information and other H.265 metadata. In particular, media content type is widely recognised as a most influential factor in the application layer for user's perceived visual quality, and thus a most common and important parameter in QoE evaluation and modelling as proved in previous studies through subjective video quality tests. Currently, H.265-specific QoE modelling is largely missing. Nightingale et al. (2014b) described a function to quickly approximate H.265-coded video content type based on the semantics of the received stream especially the HEVC quadtree partitioning and prediction mode decisions made by the encoder. This work on HEVC content type classification can serve as a starting point towards an effective model for evaluating and predicting QoE of H.265-coded video streaming in real time.

Optimised MCCN Content Distribution and Access

Finally, the proposed integrated architecture considers optimised MCCN video content distribution and user access with service mobility support. The architecture leverages the distributed deployment of cloud domains, CDN domains, and various RANs, including the emerging cloud networking paradigm known as federated cloud, where inter-cloud collaboration is enabled. In particular, mobility- and location-aware seamless and adaptive MCCN services are proposed for mobile users in the architecture, where mobile users are able to receive cost-effective subscribed services in a visited domain. Exploring location and mobility awareness in service delivery can contribute to optimising MCCN service routing and rerouting, load balancing video application traffic, and thus enhancing users' roaming experience in terms of bandwidth and delay, which are especially important to support mobile streaming users. Therefore, the integrated architecture aims to take advantage of the geographically distributed cloud service provision, coupled with real-time positioning and context awareness, to achieve cloud service-level mobility across distributed cloud service domains through inter-cloud cooperation. This will add another dimension to the conventional network-level mobility, and enable the mobile cloud service users to enjoy pervasive and smooth services on the move.

To sum up, the envisioned next-generation mobile cloud video streaming framework would seamlessly integrates the latest video coding standard H.265 and/or its extensions such as SHVC, the new streaming standard MMT being defined, security and robustness by design, media- and EEE-aware resource management, QoE-driven adaptation with context and content awareness, and optimised MCCN content distribution and access. It is noted that this forward-looking advanced framework includes a number of emerging technologies that entail further research and development to fully achieve the expected potential. Clearly, in the proposed components, there are still a number of challenges and constraints, some of which are further highlighted in the following section.

FUTURE RESEARCH DIRECTIONS

This section offers a vision into future research trends on related topics from both the perspectives of H.265 video applications and MCCN.

Perspective from H.265 Video Streaming

Based on the critical review of the state of the art, it is evident that the research and development in the field of H.265-based video networking is still in its very early stage, not just H.265 video over mobile cloud networks but also in other kinds of wired or wireless networks. In light of the importance of H.265 as the next-generation video coding standard to substantially improve the efficiency in video encoding, storage and transmission, both the video signal processing and the networking/cloud computing communities should intensify (and coordinate through collaboration) their research and development activities in the design, implementation, testing and evaluating H.265-coded video applications and apps in various networking scenarios including but not limited to mobile cloud networks.

In particular, more extensive work is called for in-depth research, practical implementations and empirical performance evaluation of the emerging standards such as SHVC and MMT, which are expected to play a significant role in delivering scalable, adaptive, efficient and robust video streaming in the evolving Internet. Both SHVC and MMT standardisation is expected to be completed in 2014, which will boost the worldwide investigation and early deployment of these technologies.

Moreover, there are still many challenges to be overcome before parallel H.265 encoding can be effectively performed in the MCCN environment. Firstly the spatial and temporal dependencies in Inter encoding must be considered carefully when deciding how to split a video into parallel work streams. A two-pass encoding system similar to the suggestion by Barlas (2012) may need to be employed. However, the second and possibly more challenging problem is that of managing resources and work queues in a highly parallel environment where jobs may be distributed at the Tile level (or even at the CU level) to individual nodes.

Further development and optimisation of H.265 and its extensions, beyond the built-in parallelisation tools, for (mobile) cloud processing operations will help facilitate the integration of H.265 video coding standards and (mobile) cloud computing and networking paradigms, and accelerate the adoption of H.265 applications/apps by mobile cloud users. In addition, efficient methods and tools (including APIs that are compatible with major public cloud platforms) are highly desired to enable fast mobile cloud video service creation, validation and deployment.

Regarding large-scale practical deployment, it is envisioned that various streaming systems built upon different standards including DASH, MMT as well as the current MPEG-TS and other non-standard-based solutions etc., apart from the different encoders and transcoders employed, will co-exist for a number of years to come and their cost-effective and seamless inter-working is essential for ubiquitous streaming service access and enriched user experience for mobile clients.

In addition, meeting end users' growing QoE requirements is challenging yet crucial for the successful system operation and service provision. New QoE models optimised or specifically designed for H.265-based streaming services over mobile cloud networks are demanded, including but not limited to cross-layer QoS and QoE mapping, or the mapping from one or more objective visual quality metric to approximate a subjective QoE metric. Users' total experience beyond the visual quality experience may have to be taken into account. Based on practical QoE models, real-time QoE monitoring and prediction algorithms can be designed for QoE management and adaptive QoE-oriented streaming.

Perspective from Mobile Cloud Computing and Networking

From the cloud network infrastructure's view, large-scale MCCN paradigms based on federated clouds are expected to come into play for world-wide ubiquitous mobile cloud applications beyond the current cloud bursting model, which combines private and public clouds for a hybrid system. Such paradigms will integrate various existing distributed clouds and other virtualised or physical networks including various wired and wireless networks. Real-time applications such as the concerned video coding (and other signal processing) and streaming require a seamless integration and operation of heterogeneous mobile cloud architectures and platforms in a software-defined federated cloud computing and networking environment. Ideally, a user (including service providers) may only have to roughly indicate the (video) application's key requirements and the budget, and the system (represented e.g., by an infrastructure provider agent) will then automatically construct an end-to-end, on-demand, software-defined virtual network that may be based on (a part of) a federated MCCN paradigm to meet the user's overall requirements.

Integrated into such federated clouds, clouds in various formats such as cloudlets, ad hoc network-based clouds and personal clouds can complement the Internet-centric clouds by offering localised, opportunistic, follow-me, or highly personalised cloud services. Distributed resource and security/trust management schemes are essential for these kinds of mobile cloud systems to be practically deployed. Moreover, fast intelligent cloud service selection algorithms have to be devised since multiple cloud services may be collocated and available to a mobile cloud user. These algorithms will allow the user to determine which cloud service(s) should be switched to in order to maximise his/her QoE given the budget, or allow the service provider to optimise the overall system management in the region whilst complying with the existing Service Level Agreement (SLA) with the user. In addition, with the trend of increasing smart devices and connections, more sophisticated interactions are expected between the cloud and a mobile cloud client (smart device) for more complex MCCN operations. Such interactions should be transparent to the end user and will need to be addressed to meet the requirements of more complicated and demanding (video) applications/apps, whilst optimising the overall performance-cost trade-off may be targeted.

Moreover, efficient, scalable and real-time context awareness throughout the whole system is desired to be established to assist system-level management and adaptation. This task is challenging taken into account the potentially wide range of related context parameters for different management and adaptation functionality, the time/location-varying and -sensitive feature of most context parameters and the corresponding time constraints and sheer volume of context measurements and messages, and a uniform definition and interpretation of common context parameters in heterogeneous MCCN environments. Interestingly, the challenges may be mitigated by exploring the MCC paradigm itself considering the required computation and storage power.

CONCLUSION

This chapter addresses video streaming in mobile cloud networks, with a focus on context-aware adaptive H.265-coded streaming, based on emerging standards such as SHVC, DASH and MMT. Although the mobile cloud computing and networking (MCCN) paradigm offers a powerful processing and storage platform for ubiquitous and on-demand video service provisioning, there are numerous challenges in the end-to-end video distribution chain to meet the QoE of end users and the requirements for secure, robust and real-time video processing and delivery, whilst H.265 video networking is in its infancy. The latest advances in this area have been critically surveyed, and extensions to the emerging streaming standards have been presented to incorporate MCCN and context awareness functionality into the architectures. The most promising standards and approaches are recommended and integrated in a proposed reference framework to inspire further research on H.265 video networking, which is expected to gain increasing momentum.

ACKNOWLEDGMENT

This work was partially funded by the UK Engineering and Physical Sciences Research Council (EPSRC) under grant number EP/J014729/1: Enabler for Next-Generation Mobile Video Applications.

REFERENCES

Aggarwal, V., Gopalakrishnan, V., Jana, R., Ramakrishnan, K. K., & Vaishampayan, V. (2013). Optimizing cloud resources for delivering IPTV services through virtualization. *IEEE Transactions on Multimedia*, *15*(4), 789–801. doi:10.1109/TMM.2013.2240287

Alasaad, A., Shafiee, K., Behairy, H., & Leung, V. (2014). Innovative schemes for resource allocation in the cloud for media streaming applications. *IEEE Transactions on Parallel and Distributed Systems*, *9219*(c), 1–1. doi:10.1109/TPDS.2014.2316827

Alcaraz Calero, J. M., & Gutierrez Aguado, J. (2014). *MonPaaS: An adaptive monitoring platform as a service for cloud computing infrastructures and services*. IEEE Transactions on Services Computing. doi:10.1109/TSC.2014.2302810

Bae, S.-H., Kim, J., Kim, M., Cho, S., & Choi, J. S. (2013). Assessments of subjective video quality on HEVC-encoded 4K-UHD video for beyond-HDTV broadcasting services. *IEEE Transactions on Broadcasting*, *59*(2), 209–222. doi:10.1109/TBC.2013.2247171

Barlas, G. (2012). Cluster-based optimized parallel video transcoding. *Parallel Computing*, *38*(4-5), 226–244. doi:10.1016/j.parco.2012.02.001

Bossen, F., Bross, B., Member, S., Karsten, S., & Flynn, D. (2012). HEVC complexity and implementation analysis. *IEEE Transactions on Circuits and Systems for Video Technology*, *22*(12), 1685–1696. doi:10.1109/TCSVT.2012.2221255

Casas, P., & Schatz, R. (2014). Quality of experience in cloud services: Survey and measurements. *Computer Networks*, 1–17. doi:10.1016/j.comnet.2014.01.008

Chang, S.-Y., Lai, C.-F., & Huang, Y.-M. (2012). Dynamic adjustable multimedia streaming service architecture over cloud computing. *Computer Communications*, *35*(15), 1798–1808. doi:10.1016/j.comcom.2012.06.001

Chen, J., Boyce, J., Ye, Y., & Hannuksela, M. (2013). *Scalable HEVC (SHVC) test model 4 (SHM 4). JCT-VC of ITU-T SG 16 WP 3 and ISO/IEC JTC 1/SC 29/WG 11, JCTVC-O1007_v1. 15th Meeting*: Geneva.

Chen, Y. W., & Jiang, W. (2013). Low-complexity transcoding from H.264 to HEVC based on motion vector clustering. *Electronics Letters*, *49*(19), 1224–1226. doi:10.1049/el.2013.0329

Choi, K., & Jang, E. (2012). Industry and standards leveraging parallel computing in modern video coding standards. *IEEE MultiMedia*, *19*(Jul-Sept), 7–11. doi:10.1109/MMUL.2012.36

Cisco. (2014). *Cisco visual networking index: Global mobile data traffic forecast update, 2013–2018*. Retrieved May 18, 2014, from http://www.cisco.com/en/US/solutions/collateral/ns341/ns525/ns537/ns705/ns827/white_paper_c11-520862.html

Correa, G., Assuncao, P., Agostini, L., & Cruz, L. (2011). Complexity control of high efficiency video encoders for power-constrained devices. *IEEE Transactions on Consumer Electronics*, *57*(4), 1866–1874. doi:10.1109/TCE.2011.6131165

Correa, G., Assuncao, P., Agostini, L., & Cruz, L. D. S. (2013). Coding tree depth estimation for complexity reduction of HEVC. In *Proc. 2013 Data Compression Conference*. IEEE. doi:10.1109/DCC.2013.12

Dean, J., & Ghemawat, S. (2008). MapReduce: Simplified data processing on large clusters. *Communications of the ACM*, *51*(1), 107–113. doi:10.1145/1327452.1327492

Diaz-Sanchez, D., Sanchez, R., Lopez, A., Almenares, F., & Arias, P. (2012). A H.264 SVC distributed content protection system with flexible key stream generation. In *Proc. 2012 IEEE 2nd International Conference on Consumer Electronics - Berlin (ICCE-Berlin)*. IEEE. doi:10.1109/ICCE-Berlin.2012.6336520

Do-kyoung, K., & Budagavi, M. (2013). Combined scalable and mutiview extension of high efficiency video coding (HEVC). In *Proc. Picture Coding Symposium (PCS) 2013* (pp. 414–417). PCS.

Fang, J., Chen, Z., Liao, T., & Chang, P. (2014). A fast pu mode decision algorithm for h.264/avc to hevc transcoding. In *Proc. Second International Conference on Signal, Image Processing and Pattern Recognition (SIPP 2014)*. Academic Press. doi:10.5121/csit.2014.4218

Fernando, N., Loke, S. W., & Rahayu, W. (2013). Mobile cloud computing: A survey. *Future Generation Computer Systems*, *29*(1), 84–106. doi:10.1016/j.future.2012.05.023

Fraunhofer-HHI. (2014a). *HEVC 4K real-time software decoder*. Retrieved May 18, 2014, from http://www.hhi.fraunhofer.de/fields-of-competence/image-processing/solutions/hevc-software-and-hardware-solutions/hevc-4k-real-time-decoder.html

Fraunhofer-HHI. (2014b). *Real-time software encoding up to 1080p60*. Retrieved May 18, 2014, from http://www.hhi.fraunhofer.de/fields-of-competence/image-processing/solutions/hevc-software-and-hardware-solutions/hevc-real-time-software-encoder.html

Garcia, R., & Kalva, H. (2014). Subjective evaluation of HEVC and AVC/H.264 in mobile environments. *IEEE Transactions on Consumer Electronics*, *60*(1), 116–123. doi:10.1109/TCE.2014.6780933

Gartner. (2013). *Gartner identifies the top 10 strategic technology trends for 2014*. Retrieved May 18, 2014, from http://www.gartner.com/newsroom/id/2603623

Guan, X., & Choi, B.-Y. (2014). Push or pull? Toward optimal content delivery using cloud storage. *Journal of Network and Computer Applications*, *40*, 234–243. doi:10.1016/j.jnca.2013.09.003

Hazari, G., Karandikar, P., & Sanghvi, H. (2014). Performance estimation and architecture exploration of a video IP design in a smart phone SoC context. In *Proc. 2014 IEEE International Conference on Electronics, Computing and Communication Technologies (IEEE CONECCT)*. IEEE.

He, J., Wen, Y., Huang, J., & Wu, D. (2014). On the cost – QoE tradeoff for cloud-based video streaming under Amazon EC2's pricing models. *IEEE Transactions on Circuits and Systems for Video Technology*, *24*(4), 1–3. doi:10.1109/TCSVT.2013.2283430

He, J., Wu, D., Zeng, Y., Hei, X., & Wen, Y. (2013). Toward optimal deployment of cloud-assisted video distribution services. *IEEE Transactions on Circuits and Systems for Video Technology*, *23*(10), 1717–1728. doi:10.1109/TCSVT.2013.2255423

He, Y., Kunstner, M., Gudumasu, S., Ryu, E., Ye, Y., & Xiu, X. (2013). Power aware HEVC streaming for mobile. In Proc. Visual Communications and Image Processing (VCIP) 2013. Academic Press.

Hellge, C., Gómez-barquero, D., Schierl, T., & Wiegand, T. (2011). Layer-aware forward error correction for mobile broadcast of layered media. *IEEE Transactions on Multimedia*, *13*(3), 551–562. doi:10.1109/TMM.2011.2129499

HM. (2014). *HEVC reference software*. Retrieved May 22, 2014, from https://hevc.hhi.fraunhofer.de/

Hsueh, S., Lin, J., & Lin, M. (2011). Secure cloud storage for convenient data archive of smart phones. In *Proc. 2011 IEEE 15th International Symposium on Consumer Electronics (ISCE)* (pp. 156–161). IEEE. doi:10.1109/ISCE.2011.5973804

Hu, M., Luo, J., Wang, Y., & Veeravalli, B. (2014). Practical resource provisioning and caching with dynamic resilience for cloud-based content distribution networks. *IEEE Transactions on Parallel and Distributed Systems*, *25*(8), 2169–2179. doi:10.1109/TPDS.2013.287

Hu, N., & Yang, E. (2014). Fast motion estimation based on confidence interval. *IEEE Transactions on Circuits and Systems for Video Technology*, *24*(8), 1310–1322. doi:10.1109/TCSVT.2014.2306035

Irondi, I., Wang, Q., & Grecos, C. (2014). Empirical evaluation of H.265/HEVC based dynamic adaptive video streaming over HTTP (HEVC-DASH). In *Proc. SPIE Photonics Europe 2014: Real-Time Image and Video Processing (Conference EPE115)* (Vol. 2). SPIE.

Islam, S., & Grégoire, J.-C. (2012). Giving users an edge: A flexible cloud model and its application for multimedia. *Future Generation Computer Systems*, *28*(6), 823–832. doi:10.1016/j.future.2012.01.002

ISO/IEC (2007). *Information technology — Generic coding of moving pictures and associated audio information: Part 1: Systems.* International Standard 13818-1:2007.

ISO/IEC (2014a). *Information technology — Dynamic Adaptive Streaming over HTTP (DASH) — Part 1: Media presentation description and segment formats.* International Standard 23009-1:2014.

ISO/IEC (2014b). *Information technology — High efficiency coding and media delivery in heterogeneous environments — Part 1: MPEG media transport (MMT).* Final Draft International Standard (FDIS) 23008-1:2014.

Itani, W., Kayssi, A., & Chehab, A. (2010). Energy-efficient incremental integrity for securing storage in mobile cloud computing. In *Proc. 2010 International Conference on Energy Aware Computing (ICEAC)*. Academic Press. doi:10.1109/ICEAC.2010.5702296

ITU-T (2012). *Advanced video coding for generic audiovisual services.* ITU-T Recommendation H.264.

ITU-T (2013). *High efficiency video coding.* ITU-T Recommendation H.265.

Jarschel, M., Schlosser, D., Scheuring, S., & Hoßfeld, T. (2013). Gaming in the clouds: QoE and the users' perspective. *Mathematical and Computer Modelling*, *57*(11-12), 2883–2894. doi:10.1016/j.mcm.2011.12.014

Jia, W., Zhu, H., Cao, Z., Wei, L., & Lin, X. (2011). SDSM: A secure data service mechanism in mobile cloud computing. In *Proc. 2011 IEEE Conference on Computer Communications Workshops (INFOCOM WKSHPS)* (pp. 1060–1065). IEEE. doi:10.1109/INFCOMW.2011.5928784

JM. (2014). *H.264/AVC reference software*. Retrieved May 22, 2014, from http://iphome.hhi.de/suehring/tml/index.htm

Jokhio, F., Ashraf, A., Lafond, S., Porres, I., & Lilius, J. (2013). Prediction-based dynamic resource allocation for video transcoding in cloud computing. In *Proceedings of 2013 21st Euromicro International Conference on Parallel, Distributed, and Network-Based Processing*. Academic Press. doi:10.1109/PDP.2013.44

Khan, A. N., Mat Kiah, M. L., Khan, S. U., & Madani, S. (2013a). Towards secure mobile cloud computing: A survey. *Future Generation Computer Systems*, *29*(5), 1278–1299. doi:10.1016/j.future.2012.08.003

Khan, A. U., Orioe, M., & Kiran, M. (2013b). Threat methodology for securing scalable video in the cloud. In *Proc. 8th International Conference for Internet Technology and Secured Transactions (ICITST-2013)* (pp. 428–436). Academic Press. doi:10.1109/ICITST.2013.6750237

Khan, M. U. K., Shafique, M., & Henkel, J. (2014). Software architecture of High Efficiency Video Coding for many-core systems with power-efficient workload balancing. *Design, Automation, & Test in Europe Conference & Exhibition*, *2014*, 1–6. doi:10.7873/DATE.2014.232

Lao, F., Zhang, X., & Guo, Z. (2012). Parallelizing video transcoding using map-reduce-based cloud computing. In *Proceedings of 2012 IEEE International Symposium on Circuits and Systems* (pp. 2905–2908). IEEE. doi:10.1109/ISCAS.2012.6271923

Lasserre, S., Le Leannec, F., Taquet, J., & Nassor, E. (2014). Low-complexity intra coding for scalable extension of HEVC based on content statistics. *IEEE Transactions on Circuits and Systems for Video Technology*, *24*(8), 1375–1389. doi:10.1109/TCSVT.2014.2305513

Li, B., Xu, J., Li, H., & Wu, F. (2011). Optimized reference frame selection for video coding by cloud. In *Proceedings of 2011 IEEE 13th International Workshop on Multimedia Signal Processing* (pp. 1–5). IEEE. doi:10.1109/MMSP.2011.6093770

Li, Z., Mitra, K., Zhang, M., Ranjan, R., Georgakopoulos, D., Zomaya, A. Y., & Sun, S. (2014). Towards understanding the runtime configuration management of do-it-yourself content delivery network applications over public clouds. *Future Generation Computer Systems*, *37*, 297–308. doi:10.1016/j.future.2013.12.019

Liang, F., Peng, X., & Xu, J. (2013). A light-weight HEVC encoder for image coding. In Proc. Visual Communications and Image Processing (VCIP) 2013. Academic Press. doi:10.1109/VCIP.2013.6706448

Lin, S., Zhang, X., Yu, Q., Qi, H., & Ma, S. (2013). Parallelizing video transcoding with load balancing on cloud computing. In *Proceedings of 2013 IEEE International Symposium on Circuits and Systems (ISCAS2013)* (pp. 2864–2867). IEEE. doi:10.1109/ISCAS.2013.6572476

Liu, F., Shu, P., Jin, H., Ding, L., Yu, J., Niu, D., & Li, B. (2013, June). Gearing resource-poor mobile devices with powerful clouds: architectures, challenges, and applications. *IEEE Wireless Communications*, 14–22.

Liu, X., Liu, Y., Yang, W., & Yang, L. T. (2014). High-efficiency mode decision procedure for H.264/AVC under cloud computing environments. *IEEE Systems Journal*, *8*(1), 322–332. doi:10.1109/JSYST.2013.2260642

Live555. (2014). *Live555 streaming media project*. Retrieved May 22, 2014, from http://www.live555.com/liveMedia/

Manvi, S. S., & Krishna Shyam, G. (2013). Resource management for infrastructure as a service (IaaS) in cloud computing: A survey. *Journal of Network and Computer Applications*, 1–17. doi:10.1016/j.jnca.2013.10.004

MCN. (2014). *EU FP7 mobile cloud networking (MCN) project*. Retrieved May 22, 2014, from http://www.mobile-cloud-networking.eu/site/

MonPaaS. (2014). Retrieved May 25, 2014, from http://sourceforge.net/projects/monpaas/

MultiCoreWare. (2014). Retrieved May 25, 2014, from http://x265.org/about.html

Nagios. (2014). Retrieved May 25, 2014, from http://www.nagios.org/

Nakasu, E. (2012, April). A future TV system that conveys an enhanced sense of reality and presence. *IEEE Consumer Electronics Magazine*.

Nightingale, J., Wang, Q., & Grecos, C. (2012). HEVStream : A framework for streaming and evaluation of high efficiency video coding (HEVC) content in loss-prone networks. *IEEE Transactions on Consumer Electronics*, *58*(2), 404–412. doi:10.1109/TCE.2012.6227440

Nightingale, J., Wang, Q., & Grecos, C. (2013). Scalable HEVC (SHVC)-based video stream adaptation in wireless networks. In *Proc. IEEE 24th Annual International Symposium on Personal, Indoor, and Mobile Radio Communications (IEEE PIMRC'13)*. IEEE. doi:10.1109/PIMRC.2013.6666769

Nightingale, J., Wang, Q., Grecos, C., & Goma, S. (2013). Subjective evaluation of the effects of packet loss on HEVC encoded video streams. In *Proceedings of 2013 IEEE Third International Conference on Consumer Electronics - Berlin (ICCE-Berlin)* (pp. 358–359). IEEE. doi:10.1109/ICCE-Berlin.2013.6698055

Nightingale, J., Wang, Q., Grecos, C., & Goma, S. (2014a). Evaluation of in-network adaptation of scalable high efficiency video coding (SHVC) in mobile environments. In *Proc. SPIE Conference on Mobile Devices and Multimedia: Enabling Technologies, Algorithms, and Applications 2014 (SPIE Conference 9030)*. SPIE.

Nightingale, J., Wang, Q., Grecos, C., & Goma, S. (2014b). Deriving video content type from H.265/HEVC bitstream semantics. In *Proc. SPIE Photonics Europe 2014: Real-Time Image and Video Processing (Conference EPE115)*. SPIE.

OpenStack. (2014). Retrieved May 25, 2014, from https://www.openstack.org/

Oztas, B., Pourazad, M. T., Nasiopoulos, P., Sodagar, I., & Leung, V. C. M. (2014). A rate adaptation approach for streaming multiview plus depth content. In *Proc. 2014 International Conference on Computing, Networking and Communications (ICNC)* (pp. 1006–1010). Academic Press. doi:10.1109/ICCNC.2014.6785475

Peixoto, E., Shanableh, T., & Izquierdo, E. (2014). H.264 / AVC to HEVC video transcoder based on dynamic thresholding and content modeling. *IEEE Transactions on Circuits and Systems for Video Technology*, *24*(1), 99–112. doi:10.1109/TCSVT.2013.2273651

Pereira, R., Azambuja, M., Breitman, K., & Endler, M. (2010). An architecture for distributed high performance video processing in the cloud. In *Proceedings of 2010 IEEE 3rd International Conference on Cloud Computing* (pp. 482–489). IEEE. doi:10.1109/CLOUD.2010.73

Pinol, P., Torres, A., Lopez, O., Martinez, M., & Malumbres, M. (2013). Evaluating HEVC video delivery in VANET scenarios. In Proc. 2013 IFIP Wireless Days (WD). IFIP. doi:10.1109/WD.2013.6686539

Qi, G.-J., Tsai, M.-H., Tsai, S.-F., Cao, L., & Huang, T. S. (2012). Web-scale multimedia information networks. *Proceedings of the IEEE*, *100*(9), 2688–2704. doi:10.1109/JPROC.2012.2201909

Red5. (2014). *Red5 media server project*. Retrieved May 22, 2014, from http://www.red5.org/

Sardis, F., Mapp, G., Loo, J., Aiash, M., & Vinel, A. (2013). On the investigation of cloud-based mobile media environments with service-populating and QoS-aware mechanisms. *IEEE Transactions on Multimedia*, *15*(4), 769–777. doi:10.1109/TMM.2013.2240286

Schierl, T., Hannuksela, M. M., Wang, Y., & Wenger, S. (2012). System layer integration of high efficiency video coding. *IEEE Transactions on Circuits and Systems for Video Technology*, *22*(12), 1871–1884. doi:10.1109/TCSVT.2012.2223054

Schulzrinne, H., Casner, S., Frederick, R., & Jacobson, V. (2003). *RTP: A transport protocol for real-time applications*. IETF RFC 3550.

Schulzrinne, H., Rao, A., Lanphier, R., Westerlund, M., & Stiemerling, M. (2013). *Real time streaming protocol 2.0 (RTSP)*. IETF Internet Draft, draft-ietf-mmusic-rfc2326bis-36.

Sebestyen, G., Hangan, A., Sebestyen, K., & Vachter, R. (2013). Self-tuning multimedia streaming system on cloud infrastructure. *Procedia Computer Science*, *18*, 1342–1351. doi:10.1016/j.procs.2013.05.301

Shahid, Z., & Puech, W. (2014). Visual protection of HEVC video by selective encryption of CABAC binstrings. *IEEE Transactions on Multimedia*, *16*(1), 24–36. doi:10.1109/TMM.2013.2281029

Shanableh, T., Peixoto, E., & Izquierdo, E. (2013). MPEG-2 to HEVC video transcoding with content-based modeling. *IEEE Transactions on Circuits and Systems for Video Technology*, *23*(7), 1191–1196. doi:10.1109/TCSVT.2013.2241352

Shen, T., Lu, Y., Wen, Z., Zou, L., Chen, Y., & Wen, J. (2013). Ultra Fast H.264/AVC to HEVC Transcoder. In *Proc. 2013 Data Compression Conference* (Vol. 92093). IEEE. doi:10.1109/DCC.2013.32

Shi, Z., Sun, X., & Wu, F. (2012). Spatially scalable video coding for HEVC. *IEEE Transactions on Circuits and Systems for Video Technology*, *22*(12), 1813–1826. doi:10.1109/TCSVT.2012.2223031

Sitaram, D., & Manjunath, G. (2012). Future trends and research directions. In Moving to the cloud. Academic Press. doi:10.1016/B978-1-59749-725-1.00010-X

Sullivan, G. J., Boyce, J. M., Chen, Y., Ohm, J., Segall, C. A., & Vetro, A. (2013). Standardized extensions of high efficiency video coding (HEVC). *IEEE Journal of Selected Topics in Signal Processing*, *7*(6), 1001–1016. doi:10.1109/JSTSP.2013.2283657

Van Wallendael, G., Dooms, A., De Cock, J., Braeckman, G., Boho, A., Preneel, B., & Van De Walle, R. (2013). End-to-end security for video distribution. *IEEE Signal Processing Magazine*, (March): 97–107.

Van Wallendael, G., Staelens, N., Janowski, L., De Cock, J., Demeester, P., & Van De Walle, R. (2012). No-reference bitstream-based impairment detection for high efficiency video coding. In *Proceedings of 2012 Fourth International Workshop on Quality of Multimedia Experience (QoMEX)* (pp. 7–12). Academic Press. doi:10.1109/QoMEX.2012.6263845

Viitanen, M., Vanne, J., Hämäläinen, T. D., & Lainema, J. (2012). Complexity analysis of next-generation HEVC decoder. In *Proc. 2012 IEEE International Symposium on Circuits and Systems (ISCAS)*. IEEE. doi:10.1109/ISCAS.2012.6272182

Wang, H., Wu, S., Chen, M., & Wang, W. (2014). Security protection between users and the mobile media cloud. *IEEE Communications Magazine*, *52*(March), 73–79. doi:10.1109/MCOM.2014.6766088

Wang, Y.-K., Even, R., Kristensen, T., & Jesup, R. (2011). *RTP payload format for H.264 video*. IETF RFC 6184.

Wu, Y., Zhang, Z., Wu, C., Li, Z., & Lau, F. C. M. (2013). CloudMoV: Cloud-based mobile social TV. *IEEE Transactions on Multimedia*, *15*(4), 821–832. doi:10.1109/TMM.2013.2240670

x264. (2014). *H.264/AVC encoder*. Retrieved May 22, 2014, from http://www.videolan.org/developers/x264.html

Xiong, J., Li, H., Wu, Q., & Meng, F. (2014). A fast HEVC inter CU selection method based on pyramid motion divergence. *IEEE Transactions on Multimedia*, *16*(2), 559–564. doi:10.1109/TMM.2013.2291958

Yan, C., Zhang, Y., Xu, J., Dai, F., Li, L., Dai, Q., & Wu, F. (2014). A highly parallel framework for HEVC coding unit partitioning tree decision on many-core processors. *IEEE Signal Processing Letters*, *21*(5), 573–576. doi:10.1109/LSP.2014.2310494

Yang, J., Wang, H., Wang, J., Tan, C., & Yu, D. (2011). Provable data possession of resource-constrained mobile devices in cloud computing. *Journal of Networks*, *6*(7), 1033–1040. doi:10.4304/jnw.6.7.1033-1040

Yue, H., Sun, X., Yang, J., & Wu, F. (2013). Cloud-based image coding for mobile devices — Toward thousands to one compression. *IEEE Transactions on Multimedia*, *15*(4), 845–857. doi:10.1109/TMM.2013.2239629

Zeng, L., Veeravalli, B., & Wei, Q. (2014). Space4time: Optimization latency-sensitive content service in cloud. *Journal of Network and Computer Applications*, *41*, 358–368. doi:10.1016/j.jnca.2014.02.002

Zhao, Y., Song, L., Wang, X., Chen, M., & Wang, J. (2013). Efficient realization of parallel HEVC intra encoding. In *Proc. 2013 IEEE International Conference on Multimedia and Expo Workshops (ICMEW)* (pp. 4–9). IEEE.

Zhu, W., Au, O. C., Yang, H., Dai, W., Zhang, H., & Zhang, X. (2013). Simplified generalized residual prediction in scalable extension of HEVC. In Proc. Visual Communications and Image Processing (VCIP) 2013 (Vol. 16). Academic Press. doi:10.1109/VCIP.2013.6706450

Zhu, Z., Gupta, P., Wang, Q., Kalyanaraman, S., Lin, Y., & Franke, H. (2011). Virtual base station pool: Towards a wireless network cloud for radio access networks categories and subject descriptors. In *Proc. 8th ACM International Conference on Computing Frontiers*. ACM.

ADDITIONAL READING

Abolfazli, S., Sanaei, Z., Ahmed, E., Gani, A., & Buyya, R. (2014). Cloud-Based Augmentation for Mobile Devices: Motivation, Taxonomies, and Open Challenges. *IEEE Communications Surveys and Tutorials*, *16*(1), 337–368. doi:10.1109/SURV.2013.070813.00285

Aceto, G., Botta, A., de Donato, W., & Pescapè, A. (2013). Cloud monitoring: A survey. *Computer Networks*, *57*(9), 2093–2115. doi:10.1016/j.comnet.2013.04.001

Adzic, V., Kalva, H., & Furht, B. (2012). Optimizing Video Encoding for Adaptive Streaming over HTTP. *IEEE Transactions on Consumer Electronics*, *58*(2), 397–403. doi:10.1109/TCE.2012.6227439

Al-Zaiti, S. S., Shusterman, V., & Carey, M. G. (2013). Novel technical solutions for wireless ECG transmission & analysis in the age of the internet cloud. *Journal of Electrocardiology*, *46*(6), 540–545. doi:10.1016/j.jelectrocard.2013.07.002 PMID:23992916

Broberg, J., Buyya, R., & Tari, Z. (2009). MetaCDN: Harnessing "Storage Clouds" for high performance content delivery. *Journal of Network and Computer Applications*, *32*(5), 1012–1022. doi:10.1016/j.jnca.2009.03.004

Buyya, R. (2013). Cloud Applications. In Mastering Cloud Computing (pp. 353–371). Morgan Kaufmann. doi:10.1016/B978-0-12-411454-8.00010-3

Cabarcos, P. A., Mendoza, F. A., Guerrero, R. S., López, A. M., & Díaz-sánchez, D. (2012). SuSSo : Seamless and Ubiquitous Single Sign-on for Cloud Service Continuity across devices. *IEEE Transactions on Consumer Electronics*, *58*(4), 1425–1433. doi:10.1109/TCE.2012.6415016

Calyam, P., Rajagopalan, S., Seetharam, S., Selvadhurai, A., Salah, K., & Ramnath, R. (2014). VDC-Analyst: Design and verification of virtual desktop cloud resource allocations. *Computer Networks*, *68*, 110–122. doi:10.1016/j.comnet.2014.02.022

Cheng, L., & Wang, C.-L. (2013). Network performance isolation for latency-sensitive cloud applications. *Future Generation Computer Systems*, *29*(4), 1073–1084. doi:10.1016/j.future.2012.05.025

Chi, C. C., Alvarez-mesa, M., Juurlink, B., Clare, G., Henry, F., Pateux, S., & Schierl, T. (2012). Parallel Scalability and Efficiency of HEVC Parallelization Approaches. *IEEE Transactions on Circuits and Systems for Video Technology*, *22*(12), 1827–1838. doi:10.1109/TCSVT.2012.2223056

De Cicco, L., Mascolo, S., & Calamita, D. (2013). A resource allocation controller for cloud-based adaptive video streaming. In *Proc. 2013 IEEE International Conference on Communications Workshops (ICC)* (pp. 723–727). Ieee. doi:10.1109/ICCW.2013.6649328

Elgazzar, K., Hassanein, H. S., & Martin, P. (2013). DaaS: Cloud-based mobile Web service discovery. *Pervasive and Mobile Computing*. doi:10.1016/j.pmcj.2013.10.015

Flores, H., & Srirama, S. N. (2013). Mobile Cloud Middleware. *Journal of Systems and Software*. doi:10.1016/j.jss.2013.09.012

Gurkok, C. (2014). Securing Cloud Computing Systems. In Network and System Security (pp. 83–126). doi:10.1016/B978-0-12-416689-9.00004-6

Jiao, Y., Zhang, S., Li, Y., Wang, Y., & Yang, B. (2013). Towards cloud Augmented Reality for construction application by BIM and SNS integration. *Automation in Construction*, *33*, 37–47. doi:10.1016/j.autcon.2012.09.018

Jula, A., Sundararajan, E., & Othman, Z. (2014). Cloud computing service composition: A systematic literature review. *Expert Systems with Applications*, *41*(8), 3809–3824. doi:10.1016/j.eswa.2013.12.017

Kaewpuang, R., Niyato, D., Wang, P., & Hossain, E. (2013). A Framework for Cooperative Resource Management in Mobile Cloud Computing. *IEEE Journal on Selected Areas in Communications*, *31*(12), 2685–2700. doi:10.1109/JSAC.2013.131209

Khan, R., Othman, M., Madani, S. A., & Khan, S. U. (2014). A Survey of Mobile Cloud Computing Application Models. *IEEE Communications Surveys and Tutorials*, *16*(1), 393–413. doi:10.1109/SURV.2013.062613.00160

Kousiouris, G., Menychtas, A., Kyriazis, D., Gogouvitis, S., & Varvarigou, T. (2014). Dynamic, behavioral-based estimation of resource provisioning based on high-level application terms in Cloud platforms. *Future Generation Computer Systems*, *32*, 27–40. doi:10.1016/j.future.2012.05.009

Kovachev, D., Yu, T., & Klamma, R. (2012). Adaptive Computation Offloading from Mobile Devices into the Cloud. *2012 IEEE 10th International Symposium on Parallel and Distributed Processing with Applications*, 784–791. doi:10.1109/ISPA.2012.115

Li, X., Qian, Z., You, I., & Lu, S. (2013). Towards cost efficient mobile service and information management in ubiquitous environment with cloud resource scheduling. *International Journal of Information Management*, 1–10. doi:10.1016/j.ijinfomgt.2013.11.007

Liu, Y., Wang, S., & Dey, S. (2014). Content-Aware Modeling and Enhancing User Experience in Cloud Mobile Rendering and Streaming. *IEEE Journal on Emerging and Selected Topics in Circuits and Systems*, *4*(1), 43–56. doi:10.1109/JETCAS.2014.2298921

Ma, X., Zhao, Y., Zhang, L., Wang, H., & Peng, L. (2013). When Mobile Terminals Meet the Cloud: Computation Offloading as the Bridge. *IEEE Network*, *27*(Sept/Oct), 28–33. doi:10.1109/MNET.2013.6616112

Makris, P., Skoutas, D. N., & Skianis, C. (2013). A Survey on Context-Aware Mobile and Wireless Networking : On Networking and Computing Environments' Integration. *IEEE Communications Surveys and Tutorials*, *15*(1), 362–386. doi:10.1109/SURV.2012.040912.00180

Marinescu, D. (2013a). Cloud Computing: Applications and Paradigms. In Cloud Computing (pp. 99–130). Morgan Kaufmann. doi:10.1016/B978-0-12-404627-6.00004-X

Marinescu, D. (2013b). Cloud Application Development. In Cloud Computing (pp. 317–359). doi:10.1016/B978-0-12-404627-6.00011-7

Marinescu, D. (2013c). Cloud Resource Management and Scheduling. In *Cloud Computing* (pp. 163–203). Morgan Kaufmann; doi:10.1016/B978-0-12-404627-6.00006-3

Meera, a., & Swamynathan, S. (2013). Agent based Resource Monitoring System in IaaS Cloud Environment. *Procedia Technology, 10*, 200–207. doi:10.1016/j.protcy.2013.12.353

Miller, K., Quacchio, E., Gennari, G., & Wolisz, A. (2012). Adaptation algorithm for adaptive streaming over HTTP. *2012 19th International Packet Video Workshop (PV)*, 173–178. doi:10.1109/PV.2012.6229732

Ohm, J., & Sullivan, G. J. (2013). High Efficiency Video Coding: The Next Frontier in Video Compression. *IEEE Signal Processing Letters*, *30*(January), 152–158. doi:10.1109/MSP.2012.2219672

Paul, S., Jain, R., Samaka, M., & Pan, J. (2014). Application delivery in multi-cloud environments using software defined networking. *Computer Networks*, *68*, 166–186. doi:10.1016/j.comnet.2013.12.005

Pu, W., Zou, Z., & Chen, C. W. (2011). Dynamic Adaptive Streaming over HTTP from Multiple Content Distribution Servers. *2011 IEEE Global Telecommunications Conference - GLOBECOM 2011*, 1–5. doi:10.1109/GLOCOM.2011.6134143

Rodrigues, J. J. P. C., Zhou, L., Mendes, L. D. P., Lin, K., & Lloret, J. (2012). Distributed media-aware flow scheduling in cloud computing environment. *Computer Communications*, *35*(15), 1819–1827. doi:10.1016/j.comcom.2012.03.004

Schierl, T., Sanchez de la Fuente, Y., Globisch, R., Hellge, C., & Wiegand, T. (2010). Priority-based Media Delivery using SVC with RTP and HTTP streaming. *Multimedia Tools and Applications*, *55*(2), 227–246. doi:10.1007/s11042-010-0572-5

Shi, W., Lu, Y., Li, Z., & Engelsma, J. (2011). SHARC: A scalable 3D graphics virtual appliance delivery framework in cloud. *Journal of Network and Computer Applications*, *34*(4), 1078–1087. doi:10.1016/j.jnca.2010.06.005

Shiraz, M., Gani, A., Khokhar, R. H., & Buyya, R. (2013). A Review on Distributed Application Processing Frameworks in Smart Mobile Devices for Mobile Cloud Computing. *IEEE Communications Surveys and Tutorials*, *15*(3), 1294–1313. doi:10.1109/SURV.2012.111412.00045

Sjöberg, R., Chen, Y., Fujibayashi, A., Hannuksela, M. M., Samuelsson, J., Tan, T. K., & Wenger, S. (2012). Overview of HEVC High-Level Syntax and Reference Picture Management. *IEEE Transactions on Circuits and Systems for Video Technology*, *22*(12), 1858–1870. doi:10.1109/TCSVT.2012.2223052

Subashini, S., & Kavitha, V. (2011). A survey on security issues in service delivery models of cloud computing. *Journal of Network and Computer Applications*, *34*(1), 1–11. doi:10.1016/j.jnca.2010.07.006

Winkler, V. (2013). Evaluating Cloud Security : An Information Security Framework. In D. Rountree & I. Castrillo (Eds.), *The Basics of Cloud Computing* (pp. 101–121). Syngress; doi:10.1016/B978-0-12-405932-0.00006-2

Wu, T.-Y., Chen, C.-Y., Kuo, L.-S., Lee, W.-T., & Chao, H.-C. (2012). Cloud-based image processing system with priority-based data distribution mechanism. *Computer Communications*, *35*(15), 1809–1818. doi:10.1016/j.comcom.2012.06.015

Yang, M., Cai, J., Wen, Y., & Foh, C. H. (2011). Complexity-rate-distortion evaluation of video encoding for cloud media computing. *2011 17th IEEE International Conference on Networks*, 25–29. doi:10.1109/ICON.2011.6168501

Zheng, L., Tian, L., & Wu, Y. (2011). A rate control scheme for distributed high performance video encoding in cloud. *2011 International Conference on Cloud and Service Computing*, 131–133. doi:10.1109/CSC.2011.6138510

Zhu, X., Zhu, J., Pan, R., Prabhu, M. S., & Bonomi, F. (2012). Cloud-Assisted Streaming for Low-Latency Applications. In *2012 International Conference on Computing, Networking and Communications (ICNC)* (pp. 949–953). doi:10.1109/ICCNC.2012.6167565

Zhuang, Y., Jiang, N., Wu, Z., Li, Q., Chiu, D. K. W., & Hu, H. (2014). Efficient and robust large medical image retrieval in mobile cloud computing environment. *Information Sciences*, *263*, 60–86. doi:10.1016/j.ins.2013.10.013

Zhuang, Z., & Guo, C. (2012). Building cloud-ready video transcoding system for Content Delivery Networks (CDNs). *2012 IEEE Global Communications Conference (GLOBECOM)*, 2048–2053. doi:10.1109/GLOCOM.2012.6503417

KEY TERMS AND DEFINITIONS

Adaptive Streaming: Streaming that is able to adapt to the context.

Cloud-Based Video Applications: Video applications that utilise the resources provided by a cloud.

Content Awareness: The capability of being aware of the media (e.g., video) content payload, header, and/or related metadata or semantics.

Context Awareness: The capability of being aware of the contextual parameters related to the application, the network conditions, the device's capabilities and constraints, the user's profiles/preferences and so on.

H.265/HEVC: The latest standard for video compression and decompression.

Mobile Cloud Computing and Networking (MCCN): Cloud computing and networking for mobile users.

Next-Generation Video Technologies: Technologies related to video coding, processing and networking based on H.265/HEVC and other emerging standards.

Quality of Experience (QoE): The perceived (subjective) quality by an end user.

Section 4

Network and Service Virtualization

This section outlines the fundamental concepts and issues tangible to the network and service virtualization techniques. It initially presents the evolution of the cloud computing paradigm and its applicability in various sections of the computing and networking/telecommunications industry, such as cloud networking, cloud offloading, and network function virtualization. It then elaborates on ubiquitous and adaptive Web-based multimedia communications via the cloud, as well as a resource prediction mechanism in network-aware delivery clouds for user-centric media events.

Chapter 10
Virtualization Evolution:
From IT Infrastructure Abstraction of Cloud Computing to Virtualization of Network Functions

Harilaos Koumaras
NCSR Demokritos, Greece

George Xilouris
NCSR Demokritos, Greece

Christos Damaskos
NCSR Demokritos, Greece

Georgios Gardikis
NCSR Demokritos, Greece

George Diakoumakos
NCSR Demokritos, Greece

Vaios Koumaras
NCSR Demokritos, Greece

Michail-Alexandros Kourtis
NCSR Demokritos, Greece

Thomas Siakoulis
NCSR Demokritos, Greece

ABSTRACT

This chapter discusses the evolution of the cloud computing paradigm and its applicability in various sections of the computing and networking/telecommunications industry, such as the cloud networking, the cloud offloading, and the network function virtualization. The new heterogeneous virtualized ecosystem that is formulated creates new needs and challenges for management and administration at the network part. For this purpose, the approach of Software-Defined Networking is discussed and its future perspectives are further analyzed.

INTRODUCTION

The latest years, cloud computing, as a technology, has exhibited significant growth and in acceptance, being a primary trend for deploying and developing IT services. Cloud computing supports flexible and scalable management of IT resources, through the respective abstraction of the IT resources, which lower the barriers to future changes, with reduced capital expense risk and pay-as-you-go (i.e. usage-based) pricing models (Ernst & Young, 2011). The elasticity that the cloud computing environment offers, creates an opportunity for the evolutionary upgrade of legacy data centers in order to support

DOI: 10.4018/978-1-4666-8225-2.ch010

innovative business models either in the field of pricing or resource utilization, reducing operational expenditures and minimizing market entrance costs, while at the same time the cloud computing technology maximizes the return of investment and the internal return rate.

The success of the cloud computing platforms have expanded their usage in the mobile communication industry as well, where Mobile Cloud Computing (Mousicou, Mavromoustakis, Bourdena, Mastorakis, & Pallis, 2013) refers to an infrastructure where both the data storage and data processing are offloaded outside of the mobile device, supporting therefore innovative services and applications. Mobile devices have recently become so popular that they are increasingly replacing personal computers. However, due to limited resources, mobile devices cannot offer the same performance as the personal computers. One approach to overcome both computational and storage limitation is offloading mobile-related recourses to the cloud. In this case, and with the help of offloading, the mobile device runs only a thin layer of software which interfaces with application-specific services in the cloud. This trend is called Networking Cloud and supports cloud applications that move the computing power and data storage away from the mobile devices into powerful and centralized computing platforms located in clouds. However, such an approach requires that source data are available to the remote service and this might require transferring data from the mobile device to the cloud, therefore transferring the resource availability issue for the support of sophisticated applications at the network side.

Following the paradigm of the cloud computing success in the abstraction of IT infrastructures both in the mobile and computing industry, the virtualization trend has recently expanded its field of application in the networking industry as well.

Current networking infrastructures basically rely on hardware-based devices as their building elements; most in-network functionalities (routing/switching, filtering, analysis, adaptation, signaling control, security provision etc.) are carried out by stand-alone hardware appliances. This approach, while having worked well for several decades, is now seen as a major factor which contributes to the so-called "ossification" of the Internet. Solely relying on hardware platforms with fixed resources/capabilities, significantly slows down and hampers the introduction of new network services. The advent of network innovations in the context of Future Internet (new protocols, algorithms and standards) calls for continuous upgrades (or even replacement) of the existing appliances in a much faster pace than their average lifetime.

Although modern networking appliances exhibit remarkable performance in transmission speeds and spectrum efficiency as well as satisfactory interoperability in terms of compliance to network protocols (TCP, IP, HTTP etc.), their deployment as "closed", heterogeneous hardware platforms presents several key limitations, such as manual establishment and configuration of networking services, especially across heterogeneous domains (e.g. mobile/terrestrial), thus involving considerable setup and reconfiguration delays. New network technologies, algorithms and protocols cannot be rapidly introduced into the market since they involve time-consuming and costly hardware upgrades and are thus associated with significant CAPEX investments. Network resources are assigned statically to each user, without the capability to automatically up/down scale according to user's needs, which would also assume new, flexible billing models.

A promising solution to alleviate the aforementioned limitations in all infrastructure technologies is the Network Function Virtualization (NFV) model. Following the paradigm of the Cloud Computing for the virtualization of computing and storage resource, the concept of NFV is being used in the literature as well as in the market with various meanings in order to efficiently support the transferring of cloud computing advantages to the network. Depending on the context, NFV can be used to refer to the interconnection of remote data centers so as to federate their IT resources, or the diffusion of IT cloud assets (i.e., servers, storage) into the network in a CDN-like manner so as to bring them "closer" to the end user. It can also refer to the virtualization and abstraction of network resources (i.e., links, nodes and functionalities) and their provision to the end-user as-a-Service, in a cloud-like manner, featuring dynamic resource pooling and elasticity.

The term NFV is being used in the literature as well as in the market with various meanings. Depending on the context, it can be used to refer to the interconnection of remote data centers so as to federate their IT resources, or the diffusion of IT cloud assets (i.e., servers, storage) into the network in a CDN-like manner so as to bring them "closer" to the end user. It can also refer to the virtualization and abstraction of network resources (i.e., links, nodes and functionalities) and their provision to the end-user as-a-Service, in a cloud-like manner, featuring dynamic resource pooling and elasticity. In this context, Network Functions Virtualisation (NFV) appears as an emerging aspect in the networking domain, which has the potential to radically redefine the substance of what is referred to as "network infrastructure". NFV refers to the virtualization of network functions carried out by specialized hardware devices and their migration as software-based appliances, which are deployed on top of commodity IT (including Cloud) infrastructures.

NFV should not considered as a single technology. Instead, the realization of the cloud network concept relies on the synergistic application of specific component technologies, which are supported by the current trend of Network Virtualization. Management issues of the various virtualized appliances and the virtualized network functions are adequately addressed by the Software Defined Networking (SDN), which offers an integrated and unified management approach of the virtualized ecosystem.

These enabling technologies for cloud networking are briefly overviewed in the sections to follow.

BACKGROUND

During the recent years, cloud computing architectures have become popular as a method of deployment of workloads and for delivering of computing applications as a service rather than a product (Bourdena, Kormentzas, Skianis, Pallis, & Mastorakis, 2011). The concept of "clouds" has demonstrated commercial success, while it is expected to attain an even larger part in the Information and Communications Technology (ICT) domain over the next decade (see, e.g., (Group, 2010), (Gartner, 2014), (IDC, 2014). The potential of clouds is leveraged by the fact that it allows the reduction of entry cost for new services. Therefore, cloud computing minimizes the business establishment cost, the investments on new infrastructure and optimally lowers the risk of launching a new service, platform or product.

The foundation of the idea of cloud computing began in the 1960s. John McCarthy conceived the notion that "computation may someday be organized as a public utility" (Parkhill, 1966). In 1966, Douglas Parkhill wrote the book "The challenge of the Computer Utility" which thoroughly explores all modern-day characteristics of cloud computing such as offered as a utility, elastic provision, seemingly to infinite supply and online as a comparison to electricity (Parkhill, 1966). Other scholars maintain that the roots of cloud computing were back in the 1950s when Herb Grosch (creator of Grosch's Law) predicted that one day the entire world would function on dumb terminals powered by as few as fifteen mega data centers. (Grosch, 1950). The very first development was in 1999 with the arrival of Salesforce.com which pioneered the concept of delivering enterprise applications through a simple website.

The federation of homogeneous and heterogeneous data centers formulates a cloud computing. The basic idea of cloud computing is using remote servers on the internet to manage, store and process data instead of using a personal computer. When a cloud is made available in a pay-as-you-go manner to the general public, they call it a public cloud; the service being sold is utility computing. They use the term private cloud to refer to internal data centers of a business or other organization, not being available to the general public.

From a hardware provisioning and pricing point of view, cloud computing concept introduces the following new concepts and models:

- The appearance of elastic computing resources available on demand, quickly enough to follow load surges, thereby eliminating the need for users to plan far ahead for provisioning.
- The elimination of an hardware CAPEX and OPEX, thereby allowing companies to start small and increase hardware resources only when there is an increase in their needs.
- The ability to pay for use of computing resources on a short-term basis as needed and release them as needed, thereby rewarding conservation by releasing machines and storage when they are no longer useful.

Cloud computing represents a model for enabling ubiquitous and on-demand network access to a shared pool of configurable, computing resources (e.g., networks, servers, storage, applications, services, etc.) that can be rapidly provisioned and released with reduced management effort and service provider interaction (Cloud, 2014). In this concept, as Figure 1 depicts, cloud computing mainly provides three different types of services: Software as a Service (SaaS) (e.g., SalesForce (Company, 2014), Basecamp (software, 2014), GoogleApps (Business, 2014), Platform as a Service (PaaS) (e.g., Windows Azure (Microsoft, Windows Azure Platform, 2014), Force.com (Resources, 2014), Google App Engine (Google,

Figure 1. The IaaS/PaaS/SaaS layered architecture of a cloud

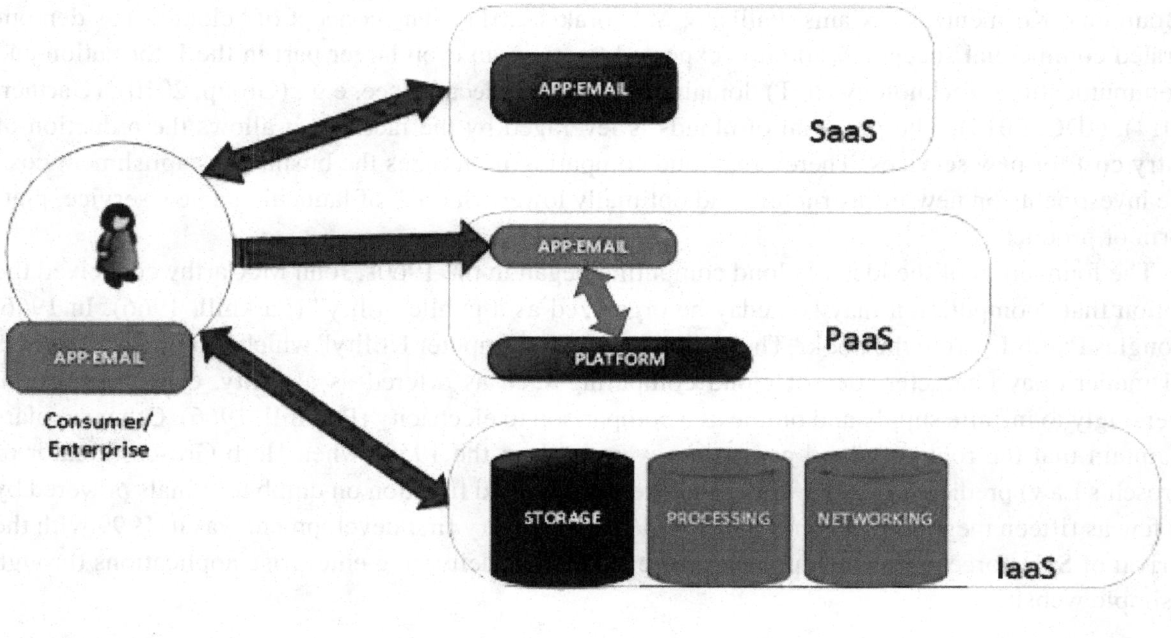

2014), and Infrastructure as a Service (IaaS) (e.g., Amazon AWS (Amazon, 2014), Rackspace.com (Rackspace, 2014), Cloud Hosting (Solutions., 2014)). None of the three types of services requires end-user knowledge of the physical location and the configuration of the cloud that delivers the services. The three segments are Infrastructure-as-a-Service (IaaS), Platform-as-a-Service (PaaS), and Software-as-a-Service (SaaS) (Ernst & Young, 2011).

Infrastructure as a Service (IaaS)

It is the demanded infrastructure for the provisioning of cloud servers. Basically it is virtual server instances with unique IP addresses and blocks of storage on demand. Customers use the provider's application program interface (API) in order to start, stop or access and configure their virtual servers and storage.

Platform as a Service (PaaS)

PaaS provides the entire infrastructure needed to run applications over the Internet. It is a set of software and product development tools hosted on the provider's infrastructure. Developers create applications on the provider's platform over the Internet.

Software as a Service (SaaS)

At this cloud model, the vendor supplies the hardware infrastructure, the software product and interacts with the user through a front-end portal. Because the service provider hosts both the application and the data, the end user is free to use the service from anywhere.

The use of the cloud computing can be summarized considering the following advantages:

- **Cost Efficient:** Desktop software costs a lot more than cloud services since there are different payment methods a company can select for its cloud storage.
- Elastic storage and processing power.
- **Backup and Recovery:** All data is stored in the cloud, which makes it easier to back it up and restore it than on a physical device.
- **Easy Access to Information:** By the time anyone registers in the cloud, he can access his files or anything he has stored in it from anywhere, anyhow and anytime.
- **Quick Development:** Easy for the whole system to be fully functional in a matter of time (depends on the needs of the business).

On the other hand, the use of cloud computing may involve various disadvantages, which are summarized as following:

- Security and privacy in the Cloud.
- Great concern for the company while putting private data and information in the cloud. It is up to the service provider to ensure the protection of such documents.
- Dependency and vendor lock-in.
- The difficulty on moving from your current provider to another.
- Technical difficulties and downtime.

- The whole setup of a cloud service depends on Internet connection, so depending on the ISP of every company there might be a delay or any downtime.
- Limited admin, control and flexibility.
- Increased vulnerability.
- Cloud based services are "exposed" to the public internet and are a more vulnerable target for hackers.

The current cloud platforms (e.g., VMware vSphere (VMware, 2014), Microsoft Hyper-V (Microsoft., 2014), Real Hat KVM (Hat, 2014) virtualize the host's physical resources (through the use of specific software called hypervisor) and make them available to multiple guest virtual machines. These virtual machines share the various cloud platforms' resources concurrently. The most of the cutting-edge cloud management solutions (e.g., vCloud Director (VMware., 2014), Abiquo (Abiquo, 2014), DynamicOps (DynamicOps, 2014), Gale Technologies (Technologies, 2014), Platform Computing (Computing, 2014)) create resource pools and automatically allocate resources among virtual machines based on pre-defined rules and policies. The resources (e.g., processor usage, memory usage, storage, etc.) are managed at the cloud level rather than the machine-by-machine level. Also, all the resource allocation policies proposed so far are static and can be executed only at the initialization phase of the virtual machines. Finally, all available solutions are proprietary, and there are no widely accepted standards or de facto open source reference implementations for cloud management applications.

The first step for succeeding elastic scalability in cloud environments is the resource discovery and the proper monitoring of the cloud resources. Traditional monitoring technologies for single machines or clusters are restricted to locality and homogeneity of monitored objects and therefore, cannot be applied in the cloud in an appropriate manner (Vincent, 2012). There are lots of third-party collectors of cloud statists which provide monitoring facilities (e.g., Cloudkick (Cloud monitoring & management, 2014), Nimsoft Monitor (nimsoft, 2014), Monitis (monitis, 2014), Opnet (OPNET, 2014), RevealCloud (Copperegg, 2014), etc.). All of them are proprietary solutions and do not aim at defining a standard for cloud monitoring. Due to this fact, the QoE4CLOUD project aims to extend Open Cloud Computing Interface (OCCI) for supporting cloud monitoring and contribute to relevant standardization activities.

The next step towards elastic scalability is the modelling of computing resources and the definition of QoE requirements of different cloud entities. In the case of cloud environments, it is crucial that the resource modelling is able to represent virtual resources, virtual networks, and virtual applications. Therefore, the existing service architectures should be expanded to include the virtual resources, described in terms of properties and functionalities (Houidi, Louati, & Zeghlache, Virtual Resource Description and Clustering for Virtual Network, 2009).

Publication (Lodi, Panzieri, Rossi, & Turrini, 2007) proposes a middleware architecture for enabling SLA-driven clustering of QoS-aware application servers. After applying load balancing techniques, the resource usage of application servers is optimized, and the application hosting SLA is fulfilled without creating resource over-provisioning costs.

References (Stantchev & Schröpfer, 2009), (Wang, 2010), (Xiao, Lin, & Jiang, 2010), (Li, QinfenHao, Xiao, & Li, 2009), and (Ye, Jain, & Xia, 2010) provide stable service levels for applications and platforms being hosted in a cloud ecosystem, as described in their SLA agreements. In particular, (Stantchev & Schröpfer, 2009) proposes a three-step approach to map SLA and QoS requirements of business processes to cloud infrastructures. When a performance gap occurs, translucent replication of services is employed. From another point of view, (Wang, 2010) prioritizes Video-on-Demand (VoD) traffic considering the respective charging model. The total revenue of the service provider is maximized, through the definition of a proper optimization problem. The pay-as-you-go billing approach adopted in Cloud computing challenges resource provisioning for service providers. In this context, (Xiao, Lin, & Jiang, 2010) based on the Dirichlet multinomial model presents an efficient reputation-based QoS provisioning scheme. The cost of computing resources is minimized, while the desired QoS metrics are satisfied. Publication (Li, QinfenHao, Xiao, & Li, 2009) applies feedback control theory to present a Virtual Machine (VM)-based architecture for adaptive management of virtualized resources in cloud computing. Moreover, it models an adaptive controller that dynamically adjusts multiple virtualized resources utilization to achieve application SLA in cloud computing. Unlike the previous counterparts, (Ye, Jain, & Xia, 2010) considers also power management issues, since it studies a service cloud environment with mobile devices.

As it was emphasized previously, one of the most important benefits of cloud ecosystem is its ability to allow the use of on demand resources. This feature leads to dynamically scalable systems and platforms. To take full advantage of the benefits of dynamic scaling, a cloud client (user or middleware) needs to be able to make accurate decisions on when to scale up and down. The scaling decisions must be done in advance to compensate for the overhead of using virtual resources, specifically their setup time. Therefore, a prediction method is usually used, as it best suits this task. Article (Caron & Desprez, 2011) presents a new approach to the auto-scaling problem based on identifying past patterns that are similar to the present use of the system.

CLOUD PROCESSING

Cloud-based processing (often called also as Computation Offloading) is another technology in the field of cloud computing that helps especially in the saving of energy. It is a crucial technology that is going to be extensively used in the forthcoming years in the IT industry.

The idea of computation offloading is to load a section of application execution to powerful processing units such as servers or clouds, in order to improve the performance, increase the quality of service (Bourdena, Pallis, Kormentzas, Skianis, & Mastorakis, 2012), achieve more stringent real-time performance requirement, and extend the battery life. Offloading is a solution to augment system's capabilities by migrating computation to more resourceful computers. This is different form the traditional client-server architecture, where a thin client always migrates computation to a server. Computation offloading is also different from the migration model used in multiprocessor systems and grid computing, where a process may be migrated for load balancing. The key difference is that computation offloading migrates programs to servers outside of the users' immediate computing environment.

The main motivation for using computation offloading is the saving of energy. Computation offloading is a reliable and effective way to achieve this goal. However, one of the most challenging tasks in mobile offloading is to decide, when it is needed. Generally, offloading is beneficial, whenever the gained efficiency outweighs the costs involved. The difficult part is to define the indicators of efficiency and their related costs, observe their realization and optimize the corner cases where the counterparts compensate each other. One of the key reasons to the difficulty is that mobile environment is much more dynamic than any desktop or server environment. There are generally three different types of decision schemes: static, dynamic and their combination, which we call hybrid. In addition to them, these can be further spllited into automated and human-made decisions.

There are three basic architectural models for computational offloading. The feature offloading, the method offloading, the image offloading. To begin with, in feature offloading, the mobile software prepares the dataset that is sufficient in solving the computational problem in question. Then the software sends the dataset to his cloud, where the actual computation is done. The mobile software eventually receives the result dataset and acts accordingly. To continue, the method offloading, stands for transfer of execution of subroutines. It is similar to feature offloading. The only difference is that the computation split of the code happens on a semantic rather than a logical level. Therefore offloading decisions may also be based on purely computational statistics. Finally, the image offloading, is an intuitive yet difficult-sounding approach towards offloading computation. The image of the program code is offloaded to a virtualized environment and the state of the machine is maintained to correspond to the one of mobile device's processes. Regarding the logical context of offloading, there is a variety of ways to improve the user experience and energy efficiency in the mobile device.

The economic model for offloading, by renting computation, is provided by virtualization and cloud computing. As the various connected devices become more widespread in their deployment, offloading techniques that can take advantage of cloud computing will become increasingly relevant. More applications based on "offloadable" computation will be designed and developed and computation offloading will become really popular.

CLOUD NETWORKING

Cloud-based networking is the combination of cloud computing and networks, especially mobile, to bring benefits for mobile users, network operators, as well as cloud computing providers. The ultimate goal of Cloud Networking is to enable execution of rich applications on a plethora of mobile devices, with a rich user experience. Cloud Networking provides business opportunities for mobile network operators as well as cloud providers. More comprehensively, Cloud Networking can be defined as "a rich mobile computing technology that leverages unified elastic resources of varied clouds and network technologies toward unrestricted functionality, storage, and mobility to serve a multitude of mobile devices anywhere, anytime through the channel of Ethernet or Internet regardless of heterogeneous environments and platforms based on the pay-as-you-use principle.

Cloud Networking and Mobile Data Offloading – often called Wi-Fi offload – is so much more than just offloading 3G/4G mobile users to the Wi-Fi network, which at many locations is a more cost-effective access method for mobile broadband. As both subscribers and devices tend to connect to Wi-Fi whenever it is in reach, mobile operators need to follow their subscribers into the Wi-Fi environment. Hence the business case for Wi-Fi offload is both about saving on costs and reducing churn. This is why many mobile operators are starting to integrate Wi-Fi simply as another radio network to their 3GPP mobile core; it is all about building a heterogeneous network.

For years mobile subscribers have been used to mobile broadband at an affordable price, in many markets even for a flat fee per month regardless of usage. That worked well until the start of the "iPhone time." According to the Cisco Visual Networking Index (VNI), the normal cell phone movement about tripled from 2010 to 2011 (now 150 MB/month) and the worldwide portable information activity will expand 18-fold between 2011 and 2016.

Also, more gadgets, for example, laptops and tablets like the iPad come with mobile data broadband capabilities built-in, as they are designed to download e.g. HD video from anyplace, at any time. While some portable administrators direly require a financially savvy method for fulfilling clients' steadily expanding crave more transfer speed, this is by all account not the only driver for Wi-Fi offload. As gadgets with implicit Wi-Fi perform better in Wi-Fi systems (with rates up to 300 Mbit/s) than in 3g/4g – particularly inside – portable administrators need to have the capacity to convey a great Wi-Fi-based end-client experience. Moreover, with more new sorts of gadgets being planned particularly as "Wi-Fi just," the administrator can diminishing stir and make endorsers more "sticky" by offering Wi-Fi.

Offloading is going to be really important in the forthcoming years. In the past few years, two important trends have occurred:

- **Sensor Deployment:** Sensors are widely deployed for monitoring the environment or for security. These sensors acquire large amounts of data but the sensors have limited computing capabilities.
- **Growth in Smartphones:** Smartphones have become the primary computing platforms for millions of people. Mobile platforms generate large amounts of multimedia data and most of the data are stored on-line on cloud servers.

As the number of connected devices—including mobile phones, tablets, laptops, and sensors—grow, the demand for increased functionalities will continue. In the next few years, we will see pressing needs for personalized management of multimedia data. This would be a natural progression of the Internet. As the amounts of multimedia data grow, users need better ways to manage their data than relying on file names, dates, and directories. It would be inconvenient to ask users to describe every image and every video by a set of keywords and then use keyword-based search. This will lead to a rapid growth in recognition and data management technologies on these connected devices.

Many of these technologies can provide large speedups with parallelism, since multimedia processing offers many opportunities for both code and data parallelism. Computing speeds of these connected devices however, will not grow at the same pace as servers' performance. This is due to several constraints, including

- **Form Factor:** Users want devices that are smaller and thinner; yet they also want devices with more computational capability.
- **Power Consumption:** Current battery technology constrains the clock speed of processors since doubling the clock speed approximately octuples the power consumption. It becomes difficult to offer long battery lifetimes with high clock speeds. These factors indicate that mobile computing speeds will not grow as fast as the growth in data, and applications' computational requirements. As a result of the above on one hand, we have a massive growth in mobile data in both types and volumes, and in the computational requirements of mobile applications. On the other hand, the computational capabilities of the devices—that acquire and store the data, and provide applications for the user—will be unlikely to grow at the same pace. Offloading computation is a natural solution to this problem.

The economic model for offloading, by renting computation, is provided by virtualization and cloud computing. As the various connected devices become more widespread in their deployment, offloading techniques that can take advantage of cloud computing will become increasingly relevant. Applications on these connected devices will start to be designed such that they have "offloadable" computation—and such design of applications can benefit from the various techniques and solutions surveyed in this paper.

There are two different types of offloading:

First of all we have the on-the-spot offloading. In this type of offloading there is usage of spontaneous connectivity to Wi-Fi and transfer data on the spot. Moreover, when the user leaves Wi-Fi coverage, offloading terminates and unfinished actions are transferred through cellular networks. Finally, nowadays smartphones for example already give priority to Wi-Fi than cellular interface.

The second type of offloading is the delayed offloading. In this type each data transfer is given a "deadline" in order to be sent out. Furthermore, it sends the data piece by piece as a user enters and exits different Wi-Fi areas and finally if the data is not sent out before the deadline, then it is finished by using the cellular networks. There are three basic key aspects of Wi-Fi offloading that need to be addressed in order for service providers to benefit from offloading data traffic from 3G/LTE to Wi-Fi. To begin with, there is the building of a Wi-fi footprint that is adapted for offloading. Secondly, an issue that needs to be taken into consideration is how to get devices to select Wi-Fi and automatically authenticate for a seamless user experience. Finally, another problem is how to interact with the mobile core for policies and charging.

As it is evident, the offloading gives many benefits to the users and network providers. By using the Wi-Fi to offload data lowers the cost of data transfers. Also, there is a lowered subscription prices due to lowered costs, which is a great benefit for the users. Finally, the proper use of data transfer delays via delayed offloading can help users to select more specific and detailed plans.

By offloading clients from the 3g/4g system to Wi-Fi systems, portable drivers can include more capacity in a moderate and adaptable way. We have seen administrators that have assembled Wi-Fi offload arranges proactively in ranges with substantial versatile broadband use, for example, colleges – and harvested the prizes of decreased cost and more level beat because of a superior client experience.

Alternative offload results that just concentrate on bypassing the parcel center passages in the versatile center will just diminishing the heap on these hubs and not offload the whole system including the Radio Access Network (RAN). Using femtocells for offloading is a technique for building the 3G radio framework cost-satisfactorily, yet femtocells don't give an option of stretching the foot formed impression quickly through accessories the way that Wi-Fi does.

Also most Wi-Fi-empowered gadgets attempt to build a Wi-Fi association as the first decision at whatever point accessible. A few provisions must be utilized on Wi-Fi. It is no amaze that bearer-class Wi-Fi has quickly picked up investment and Wi-Fi offload has turned into a necessity around mobile operators globally.

NETWORK FUNCTION VIRTUALIZATION

Network Functions Virtualisation (NFV) appears as an emerging aspect in the networking domain, which has the potential to radically redefine the substance of what is referred to as "network infrastructure". NFV refers to the virtualization of network functions, as Figure 2 depicts, carried out by specialized hardware devices and their migration as software-based appliances, which are deployed on top of commodity IT (including Cloud) infrastructures.

Figure 2. The Network Functions Virtualisation (NFV) concept

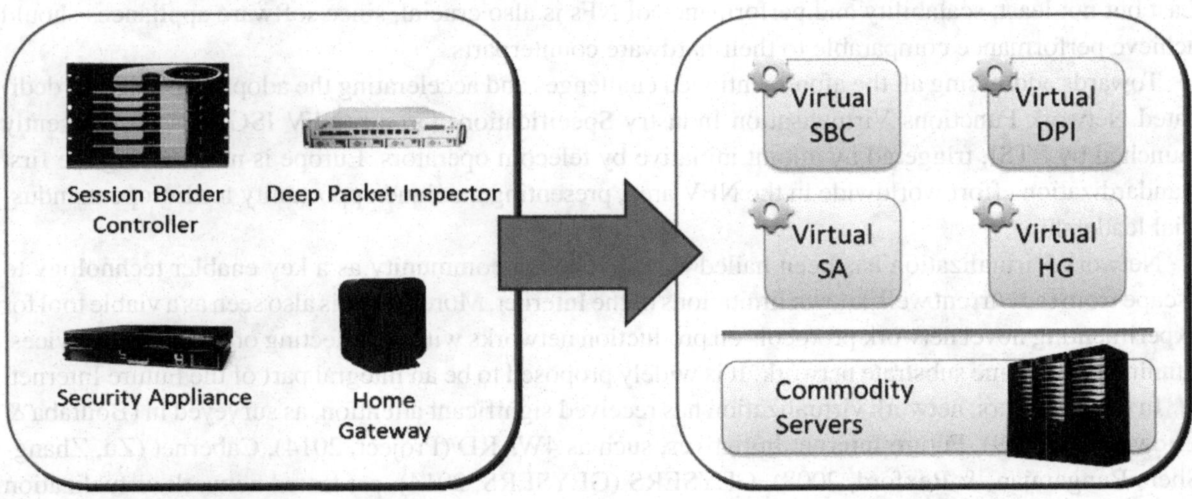

The NFV approach introduces key benefits for network operators/service providers, such as:

- Consolidation of hardware resources, leading to *reduced equipment investment and maintenance costs* (reduction of both CAPEX and OPEX) *and power consumption.*
- *Sharing of resources* among different network functions and users.
- *Up- and down-scaling of resources* assigned to each function.
- *Rapid introduction of novel network functions* (including upgrading of existing ones) at much lower cost and lower risk, leading to significant decrease of Time-To-Market (TTM) for new solutions. New experimental services can co-exist in the same infrastructure with "production" ones.
- Promotion of innovation, by opening a part of the networking market and transforming it to a *novel virtual appliance market, facilitating the involvement of software entrants,* including SMEs and even academia

While, leveraging the aforementioned benefits, several vendors are already offering virtualised appliances and middleboxes as commercial products, NFV presents several critical challenges when it comes to the automated and large-scale deployment of virtualized appliances within an operational infrastructure. While state-of-the-art IaaS cloud management platforms have proved very effective in deploying Virtual Machines (VMs) for hosting user applications, the automated deployment of virtualised network appliances instead is a much more challenging task, since it implies joint management of IT and networking resources within the same infrastructure, in order to couple the existing network connectivity services with the deployed NFs. A scalable and at the same time efficient management solution should achieve NF deployment and resource management, while also taking into account the established network topology. Fault resilience and availability are also critical issues, since the malfunction of a virtual network function may affect the entire network service. What is more, a NFV solution should be compatible with existing network management infrastructures (including OSS/BSS platforms) enabling a smooth migration path towards a fully virtualised infrastructure. It should also be as generic and universal as possible, supporting both virtual appliances and underlying hardware assets from different vendors. Last but not least, scalability and performance of NFs is also crucial, since software appliances should achieve performance comparable to their hardware counterparts.

Towards addressing all the aforementioned challenges and accelerating the adoption of NFV, a dedicated Network Functions Virtualisation Industry Specifications Group (NFV ISG) has been recently launched by ETSI, triggered by a joint initiative by telecom operators. Europe is now driving the first standardization effort worldwide in the NFV area, presenting a unique opportunity for European industrial leadership.

Network Virtualization has been hailed by the research community as a key enabler technology to escape from the current well-known limitations of the Internet. Moreover, it is also seen as a viable tool for experimenting novel network protocols on production networks without affecting other critical services, running of the same substrate network. It is widely proposed to be an integral part of the Future Internet.

In the past years, network virtualization has received significant attention, as surveyed in (Boutaba & Chowdhury, 2009). Future Internet Initiatives, such as 4WARD (Project, 2014), Cabernet (Zu, Zhang-Shen, Rangarajan, & Rexford, 2008), GEYSERS (GEYSERS, 2014), presented network virtualization architectures with emphasis on the business roles and the interfaces required for the provisioning and management of virtual networks across multiple domains. (Schaffrath, et al., 2009), (Werle, et al., 2011) presented early prototype implementations which realize several components of the 4WARD network virtualization architecture, while their work continued in (Papadimitriou, et al., 2012) showed that this architecture is technically feasible and robust. Several platforms have been deployed, assisting network operators to deploy virtual networks on their own infrastructure (Nogueira, Melo, Carapinha, & Sargento, A platform for Operator-driven Network Virtualization, 2011). Also (Peng, A Network Virtualisation Framework for IP Infrastructure Provisioning, 2011) project proposes an architecture for Network-Infrastructure-as-a-Service but without accommodating in-network services. Other initiatives arw also addressing network virtualisation, via the so-called Network Information and Control (NetIC) Generic Enabler (FI-WARE, 2014). NetIC is intended to provide access to network operation to higher-layer entities. It is more focused on Virtual Network provisioning, while programmability is supported by applying the SDN paradigm to allow the users to develop applications for network management.

In terms of virtual network embedding, most existing algorithms (e.g., (Zhang, Qian, Guo, & Lu, 2011), (Masti & Raghavan, 2012), (Yu, 2012), (Sarsembagieva, Gardikis, Xilouris, Kourtis, & Demestichas, 2013) consider a single substrate provider and require full knowledge of the available resources and the underlying network topology. Recent work (Chowdhury, Rahman, & Boutaba, 2012) presents a multi-domain VN embedding framework. This approach consists in relaying VN requests across Infrastructure Providers till the embedding has been completed. However, this VN embedding approach lacks of algorithms for resource assignment and allocation and it has not been evaluated. Hence, it is unclear how fast it converges to a complete VN embedding. (Houidi, Louati, Bean-Ameur, & Zeghlache, 2011) provides a set of algorithms for multi-domain VN embedding. Resource planning becomes more complicated if computing constraints on the network elements are also to be taken into account (Nogueira, Melo, Carapinha, & Sargento, Network Virtualization System Suite: Experimental Network Virtualization Platform, 2011), (Nogueira, Melo, Carapinha, & Sargento, Virtual Network Mapping into Heterogeneous Substrate Networks, 2011).

With regard to node virtualisation, advances on server (e.g., (Barham, et al., 2003) and link (e.g., (Rekhter & Rosen, 1999)) virtualization provide the technological ingredients needed to deploy virtual networks at global scale. In addition, (Egi E., et al., 2008) showed that virtual routers on commodity hardware have the capability to forward minimum-sized packets at several Gbps, while offering a high level of programmability (Egi N., et al., 2011). Platforms, such as VINI (Bavier, Feamster, Huang, Peterson, & Rexford, 2006) and Trellis (Bhatia, et al., 2008), synthesize server and link virtualization technologies to build simple virtual networks, mainly used for experimentation. In most cases, a virtual router provides an illusion of isolation, rather than a real isolation, as it lacks dedicated memory, processing and I/O resources (Carapinha & Jimenez, 2009).

Some recent activities also expand the network virtualisation concept to cover also the operations of the lower layers (PHY/MAC). In this context, the recently launched FP7 iJoin [IJOIN] and TROPIC [TROPIC] projects focus on the cloud-based virtualization of the cellular Radio Access Network (RAN) aiming at efficient resource management for small cells. Similarly and with a more extended scope, Mobile Cloud Networking [MCN] proposes a framework to fully virtualize a mobile network on end-to-end basis, from the RAN to the application server domains. For this purpose, MCN embraces the concept of Network Function virtualization, however specifically targeting to mobile network components.

The Network Function lifecycle comprises eight stages, as depicted in Figure 3.

Development of Functions is performed by Function Developers, which can be the Service Providers or third-party entities. NFs are published and aggregated in the Function Store.

Validation and debugging is also an important procedure, to ensure that the developed function works as expected. Buggy function code can have severe impact on the stability of the service. Function code and VMs will be digitally signed to ensure authenticity and, in any case, each service provider reserves the right to disallow the deployment of certain third-party functions into the network infrastructure. Although network traffic analysed by the NFs will correspond to a portion of the total network traffic, as the Orchestrator and SDN functions will only forward specifically selected flows towards each NF.

Publication of functions is performed at the Function Store, whose repository will host both the function image (as stand-alone application or integrated VM) and the associated description/metadata.

Function *Brokerage* is undertaken by the brokerage platform, which will be able to match user "high-level" service requirements with the specific technical specifications of the NFs, ensuring that the resources required for NF deployment are available.

Upon NF S*election* by the user, the *Deployment* phase includes the transfer of the VM image containing the function from the Store to in-network cloud infrastructure and the VM instantiation. The Orchestrator utilises the SDN control plane for network reconfiguration and the connection of the deployed NF with the customer vNet (network service injection).

Figure 3. Network Function lifecycle

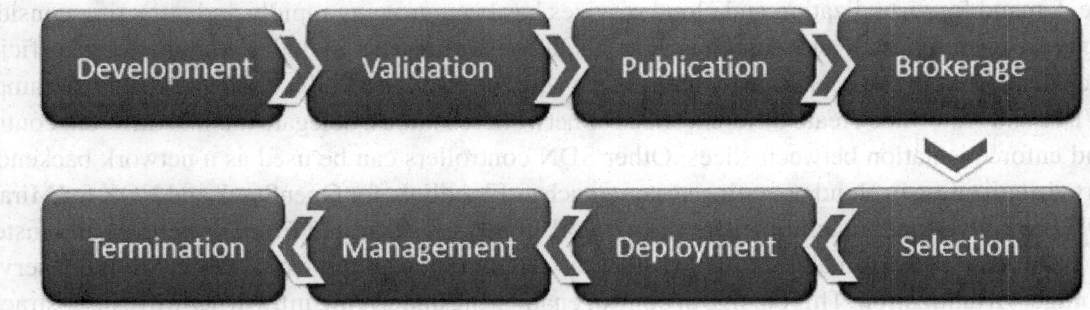

After instantiation, to facilitate *Management,* the function will expose, as aforementioned, an open NF Control API for uniform NF configuration and parameterisation by operator, the customers and also by their applications.

Function *Termination* involves the removal of the NF instance from the virtualised infrastructure, also involving the necessary network re-configuration.

A critical issue in programmable architectures is security; deploying a third-party network appliance on a programmable network raises several security issues and may cause severe network malfunction due to either buggy code or malicious actions. This issue is of particular importance in SDN-as-a-Service (SDNaaS) platforms, where users are enabled to deploy arbitrary network applications for controlling network slices. To address this issue, this chapter proposes a three-tier approach:

- First, the overall concept itself foresees that network functions to be deployed are only chosen among the pre-developed ones already available at the Store, and does not fully expose the control API, which would allow each user to apply arbitrary control code into the network.
- Second, each new function published on the Function Store can be validated by the operator (using established auditing procedures which are out of the scope of the project), who may allow or disallow its deployment on the domain. In this sense, each operator deploys solely functions which have been validated and authorised. Authenticity of function code and associated VMs will be assured via the use of digital certificates.
- Third, the cloud-based management approach achieves deployment of function code into isolated virtual machines with controlled resources. In this way, any anomalies within a function code do not drain the computing resources of other co-located NFs.

SOFTWARE DEFINED NETWORKING

The huge growth of virtualisation and cloud computing in the market, as the previous sections have analysed, prompt the IT industry to revise their opinions about current traditional network architectures. The majority of traditional networks are built with Ethernet switches, which are arranged in a tree structure. This design was adequate in the time that client-server computing was at the forefront. But currently things have changed and the concept of virtualisation has entered at various layers of the computing industry, spanning from the application/service layer down to networking and function virtualisation. This virtualised heterogeneity creates new needs for management and administration, capable of handling the new virtualised functions and optimizing the respective resource availability. This new technology is called Software Defined Networking (SDN).

The demand for virtualization and cloud services has been growing rapidly and attracting considerable interest from industry and academia. The challenges it presents includes among others: efficient resource management and scalability, which can be addressed using SDN's control model. For example, FlowVisor and AutoSlice create different slices of network resources, delegate them to different controllers and enforce isolation between slices. Other SDN controllers can be used as a network backend to support virtualization in cloud operating systems such as Floodlight for OpenStack and NOX for Mirage.

SDN is a network architecture where the network control is separated from forwarding and instead of this is directly programmable as Figure 4 depicts. SDN was inspired from the new trend in servers and storage, virtualization. This change of control enables the underlying infrastructure to be abstracted for various applications and network services and as a consequence of this the network can be treated as a logical or virtual entity. With SDN system, administrators have the opportunity to convert network services much easier into virtual services and as a result of this manually configuration of hardware is replaced, as it is no longer essential. Furthermore, SDN gives the chance to administrators to have central control of network traffic without even requiring physical access to hardware devices. These elements are called the control plane and the data plane. SDN separates the system into the control plane and the data plane. The majority of IT specialists believe that SDN technology makes networking much simpler. Many companies like Google or Facebook have already begun to use SDN and Openflow protocol.

There are many reasons why SDN technology was needed to be introduced. To begin with, there is the change of traffic patterns. Within the enterprise data center, traffic patterns have changed significantly. In contrast to client-server applications where the majority of the communication occurs between one client and one server, today's applications access different databases and servers. Furthermore, another key reason to use the SDN technology is the ability to incorporate faster and more powerful hardware. For example, a network switch can be used to handle the forwarding of data packets, while a separate virtual server can be configured to run the network control plane. This split configuration permits the network development and runtime environment to be located on a more advanced and faster platform, rather than being relegated to the lower-end and slower management processors used on hardware switches and routers. Moreover, another reason is the "consumerization" of the IT. Users are increasingly using mobile devices such as smartphones or tablets to access the corporate network. Furthermore, another important reason is the big rise of cloud services. Public and private cloud services have become significantly popular. Finally, the "big data" means more bandwidth and SDN is here to provide it. All the above, along with some limitations that exists in current networks such as complexity, inconsistent policies, inability to scale and vendor performance, force the IT industry to the development of the SDN technology. A very effective way to understand and get familiar with the SDN technology is to analyze the four Software Networking layers that are depicted in Figure 5. In this way it is easier to understand the features and the benefits that SDN provides.

- **Forwarding:** It is also commonly known as the Data Plane. It is the bottom layer and probably the most important of all. It is responsible for the effective and fast movement of data.
- **Control:** It is the layer where the traffic is handled. It works upon the topology of a network and is responsible to identify and acknowledge networks by interacting with other devices.
- **Services:** It appears more often in devices like firewalls and routers. Its responsibility is to perform advanced operations upon networking data when Forwarding cannot perform these operations.
- **Management:** It is also named as the control plane layer. In this layer the network devices can be configured. It is also responsible for providing basic guidelines of how each part of the network can correspond with each other.

Generally there are two types of SDN interfaces, Northbound and Southbound. These interfaces in theory can be applied to almost any type of network, OS or computer system but more recently they have been used successfully in accordance with Application Program Interfaces (APIs) in SDN.

Figure 4. SDN controller

Figure 5. SDN layering

- **Northbound APIs:** In SDN, the northbound API interface on the controller enables applications and the overall management system to program the network and request services from it. This application tier often includes global automation and data management applications, as well as providing basic network functions such as data path computation, routing and security. Nowadays, no formalized standards have been ratified for northbound APIs with several dozen open and proprietary protocols being developed using different northbound APIs. This lack of standard APIs is caused by the varied nature of applications sitting above the controller. Nevertheless, a lot of vertical applications are currently using northbound APIs such as OpenStack.
- **Southbound APIs:** When we are referring to southbound APIs OpenFlow is the most important thing. Although it is not explicitly required by SDN, OpenFlow is a protocol often used as the southbound API that defines a set of open commands for data forwarding. These commands allow routers to discover the network's topology and define the behavior of physical and virtual switches based on application requests sent via the northbound APIs.

OpenFlow is the first communication interface recognized in the SDN architecture. With OpenFlow direct access and manipulation of network devices are permitted. One of the main problems of existing networks is the absence of an open interface and that is why the need of OpenFlow is so huge. The OpenFlow protocol is implemented not only in the interface of network devices, but also in the interface of SDN control software. OpenFlow protocol uses the concept of flows to examine network traffic and it also allows to the IT to determine how much traffic can flow through the network devices, whereas the current IP-based routing does not provide this level of control, as all flows between two endpoints should follow exactly the same path through the network, regardless of their different requirements.

Openflow is a key issue of SDN architecture and until now is the only standardized SDN protocol allowing direct manipulation of the network devices. OpenFlow can be deployed even on existing networks, both physical and virtual as it is depicted in Figure 6. Network devices can fully support OpenFlow-based forwarding as well as traditional forwarding, and in this way it makes it very easy and convenient for enterprises and carriers to progressively introduce OpenFlow technologies. A lot of efforts are made to standardize OpenFlow and ensure interiperability between network devices and control software from different vendors. Moreover, crucial is, that OpenFlow architecture can integrate seamlessly with an enterprise or carrier's existing infrastructure and provide a simple migration path for those segments of the network that need SDN functionality the most. SDN technologies based on the OpenFlow give us the opportunity to reduce operations and make the management of networks much simplier. Some of the benefits of OpenFlow are: centralized control of multi-vendor environments, reduced complexity through automation, increased network reliability and security, more granular network control and finally much better user experience.

Figure 6. SDN OpenFlow Architecture

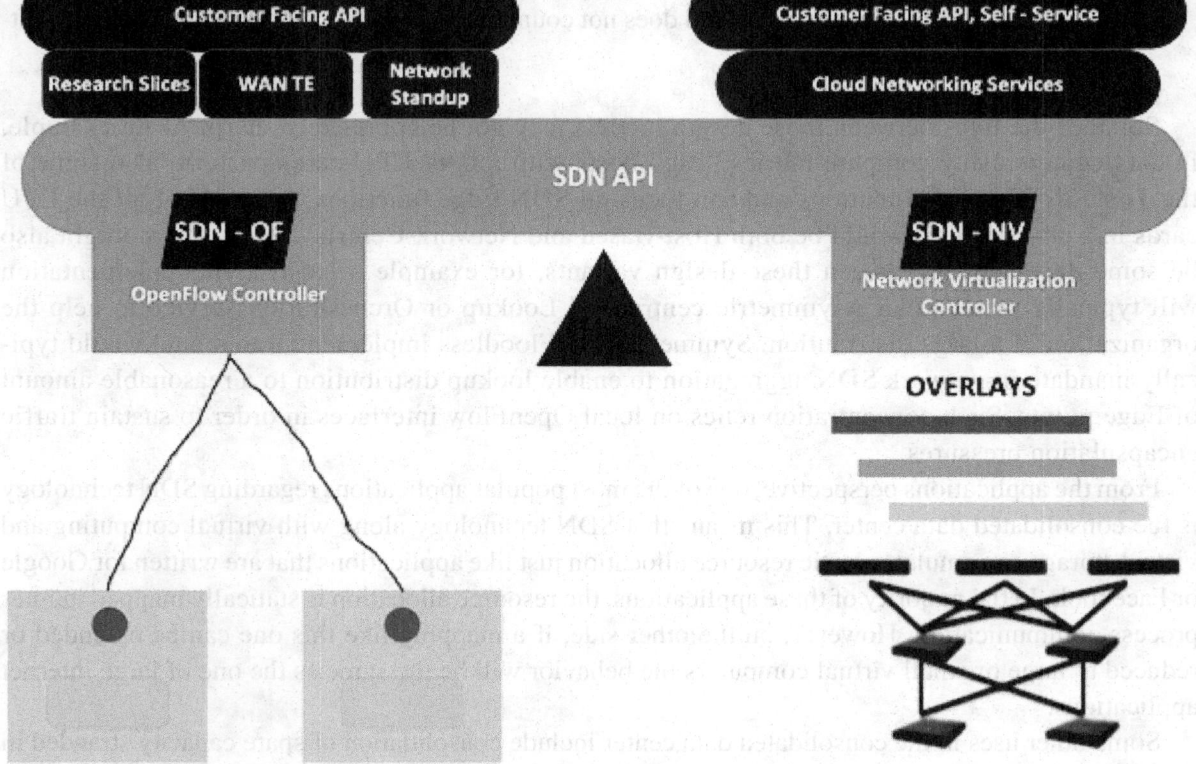

SDN can be deployed at various models, which are described and analyses hereafter:

- **Symmetric vs. Asymmetric:** As far as asymmetric model is concerned, SDN information is centralized and edge driving is distributed. However, on the other side, a lot of question are raised due to scale-out, simplicity doubts, etc. As far as the symmetric model is concerned, efforts are made to increase global information distribution capability and SDN aggregation performance, in order to achieve that the SDN elements will be basically one type of component.
- **Floodless vs Flood-Based:** When we are referring to a flood-based model, a big amount of global information sharing is achieved by using broadcast and multicast techniques. In this way SDN models become more symmetric, and strengthen the already existing principles, in order to achieve global awareness and identity learning. However, one drawback of this is that more locations are added and as a result of this scalability is degraded. In the Floodless model, on the other side, all the forwarding process is based on global exact match, which is most commonly achieved by using distributed hashing and distributed caching of SDN lookup tables.
- **Host-Based vs. Network-Centric:** Regarding host-based model an assumption is made as far as use of SDN in data-centers is concerned, as we have a lot of virtual machines moving to enable electricity. Taking into consideration this assumption, the SDN encapsulation processing is already done at the host HyperVisor on behalf of the virtual machines. By this design, SDN edge traffic is reduced. On the other hand, in a NetworkCentric design a much clearer demarcation is made between the network edge and the end points. An SDN edge like this one is associated with the access of Top of Rack device and outside the host end points. Clearly, this is a much more traditional approach to networking and does not count on end points to perform any possible routing operation.

Some of the lines between these design models may not be completely sharp. As an example, in data-centers using compute fabrics "Big" hosts with lots of CPU cards perform also some of the TopOfRack access functions and can focus on SDN Edge functions on behalf of all the CPU cards in a chassis. This would be both Host-Based and Network-Centric design. There might also be some dependency between these design variants, for example a HostBased implementation will typically mandate an Asymmetric centralized Lookup or Orchestration service to help the organization of a large distribution. Symmetric and Floodless implementation model would typically mandate in-network SDN aggregation to enable lookup distribution to a reasonable amount of Edge points. Such concentration relies on local OpenFlow interfaces in order to sustain traffic encapsulation pressures.

From the applications perspective, one of the most popular applications regarding SDN technology is the consolidated data center. This means that SDN technology along with virtual computing and virtual storage can emulate elastic resource allocation just like applications that are written for Google or Facebook. In the majority of these applications, the resource allocation is statically mapped in inter process communication. However, on the other side, if a mapping like this one can be extended or reduced to large or small virtual computers the behavior will be the same as the one of large internet applications.

Some other uses in the consolidated data center include consolidation of spare capacity stranded in static partition of racks to pods. As a result of pooling these spare capacities we have a considerable reduction of computing resources.

The use of SDN distributed and global edge control also includes the capability to balance load on lots of links leading from the racks to the switching spine of the data-center. Without SDN this task could only be done by using traditional link-state updates that update all locations upon change in any possible location. Distributed global SDN measurements might extend the cap on the scale of physical clusters. Other data-center uses being listed are distributed application load balancing, distributed firewalls, and similar adaptations to original networking functions that arise from dynamic, any location or rack allocation of compute resources.

SDN is also used for addressing the traditional and geo-distributed campus network regarding enterprise and carrier managed network services. These specific environments were always challenged by a lot of complexities of moves-adds-changes and movement of users. However with the growth and use of SDN, it is expected that these challenges could be addressed using global definitions and being separated from the physical interfaces of the network infrastructure.

It has been observed that this "overlay" approach might lead to inefficiency and low performance, because characteristics of the underlying infrastructure are ignored. Hence, carriers have identified the gaps in overlays and asked for them to be filled by SDN solutions that take traffic, topology, and equipment under consideration. Accordingly, there exists the opinion regarding SDN, that exposes network resources so they can be continually optimized and that traffic demands can be handled in a much more predictable way.

Furthermore another application is the Application Performance Management (APM) – organizations like Compuware, Fluke etc. that accept information and data via tap either SPAN ports are looking at the state of applications on the network. Moreover, another applications are the IPAM (includes physical and virtual nodes), the Security Information Event Management (SIEM) –integrates products and tools that have an overall view of the security events occurring in a network with an SDN controller- and finally the call processor such as an IP PBX or Call Manager that will totally understand when voice and video calls are due to set up.

As it is evident from all the above SDN is here to stay and from the development and the usage of SDN technology derive some basic benefits that will prompt the users and service providers to use extensively the SDN technology in the forthcoming years. However, the IT industry has been focused until recently just on technical details and not on the value that SDN can bring to the forefront.

- Decoupling of control data plane,
- Enables treatment as logical/virtual entities,
- Make them easily programmable in the Application layer,
- Exists higher rate of innovation,
- Anywhere access to information via the cloud,
- Network management,
- Resource utilization,
- Security,
- Network Functions Virtualization,
- Network service chaining,
- Bandwidth calendaring,
- Energy management,
- Improve network efficiency,
- Improve IT agility and network customization,
- Provide advanced analytics.

On the other hand, however, there are concerns about taking the decision to develop and use the SDN technology. Many IT specialists argue that the current state of new versions of APIs (such as OpenFlow) being released is perhaps occurring too quickly, without allowing for innovations to drive the market. Furthermore, SDN is faced with a major challenge from traditional networking vendors, which have long relied on sales of their proprietary networking hardware and software and could see a significant decline in the sales if SDN is rapidly adopted. Moreover, many organizations simply do not have the time, expertise, or capital to invest in a completely new networking architecture. Still, as a result of the industry's activities surrounding SDN, there is plenty of positive buzz regarding SDN technology.

SDN applicability is not limited to the wired networking, but it has also positive impact in the field of wireless networking. As mobile networks are becoming the major channel to access Internet services, there is an urgent need to keep us with the pace of user growth and the scale of services. For example, the recent demand of network capacity for mobile data traffic is far exceeding the supply of current networks. At the same time, services also evolve in both variety and complexity. For this reason SDN is currently becoming really useful for mobile networks and there are many solutions that this technology offers to us for the wireless mobile networks such as:

- **Cellular Networks:** The existing cellular infrastructure has been criticized as being expensive and inflexible, suffering from complex control plane protocols and vendor-specific configuration interfaces. In order to simplify the management of cellular data networks, the project CellSDN proposes a SDN design for the cellular core infrastructure. Because applying SDN to cellular environment needs to meet several challenges, like user mobility and real-time adaption, a set of necessary extensions are identified for the key elements of CellSDN architecture. For example, policies of subscriber attributes are translated into swtich rules that match on packet headers and a local control agent is introduced on the switch to alleviate the scalability issue of central controlling by performing localized actions guided by the control platform.
- **WLAN Environment:** OpenRoads is the first SDN solution that is deployed on campus using OpenFlow and virtualization to decouple mobility from physical network and allow multiple providers to control and configure underlying infrastructure concurrently. The OpenRoads platform aims at enabling experimental research by using open-source controller and extend it to control and capture wireless events such as hos-AP association. The greatest feature is its openness that all the tools used and developed in the project are freely available.

However, one of the main concerns of SDN, especially by the industry, is the SDN security aspects. Currently a lot of research has been done regarding SDN security. The proposed solutions have been categorized into four groups in terms of their target environment: enterprise networks, cloud and data center, home and edge access, and general design.

Regarding enhanced security in wireless mobile networks with SDN, network convergence is the trend where operators will integrate diverse wireless technologies like 4G or WiFi to the network infrastructure. This creates a challenge toward interoperability as how to manage the multi-vendor physical devices that use different configurations under various policy and security requirement in a multi-operator environment. SDN provides the virtualized abstraction that gives a convenient way to hide the complexity of various wireless protocols and topology. The programmability and flow model of SDN also facilitate granular policy control, flexible traffic aggregation and partition. These functional features and its openness make SDN suitable for the upcoming wireless mobile environment. As it is evident until now, there is not so much research on the security of the SDN technology regarding mobile networks. For this reason it is essential for the IT industry to ensure that no serious security issues will exist from the usage of the SDN technology.

The future of SDN is still on-going. Due to the fact that SDN becomes more widely adopted and protocols such as OpenFlow are further defined, new solutions are further defined, new solutions are proposed and new challenges arise such as: controller and switch design, scalability and performance issues, controller-service interfacing, virtualization and cloud service interfacing, virtualization and cloud service applications, information centric networking and enabling heterogeneous networking with SDN.

To sum up, SDN has great potential to change the way networks operate and OpenFLow in particular has been routed as a radical new idea in networking with great potentials that will change the whole current networking architectures.

FUTURE RESEARCH DIRECTIONS

The joint management of cloud and network resources has become a hot topic in research since allocation and reconfiguration of resources in an integrated way has become mandatory. Moreover, resource monitoring and fault detection is essential for these processes. In order to facilitate resource discovery and mapping, there exist several resource description frameworks and schemas so as to separately describe network resources and cloud/IT ones –some of them are mentioned in (Peng, A Network Virtualisation Framework for IP Infrastructure Provisioning, 2011). However, at present, there is no separate entity for infrastructure description which is required for resource advertisement. (Koslovski, Vicat, & Primet, 2008) and (Medhioub, Houidi, Louati, & Zeghlache, 2011) present work on network resource description that is being extended to the cloud (resources and services). In this context, future research directions will include the establishment of a common resource description schema for composite in-network assets, as required for resource advertisement and efficient service mapping.

Following the description phase, the provisioning of resources in a joint cloud/network architecture system should be done taking into account computing resources (e.g. CPU, HDD, RAM) as well as typical network resources (e.g. bandwidth, latency). The subject is tackled today mostly in an individual way in the different areas of resource management. (Bouyoucef, Limam-Bedhiaf, & Cherkaoui, 2010), (Csorba, Meling, & Heegaard, 2010), and (Houidi, Louati, Zeghlache, Papadimitriou, & Mathy, Adaptive virtual network provisioning, 2010) are works that address the allocation of cloud computing resources, i.e., virtual machines (VMs). (Osana & Kuribayashi, 2010) presents a fair joint multiple resource (computational and network) allocation, however it makes a clear separation between network and computing resources. (Soares, Carapinha, Melo, Monteiro, & Sargento, 2012), on the other hand, envisions a full integration of the Cloud and the network, particularly addressing the resource allocation problem through joint virtualization of network and cloud resources, by proposing an algorithm to allocate cloud and network resources in an integrated way. (Rui, Li, Ghanem, & Yike, 2012) considers the elastic resource provisioning as a key feature of cloud computing and proposes a lightweight approach to enable cost-effective elasticity for cloud application by providing fine-grained scaling and resource management at the resource level itself (CPUs, memory, I/O) in addition to VM-level scaling. Finally, (Fajjari, Aitsaadi, Pujolle, & Zimmermann, 2012) tackles the fundamental challenge of efficient resource allocation within Cloud's backbone network and investigates a new dynamic adaptive virtual network resource allocation strategy named Backtracking-VNE which guarantees an efficient resources share between embedded virtual links with respect to their occupancy.

Despite the attention, the work in joint cloud/network resource management is still in its early stage. A common need, addressed by many research efforts, is the joint provision of cloud and network assets in order to offer cloud IT services with adequate network Quality of Service (Javier Carmona-Murillo, 2014). For providing Moreover, several research efforts are preliminarily addressing the utilisation of technologies such as OpenFlow for the provision of virtual networks within a data centre to support the cloud infrastructure (Matias, Jacob, Sanchez, & Demchenko, 2011), (Matias, Tornero, Mendiola, Jacob, & Toldeo, 2012). However, such solutions are only at preliminary stage and further future research is necessary towards a deeper and more sophisticated framework.

CONCLUSION

Cloud computing is a promising technology for organizations, notably to address growing demands for storage and real-time data processing, creating a unique opportunity for modern businesses to streamline their IT requirements in a very flexible and cost effective way. This has been motivated mainly by the need to reduce Capex, while keeping control of Opex. IT workloads have increasingly migrated to "cloud" infrastructures, i.e., homogeneous x86 compute fabrics built from commodity servers, interconnected by Ethernet fabrics and supported by NAS and SAN storage backends, managed by control software such as OpenStack and Eucalyptus.

Moving forward from the already successful Cloud Computing, the trend of cloud and virtualization was further expanded to new fields, such as the processing and the networking, creating a layered ecosystem of cloud resources, based on virtualization. For example the Network Functions Virtualisation (NFV) is an emerging concept, which refers to the migration of certain network functionalities, traditionally performed by hardware elements, to virtualized IT infrastructures, where they are deployed as software components. NFV leverages commodity servers and storage, including cloud platforms, to enable rapid deployment, reconfiguration and elastic scaling of network functionalities.

The new multi-layered cloud-based ecosystem creates new challenges especially in the field of management and administration, which is not feasible any more by the traditional and already widely used techniques and methods. Software Defined Networking (SDN) provides a new network architecture that brings with it many positive results. OpenFlow architecture abstracts the underlying infrastructure from the applications that use it and in this way allows to the network to become much more programmable, manageable and scalable. SDN prompts IT specialists to manage their servers, applications, networks and storage with a simple approach and tool set. Generally, SDN can improve network agility and scalability.

Networking will rely in the future more and more on software, which will make pace of innovation for networks much faster. SDN can make today's networks more flexible and allocate the resources dynamically. It also promises to secure cloud environments and provide higly automated operations. Of course the SDN revolution today is extremely turbulent. Presently, its development is focused heavily on the large data center and virtualization space. It may very well evolve into a useful tool for the enterprise and service provider space in the future, but there's a lot of work that needs doing by everyone involved before that can happen.

To conclude, SDN with its many advantages is on the way to become the new trend for network and technologies and it is believed that it is going to be used extensively in the forthcoming years.

REFERENCES

Abiquo. (2014). *Virtualization, cloud services, software - Cloud computing platform*. Retrieved from http://www.abiquo.com

Amazon. (2014). *Amazon web services*. Retrieved from http://aws.amazon.com

Amazon Web Services. (n.d.). Retrieved from http://aws.amazon.com/

Application and Network Performance with OPNET. (n.d.). Retrieved from http://www.opnet.com

Barham, P., Dragovic, B., Fraser, K., Hand, S., Harris, T., Ho, A., & Warfield, A. et al. (2003). Xen and the art of virtualization. In *Proc. 19th ACM Symposium on OS Principles*. ACM.

Bavier, A., Feamster, N., Huang, M., Peterson, L., & Rexford, J. (2006). In VINI veritas: Realistic and controlled network experimentation. In *Proc. ACM SIGCOMM*. ACM.

Bhatia, S., Motiwala, M., Muhlbauer, W., Mundada, Y., Valancius, V., Bavier, A., & Rexford, J. et al. (2008). Trellis: A platform for building flexible, fast virtual networks on commodity hardware. In *Proc. 3rd ACM Workshop on Real Overlays and Distributed Systems*. ACM.

Bourdena, A., Kormentzas, G., Skianis, C., Pallis, E., & Mastorakis, G. (2011). *Real-time TVWS trading based on a centralized CR network architecture*. IEEE GLOBECOM Workshops. doi:10.1109/GLOCOMW.2011.6162600

Bourdena, A., Pallis, E., Kormentzas, G., Skianis, C., & Mastorakis, G. (2012). *QoS provisioning and policy management in a broker-based CR network architecture*. Anaheim, CA: IEEE Globecom. doi:10.1109/GLOCOM.2012.6503383

Boutaba, N., & Chowdhury, R. (2009). Network virtualization: State of the art and research challenges. *IEEE Communications Magazine*, *47*(7), 20–26. doi:10.1109/MCOM.2009.5183468

Bouyoucef, K., Limam-Bedhiaf, I., & Cherkaoui, O. (2010). Optimal allocation approach of virtual servers in cloud computing. In *Proc. 6th EURO-NF Conference on Next Generation Internet* (NGI). Academic Press. doi:10.1109/NGI.2010.5534467

Business, G. A. (2014). *Google apps for business*. Retrieved 7 11, 2014, from http://www.google.com/apps/intl/en/business/index.html

Carapinha, J., & Jimenez, J. (2009). Network virtualization – A view from the bottom. In *Proc. ACM SIGCOMM VISA'2009 Workshop*. ACM.

Caron, E., & Desprez, F. (2011). Forecasting for cloud computing on-demand resources based on pattern matching. *Journal of Grid Computing*.

Chowdhury, M., Rahman, M., & Boutaba, R. (2012). ViNEYard: Virtual network embedding algorithms with coordinated node and link mapping. *IEEE/ACM Transactions on Networking*, *20*(1), 203–226. doi:10.1109/TNET.2011.2159308

Cloud, N. (2014). Retrieved from http://csrc.nist.gov/publications/nistpubs/800-145/SP800-145.pdf

Cloud Computing, Managed Hosting, Dedicated Server Hosting by Rackspace. (n.d.). Retrieved from http://www.rackspace.com/

Cloud Hosting | Webair Cloud Server Solutions. (n.d.). Retrieved from http://www.webair.com/web-hosting-cloud-servers.html

Cloud Monitoring & Management. (2014). Retrieved from http://cloudkick.com

Cloud Monitoring & Management. (n.d.). Retrieved from http://cloudkick.com

Company. (2014). Retrieved from http://www.salesforce.com

Computing, P. (2014). *Clusters, grids, clouds*. Retrieved from http://www.platform.com

Copperegg. (2014). *Uncover and resolve performance issues with cloud performance monitoring*. Retrieved from http://www.copperegg.com/product/cloud-monitoring/

CRM - The Enterprise Cloud Computing Company. (n.d.). Retrieved from http://www.salesforce.com

Csorba, M., Meling, H., & Heegaard, P. (2010). Ant system for service deployment in private and public clouds. In *Proceeding of the 2nd worKshop on Bio-Inspired Algorithms for Distributed Systems*. ACM. doi:10.1145/1809018.1809024

Developer Force: Salesforce.com & Force.com Developer Resources. (n.d.). Retrieved from http://developer.force.com/

DynamicOps. (2014). *Operations virtualization, cloud automation, cloud management, VDI, private cloud*. Retrieved from http://www.dynamicops.com

Egi, E., Greenhalgh, A., Handley, M., Hoerdt, M., Huici, F., & Mathy, L. (2008). Towards high performance virtual routers on commodity hardware. In *Proc. ACM CoNEXT 2008*. ACM. doi:10.1145/1544012.1544032

Egi, N., Greenhalgh, A., Handley, M., Hoerdt, M., Huici, F., Mathy, L., & Papadimitriou, P. (2011). A platform for high performance and flexible virtual routers on commodity hardware. *ACM SIGCOMM Computer Communication Review Archive, 40*(1), 127-128.

Emeakaroha, V. C., Netto, M. A., Calheiros, R. N., Brandic, I., Buyya, R., & Rose, C. A. (2011). Towards autonomic detection of SLA violations in cloud infrastructures. *Future Generation Computer Systems*.

Ernst & Young. (2011). *Cloud computing issues and impacts*. Ernst and Young.

Fajjari, I., Aitsaadi, N., Pujolle, G., & Zimmermann, H. (2012). An optimised dynamic resource allocation algorithm for cloud's backbone network. In *Proceedings of IEEE 37th Conference on Local Computer Networks* (LCN). IEEE.

FI-WARE. (2014). *FI-WARE interface to networks and devices (I2ND)*. Retrieved from http://forge.fi-ware.eu/plugins/mediawiki/wiki/fiware/index.php/FI-WARE_Interface_to_Networks_and_Devices_(I2ND)

Gartner. (2014). Retrieved from http://www.gartner.com/it/page.jsp?id=1389313

GEYSERS. (2014). *Generalised architecture for dynamic infrastructure services*. Retrieved from http://www.geysers.eu/

Google. (2014). *Google app engine*. Retrieved from http://code.google.com/intl/el-GR/appengine

Google App Engine. (n.d.). Retrieved from http://code.google.com/intl/el-GR/appengine/

Google Apps for Business. (n.d.). Retrieved from http://www.google.com/apps/intl/en/business/index.html

Grosch, H. (1950). *Proceedings of the 1948 scientific computation forum*. IBM.

Group, E. (2010). *The future of cloud computing: Opportunities for European cloud computing beyond 2010*. Author.

Hat, R. (2014). *Red hat KVM*. Retrieved from http://www.redhat.com/virtualization/rhev

Houidi, I., Louati, W., Bean-Ameur, W., & Zeghlache, D. (2011). Virtual network provisioning across multiple substrate networks. *Computer Networks*, *55*(4), 1011–1023. doi:10.1016/j.comnet.2010.12.011

Houidi, I., Louati, W., & Zeghlache, D. (2009). Virtual resource description and clustering for virtual network. In *Proc. IEEE ICC, Workshop Network of the Future*. IEEE. doi:10.1109/ICCW.2009.5207979

Houidi, I., Louati, W., Zeghlache, D., Papadimitriou, P., & Mathy, L. (2010). Adaptive virtual network provisioning. In *Proc. of the Second ACM SIGCOMM Workshop on Virtualized Infrastructure Systems and Architectures (VISA '10)*. ACM. doi:10.1145/1851399.1851407

IDC. (2014). Retrieved from http://www.idc.com/research/cloudcomputing/index.jsp

IT Monitoring. (n.d.). Retrieved from http://portal.monitis.com/

ITSM- Network Monitoring + Service Desk Management. (n.d.). Retrieved from http://www.nimsoft.com

Javier Carmona-Murillo, J.-L. G.-S.-P.-J.-P. (2014). QoS in next generation mobile networks: An analytical study. In Resource management in mobile computing environments (pp. 25-41). Springer.

Koslovski, G., Vicat, P., & Primet, B. (2008). VXDL: Virtual resources and interconnection networks description language. In *Proc. GridNets 2008*. Academic Press.

Li, Q., Xiao, L., & Li, Z. (2009). Adaptive management of virtualized resources in cloud computing using feedback control. In *Proceedings of the 2009, First IEEE International Conference on Information Science and Engineering* (pp. 99 - 102). Nanjing, China: IEEE.

Lodi, G., Panzieri, F., Rossi, D., & Turrini, E. (2007). *SLA-driven clustering of QoS-aware application servers*. Academic Press.

Masti, S., & Raghavan, S. (2012). VNA: An enhanced algorithm for virtual network embedding. In *Proceedings of 21st International Conference on Computer Communication Networks* (ICCCN). Academic Press. doi:10.1109/ICCCN.2012.6289180

Matias, J., Jacob, E., Sanchez, D., & Demchenko, Y. (2011). An OpenFlow-based network virtualization framework for the cloud. In *Proc 3rd IEEE Int.Conf on Cloud Computing Technology and Science*. IEEE. doi:10.1109/CloudCom.2011.104

Matias, J., Tornero, B., Mendiola, A., Jacob, E., & Toldeo, N. (2012). Implementing layer 2 network virtualization using OpenFlow: Challenges and solutions. In *Proceedings of European Workshop on Software Defined Networking* (EWSDN). Academic Press. doi:10.1109/EWSDN.2012.18

Medhioub, H., Houidi, I., Louati, W., & Zeghlache, D. (2011). Design, implementation and evaluation of virtual resource description and clustering framework. In *Proceedings of IEEE International Conference on Advanced Information Networking and Applications* (AINA). IEEE. doi:10.1109/AINA.2011.46

Microsoft. (2014a). *Windows Azure platform*. Retrieved from http://www.microsoft.com/windowsazure

Microsoft. (2014b). *Microsoft Hyper-V*. Retrieved from http://www.microsoft.com/servers/hyper-v-server/default.mspx

Microsoft. (n.d.). *Windows Azure platform*. Retrieved 2011 from http://www.microsoft.com/windowsazure/

monitis. (2014). *IT monitoring*. Retrieved from http://portal.monitis.com/

Mousicou, P., Mavromoustakis, C., Bourdena, A., Mastorakis, G., & Pallis, E. (2013). Performance evaluation of dynamic cloud resource migration based on temporal and capacity-aware policy for efficient resource sharing. In *Proceedings of the 2nd ACM Workshop on High Performance Mobile Opportunistic Systems*. ACM. doi:10.1145/2507908.2507917

nimsoft. (2014). *ITSM- Network monitoring and service desk management*. Retrieved from http://www.nimsoft.com

NIST. (2014). *NIST cloud definition*. Retrieved from http://csrc.nist.gov/publications/nistpubs/800-145/SP800-145.pdf

Nogueira, J., Melo, M., Carapinha, J., & Sargento, S. (2011). A platform for operator-driven network virtualization. In *Proc. IEEE EUROCON - International Conference on Computer as a Tool*. IEEE. doi:10.1109/EUROCON.2011.5929325

Nogueira, J., Melo, M., Carapinha, J., & Sargento, S. (2011). Network virtualization system suite: Experimental network virtualization platform. In *Proceedings of International Conf. on Testbeds and Research Infrastructures for the Development of Networks and Communities*. Academic Press.

Nogueira, J., Melo, M., Carapinha, J., & Sargento, S. (2011). Virtual network mapping into heterogeneous substrate networks. In *Proc. IEEE ISCC*. Academic Press. doi:10.1109/ISCC.2011.5983876

OPNET. (2014). *Application and network performance with OPNET*. Retrieved from http://www.opnet.com

Osana, Y., & Kuribayashi, S. (2010). Enhanced fair joint multiple resource allocation method in all-IP networks. In *Proc. 24th IEEE Int. Conf. on Advanced Information Networking and Applications Workshops (WAINA)*. IEEE. doi:10.1109/WAINA.2010.33

Papadimitriou, P., Houidi, I., Louati, W., Zeghlache, D., Werle, C., Bless, R., & Mathy, L. (2012). *Towards large-scale network virtualization*. Santorini: IFIP WWIC.

Parkhill, D. (1966). *The challenge of the computer utility*. Addison-Wesley.

Peng, B. (2011). A network virtualisation framework for IP infrastructure provisioning. In *Proc 3rd IEEE Int.Conf on Cloud Computing Technology and Science*. IEEE.

Project 4. (2014). *4WARD project*. Retrieved from http://www.4ward-project.eu/

Project Management Software, Online Collaboration: Basecamp. (n.d.). Retrieved from http://basecamphq.com/

Rackspace. (2014). *Cloud computing, managed hosting, dedicated server hosting by rackspace*. Retrieved from http://www.rackspace.com

Rekhter, E., & Rosen, Y. (1999). *BGP/MPLS VPNs, RFC 2547*. IETF.

Resources, D. F. (2014). *Developer force: Salesforce.com & force.com developer resources*. Retrieved from http://developer.force.com

Rui, H., Li, G., Ghanem, M., & Yike, G. (2012). Lightweight resource scaling for cloud applications. In *Proceedings of 12th IEEE/ACM International Symposium on CLuster, Cloud and Grid Computing* (CCGrid). IEEE.

Sarsembagieva, K., Gardikis, G., Xilouris, G., Kourtis, A., & Demestichas, P. (2013). Efficient planning of virtual network services. In *Proceedings of IEEE Region 8 EuroCon Conference*. IEEE.

Schaffrath, G., Werle, C., Papadimitriou, P., Feldmann, A., Bless, R., Greenhalgh, A., & Mathy, L. et al. (2009). Network virtualization architecture: Proposal and initial prototype. In *Proc. ACM SIGCOMM VISA*. ACM.

Soares, J., Carapinha, J., Melo, M., Monteiro, R., & Sargento, S. (2012). Resource allocation in the network operator's cloud: A virtualization approach. In *Proceedings of IEEE Symposium on Computers and Communications* (ISCC). IEEE.

Software. P. M. (2014). Retrieved from http://basecamphq.com

Solutions, W. C. (2014). *Cloud hosting*. Retrieved from http://www.webair.com/webhosting-cloud-servers.html

Stantchev, V., & Schröpfer, C. (2009). Negotiating and enforcing QoS and SLAs in grid and cloud computing. In *Proceedings of the 4th International Conference on Advances in Grid and Pervasive Computing*. Academic Press. doi:10.1007/978-3-642-01671-4_3

Technologies, G. (2014). *Automation, orchestration, and provisioning*. Retrieved from http://www.galetechnologies.com

Uncover and Resolve Performance Issues with Cloud Performance Monitoring. (n.d.). Retrieved from http://www.copperegg.com/product/cloud-monitoring/

Vincent, E. (2012). Towards autonomic detection of SLA violations in cloud infrastructures. *Future Generation Computer Systems*, *28*(7), 1017–1029. doi:10.1016/j.future.2011.08.018

VMware. (2014). *VMware vSphere: Private cloud computing for mid-size & enterprises businesses*. Retrieved from http://www.vmware.com/products/vsphere/mid-size-and-enterprise-business/overview.html

VMware. (2014). *VMware vCloud director: Secure private clouds, infrastructure as a service.* Retrieved from http://www.vmware.com/products/vcloud-director/overview.html

Wang, X. (2010). An adaptive QoS management framework for VoD cloud service centers. In *Proc. 2010 International Conference on Computer Application and System Modeling*. Academic Press.

Werle, C., Papadimitriou, P., Houidi, I., Louati, W., Zeghlache, D., Bless, R., & Mathy, L. (2011). Building virtual networks across multiple domains. In *Proc. ACM SIGCOMM 2011*. ACM. doi:10.1145/2018436.2018495

Xiao, Y., Lin, C., & Jiang, Y. (2010). Reputation based QoS provisioning in cloud computing via dirichlet multinomial model. In *Proceedings of 2010 IEEE International Conference on Communications (ICC)*. IEEE. doi:10.1109/ICC.2010.5502407

Ye, Y., Jain, N., & Xia, L. (2010). A framework for QoS and power management in a service cloud environment with mobile devices. In *Proceedings of 2010 Fifth IEEE International Symposium on Service Oriented System Engineering (SOSE)* (pp. 236 - 243). IEEE. doi:10.1109/SOSE.2010.53

Yu, J. (2012). Solution for virtual network embedding problem based on simulated annealing genetic algorithm. In *Proceedings of the 2nd International Conference on Consumer Electronics, Communications and Networks* (CECNet). Academic Press.

Zhang, S., Qian, Z., Guo, S., & Lu, S. (2011). FELL: A flexible virtual network embedding algorithm with guaranteed load balancing. In *Proc. 2011 IEEE International Conference on Communications (ICC)*. IEEE. doi:10.1109/icc.2011.5962960

Zu, Y., Zhang-Shen, R., Rangarajan, S., & Rexford, J. (2008). Cabernet: Connectivity architecture for better network services. In *Proc. ACM ReArch '08*. ACM.

KEY TERMS AND DEFINITIONS

IaaS: Infrastructure as a Service is a cloud computing segment, which is based on the abstraction of infrastructure.

NFV: Network Functions Virtualization is the concept of virtualising specific network functions/services.

PaaS: Platform as a Service is a cloud computing segment, which is based on the abstraction of a platform.

SaaS: Software as a Service is a cloud computing segment, which is based on the provision of a specific software/application as a service.

SDN: Software Defined Networking is a trend to computer networking that offers network management of network services through abstraction of layer 2 functionalities.

SDNaaS: SDN-as-a-Service is the provision of SDN capabilities over a cloud computing environment.

VM: Virtual Machine is the emulation of a particular computer system.

Chapter 11
Towards Ubiquitous and Adaptive Web-Based Multimedia Communications via the Cloud

Spyros Panagiotakis
Technological Educational Institute of Crete, Greece

Andreas Stamoulias
Technological Educational Institute of Crete, Greece

Ioannis Vakintis
Technological Educational Institute of Crete, Greece

Kostas Kapetanakis
Technological Educational Institute of Crete, Greece

Haroula Andrioti
Technological Educational Institute of Crete, Greece

Athanasios Malamos
Technological Educational Institute of Crete, Greece

ABSTRACT

This chapter at first surveys the Web technologies that can enable ubiquitous and pervasive multimedia communications over the Web and then reviews the challenges that are raised by their combination. In this context, the relevant HTML5 APIs and technologies provided for service adaptation are introduced and the MPEG-DASH, X3Dom, and WebRTC frameworks are discussed. What is envisaged for the future of mobile multimedia is that with the integration of these technologies one can shape a diversity of future pervasive and personalized cloud-based Web applications, where the client-server operations are obsolete. In particular, it is believed that in the future Web cloud-based Web applications will be able to communicate, stream, and transfer adaptive events and content to their clients, creating a fully collaborative and pervasive Web 3D environment.

DOI: 10.4018/978-1-4666-8225-2.ch011

INTRODUCTION

So far, real time multimedia communications between various client devices, either one-way (streaming) or bidirectional (chat or conference), were, more or less, a static and monolithic operation dominated by several platform-specific solutions. In particular, the streaming of media required the setup of dedicated streaming servers, the installation of the appropriate standalone applications at client side and, obviously, the support of the corresponding streaming protocols for transferring the streamed packets.

With respect to communicating at real time via the web, until recently the streaming of media over HTTP was just a myth, while the receipt of streaming media via web could be accomplished only with the installation of the appropriate third party software (browser plug-ins) to receive and process the data streamed from the server. Additionally, the popular media players provide plug-ins for most browsers to allow video and audio streams to be played back over the web. Web chatting and conferencing is also possible only via plug-ins. SIP (Session Initiation Protocol) and XMPP (eXtensible Messaging and Presence Protocol) are the most popular protocols for such uses.

However, the emergence of HTML5 (Berjon et al., 2014), early in 2008, and of other intriguing web technologies have drastically changed the whole view to a dynamic, browser-friendly and platform independent approach. This is due to the fact that HTML5 introduced several extended functionalities to web browsers changing the way data are transferred, visualizations are displayed and graphics are processed. This is mostly accomplished via several JavaScript libraries and custom JavaScript programming which allow to web-pages to gain access to various device features provided for media access and customization. In that context, the installation of flash player is not mandatory for video streaming any more, since HTML5 provides an element with the tag name "video" that can substitute the requirement for any such plug-in. Furthermore, images can be loaded in an element with the tag name "canvas", a container which can be used to draw graphics on the fly with JavaScript. The canvas element is supported anymore by the most popular desktop and mobile browsers. Technologies such as WebGL (Web Graphics Library), SVG (Scalable Vector Graphics) and Quartz 2D can be combined with a canvas element to draw 2D and 3D graphics with support for user interaction. More critical, the Media Capture and Streams API (Burnett et al., 2013), part of the general Device APIs, enables access via the web to a user's microphone and camera device. To this end the GetUserMedia method is defined. Hence, the live streaming of media, audio and video, from a user over the web can be now a reality.

Additionally, an innovative approach takes place in the recent browser releases with respect to the data transferring protocols over TCP/IP. WebSockets (RFC6455, 2011) use standard HTTP signaling to establish a persistent bidirectional TCP connection and transfer data, in the form of WebSockets frames, between web clients and web servers. With WebSockets web push, that is pushing data from a web server to its clients, can be a reality. In many web servers, WebSockets are ready and tested, following the introduction of the new HTML5 APIs. WebSockets Servers can be found written in many programming languages including C, Python and Java.

In the same context, WebRTC (Bergkvist et al., 2014) is an open project supported by Google, Mozilla and Opera that aims to bring high quality Web Real Time Communications between browsers using simple JavaScript and HTML5. WebRTC uses the aforementioned getUserMedia method to access a peer's microphone and camera and stream media data to another peer browser and vice versa. The peer-to-peer connections are established via the PeerConnection API, which implements JSEP (JavaScript Session Establishment Protocol). JSEP signaling is used in the WebRTC framework as SDP in SIP-based communications that is to describe and negotiate a session between two browsers via the mediating session managers. WebRTC does not mandate the use of any session protocol, such as SIP or XMPP, enabling implementation differentiation. Ericsson labs presented the first implementation of WebRTC in 2011.

With respect to streaming and progressive downloading via the web, MPEG-DASH (DASH Industry Forum) is the innovative technology to provide Dynamic Adaptive Streaming over HTTP of multimedia data to the clients. In MPEG-DASH a web server hosts segments of a video in a variety of quality encodings. On the other hand, the client is provided with a description file, known as MPD, in order to acquire the most suitable version of the segments for downloading and play back. The MPD provides details and URIs for the video segments. Whenever the environment of the client supports higher quality video, the source switches to the corresponding segments. This adaptation takes place on the fly.

In this advanced and web-friendly environment that has been shaped, the XML-based X3D (eXtensible 3D) graphics (ISO/IEC 19775:2004 Extensible 3D (X3D)) adopt all the advantages a text file can provide. These include: web-friendly files, DOM implementation and a significant amount of compression. An X3D file can hold all the necessary data to describe a 3D world along with scripts for user interaction or animation. The HTML5 adopts the advantages of this file structure implementing the DOM and providing compatibility with X3D as it is introduced by X3Dom (Behr et al., 2009). X3Dom, which has recently joint the W3C, is an experimental open source framework and runtime environment that takes advantage of the scalability of X3D graphics to produce rich 3D environments on HTML5 web pages with no use of plug-ins or other third party software. X3Dom is the state of the art technology to embed X3D graphics on the canvas element of HTML5.

Hence, web-browsers that support HTML5 and WebGL can display 3D graphics without the requirement for additional software installation. Furthermore, thanks to the hardware acceleration techniques, the network traffic remains low since the terminal devices undertake all the process to produce graphics and the networks carry just text (XML) information. A simple X3D file is downloaded from a web server and the JavaScript libraries provided by X3Dom undertake to translate the X3D models into WebGL and display them on a canvas. Additional functionality can be also supported, just like a common 3D player has. A user within such a 3D world can interact with the 3D surrounding in a variety of ways including viewing of 3D models, walking or flying in the scene or even altering the displayed models. Interactions can take place either in the main 3D world or in the wider HTML5 environment. Ajax technology can be also implemented (Ajax3D), so actions performed by a user in an HTML5 page are taken into account updating just the involved parts of the 3D world and not the whole page or 3D world. Additionally, multimedia streams can be converted into BLOBs (Binary Large Objects) using the File API (Ranganathan et al., 2013). BLOB objects can be transferred and manipulated just like other binary data via WebSockets enabling web streaming and/or conferencing.

What is envisaged for the future of mobile multimedia is that with the integration of HTML5, MPEG-DASH, WebRTC, WebSockets, and X3Dom, along with various other relevant web APIs and technologies provided for service adaptation, one can shape a diversity of future pervasive and personalized cloud-based web applications, where the client-server operations are obsolete. In particular, it is believed that in the future web; cloud-based web applications will be able to communicate, stream and transfer adaptive events and content to their clients, and vice-versa, creating a fully collaborative and pervasive web 3D environment. This chapter at first surveys the state of the art technologies related to ubiquitous and pervasive multimedia communications over the web and then reviews the challenges raised by their combination. The rest of the chapter is organized as follows: the next section introduces to the relevant HTML5 APIs and technologies and discusses the MPEG-DASH, X3Dom and WebRTC frameworks. Then, some related works are presented and the chapter concludes with the authors' envisioning for the future web and their future research directions.

RELATED TECHNOLOGIES

HTML5 APIs That Enable Pervasive and Adaptive Multimedia over the Web

HTML is the universal language of the World Wide Web. In the early years, HTML had limited potentialities and was designed just for describing static web content. But with the course of time, the language has been dramatically evolved, offering real challenges to developers. Its latest version, HTML5 has completely changed the status in the IT firmament with the breaking through technologies it introduces. For example video files do not require any more external plugins like flash in order to be played back in a browser, as HTML5 with its <video> tag embeds such functionalities, as play, stop/pause, move back/forward, directly into the body of the language. Essentially, HTML5 is not anymore a simple language for describing web pages, but a combination of HTML, CSS and many Javascipt APIs, which makes it a powerful platform with rich capabilities. In the following, the attention will be paid on these Javascipt APIs, available with the 5th edition of HTML that can enable the provision of pervasive, ubiquitous and adaptive web applications to end users. Because with these APIs web sites and web applications are offered an insight to the personal context and ambient environment of the end users, static or mobile, enabling capabilities for personalized, customized and anticipatory service provisioning.

Sensors and Hardware Integration

Modern mobile devices of smartphone and tablet style embed a rich variety of sensors. In order applications to have access to the data from sensors, normally a middleware tool needs to mediate to facilitate the communication. Special-purpose Application Programming Interfaces (APIs) expose sensor data to the mobile web developers. Table 1 summarizes some critical sensors and hardware APIs from W3C as they are included in (Mobile-web-app-state, 2014).

Table 1. Sensors and Hardware APIS

	Feature	Working Group	Maturity	Current Implementation
1	Geolocation	Geolocation	W3C Recommendations	Widely deployed
2	Motion sensors		Last Call Working Drafts	Well deployed
3	Battery status	Device API s	Candidate Recommendations	Very limited
4	Proximity sensors		Candidate Recommendations	Very limited
5	Ambient light sensor		Candidate Recommendations	Very limited
6	Networking information API		Discontinued	Very limited
7	Camera & Microphone streams	Device APIs and Web Real-Time Communications	Working Drafts	Limited but growing

Geolocation API

Geolocation API (Popescu, 2013) allows the client-side device to provide geographic positioning information to javascript web applications. Geolocation API offers to mobile users the possibility to share their location with anyone they trust (individuals or web sites). The Geolocation API returns the geographical coordinates of the user device in a geodetic datum, that is in the form of latitude and longitude. In order them to be understandable or valuable for the end user, later this information must be translated to something like a city or street name or the name of a favorite area (e.g. my mother's place, my office, my gym), since the user understands better the civil datum. Online services such as Google and Bing maps, can undertake such transformations. Apart from latitude and longitude, the geolocation API can also return additional information such as the user's altitude, heading and speed and the altitude accuracy.

There isn't a standard positioning technology with which the Geolocation API finds the user location; it rather uses any available method offered by the device. Hence, there is no guarantee about the accuracy of the returned data. Several positioning technologies can be used and combined to this end including:

- **Global Positioning System (GPS):** A very promising way to return the location when outdoors but with very bad results when indoors. GPS takes the signal from many GPS satellites (and the serving cellular network in the form of A-GPS) to calculate the final location. Its disadvantages include the draining of devices from power and the need for enough time to yield results especially at start up.
- **Wi-Fi:** The location is found by triangulating the location estimations from several Wi-Fi hot spots. The accuracy depends on the density of the access points in the surroundings of the user.
- **GSM and UMTS Cell IDs:** Similar to the WiFi method the results are estimated by triangulating the location measurements from the serving cellular network's towers near the user. The accuracy depends on the density of the base stations in the surroundings.
- **IP Address:** It is considered an unreliable means to return the location of the user due to the fact that it is greatly based on the ISP provider, which could be far away from the physical address.

Taking into account that user location is included in the personal and sensitive information and with respect to the user privacy; the Geolocation API requires the confirmation of the user before sharing his or her location with any application or individual.

How It Works

The Geolocation API uses the navigator.geolocation property which returns a Geolocation object. The Geolocation object contains the location of the user represented in latitude and longitude coordinates. In particular, the Geolocation object has 3 methods, the getCurrentPosition, the watchPosition and the clearWatch, as Table 2 depicts.

The *getCurrentPosition* gets the user location only once. Its successful callback returns a *Position object* as argument, and its fail callback returns an error. The Position object consists of several properties, the most critical of which are the coords.latitude and coords.longitude. Table 3 enlists the properties of a Position object.

The *watchPosition* method gets user location as the user moves. This function is iteratively called as the user location changes so the web application is always provided with updated location information. It returns the same arguments as the getCurrentPosition. In addition, it returns an ID number to ensure the uniqueness of the user. The third method of Geolocation object, *clearWatch*, uses this ID number to stop polling the user location.

Table 2. Geolocation API methods

Method	Description
getCurrentPosition	Gets the user location once
watchPosition	Keeps polling for user position and returns an associated ID.
clearWatch	Stops polling for user position

Table 3. Position object properties

Property	Unit
coords.latitude	degrees
coords.longitude	degrees
coords.altitude	meters
coords.accuracy	meters
coords.altitudeAccuracy	meters
coords.heading	degrees clockwise
coords.speed	meters/second
timestamp	like the Date object

Table 4. Orientation API methods

Event	Description
DeviceOrientation	It fires whenever a significant change in orientation occurs
CompassNeedsCalibration	It fires when the user agent determines that a compass used to obtain user orientation needs calibration
DeviceMotion	It fires regularly with information about the motion of the device

Figure 1. The DeviceOrientation event properties

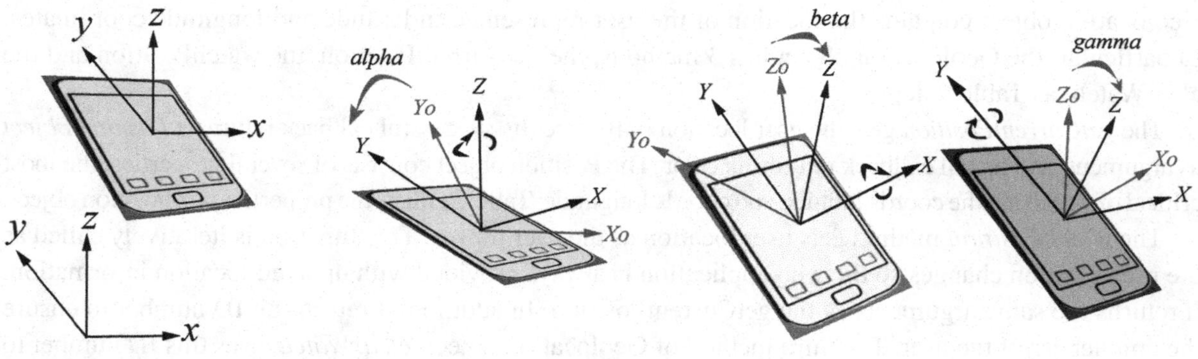

Table 5. Device orientation event properties

Property	Description
Alpha	Denotes the direction the device is facing according to the compass
Beta	Denotes the angle in degrees the device is tilted front-to-back
Gamma	Denotes the angle in degrees the device is tilted left-to-right

Table 6. Device motion event properties

Property	Description
Acceleration	Provides acceleration data, in m/s^2 for each of the x, y, and z axes
AcceleratonIncludingGravity	Provides same data as above, but with effects due to the Earth's gravity included
RotationRate	Provides the rate of rotation in deg/s around each of the axes
Interval	Time in milliseconds between samples

Browser Support: Currently the Geolocation API is supported by the Mozilla Firefox, Chrome, Opera, Internet Explorer, Safari, and the native Android and Blackberry browsers.

Device Orientation API

The most modern mobile devices are equipped with plenty of motion sensors. Motion sensors include accelerometers, gyroscopes and compasses. The HTML5 Device Orientation API (Block & Popescu, 2011) provides developers with access to underlying motion sensors and to associated data from the orientation and movement of the device. The API specifies the events listed in Table 4.

The *DeviceOrientation* event exposes all the orientation changes. It returns the properties, alpha, beta and gamma that are explained in Table 5.

Figure 1 visualizes the values of the *DeviceOrientation* event.

The *DeviceMotion* event exposes the acceleration and rotation rates of the device. It takes 4 properties, acceleration, acceleratonIncludingGravity, rotationRate and interval. Table 6 details on them.

Browser Support: Currently the Device Orientation API is supported by the Mozilla Firefox, Chrome, Opera, Internet Explorer, Safari, and the native Android and Blackberry browsers.

Battery Status API

Normally, mobile devices have a life time of 9 to 10 hours of active usage before battery drains all its energy. The Battery Status API (Kostiainen & Lamouri, 2012) can make the web applications smarter and energy-friendly. It uses the navigator.battery property to create a BatteryObject. Table 7 depicts the basic properties of a BatteryObject.

Browser Support: Currently the Battery Status API is only supported by Mozilla Firefox.

Proximity Sensor API

The Proximity Sensor API detects the distance between the mobile device and the user or an object. The API (Kostiainen & Tran, 2013) has the two methods of Table 8 to work with:

Table 7. Battery Status API properties

Properties	Description
navigator.battery.level	Obtains the charging level of the battery. Returns a value between 0 and 1.
navigator.battery.charging	Informs if the device is currently charging or not. Returns true or false.
navigator.battery.chargingTime	The remaining time in seconds until charging level reaches 100%.
navigator.battery.dischargingTime	The time in seconds before the battery is completely discharged and the device shuts down.

Table 8. Proximity Sensor API methods

Method	Description
Device proximity	Measures the distance in centimeters
User proximity	Informs the user if an object is near or not

Table 9. LightLevelEvent values

Light Level	Ambient Characterization
<50 lux	Dim Environment
50 ~ 10000 lux	Normal
> 10000 lux	Bright

The *deviceProximityEvent* property measures the distance in centimeters but the minimum and maximum distance a proximity sensor supports varies. Usually the value ranges from 0 to 10cm. The *userProximityEvent* property returns a Boolean value (true or false) which inform the user if an object is near or far.

Browser Support: Currently the Proximity Sensor API is only supported by Mozilla Firefox.

Ambient Light Sensor API

The Ambient Light Sensor API (Turner & Kostiainen, 2014) senses the environment of the device to provide web applications with the measured luminosity in lux units. The values range from 0 to 10000 lux. Obviously an embedded Light Sensor is required. When a light change is detected, the *DeviceLightEvent* provides applications with the updated value of luminosity. A second interface is the *LightLevelEvent*, which provides less accurate characterization of the ambient light. In particular it categorizes the light level into 3 categories. The first category is the "Dim" environments with light values below 50 lux, the second is the "Normal" environments with values ranging from 50 to 10000 lux and the third is the "Bright" environments with light values greater than 10000 lux. Table 9 includes this categorization.

Browser Support: Currently the Ambient Light Sensor API is only supported by Mozilla Firefox.

Media Capture and Streams API

The Media Capture and Streams API (or GetUserMedia API) (Burnett et al., 2013) offers to web applications access to multimedia streams, such as video and audio, from local devices (webcam or microphone) through a browser. It then capitalizes on the HTML5 <video> and <audio> elements to play them back. In terms of user privacy, the Media Capture and Streams API behaves similar to the Geolocation API. Whenever an application attempts to access the local media devices the browser asks the user for his permission. The revolutionary with this API is that access to the local media devices takes place without any need for plugins installation. Below is an example of how access to camera and microphone can be achieved.

```
If (navigator.getUserMedia)
{
  navigator.getUserMedia({audio: true, video: true}, successCallback, error-
Callback);
 }
```

The method *navigator.getUserMedia()* takes three arguments: *constraints, successCallback and errorCallback*. In *constrains* the type of media that will be accessed (video, audio or both) are defined. In *successCallback* the success scenario is defined. Hence, when video and audio are loaded; the captured media streams are put in a <video> element identifying the object of the *LocalMediaStream* via a BLOB URL (Ranganathan et al., 2013).

```
function successCallback (MediaStream) {
 video.src = window.URL.createObjectURL(MediaStream);
}
```

In *errorCallback* three cases for failure can occur, in general: i) Permission denied by the user, ii) No media tracks are found, iii) The browser does not support the specific constrain. Hence an alternative solution should be offered to the user:

```
function errorCallback (e) {
  video.src = 'fallbackvideo.webm';
}
```

Browser Support: Currently the Media Capture and Streams API is supported by the Mozilla Firefox, Chrome, Opera and Blackberry browsers.

Performance Characteristics

Performance is a critical part in web applications development. To this end, several tools for web applications performance optimization can be found. Especially for mobile web applications, their limitations in terms of battery, networking, memory and CPU need to be taken into consideration during development and provision. HTML5 provides tools capable to measure various aspects of mobile resources. These include the Network Information API, the Resource Timing API, the High Resolution Time API and the User Timing API.

Table 10. Network Information API properties

Properties	Description
Bandwidth	It estimates the current bandwidth. Zero means an offline user.
Metered	A connection is characterized as "metered" when the user's connection is subject to a limitation from the Internet Service Provider. Hence the web applications are requested to be careful with the bandwidth usage. It returns a Boolean value.

Network Information API

The Network Information API (Lamouri, 2014) measures the available bandwidth and offers to the developers the ability to adapt web media elements, as images, videos, audios and fonts, accordingly for a better user experience with multimedia content. The navigator.connection method provides an object with the two properties, bandwidth and metered, of Table 10.

Despite its obvious value, the development of Network Information API has been discontinued currently. In the following, the Resource timing API will be presented, which is in a stable status of development and can provide developers with similar information.

Browser Support: When discontinued the Network Information API was only supported by the native Android and Blackberry browsers.

Resource Timing API

A factor that affects user experience in web application is latency. Network latency refers to the delay data packets experience as they are transferred from the sender to the receiver. The Resource Timing API (Jain et al., 2014) measures the time needed for various resources of a web page to be loaded in a browser. During the development phase of a mobile web application, such debugging information can let the developer think and incorporate into his application design various intelligent methodologies for adapting appropriately the application and offering greater user experience to poor execution environments. Some of the networking information that can be retrieved by this API is the time for redirect, cache, access to DNS, opening a TCP session, transmitting a request and receiving a response. Figure 2 illustrates the measured times from the Resource Timing API.

Apart from time-sensitive networking information, the Resource Timing API can also measure the delays from other critical components for most web applications such as the performance of various third part assets including Javascipt libraries, social widgets and CSS frameworks.

Browser Support: Currently the Resource Timing API is supported by the Chrome and Internet Explorer browsers.

The High Resolution Time and the User Timing API

The High Resolution Time API (Mann, 2012) measures the internal time performance of a web application in terms of function calls, interface callbacks, variable assignments, etc. As it is described in W3C it is "a JavaScript interface that provides the current time in sub-millisecond resolution and such that it is not subject to system clock skews or adjustments." The API uses the *Performance interface* which

Figure 2. Timing attributes of the Resource Timing API

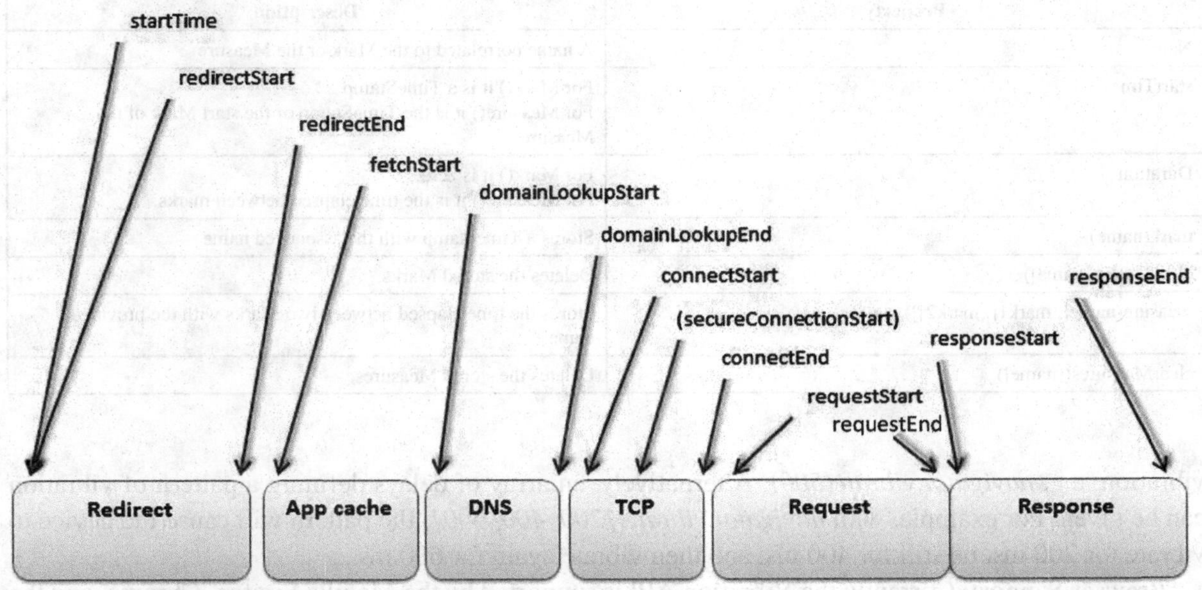

exposes only the method *now()*. Now() returns a *DOMHighResTimeStamp* object which represents the current time in milliseconds. Performance.now() is similar to the Javascipt function Date.now() with the difference that the former is far more accurate with a precision to a thousandth of a millisecond.

Similar to the High Resolution Time API, the User Timing API (Mann, Wang et al., 2013) also measures the internal performance of web applications. However, the former API has the drawback that if someone needs to measure the performance in different files of an application he has to insert global variables. The User Timing API facilitates such situations by offering to web developers access to high precision timestamps. In particular it implements the *PerformanceEntry* interface, which includes the *PerformanceMark* and *PerformanceMeasure* interfaces. The *mark()* method stores a timestamp which is available across all files of the application. In addition, with *mark()* someone can differentiate the time it starts measuring by the time the "*mark*" timestamp was posed in the application. Then, with the *measure()* method the time between marks can be measured. Table 11 includes the properties of the User Timing API and elaborates further on them.

Browser Support: Currently the High Resolution Time and the User Timing APIs are supported by the Chrome, Internet Explorer and the native Android browsers.

Various HTML5 APIs Enabling Pervasiveness and Service Adaptation

Vibration API

Vibration is synonym to Mobile devices. Hereafter, this capability is extended to the Web applications. The Vibration API (Kostiainen, Vibration API, 2014) uses the *navigator.vibrate* method to enable vibrations. *Navigator.vibrate()* takes as argument a number in milliseconds denoting the duration of the

Table 11. User Timing API properties

Property	Description
Name	A name correlated to the Mark or the Measure
startTime	For Mark() it is a TimeStamp For Measure() it is the TimeStamp of the start Mark of the Measure.
Duration	For Mark() it is zero. For Measure() it is the time elapsed between marks.
mark(name)	Stores a TimeStamp with the associated name
clearMarks([name])	Deletes the stored Marks.
measure(name[, mark1[, mark2]])	Stores the time elapsed between two Marks with the provided name.
clearMeasures([name])	Deletes the stored Measures.

vibration, e.g. *navigator.vibrate(500)*; Alternatively, an array of delays defining a pattern of vibration can be given. For example, with *navigator.vibrate([200, 400, 600])* the pattern will cause the device to vibrate for 200 ms, be still for 400 ms, and then vibrate again for 600 ms.

Browser Support: Currently the Vibration API is supported by the Mozilla Firefox, Chrome, and the native Android and Blackberry browsers.

Full Screen API

The Fullscreen API (Van Kesteren & Çelik, 2012) allows web developers to tag elements in web applications (or documents) for viewing in full-screen mode. Instead of using the F11 keyboard button this can be enabled by simply pressing above the web element. Exiting from the full-screen mode is achieved by clicking again on the web element. It is mostly used with images and videos.

Browser Support: Currently the Full Screen API is supported by the Mozilla Firefox, Chrome, Internet Explorer and the native Blackberry browsers.

Page Visibility API

The Page Visibility API (Mann & Jain, 2013) provides the web developer with the capability to offer better user experience by applying the visibility or not state into their web application. An application will have different behavior when it is visible and different when it is hidden. It can be used to adapt the usage of resources to the need of the Web application, for instance by reducing network activity when a page is minimized. Furthermore, it can have a great impact on the mobile devices because they can save energy from battery.

The API has two properties the *Hidden* and the *VisibilityState*. The *Hidden* is a Boolean property, which with True indicates a hidden document and with False a visible one. The *VisibilityState* has four options: "*hidden*", "*visible*", "*prerender*", and "*unloaded*". Table 12 elaborates on them. Finally, the API contains the *visibilityChange* event which fires whenever the visibility state of a Document changes.

Browser Support: Currently the Page Visibility API is supported by the Mozilla Firefox, Chrome, Opera, Internet Explorer, Safari, and the native Android and Blackberry browsers.

Table 12. VisibilityState values

Values	Description
Hidden	The document is totally hidden.
Visible	The document is visible.
Prerender	Optional. The document contained by the top level browser tab is loaded off-screen and is not visible.
Unloaded	Optional. The User Agent is to unload the document contained by the top level browser tab.

Other Html5 Enabling Technologies

Web Workers

Javascipt is a single-threated language, which means that javascript-based web applications can handle only one script at a time. This can do web applications unresponsive offering a poor user experience. HTML5 attempts to solve this problem by introducing the Web workers API (Hickson, 2012 (Web Workers)). Web Workers are scripts running in the background without influencing the main UI, offering, thus, a concurrent execution.

Web Workers are executed in different files, which are called from the main script with a *postMessage*() method. The *postMessage*() method accepts either a string or a JSON object as argument. The Web Workers handles the Messages from the main page with the *onmessage* handler. The data between the main thread and the Worker are copied and not shared minimizing, thus, the time required for a large file to be transferred. The Web Workers can transfer different type of objects such as Files, BLOBs, ArrayBuffers, and JSON objects. However, Web Workers have currently some limitations. Table 13 enlists the objects a Worker can and cannot have access.

Table 13. Web Workers capabilities and limitations

DO Have Access	DO NOT Have Access
The navigator object	The DOM (it's not thread-safe)
The location object (read-only)	The "window" object
XMLHttpRequest	The "document" object
setTimeout()/clearTimeout() setInterval()/ clearInterval()	The "parent" object
The Application Cache	The local name space. Web Workers will not work if a web page is being served directly from the local filesystem (using file://)
Importing external scripts using the *importScripts*() method	All Worker scripts must be served from the same domain and protocol as the script that creates the worker.
Spawning other web workers	

Web Storage

HTML5 introduces new methodologies for the storage of data by Web applications. In the past, data were stored exclusively in the web server but with the Web storage capability (Hickson, 2013 (Web Storage)) this has changed. The data can now be stored in the mobile device and be later synchronized with the server. This provides, at first, offline usage of data and, at second, improves the application performance. There are two main web storage types: Local Storage and Session Storage. The Local Storage stores data for ever without to be lost. On the other hand, the Session Storage stores data only for the duration of a session.

The values on the local Storage are stored as key-value pairs, hence whenever the application wants to access the values it must use the respective key. Only strings can be stored via the Storage API. In most browsers, storing of different data types results in automatic conversion of them to a string format. Conversion into JSON, however, allows for effective storage of JavaScript objects. Local Storage has an upper limit at the storage space it can access, which varies from browser to browser (5 Megabytes for Google Chrome, Mozilla Firefox and Opera), but it is definitely far better than the 4 Kilobytes of cookies.

Web Intents

Web Intents (Billock et al., 2013) is a framework for service discovery and inter-application communication enabling information sharing between web applications. Most users use specific web applications such as facebook, twitter, google+, viber, skype, dropbox, each with its own API. With Intents, web developers do not need to deal with each of them because web Intents unify access to them incorporating them to the logic of a web application. Web Intents enable to several different applications to work together. Via Intents several actions can be performed, such as sharing, editing, viewing, picking, subscribing or saving of a document. Also, web Intents are mobile friendly and can be used in a variety of mobile operating systems such as Android and iOS.

Web Intents function similar to web services. Essentially, it is transfer of the well-known publish-subscribe model to the web. The life cycle of a Web Intent consists of 5 stages: registration, invocation, selection, delivery and response (Billock et al., 2013). At first, a User Agent is being informed by a web application that it is able to handle Intents for specific actions. Whenever a client page sends to the agent such Intents for handling, the User Agent selects this application as appropriate for the Intent. Then the User Agent delivers the Intent to the application, which responds by passing data to the client page.

A Web Intent object can contain several parameters. The most important parameters are *action* and *type* that cannot be empty. The *action* parameter indicates the action type of the Intent, for example edit. The *type* parameter indicates the type of the data payload. *Data* parameter is optional and it refers to any data including transferables. The next example demonstrates an application submitting Intent for an appropriate service to share a list of images designated via urls.

```
var intent = new Intent({"action":"http://webintents.org/share",
                        "type":" text/uri-list ",
                        "data":getPublicURIForImage(...)});
```

WebSockets

The WebSocket protocol (RFC6455, 2011), provides a bidirectional communication channel using a single TCP connection. It has been designed for implementation in both browsers and web-servers and its API (Hickson, 2012 (WebSockets)) has being standardized by the W3C. WebSocket connections are established over the regular TCP port 80, which ensures that the system can run behind firewalls. The life-cycle of a WebSocket session is depicted in Figure 3. At first the client, a browser that supports the WebSocket protocol, requests a server to establish a WebSocket connection. The positive response from the server denotes the start of such a connection. The connection remains open for the whole session, until any endpoint requests its release with the specified procedure. As a WebSocket remains active; WebSocket frames can be transferred from server to client and vice versa with no preceding request. In an indicative implementation the WebSockets server may also host the service logic of a web-application, which might be responsible for maintaining a listing of the clients with active WebSockets and session management. Although logical separated, the web server, the service logic and the WebSockets server could run on the same physical entity.

As it is depicted in Figure 3 the HTTP is initially used to establish the WebSocket connection between a compatible browser and a server. When the bidirectional connection is established, the application may transfer data to the server using this dedicated socket. The added value appears in the case that a server needs to push data to the client, which can take place asynchronously. Prior to websockets, a client-sided mechanism to request any updated data from the server should be used, a technique that consumes unnecessarily the network resources.

As it is described in (RFC6455, 2011), a WebSocket session consists of two parts, the handshake and the data transfer. The handshake is based on HTTP signaling, extended with websocket headers. The HTTP GET message, as it is depicted below, holds information about the websocket server (*host*)

Figure 3. Life-cycle of a WebSocket session

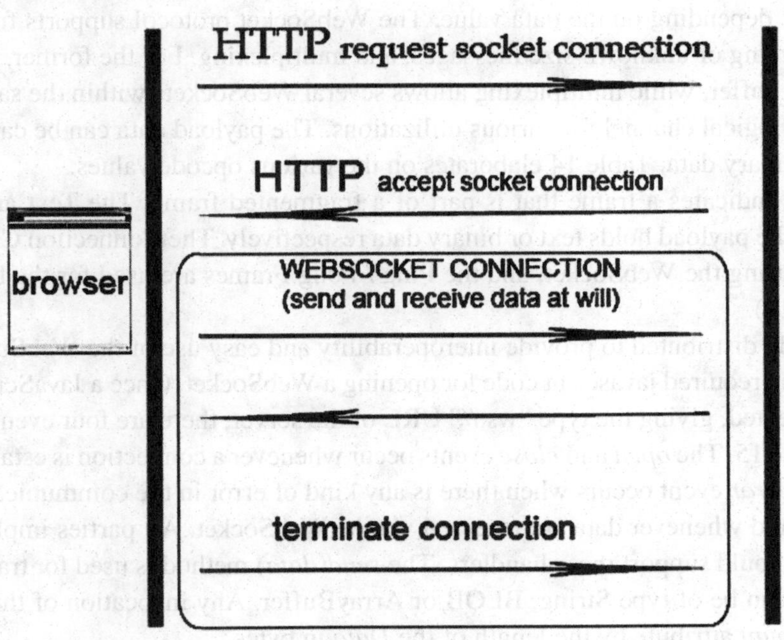

and the originating web application (*origin*), as well as the *upgrade* header that indicates a request for switching to a websocket connection. The *sec-websocket* values include information related to security, subprotocols and versioning respectively.

```
GET /chat HTTP/1.1
Host: server.example.com
Upgrade: websocket
Connection: Upgrade
Sec-WebSocket-Key: dGhlIHNhbXBsZSBub25jZQ==
Origin: http://example.com
Sec-WebSocket-Protocol: chat, superchat
Sec-WebSocket-Version: 13
```

The HTTP response from the server acknowledges the transfer of the connection to a websocket and includes the required headers for security verification.

```
HTTP/1.1 101 Switching Protocols
Upgrade: websocket
Connection: Upgrade
Sec-WebSocket-Accept: s3pPLMBiTxaQ9kYGzzhZRbK+xOo=
    Sec-WebSocket-Protocol: chat
```

Once the handshake procedure has been completed successfully, all data between a client and a server are transferred via the WebSocket in the form of WebSocket frames. According to the specification each such frame is defined with three mandatory values; the *opcode*, which defines the type of the payload, the *payload length*, and the *payload data*. The *opcode* has a length of 4 bits, while the size for *payload length* and *data* may vary depending on the data value. The WebSocket protocol supports frame fragmentations to allow streaming of unknown size messages, and multiplexing. For the former, the server chooses a reasonable size buffer, while multiplexing allows several WebSockets within the same origin and host to share a single logical channel for various utilizations. The payload data can be carried both as Text (UTF-8 text) or Binary data. Table 14 elaborates on the various opcode values.

A continuation Frame indicates a frame that is part of a fragmented frame. The Text and Binary Frames indicate whether the payload holds text or binary data respectively. The Connection Close value starts the signaling for closing the WebSocket, and the Ping / Pong Frames are used for the keep-alive process (shown in Table 14).

Frameworks are already distributed to provide interoperability and easy use of the WebSocket API. The Listing 1 illustrates the required javascript code for opening a WebSocket. Once a JavaScript object named *socket* has been created, giving the type "ws://" URL of the server, there are four event handlers to be used as listed in Table 15. The *open* and *close* events occur whenever a connection is established or closed, respectively. The *error* event occurs when there is any kind of error in the communication. The *message* handler is triggered whenever data are received via the WebSocket. All parties implementing the WebSocket interface should support these handlers. The *send*(*data*) method is used for transmitting data via the socket. Data can be of type String, BLOB or ArrayBuffer. Any invocation of this method increases the *bufferedAmount* attribute by the length of the *Data* in bytes.

Listing 1.

```
<!DOCTYPE HTML>
<html>
<head>
<script type="text/javascript">
var socket = new WebSocket('ws://game.example.com:12010/updates');
socket.onopen = function () {
  setInterval(function() {
    if (socket.bufferedAmount == 0)
      socket.send(getUpdateData());
  }, 50);
};
socket.onmessage = function (evt)
    {
        var received_msg = evt.data;
        console.log("received message: "+received_msg);
    };
socket.onclose = function()
    {
  console.log("Connection is closed...");
    };
</script>
</head>
</html>
```

Table 14. Opcode values for WebSockets

Opcode	Meaning
0	Continuation Frame
1	Text Frame
2	Binary Frame
8	Connection Close
9	Ping
10	Pong

Table 15. Event handlers for WebSockets

Event	Event Handler
Open	Socket.onopen
Message	Socket.onmessage
Error	Socket.onerror
Close	Socket.onclose

Applications Scenarios

The combination of the above APIs can provide very interesting pervasive applications, which keep undiminished the interest of the user. The rapid growth of smartphones, with all these advanced sensing and networking capabilities, creates the appropriate infrastructure for HTML5 to thrive.

An interesting such scenario would be a web application that uses the light sensor of a smartphone to detect the luminance in the usage environment and then to dynamically adapt the background of a web page to enhance readability. A variant of this application would be another one that changes the graphics of a webpage based on instantaneous network information. Another intriguing scenario would be a web application using WebSockets to send notifications to its subscribers and upon their receipt a phone to vibrate. In the same context, crowd sensing application is now easy to be implemented. Sensors APIs mine periodically the data from the phone and WebSockets send the valuable information to the central server to analyze and visualize the data creating useful maps.

MPEG DASH: The MPEG Standard for Dynamic Adaptive Streaming over HTTP

Introduction

The content adaptation is an almost mandatory procedure for application distribution over ubiquitous environments and heterogeneous devices. Web applications can make use of the aforementioned HTML5 techniques to dynamically modify content and/or user interfaces. Another level of web content adaptation considers the adaptation of web video streams based on the available resources. The MPEG-DASH standard, which stands for Dynamically Adaptive Streaming over HTTP, provided by the DASH-IF (DASH Industry Forum), provides a mechanism to enable adaptive video streaming by requesting the most suitable representation of media content over the time. The initialization process for a DASH execution scenario requires an MPD (Media Presentation Description) file. The MPD, which conforms to the XML document format, describes the available representations of media for streaming. The DASH player is responsible to monitor the resources availability over the time and switch between the available representations to provide the most suitable media file. In the case, for instance, of a video streaming application that is based on network traffic, the MPD should include information regarding the requested video file, such as the URLs for the available representations, the requirement for bandwidth by each one, and the available languages for subtitling. In DASH are defined both static and dynamic profiles for Video on Demand and Live Stream services, respectively. Media for streaming is chopped into individual particles named segments. Each video segment is hosted in a web server, is requested by the player and is delivered over HTTP similar to the principles of progressive downloading. The player estimates the available bandwidth during each delivery and decides if the next request will be also for the same representation or not. When a video segment arrives, it is smoothly appended to the previous one, providing a seamless playback of the video for better Quality of Experience (QoE). The segments are divided by representations and each representation corresponds to a different video quality in terms of frame resolution. Therefore, for better QoE, the selected representations should maintain a good frame-rate while altering the resolution, according to the research in (Zinner et al., 2010). Since MPEG-DASH is an HTTP-based standard, in the MPD file the available segments are identified via HTTP-URLs.

The DASH-IF in (ISO/IEC 23009-1, 2014) describes all the required information for streaming multimedia content over the web, while supporting multiple representations for dynamically switching between qualities. On the other hand, the HTML5 introduces features which provide efficient media playback in a browser. DASH and HTML5 are complementing technologies. In this context, the DASH-IF developed and delivered a reference JavaScript DASH player that runs on top of web browsers (DASH. JS). The JavaScript player parses the MPD file and determines the bandwidth availability. Running some decision making algorithms, the client requests video segments from the corresponding servers. Finally, the player is responsible to playback the buffered data and to adapt seamlessly the different received video qualities during playback.

In Figure 4 the lifecycle of a MPEG-DASH streaming service is depicted. The MPD file, which is delivered through a common HTTP messages exchange, holds the available representations and the URLs of the media resources that can be requested by the clients. The DASH Control Engine reads the description file and based on the available resources determines the most suitable representation to request segments. Additionally, the Media Engine combines the received segments to deliver smooth adaptation and playback. The client may be developed in any platform with support for HTTP and can perform video decoding and merging of the segments.

MPD Analysis

Structure

Understanding the hierarchy in the MPD files (Figure 5) is the required step towards familiarization with MPEG-DASH implementations. The structure of an MPD file is described in ISO/IEC 23009-1:2012. According to this ISO/IEC standard, companies and individuals are allowed to provide custom profiles / interoperability points for their needs for media representation. An MPD file starts with the required

Figure 4. The MPEG DASH architecture

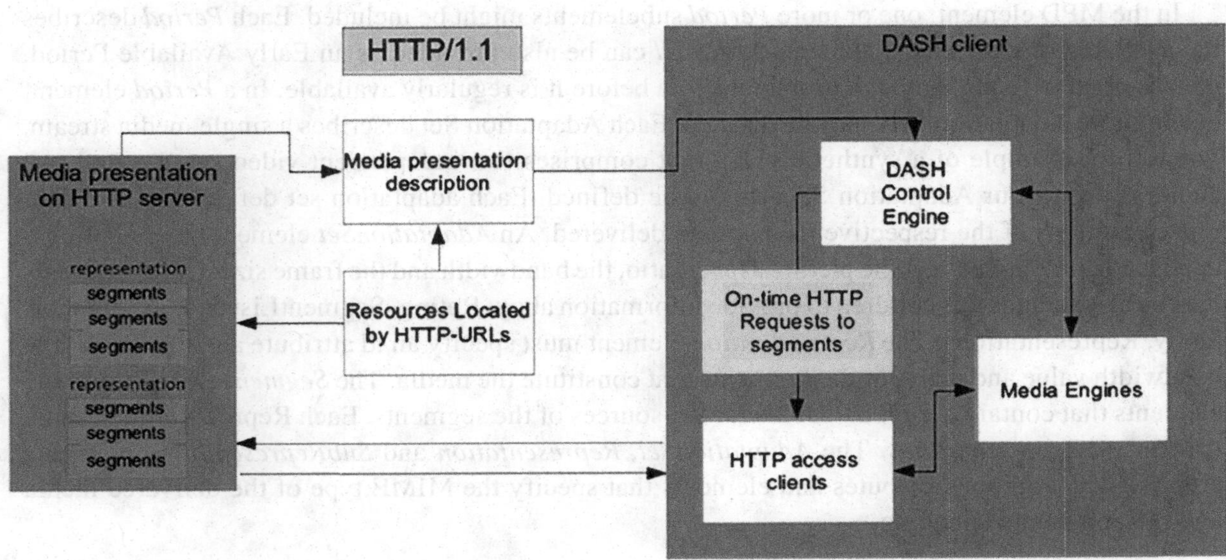

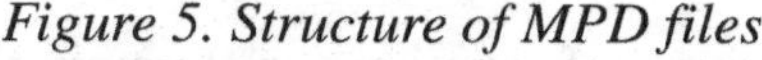

Figure 5. Structure of MPD files

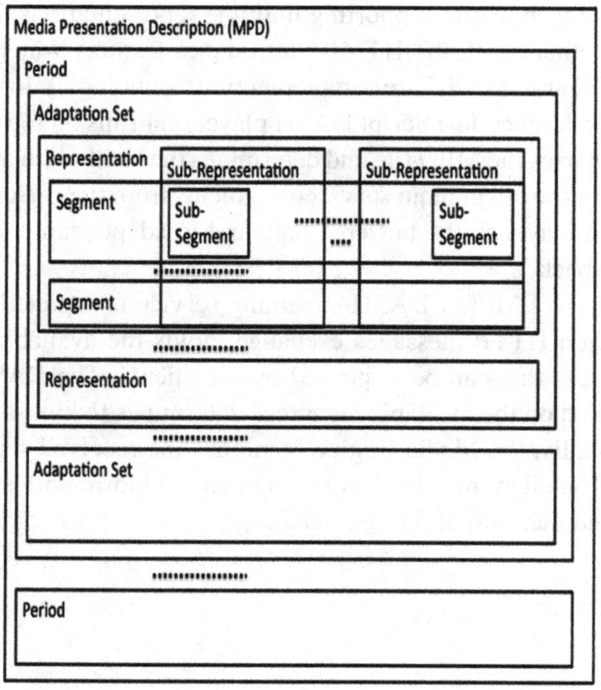

declarations of name-spaces, including the type of the MPD, the profile that sets the boundaries for the elements included in the file and the type of the media to be delivered. Several profiles are defined in the DASH standard. In case of a static MPD (profile: video on demand), the media presentation duration must be included. In case of a dynamic MPD (profile: live streaming), the starting time is set using the corresponding attribute and optionally, the end time. The duration value is described in the *minBufferTime* attribute.

In the MPD element, one or more *Period* subelements might be included. Each *Period* describes the available sets for media content. A *Period* can be also provided as an Early Available Period, in case of advertising that is to promote media before it is regularly available. In a *Period* element, one or more Adaptation Sets may be defined. Each Adaptation Set describes a single media stream. In case, for example of a synthetic video that comprises two independent video streams and two audio streams, four Adaptation Sets should be defined. Each adaptation set defines the available representations of the respective media to be delivered. An *AdaptationSet* element has as optional attributes the content type, the picture aspect ratio, the bandwidth and the frame size. Other elements may be also included as children to provide information about Rating, SegmentList and, most importantly, Representations. The *Representation* element must specify an id attribute and the applicable bandwidth value and includes the segments that constitute the media. The *Segment* elements are the elements that contain the HTTP-URLs for the sources of the segments. Each Representation can be split in *subRepresentations*. The *AdaptationSet*, *Representation* and *SubRepresentation* elements are assigned common attributes and elements that specify the MIME type of the delivered media and the applicable encoding.

MPD Types

- **Static Type for Video on Demand:** An example MPD file of static type, describing the simple scenario of an mp4 movie stream, is depicted in Listing 2. The movie comprises three Adaptation Sets: one for the video stream, one for the audio stream and one for subtitles. For the two first, several representations are defined for various values of bandwidth. The attributes in the MPD element describe the namespaces, the MPD type, the duration, and the minimum buffer time. The MPD profile is set to video on demand (see Listing 2).

The Base URL provides the HTTP path for the representations and is used as prefix for the representations' URL. In this example that two different servers with the same movie instance are provided, the client may pick the closest one and can, then, switch to the other in case of unavailability.

In the Period element the AdaptationSets contain the attributes that define the MIMEtype of the nested representations, the codecs and the language. The *segmentAlignment* attribute denotes whether the segments are overlapping, to allow the client to switch between representations before the previous representation has finished. The *segmentStartsWithSAP* clarifies if there is a stream access point, helpful to be used when the user navigates back and forth in a video playback. The value "1" is used to define random access of media presentation; the value "2" defines the ability to switch between two representations. As a child element in an AdaptationSet lies the Representation element which holds attributes for the id, the width and height of the video aspect ratio and the required bandwidth. The bandwidth value determines the minimum bandwidth which should be available in order to pick a client the corresponding representation. The BaseURL element, depicted as child in the Representation node, complements the URL for the described representation that can be, for example: "http://cdn1.example.com/3463275477.mp4a". In this example segments are not defined within representations, which mean that each representation comprises just one segment. Obviously, this is due to the short duration of the stream (less than six minutes as it is defined in the corresponding attribute). Several more attributes are described in the DASH specification.

- **Dynamic Type for Live Video Streaming:** An example MPD file of dynamic type, describing the simple scenario of an mp4-encoded live stream, is depicted in Listing 3. Here, one Adaptation Set is defined for the video stream and two for the audio, each at a different language. For the video stream three alternative Representations are defined according to bandwidth. Similar to the static type, the attributes in the MPD element describe the namespaces, the MPD type and the minimum buffer time. The MPD profile is now set to live streaming. Taking into account that the duration of a live streaming cannot be fixed, several attributes related to timing and scheduling are also defined, including the minimum update period, the time shift buffer depth and the time the media will be available (Listing 3).

The AdaptationSet includes the mime type, codecs, language, frame rate, segment alignment and segment start with SAP attributes. In a *SegmentTemplate* element, the path that complements the HTTP URL defined in the *BaseURL* element is given. However, due to the unknown duration of a live streaming, it is defined as a parameterized URL. In the depicted example, the symbols "$" and "%" are used as markers to be overwritten by other values, as it is described in the segmentTemplate element, and form the HTTP URL for each segment in a representation. For example, as it concerns the video segments, within the "video/" folder, defined in the *BaseURL* element, three different folders shall be created; each for one of the

Listing 2.

```
<MPD
  xmlns:xsi="http://www.w3.org/2001/XMLSchema-instance"
  xmlns="urn:mpeg:DASH:schema:MPD:2011"
  xsi:schemaLocation="urn:mpeg:DASH:schema:MPD:2011 DASH-MPD.xsd"
  type="static"
  mediaPresentationDuration="PT325S"
  minBufferTime="PT1.2S"
  profiles="urn:mpeg:dash:profile:isoff-on-demand:2011">
  <BaseURL>http://cdn1.example.com/</BaseURL>
  <BaseURL>http://cdn2.example.com/</BaseURL>
  <Period>
    <AdaptationSet mimeType="audio/mp4" codecs="mp4a.40.2" lang="fr"
      segmentAlignment="true" segmentStartsWithSAP="1">
      <Representation id="3" bandwidth="64000">
        <BaseURL>3463275477.mp4a</BaseURL>
      </Representation>
      <Representation id="4" bandwidth="32000">
        <BaseURL>5685763463.mp4a</BaseURL>
      </Representation>
    </AdaptationSet>
    <AdaptationSet mimeType="application/ttml+xml" lang="de">
      <Representation id="5" bandwidth="256">
        <BaseURL>796735657.xml</BaseURL>
      </Representation>
    </AdaptationSet>
    <AdaptationSet mimeType="video/mp4" codecs="avc1.4d0228"
segmentAlignment="true" segmentStartsWithSAP="1">
      <Representation id="6" bandwidth="256000" width="320" height="240">
        <BaseURL>8563456473.mp4v</BaseURL>
      </Representation>
      <Representation id="7" bandwidth="512000" width="320" height="240">
        <BaseURL>56363634.mp4v</BaseURL>
      </Representation>
      <Representation id="8" bandwidth="1024000" width="640" height="480">
        <BaseURL>562465736.mp4v</BaseURL>
      </Representation>
      <Representation id="9" bandwidth="1384000" width="640" height="480">
        <BaseURL>41325645.mp4v</BaseURL>
      </Representation>
    </AdaptationSet>
      </Period>
  </MPD>
```

Listing 3.

```
<MPD
  xmlns:xsi="http://www.w3.org/2001/XMLSchema-instance"
  xmlns="urn:mpeg:DASH:schema:MPD:2011"
  xsi:schemaLocation="urn:mpeg:DASH:schema:MPD:2011 DASH-MPD.xsd"
  type="dynamic"
  minimumUpdatePeriod="PT2S"
  timeShiftBufferDepth="PT30M"
  availabilityStartTime="2011-12-25T12:30:00"
  minBufferTime="PT4S"
  profiles="urn:mpeg:dash:profile:isoff-live:2011">
  <BaseURL>http://cdn1.example.com/</BaseURL>
  <BaseURL>http://cdn2.example.com/</BaseURL>
  <Period>
    <!-- Video -->
    <AdaptationSet mimeType="video/mp4" codecs="avc1.4D401F" frameR-
ate="30000/1001"
      segmentAlignment="true" segmentStartWithSAP="1">
      <BaseURL>video/</BaseURL>
      <SegmentTemplate timescale="90000" initialization="$Bandwidth%/init.
mp4v"
        media="$Bandwidth%/$Time$.mp4v">
        <SegmentTimeline>
          <S t="0" d="180180" r="432"/>
        </SegmentTimeline>
      </SegmentTemplate>
      <Representation id="v0" width="320" height="240" bandwidth="250000"/>
      <Representation id="v1" width="640" height="480" bandwidth="500000"/>
      <Representation id="v2" width="960" height="720" bandwidth="1000000"/>
    </AdaptationSet>
    <!-- English Audio -->
    <AdaptationSet mimeType="audio/mp4" codecs="mp4a.0x40" lang="en" segmen-
tAlignment="0"
      segmentStartWithSAP ="1">
      <SegmentTemplate timescale="48000" initialization="audio/en/init.mp4a"
media="audio/en/$Time$.mp4a">
        <SegmentTimeline>
          <S t="0" d="96000" r="432"/>
        </SegmentTimeline>
      </SegmentTemplate>
      <Representation id="a0" bandwidth="64000" />
```

continued on following page

Listing 3. Continued

```
    </AdaptationSet>
    <!-- French Audio -->
    <AdaptationSet mimeType="audio/mp4" codecs="mp4a.0x40" lang="fr" segmen-
tAlignment="0"
       segmentStartWithSAP ="1">
      <SegmentTemplate timescale="48000" initialization="audio/fr/init.mp4a"
media="audio/fr/$Time$.mp4a">
        <SegmentTimeline>
           <S t="0" d="96000" r="432"/>
        </SegmentTimeline>
      </SegmentTemplate>
      <Representation id="a0" bandwidth="64000" />
    </AdaptationSet>
  </Period>
</MPD>
```

defined Bandwidth values (250000, 500000, 1000000) for representations. Within these folders shall be put the segments for the respective representation. Each such folder shall include a segment named "init.mp4v" for initialization and several .mp4v segments with names including the word "Time". The same occurs for the audio segments (.mp4a files) that shall be put within the folders "audio/en" and "audio/fr" respectively.

The SegmentTimeline element expresses the duration of each segment in units based on the timescale attribute. Several more attributes are described in the DASH specification.

The Table 16 summarizes the MPD structure and denotes the most important elements and attributes it includes up to the representation level.

Table 16. Elements and attributes of an MPD file

Element or Attribute Name	Description
MPD	The root Element of Media Presentation Description
@profiles	Specifies a list of profiles to enable interoperability
@mediaPresentationDuration	The duration of the entire presentation
@minBufferTime	A common duration used in representation. The playout begins after minbufferTime * bandwidth bits
Period	Information of a period
BaseURL	The url to be used for reference or alternative url
AdaptationSet	At least one in each period to specify the available sets for adaptation
Representation	The representation information in an adaptation set
@id	Unique identifier for the representation
@bandwidth	data to calculate when enough data are delivered for starting continues playout
@mimeType	The MIME type of the segment
@codecs	The codecs in the representation

3D Content over the Web: From VRML to X3D and X3Dom

Introduction

The ability to render 3D content in real-time over the web seems to be the next step since the introduction of 2D multimedia content in HTML pages. All started back in 1995, when HyperText Markup Language (HTML) inspired and proposed a text based meta-language for the representation of 3D scenes over the web, the so-called Virtual Reality Modeling Language (VRML). Two years later, in 1997, a newer version of VRML, the so-called VRML97 (ISO/IEC 14772-1, 1997), also known as VRML 2.0, became the first ISO standard for representing interactive 3D vector graphics for the web. VRML is a text file format that describes 3D geometrical shapes, by defining vertices and edges along with additional information for colours and textures. VRML technology could also create and define animations, sounds and lightings triggered by external events and timers via Java or ECMA-Script functions defined in a script node of the VRML file.

VRML was accepted with much interest by the end users as well as by many companies that either implemented the WRL extension into their 3D modeling programs, in order to import/export/save to that specific file format, or contributed to the VRML standard by improving its quality level. Since then and for the last 20 years, there have been developed various solutions, most of them being disappeared over the time, that either followed the traditional plugin-based method or a method of a direct integration of the rendering system into the browser's architecture. The former required the installation of a platform specific plug-in for the rendering of the scene, such as Flash, Silverlight, ShockWave and Quicktime, but, recently, X3D/X3Dom changed the way of implementing 3D into the web.

Authoring tools such as Director that natively supported 3D graphics made it possible to embed 3D content on the web via Shockwave and Flash plugins. But as its implementation was based on 2D vector shapes, it was not accepted as a proper solution for 3D scenes on the web, as it could not support complex 3D objects. Flash technology of fake 3D, later lead to projects like PaperVision3D (Papervision3D). The latter, despite its very impressive results, did not manage to earn the users' interest in long term, as it was not able to support complex 3D shapes and visual effects. In the same context, other companies like Microsoft tried to develop a web plugin that would enable the developers to create a rich multimedia environment using vector graphics, animations and even fake 3D objects by a perspective transformation of 2D content. Later another graphics API for interactive 3D web applications was presented by Google, namely O3D (WebGL implementation of O3D). O3D is an open source JavaScript API started in 2009 as a framework for use in the development process of games, advertisements, simulations, engineering applications and massive online virtual worlds. O3D is composed of two layers: the lower layer implemented in C/C++ that provides a geometry and shader abstraction using WebGL or DirectX and the higher layer API implemented in JavaScript, which provides the scene-graph API. O3D is similar to the current standard X3D, in respect to the scene-graph model, but it does not provide a declarative way of defining its contents and all its scenes' content building processes should be performed using JavaScript. Finally in 2009 an XML-based Markup Language was introduced, namely 3DMLW (3D Markup Language for the Web) (3DMLW), for the representation of interactive 2D/3D content over the web. 3DMLW is developed by 3D Technologies R&D in order to provide a fast and powerful tool for creating rich and intuitive visual applications. The 3DMLW platform consists of an open source software suite, with its own scripting language, a renderer based on standard OpenGL for cross-platform compatibility, a plugin interface for managing input/output events and a server toolset that provides an automatic conversion process of 3D models and textures of several file formats to the 3DMLW format.

WebGL

Currently the only backend renderer that does not require a plugin is that of WebGL (Web Graphics Library) (Jackson, 2014 (webgl 1.0)). WebGL is a 2D rendering API designed as a drawing/rendering context for the HTML5 Canvas element. WebGL provides rendering functionalities similar to OpenGL ES 2.0 by giving access to the hardware accelerated graphics GPU via JavaScript. What started as Canvas 3D experiments back in 2006 by Vladimir Vukićević, now represents the leading rendering technology in web 3D graphics. This novel variation of OpenGL modified for browser compatibility and wrapped for the web is designed and maintained by the non-profit Khronos Group. OpenGL ES 2.0 is a shader-based OpenGL dialect that was designed and developed for portable devices such as smartphones and tablets that have graphics chips less powerful than the ones used by desktop computers. The ability to render 3D content in a HTML5 canvas element using WebGL is enabled via the *WebGLRenderingContext* which provides its own special properties and methods for the interaction and manipulation of the content. WebGL makes use of the HTML5 Canvas, as it provides a destination for programmatic rendering in web pages and allows the use of different rendering APIs for this task. Canvas specification comes only with the *CanvasRenderingContent2D* Interface which defines a 2D drawing context for the HTML5 canvas element that enables the user to draw and manipulate graphics with the provided methods and properties.

WebGL in its core is composed of scripts known as shaders, responsible for the visual representation of the 3D content. Multiple scripts are being used in order to render a scene, but are being separated in only two categories, namely Vertex Shader (VS), and Fragment Shader (FS). The VS is responsible for the vertex coordinate transformations and the final vertex position, which represent the position of the object stored internally into the GPU in order to be passed afterwards at the FS scripts. Actually the two shaders, VS and FS, work together for the final rendering but if needed the values passed from the VS can be overridden. FS is responsible for the final color of each pixel of the rendered output image, but in cases of obscured objects in the scene, based on the viewpoint projection matrix and dimension, FS can optionally discard some fragments of the vertex position data send by the VS.

Since WebGL technology is based on OpenGL ES 2.0, the OpenGL graphics rendering API for 2D/3D hardware accelerated graphics via GPU for mobile browsers and embedded systems, like smartphones, tablets and game consoles, started to support WebGL capabilities. Browsers for portable devices, like Firefox, Internet Explorer, Google Chrome, and Opera Mobile, already support this technology in some devices, as WebGL availability depends on their hardware and especially the GPU. Since WebGL became available for mobiles and tablets, more and more interactive, multimedia-heavy, web-based applications start to be developed. Such multimedia applications are possible today but are still evolving as technology emerges, new rendering APIs are being developed and hardware in portable devices is getting better. Khronos Group rushes towards the technological evolution and since 2013 it is under the development of the WebGL 2.0 specification (Jackson, 2014 (webgl 2.0)) that is based on the OpenGL ES 3.0 API and will allow additional rendering functionalities. The WebGL 2 is an extension of WebGL 1 and will be compatible with it. The latter means that all existing content will run in WebGL 2 without any modification, but in order to access the new functionalities provided by the new *WebGL2RenderingContext* it has to be explicitly requested by the content.

X3D

The X3D (Daly & Brutzman, 2007) is a standardised XML-based file format for representing real-time and interactive 3D computer graphics on the web, first approved by ISO in 2004. Its initial efforts started by the Web3D Consortium, who designed the language to be the successor of VRML. X3D was developed as a royalty-free specification for broad 3D graphics, with multiple levels of functionalities, that defines various data-encoding formats, but would still maintain a compatibility with predecessor technology. There are three ISO documents that comprise the X3D specification, namely the Abstract Functionality (ISO/IEC 19775, 2004), the Encodings (ISO/IEC 19776, 2007) and the Language Bindings (ISO/IEC FDIS 19777-1, 2005; ISO/IEC FDIS 19777-2, 2005). The first document defines the architecture and abstract definitions of all X3D components alongside the abstract API of X3D. The second defines the three different types of file encoding, namely XML, classic VRML and Binary, and finally the third document defines the X3D language API bindings, which is separated in ECMA-Script API to Scene Access Interface (SAI) and Java API to SAI.

X3D is being used for a variety of purposes by the 3D community, from simple use cases to complex applications, as it supports multi-texture rendering, real-time reflection and lighting, shaders with texture, normalmap, lightmap, movietexture and a deferred rendering architecture. Also it supports animation, interchangeable humanoid animation (H-Anim), geospatial position and the IEEE Distributed Interactive Simulation (DIS) network protocol. The functionalities provided by the low level rendering engines of OpenGL and DirectX provide cross-platform interoperability in X3D visual functionalities, such as rendering, texturing and modeling. The geometric modeling functionalities in X3D are composed of geometric primitives like box, sphere, cylinder and cone. It also supports a triangle-definition node for the representation of any object and even more complex geometric nodes, like elevation grid and non-uniform rational basis spline (NURBS) nodes, that represent curves and surfaces. X3D describes nodes that capture the user's events from standard input interface devices like keyboard and mouse. Interactivity with objects can be enhanced with simple animations using linear interpolators that control the objects position and rotation, but also with complex animations using SAI functionalities either using ECMA-Script or Java.

X3D was created in order to deliver lightweight and balanced web applications. To this end, Web3D Consortium introduced a profile system that is being used for the specification of the components used in an X3D world. This component-based architecture of X3D is composed of several profiles including the Core, Interchange, Interactive, Immersive, Full, MPEG-4 Interactive, CDF (CAD Distillation Format) and Medical-Interchange profiles. Each profile declares the functions needed in the development and rendering process of an X3D world, which in turn control the components used and their associated nodes. Such an architecture can lead in advancement as the development of one area doesn't affect or slow others. Furthermore, authors can extend the X3D using a prototyping mechanism that allows them to create and describe new prototype nodes or re-use and alter previously defined ones, by introducing new features that support a new technology.

X3D has already been proposed in the HTML5 specification as the technology for declarative 3D scenes, meaning that it has already been defined how such X3D data should be included into the DOM (Document Objet Model). However, HTML5 does not define the structure of the DOM integration nor the scene graph accessing methods. Nowadays, there are 3D software packages, game engine plugins and 3D rendering plugin-based systems, just like X3D, which can cooperate with the browser and create a rich media environment. But most of these suffer from two major drawbacks: At first, these systems manage interactions, communications and rendering internally, which means that developers have to deal with the synchronization between the DOM and the plugin, along with familiarization with the program's API. At second, since it is a plugin system, an installation process by the end user is required that may introduce security and incompatibility issues.

X3Dom

Based on the above technologies of X3D and HTML5, a new integration model was proposed, named X3Dom (X3Dom; Behr et al., 2009) (pronounced X-Freedom). X3Dom can be described as the "product" of the discussions in both Web3D and W3C communities, for the development of a JavaScript based interface for X3D. This integration model was developed by Fraunhofer research organization, a Web3D Consortium member, as an experimental open source framework and client-side rendering API with no requirement for external plug-ins, based on the HTML5 specification for declarative 3D content (using X3D elements as part of the HTML5 DOM tree). The X3D elements are directly integrated as DOM elements and all scene manipulations are done using DOM-based scripting interfaces. The main goal of X3Dom is to support HTML5 content that includes X3D data inside the browser's DOM tree in a separate namespace. For this purpose X3Dom proposed the removal of the X3D prefix from all the nodes belonging to the X3D world. The following code examples (Behr et al., 2009) demonstrate the inclusion of an XML-encoded X3D world into an XHTML file with the usage of the X3D prefix (Listing 4) and how the same X3D scene could look like without it, as proposed by X3Dom (Listing 5).

Listing 4.

```
<?xml version='1.0' encoding='UTF-8'?>
<!DOCTYPE html PUBLIC "-//W3C//DTD XHTML 1.0 Strict//EN" "http://www.w3.org/
TR/xhtml1/DTD/xhtml1-strict.dtd">
<html xmlns='http://www.w3.org/1999/xhtml'>
   <head>
      <title>X3D DOM INTEGRATION AND MANIPULATION</title>
   </head>
   <body>
      <h1>X3D DOM INTEGRATION AND MANIPULATION</h1>
      <x3d:x3d xmlns:x3d="http://www.web3d.org/specifications/x3d-3.2.xsd">
            <x3d:Scene>
                  <x3d:Shape>
                        <x3d:Box x3d:size="5 5 5" />
                  </x3d:Shape>
            </x3d:Scene>
      </x3d:x3d>
   </body>
```

Listing 5

```
</html>
<?xml version='1.0' encoding='UTF-8'?>
<!DOCTYPE html PUBLIC "-//W3C//DTD XHTML 1.0 Strict//EN" "http://www.w3.org/
TR/xhtml1/DTD/xhtml1-strict.dtd">
<html xmlns='http://www.w3.org/1999/xhtml'>
    <head>
        <title>X3D DOM INTEGRATION AND MANIPULATION</title>
    </head>
    <body>
        <h1>X3D DOM INTEGRATION AND MANIPULATION</h1>
        <x3d xmlns="http://www.web3d.org/specifications/x3d-3.2.xsd">
                <Scene>
                        <Shape>
                                <Box size="5 5 5"/>
                        </Shape>
                </Scene>
        </x3d>
    </body>
</html>
```

Throughout their improvements, Fraunhofer proposed a common event model for the two standards XHTML and X3D, as they had already defined different event models for common events based on their application domains. Based on that common event model, one of the changes and improvements proposed by the X3Dom was the integration of the *id* attribute that is being used by the XHTML profile for defining elements in the DOM the same way as the X3D's *DEF* attribute defines nodes. The proposed attribute is not aiming at replacing the *DEF* attribute but rather proposing an alternative/supplementary solution. Additionally, X3Dom proposed the introduction of a new attribute named *USE* that could enable the re-usability of a node and also create a multi-parent relationship within the XHTML tree (as it was defined in an X3D tree). In Listing 6, the aforementioned *id* and *USE* attributes, introduced by X3Dom into the X3D, are demonstrated. The *id* attribute is being used by X3Dom the same way it handles the *DEF* attribute. Retrieving the element that is defined by an *id*, can be performed using the *document.getElementById*("*id* name") method, similar to the *document.getElementsByTagName*("*DEF* name") method for retrieving an element using its *DEF* attribute. At the same example, a second transform element inside the X3D scene is defined that uses the aforementioned *USE* attribute. The *USE* attribute is used to create a clone of an element defined by the same *DEF* name somewhere earlier in the scene. In the example scene, the shape defined within the first transform element is being cloned and re-rendered for a second time inside the canvas in its new position defined by the translation attribute. The *USE* attribute can be used in most X3D elements, a procedure that can simplify the scene construction process.

Also X3Dom's architecture was developed as a connector between the browser frontends and the X3D backend. That connector is responsible for monitoring DOM updates and the synchronization between the two technologies, by creating a DOM/X3D adapter that can support different frontends and

Listing 6.

```
<?xml version='1.0' encoding='UTF-8'?>
<!DOCTYPE html PUBLIC "-//W3C//DTD XHTML 1.0 Strict//EN" "http://www.w3.org/
TR/xhtml1/DTD/xhtml1-strict.dtd">
<html xmlns='http://www.w3.org/1999/xhtml'>
   <head>
      <title>X3Dom INTEGRATION</title>
   </head>
   <body>
      <h1>X3Dom INTEGRATION</h1>
      <x3d xmlns="http://www.web3d.org/specifications/x3d-3.2.xsd">
            <Scene>
                  <Transform id="myBoxID" DEF="myBox" translation="0 10 0"
rotation="0 0 1 0">
                        <Shape>
                              <Box size="5 5 5"/>
                        </Shape>
                  </Transform>
                  <Transform id="myBoxID2" USE="myBox" translation="0 0 0"
rotation="0 0 1 0">
            </Scene>
      </x3d>
   </body>
</html>
```

backends. Alongside the connector, the X3Dom architecture specifies the User Agent as responsible for composing the final rendering output and also providing the methods for accessing the multimedia content and holding the DOM tree. The final part that completes the X3Dom architecture is that of the X3D runtime, which is responsible for updating and rendering the scene, offering also user interaction-like navigation and picking. X3Dom is able to support multiple X3D runtimes, one for every different backend described in the fallback model. The framework is able to detect what backend is needed by checking the requested profile. The X3Dom implementation supports the X3D/SAI plugins and the WebGL as backend, but may fallback to Flash in cases of browser incompatibilities.

Using WebGL as backend renderer, the 3D content is instantiated inside the HTML5 canvas element, via a JavaScript request to the OpenGL context using the *canvas.getContext*('webgl') method. In X3Dom the backend does not collect the objects to render by traversing the DOM elements directly, but rather it constructs a scene-graph hierarchy of the X3D nodes, in order to achieve both flexibility and performance. That extra scene-graph is flexible enough as it parses the X3D elements using the *X3Dom.fields* math library that comes handy for development purposes, but also is less performance costly as it only updates the initial values and synchronizes them when DOM mutation events occur. The latter is faster than the per frame parsing of multiple elements' attributes that should had followed in case of an alternative solution. That mapping between DOM and X3D nodes is not an one-to-one connection as one could think, but in many cases an X3D node can link to multiple DOM nodes, using the USE/DEF attribute, a case that never applies to DOM, where every DOM node always links to one X3D node. The X3D scene is at first rendered on load and then is re-rendered upon scene changes either when an interpolator is used or an external script is changing the scene. The rendering process is a resource consuming procedure as it enables and instructs the backend renderer to collect all the Shape objects, each of which has geometry and appearance, calculate their position using their Transform grouping nodes and then, using the viewport direction, to sort them back to front. WebGL shaders then calculate each pixel's color based on depth, shadow, transparency, occlusion, lighting and camera angle in order to produce the final image.

X3Dom's efforts focus on a tight integration of X3D and HTML5 technologies and so far their proposed architecture and implementation have been successfully accepted by both Web3D and W3C communities. Their goal is to fulfil the HTML5 promise for 3D everywhere and for everyone by creating for the X3D an equivalent to the SVG success in 2D graphics.

WEBRTC: Enabling Real Time Communications over the Web

Introduction

Over the years the Web has managed to overcome several obstacles from the past developing and introducing implementations that can enable synchronous communications over the web. One of the challenges that the developers had to overcome was the ability to transfer video, audio and data over the web without using plugins, such as Flash, Java Applets, etc. To this end, the IETF (Internet Engineering Task Force) and the W3C (World Wide Web Consortium) worked together and developed the WebRTC (Web Real-Time Communication) technology. In this alliance, the IETF specifies the networking protocols and the W3C the JavaScript APIs including access to local media devices such as microphones and web cameras (Alvestrand, H., 2014). The JavaScript APIs of WebRTC are compatible with any browser that supports WebRTC, so users can establish communication for audio, video and generic data.

WebRTC is an open project supported by Google, Mozilla and Opera. The goal of WebRTC is to enable real-time communication among browsers in a peer-to-peer communication utilizing JavaScript and HTML5 without the use of plugins. For instance, applications such as video calls, video-conferencing, text chat, online games, etc. are some of the applications that can be supported with this real-time communication technology. A general overview of WebRTC for audio, video and data transfer between browsers and other applications is given in (Loreto & Romano, 2012; Jennings et al., 2013).

WebRTC is characterized mainly by its architecture where it includes session management and signaling, Peer Connection, audio and video engines and data transport. In this section a brief review of the WebRTC architecture will be presented including the necessary technical detail related to APIs, topologies and codecs.

The WebRTC Architecture

The WebRTC Browser architecture is based on two core interfaces as Figure 6 depicts. The first interface refers to the *Protocols* that browsers apply in order to have a direct peer-to-peer connection between them without servers to intervene. The second interface refers to the *APIs* that browsers provide to JavaScript applications so they benefit by the underlying WebRTC infrastructure.

Figure 6. WebRTC Browser Model

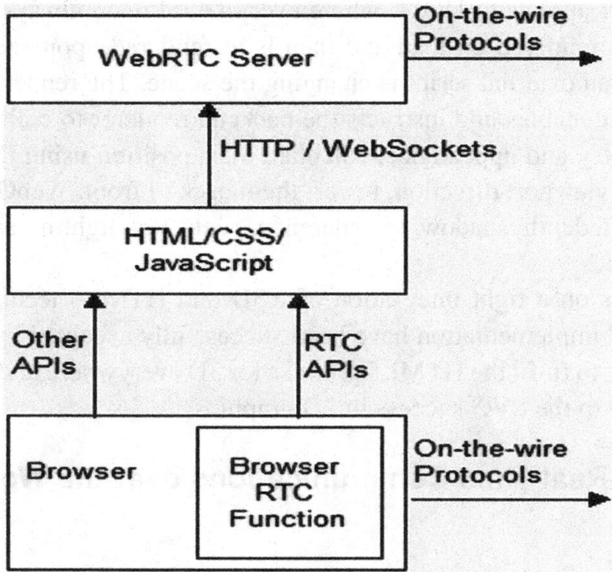

The trapezoid model of the generic WebRTC architecture, shown in Figure 7, is inspired by the SIP (Session Initiation Protocol) based communications. As it is depicted, each browser is associated with a WebRTC server, situated in its network domain, which is responsible for session initialization and negotiation with its opposite server. We assume that each browser has downloaded via a web server a Javascript web application exploiting the local WebRTC APIs. Upon successful session establishment, a media and data path connecting directly the two browsers opens. Signaling messages exchanged between browsers and servers and/or between servers are responsible for the management and closing of such sessions. WebRTC servers can modify, translate and manage the messages as required. Between browsers and WebRTC servers various protocols can be used for their communication including HTTP, and WebSockets.

In the following sections, attention will be paid on the required signaling and how WebRTC embodies it. Next, the main APIs will be discussed and the enabling STUN, TURN and ICE network protocols will be analyzed. Then, the potential topologies will be presented and, finally, information will be provided about the Codecs that WebRTC uses.

Signaling

Signaling refers to a mechanism to coordinate session management and send control messages. Signaling methods and protocols are not specified by WebRTC, hence any relevant protocol can be used as carrier (e.g. SIP or XMPP). It exchanges three types of information: session control messages, network configuration and media capabilities (Dutton, 2012).

Signaling is used during session establishment or update to exchange an offer and an answer between browsers. SDP (Session Description Protocol) is the legacy protocol that can be used to this end. For example, the SDP protocol can be used for the capabilities negotiation between browsers while setting up or updating a peer connection. As an alternative to SDP the WebRTC specifies JSEP (JavaScript

Figure 7. Generic WebRTC architecture

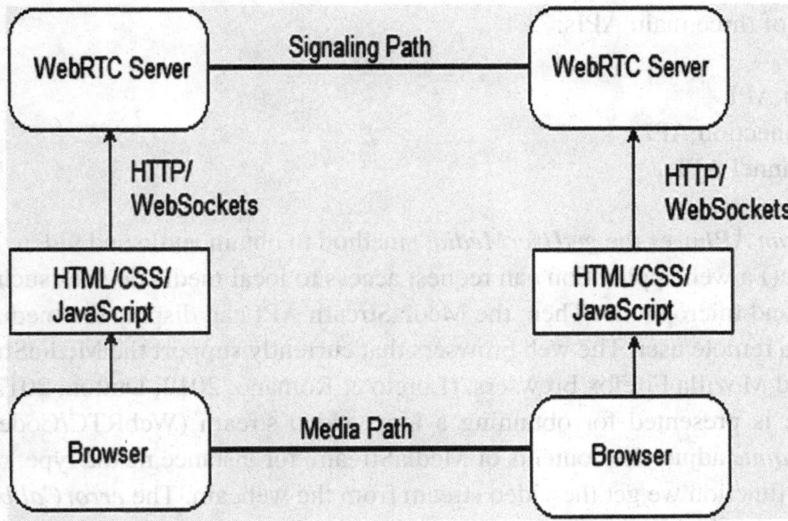

Session Establishment Protocol) for implementing such offer/answer exchanges. JSEP signaling (see Figure 8) can be used in the WebRTC framework as SDP in SIP-based communications that is to describe and negotiate a session between two browsers via the mediating session managers. Once session is established, media and data can be transferred directly between the two browser peers. To illustrate how open and flexible the WebRTC architecture is, JSEP signaling can be transferred from a browser to a WebRTC server via websockets or HTTP and then to be translated to SIP/SDP signaling, enabling thus communication between a browser and a VoIP phone.

Figure 8. JSEP architecture

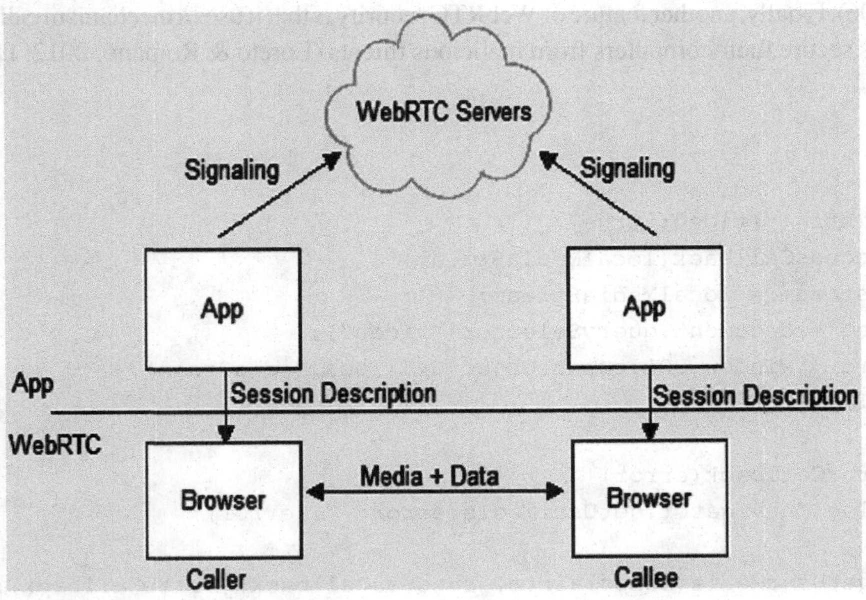

WebRTC Main APIs

WebRTC consists of three main APIs:

1. MediaStream API,
2. RTCPeerConnection API,
3. RTCDataChannel API.

The *MediaStream API* uses the *getUserMedia()* method to obtain audio and video. In more specific, with getUserMedia() a web application can request access to local media devices such as, for instance, the user's camera and microphone. Then, the MediaStream API can display the media streaming content and send it to a remote user. The web browsers that currently support the MediaStream API are the Chrome, Opera and Mozilla Firefox browsers. (Loreto & Romano, 2012; Dutton, 2012)

A sample code is presented for obtaining a local video stream (WebRTC/Codelab - Bitbucket) (Listing 7). *Constraints* adjust the contents of MediaStream, for instance media type, resolution, etc. In *successCallback()* function we get the video stream from the webcam. The *errorCallback()* function is used if an error appears. Finally, on the last line, *getUserMedia()* is called having three parameters: The constraint object and the two functions mentioned above, successCallback and errorCallback.

The *RTCPeerConnection API* is used for session management, audio and video communication between peers and the provision of stable and efficient communication of streaming media. The RTCPeerConnection API at first implements session negotiation via the serving WebRTC servers and upon successful establishment of the session, it provides orchestration of audio and video calling (including signal processing and codec handling), media encryption and bandwidth management. Finally, it enables the browser-to-browser communication.

Security and user privacy is seriously taken into account by WebRTC. Hence it takes care to protect users and devices. Specifically, the encryption for media and data is mandatory using protocols such as Secure Real Time Protocol (SRTP) and Datagram Transport Layer Security (DTLS). SRTP provides encryption, integrity and authentication messages. DTLS defines communication privacy for datagram protocols (RFC4347, 2006). Finally, another feature of WebRTC security is that it uses a mechanism called sandboxing that helps users secure their computers from malicious threats (Loreto & Romano, 2012; Dutton, 2012).

Listing 7.

```
var constraints = {video: true};
function successCallback(localMediaStream) {
    window.stream = localMediaStream;
    var video = document.querySelector("video");
    video.src = window.URL.createObjectURL(localMediaSream);
    video.play();
}
function errorCallback(error){
   console.log("navigator.getUserMedia error: ", error);
}
 navigator.getUserMedia(constraints, successCallback, errorCallback);
```

Figure 9. STUN network architecture

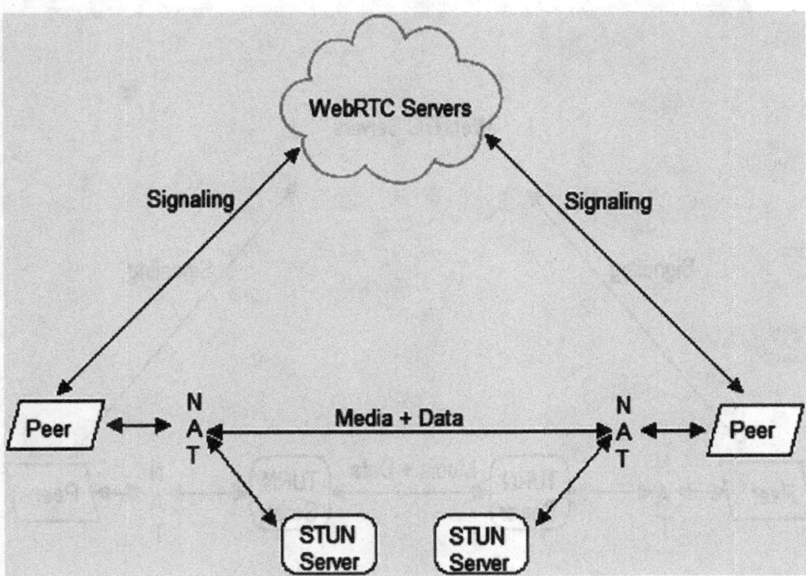

The *RTCDataChannel API* empowers the interchange of arbitrary data between peers providing low latency and high throughput. Data exchange takes place over bidirectional Data Channels where incoming and outgoing user data are encapsulated within SCTP (Stream Control Transmission Protocol) packets. SCTP has been selected as the transport protocol for Data Channels. The RTCDataChannel API can be used in gaming applications, file transfer, remote desktop applications, real-time text chat, etc. Furthermore, the RTCDataChannel API has the same API as WebSockets, is fast and can be secure (over DTLS) (Loreto & Romano, 2012; Dutton, 2012).

WebRTC Network Protocols

NAT (Network Address Translation) give the opportunity to each device in a private local network to get a public IP address. However, WebRTC cannot be used without a public IP address at the session negotiation phase (Dutton, WebRTC in the real world: STUN, TURN and Signaling - HTML5 Rocks, 2013). Hence, to achieve NAT traversal WebRTC uses three different types of network protocols, namely:

1. STUN,
2. TURN,
3. ICE.

STUN stands for Session Traversal Utilities for NAT and is a client-server protocol. The server part sits behind a NAT so it discovers the user's public IP address and TCP port and let the STUN client be aware of them. This procedure helps a WebRTC peer to get its public IP address and port, and passes them via WebRTC signaling to the other peer (see Figure 9) (Dutton, WebRTC in the real world: STUN, TURN and Signaling - HTML5 Rocks, 2013). Hence, STUN gives permission to the WebRTC media and data flows (for instance real-time voice, video, and messaging) between peers.

Figure 10. TURN network architecture

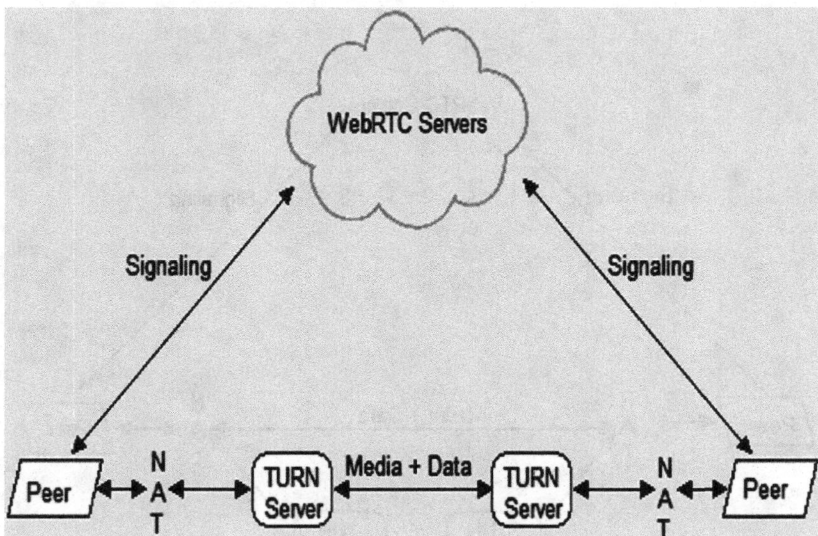

TURN stands for Traversal Using Relays around NAT and is used as a fallback solution to STUN when STUN cannot be used. A TURN server is used as a relay for the audio, video and data streams between peers (see Figure 10) (Dutton, 2013). In particular, it offers to a WebRTC peer the required public IP address for communication outside its LAN.

ICE stands for Interactive Connectivity Establishment and is a framework for connecting peers. The mission of ICE is to try finding the best solution for WebRTC peers choosing between STUN and TURN.

At first, ICE tries to connect peers directly via STUN. If that fails, then ICE uses a TURN relay server (Dutton, 2013).

Network Topologies

WebRTC is very flexible to support any network configuration. Depending on the application and the number of the participating peers in a WebRTC session, several types of network topologies can be established.

The simplest connection that concerns the communication between just two peers is the direct *peer-to-peer connection* between the two endpoints (see Figure 11).

Figure 11. Peer-to-peer connection

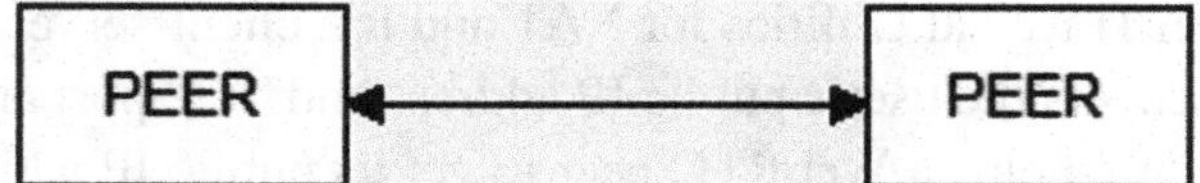

Figure 12. Mesh topology

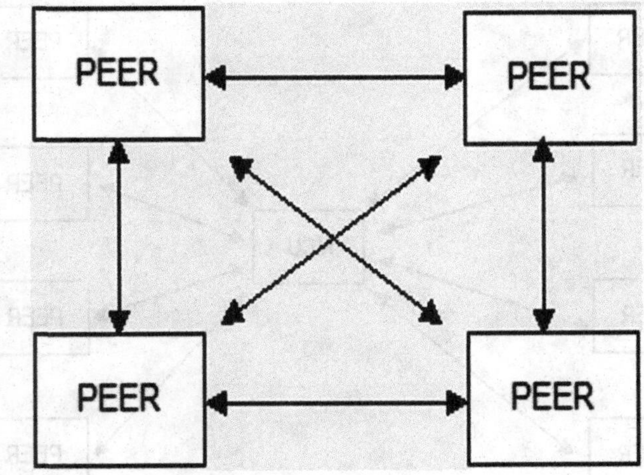

For conference-like WebRTC sessions, where more than two peers participate, *mesh*, *star* and *MCU* topologies can be set up. In a *Mesh topology* each peer connects directly to all other available peers maintaining several peer-to-peer connections (Figure 12). A Mesh topology is easy to be established. The disadvantages are that it can be used for limited peers and that it requires from the application to multiplex media and data from all open connections so a conference is enabled.

In a *Star topology* one peer is assigned the role of coordinator and maintains the connections with any other peer. The central peer is also responsible to send the multiplexed data to all the other peers (Figure 13). The disadvantage is that the central peer should be robust enough to undertake this load, while there are not special requirements from the other peers.

Figure 13. Star topology

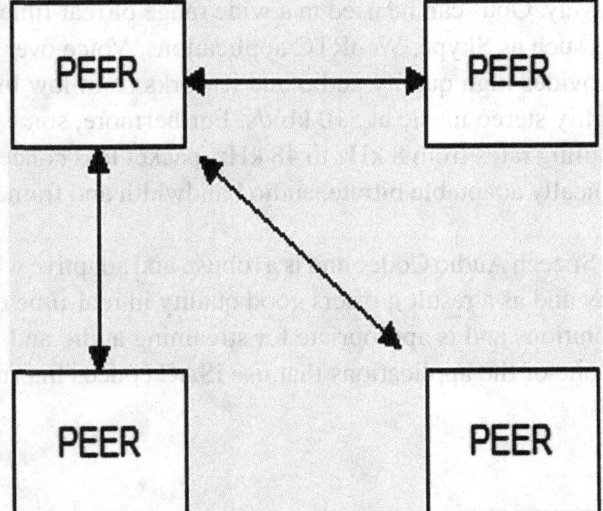

Figure 14. MCU topology

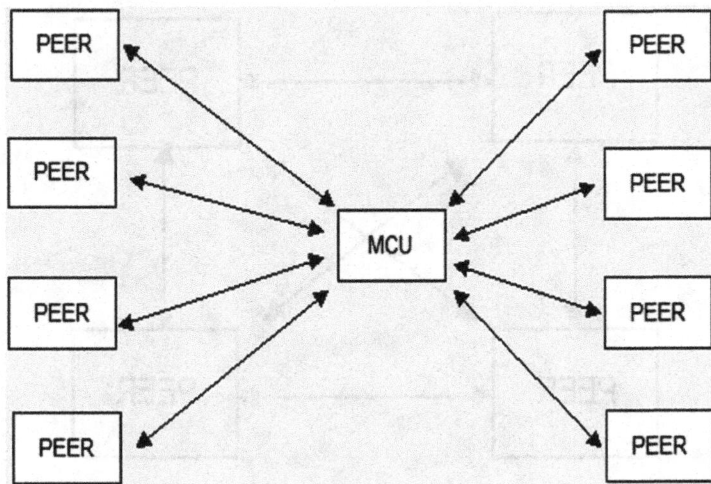

The most robust network topology for conference-style communications is the *MCU* (Multipoint Control Unit) (Figure 14). MCU is a mediating server that can maintain connections with a great number of participants and distribute multiplexed media content to them. Whenever a peer decides to leave a conference the MCU simply terminates this connection. A MCU can handle different resolutions and codecs to enable interoperability between different peers. It is mainly used for video conferencing (Dutton, 2012).

WebRTC Codecs

Currently WebRTC supports the Opus, iSAC and iLBC audio codecs as well as the VP8 video codec.

Opus is an open source and royalty free audio codec developed by IETF and standardized as RFC 6716 in 2012 (RFC6716, 2012). It can be used in both, speech interaction and music transmission via the Internet. In order to create Opus, Skype and Xiph.org collaborated offering their SILK and CELT codecs technology respectively. Opus can be used in a wide range of real-time communications including interactive applications such as Skype, WebRTC applications, Voice over IP, chat in games, video-conferencing, etc. Opus provides high quality audio and it works from low bitrate narrowband speech at 6 kbit/s to very high quality stereo music at 510 kbit/s. Furthermore, some of the features that Opus provides are: different sampling rates from 8 kHz to 48 kHz, packet loss concealment, frame sizes from 2.5 ms up to 60 ms, dynamically adaptable bitrate, audio bandwidth and frame size, up to 255 channels (Opus Codec).

iSAC stands for internet Speech Audio Codec and is a robust, and adaptive wideband audio and speech codec. It provides low delay and as a result it offers good quality in real-time communications. iSAC is developed by Global IP Solutions and is appropriate for streaming audio and Voice over IP (VoIP) applications. Google Talk is one of the applications that use iSAC codec (Internet Speech Audio Codec; Le Grand et al., 2013).

iLBC stands for internet Low Bitrate Codec and is a royalty free narrow band speech codec. It was developed by Global IP Solutions and is used in many Voice over IP (VoIP) and streaming audio applications (WebRTC - iLBC Freeware).

VP8 is a highly efficient video compression technology that was developed by On2 Technologies. In 2010, Google acquired On2 and made VP8 available as part of the WebM Project. WebM is a royalty-free media file format designed for the web and defines the file container structure for both video and audio streams. The structure of WebM files is based on Matroska container (The WebM Project).

RELATED WORKS

HTML5 and Real-Time Participatory Sensing Services

The rapid evolution of mobile phones in recent years has brought great impact on people's daily lives. From simple calling devices they have become powerful platforms with features such as access to the internet, barcodes scanners, embedded sensors (e.g., GPS, accelerometer, gyroscope, light, video, microphone, etc.). Also, they can communicate with external sensors through network protocols such as Bluetooth. Apart from the evolution of mobiles, Web, also, currently lives its evolutionary phase with HTML5. Thus, several Web applications have been mobilized and many Web sites are now responsive. HTML5 is the definite "software glue" which fills the gap between mobiles and Web and becomes the key to any future development. All these mobile features can be used combinatorial to the advanced features of HTML5 for enabling valuable distributed participatory sensing applications.

The participatory sensing applications can be extended to many fields of the daily life, namely: transportation and civil infrastructure monitoring, environmental monitoring, health and fitness, urban sensing and traffic monitoring. In the following some characteristic participatory sensing applications from various domains will be discussed.

Road and Traffic Monitoring

A problem that concerns a lot of people is the monitoring of road and traffic conditions in a city. In (Mohan at al., 2008) the authors present an application for monitoring road and traffic conditions using smartphones. They use the built-in sensors of smartphones such as accelerometer, microphone, and GPS to detect potholes, bumps, braking, and honking. Another similar paper is the Pothole patrol (Eriksson et al., 2008). It uses some sensor-equipped vehicles (e.g. taxis) to gather data from the streets of Boston and then train the detector, a decision-making process, so it reaches to final conclusions. Four years later and 12245.77 kilometers away in the streets of Mumbai Wolverine, the authors of (Bhoraskar et al., 2012) tried also to identify road conditions using the accelerometer, magnetometer and GPS from their smartphones. Compared to the two previous papers they promise more accurate results. Bikestatic (Reddy et al., 2010) is an application for improving the daily life of a cyclist. It documents routes using an Android application and the built-in sensors and then records the roughness and noisiness of a road. Then, the user can share the information and see visualizations of the data.

Health

The monitoring of patients and the progress of their health is a very important issue for their relatives. Ambulation (Ryder et al., 2009) is a tool for detecting the movement of patients who suffer from chronic diseases such as Multiple Sclerosis, Parkinson's, and Muscular Dystrophy. It runs as a service at the background of Android and Nokia N95 mobile phones and sends the collected data to a web server for visualization. AndWellness (Hicks et al., 2010) is a web platform for health that uses mobile devices as real-time sensor data collectors. The evaluation of the platform was made from people who survive from breast cancer and young moms. Except from monitoring the health of a sick people there are applications for healthy people who want to improve their lives by maintaining a healthier lifestyle. BeWell (Lane et al., 2011) tracks the everyday behavior of people by absorbing sensor data from a variety of multiple embedded smartphone sensors. It promotes wellbeing by monitoring daily activities such as sleep, physical activity and social interactions.

Environmental Monitoring

In recent years several researches have been carried out in the field of environmental monitoring. Ikarus (Von Kaenel et al., 2011) is a flight recording device that collects sensor data from cross-country flights measuring thermal atmospheric conditions. The application provides thermal maps using GPS and barometer pressure values taken from mobile devices. The total results have been taken from more than 30,000 flights. In the same context, GasMobile (Hasenfratz et al., 2012) provides information about air quality and pollution using an Android client application and displaying the data in a high-resolution air pollution map. To collect the data it uses an external sensor which is capable to measure the carbon dioxide values.

MPEG-DASH and Websockets Streaming

QoE is a term that defines how well a system or an application operates in order to meet the user's requirements. Essentially it is a high-level redefinition of Quality of Sevice (QoS) to include user requirements. The term QoE is currently met in a large variety of research domain ranging from mobile networks to media streaming applications (Bourdena et al, 2013; Carmona-Murillo et al, 2014; Narayanan, 2014). In particular as video delivery over HTTP is concerned, it is evolving rapidly.

MPEG-DASH players include a custom logic to estimate the adaptation level and a separate algorithm to achieve a transparent quality switch in real-time. A novel throughput estimation method for audiovisual content streaming was introduced by Thang et al. in (Thang et al., 2012), which was used to calculate the best possible quality. The measurements they conducted also proved that, in case of bottlenecks, a single connection is better than two. Another such algorithm was presented in (Miller et al., 2012]. In their study the authors additionally examined the effect of delay between the users requests and the start of the playback.

As Sánchez et al. describe in (Sánchez et al., 2011), the diversity of modern devices hosting video players, in addition to the availability of several video representations in a variety of bit rates and qualities, point out Scalable Video Coding (SVC) as a key technology to serve the future video delivery to mobile and immobile internet devices. They study the streaming of SVC media according to the DASH paradigm.

Researcher in (Zorrilla M., 2012) is experimented with remotely rendered 3D content delivered to clients using various streaming protocols. His measurements showed dependency on the segmentation size. Thus, dynamic adaptation using MPEG-DASH proved to be the wisest solution for live video streaming applications. The latters included real-time graphics generation, for which the system could manage the segment size dynamically.

As it is mentioned in (Iacono et al., 2014), web applications using the WebSockets protocol can provide resources and cost efficiency. However, processing content from several sources simultaneously may result in a performance degradation of the web application as it is pointed out in (Zhanikeev M., 2013 (COMPSACW)). Hence, the decision whether to use WebSockets depends rather on the use-case scenario and the main application architecture.

As live video streaming over HTTP is concerned, in (Zhanikeev M., 2013 (IEICE)) the author measures the bounds of throughput an HTML5 application can achieve in practice. The study underlines that browsers using WebSockets can support video streams with very high throughput. Also, aggregation of data using multiple parallel substreams, coordinated via webworkers and WebSockets, can further improve throughput.

WebRTC and X3D

According to the official WebRTC website (WebRTC), more than 1,000,000,000 users have made use of WebRTC open source technology so far. Ericsson Labs was the first that implemented a WebRTC application in 2011 (Persson, 2011). In 2013, Mozilla in cooperation with Google presented the successful connection between Firefox and Chrome browsers using the WebRTC RTCPeerConnection API without the need for plugins (Reavy & Nyman, 2013).

Nowadays, we can find several open platforms based on the WebRTC technology that provide users with the ability to customize the platform according to their needs. The application domains can vary from telemedicine and education to media, entertainment and video conference. Tokbox (TokBox), BlueJeans (BlueJeans), Zingaya (Zingaya) are some of these platforms. In addition, GearCloud Labs has recently presented a platform called Mixology that provides multiple live video streams and interactive graphics in real-time (Gearcloud Labs). Furthermore, Google has added a plugin called Google Hangouts which is based on WebRTC technology and offers to users plenty features such as group conversations and more (Roettgers, 2011; Google+ Hangouts).

It is worth presenting, here, some scientific works in order to observe not only the improvements but also the potentials that WebRTC can provide. The authors of (Becke et al., 2013) examine the performance of RTCWeb protocol on top of SCTP for non-media data transfer. By using several congestion control algorithms for SCTP, they propose how the SCTP protocol can be more delay tolerant by applying an appropriate stream scheduler and support for the interleaving of user messages.

In the world of gaming, several Web games are developed using mainly 3D graphics in order to implement virtual worlds, etc. Some of the latest technologies that are used are WebGL and X3Dom. In fact, the X3Dom technology is friendly to use with many potentials. For instance, authors in (Jung at al., 2011), after having realized that the major driving technology for the documentation and presentation of culture driven media is real-time 3D content, they employed the virtual museum (VM) model for communication needs. Real-time 3D content is delivered through web browsers within the X3Dom framework. The authors describe application scenarios and measure technological requirements, so as to present virtually, via the web, the cultural heritage artifacts kept in museums.

Authors in (Mao et al., 2012), present a framework for visualizing 3D city models online via browsers. The framework is based on City Geography Markup Language (CityGML) and X3D and is supported by HTML5. The authors propose several methods and structures in different scales (blocks, buildings, and facades) in order to display detailed 3D city models and handle the big amount of data. The outcome shows that the applied methodology exhibits visual resemblance of the original 3D city models.

Related Developments by the Authors

The Multimedia Content Laboratory or MCLab (http://www.medialab.teicrete.gr/) was established early in 2004 in the Department of Informatics Engineering of the Technological Educational Institute of Crete. Since then it has been involved in a variety of research and development projects on various aspects of multimedia, including interactive web, modeling and representation of 3D content, multimedia networking and communications. Over the last three years the research efforts emphasize on the integration of 3D content with web technologies exploiting the HTML5 and W3C web APIs.

The involvement of MCLab with HTML5 and other W3C web APIs started early in 2011 as part of experimentations with websockets for the delivery of 3D animations over the web (Kapetanakis, Panagiotakis, 2012 (TEMU)). In that context, using Java, X3D, Ajax and WebSockets, two discrete instances of a server-side rendering system were developed. An X3Dom equivalent scenario utilizing X3D and HTML5 / WebGL technologies was also implemented, to emulate client-side rendering on the same environment. The three implementations were evaluated in terms of battery and memory consumption, latency in graphics display and required network resources.

In order to measure the battery consumption in mobile devices and enable energy efficient provision of mobile multimedia, an innovative methodology for evaluation of energy and resource consumption in mobile devices was introduced. The latter did not require any external metering device but exploited the advanced software and hardware features of modern smartphones to this end. In particular, a mobile application was developed that exploited the Battery Manager and the resource auditing capabilities of the Android OS to log the charging level of device's battery, CPU utilization and the signal strength of all connected networks as the device executed various operations. With this test-bed energy consumption and CPU utilization in various tests, carried out under controlled conditions, were evaluated including multimedia playback, phone calling and connection to various networks (Kapetanakis, Panagiotakis, 2012 (MDSD)) (Mastorakis et al., 2014).

Continuing experimentation with websockets and the Media Capture and Streams API of HTML5, MClab introduced in (Panagiotakis et al., 2013) an architecture that capitalizes on the above technologies to enable real time communications over the web via third party access to multimedia streams from local devices. With such an implementation a web application can communicate, stream and transfer media or other data to its clients at real time to support a fully collaborative environment. Also, the web applications developed in this context for live video streaming and web video chat, without any requirement for plug-in installation, were demonstrated. In addition, a websockets-based messenger for text and live image exchange between browser peers was also developed (Websockets-based messenger for text and live image exchange between browser peers).

Encouraged by the first results, experimentations with the delivery of 3D content over websockets in a more demanding communication scenario were attempted. Hence, in (Kapetanakis, Panagiotakis et al., 2013; Collaborative 3D web-application for preschool children's education) an architecture for interactive 3D scenes streaming over the web was introduced. In this paper a collaborative 3D web-application for preschool children's education that capitalizes on the above technologies was also demonstrated. Small classes, real or virtual, can be arranged around an instructor who can control the main 3D scenery. The application provides a positive and encouraging environment for toddlers to interact with computers while recognizing and playing with 3D animated models of favorite animals.

In the same context, a methodology for browsers' performance evaluation in terms of their ability to display 3D graphics has been recently introduced (Workbench for browsers' performance evaluation in terms of their ability to display 3D graphics). The methodology uses a JavaScript function to increase the 3D scene by certain triangles per second and then to automatically collect the achieved fps. A series of experiments using different browsers on a variety of operating systems have been conducted so far, that underline the performance differences among browsers.

Apart from the research projects above, 3D, HTML5 and web APIs have also been integrated in a variety of R&D projects:

I-promotion is a Partnership of MCLab with other research laboratories and companies that develop a platform for Big Data distribution including 3D content, clustered remote rendering mechanisms and client side 3D representations (Web page for the i-promotion project; Zampoglou, Spala et al., 2013; Zampoglou, Malamos et al., 2013). In that context, multimedia content and metadata, attached to MPEG-4 and MPEG-7 containers respectively, are distributed between modules of a cluster while a remote renderer is instructed to adaptively deliver final content, in terms of rendered images, to its clients. As a result, the platform personalizes and visualizes complex high-end realistic 3D, multimedia and mixed reality content. Additionally, it provides an interface between heterogeneous distributed peers including Digital TV broadcasters, desktop PCs and portable devices.

Opencourses is another funded project MClab is currently carrying out. Using HD video cameras installed in classrooms of the Technological Institute of Crete we deliver live and on demand video stream from the classes enabling distance learning. The recorded courses are delivered via MPEG-DASH, hence content can be played back at client side with no plug-in requirement. More impressively, an attractive virtual 3D classroom has been embedded in the associated web page for displaying synchronized slides and video streams from the courses (Virtual 3D classroom). Very soon, in this virtual world it will be also integrated the extension that have been developed by MCLab for X3Dom providing MPEG-DASH video streams on *MovieTexture* elements (Kapetanakis, et al., 2014; Mini page with the use of MPEG-DASH as 3D model's texture for X3Dom).

Last but not least, a state of the art combination of 3D technologies, semantic annotation and case-based reasoning with application in interior design and decoration. MCLab is currently working on a virtual reality platform that implements Artificial Intelligence (AI) algorithms to suggest various room representations according to the users' input. The system is self-trained and proposes more accurate solutions over the time. The environment where the collaboration takes place is an interactive 3D virtual room, which is formed as the user designs the blueprints of the room (Malamos, Sympa et al., 2009).

FUTURE RESEARCH DIRECTIONS

What the authors are envisioning for the future of mobile multimedia is that with the integration of HTML5, MPEG-DASH, WebRTC, WebSockets, and X3Dom, along with various other relevant web APIs and technologies provided for service adaptation, one can shape a diversity of future pervasive and personalized cloud-based web applications, where the client-server operations are obsolete. In particular, it is believed that in the future web; cloud-based web applications will be able to communicate, stream and transfer adaptive events and content to their clients, creating a fully collaborative and pervasive web 3D environment.

For example, in the past MCLab developed, using Internet friendly technologies and 3D graphics, a large scale platform for educational multiplayer gaming named Evie-m (Malamos, Mamakis et al., 2009; Kapetanakis et al., 2013; Pachoulakis et al., 2012; Malamos, Kotanitsi et al., 2008; Malamos, Mamakis et al., 2008; Malamos et al., 2007). The main target was to be provided an interoperable platform for 3D visual representations in a collaborative environment. Mathematics for high-school students were selected as the first use case scenario. The scenario of the game was as follows: The students, separated into groups, joined a virtual world. The on screen panel of the game enabled the players to add virtual 3D objects on the main terrain. The goal for each student was to maximize each contribution to the building of a virtual city. Each construction request triggered a module which picked a question with multiple possible answers according to a predefined educational objective. The player should correctly answer the question before he was able to gain the requested construct. Another interesting module was the chat, which was giving to students and tutors the ability for real-time text communication between them via the platform during the game. The Evie-m platform had a main core application based on X3D graphics and its logic was written in Java. The communication between the connected computers was taking place Peer-to-Peer to synchronize data among them and deliver a complete collaborative 3D environment. The Evie-m platform was structured by autonomous software modules so its core logic and/or the interfaces can be easily updated. For example, in the view of the future web that authors are envisaged, one can easily develop and integrate new web and browser friendly solutions based on the HTML5 based web APIs and technologies to transform Evie-m to a collaborative and pervasive web 3D platform for educational gaming.

But educational gaming is just an example application for such architectures. Collaborative and pervasive web 3D environments can ideally fit any scenario from education and entertainment to health and communications. Another example multipurpose platform that authors are envisioning that can be also based on the same technologies as Evie-m, is a smartphone-friendly framework which would provide users with a complete control of their mobile devices over a remote web interface. In such a "smartphone everywhere" system, the user would be able to leave (or forget) his smartphone at home, but still receiving calls, messages and accessing all of his data via a 3D web interoperable environment. Combining web3D technologies with data representation it could raise the "wow" factor. Another asset for such an implementation is the "stolen mobile" case. Whenever a thief attempts to use the mobile and connects to the Internet, the owner of the mobile may use completely the device and gain access to track it. To respect user privacy, the system would lock the device while operating from remotely, displaying a custom 3D animated logo on the smartphone, so that other users might not have access to the smartphone.

Definitely, the open issues that such implementations include, so that a reliable and robust combination of technologies is selected in order to be delivered a complete multipurpose environment for 3D collaboration, are many. For instance a series of, compatible or not, mature or not, technologies will need to be implemented, integrated and evaluated including: 3D rendering on smartphone devices, web applications able to manipulate Big Data using cloud and cluster technologies, networking for real time peer-to-peer communication based on WebRTC, streaming multimedia data using MPEG-DASH and WebSockets, performance evaluations of various networking technologies, etc. However, its preceding R&D expertise on web 3D graphics, HTML5 and web technologies endorses MCLab with a strong belief to develop collaborative platforms exploiting the new advanced browser- and smartphone-friendly technologies.

In this context, several on-going research projects are running on this idea investigating the integration of the technologies above and proposing optimal solutions that will facilitate the completion of the Big Picture:

The first investigates the applicability and integration of WebRTC and/or websockets as the communication mechanism for a collaborative and P2P platform such as Evie-m. In such an architecture fast and reliable data transfer between peers is required, as well as a synchronization mechanism to update the virtual world that each peer displays. Hence this research examines if these two communication technologies can be used for the transfer of the textual descriptors of 3D virtual worlds between peer browsers.

The second is on pervasive and crowdsourcing computing and implements a middleware web platform, named RTP2S (Real-Time Participatory Sensing Services). The latter, collects various sensor data from its mobile clients in order to broker them on demand via RESTful web APIs to interesting third party web applications that are not, hence, required to maintain any access to mobile devices. The platform will be totally based on HTML5 and web APIs exploiting features such as mobile workers, web intents, websockets, browser sensor APIs, etc. Such a middleware can be also the basis for what is called "games with purpose", where a platform collects useful data using the input that a user gives while playing a customized game.

The third investigates various methods for packaging and delivery of virtual reality 3D worlds over the Internet, so they are directly reproduced in a browser. In particular it is examined the potentiality for integration of the XML-based MPEG-4 scene descriptions in the HTML context, to allow the play back of MPEG-4 3D scenes within web browsers. In order this to be achieved, the gap between X3D and MPEG-4 needs to be bridged and then to take advantage of the X3Dom framework for the display of MPEG-4 3D scenes within browsers. The proposed solution will be based on XSLT transformations for the automatic translation of MPEG-4 3D descriptions to X3D ones.

In the same context, the fourth project examines the applicability of MPEG-DASH for the streaming of 3D content over the web proposing the required adaptations in the MPEG-DASH architecture to this end. In the context of this project, MCLab achieved recently to contribute a bridge between MPEG-DASH and X3Dom, so developers are able to stream HD video as the texture of a 3D model (Kapetanakis, et al., 2014; Mini page with the use of MPEG-DASH as 3D model's texture for X3Dom). In addition, work on cloud computing and map reduce techniques and algorithms is currently carried out to create MPEG-DASH-friendly chunks of 3D meshes and achieve their progressive representation at client side to increase quality of experience. A new profile for MPEG-DASH will be finally proposed to include adaptive delivery of web3D content.

As far as it concerns game development for the web, physics-based realism is hardly supported in X3D standalone players, while they are completely ignored in X3Dom. Hence, the fifth ongoing project in MCLab examines exactly the implementation and integration of physics in a virtual X3Dom world. Based on the X3D specification and the Bullet.js physics library, a mechanism that applies laws of physics to a web 3D scene has been contributed to the X3Dom framework. This is regarded that will enable web developers to create rich 3D and high quality interactive web games with smooth and realistic animations.

The results from these five projects will be integrated finally, in a collaborative and pervasive web 3D platform, which will assure portability of the developed solutions across other similar platforms and mobile environments.

CONCLUSION

What the authors of this chapter are envisaged for the future of mobile multimedia is that with the integration of HTML5, MPEG-DASH, WebRTC, WebSockets, and X3Dom, along with various other relevant web APIs and technologies provided for service adaptation, one can shape a diversity of future pervasive and personalized cloud-based web applications, where the client-server operations are obsolete. In particular, the authors believe that in the future web; cloud-based web applications will be able to communicate, stream and transfer adaptive events and content to their clients, and vice-versa, creating a fully collaborative and pervasive web 3D environment. This is also propelled and underlined by the recent efforts of Intel engineers (Correia Edward J., 2014) to increase performance of browser-based applications by accessing via Javascript the SIMD (Single-Instruction, Multiple Data) instructions resident on the host processor. Such an achievement would make HTML5 apps run as if they were native. This chapter at first surveyed the state of the art technologies related to ubiquitous and pervasive multimedia communications over the web and then reviewed the challenges raised by their combination.

REFERENCES

3DMLW. (3D Markup Language for Web). (n.d.). *An open source platform for creating rapidly interactive 3D and 2D applications for web or desktop*. Retrieved July 12, 2014, from http://www.3dtech-rd.net/3dmlw/

Ajax3D. (n.d.). Retrieved July 12, 2014, from http://sourceforge.net/projects/ajax3d/

Alvestrand, H. (2014). *Overview: Real time protocols for browser-based applications*. Retrieved July 12, 2014, from http://tools.ietf.org/html/draft-ietf-rtcweb-overview-10

Becke, M., Rathgeb, E. P., Werner, S., Rungeler, I., Tuxe, M., & Stewart, R. (2013, April). Data Channel Considerations for RTCWeb. *Communications Magazine, IEEE, 51*(4), 34–41. doi:10.1109/MCOM.2013.6495758

Behr, J., Eschler, P., Jung, Y., & Zöllner, M. (2009). X3Dom: A DOM-based HTML5/X3D integration model. In *Proceedings of the 14th International Conference on 3D Web Technology* (pp. 127-135). ACM. doi:10.1145/1559764.1559784

Bergkvist, A., Burnett, D. C., Jennings, C., & Narayanan, A. (Eds.). (2014, July 1). *WebRTC 1.0: Real-time communication between browsers - W3C*. Retrieved July 13, 2014, from: http://dev.w3.org/2011/webrtc/editor/webrtc.html

Berjon, R., Faulkner, S., Leithead, T., Navara, E. D., O'Connor, E., Pfeiffer, S., & Hickson, I. (Eds.). (2014, July 31). HTML5 - A vocabulary and associated APIs for HTML and XHTML. *W3C Candidate Recommendation.* Retrieved July 31, 2014, from: http://www.w3.org/html/wg/drafts/html/CR/

Bhoraskar, R., Vankadhara, N., Raman, B., & Kulkarni, P. (2012). Wolverine: Traffic and road condition estimation using smartphone sensors. In *Proceedings of Communication Systems and Networks (COMSNETS)* (pp. 1-6). IEEE. doi:10.1109/COMSNETS.2012.6151382

Billock, G., Hawkins, J., & Kinlan, P. (Eds.). (2013, May 23). *Web intents W3C working group note*. Retrieved July 12, 2014, from http://www.w3.org/TR/web-intents/

Block, S., & Popescu, A. (Eds.). (2011, December 1). *DeviceOrientation event specification, W3C working draft*. Retrieved July 12, 2014, from http://www.w3.org/TR/orientation-event/

BlueJeans. (n.d.). Retrieved July 12, 2014, from http://bluejeans.com/

Bourdena, A., Kormentzas, G., Pallis, E., & Mastorakis, G. (2013, June). Radio resource management algorithms for efficient QoS provisioning over cognitive radio networks. In *Proceedings of Communications* (ICC) (pp. 2415-2420). IEEE. doi:10.1109/ICC.2013.6654893

Burnett, D. C., Bergkvist, A., Jennings, C., & Narayanan, A. (Eds.). (2013, September 3). *Media capture and streams, W3C working draft*. Retrieved July 12, 2014, from http://www.w3.org/TR/mediacapture-streams/

Carmona-Murillo, J., González-Sánchez, J. L., Cortés-Polo, D., & Rodríguez-Pérez, F. J. (2014). QoS in next generation mobile networks: An analytical study. In Resource management in mobile computing environments (pp. 25-41). Springer International Publishing.

Collaborative 3D Web-Application for Preschool Children's Education. (n.d.). Retrieved July 12, 2014, from http://www.medialab.teicrete.gr/minipages/x3dws/

Correia Edward, J. (2014). SIMD + JavaScript = Faster HTML5 apps, insights from Intel visionary Moh Haghighat. *Intel Software Adrenaline*. Retrieved July 13, 2014, from: https://software.intel.com/sites/billboard/article/simd-javascript-faster-html5-apps

Daly, L., & Brutzman, D. (2007, November). X3D: Extensible 3D graphics standard. *Signal Processing Magazine, IEEE, 24*(6), 130–135. doi:10.1109/MSP.2007.905889

DASH.JS. (n.d.). Retrieved July 12, 2014, from https://github.com/Dash-Industry-Forum/dash.js

Industry Forum, D. A. S. H. (n.d.). Retrieved July 12, 2014, from http://dashif.org/

Dutton, S. (2012, July 23). *Getting started with WebRTC - HTML5 rocks*. Retrieved July 12, 2014, from http://www.html5rocks.com/en/tutorials/webrtc/basics/

Dutton, S. (2013, November 4). *WebRTC in the real world: STUN, TURN and signaling - HTML5 rocks*. Retrieved July 12, 2014, from http://www.html5rocks.com/en/tutorials/webrtc/infrastructure

Eriksson, J., Girod, L., Hull, B., Newton, R., Madden, S., & Balakrishnan, H. (2008). The pothole patrol: Using a mobile sensor network for road surface monitoring. In *Proceedings of the 6th International Conference on Mobile Systems, Applications, and Services* (pp. 29-39). ACM. doi:10.1145/1378600.1378605

Labs, G. (n.d.). Retrieved July 12, 2014, from http://gearcloudlabs.com/video/

Google + Hangouts. (n.d.). Retrieved July 12, 2014, from http://www.google.com/+/learnmore/hangouts/

Hasenfratz, D., Saukh, O., Sturzenegger, S., & Thiele, L. (2012). Participatory air pollution monitoring using smartphones. In *Proceedings of 2nd International Workshop on Mobile Sensing*. Academic Press.

Hicks, J., Ramanathan, N., Kim, D., Monibi, M., Selsky, J., Hansen, M., & Estrin, D. (2010). *AndWellness: An open mobile system for activity and experience sampling*. New York, NY: ACM. doi:10.1145/1921081.1921087

Hickson, I. (Ed.). (2012, September 20). *The WebSocket API - W3C*. Retrieved July 13, 2014, from W3C Candidate Recommendation: http://www.w3.org/TR/2012/CR-websockets-20120920/

Hickson, I. (Ed.). (2012, May 1). *Web workers*. Retrieved July 12, 2014, from W3C Candidate Recommendation: http://www.w3.org/TR/workers/

Hickson, I. (Ed.). (2013, July 30). *Web storage*. Retrieved July 12, 2014, from Web Storage, W3C Recommendation: http://www.w3.org/TR/webstorage/

Lo, I. L., & Santano, G. S. (2014). Web-native video live streaming. In *Proceedings of the Second IARIA International Conference on Building and Exploring Web Based Environments (WEB 2014)* (pp. 14-19). Chamonix, France: IARIA.

Internet Speech Audio Codec. (n.d.). Retrieved July 12, 2014, from http://en.wikipedia.org/wiki/Internet_Speech_Audio_Codec

ISO/IEC 14772-1:1997. (n.d.). *Information technology -- Computer graphics and image processing -- The virtual reality modeling language -- Part 1: Functional specification and UTF-8 encoding*.

ISO/IEC 19775:2004. (n.d.). *Information technology — Computer graphics and image processing — Extensible 3D (X3D)*.

ISO/IEC 19776:2007. (n.d.). *Information technology — Computer graphics and image processing — Extensible 3D (X3D) encodings*.

ISO/IEC FDIS 19777-1:2005. (n.d.). *Information technology — Computer graphics and image processing — Extensible 3D (X3D) language bindings — Part 1: ECMAScript*.

ISO/IEC FDIS 19777-2:2005. (n.d.). *Information technology — Computer graphics and image processing — Extensible 3D (X3D) language bindings — Part 2: Java*.

ISO/IEC 23009-1:2014. (n.d.). *Information technology -- Dynamic adaptive streaming over HTTP (DASH) -- Part 1: Media presentation description and segment formats*.

Jackson, D. (Ed.). (2014, July 1). *WebGL specification*. Retrieved July 12, 2014, from WebGL Specification, Khronos Group, Editor's Draft: http://www.khronos.org/registry/webgl/specs/latest/1.0/

Jackson, D. (Ed.). (2014, July 2). *WebGL 2 specification*. Retrieved July 12, 2014, from WebGL 2 Specification, Khronos Group, Editor's Draft: http://www.khronos.org/registry/webgl/specs/latest/2.0/

Jain, A., Mann, J., Wang, Z., & Quach, A. (Eds.). (2014, June 24). *Resource timing, W3C candidate recommendation*. Retrieved July 12, 2014, from http://www.w3.org/TR/resource-timing/

Jennings, C., Hardie, T., & Westerlund, M. (2013, April). Real-time communications for the web. *Communications Magazine, IEEE, 51*(4), 20–26. doi:10.1109/MCOM.2013.6495756

Jung, Y., Behr, J., & Graf, H. (2011). X3Dom as carrier of the virtual heritage. In *Proceedings of the 4th ISPRS International Workshop 3D-ARCH*. Academic Press.

Kapetanakis, K., & Panagiotakis, S. (2012). Efficient energy consumption's measurement on android devices. In *Proceedings of the 2nd International Workshop on Mobile Device Software Development and Web Development – MDSD 2012 (in Conjunction with the 16th PanHellenic Conference on Informatics - PCI 2012)*. Piraeus, Greece: MDSD. doi:10.1109/PCi.2012.29

Kapetanakis, K., & Panagiotakis, S. (2012). Evaluation of techniques for web 3D graphics animation on portable devices. In *Proceedings of the 5th IEEE International Conference on Telecommunications and Multimedia (TEMU) 2012*. Heraklion, Greece: IEEE. doi:10.1109/TEMU.2012.6294708

Kapetanakis, K., Andrioti, H., Vonorta, H., Zotos, M., Tsigkos, N., & Pachoulakis, I. (2013). Collaboration framework in the EViE-m platform. In *Proceedings of the 14th European Association for Education in Electrical and Information Engineering (EAEEIE)*. Chania, Greece: EAEEIE. doi:10.1109/EAEEIE.2013.6576525

Kapetanakis, K., Panagiotakis, S., & Malamos, A. G. (2013). HTML5 and WebSockets: Challenges in network 3D collaboration. In *Proceedings of the 3D International Workshop on Mobile Device Software Development and Web Development – MDSD 2013 (in Conjunction with the 17th PanHellenic Conference on Informatics - PCI 2013)*. Thessaloniki, Greece: MDSD. doi:10.1145/2491845.2491888

Kostas, K., Panagiotakis, S., Malamos, A. G., & Zampoglou, M. (2014) Special session on "3D multimedia transmission over future networks," adaptive video streaming on top of Web3D: A bridging technology between X3DOM and MPEG-DASH. In *Proceedings of 2014 International Conference on Telecommunications and Multimedia (TEMU)*. Academic Press.

Kostiainen, A. (Ed.). (2014, June 19). *Vibration API*. Retrieved July 12, 2014, from Vibration API, W3C Last Call Working Draft: http://www.w3.org/TR/vibration/

Kostiainen, A., & Lamouri, M. (Eds.). (2012, May 8). *Battery status API*. Retrieved July 12, 2014, from Battery Status API, W3C Candidate Recommendation: http://www.w3.org/TR/battery-status/

Kostiainen, A., & Tran, D. D. (Eds.). (2013, October 1). *Proximity events*. Retrieved July 12, 2014, from Proximity Events, W3C Candidate Recommendation: http://www.w3.org/TR/proximity/

Lamouri, M. (Ed.). (2014, April 10). *The network information API, W3C working group note*. Retrieved July 12, 2014, from http://www.w3.org/TR/netinfo-api/

Lane, N. D., Mohammod, M., Lin, M., Yang, X., Lu, H., & Ali, S. (2011). BeWell: A smartphone application to monitor, model and promote wellbeing. In *Proceedings of 5th International ICST Conference on Pervasive Computing Technologies for Healthcare*. Academic Press. doi:10.4108/icst.pervasivehealth.2011.246161

Le Grand, T., Jones, P., Huart, P., & Shabestary, T. (2013). *RTP payload format for the iSAC codec*. Retrieved July 12, 2014, from IETF: http://tools.ietf.org/html/draft-ietf-avt-rtp-isac-04

Loreto, S., & Romano, S. P. (2012). Real-time communications in the web: Issues, achievements, and ongoing standardization efforts. *IEEE Internet Computing*, *16*(5), 68–73. doi:10.1109/MIC.2012.115

Malamos, A. G., Kotanitsi, E., Sympa, P. V., Mamakis, G., Lopez, A. Z., & Crespo, A. J. (2008). *EVIE-m: Utilizing web 3D technologies in mathematics education*. Paper presented at TEMU Conference 2008, Ierapetra, Greece.

Malamos, A. G., Mamakis, G., Sympa, P., Kotanitsi, E., Crespo, A. J., & Lopez, A. Z. (2008). Technical aspects in using X3D in virtual reality mathematics education (EViE-m platform). In *Proceedings of the 12th WSEAS CSCC Multiconference*. Heraklion, Greece: WSEAS.

Malamos, A. G., Mamakis, G., Sympa, P., Kotanitsi, E., Kaliakatsos, Y., Kladis, D., & Lopez, A. Z. (2009). Extending X3D-based educational platform for mathematics with multicast network capabilities. In *Proceedings of WBE2009*. Phuket, Thailand: Academic Press.

Malamos, A. G., Sympa, P. V., & Mamakis, G. S. (2009). XML annotation of conceptual characteristics in interior decoration. In *Proceedings of 6th International Conference, New Horizons in Industry, Business and Education (NHIBE 2009)*. Santorini: Academic Press.

Malamos, A. G., Sympa, P. V., Mamakis, G., & Kaliakatsos, Y. (2007). Evie-m (educational virtual environment mathematics): An alternative approach for an educational strategy game for mathematics. In Proceedings of CBLIS 2007. Heraklion, Greece: Academic Press.

Mann, J. (Ed.). (2012, December 17). *High resolution time*. Retrieved July 12, 2014, from High Resolution Time, W3C Recommendation: http://www.w3.org/TR/hr-time/

Mann, J., & Jain, A. (Eds.). (2013, October 29). *Page visibility* (2nd ed.). Retrieved July 12, 2014, from Page Visibility (Second Edition), W3C Recommendation: http://www.w3.org/TR/page-visibility/

Mann, J., Wang, Z., & Quach, A. (Eds.). (2013, December 12). *User timing*. Retrieved July 12, 2014, from User Timing, W3C Recommendation: http://www.w3.org/TR/user-timing/

Mao B., Cao J., & Wu Z. (2012). *Web-based visualisation of the generalised 3D city models using HTML5 and X3Dom*. doi:10.6029/smartcr.2012.05.005

Mastorakis, G., Panagiotakis, S., Kapetanakis, K., Dagalakis, G., Mavromoustakis, C. X., Bourdena, A., & Pallis, E. (2014). Energy and resource consumption evaluation of mobile cognitive radio devices. In C. Mavromoustakis, E. Pallis, & G. Mastorakis (Eds.), Resource management in mobile computing environments. Springer. doi:10.1007/978-3-319-06704-9_16

Miller, K., Quacchio, E., Gennari, G., & Wolisz, A. (2012). Adaptation algorithm for adaptive streaming over HTTP. In *Proceedings of the IEEE International Packet Video Workshop (PV)* (pp. 173—178). IEEE. doi:10.1109/PV.2012.6229732

Mini Page with the Use of MPEG-DASH as 3D Model's Texture for X3Dom. (n.d.). Retrieved July 12, 2014, from http://www.medialab.teicrete.gr/minipages/dash3d/

Mobile-Web-App-State. (2014, April). *Standards for web applications on mobile: Current state and roadmap*. W3C Document. Retrieved July 12, 2014, from http://www.w3.org/2014/04/mobile-web-app-state/

Mohan, P., Padmanabhan, V. N., & Ramjee, R. (2008). Nericell: Rich monitoring of road and traffic conditions using mobile smartphones. In *Proceedings of the 6th ACM Conference on Embedded Network Sensor Systems* (pp. 323-336). ACM. doi:10.1145/1460412.1460444

Narayanan, R. G. L. (2014). Mobile video streaming resource management. In Resource management in mobile computing environments (pp. 461-480). Springer International Publishing.

O3D WebGL Implementation of 03D. (n.d.). Retrieved July 12, 2014, from https://code.google.com/p/o3d/

Codec, O. (n.d.). Retrieved July 12, 2014, from http://www.opus-codec.org/

Pachoulakis, I., Profit, A. N., & Kapetanakis, K. (2012). The question manager and tutoring module for the EViE-m platform. In *Proceedings of International Conference on Telecommunications and Multimedia (TEMU '12)*. Heraklion, Greece: Academic Press. doi:10.1109/TEMU.2012.6294716

Panagiotakis, S., Kapetanakis, K., & Malamos, A. G. (2013). Architecture for real time communications over the web. *International Journal of Web Engineering*, *2*(1), 1–8. doi:10.5923/j.web.20130201.01

Papervision3d, Open Source Realtime 3D Engine for Flash. (n.d.). Retrieved July 12, 2014, from https://code.google.com/p/papervision3d/

Persson, P. (2011, November 9). *A web RTC tutorial | Ericsson Blog Ericsson research blog*. Retrieved July 12, 2014, from http://www.ericsson.com/research-blog/context-aware-communication/web-rtc-tutorial/

Popescu, A. (Ed.). (2013, October 24). *Geolocation API specification, W3C recommendation*. Retrieved July 12, 2014, from http://www.w3.org/TR/geolocation-API/

Ranganathan, A., & Sicking, J. (Eds.). (2013, September 12). *File API - W3C*. Retrieved July 13, 2014, from File API - W3C Last Call Working Draft: http://www.w3.org/TR/FileAPI/

Reavy, M., & Nyman, R. (2013, February 4). *Hello Chrome, it's Firefox calling! Mozilla hacks – The web developer blog*. Retrieved July 12, 2014, from https://hacks.mozilla.org/2013/02/hello-chrome-its-firefox-calling/

Reddy, S., Shilton, K., Denisov, G., Cenizal, C., Estrin, D., & Srivastava, M. (2010). Biketastic: Sensing and mapping for better biking. In *Proceedings of the SIGCHI Conference on Human Factors in Computing Systems* (pp. 1817-1820). ACM. doi:10.1145/1753326.1753598

RFC4347 - Datagram Transport Layer Security. (2006, April). Retrieved July 12, 2014, from IETF http://tools.ietf.org/html/rfc4347

RFC6455 - The WebSocket Protocol. (2011, December). Retrieved July 12, 2014, from Internet Engineering Task Force (IETF): http://tools.ietf.org/html/rfc6455

RFC6716 - Definition of the Opus Audio Codec. (2012, September). Retrieved July 12, 2014, from Internet Engineering Task Force (IETF): http://tools.ietf.org/html/rfc6716

Roettgers, J. (2011, June 30). *The technology behind Google+ hangouts – Tech news and analysis*. Retrieved July 12, 2014, from https://gigaom.com/2011/06/30/google-hangouts-technology/

Ryder, J., Longstaff, B., Reddy, S., & Estrin, D. (2009). Ambulation: A tool for monitoring mobility patterns over time using mobile phones. In *Proceedings of Computational Science and Engineering*. IEEE. doi:10.1109/CSE.2009.312

Sánchez, Y., Hellge, C., Schierl, T., Van Leekwijck, W., & Le Louédec, Y. (2011). Scalable video coding based DASH for efficient usage of network resources. In *Proceedings of the Third W3C Web and TV Workshop* (pp. 19-20). Academic Press.

Thang, T., Ho, Q., Kang, J., & Pham, A. (2012, February). Adaptive streaming of audiovisual content using MPEG DASH. *IEEE Transactions on Consumer Electronics*, *58*(1), 78–85. doi:10.1109/TCE.2012.6170058

The WebM Project. (n.d.). Retrieved July 12, 2014, from http://www.webmproject.org/

TokBox. (n.d.). Retrieved July 12, 2014, from Add live, face-to-face video with the OpenTok platform - TokBox: http://tokbox.com/

Turner, D., & Kostiainen, A. (Eds.). (2014, June 19). *Ambient light events, W3C last call working draft*. Retrieved July 12, 2014, from http://www.w3.org/TR/ambient-light/

Van Kesteren, A., & Çelik, T. (Eds.). (2012, July 3). *Fullscreen, W3C working draft*. Retrieved July 12, 2014, from http://www.w3.org/TR/fullscreen/

Virtual 3D Classroom. (n.d.). Retrieved July 12, 2014, from http://opencourses.teicrete.gr/index.php/el/vrclass

Von Kaenel, M., Sommer, P., & Wattenhofer, R. (2011). Ikarus: Large-scale participatory sensing at high altitudes. In *Proceedings of the 12th Workshop on Mobile Computing Systems and Applications* (pp. 63-68). ACM. doi:10.1145/2184489.2184503

Web Page for the i-Promotion Project. (n.d.). Retrieved July 12, 2014, from http://translate.google.com/translate?sl=el&tl=en&js=n&prev=_t&hl=en&ie=UTF-8&u=http%3A%2F%2Fwww.ipromotion.gr%2Findex.php%2Fhomepage&act=url

WebRTC. (n.d.). Retrieved July 12, 2014, from http://www.webrtc.org/

WebRTC - iLBC Freeware. (n.d.). Retrieved July 12, 2014, from http://www.webrtc.org/ilbc-freeware

WebRTC / Codelab - Bitbucket. (n.d.). Retrieved July 12, 2014, from https://bitbucket.org/webrtc/codelab

Websockets-Based Messenger for Text and Live Image Exchange between Browser Peers. (n.d.). Retrieved July 12, 2014, from http://medialab.teicrete.gr:8080/WebSocketsJetty/

Workbench for Browsers' Performance Evaluation in Terms of their Ability to Display 3D Graphics. (n.d.). Retrieved July 12, 2014, from http://www.medialab.teicrete.gr/minipages/x3domwb/

X3Dom Website. (n.d.). Retrieved July 13, 2014, from http://www.x3dom.org/

Zampoglou, M., Malamos, A. G., Sardis, E., Doulamis, A., Kapetanakis, K., Kontakis, K., & Vafiadis, G. (2013). A content-aware cloud platform for virtual reality web advertising. In Proceedings of Workshop Cloud-of-Things 2013 (CoT '13). Athens, Greece: Academic Press.

Zampoglou, M., Spala, P., Kontakis, K., Malamos, A. G., & Ware, J. A. (2013). Direct mapping of x3d scenes to mpeg-7 descriptions. In *Proceeding of the 18th International Conference on 3D Web Technology*. San Sebastian, Spain: Academic Press. doi:10.1145/2466533.2466540

Zhanikeev, M. (2013a). A practical software model for content aggregation in browsers using recent advances in HTML5. In Proceedings of Computer Software and Applications Conference Workshops (COMPSACW) (pp. 151 – 156). Academic Press. doi:10.1109/COMPSACW.2013.18

Zhanikeev, M. (2013b). Experiments with application throughput in a browser with full HTML5 support. *IEICE Communications Express, 2*(5), 167-172.

Zinner, T., Hohlfeld, O., Abboud, O., & Hoßfeld, T. (2010). Impact of frame rate and resolution on objective QoE metrics. In *Proceedings of Quality of Multimedia Experience (QoMEX)*. Trondheim, Norway: Academic Press. doi:10.1109/QOMEX.2010.5518277

Zingaya. (n.d.). Retrieved July 12, 2014, from Online call – Let the visitors call you without a phone: http://zingaya.com/

Zorrilla, M. (2012). End to end solution for interactive on demand 3D media on home network devices. In *Proceedings of Broadband Multimedia Systems and Broadcasting (BMSB)*. IEEE. doi:10.1109/BMSB.2012.6264228

KEY TERMS AND DEFINITIONS

HTML5: The latest update of HTML. It provides a great set of intriguing web technologies that drastically transform web to a browser-friendly and platform independent service. This is due to the fact that HTML5 introduces several functionalities to web browsers (mostly accomplished via several JavaScript APIs) changing the way data are transferred, visualizations are displayed and graphics are processed. Hence, web-pages can gain access to various features provided for media access and applications customization.

MPEG-DASH: It enables adaptive media streaming over HTTP by requesting the most suitable representation of media content over the time. The initialization process for a DASH execution scenario requires an MPD file. The MPD, which conforms to the XML document format, describes the available representations of media for streaming. The DASH player is responsible to monitor the resources availability over the time and switch between the available representations to provide users with the most suitable media file.

Pervasive Computing: Also known as ubiquitous computing. Essentially it is a dynamic implementation of the cycle: monitoring-decision-execution, so adaptive, customized, personalised and ubiquitous service provision is offered to a service consumer wherever he is situated in, whatever device he carries with, whenever he connects to a service. Ubiquitous computing touches on a wide range of research topics, including distributed computing, mobile computing, location computing, mobile networking, context-aware computing, sensor networks, human-computer interaction, and artificial intelligence.

WebRTC: The goal of WebRTC is to enable real-time communication among browsers in a peer-to-peer communication utilizing JavaScript and HTML5 without the use of plugins. Applications such as video calls, video-conferencing, text chat, online games, etc. are some of the applications that can be supported with this web technology. IETF specifies the networking protocols and the W3C the JavaScript APIs for WebRTC.

WebSockets: The WebSocket protocol provides a bidirectional communication channel using a single TCP connection. It has been designed for implementation in both browsers and web-servers and its API has being standardized by the W3C. WebSocket connections are established over the regular TCP port 80, which ensures that the system can run behind firewalls. Upon establishment the WebSocket remains open for the whole session, until any endpoint requests its release with the specified procedure. As a WebSocket remains active; WebSocket frames can be transferred from server to client and vice versa with no preceding request. The added value appears in the case that a server needs to push data to the client, which can take place asynchronously.

X3D: A standardised XML-based file format for representing real-time and interactive 3D computer graphics on the web. X3D can be used from simple use cases to complex applications, as it supports multi-texture rendering, real-time reflection and lighting, shaders with texture, normalmap, lightmap, movietexture and a deferred rendering architecture. The functionalities provided by the low level rendering engines of OpenGL and DirectX provide cross-platform interoperability in X3D visual functionalities, such as rendering, texturing and modeling.

X3Dom: The "product" of discussions between Web3D and W3C communities for the development of a JavaScript-based interface for X3D. This is an experimental open source framework and client-side rendering API with no requirement for external plug-ins, based on the HTML5 specification, for declarative 3D content. The X3D elements are directly integrated as DOM elements and all scene manipulations are done using DOM-based scripting interfaces.

Chapter 12
A Resource Prediction Engine for Efficient Multimedia Services Provision

Yiannos Kryftis
University of Nicosia, Cyprus

Jordi Mongay Batalla
National Institute of Telecommunications, Poland & Warsaw University of Technology, Poland

George Mastorakis
Technological Educational Institute of Crete, Greece

Athina Bourdena
University of Nicosia, Cyprus

Constandinos X. Mavromoustakis
University of Nicosia, Cyprus

Evangelos Pallis
Technological Educational Institute of Crete, Greece

ABSTRACT

This chapter presents a novel network architecture for optimal and balanced provision of multimedia services. The proposed architecture includes a central Management and Control (M&C) plane, located at Internet provider's premises, as well as distributed M&C planes for each delivery method, including Content Delivery Networks (CDNs) and Home Gateways. As part of the architecture, a Resource Prediction Engine (RPE) is presented that utilizes novel models and algorithms for resource usage prediction, making possible the optimal distribution of streaming data. It also enables for the prediction of the upcoming fluctuations of the network that provide the ability to make the proper decisions in achieving optimized Quality of Service (QoS) and Quality of Experience (QoE) for the end users.

INTRODUCTION

The continuously increasing users' network activities and the escalating amount of information that they generate within the Internet have set the basis for the convergence between networks and media, paving the way towards the Future Media Internet ("Consumer Internet Traffic 2012-2017," 2014). As a result of this on-going convergence, citizens are already witnessing profound transformations on the

DOI: 10.4018/978-1-4666-8225-2.ch012

way they communicate and interact among each other, as well as with various entities that constitute their living/working environments. For the first time, human relationships that were fostered in face-to-face interactions – which predominantly provided the building blocks of social structure – are nowadays complemented by communications that occur in virtual environment (cyberspace) at a much faster pace. Driving forces are the recent advances in connected media technologies and social networks, supported by the widespread deployment of broadband infrastructures and Cloud Computing facilities, along with a new breed of user-equipment that integrates communication and computation capabilities. All of them are rapidly transforming the environment(s) that citizens are surrounded by, as they introduce new kinds of interactions between humans and objects. Hence, in this evolving Future Media environment, it is normal for citizens to demand the kind of experiences that they are accustomed to in their daily/real lives, i.e., no longer interact with only their own media in a "user-centric" approach, but be able to form groups in an ad-hoc manner and interact each other for sharing their experiences in a "community-centric" approach. Altogether, a community-centric media ecosystem emerges as a cross-breeding of networked/connected media and social networks, where citizens can create, share, or even trade their experiences (be called "Media Events"), within different contexts (e.g., home, business, mobile, etc.) and with maximum possible (i.e., better-than-best-effort) Quality of Experience (QoE).

Within the term "Media Event", it is anticipated not only real-world events that citizens experience in their daily lives (i.e. entertainment, sports, educational, emergency, cultural services/applications, etc.), but also implicitly and possibly automatically generated virtual ones, stemming from citizens' social network activity (within cyberspace), which may often be highly correlated with their real-life experiences. In this respect, every Media Event is the synthesis of a number of content, service, network/IT and social elements – each one with its intrinsic rules and characteristics – which citizens administrate and coordinate through an interactive process. Towards conveying Media Events following a user/community-centric approach with maximum possible Quality of Experience, Media Delivery plays a key role. Media Delivery is the assembly of communication protocols and mechanisms, through which Media Events are delivered over a given medium. Media Delivery calls for new architectures, associated technologies (i.e. functionalities and mechanisms) supporting their synergy, in order to meet emerging requirements and increase the quality that citizens experience, either individually or as part of a community group.

In addition, the current Media Distribution Systems, also known as Content Delivery Networks (CDNs), increasingly generate the vast majority of Internet traffic so their architecture has great impact in the design of the Future Media Internet. Recently, the convergence between traditional CDNs, peer-to-peer and geographically distributed Cloud-based video streaming approaches are emerging a new era for network-aware media distribution technologies. Based on this convergence and by taking into account recent advances both in the P2P (Andreou, Mavromoustakis, Mastorakis, Bourdena, & Pallis, 2014) and CDN sectors, this chapter elaborates on a communication landscape, where media-distribution follows a network-aware approach. Towards these, the chapter proposes an innovative scalable media predictive distribution and control architecture that optimizes the requirements of throughput on media-providing nodes, by optimally exploiting the uploading capacity between Conventional Cloud media servers, CDN media servers and Home Gateways, without compromising quality in distribution of each Media Event. End-to-end coordination of all involved entities is carried out by the software at the operator's level that estimates and reserves in-advance the required network assets in accordance with the Media Event's Quality of Service (QoS) requirements and users' QoE expectations. Towards minimum intervention onto the physical infrastructure of the involved networked entities, a prototype of the Media Distribution Middleware is foreseen, able to reserve in-advance the required network assets as a matter of Media

Events QoS requirements and users' QoE expectations, available at any Resource Provider level (i.e., CDN operators, Cloud providers, Network Providers or even custom users utilising Home Gateways). In this way, these Resource Providers maintain control of their assets, besides being responsible for applying any resource reservation requests onto their infrastructure. Furthermore, this chapter aims to present the design and implementation of an innovative, scalable and cost effective system, based on the cooperation of three technologies: Cloud Computing, CDNs and P2P. The proposed solution offers flexible delivery configurations, exploiting a novel resource reservation scheme, according to the media delivery chain actors' requirements and their business plans. The chapter also includes the study and design of a Resource Prediction Engine (RPE) based on a predictive model, to support the resource allocation and the traffic-aware accountability in the media-sharing process. The RPE takes advantage of well-established workload and traffic prediction, on one hand, as well as of forecasting algorithms, on the other hand, in order to provide timely small-term and mid-term estimation of the required resources needed to accommodate an anticipated demand. It dynamically and proactively computes the optimal amount of bandwidth that has to be allocated, towards a stable and effective real time media distribution. Finally, the chapter presents the design and development of a novel resource reservation mechanism for both unicast and multicast streaming, by proactively assigning resources based on an auto scaling algorithm, thanks to the RPE. The resource management service is able to exploit resources from Conventional Cloud media servers, CDN media servers and Home Gateways and to dynamically optimise their usage during Media Events delivery, as a matter of QoS requirements and user's QoE expectations. In case of Cloud/CDN, it instructs the appropriate resource reservation service, multicast optimization decisions and auto-scaling commands at Cloud/CDN native management entities. In case of the P2P delivery, there is a management for scaling the upload bandwidth of each End-User, participating in the Home Gateways cloud through their Home Gateways.

BACKGROUND

Content Delivery Networks

A content delivery network (CDN) is generally understood as a system of multiple computers, working as servers deployed across different networks and/or data centers, often geographically dispersed. The content is distributed across these servers/data centers, while it is accessed, depending on several main parameters, i.e., geographical location, type of content (e.g., media content requires special software installed on the server, which other type of content usually does not need to operate) and the origin of a website (Nygren, Sitaraman, & Sun, 2010). It is outmost important to have a CDN thoughtfully and appropriately designed, as it can significantly accelerate access to web pages, as well as to different types of media content, like music and video streams and other downloadable content available via the Internet. The CDN can benefit the two major stakeholders of the Internet content below, if it is properly designed:

- **Content Providers:** Offloading the traffic from one origin hosting server/servers structure to multiple, dispersed localizations usually results in significant cost reduction in hosting and bandwidth consumption;
- **Content Consumers:** Improving the performance of content delivery, resulting in better quality and availability of the content and the speed of its delivery.

Functionally, CDN works through replicating the content originally uploaded by the content provider in the so called "caching servers", which are usually placed across different geographical locations. This enables to cut the distance between the nodes, which increases the speed and the quality of content delivery ("PC MAG," 2014). Additionally, CDN may support peer-to-peer processing. This can be achieved through a multiple ISP connections, which have a peering relationship with other ISP backbones. This chapter aims to deliver the best performing optimization mechanism that will enable to further leverage the efficiency of CDN, gathering information about various quality metrics from the system modules. Specifically, the presented proposal enables to feed the CDN with extended information gathered from different points of underlying network that improves the decision making process with regards to the choice of a server in the CDN. Furthermore, the processing of data in real time, enables immediate adaptation of signal streaming based on advanced factors monitored and fed into the CDN. This information also enables the more efficient communication with media servers. That results a more effective server choice and optimization. Effectively, this enables to provide the best possible user experience, while streaming the video content and more cost-effective stream delivery.

Conventional Cloud

Cloud Computing has recently emerged as a new paradigm for hosting and delivering services over the Internet. EU Cloud Computing Expert Working Group (Lutz Schubert, 2012) adopted definition provided by the National Institute of Standards and Technology (NIST): "Cloud Computing is a model for enabling ubiquitous, convenient, on-demand network access to a shared pool of configurable computing resources (e.g., networks, servers, storage, applications and services) that can be rapidly provisioned and released with minimal management effort or Service Provider interaction". The cloud model is composed of five essential characteristics, three service models (software / platform / infrastructure as a service) and four deployment models, whereas the five characteristics are: on-demand self-service, broad network access, resource pooling, rapid elasticity and measured service. The deployment models include private, community, public and hybrid cloud (Mell & Grance, 2011). The main advantage of Cloud Computing is a new computing model, in which resources (e.g., CPU and storage) are provided as general utilities that can be leased and released by users through the Internet in an on-demand fashion (such as hosted software). Clouds are generally accessible through the Internet and use the Internet as a service delivery network. They can also be accessed by mobile devices (Saleem, Salim, & Rehmani, 2014). Additionally, to achieve high network performance, many of the recent clouds are based on Data Centers infrastructures located all around the globe. A Service Provider can easily leverage geo-diversity to achieve maximum service utility. Other distinguish feature of a cloud is the multi-tenancy. Cloud services are typically divided into the following three categories:

- **Infrastructure as a Service (IaaS):** Refers to on-demand provisioning of infrastructural resources, usually in terms of VMs. Examples of IaaS providers include Amazon EC2 ("Amazon Elastic Computing Cloud," 2014), Flexiscale ("FlexiScale Cloud Comp and Hosting," 2014);
- **Platform as a Service (PaaS):** Refers to providing platform layer resources, including operating system support and software development frameworks. Examples of PaaS providers include Google App Engine ("Google App Engine," 2014), Microsoft Windows Azure ("Windows Azure," 2014);

- **Software as a Service (SaaS):** Refers to providing on-demand applications over the Internet. Examples of SaaS providers include Salesforce.com ("Salesforce CRM," 2014).

Media clouds (Mousicou, Mavromoustakis, Bourdena, Mastorakis, & Pallis, 2013; Papanikolaou, Mavromoustakis, Mastorakis, Bourdena, & Dobre; Poehlein, Saxena, Willis, Fedders, & Guttmann, 2010) are platforms based on servers infrastructures that are directed to share multimedia content ("MediaCloud systems," 2014; "Vodafone Media Cloud," 2014). They are a step forward from the classical Content Delivery Networks, representing a potential business for Cloud Providers, since they are cost-effective when creating, storing, sharing and delivering digitized content ("Moving to the Media Cloud," 2014). However, in practice, media clouds are not so efficient in content delivery. They confine themselves to similar CDN approach (i.e. put the content close to the End-Users thanks to Data Centers located all around the globe). This approach is only efficient for popular content, as it requires a large investment to bring the infrastructure close to the users, while many other multimedia use-cases (e.g., ad-hoc users' requests) cannot be efficiently served. The reason is that the media clouds do not take into consideration many of the advanced research results appeared in the last years (e.g., information/content-centric orientation trend recognized in Future Internet). New concepts (partially overlapping) and architecture proposals, like Information Centric Networking (ICN) and Content-Oriented/Centric/Aware Networking (CON/CCN/CAN) (Choi, Han, Cho, Kwon, & Choi, 2011) have emerged for improving content aware Media Delivery (Choi et al., 2011; Detti, Blefari Melazzi, Salsano, & Pomposini, 2011; Jacobson et al., 2009; Katsaros, Xylomenos, & Polyzos, 2011; Koponen et al., 2007; Koumaras et al., 2011).

The difficulties to adopt the proposed mechanisms and algorithms by the media clouds come from the fact that these solutions build complex architectures and assume strong cooperation between involved actors, which has been relegated only for some specific cases. This is when one unique actor is responsible for content creation, storage and delivery (e.g., big Network Operators or big CDN). Akamai also introduced the concept of controlled network resources for improvement of content delivery in its services (Su, Choffnes, Kuzmanovic, & Bustamante, 2009). Some media clouds have deployed a few of the proposed (ICN-like) mechanisms (e.g., ("Sony Ci," 2014) real-time transcoding) but these mechanisms are not strictly related with the delivery phase, which is crucial for Media Event QoE. The current media clouds consider the Internet as a connectivity platform, providing best effort services, thus not being able to offer QoE-based delivery. This chapter aims to introduce a solution for QoE-based delivering media, which decisively increases the current potential of the media cloud approach.

Home Media Gateway Cloud

The fast spread of high-speed broadband access has enabled home users to consume a number of services over the Internet, ranging from legacy communication services, such as TV and telephony to video-on-demand (VoD), online gaming and home automation (Ciobanu, Comaneci, Dobre, Mavromoustakis, & Mastorakis; Kwon & Yeom, 2002). Users commonly access the Internet and its services via a home gateway that manages all network connectivity in the home. TVs and other devices without native network support are typically connected through a set-top box (STB), which is responsible for transcoding the content so that it can be properly displayed on the end-device. For security reasons, as well as due to digital rights management and marketing matters, most STBs are closed platforms, thus limiting the set of services that can be run on them. ISPs generally provide one STB with a small number of services and users have to acquire additional boxes to expand their service portfolio. From the users' point of view, dealing with multiple physical devices is not necessarily easy. Regarding the ISPs, they see this as a lost opportunity to increase their revenues in these external services. The solution that ISPs have put in place to solve both problems consists of hosting services in the cloud and delivering them through a simple (and cheap) STB. This approach has two main advantages for the ISP: 1) it allows service personalization without any physical intervention and 2) it simplifies the management of the services. On the customer side, it simplifies installation, configuration and utilization of the service portfolio.

Cloud-based applications and services have become common place. Cloud computing allows service providers to run application logic on huge data centers, where CPU, memory and storage resources are orders of magnitude larger than those present in mobile devices or in the home network. Cloud-based applications are enabling End-Users to access and make use of these remote-computing capabilities. Cloud applications (thus the End-Users) benefit from many advantages such as lower computing costs, performance improvement, instantaneous software updates, group collaboration and even unlimited storage capacity (all of these services often coming along with fees). However, this cloud-based approach has critical limitations. The cloud adds potentially large network delays and creates a dependency on the availability of the network connectivity, due to the required communication between end users' devices and the remote servers located in the data centers. Also, it does not exploit local storage and caching at home. Besides, it is unlikely that a single cloud will offer all services a user might want, or that a user will accept, contacting his ISP anytime he wants a new service. Thus, only an ISP managed cloud can control the complete network path to the user. Therefore, accessing multiple clouds comes at the risk of poor service quality and poor quality of experience. This represents another challenge in such a multi-cloud environment.

Some works (Sappington, 2013; Wei, Li, Yang, & Jia, 2010; Whiteaker et al., 2012) propose leveraging the home gateway as a proxy to the cloud to solve the issues identified above. The entity is referred as a service-hosting gateway (SHG). The SHG acts as a flexible, always-on platform located inside the home. It can be used to improve interaction, cache data, allowing the user to deploy new services locally. These services can be made available to users through an application store model. The SHG can also act as a home hub, coordinating devices such as smartphones, tablets and home sensors to provide a unified interface to the user. Moreover, the gateway lies at the border between the Internet and the home network. This unique position allows the SHG to perform advanced network resource management and troubleshooting, increasing the Quality of Experience for the user. On the negative side, the SHG represents additional upfront hardware cost and management complexity for the ISP. In some sense, the proposed Enhanced Home Gateway (EHG) could be considered as a new SHG and could be of a real use for existing cloud-based services. Acting as a cloud proxy, the EHG allows these cloud-based services to maintain their data center architectures, performing application specific tasks such as content buffering, caching, pre-fetching, QoS/QoE-based video transcoding/server-switching, replicating and many more. On the other hand, there is a noticeable difference between the SHG and the proposed EHG. A set of interconnected EHGs represents a cloud entity, providing the capabilities discussed above to the end users. Using some new and innovative streaming solutions that consider the numerous present EHGs, the EHG cloud serves home and mobile devices with multimedia contents. While conventional clouds are distant (in a network sense) from the end users, the EHG cloud entity is located as close as possible from the home devices, towards minimizing network latencies and bandwidth limitations and improving the overall QoS, as well as QoE.

Network Architectures for Hybrid Delivery Systems and Resource Prediction Engines

There are many existing research attempts to combine different delivery methods, in order to achieve better QoE for the users. One proposal could be the CDN-P2P hybrid architecture for cost-effective streaming media distribution that combines the advantages of using CDN for providing high QoE with the low cost of using P2P-based stream (Xu, Kulkarni, Rosenberg, & Chai, 2006). A similar approach by Yin et al. (Yin et al., 2009) on the design and deployment of a Hybrid CDN-P2P System for Live Video Streaming demonstrated the improvement in startup delay time and in stability. Current research approaches focus on how to benefit from the combination of the different delivery methods but they do not take consideration of handling each resource separately. This chapter goes beyond the current state of the art, by handling each resource (i.e. streaming channel) based on the prediction of the future demand for each resource, as well as the current and predicted network metrics. Towards providing to the users the desired Quality of Experience (QoE) during the multimedia services provision process, there is a need of implementing a resource usage prediction engine that provides the ability to predict future demands of the network resources. This gives the opportunity through a management plane to trigger the proper actions for keeping the desired quality for the streaming sessions. The resource prediction engine has to be developed based on novel models, able to efficiently predict and plan the needed bandwidth capacity based on bandwidth auto-scaling functions, automatically accommodating the fluctuations of the network resources for a certain multimedia event provision. In this direction, Niu et al (Niu, Liu, Li, & Zhao, 2011) presented some of the issues of demand forecast and performance prediction in peer-assisted Video-on-Demand (VoD) services. They used the Box-Jenkins approach (Box, Jenkins, & Reinsel, 2013) to predict the future population of each video channel based on a given time series of the population of the video channel in the past. They avoid periodicity, by using regression methods and more specifically the seasonal ARIMA (autoregressive integrated moving average) model. They infer the initial population of a new released video channel, using machine learning techniques. They also utilize pass data from newly released video channels as training data to make a prediction, based on statistical models and of the channels release time. The ARMA (autoregressive moving-average) model (Box et al., 2013) was used to predict the server bandwidth demands by a video channel at future time. The entire procedure was proven to have reasonable computation cost. In (Niu, Xu, Li, & Zhao, 2012), Niu et al. proposed a predictive cloud bandwidth auto-scaling system for VoD providers. Based on the history of the bandwidth demand in each video channel, derived by the cloud monitoring services, it estimates the expectations for near future demands. By doing so, it provides quality assurance, deciding the minimum bandwidth reservation to satisfy the demand. Additionally, the system makes load direction between data centers for minimizing the bandwidth needs.

Wu and Lui (Wu & Lui, 2012) presented a system architecture for modeling and optimization of the replication strategy in P2P-VoD systems. They showed that conventional proportional replication strategy is not optimal, by proposing a passive replacement strategy for the decision of the content that should be deleted when a local storage is full and an active replication algorithm to aggressively push data to peers in order to achieve the desired replication ratios. They validated their results with simulations. A similar approach to the optimal content placement for a large-scale VoD system is presented in (Wu & Lui, 2012) In (Suh et al., 2007), the Push-to-Peer approach was presented that proactively pushes content to peers, in order to increase content availability and to improve use of the peer uplink bandwidth. It allows performance analysis of the push policies, distributed load balancing strategies for the initial selection of serving peers and distributed strategies to cope with dynamic uplink bandwidth. A different approach for achieving efficient content delivery is the use of Content Oriented Networking-CON (Choi et al., 2011). In an energy consumption based approach, Mavromoustakis et al. (Mastorakis, Pallis, Mavromoustakis, & Bourdena, 2014; C. Mavromoustakis, Dimitriou, & Mastorakis, 2013; C. X. Mavromoustakis, Pallis, & Mastorakis, 2014) faced the issue of optimization of the energy efficiency on mobile cloud applications, presenting a framework (Bourdena, Mastorakis, Pallis, Arvanitis, & Kormentzas, 2012; Bourdena, Mastorakis, Pallis, Karditsis, & Kormentzas, 2012) that utilizes resource offloading techniques that are proven to optimize the energy consumption in the mobile devices. The wireless devices introduce some special features that have to be handled for efficient content delivery, like the optimization of energy consumption and the optimization of radio resource management (Bourdena et al., 2014; Dimitriou, Mavromoustakis, Mastorakis, & Pallis, 2013; Mastorakis, Mavromoustakis, Bourdena, Kormentzas, & Pallis, 2013; Mastorakis, Mavromoustakis, Bourdena, & Pallis, 2013; Mastorakis, Mavromoustakis, et al., 2014; Mastorakis, Panagiotakis, et al., 2014; C. Mavromoustakis et al., 2014). There is a plethora of research papers about the wireless resource management that can be achieve, by using energy aware routing and optimum scheduling (Bourdena et al.; Mastorakis, Mavromoustakis, Bourdena, Pallis, & Sismanidis, 2013; C. Mavromoustakis, Dimitriou, & Mastorakis, 2012; C. X. Mavromoustakis et al.; C. X. Mavromoustakis, Dimitriou, Mastorakis, Bourdena, & Pallis, 2014; C. X. Mavromoustakis, Dimitriou, Mastorakis, & Pallis, 2013). These research approaches indicate that although some work has been done and the related tools where developed, there is a lack of a system that combines the ability to predict future demands, by taking advantage of that prediction to automatically accommodate the fluctuations of the network resources for the optimal provision of the desired Quality of Service (QoS) and QoE to the end users. In this context, this chapter proposes a network architecture that predicts the future content delivery demands and the future network usage, performing all the necessary adaptations to deliver the content in an optimal and balanced way.

PROPOSED SYSTEM ARCHITECTURE

Media/content distribution generates today a significant part of the global Internet traffic and the amount of this traffic is expected to increase in near future. Different technologies of great interest have already been deployed for Media Distribution Systems: Content Delivery Networks (CDNs), Peer-to-Peer systems, Over-the-Top (OTT) solutions and other operators' proprietary solutions. The architecture of such systems has significant impact in the design of the Future Internet. Several features are required for these systems:

- Efficiency, aiming at the highest possible utilization of the heterogeneous and geographically distributed network resources, in order to minimize the delivery cost and, in turn, to achieve their wide adoption by the users;
- Stability and availability of the system (uninterrupted service) in the presence of dynamic conditions (dynamic user requests, changes in underlying network conditions, users' behaviour change, etc.);
- Performance and QoS/QoE, which, for a given set of QoS/QoE policies, the overall system should offer guarantee within the levels specified and agreed within Service Level Agreements (SLAs) between the users and providers;
- Scalability, which is measured by the amount of resources, while bandwidth and processing overhead have to contribute as the number of participating users grows.

In the roadmap towards these goals, a very promising solution is the synergy among traditional CDNs, P2P and geographically distributed Cloud-based streaming approaches. This solution can fully utilize the stable edge transport capability of CDN, the scalable last-mile transport capability of P2P and the resource elasticity offered by the Cloud computing, while avoids excessive use (geographic inter-domain span) of P2P delivery, which is ISP-unfriendly. Based on the above, this chapter elaborates on an innovative and scalable Media Distribution System, for mediating resource reservation requests to the underlying physical resource infrastructures (i.e., Cloud Data Centres, Telecommunication infrastructures including CDNs, as well as User created Media Home Gateways Cloud), able to correlate the architectural solution with the target number of users and Media Events to be accommodated. The geographic span and business aspects of the system will also be considered, aiming to support providers' business extension and produce better Return On Investment (ROI). The anticipated user-driven QoE enhancement calls for technologies that can offer optimised delivery of Media Events in an end-to-end approach, even over highly heterogeneous network environments, making imperative the use of real time interaction mechanisms, via which users can enhance their QoE under various contexts or diversified operating conditions (home, work, mobile, etc.). The proposed network architecture is depicted in Fig. 1 with an upper layer (called Central M&C plane) that coordinates such a collaboration environment. The proposed architecture distinguishes four separated planes detailed below.

The Central Management and Control (M&C) plane is a central point of the proposed system. It is placed in Telco's domain, coordinating the optimal exploitation of the resources that are available at each Resources Provider (Telecommunication Network operators, CDN providers, Conventional Cloud operators, users' Home Gateways). The coordination process is dynamic and continuous, taking into consideration not only all the ongoing streaming sessions, but also all the potential upcoming ones. For this purpose, M&C plane monitors quality parameters of all domain access points involved in the system, as well as the content requests issued by the users.

Figure 1. The proposed overall network architecture

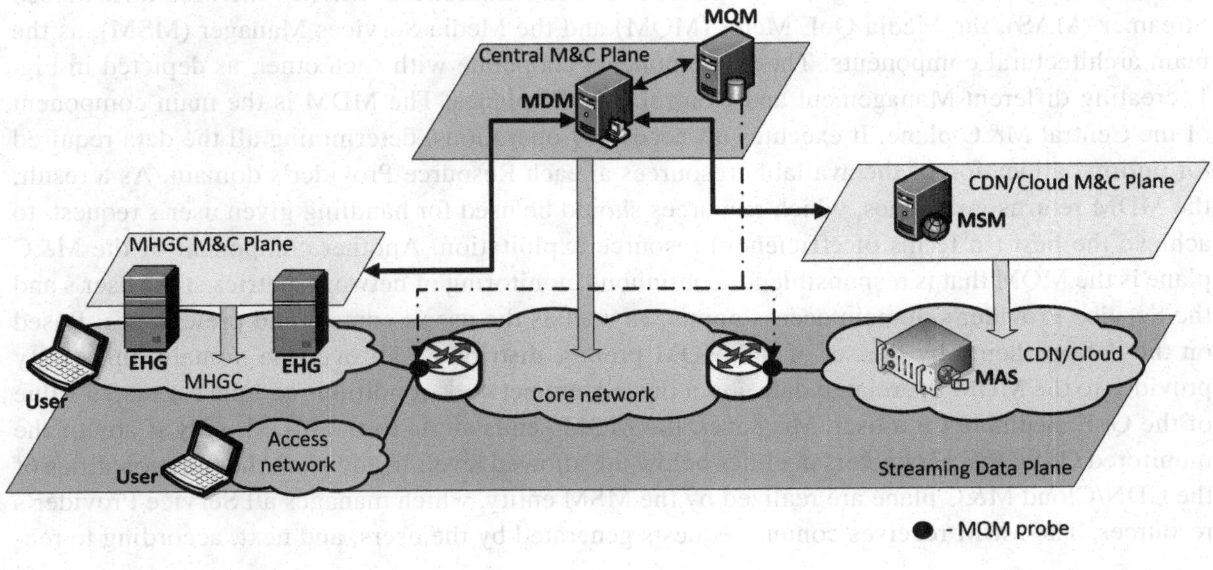

The CDN/Cloud M&C plane is placed in the Service Provider premises. It handles user's requests, making decisions about what and how to perform the streaming and adaptation functionalities (e.g., at which bitrate and from which servers). The decision process is supported by the data acquired from the Main M&C plane, related with the quality level of the CDN/Cloud domain access points and the knowledge about resources available at this domain. The CDN/Cloud M&C plane is also responsible for the proper distribution of content replicas on CDN/Cloud resources, based on guidelines provided by the main M&C plane.

The MHGC M&C plane is responsible for the establishment and management of a MHGC ad-hoc system. Similarly to the CDN/CC M&C plane, it handles user's requests, taking into account information received from the Main M&C plane about what and how to perform the streaming, as well as the adaptation functionalities (e.g., at which bitrate and from which peers). Moreover, this plane cooperates with the CDN/CC M&C plane to provide access to the media content, which is not available in the given MHGC domain.

The Streaming Data plane is in charge of the delivery of the requested multimedia content towards the user's application, in accordance with the rules worked out by the CDN/Cloud M&C (or MHGC M&C) plane. The content delivery realized by this plane is based on adaptive streaming mechanisms that dynamically exploit the available bandwidth and media rendering conditions. In particular, emerging media delivery approaches such as the Dynamic Adaptive Streaming over HTTP (DASH) (Sodagar, 2011) and the Web Real-Time Communication (WebRTC) ("Web browsers with Real-Time Communications - WebRTC initiative," 2014) are under investigation.

Entities into the Different Planes

The proposed Media Delivery solution is innovative, scalable and predictive based on a novel Network-Aware Delivery architecture that efficiently exploits users' resources (i.e., Home Gateways), CDN assets and Conventional Cloud properties, by customising their usage via dynamic resource reservation schemes and proactive auto-scaling mechanisms, for the Media Events delivery in respect to user QoE. This overall solution is made possible through the realization of a novel Media Distribution System, including the Media Distribution Middleware (MDM), the Media Advanced Streamer (MAS), the Media QoE Meter (MQM) and the Media Services Manager (MSM), as the main architectural components. These components cooperate with each other, as depicted in Fig. 1, creating different Management and Control (M&C) planes. The MDM is the main component of the Central M&C plane. It executes all necessary operations, determining all the data required for optimal allocation of the available resources at each Resource Provider's domain. As a result, the MDM returns guidelines, which resources should be used for handling given user's request, to achieve the best (in terms of efficiency) resource exploitation. Another component of the M&C plane is the MQM that is responsible for continuous monitoring of network metrics at the user's and the Service Provider's domain access points, as well as the user's context and preferences. Based on the data gathered by the set of the MQM probes, distributed all over the domain, this entity provides to the MDM the related data about the current network conditions and the estimated value of the QoE available for a user. Moreover, the MQM sends alerts to the MDM, only if any of the monitored QoS/QoE parameters declines below the allowed level. In addition, the functionalities of the CDN/Cloud M&C plane are realized by the MSM entity, which manages all Service Provider's resources. The MSM receives content requests generated by the users, and next, according to recommendations received from the MDM, takes a decision, on which server should stream requested media and with which bitrate. In this way, the MSM, contrary to existing solutions, performs adaptation decision, taking into account not only the available bandwidth, but also considering other important information addressed by the MDM, such as the estimated QoE value and the prediction of potential upcoming streaming sessions. Although conceptually, the MSM is one entity, which manages the whole Service Provider domain, its functionality can be distributed between several physical machines (for example, related with different streaming protocols), but interconnected to form one coherent component.

The EHG entity is placed at the user's premises. In this way, the control modules of EHGs realize functionalities of the Media Home Gateway Cloud (MHGC) M&C plane that are responsible for creating the MHGC ad-hoc system from a set of peer-to-peer connected EHGs. Similarly to the MSM, the EHG receives content requests from the users. It then asks the MDM about information which MHGC peers should be involved, in order to efficiently deliver the requested content. EHG collaborates with MSM entities to obtain media content requested by the user, if this content (or part of it) is not stored on any of EHGs belonging to given MHGC. In addition, the MAS entity resides in the CDN/Cloud domain as a standalone component, whereas in case of the MHGC, its functionalities are provided by the EHG. Streaming process realized by the MAS is performed, in accordance with instructions received from the MSM/EHG entity.

Resource Prediction Engine for Optimal and Balanced Multimedia Services Provision

The internal architecture of the MDM component is presented in Figure 2. The QoS/QoE Politics Traffic Data History component gathers the monitoring data that comes from the MQM, using them as input to the Media Traffic Forecast that generates the long-time prediction for the traffic in the network. The Resource allocator/scheduler uses the monitoring data for short-term prediction, feeding the MSM component with the optimal methods of the content delivery. At the same time, the Bandwidth Allocation Optimizer calculates the optimal bandwidth allocation for the peer-to-peer delivery among MHGC devices. The optimizer is an online system that takes into consideration the network metrics, which come from the MQM, delivering that information to the MHGC devices.

The MDM adopts a resource prediction engine, in order to be able to predict future demands for resources. The prediction is divided in a short-term and long-term prediction. The long-term prediction takes as input the demand for each resource in the past, exploiting some statistical methods to predict future demands. This gives the chance to the system to make the optimal distribution of the data in CDNs and EHGs based on the prediction before the actual need. More specifically, Figure 3 presents an overview of the proposed resource prediction system used for the prediction of the future demands for streaming of video channels. The Monitoring Service provides a measurement stream, by sampling an attribute. This is used as an input to the Predictor, which presents the prediction as a vector of the next values of the measurement stream, each one associated with an estimated error. The Prediction Stream is the output of the Predictor and applications can directly subscribe to the stream to use the data. The Buffer keeps a short history of the Prediction Stream, in order to allow asynchronous communication with applications when needed. The Evaluator is an optional component that constantly monitors the performance of the predictor, by comparing the predicted value with the real measured value and refits the model.

Figure 2. Media Distribution Middleware internal architecture

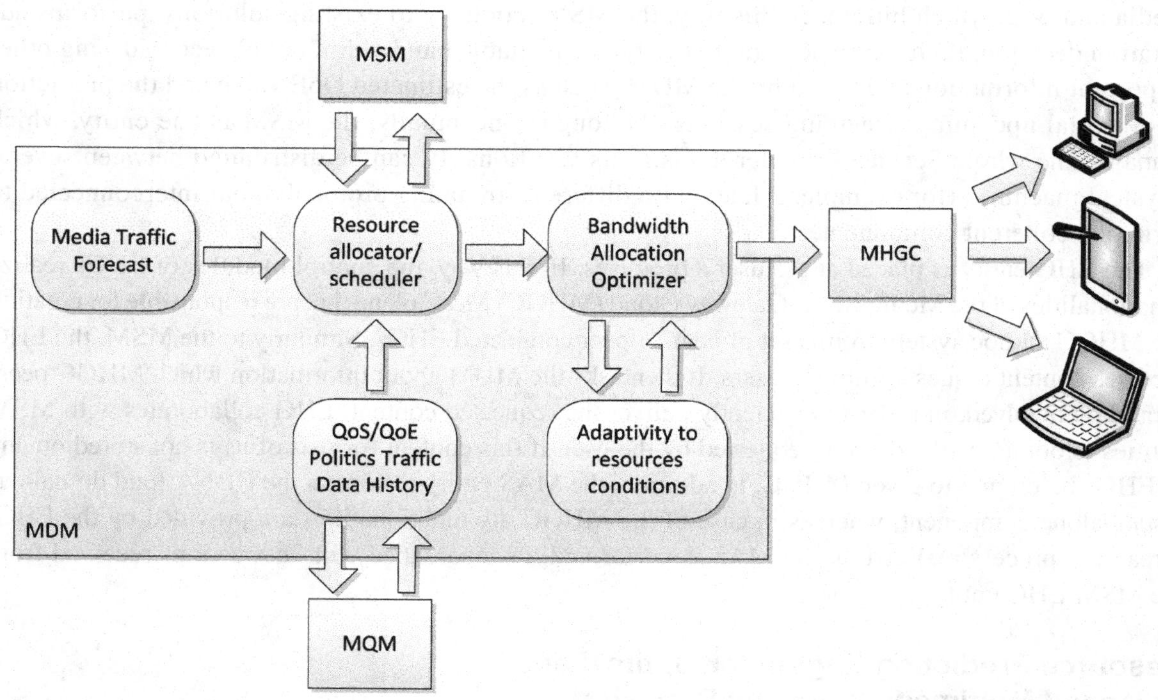

Figure 3. Overview of the proposed online resource prediction system

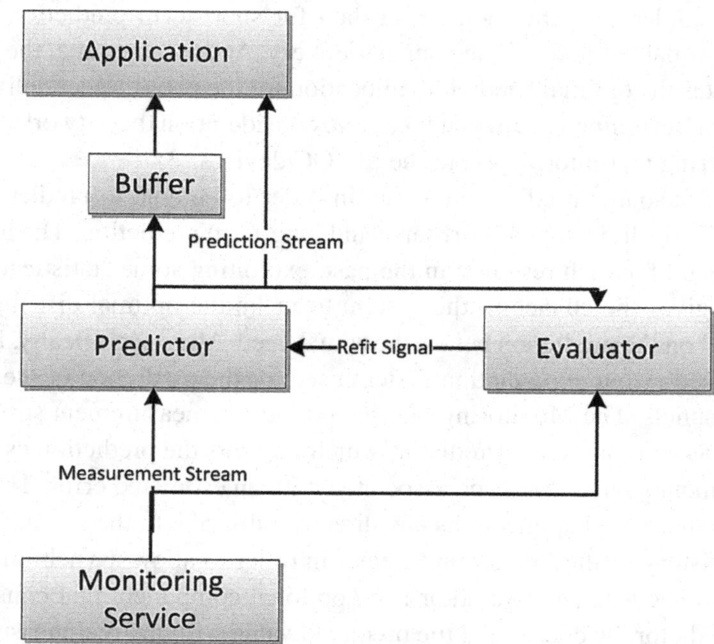

The prediction engine can be implemented in a high level programming language (i.e. Java, C++, etc), utilizing the functionality of special software environments for statistical computing and graphics that include multiple time series models and prediction methods like the R-system (Team, 2014), or the RPS toolkit ("RPS toolkit," 2014). RPS (Dinda, 2006) is a publicly available toolkit that allows the creation of online and offline resource prediction systems. It includes its own monitoring facilities but it also provides the ability to use monitoring data that comes from other sources. Part of the system is the wavelet toolkit (Skicewicz, Skicewicz, & Dinda, 2003) that supports analysis of the signals. R (Team, 2014) is a very popular free software environment for statistical computing and graphics. The forecast package ("CRAN-forecast package," 2014; Hyndman & Khandakar, 2007) of R implements automatic forecasting with multiple methods including ARIMA models, exponential smoothing methods, Theta method (Assimakopoulos & Nikolopoulos, 2000), cubic splines (Hyndman, King, Pitrun, & Billah, 2005) and many others. Hyndman and Khandakar presented the implementation of exponential smoothing methods and the ARIMA modelling approach in the forecast package. The proposed prediction engine uses the aforementioned packages, extending them in order to achieve optimal prediction. If a long-term (i.e. for the next hour) prediction has to be achieved for the needed bandwidth of a specific Video On Demand (VoD), the prediction engine needs to exploit the history of the bandwidth reservation for the specific VoD. The history data will be used to fit in the proper statistical model, suitable for the specific VoD. The forecast function will then be used to make the prediction. The result will be the estimated need for bandwidth for the specific VoD after one hour. This value will be used by the Resource allocator/scheduler to decide how to serve the estimated future need.

The MDM component uses the predicted future values for the metrics, in order to take the decisions for delivery of the requested media, which may be streamed: 1) directly from the Cloud, 2) through deployed surrogate servers of the CDN, 3) by establishing a Media Home Gateway Cloud (MHGC) ad-hoc system and using a combined P2P-based technology of distribution with multi-source, multi-destination congestion control algorithms, or 4) a combination of parts or all of them (thanks to stream-switching adaptation technique). The results are forwarded to the MSM component that is responsible for the actual streaming of the data to the user. A simple selection algorithm for the delivery method could use the higher value taken among the current (as received from MQM) and the predicted (as forecasted by the RPE) bandwidth need. If it is below a preset limit (based on administrative high level decisions and network status), only the Cloud delivery will be used. If it is above the limit, CDNs will be used, while the number of CDNs used is increasing according the demand. After the top limit is reached, a P2P delivery method is exploited. This algorithm provides the advantage that the data is not distributed before the actual need. In the case of a VoD with low customers demand, the CDNs will not been used for its distribution. On the other hand, if a popular VoD is requested, an early prediction will occur, while the number of CDNs, distributing the VoD will rapidly increase based on the demand. Finally, the P2P delivery method will be used, only when needed, while at the time that this happens, the number of the users already possessing the specific video will be satisfactory with those users, acting as seeders to distribute the VoD to the others.

SOLUTIONS AND RECOMMENDATIONS

Existing cloud resource reservation techniques are based, either on a "fixed-price" model, so as to accommodate the anticipated peak demand but with low resource utilization during non-peak times, or on a "pay-as-you-go" model, where the cost is estimated for the total amount of bytes transferred, but subject to variation due to contention from other applications in the Conventional Cloud Data Centre. This solution goes a step beyond, by elaborating on a novel resource reservation and provision scheme (through the MDM), based on the recently proposed bandwidth auto-scaling algorithms, leading to both high resource utilization and quality guarantees. It covers both delivery configurations, i.e. Conventional Cloud Users (e.g., for OTT players), or CDN Users (e.g., Telcos may utilise it too), as well as the distribution between User's Home Gateways, interconnected as Media Home Gateways Cloud.

Towards enabling every user access in any context and in a hybrid fashion, i.e., simultaneous usage and seamless switching of users (e.g., in a social network scenario), devices (e.g., desktop PCs, laptops, TVs, tablets, e-book readers, or even home entertainment and household appliances), operating platforms (e.g., iOS, Android, Linux, Windows), and access technologies (e.g., fixed, mobile, broadcast, broadband), interoperability arises as a very critical issue. An answer to this challenge could be the exploiting of recent advances in Web technologies for harmonizing the 'one-to-many' and 'many-to-many' communication paradigms into a common and open-to-all-users interoperable solution, enabling ubiquitous access for both media entertainment (in real-time or not) and real-time communication services. In particular, it paves the way towards harmonizing emerging multimedia system approaches such as MPEGs' Dynamic Adaptive Streaming over HTTP (DASH) and W3Cs'/IETFs' Web Real-Time Communication (WebRTC)/Real-Time Communication in Web-browsers (RTCWEB) into a common approach (i.e., the MAS), having the ability to seamlessly integrate any existing system and ensure uncompromised user experience. Thanks to the MDM and the MQM, the mechanism dynamically detects the requirements needed for efficient streaming (by considering parameters such as the available bandwidth and media rendering conditions), in order to launch the MAS, which will achieve adaptation, in addition to streaming functionalities. The solution offers a new experience of seamless video delivery, adapting and enriching the quality of the streamed media across the whole distribution chain.

FUTURE RESEARCH DIRECTIONS

This chapter presented a network architecture that provides a better control on the process of multimedia content delivery. Each component constituting the complete architecture could be studied and developed further. The MQM could be extended to raise alert signals, in order to trigger the MDM and the other relevant entities of the system, towards taking actions to guarantee the best possible QoE to the user, given the current and predicted state of the network. The MAS could perform "on-the-fly" transcoding of the media content to obtain media that best fits current user and network capabilities. The EHG can allow context-aware service discovery and requesting from user terminals. Future directions in the MDM could include the development of a load balancing algorithm that combines the delivery method and the load balancing under one scheme or multiple schemes that not only use the predicted values but the error estimations of the predictions as well. Also, the Resource Prediction Engine could be extended to use more advanced algorithms and prediction methods, based on novel models that can describe the resource usage in such networks.

CONCLUSION

This chapter presents a novel network architecture for optimal selection of multimedia content delivery methods. It also presents a novel resource prediction engine utilized for balanced delivery load. The proposed system based on a resource prediction engine performs all necessary adaptations to deliver the content in an optimal and balanced way, in order to keep a high QoS and QoE for the end users. The proposed architecture exploits recent advances in Networked Media and Cloud Computing technologies, by progressing beyond the current state-of-the-art through the elaboration on their convergence, into a unified system, where users exchange Media Events, by exploiting servers' infrastructures available in Conventional Clouds (public or private infrastructure configurations, usually offered by Over-the-Top providers), Content Delivery Networks (CDNs) and Media Distribution Community Clouds (Home Gateways/Community Gateways configurations, exploited in Peer-to-Peer mode).

The proposed Media Distribution Middleware (MDM) dynamically reallocates the necessary resources on the access to the infrastructures (belonging to one or more owners), answering to the users requests. The system is proposing customized unicast/multicast transmission for QoE-based Media Delivery, thanks to the predictive model exploited by the MDM for resources allocation. It introduces new features for the Network Provider, which focuses on allocating on demand, the requested resources by collaborating with the Media Service Providers owning infrastructures of servers (e.g., a conventional Cloud Provider, CDNs or Media Home Gateway Cloud). Such collaboration is assumed to be based on Service Level Agreements (SLA) with different infrastructures' owners (e.g., other Cloud/CDN Providers) to use their servers for Media delivery.

REFERENCES

Amazon Elastic Computing Cloud. (2014). Retrieved from http://aws.amazon.com/ec2

Andreou, A., Mavromoustakis, C. X., Mastorakis, G., Bourdena, A., & Pallis, E. (2014). Adaptive heuristic-based P2P network connectivity and configuration for resource availability. In Resource management in mobile computing environments (pp. 221-240). Springer.

Assimakopoulos, V., & Nikolopoulos, K. (2000). The theta model: A decomposition approach to forecasting. *International Journal of Forecasting*, *16*(4), 521–530. doi:10.1016/S0169-2070(00)00066-2

Bourdena, A., Makris, P., Skoutas, D. N., Skianis, C., Kormentzas, G., Pallis, E., & Mastorakis, G. (n.d.). *Joint radio resource management in cognitive networks: TV white spaces exploitation paradigm*. Academic Press.

Bourdena, A., Mastorakis, G., Pallis, E., Arvanitis, A., & Kormentzas, G. (2012). *A dynamic spectrum management framework for efficient TVWS exploitation*. Paper presented at the Computer Aided Modeling and Design of Communication Links and Networks (CAMAD). doi:10.1109/CAMAD.2012.6335377

Bourdena, A., Mastorakis, G., Pallis, E., Karditsis, E., & Kormentzas, G. (2012). *A radio resource management framework for TVWS exploitation under the RTSSM policy*. Paper presented at the Telecommunications and Multimedia (TEMU). doi:10.1109/TEMU.2012.6294718

Bourdena, A., Mavromoustakis, C. X., Kormentzas, G., Pallis, E., Mastorakis, G., & Yassein, M. B. (2014). A resource intensive traffic-aware scheme using energy-aware routing in cognitive radio networks. *Future Generation Computer Systems*, *39*, 16–28. doi:10.1016/j.future.2014.02.013

Box, G. E., Jenkins, G. M., & Reinsel, G. C. (2013). *Time series analysis: Forecasting and control.* John Wiley & Sons.

Choi, J., Han, J., Cho, E., Kwon, T., & Choi, Y. (2011). A survey on content-oriented networking for efficient content delivery. *Communications Magazine, IEEE*, *49*(3), 121–127. doi:10.1109/MCOM.2011.5723809

Ciobanu, N.-V., Comaneci, D.-G., Dobre, C., Mavromoustakis, C. X., & Mastorakis, G. *OpenMobs: Mobile broadband internet connection sharing*. Academic Press.

Consumer Internet Traffic 2012-2017. (2014). Retrieved from http://www.cisco.com/web/solutions/sp/vni/vni_forecast_highlights/index.html

CRAN-Forecast Package. (2014). Retrieved from http://CRAN.R-project.org/package=forecasting

Detti, A., Blefari Melazzi, N., Salsano, S., & Pomposini, M. (2011). *CONET: A content centric internetworking architecture.* Paper presented at the ACM SIGCOMM Workshop on Information-Centric Networking. doi:10.1145/2018584.2018598

Dimitriou, C. D., Mavromoustakis, C. X., Mastorakis, G., & Pallis, E. (2013). *On the performance response of delay-bounded energy-aware bandwidth allocation scheme in wireless networks.* Paper presented at the Communications Workshops (ICC). doi:10.1109/ICCW.2013.6649310

Dinda, P. A. (2006). Design, implementation, and performance of an extensible toolkit for resource prediction in distributed systems. *IEEE Transactions on Parallel and Distributed Systems*, *17*(2), 160–173.

FlexiScale Cloud Comp and Hosting. (2014). Retrieved from http://www.flexiscale.com

Google App Engine. (2014). Retrieved from http://code.google.com/appengine

Hyndman, R. J., & Khandakar, Y. (2007). *Automatic time series for forecasting: The forecast package for R.* Monash University, Department of Econometrics and Business Statistics.

Hyndman, R. J., King, M. L., Pitrun, I., & Billah, B. (2005). Local linear forecasts using cubic smoothing splines. *Australian & New Zealand Journal of Statistics*, *47*(1), 87–99. doi:10.1111/j.1467-842X.2005.00374.x

Jacobson, V., Smetters, D. K., Thornton, J. D., Plass, M. F., Briggs, N. H., & Braynard, R. L. (2009). *Networking named content.* Paper presented at the 5th International Conference on Emerging Networking Experiments and Technologies. doi:10.1145/1658939.1658941

Katsaros, K., Xylomenos, G., & Polyzos, G. C. (2011). MultiCache: An overlay architecture for information-centric networking. *Computer Networks*, *55*(4), 936–947. doi:10.1016/j.comnet.2010.12.012

Koponen, T., Chawla, M., Chun, B.-G., Ermolinskiy, A., Kim, K. H., Shenker, S., & Stoica, I. (2007). A data-oriented (and beyond) network architecture. *Computer Communication Review*, *37*(4), 181–192. doi:10.1145/1282427.1282402

Koumaras, H., Negru, D., Borcoci, E., Koumaras, V., Troulos, C., Lapid, Y., & Gardikis, G. (2011). *Media ecosystems: A novel approach for content-awareness in future networks*. Springer.

Kwon, J. B., & Yeom, H. Y. (2002). Providing VCR functionality in staggered video broadcasting. *IEEE Transactions on Consumer Electronics, 48*(1), 41–48.

Lutz Schubert, K. J. (2012). *Advances in clouds: Report from the cloud computing expert working group*. Academic Press.

Mastorakis, G., Mavromoustakis, C. X., Bourdena, A., Kormentzas, G., & Pallis, E. (2013). *Maximizing energy conservation in a centralized cognitive radio network architecture.* Paper presented at the Computer Aided Modeling and Design of Communication Links and Networks (CAMAD). doi:10.1109/CAMAD.2013.6708112

Mastorakis, G., Mavromoustakis, C. X., Bourdena, A., & Pallis, E. (2013). *An energy-efficient routing scheme using backward traffic difference estimation in cognitive radio networks.* Paper presented at the World of Wireless, Mobile and Multimedia Networks (WoWMoM). doi:10.1109/WoWMoM.2013.6583446

Mastorakis, G., Mavromoustakis, C. X., Bourdena, A., Pallis, E., & Sismanidis, G. (2013). *Optimizing radio resource management in energy-efficient cognitive radio networks.* Paper presented at the 2nd ACM Workshop on High Performance Mobile Opportunistic Systems. doi:10.1145/2507908.2507920

Mastorakis, G., Mavromoustakis, C. X., Bourdena, A., Pallis, E., Sismanidis, G., Stratakis, D., & Papadakis, S. (2014). Energy-efficient routing in cognitive radio networks. In *Resource management in mobile computing environments* (pp. 323–340). Springer; doi:10.1007/978-3-319-06704-9_14

Mastorakis, G., Pallis, E., Mavromoustakis, C. X., & Bourdena, A. (2014). Efficient resource management utilizing content-aware multipath routing. In *Resource management in mobile computing environments* (pp. 389–395). Springer; doi:10.1007/978-3-319-06704-9_17

Mastorakis, G., Panagiotakis, S., Kapetanakis, K., Dagalakis, G., Mavromoustakis, C. X., Bourdena, A., & Pallis, E. (2014). Energy and resource consumption evaluation of mobile cognitive radio devices. In *Resource management in mobile computing environments* (pp. 359–388). Springer; doi:10.1007/978-3-319-06704-9_16

Mavromoustakis, C., Andreou, A., Mastorakis, G., Papadakis, S., Bourdena, A., & Stratakis, D. (2014). *Energy consumption optimization through pre-scheduled opportunistic offloading in wireless devices.* Paper presented at the EMERGING 2014, the Sixth International Conference on Emerging Network Intelligence.

Mavromoustakis, C., Dimitriou, C. D., & Mastorakis, G. (2012). *Using real-time backward traffic difference estimation for energy conservation in wireless devices.* Paper presented at the AP2PS 2012, the Fourth International Conference on Advances in P2P Systems.

Mavromoustakis, C., Dimitriou, C. D., & Mastorakis, G. (2013). On the real-time evaluation of two-level BTD scheme for energy conservation in the presence of delay sensitive transmissions and intermittent connectivity in wireless devices. *International Journal on Advances in Networks and Services, 6*(3 and 4), 148-162.

Mavromoustakis, C. X., Andreou, A., Mastorakis, G., Bourdena, A., Batalla, J. M., & Dobre, C. (n.d.). *On the performance evaluation of a novel offloading-based energy conservation mechanism for wireless devices*. Academic Press.

Mavromoustakis, C. X., Dimitriou, C., Mastorakis, G., Bourdena, A., & Pallis, E. (2014). Using traffic diversities for scheduling wireless interfaces for energy harvesting in wireless devices. In *Resource management in mobile computing environments* (pp. 481–496). Springer.

Mavromoustakis, C. X., Dimitriou, C. D., Mastorakis, G., & Pallis, E. (2013). *Real-time performance evaluation of F-BTD scheme for optimized QoS energy conservation in wireless devices*. Paper presented at the Globecom Workshops (GC Wkshps). doi:10.1109/GLOCOMW.2013.6825148

Mavromoustakis, C. X., Pallis, E., & Mastorakis, G. (2014). Resource management in mobile computing environments. In *Modeling and optimization in science and technologies*. Retrieved from https://www.mediacloud.cc

Mell, P., & Grance, T. (2011). *The NIST definition of cloud computing*. NIST.

Mousicou, P., Mavromoustakis, C. X., Bourdena, A., Mastorakis, G., & Pallis, E. (2013). *Performance evaluation of dynamic cloud resource migration based on temporal and capacity-aware policy for efficient resource sharing*. Paper presented at the 2nd ACM Workshop on High Performance Mobile Opportunistic Systems. doi:10.1145/2507908.2507917

Niu, D., Liu, Z., Li, B., & Zhao, S. (2011). *Demand forecast and performance prediction in peer-assisted on-demand streaming systems*. Paper presented at the INFOCOM. doi:10.1109/INFCOM.2011.5935196

Niu, D., Xu, H., Li, B., & Zhao, S. (2012). *Quality-assured cloud bandwidth auto-scaling for video-on-demand applications*. Paper presented at the INFOCOM. doi:10.1109/INFCOM.2012.6195785

Nygren, E., Sitaraman, R. K., & Sun, J. (2010). The akamai network: A platform for high-performance internet applications. *Operating Systems Review*, *44*(3), 2–19. doi:10.1145/1842733.1842736

Papanikolaou, K., Mavromoustakis, C. X., Mastorakis, G., Bourdena, A., & Dobre, C. (n.d.). *Energy consumption optimization using social interaction in the mobile cloud*. Academic Press.

PC MAG. (2014). Retrieved from http://www.pcmag.com/encyclopedia/term/39466/cdn

Poehlein, S., Saxena, V., Willis, G., Fedders, J., & Guttmann, M. (2010). *Moving to the media cloud: Available RPS toolkit*. Retrieved from http://www.cs.northwestern.edu/~RPS/

Saleem, Y., Salim, F., & Rehmani, M. H. (2014). Resource management in mobile sink based wireless sensor networks through cloud computing. In *Resource management in mobile computing environments* (pp. 439–459). Springer.

Salesforce, C. R. M. (2014). Retrieved from http://www.salesforce.com/platform

Sappington, B. (2013). *Residential gateway trends: Bringing value home*. Academic Press.

Skicewicz, J., Skicewicz, J. A., & Dinda, P. A. (2003). *Tsunami: A wavelet toolkit for distributed systems*. Academic Press.

Sodagar, I. (2011). *Industry and standards*. Academic Press.

Sony Ci. (2014). Retrieved from https://www.sonymcs.com/

Su, A.-J., Choffnes, D. R., Kuzmanovic, A., & Bustamante, F. E. (2009). Drafting behind Akamai: Inferring network conditions based on CDN redirections. *IEEE/ACM Transactions on Networking*, *17*(6), 1752–1765. doi:10.1109/TNET.2009.2022157

Suh, K., Diot, C., Kurose, J., Massoulie, L., Neumann, C., Towsley, D., & Varvello, M. (2007). Push-to-peer video-on-demand system: Design and evaluation. *IEEE Journal on Selected Areas in Communications*, *25*(9), 1706–1716.

Team, R. C. (2014). *R: A language and environment for statistical computing*. Academic Press.

Vodafone Media Cloud. (2014). Retrieved from http://www.mediacloud.tv/

Web Browsers with Real-Time Communications - WebRTC Initiative. (2014). Retrieved from http://www.webrtc.org/

Wei, Z., Li, J., Yang, Y., & Jia, D. (2010). *A residential gateway architecture based on cloud computing*. Paper presented at the Software Engineering and Service Sciences (ICSESS). doi:10.1109/ICSESS.2010.5552422

Whiteaker, J., Schneider, F., Teixeira, R., Diot, C., Soule, A., Picconi, F., & May, M. (2012). Expanding home services with advanced gateways. *Computer Communication Review*, *42*(5), 37–43. doi:10.1145/2378956.2378962

Windows Azure. (2014). Retrieved from http://www.microsoft.com/azure

Wu, W., & Lui, J. (2012). Exploring the optimal replication strategy in P2P-VoD systems: Characterization and evaluation. *IEEE Transactions on Parallel and Distributed Systems*, *23*(8), 1492–1503.

Xu, D., Kulkarni, S. S., Rosenberg, C., & Chai, H.-K. (2006). Analysis of a CDN–P2P hybrid architecture for cost-effective streaming media distribution. *Multimedia Systems*, *11*(4), 383–399. doi:10.1007/s00530-006-0015-3

Yin, H., Liu, X., Zhan, T., Sekar, V., Qiu, F., Lin, C., . . . Li, B. (2009). *Design and deployment of a hybrid CDN-P2P system for live video streaming: Experiences with LiveSky*. Paper presented at the 17th ACM International Conference on Multimedia.

KEY TERMS AND DEFINITIONS

Content Delivery Network (CDN): A large distributed system of servers deployed in multiple data centers across the Internet.

Multimedia Services System: A system that provides any type of multimedia services to the end users.

Quality of Experience (QoE): A measure of a customer's experiences with a service. It focuses on the entire service experience. It is a more holistic evaluation.

Quality of Service (QoS): The overall performance of a computer network. It is particularly the performance seen by the users of the network.

Resource Prediction Engine (RPE): A system used for the prediction of future values of a resource, based on previous values of that resource.

Compilation of References

3DMLW. (3D Markup Language for Web). (n.d.). *An open source platform for creating rapidly interactive 3D and 2D applications for web or desktop*. Retrieved July 12, 2014, from http://www.3dtech-rd.net/3dmlw/

Abdelzaher, T., Diao, Y., Hellerstein, J. L., Lu, C., & Zhu, X. (2008). *Introduction to control theory and its application to computing systems* (pp. 185–215). Annapolis, MD: Academic Press. doi:10.1007/978-0-387-79361-0_7

Abiquo. (2014). *Virtualization, cloud services, software - Cloud computing platform*. Retrieved from http://www.abiquo.com

Abolfazli, S., Sanaei, Z., Ahmed, E., Gani, A., & Buyya, R. (2013). Cloud-based augmentation for mobile devices: Motivation, taxonomies, and open challenges. *IEEE Communications Surveys and Tutorials*, (July), 1–32.

Abolfazli, S., Sanaei, Z., Gani, A., Xia, F., & Yang, L. T. (2013). Rich mobile applications: Genesis, taxonomy, and open issues. *Journal of Network and Computer Applications*.

Aepona. (2010). *Mobile cloud computing solution brief.* White Paper. Author.

Agarwal, B., Chitnis, P., Dey, A., Jain, K., Navda, V., Padmanabhan, V. N., . . . Spring, N. (2010). Stratus: Energy-efficient mobile communication using cloud support. In S. Kalyanaraman, V. N. Padmanabhan, K. K. Ramakrishnan, R. Shorey & G. M. Voelker (eds.), SIGCOMM (pp. 477-478). ACM. doi:10.1145/1851182.1851272

Aggarwal, V., Gopalakrishnan, V., Jana, R., Ramakrishnan, K. K., & Vaishampayan, V. (2013). Optimizing cloud resources for delivering IPTV services through virtualization. *IEEE Transactions on Multimedia*, *15*(4), 789–801. doi:10.1109/TMM.2013.2240287

Ajax3D. (n.d.). Retrieved July 12, 2014, from http://sourceforge.net/projects/ajax3d/

Akhshabi, S., Begen, A. C., & Dovrolis, C. (2011). An experimental evaluation of rate-adaptation algorithms in adaptive streaming over http. In *Proceedings of ACM MMSys*. ACM.

Akhshabi, S., Anantakrishnan, L., Dovrolis, C., & Begen, A. C. (2012). What happens when HTTP adaptive streaming players compete for bandwidth? In *Proc. NOSSDA*. Academic Press.

Akoush, S., Sohan, R., Rice, A., Moore, A. W., & Hopper, A. (2010, August). Predicting the performance of virtual machine migration. In *Proceedings of Modeling, Analysis & Simulation of Computer and Telecommunication Systems* (MASCOTS) (pp. 37-46). IEEE. doi:10.1109/MASCOTS.2010.13

Akyildiz, I. F., Lee, W.-Y., Vuran, M. C., & Mohanty, S. (2008). A survey on spectrum management in cognitive radio networks. *IEEE Communications Magazine*, *46*(4), 40-48.

Al Noor, S., Mustafa, G., Chowdhury, S. A., Hossain, M. Z., & Jaigirdar, F. T. (2010). A proposed architecture of cloud computing for education system in Bangladesh and the impact on current education system. *International Journal of Computer Science and Network Security*, *10*(10), 7–13.

Alabbadi, M. M. (2011, September). Cloud computing for education and learning: Education and learning as a service (ELaaS). In *Proceedings of Interactive Collaborative Learning* (ICL) (pp. 589-594). IEEE.

Alasaad, A., Shafiee, K., Behairy, H., & Leung, V. (2014). Innovative schemes for resource allocation in the cloud for media streaming applications. *IEEE Transactions on Parallel and Distributed Systems, 9219*(c), 1–1. doi:10.1109/TPDS.2014.2316827

Alcaraz Calero, J. M., & Gutierrez Aguado, J. (2014). *MonPaaS: An adaptive monitoring platform as a service for cloud computing infrastructures and services.* IEEE Transactions on Services Computing. doi:10.1109/TSC.2014.2302810

Alford, T., & Morton, G. (2010). *The economics of cloud computing, addressing the benefits of infrastructure in the cloud.* Booz Allen Hamilton. Retrieved July 3, 2014 from http://www.boozallen.com/media/file/Economics-of-Cloud-Computing.pdf

Al-Hussaini, E. K. (1991). A characterization of the Burr type XII distribution. *Applied Mathematics Letters, 4*(1), 59-61.

Allman, E. (2012). Managing technical debt. *Communications of the ACM, 55*(5), 50–55. doi:10.1145/2160718.2160733

Altman, N. S. (1992). An introduction to kernel and nearest-neighbor nonparametric regression. *The American Statistician, 46*(3), 175–185.

Alvestrand, H. (2014). *Overview: Real time protocols for browser-based applications.* Retrieved July 12, 2014, from http://tools.ietf.org/html/draft-ietf-rtcweb-overview-10

Alzaghoul, E., & Bahsoon, R. (2013a). CloudMTD: Using real options to manage technical debt in cloud-based service selection. In *Proceedings of 2013 4th International Workshop on Managing Technical Debt (MTD)* (pp. 55–62). San Francisco, CA: IEEE.

Alzaghoul, E., & Bahsoon, R. (2013b). Economics-driven approach for managing technical debt in cloud-based architectures. In *Proceedings of 2013 IEEE/ACM 6th International Conference on Utility and Cloud Computing (UCC)* (pp. 239–242). Dresden: IEEE. doi:10.1109/UCC.2013.49

Alzaghoul, E., & Bahsoon, R. (2014). Evaluating technical debt in cloud-based architectures using real options. In *Proceedings of 2014 23rd Australian Software Engineering Conference (ASWEC)* (pp. 1–10). IEEE. doi:10.1109/ASWEC.2014.27

Amazon EC2. (2006). Retrieved July 27, 2014, from http://aws.amazon.com/ec2/

Amazon Elastic Compute Cloud (EC2). (n.d.). *Microsoft Azure.* Retrieved from http://www.microsoft.com/azure/

Amazon Elastic Computing Cloud. (2014). Retrieved from http://aws.amazon.com/ec2

Amazon Web Services. (n.d.). *Home page.* Retrieved July 10, 2014, from http://aws.amazon.com/

Anand, B., Thirugnanam, K., Sebastian, J., Kannan, P. G., Ananda, A. L., Chan, M. C., & Balan, R. K. (2010), Adaptive display power management for mobile games. In *Proceedings of the 9th International Conference on Mobile Systems, Applications, and Services, MobiSys '11* (pp. 57-70). New York, NY: ACM.

Andreou, A., Mavromoustakis, C. X., Mastorakis, G., Bourdena, A., & Pallis, E. (2014). Adaptive heuristic-based P2P network connectivity and configuration for resource availability. In Resource management in mobile computing environments (pp. 221-240). Springer International Publishing. doi:10.1007/978-3-319-06704-9_10

Application and Network Performance with OPNET. (n.d.). Retrieved from http://www.opnet.com

Armbrust, M., Fox, A., Griffith, R., Joseph, A. D., Katz, R., Konwinski, A., & Zaharia, M. et al. (2010, April). A view of cloud computing. *Communications of the ACM, 53*(4), 50–58. doi:10.1145/1721654.1721672

Ashkar, F., & Mahdi, S. (2006). Fitting the log-logistic distribution by generalized moments. *Journal of Hydrology, 328*(3–4), 694-703.

Assimakopoulos, V., & Nikolopoulos, K. (2000). The theta model: A decomposition approach to forecasting. *International Journal of Forecasting, 16*(4), 521–530. doi:10.1016/S0169-2070(00)00066-2

Atzori, L., Iera, A., & Morabito, G. (2010). The internet of things: A survey. *Computer Networks, 54*(15), 2787-2805.

Bae, S.-H., Kim, J., Kim, M., Cho, S., & Choi, J. S. (2013). Assessments of subjective video quality on HEVC-encoded 4K-UHD video for beyond-HDTV broadcasting services. *IEEE Transactions on Broadcasting*, *59*(2), 209–222. doi:10.1109/TBC.2013.2247171

Bahsoon, R., & Emmerich, W. (2003). ArchOptions: A real options-based model for predicting the stability of software architectures. In *Proceedings of5th International Workshop on Economic-Driven Software Engineering Research (EDSER-5)* (pp. 38–43). Portland, OR: EDSER.

Bahsoon, R., & Emmerich, W. (2004). Applying ArchOptions to value the payoff of refactoring. In *Proceedings of the Sixth ICSE Workshop on Economics-Driven Software Engineering Research (EDSER-6)* (pp. 66 – 70). Edinburgh, UK: IET. doi:10.1049/ic:20040290

Balachandran, A., Sekar, V., Akella, A., Stoica, S., & Zhang, H. (2012). *A quest for an internet video quality-of-experience metric.* Academic Press.

Balasubramanian, N., Balasubramanian, A., & Venkataramani, A. (2009). Energy consumption in mobile phones: A measurement study and implications for network applications. In FeldmannA.MathyL. (Eds.), *Internet measurement conference* (pp. 280-293). ACM. doi:10.1145/1644893.1644927

Baltoglou, G., Karapistoli, E., & Chatzimisios, P. (2012). IPTV QoS and QoE measurements in wired and wireless networks. In *Proceedings of the Global Communications Conference (GLOBECOM)* (pp. 1757-1762). IEEE. doi:10.1109/GLOCOM.2012.6503369

Barabasi, A.-L. (2005). The origin of bursts and heavy tails in human dynamics. *Nature*, *435*(7039), 207–211. doi:10.1038/nature03459 PMID:15889093

Barford, P., Kline, J., Plonka, D., & Ron, A. (2002), A signal analysis of network traffic anomalies. In *Proceedings of the 2nd ACM SIGCOMM Workshop on Internet Measurment* (IMW '02). ACM. doi:10.1145/637201.637210

Barham, P., Dragovic, B., Fraser, K., Hand, S., Harris, T., Ho, A., & Warfield, A. et al. (2003). Xen and the art of virtualization. In *Proc. 19th ACM Symposium on OS Principles*. ACM.

Barlas, G. (2012). Cluster-based optimized parallel video transcoding. *Parallel Computing*, *38*(4-5), 226–244. doi:10.1016/j.parco.2012.02.001

Bavier, A., Feamster, N., Huang, M., Peterson, L., & Rexford, J. (2006). In VINI veritas: Realistic and controlled network experimentation. In *Proc. ACM SIGCOMM*. ACM.

Bęben, A., Mongay Batalla, J., Wiśniewski, P., & Xilouris, G. (2014). A scalable and flexible packet forwarding method for future internet networks. In *Proc. IEEE Globecom*. IEEE. doi:10.1109/GLOCOM.2014.7037099

Becke, M., Rathgeb, E. P., Werner, S., Rungeler, I., Tuxe, M., & Stewart, R. (2013, April). Data Channel Considerations for RTCWeb. *Communications Magazine, IEEE*, *51*(4), 34–41. doi:10.1109/MCOM.2013.6495758

Behr, J., Eschler, P., Jung, Y., & Zöllner, M. (2009). X3Dom: A DOM-based HTML5/X3D integration model. In *Proceedings of the 14th International Conference on 3D Web Technology* (pp. 127-135). ACM. doi:10.1145/1559764.1559784

Beloglazov, A., & Buyya, R. (2010, May). Energy efficient resource management in virtualized cloud data centers. In *Proceedings of the 2010 10th IEEE/ACM International Conference on Cluster, Cloud and Grid Computing* (pp. 826-831). IEEE Computer Society. doi:10.1109/CCGRID.2010.46

Bergkvist, A., Burnett, D. C., Jennings, C., & Narayanan, A. (Eds.). (2014, July 1). *WebRTC 1.0: Real-time communication between browsers - W3C*. Retrieved July 13, 2014, from: http://dev.w3.org/2011/webrtc/editor/webrtc.html

Berjon, R., Faulkner, S., Leithead, T., Navara, E. D., O'Connor, E., Pfeiffer, S., & Hickson, I. (Eds.). (2014, July 31). HTML5 - A vocabulary and associated APIs for HTML and XHTML. *W3C Candidate Recommendation*. Retrieved July 31, 2014, from: http://www.w3.org/html/wg/drafts/html/CR/

Berman, F., Fox, G., & Hey, T. (2003). *Grid computing: Making the global infrastructure a reality*. Wiley and Sons. doi:10.1002/0470867167

Bermudez, P. Z., & Kotz, S. (2010). Parameter estimation of the generalized Pareto distribution—Part I. *Journal of Statistical Planning and Inference*, *140*(6), 1353-1373.

Bhaduri, K., Das, K., & Matthews, B. L. (2011). Detecting abnormal machine characteristics in cloud infrastructures. In *Proceedings of Data Mining Workshops (ICDMW)* (pp. 137-144). ICDMW.

Bhatia, S., Motiwala, M., Muhlbauer, W., Mundada, Y., Valancius, V., Bavier, A., & Rexford, J. et al. (2008). Trellis: A platform for building flexible, fast virtual networks on commodity hardware. In *Proc. 3rd ACM Workshop on Real Overlays and Distributed Systems*. ACM.

Bhoraskar, R., Vankadhara, N., Raman, B., & Kulkarni, P. (2012). Wolverine: Traffic and road condition estimation using smartphone sensors. In *Proceedings ofCommunication Systems and Networks (COMSNETS)* (pp. 1-6). IEEE. doi:10.1109/COMSNETS.2012.6151382

Billock, G., Hawkins, J., & Kinlan, P. (Eds.). (2013, May 23). *Web intents W3C working group note*. Retrieved July 12, 2014, from http://www.w3.org/TR/web-intents/

Bisong, A., & Rahman, S. M. (2011). An overview of the security concerns in enterprise cloud computing. *CoRR*, abs/1101.5613

Bitirgen, R., Ipek, E., & Martinez, J. F. (2008). Coordinated management of multiple interacting resources in chip multiprocessors: A machine learning approach. In *Proceedings of the 41st annual IEEE/ACM International Symposium on Microarchitecture (MICRO 41)*. IEEE Computer Society. doi:10.1109/MICRO.2008.4771801

Block, S., & Popescu, A. (Eds.). (2011, December 1). *DeviceOrientation event specification, W3C working draft*. Retrieved July 12, 2014, from http://www.w3.org/TR/orientation-event/

BlueJeans. (n.d.). Retrieved July 12, 2014, from http://bluejeans.com/

Boccuzzi, J., & Ruggiero, M. (2011). *Femtocells: Design and applications*. McGraw-Hill.

Boehm, B. W. (1981). *Software engineering economics*. Englewood Cliffs, NJ: Prentice-Hall.

Boehm, B., Abts, C., & Chulani, S. (2000). Software development cost estimation approaches - A survey. *Annals of Software Engineering*, *10*(1-4), 177–205. doi:10.1023/A:1018991717352

Bossen, F., Bross, B., Member, S., Karsten, S., & Flynn, D. (2012). HEVC complexity and implementation analysis. *IEEE Transactions on Circuits and Systems for Video Technology*, *22*(12), 1685–1696. doi:10.1109/TCSVT.2012.2221255

Bouguerra, M. S., Gautier, T., Trystram, D., & Vincent, J. M. (2010). A flexible checkpoint/restart model in distributed systems. In *Parallel processing and applied mathematics* (pp. 206–215). Springer Berlin Heidelberg. doi:10.1007/978-3-642-14390-8_22

Bourdena, A., Kormentzas, G., Pallis, E., & Mastorakis, G. (2013, June). Radio resource management algorithms for efficient QoS provisioning over cognitive radio networks. In *Proceedings of Communications* (ICC) (pp. 2415-2420). IEEE. doi:10.1109/ICC.2013.6654893

Bourdena, A., Makris, P., Skoutas, D. N., Skianis, C., Kormentzas, G., Pallis, E., & Mastorakis, G. (n.d.). *Joint radio resource management in cognitive networks: TV white spaces exploitation paradigm*. Academic Press.

Bourdena, A., Mastorakis, G., Pallis, E., Arvanitis, A., & Kormentzas, G. (2012). *A dynamic spectrum management framework for efficient TVWS exploitation*. Paper presented at the Computer Aided Modeling and Design of Communication Links and Networks (CAMAD). doi:10.1109/CAMAD.2012.6335377

Bourdena, A., Mastorakis, G., Pallis, E., Karditsis, E., & Kormentzas, G. (2012). *A radio resource management framework for TVWS exploitation under the RTSSM policy*. Paper presented at the Telecommunications and Multimedia (TEMU). doi:10.1109/TEMU.2012.6294718

Bourdena, A., Pallis, E., Kormentzas, G., & Mastorakis, G. (2013). Radio resource management algorithms for efficient QoS provisioning over cognitive radio networks. In *Proc. IEEE International Conference on Communications*. Cisco VNI Publisher. Retrieved from http://www.cisco.com/web/solutions/sp/vni/vni_forecast_highlights/index.html

Bourdena, A., Kormentzas, G., Skianis, C., Pallis, E., & Mastorakis, G. (2011). *Real-time TVWS trading based on a centralized CR network architecture*. IEEE GLOBECOM Workshops. doi:10.1109/GLOCOMW.2011.6162600

Bourdena, A., Mavromoustakis, C. X., Kormentzas, G., Pallis, E., Mastorakis, G., & Yassein, M. B. (2014). A resource intensive traffic-aware scheme using energy-aware routing in cognitive radio networks. *Future Generation Computer Systems*, *39*, 16–28. doi:10.1016/j.future.2014.02.013

Bourdena, A., Pallis, E., Kormentzas, G., Skianis, C., & Mastorakis, G. (2012). *QoS provisioning and policy management in a broker-based CR network architecture*. Anaheim, CA: IEEE Globecom. doi:10.1109/GLOCOM.2012.6503383

Boutaba, N., & Chowdhury, R. (2009). Network virtualization: State of the art and research challenges. *IEEE Communications Magazine*, *47*(7), 20–26. doi:10.1109/MCOM.2009.5183468

Bouyoucef, K., Limam-Bedhiaf, I., & Cherkaoui, O. (2010). Optimal allocation approach of virtual servers in cloud computing. In *Proc. 6th EURO-NF Conference on Next Generation Internet* (NGI). Academic Press. doi:10.1109/NGI.2010.5534467

Box, G. E., Jenkins, G. M., & Reinsel, G. C. (2013). *Time series analysis: Forecasting and control*. John Wiley & Sons.

Brazio, B., Tran-Gia, P., Akar, N., Beben, A., Burakowski, W., Fiedler, M., . . . Wittevrongel, S. (Eds.). (2006). Analysis and design of advanced multiservice networks supporting mobility, multimedia, and internetworking: COST action 279 final report. Springer. doi:10.1007/0-387-28173-8

Brown, N., Cai, Y., Guo, Y., Kazman, R., Kim, M., & Kruchten, P., … Zazworka, N. (2010). Managing technical debt in software-reliant systems. In *Proceedings of the FSE/SDP Workshop on Future of Software Engineering Research* (pp. 47–52). ACM. doi:10.1145/1882362.1882373

Buhagiar, J. K., & Debono, C. J. (2009). Exploiting adaptive window techniques to reduce TCP congestion in mobile peer networks. In *Proceedings of the 2009 IEEE conference on Wireless Communications & Networking Conference* (WCNC'09) (pp. 1962-1967). IEEE Press. doi:10.1109/WCNC.2009.4917718

Bulakci, O., Bou Saleh, A., Redana, S., Raaf, B., & Hämäläinen, J. (2013). Resource sharing in LTE-Advanced relay networks: Uplink system performance analysis. *Transactions on Emerging Telecommunications Technologies*, *24*(1), 32–48. doi:10.1002/ett.2569

BuNGee. (2010). *BuNGee: Beyond next generation mobile broadband*. Retrieved July 10, 2014, from http://cordis.europa.eu/fp7/ict/future-networks/projectsummaries/bungee.pdf

Bureau, P. (2011). Same botnet, same guys, new code. In *Proceedings of Virus Bulletin*. VB.

Burnett, D. C., Bergkvist, A., Jennings, C., & Narayanan, A. (Eds.). (2013, September 3). *Media capture and streams, W3C working draft*. Retrieved July 12, 2014, from http://www.w3.org/TR/mediacapture-streams/

Buschmann, F. (2011). To pay or not to pay technical debt. *IEEE Software*, *28*(6), 29–31. doi:10.1109/MS.2011.150

Business, G. A. (2014). *Google apps for business*. Retrieved 7 11, 2014, from http://www.google.com/apps/intl/en/business/index.html

Buyya, R., Ranjan, R., & Calheiros, R. N. (2009). Modeling and simulation of scalable Cloud computing environments and the CloudSim toolkit: Challenges and opportunities. In *Proceedings ofInternational Conference on High Performance Computing & Simulation, 2009 (HPCS'09)* (pp. 1–11). Leipzig: IEEE. doi:10.1109/HPCSIM.2009.5192685

Buyya, R., Yeo, C. S., Venugopal, S., Broberg, J., & Brandic, I. (2009). Cloud computing and emerging IT platforms: Vision, hype, and reality for delivering computing as the 5th utility. *Future Generation Computer Systems*, *25*(6), 599–616. doi:10.1016/j.future.2008.12.001

Camp, T., Boleng, J., & Davies, V. (2002). A survey of mobility models for ad hoc network research. *Wireless Communications and Mobile Computing*, *2*(5), 483-502.

Carapinha, J., & Jimenez, J. (2009). Network virtualization – A view from the bottom. In *Proc. ACM SIGCOMM VISA'2009 Workshop*. ACM.

Carmona-Murillo, J., González-Sánchez, J. L., Cortés-Polo, D., & Rodríguez-Pérez, F. J. (2014). QoS in next generation mobile networks: An analytical study. In Resource management in mobile computing environments (pp. 25-41). Springer International Publishing.

Caron, E., & Desprez, F. (2011). Forecasting for cloud computing on-demand resources based on pattern matching. *Journal of Grid Computing*.

Casas, P., & Schatz, R. (2014). Quality of experience in cloud services: Survey and measurements. *Computer Networks*, 1–17. doi:10.1016/j.comnet.2014.01.008

Chakchai, S-I. (2006). *Survey of network traffic monitoring and analysis tools*. Retrieved from https://www.researchgate.net/publication/241752391_A_Survey_of_Network_Traffic_Monitoring_and_Analysis_Tools

Challam, V., Gauch, S., & Chandramouli, A. (2007). Contextual search using ontology-based user profiles. In D. Evans, S. Furui, & C. Soulé-Dupuy (Eds.), RIAO: CID. Academic Press.

Chandola, V., Banerjee, A., & Kumar, V. (2009, July). Anomaly detection: A survey. *ACM Computing Surveys*, *41*(3), 15. doi:10.1145/1541880.1541882

Chang, S.-Y., Lai, C.-F., & Huang, Y.-M. (2012). Dynamic adjustable multimedia streaming service architecture over cloud computing. *Computer Communications*, *35*(15), 1798–1808. doi:10.1016/j.comcom.2012.06.001

Charalambous, M. C., Mavromoustakis, C. X., & Yassein, M. B. (2012). A resource intensive traffic-aware scheme for cluster-based energy conservation in wireless devices. In *Proceedings of High Perf. Comp. and Comm. & 2012 IEEE 9th Int.Conf. on Embedded Software and Systems (HPCC-ICESS)*, pp. 879-884, doi:10.1109/HPCC.2012.125

Chase, J., Irwin, D., Grit, L., Moore, J., & Sprenkle, S. (2003). Dynamic virtual clusters in a grid site manager. In *Proceedings of High Performance Distributed Computing*. IEEE. doi:10.1109/HPDC.2003.1210019

Chen, Y., Paxson, V., & Katz, R. (2010). What's new about cloud computing security. Technical Report. EECS Department, University of California, Berkeley.

Cheng, J., Balan, R. K., & Satyanarayan, M. (2005). *Exploiting rich mobile environments*. Technical Report.

Chengwei, W., Talwar, V., Schwan, K., & Ranganathan, P. (2010), Online detection of utility cloud anomalies using metric distributions. In *Proceedings ofNetwork Operations and Management Symposium (NOMS)* (pp. 96-103). IEEE.

Chengwei, W., Viswanathan, K., Choudur, L., Talwar, V., Satterfield, W., & Schwan, K. (2011). Statistical techniques for online anomaly detection in data centers. In *Proceedings of Integrated Network Management (IM)* (pp. 385-392). Academic Press.

Chen, J., Boyce, J., Ye, Y., & Hannuksela, M. (2013). *Scalable HEVC (SHVC) test model 4 (SHM 4). JCT-VC of ITU-T SG 16 WP 3 and ISO/IEC JTC 1/SC 29/WG 11, JCTVC-O1007_v1.15th Meeting*: Geneva.

Chen, Y. W., & Jiang, W. (2013). Low-complexity transcoding from H.264 to HEVC based on motion vector clustering. *Electronics Letters*, *49*(19), 1224–1226. doi:10.1049/el.2013.0329

Chester, A. P., Leeke, M., Al-Ghamdi, M., Jarvis, S. A., & Jhumka, A. (2011). *A modular failure-aware resource allocation architecture for cloud computing*. Academic Press.

Choi, J., Han, J., Cho, E., Kwon, T., & Choi, Y. (2011). A survey on content-oriented networking for efficient content delivery. *Communications Magazine, IEEE*, *49*(3), 121–127. doi:10.1109/MCOM.2011.5723809

Choi, K., & Jang, E. (2012). Industry and standards leveraging parallel computing in modern video coding standards. *IEEE MultiMedia*, *19*(Jul-Sept), 7–11. doi:10.1109/MMUL.2012.36

Chowdhury, M., Rahman, M., & Boutaba, R. (2012). ViNEYard: Virtual network embedding algorithms with coordinated node and link mapping. *IEEE/ACM Transactions on Networking*, *20*(1), 203–226. doi:10.1109/TNET.2011.2159308

Christensen, J. H. (2009). Using RESTful web-services and cloud computing to create next generation mobile applications. In *Proceedings of the 24th ACM SIGPLAN Conference Companion on Object Oriented Programming Systems Languages and Applications (OOPSLA)* (pp. 451-459). ACM. doi:10.1145/1639950.1639958

Christodorescu, M., Sailer, R., Schales, D. L., Sgandurra, D., & Zamboni, D. (2009). Cloud security is not (just) virtualization security: A short paper. In *Proceedings of the 2009 ACM Workshop on Cloud Computing Security* (CCSW '09). ACM. doi:10.1145/1655008.1655022

Chun, B. G., Ihm, S., Maniatis, P., Naik, M., & Patti, A. (2011). CloneCloud: Elastic execution between mobile device and cloud. In *Proceedings of the 6th Conference on Computer Systems (EuroSys)* (pp. 301-314). Academic Press. doi:10.1145/1966445.1966473

Chun, B. G., & Maniatis, P. (2010). Dynamically partitioning applications between weak devices and clouds. In *Proceedings of the 1st ACM Workshop on Mobile Cloud Computing and Services: Social Networks and Beyond (MCS)*. ACM. doi:10.1145/1810931.1810938

Ciobanu, N. V., Comaneci, D. G., Dobre, C., Mavromoustakis, C. X., & Mastorakis, G. (2014). OpenMobs: Mobile broadband internet connection sharing. In *Proceedings of6th International Conference on Mobile Networks and Management (MONAMI 2014)*. Wuerzburg, Germany: MONAMI.

Ciobanu, N.-V., Comaneci, D.-G., Dobre, C., Mavromoustakis, C. X., & Mastorakis, G. *OpenMobs: Mobile broadband internet connection sharing*. Academic Press.

Ciobanu, R. I., Marin, R. C., Dobre, C., Cristea, V., & Mavromoustakis, C. X. (2014). *ONSIDE: Socially-aware and interest-based dissemination in opportunistic networks*. Academic Press.

Cisco. (2013). *Cisco visual networking index: Global mobile data traffic forecast update, 2012-2017*. Cisco.

Cisco. (2014). *Cisco visual networking index: Global mobile data traffic forecast update, 2013–2018*. Retrieved May 18, 2014, from http://www.cisco.com/en/US/solutions/collateral/ns341/ns525/ns537/ns705/ns827/white_paper_c11-520862.html

Cloud Computing, Managed Hosting, Dedicated Server Hosting by Rackspace. (n.d.). Retrieved from http://www.rackspace.com/

Cloud Hosting | Webair Cloud Server Solutions. (n.d.). Retrieved from http://www.webair.com/webhosting-cloud-servers.html

Cloud Monitoring & Management. (2014). Retrieved from http://cloudkick.com

Cloud, N. (2014). Retrieved from http://csrc.nist.gov/publications/nistpubs/800-145/SP800-145.pdf

Codec , O. (n.d.). Retrieved July 12, 2014, from http://www.opus-codec.org/

Cohen, L. (1989), Time-frequency distributions-A review, *Proceedings of the IEEE*, 77(7), 941-981. doi:10.1109/5.30749

Coles, S. (2001). *An introduction to statistical modeling of extreme values*.Springer-Verlag. doi:10.1007/978-1-4471-3675-0

Collaborative 3D Web-Application for Preschool Children's Education. (n.d.). Retrieved July 12, 2014, from http://www.medialab.teicrete.gr/minipages/x3dws/

Colwell, B. (2004). We may need a new box. *Computer, 37*(3), 40-41.

Comito, C., Falcone, D., Talia, D., & Trunfio, P. (2013). Scheduling data mining applications in mobile computing environments. ERCIM News, (93).

Company. (2014). Retrieved from http://www.salesforce.com

Computing, P. (2014). *Clusters, grids, clouds*. Retrieved from http://www.platform.com

Conroy, P. (2012). Technical debt: Where are the shareholders' interests? *IEEE Software, 29*(6), 88. doi:10.1109/MS.2012.166

Consumer Internet Traffic 2012-2017. (2014). Retrieved from http://www.cisco.com/web/solutions/sp/vni/vni_forecast_highlights/index.html

Copperegg. (2014). *Uncover and resolve performance issues with cloud performance monitoring*. Retrieved from http://www.copperegg.com/product/cloud-monitoring/

Correa, G., Assuncao, P., Agostini, L., & Cruz, L. (2011). Complexity control of high efficiency video encoders for power-constrained devices. *IEEE Transactions on Consumer Electronics*, *57*(4), 1866–1874. doi:10.1109/TCE.2011.6131165

Correa, G., Assuncao, P., Agostini, L., & Cruz, L. D. S. (2013). Coding tree depth estimation for complexity reduction of HEVC. In *Proc. 2013 Data Compression Conference*. IEEE. doi:10.1109/DCC.2013.12

Correia Edward, J. (2014). SIMD + JavaScript = Faster HTML5 apps, insights from Intel visionary Moh Haghighat. *Intel Software Adrenaline*. Retrieved July 13, 2014, from: https://software.intel.com/sites/billboard/article/simd-javascript-faster-html5-apps

Cousineau, D. (2009). Fitting the three-parameter weibull distribution: review and evaluation of existing and new methods. *IEEE Transactions on Dielectrics and Electrical Insulation, 16*(1), 281-288. doi: 10.1109/TDEI.2009.4784578

CRAN-Forecast Package. (2014). Retrieved from http://CRAN.R-project.org/package=forecasting

Cranley, N., Perry, P., & Murphy, L. (2006). User perception of adapting video quality. *International Journal of Human-Computer Studies*, *64*(8), 637–647. doi:10.1016/j.ijhcs.2005.12.002

CRM - The Enterprise Cloud Computing Company. (n.d.). Retrieved from http://www.salesforce.com

Csorba, M., Meling, H., & Heegaard, P. (2010). Ant system for service deployment in private and public clouds. In *Proceeding of the 2nd worKshop on Bio-Inspired Algorithms for Distributed Systems*. ACM. doi:10.1145/1809018.1809024

Cuervo, E., Balasubramaniam, A., Cho, D. K., Wolman, A., Saroju, S., Chandra, R., & Bahl, P. (2010). Maui: Making smartphones last longer with code offload. In *Proceedings of 8th International Conference on Mobile Systems, Applications and Services*. ACM.

Cuervo, E., Balasubramanian, A., Cho, D., Wolman, A., Saroiu, S., Chandra, R., & Bahl, P. (2010). MAUI: Making smartphones last longer with code offload. In *Proceedings of the 8th International Conference on Mobile systems, applications and services* (pp. 49-62). Academic Press. doi:10.1145/1814433.1814441

Cunningham, W. (1992). The WyCash portfolio management system. In *OOPSLA '92 addendum to the proceedings on object-oriented programming systems, languages, and applications* (pp. 29–30). Vancouver, Canada: ACM. doi:10.1145/157709.157715

Curtis, B., Sappidi, J., & Szynkarski, A. (2012). Estimating the principal of an application's technical debt. *IEEE Software*, *29*(6), 34–42. doi:10.1109/MS.2012.156

Dai, J., & Zhou, Q. (2010). A PKI-based mechanism for secure and efficient access to outsourced data. In *Proceedings of 2nd International Conference on Networking and Digital Society (ICNDS)*. Academic Press.

Daly, L., & Brutzman, D. (2007, November). X3D: Extensible 3D graphics standard. *Signal Processing Magazine, IEEE*, *24*(6), 130–135. doi:10.1109/MSP.2007.905889

DASH.JS. (n.d.). Retrieved July 12, 2014, from https://github.com/Dash-Industry-Forum/dash.js

Davis, J. W. (1993). Power benchmark strategy for systems employing power management. In *Proceedings of Electronics and the Environment*. IEEE. doi:10.1109/ISEE.1993.302825

De Cicco, L. & Mascolo, S. (n.d.). *An experimental investigation of the Akamai adaptive video streaming*. HCI in Work and Learning, Life and Leisure.

De Cicco, L., Mascolo, S., & Palmisano, V. (2011). Feedback control for adaptive live video streaming. In Proceedings of MMSys'11. San Jose, CA: Academic Press. doi:10.1145/1943552.1943573

Dean, J., & Ghemawat, S. (2008, January). MapReduce: Simplified data processing on large clusters. *Communications of the ACM*, *51*(1), 1. doi:10.1145/1327452.1327492

Detti, A., Blefari Melazzi, N., Salsano, S., & Pomposini, M. (2011). *CONET: A content centric inter-networking architecture.* Paper presented at the ACM SIGCOMM Workshop on Information-Centric Networking. doi:10.1145/2018584.2018598

Developer Force: Salesforce.com & Force.com Developer Resources. (n.d.). Retrieved from http://developer.force.com/

Di Benedetto, M.-G., & Bader, F. (Eds.). (2014). *Cognitive radio and networking for heterogeneous wireless networks.* Springer.

Diaz-Sanchez, D., Sanchez, R., Lopez, A., Almenares, F., & Arias, P. (2012). A H.264 SVC distributed content protection system with flexible key stream generation. In *Proc. 2012 IEEE 2nd International Conference on Consumer Electronics - Berlin (ICCE-Berlin).* IEEE. doi:10.1109/ICCE-Berlin.2012.6336520

Dikaiakos, M. D., Katsaros, D., Mehra, P., Pallis, G., & Vakali, A. (2009). Cloud computing: Distributed internet computing for IT and scientific research. *IEEE Internet Computing, 13*(5), 10-13

Dimitriou, C. D., Mavromoustakis, C. X., Mastorakis, G., & Pallis, E. (2013, June). On the performance response of delay-bounded energy-aware bandwidth allocation scheme in wireless networks. In *Proceedings of2013 IEEE International Conference on Communications Workshops (ICC)* (pp. 631–636). Budapest: IEEE. doi:10.1109/ICCW.2013.6649310

Dinda, P. A. (2006). Design, implementation, and performance of an extensible toolkit for resource prediction in distributed systems. *IEEE Transactions on Parallel and Distributed Systems, 17*(2), 160–173.

Ding, A. Y., Han, B., Xiao, Y., Hui, P., Srinivasan, A., Kojo, M., & Tarkoma, S. (2013). Enabling energy-aware collaborative mobile data offloading for smartphones. In *Proceedings of Sensor, Mesh and Ad Hoc Communications and Networks* (SECON). IEEE.

Dinh, H.T., Lee, C., Niyato, D., & Wang, W. (2012). A survey of mobile cloud computing: Architecture, applications, and approaches. In *Wireless communications and mobile computing.* Wiley.

Dinh, H. T., Lee, C., Niyato, D., & Wang, P. (2013). A survey of mobile cloud computing: Architecture, applications, and approaches. *Wirel. Commun. Mob. Comput., 13*(18), 1587–1611. doi:10.1002/wcm.1203

Dobrian, F., Sekar, V., Awan, A., Stoica, I., Joseph, D. A., Ganjam, A., . . . Zhang, H. (2011). Understanding the impact of video quality on user engagement. In Proceedings of SIGCOMM. ACM. doi:10.1145/2018436.2018478

Doelitzscher, F., Knahl, M., Reich, C., & Clarke, N. (2013). Anomaly detection in IaaS clouds. In *Proceedings of Cloud Computing Technology and Science (CloudCom)* (vol. 1, pp. 387-394). Academic Press.

Do-kyoung, K., & Budagavi, M. (2013). Combined scalable and mutiview extension of high efficiency video coding (HEVC). In *Proc. Picture Coding Symposium (PCS) 2013* (pp. 414–417). PCS.

Doukas, C., Pliakas, T., & Maglogiannis, I. (2010). Mobile healthcare information management utilizing cloud computing and Android OS. In *Proceedings of Annual International Conference of the IEEE on Engineering in Medicine and Biology Socity (EMBC)* (pp. 1037-1040). IEEE. doi:10.1109/IEMBS.2010.5628061

Dovrolis, C., Jain, M., & Prasad, R. (n.d.). *Measurement tools for the capacity and load of internet paths.* Retrieved from http://www.cc.gatech.edu/fac/Constantinos.Dovrolis/bw-est/

Dutton, S. (2012, July 23). *Getting started with WebRTC - HTML5 rocks.* Retrieved July 12, 2014, from http://www.html5rocks.com/en/tutorials/webrtc/basics/

Dutton, S. (2013, November 4). *WebRTC in the real world: STUN, TURN and signaling - HTML5 rocks.* Retrieved July 12, 2014, from http://www.html5rocks.com/en/tutorials/webrtc/infrastructure

DynamicOps. (2014). *Operations virtualization, cloud automation, cloud management, VDI, private cloud.* Retrieved from http://www.dynamicops.com

Egi, N., Greenhalgh, A., Handley, M., Hoerdt, M., Huici, F., Mathy, L., & Papadimitriou, P. (2011). A platform for high performance and flexible virtual routers on commodity hardware. *ACM SIGCOMM Computer Communication Review Archive, 40*(1), 127-128.

Egi, E., Greenhalgh, A., Handley, M., Hoerdt, M., Huici, F., & Mathy, L. (2008). Towards high performance virtual routers on commodity hardware. In *Proc. ACM CoNEXT 2008*. ACM. doi:10.1145/1544012.1544032

Emeakaroha, V. C., Netto, M. A., Calheiros, R. N., Brandic, I., Buyya, R., & Rose, C. A. (2011). Towards autonomic detection of SLA violations in cloud infrastructures. *Future Generation Computer Systems*.

ENISA. (2012). *Report on resilience in critical cloud computing*. Retrieved July 27, 2014, from https://resilience.enisa.europa.eu/cloud-security-and-resilience/publications/critical-cloud-computing

Enomaly, Enomalism Elastic Computing Infrastructure. (n.d.). Retrieved July 10, 2014, from http://www.enomaly.com

Ercan, T. (2010). Effective use of cloud computing in educational institutions. *Procedia: Social and Behavioral Sciences*, *2*(2), 938–942. doi:10.1016/j.sbspro.2010.03.130

Ericsson White Paper. (2013). *LTE broadcast: A revenue enabler in the mobile media era*. Ericsson.

Eriksson, J., Girod, L., Hull, B., Newton, R., Madden, S., & Balakrishnan, H. (2008). The pothole patrol: Using a mobile sensor network for road surface monitoring. In *Proceedings of the 6th International Conference on Mobile Systems, Applications, and Services* (pp. 29-39). ACM. doi:10.1145/1378600.1378605

Ernst & Young. (2011). *Cloud computing issues and impacts*. Ernst and Young.

Eslami, M., Elliott, R.C., Krzymień W.A., & Al-Shalash, N. (2013). Location-assisted clustering and scheduling for coordinated homogeneous and heterogeneous cellular networks. *Transactions on Emerging Telecommunications Technologies*, *24*(1), 84–101.

Esteban, J., Benno, S., Beck, A., Guo, Y., Hilt, V., & Rimac, I. (2012). Interactions between HTTP adaptive streaming and TCP. In *Proc. NOSSDAV*. Academic Press.

EU FP7 ANIKETOS. (2012). Retrieved July 27, 2014, from http://www.aniketos.eu/

EU FP7 NEMESYS. (2012). Retrieved July 27, 2014, from http://www.nemesys-project.eu//

EU SECCRIT. (2011). Retrieved July 27, 2014, from https://www.seccrit.eu/

Fabbrizio, G. D., Okken, T., & Wilpon, J. G. (2009). A speech mashup framework for multimodal mobile devices. In *Proceedings of the 2009 International Conference on Multimodal Interfaces (ICMI-MLMI)* (pp. 71-78). Academic Press. doi:10.1145/1647314.1647329

Facebook. (n.d.). Retrieved from http://www.facebook.com

Fajjari, I., Aitsaadi, N., Pujolle, G., & Zimmermann, H. (2012). An optimised dynamic resource allocation algorithm for cloud's backbone network. In *Proceedings of IEEE 37th Conference on Local Computer Networks* (LCN). IEEE.

Fang, J., Chen, Z., Liao, T., & Chang, P. (2014). A fast pu mode decision algorithm for h.264/avc to hevc transcoding. In *Proc. Second International Conference on Signal, Image Processing and Pattern Recognition (SIPP 2014)*. Academic Press. doi:10.5121/csit.2014.4218

Fang, Z. (2010). *Resource management on cloud systems with machine learning*. (Master Thesis). Barcelona School of Informatics, Technical University of Catalonia.

Fawcelt, T. (2006). An introduction to ROC analysis. *Pattern Recognition Letters*, *27*(8), 861–874. doi:10.1016/j.patrec.2005.10.010

Fernando, N., Loke, S., & Rahayu, W. (2012, June). Mobile cloud computing: A survey. Elsevier.

Fernando, N., Loke, S. W., & Rahayu, W. (2013). Mobile cloud computing: A survey. *Future Generation Computer Systems Journal, Elsevier*, *29*(1), 84–106. doi:10.1016/j.future.2012.05.023

Ferzli, R., & Khalife, I. (2011). Mobile cloud computing educational tool for image/video processing algorithms. In *Proceedings of Digital Signal Processing Workshop and IEEE Signal Processing Education Workshop (DSP/SPE)*. IEEE.

FI-WARE. (2014). *FI-WARE interface to networks and devices (I2ND)*. Retrieved from http://forge.fi-ware.eu/plugins/mediawiki/wiki/fiware/index.php/FI-WARE_Interface_to_Networks_and_Devices_(I2ND)

FlexiScale Cloud Comp and Hosting. (2014). Retrieved from http://www.flexiscale.com

Flickr. (n.d.). Retrieved from http://www.flickr.com/

Fontugne, R., Tremblay, N., Borgnat, P., Flandrin, P., & Esaki, H., (2013). Mining anomalous electricity consumption using ensemble empirical mode decomposition. In *Proceedings of IEEE ICASSP*. IEEE.

Forman, G.H. & Zahorjan, J. (1994, April). The challenges of mobile computing. *IEEE Computer Society Magazine*.

Foster, I., & Kesselman, C. (1997). Globus: A metacomputing infrastructure toolkit. *International Journal of Supercomputer Applications*. Retrieved July 10, 2014, from http://www.globus.org/ftppub/globus/papers/globus.pdf

Foster, I., & Kesselman, C. (Eds.). (1998). *The grid – Blueprint for a new computing infrastructure*. Morgan Kaufmann.

Fowler, M. (2003, October 1). *TechnicalDebt*. Retrieved April 12, 2014, from http://www.martinfowler.com/bliki/TechnicalDebt.html

Fowler, M., Opdyke, W., & Roberts, D. (1999). *Refactoring: Improving the design of existing code*. Pearson Education India.

Fox, A., Griffith, R., Joseph, A., Katz, R., Konwinski, A., Lee, G., . . . Stoica, I. (2009). Above the clouds: A Berkeley view of cloud computing. Dept. Electrical Eng. and Comput. Sciences, University of California, Berkeley, Rep. UCB/EECS, 28, 13.

Fraunhofer-HHI. (2014a). *HEVC 4K real-time software decoder*. Retrieved May 18, 2014, from http://www.hhi.fraunhofer.de/fields-of-competence/image-processing/solutions/hevc-software-and-hardware-solutions/hevc-4k-real-time-decoder.html

Fraunhofer-HHI. (2014b). *Real-time software encoding up to 1080p60*. Retrieved May 18, 2014, from http://www.hhi.fraunhofer.de/fields-of-competence/image-processing/solutions/hevc-software-and-hardware-solutions/hevc-real-time-software-encoder.html

Freire, M., & Pereira, M. (2008). *Encyclopedia of Internet technologies and applications*. IGI Global. doi:10.4018/978-1-59140-993-9

Frey, S., & Hasselbring, W. (2010, November). Model-based migration of legacy software systems to scalable and resource-efficient cloud-based applications: The cloudmig approach. In *Proceedings of CLOUD COMPUTING 2010, The First International Conference on Cloud Computing, GRIDs, and Virtualization* (pp. 155-158). Academic Press.

Fu, Y., Lu, C., & Wang, H. (2009). Control-theoretic thermal balancing for clusters. In *Proceedings ofInternational Workshop on Feedback Control Implementation and Design in Computing Systems and Networks* (FeBID'09). Academic Press.

Fu, Y., Lu, C., & Wang, H. (2010). Robust control-theoretic thermal balancing for server clusters. In *Proceedings ofIEEE International Parallel and Distributed Processing Symposium* (IPDPS'10). IEEE. doi:10.1109/IPDPS.2010.5470480

Ganglia. (2000). *The Ganglia monitoring system*. Retrieved July 27, 2014, from http://ganglia.sourceforge.net/

Gannon, D., Bramley, R., Fox, G., Smallen, S., Rossi, A., Ananthakrishnan, R., & Govindaraju, N. et al. (2002). Programming the grid: Distributed software components, p2p and grid web services for scientific applications. *Cluster Computing*, *5*(3), 325–336. doi:10.1023/A:1015633507128

Gao, P., Liu, T., Chen, Y., Wu, X., El-khatib, Y., & Edwards, C. (2009). The measurement and modeling of a P2P streaming video service. In Proceedings of Networks for Grid Applications (LNICS). Berlin: Springer.

Garcia, R., & Kalva, H. (2014). Subjective evaluation of HEVC and AVC/H.264 in mobile environments. *IEEE Transactions on Consumer Electronics*, *60*(1), 116–123. doi:10.1109/TCE.2014.6780933

Garnaeva, M. (2012). Kelihos/Hlux botnet returns with new techniques. *Securelist*. Retrieved July 27, 2014, from, http://www.securelist.com/en/blog/655/Kelihos_Hlux_botnet_returns_with_new_techniques

Gartner. (2013). *Gartner identifies the top 10 strategic technology trends for 2014*. Retrieved May 18, 2014, from http://www.gartner.com/newsroom/id/2603623

Gartner. (2014). Retrieved from http://www.gartner.com/it/page.jsp?id=1389313

Gençay, R., Selçuk, F., & Whitcher, B. (2001). An introduction to wavelets and other filtering methods in finance and economics. Academic Press.

GEYSERS. (2014). *Generalised architecture for dynamic infrastructure services*. Retrieved from http://www.geysers.eu/

Ghobadi, M., Cheng, Y., Jain, A., & Mathis, M. (2012). Trickle: Rate limiting YouTube video streaming. In *Proc. USENIX ATC*. Academic Press.

Gkatzikis, L., & Koutsopoulos, I. (2013). Migrate or not? Exploiting dynamic task migration in mobile cloud computing systems. IEEE Wireless Communications, 20(3).

Godse, M., & Mulik, S. An approach for selecting software-as-a-service (SaaS) product. In *Proceedings of the IEEE International Conference on Cloud Computing (CLOUD '09)* (pp. 155–158). IEEE. doi:10.1109/CLOUD.2009.74

Goleva, R., & Mirtchev, S. (2010). Traffic modeling in disruption-tolerant networks. In *Proceedings of Annual Seminar of the PTT College, Modeling and Control of Information Processes*. Academic Press.

Goleva, R., Atamian, D., Mirtchev, S., Dimitrova, D., & Grigorova, L. (2013). Traffic shaping measurements and analyses in 3G network. In *Proceedings of the 2nd ACM Workshop on High Performance Mobile Opportunistic Systems HP-MOSys '13*. ACM. http://doi.acm.org/10.1145/2507908.2507916

Goleva, R., Atamian, D., Mirtchev, S., Dimitrova, D., & Grigorova, L. (2012). Traffic sources measurement and analysis in UMTS. In *Proceedings of the 1st ACM Workshop on High Performance Mobile Opportunistic Systems HP-MOSys '12* (pp. 29-32). ACM. doi:10.1145/2386980.2386987

Google App Engine. (2008). Retrieved July 27, 2014, from http://cloud.google.com/products/app-engine/

Google App Engine. (2014). Retrieved from http://code.google.com/appengine

Google Apps for Business. (n.d.). Retrieved from http://www.google.com/apps/intl/en/business/index.html

Google. (2014). *Google app engine*. Retrieved from http://code.google.com/intl/el-GR/appengine

Google + Hangouts. (n.d.). Retrieved July 12, 2014, from http://www.google.com/+/learnmore/hangouts/

Gouache, S., Bichot, G., Bsila, A., & Howson, C. (2012). Distributed and adaptive HTTP streaming. In *Proc. ICME Harmonic Mean*. Retrieved from http://en.wikipedia.org/wiki/Harmonic_mean

Grosch, H. (1950). *Proceedings of the 1948 scientific computation forum*. IBM.

Group, E. (2010). *The future of cloud computing: Opportunities for European cloud computing beyond 2010*. Author.

Gruschka, N., & Jensen, M. (2010). Attack surfaces: A taxonomy for attacks on cloud services. In *Proceedings of Cloud Computing (CLOUD)*. IEEE.

Gu, C. D., Lu, K., Wu, J. P., Fu, Y. L., Li, J. X., Xiao, C. S., . . . Liu, Z. B. (2011). The investigation of cloud computing based image mining mechanism in mobie communication WEB on Android. In *Proceedings of the 9th International Conference on Grid and Cooperative Computing (GCC)*. Academic Press.

Guan, Q., Fu, S., DeBardeleben, N., & Blanchard, S. (2013). Exploring time and frequency domains for accurate and automated anomaly detection in cloud computing systems. In *Proceedings of Dependable Computing (PRDC)*. IEEE.

Guan, X., & Choi, B.-Y. (2014). Push or pull? Toward optimal content delivery using cloud storage. *Journal of Network and Computer Applications*, *40*, 234–243. doi:10.1016/j.jnca.2013.09.003

Halas, M., Javorcek, L., & Kováč, A. (2012). Impact of SRTP protocol on VoIP call quality. In *Proceedings ofWorkshop of the 12th International Conference KTTO 2012*. Malenovice, Czech Republic: KTTO.

Harris, D. (2012). What Google compute engine means for cloud computing. In *GigaOM - Tech news, analysis and trends*. Academic Press.

Harsini, J. S., & Lahouti, F. (2012). Effective capacity optimization for multiuser diversity systems with adaptive transmission. *Transactions on Emerging Telecommunications Technologies*, *23*(6), 567–584. doi:10.1002/ett.2511

Hasenfratz, D., Saukh, O., Sturzenegger, S., & Thiele, L. (2012). Participatory air pollution monitoring using smartphones. In *Proceedings of2nd International Workshop on Mobile Sensing*. Academic Press.

Hat, R. (2014). *Red hat KVM*. Retrieved from http://www.redhat.com/virtualization/rhev

Havey, D., Chertov, R., & Almeroth, K. (2012). Receiver driven rate adaptation for wireless multimedia applications. In Proc. MMSys. Academic Press. doi:10.1145/2155555.2155582

Hay Systems. (n.d.). Retrieved from http://www.haysystems.com/

Haykin, S. (2005). Cognitive radio: Brain-empowered wireless communications. *IEEE Journal on Selected Areas in Communications*, *23*(2), 201–220.

Hazari, G., Karandikar, P., & Sanghvi, H. (2014). Performance estimation and architecture exploration of a video IP design in a smart phone SoC context. In *Proc. 2014 IEEE International Conference on Electronics, Computing and Communication Technologies (IEEE CONECCT)*. IEEE.

Hazewinkel, M. (Ed.). (2001). *Encyclopaedia of mathematics*. Kluwer.

He, Y., Kunstner, M., Gudumasu, S., Ryu, E., Ye, Y., & Xiu, X. (2013). Power aware HEVC streaming for mobile. In Proc. Visual Communications and Image Processing (VCIP) 2013. Academic Press.

He, J., Wen, Y., Huang, J., & Wu, D. (2014). On the cost – QoE tradeoff for cloud-based video streaming under Amazon EC2's pricing models. *IEEE Transactions on Circuits and Systems for Video Technology*, *24*(4), 1–3. doi:10.1109/TCSVT.2013.2283430

He, J., Wu, D., Zeng, Y., Hei, X., & Wen, Y. (2013). Toward optimal deployment of cloud-assisted video distribution services. *IEEE Transactions on Circuits and Systems for Video Technology*, *23*(10), 1717–1728. doi:10.1109/TCSVT.2013.2255423

Hellerstein, J. L., Singhal, S., & Wang, Q. (2009). Research challenges in control engineering of computing systems. *IEEE Transactions on Network and Management*, *6*(4), 206–211.

Hellerstein, J., Diao, Y., Parekh, S., & Tilbury, D. M. (2004). *Feedback control of computing systems*. John Wiley & Sons. doi:10.1002/047166880X

Hellge, C., Gómez-barquero, D., Schierl, T., & Wiegand, T. (2011). Layer-aware forward error correction for mobile broadcast of layered media. *IEEE Transactions on Multimedia*, *13*(3), 551–562. doi:10.1109/TMM.2011.2129499

Heo, J., Zhu, X., Padala, P., & Wang, Z. (2009). Memory overbooking and dynamic control of xen virtual machines in consolidated environments. In *Proceedings of the IFIP/IEEE Symposium on Integrated Management* (IM'09) (pp. 630–637). IEEE.

He, Q., Dovrolis, C., & Ammar, M. (2005). On the predictability of large transfer TCP throughput. In *Proc. ACM SIGCOMM*. ACM. doi:10.1145/1080091.1080110

Hicks, J., Ramanathan, N., Kim, D., Monibi, M., Selsky, J., Hansen, M., & Estrin, D. (2010). *AndWellness: An open mobile system for activity and experience sampling*. New York, NY: ACM. doi:10.1145/1921081.1921087

Hickson, I. (Ed.). (2012, May 1). *Web workers*. Retrieved July 12, 2014, from W3C Candidate Recommendation: http://www.w3.org/TR/workers/

Hickson, I. (Ed.). (2012, September 20). *The WebSocket API - W3C*. Retrieved July 13, 2014, from W3C Candidate Recommendation: http://www.w3.org/TR/2012/CR-websockets-20120920/

Hickson, I. (Ed.). (2013, July 30). *Web storage*. Retrieved July 12, 2014, from Web Storage, W3C Recommendation: http://www.w3.org/TR/webstorage/

Hilley, D. (2009). *Cloud computing: A taxonomy of platform and infrastructure-level offerings*. Georgia Institute of Technology. Retrieved from http://gigaom.com/cloud/what-google-compute-engine-means-for-cloud-computing/

HM. (2014). *HEVC reference software*. Retrieved May 22, 2014, from https://hevc.hhi.fraunhofer.de/

Holly, R. (2011). *How much of your phone is yours?*. Retrieved May 2014 from http://www.geek.com/mobile/how-much-of-your-phone-is-yours-1440611/

Hong, J., Suh, E., & Kim, S.-J. (2009). Context-aware systems: A literature review and classification. *Expert Systems with Applications, 36*(4), 8509–8522. doi:10.1016/j.eswa.2008.10.071

HORIZON2020. (2014). The EU framework program for research and innovation. *HORIZON, 2020*. Retrieved from http://ec.europa.eu/programmes/en

Houdaille, R., & Gouache, S. (2012). Shaping http adaptive streams for a better user experience. In Proc. MMSys. Academic Press. doi:10.1145/2155555.2155557

Houidi, I., Louati, W., Bean-Ameur, W., & Zeghlache, D. (2011). Virtual network provisioning across multiple substrate networks. *Computer Networks, 55*(4), 1011–1023. doi:10.1016/j.comnet.2010.12.011

Houidi, I., Louati, W., & Zeghlache, D. (2009). Virtual resource description and clustering for virtual network. In *Proc. IEEE ICC, Workshop Network of the Future*. IEEE. doi:10.1109/ICCW.2009.5207979

Houidi, I., Louati, W., Zeghlache, D., Papadimitriou, P., & Mathy, L. (2010). Adaptive virtual network provisioning. In *Proc. of the Second ACM SIGCOMM Workshop on Virtualized Infrastructure Systems and Architectures (VISA '10)*. ACM. doi:10.1145/1851399.1851407

Hsueh, S., Lin, J., & Lin, M. (2011). Secure cloud storage for convenient data archive of smart phones. In *Proc. 2011 IEEE 15th International Symposium on Consumer Electronics (ISCE)* (pp. 156–161). IEEE. doi:10.1109/ISCE.2011.5973804

Huang, D. (2011) Mobile cloud computing. IEEE COMSOC MMTC E-Letter, 1(4).

Huang, N. E., & Attoh-Okine, N. O. (2005). *The Hilbert-Huang transform in engineering*. CRC Taylor & Francis.

Huang, T.-Y., Handigol, N., Heller, B., McKeown, N., & Johari, R. (2012). Confused, timid, and unstable: Picking a video streaming rate is hard. In *Proc. IMC. IMC.* doi:10.1145/2398776.2398800

Huerta Canepa, G., & Lee, D. (2010). A virtual cloud computing provider for mobile devices. In *Proceedings of 1st ACM Workshop on Mobile Cloud Computing and Services: Social Networks and Beyond (MCS)*. ACM. doi:10.1145/1810931.1810937

Huerta-Canepa, G., & Lee, D. (2010). A virtual cloud computing provider for mobile devices. In *Proceedings of the 1st ACM Workshop on Mobile Cloud Computing & Services: Social Networks and Beyond* (MCS '10). ACM. http://doi.acm.org/10.1145/1810931.1810937

Huerta-Canepa, G., & Lee, D. (2010). A virtual cloud computing provider for mobile devices. In *Proceedings of the 1st ACM Workshop on Mobile Cloud Computing and Services: Social Networks and Beyond.* ACM.

Hu, F., Mostashari, A., & Xie, J. (Eds.). (2010). *Socio-technical networks: Science and engineering design.* CRC Press.

Hu, M., Luo, J., Wang, Y., & Veeravalli, B. (2014). Practical resource provisioning and caching with dynamic resilience for cloud-based content distribution networks. *IEEE Transactions on Parallel and Distributed Systems, 25*(8), 2169–2179. doi:10.1109/TPDS.2013.287

Hu, N., & Yang, E. (2014). Fast motion estimation based on confidence interval. *IEEE Transactions on Circuits and Systems for Video Technology, 24*(8), 1310–1322. doi:10.1109/TCSVT.2014.2306035

Hyndman, R. J., & Khandakar, Y. (2007). *Automatic time series for forecasting: The forecast package for R.* Monash University, Department of Econometrics and Business Statistics.

Hyndman, R. J., King, M. L., Pitrun, I., & Billah, B. (2005). Local linear forecasts using cubic smoothing splines. *Australian & New Zealand Journal of Statistics, 47*(1), 87–99. doi:10.1111/j.1467-842X.2005.00374.x

IDC. (2014). Retrieved from http://www.idc.com/research/cloudcomputing/index.jsp

Industry Forum , D. A. S. H. (n.d.). Retrieved July 12, 2014, from http://dashif.org/

Intel. (2006, June). *Dual-core Intel Xeon processor 5100 series thermal/mechanical design guide*. Retrieved June 20, 2014 from http://www.intel.com/content/dam/www/public/us/en/documents/design-guides/xeon-5100-thermal-guide.pdf

Internet Speech Audio Codec. (n.d.). Retrieved July 12, 2014, from http://en.wikipedia.org/wiki/Internet_Speech_Audio_Codec

Irondi, I., Wang, Q., & Grecos, C. (2014). Empirical evaluation of H.265/HEVC based dynamic adaptive video streaming over HTTP (HEVC-DASH). In *Proc. SPIE Photonics Europe 2014: Real-Time Image and Video Processing (Conference EPE115)* (Vol. 2). SPIE.

Isard, M., Budiu, M., Yu, Y., Birrell, A., & Fetterly, D. (2007). Dryad: Distributed data-parallel programs from sequentia building blocks. In *Proceedings of EuroSys 2007*. Academic Press.

Islam, S., & Grégoire, J.-C. (2012). Giving users an edge: A flexible cloud model and its application for multimedia. *Future Generation Computer Systems*, *28*(6), 823–832. doi:10.1016/j.future.2012.01.002

ISO/IEC (2007). *Information technology — Generic coding of moving pictures and associated audio information: Part 1: Systems*. International Standard 13818-1:2007.

ISO/IEC (2014a). *Information technology — Dynamic Adaptive Streaming over HTTP (DASH) — Part 1: Media presentation description and segment formats*. International Standard 23009-1:2014.

ISO/IEC (2014b). *Information technology — High efficiency coding and media delivery in heterogeneous environments — Part 1: MPEG media transport (MMT)*. Final Draft International Standard (FDIS) 23008-1:2014.

ISO/IEC 14772-1:1997. (n.d.). *Information technology -- Computer graphics and image processing -- The virtual reality modeling language -- Part 1: Functional specification and UTF-8 encoding*.

ISO/IEC 23009-1:2012E. (2012, April). *DASH — Part 1: Media presentation description and segment formats: Dynamic adaptive streaming over HTTP*. ISO.

ISO/IEC 23009-1:2014. (n.d.). *Information technology -- Dynamic adaptive streaming over HTTP (DASH) -- Part 1: Media presentation description and segment formats*.

IT Monitoring. (n.d.). Retrieved from http://portal.monitis.com/

Itani, W., Kayssi, A., & Chehab, A. (2010). Energy-efficient incremental integrity for securing storage in mobile cloud computing. In *Proc. 2010 International Conference on Energy Aware Computing (ICEAC)*. Academic Press. doi:10.1109/ICEAC.2010.5702296

ITSM-Network Monitoring + Service Desk Management. (n.d.). Retrieved from http://www.nimsoft.com

ITU-T (2012). *Advanced video coding for generic audio-visual services*. ITU-T Recommendation H.264.

ITU-T (2013). *High efficiency video coding*. ITU-T Recommendation H.265.

IU-ATC Project. (2008). Retrieved July 27, 2014, from http://www.iu-atc.com

Jackson, D. (Ed.). (2014, July 1). *WebGL specification*. Retrieved July 12, 2014, from WebGL Specification, Khronos Group, Editor's Draft: http://www.khronos.org/registry/webgl/specs/latest/1.0/

Jackson, D. (Ed.). (2014, July 2). *WebGL 2 specification*. Retrieved July 12, 2014, from WebGL 2 Specification, Khronos Group, Editor's Draft: http://www.khronos.org/registry/webgl/specs/latest/2.0/

Jacobson, V., Smetters, D. K., Thornton, J. D., Plass, M. F., Briggs, N. H., & Braynard, R. L. (2009). *Networking named content*. Paper presented at the 5th International Conference on Emerging Networking Experiments and Technologies. doi:10.1145/1658939.1658941

Jain, A., Mann, J., Wang, Z., & Quach, A. (Eds.). (2014, June 24). *Resource timing, W3C candidate recommendation*. Retrieved July 12, 2014, from http://www.w3.org/TR/resource-timing/

Jarschel, M., Schlosser, D., Scheuring, S., & Hoßfeld, T. (2013). Gaming in the clouds: QoE and the users' perspective. *Mathematical and Computer Modelling*, *57*(11-12), 2883–2894. doi:10.1016/j.mcm.2011.12.014

Javadi, B., Thulasiraman, P., & Buyya, R. (2012, June). Cloud resource provisioning to extend the capacity of local resources in the presence of failures. In *Proceedings of High Performance Computing and Communication & 2012 IEEE 9th International Conference on Embedded Software and Systems* (HPCC-ICESS) (pp. 311-319). IEEE. doi:10.1109/HPCC.2012.49

Javier Carmona-Murillo, J.-L. G.-S.-P.-J.-P. (2014). QoS in next generation mobile networks: An analytical study. In Resource management in mobile computing environments (pp. 25-41). Springer.

Jeffery, R., Ruhe, M., & Wieczorek, I. (2000). A comparative study of two software development cost modeling techniques using multi-organizational and company-specific data. *Information and Software Technology*, *42*(14), 1009–1016. doi:10.1016/S0950-5849(00)00153-1

Jennings, C., Hardie, T., & Westerlund, M. (2013, April). Real-time communications for the web. *Communications Magazine, IEEE*, *51*(4), 20–26. doi:10.1109/MCOM.2013.6495756

Jiang, J., Sekar, V., & Zhang, H. (2012, December). Improving fairness, efficiency, and stability in HTTP-based adaptive video streaming with FESTIN. In *Proc. CoNEXT'12. Academic Press.* doi:10.1145/2413176.2413189

Jia, W., Zhu, H., Cao, Z., Wei, L., & Lin, X. (2011). SDSM: A secure data service mechanism in mobile cloud computing. In *Proc. 2011 IEEE Conference on Computer Communications Workshops (INFOCOM WKSHPS)* (pp. 1060–1065). IEEE. doi:10.1109/INFCOMW.2011.5928784

Jin, X., & Kwok, Y. K. (2011) Cloud assisted P2P media streaming for bandwidth constrained mobile subscribers. In *Proceedings of the 16th IEEE International Conference on Parallel and Distributed Systems (ICPADS)*. IEEE.

JM. (2014). *H.264/AVC reference software*. Retrieved May 22, 2014, from http://iphome.hhi.de/suehring/tml/index.htm

Jokhio, F., Ashraf, A., Lafond, S., Porres, I., & Lilius, J. (2013). Prediction-based dynamic resource allocation for video transcoding in cloud computing. In *Proceedings of 2013 21st Euromicro International Conference on Parallel, Distributed, and Network-Based Processing*. Academic Press. doi:10.1109/PDP.2013.44

Jones, M. T. (2009). *Cloud computing with Linux*. Retrieved July 10, 2014, from http://www.ibm.com/developerworks/linux/library/l-cloud-computing/index.html

Jung, Y., Behr, J., & Graf, H. (2011). X3Dom as carrier of the virtual heritage. In *Proceedings of the 4th ISPRS International Workshop 3D-ARCH*. Academic Press.

Jung, E., Wang, Y., Prilepov, I., Maker, F., Liu, X., & Akella, V. (2010). User-profile-driven-collaborative bandwidth sharing on mobile phones. In *Proceedings of the 1st ACM Workshop on Mobile Cloud Computing & Services: Social Networks and Beyond (MCS)*. ACM.

Kai, W., Ying, W., & Bo, Y. (2012), A density-based anomaly detection method for MapReduce. In *Proceedings of Network Computing and Applications (NCA)*. IEEE.

Kakerow, R. (2003). Low power design methodologies for mobile communication. In *Proceedings of IEEE International Conference on Computer Design: VLSI in Computers and Processors*. IEEE. doi:10.1109/ICCD.2002.1106739

Kapetanakis, K., & Panagiotakis, S. (2012). Efficient energy consumption's measurement on android devices. In *Proceedings of the 2nd International Workshop on Mobile Device Software Development and Web Development – MDSD 2012 (in Conjunction with the 16th PanHellenic Conference on Informatics - PCI 2012)*. Piraeus, Greece: MDSD. doi:10.1109/PCi.2012.29

Kapetanakis, K., & Panagiotakis, S. (2012). Evaluation of techniques for web 3D graphics animation on portable devices. In *Proceedings of the 5th IEEE International Conference on Telecommunications and Multimedia (TEMU) 2012*. Heraklion, Greece: IEEE. doi:10.1109/TEMU.2012.6294708

Kapetanakis, K., Panagiotakis, S., & Malamos, A. G. (2013). HTML5 and WebSockets: Challenges in network 3D collaboration. In *Proceedings of the 3D International Workshop on Mobile Device Software Development and Web Development – MDSD 2013 (in Conjunction with the 17th PanHellenic Conference on Informatics - PCI 2013)*. Thessaloniki, Greece: MDSD. doi:10.1145/2491845.2491888

Kapetanakis, K., Andrioti, H., Vonorta, H., Zotos, M., Tsigkos, N., & Pachoulakis, I. (2013). Collaboration framework in the EViE-m platform. In *Proceedings of the 14th European Association for Education in Electrical and Information Engineering (EAEEIE)*. Chania, Greece: EAEEIE. doi:10.1109/EAEEIE.2013.6576525

Katsaros, K., Xylomenos, G., & Polyzos, G. C. (2011). MultiCache: An overlay architecture for information-centric networking. *Computer Networks, 55*(4), 936–947. doi:10.1016/j.comnet.2010.12.012

Katzela, I., & Naghshineh, M. (1996). Channel assignment schemes for cellular mobile telecommunication systems: A comprehensive survey. *IEEE Personal Communications, 3*(3), 10-31.

Katzis, K., Pearce, D. A. J., & Grace, D. (2004, February). Fixed channel allocation techniques exploiting cell overlap for high altitude platforms. In *Proceedings of the Fifth European Wireless Conference Mobile and Wireless Systems beyond 3G*. Barcelona, Spain: Academic Press.

Katzis, K., Pearce, D. A. J., & Grace, D. (2004, September). Fairness in channel allocation in a high altitude platform communication system exploiting cellular overlap. In *Proceedings ofWireless Personal Multimedia Communications Conference* (WPMC). Abano Terme, Italy: Academic Press.

Katzis, K., Papanikolaou, K., & Iakovou, M. (2013). Reinforcement learning in hierarchical cognitive radio wireless networks. In *Proceedings of the 2nd ACM Workshop on High Performance Mobile Opportunistic Systems (HP-MOSys '13)*. ACM. doi:10.1145/2507908.2507910

Keahey, K., Foster, I., Freeman, T., & Zhang, X. (2005). Virtual workspaces: Achieving quality of service and quality of life in the grid. *Sci. Program., 13*(4), 265–275.

Keahey, K., Tsugawa, M., Matsunaga, A., & Fortes, J. (2009). Sky computing. *IEEE Internet Computing Magazine, 13*(5), 43–51. doi:10.1109/MIC.2009.94

Kemp, R., Palmer, N., Kielmann, T., & Bal, H. (2012). Cuckoo: A computation offloading framework for smartphones mobile computing, applications, and services. In Proceedings of Social Informatics and Telecommunications Engineering (LNICS), (vol. 76, pp. 59–79). Springer.

Kerievsky, J. (2005). *Refactoring to patterns*. Pearson Deutschland GmbH.

Khajeh-Hosseini, A., Sommerville, I., Bogaerts, J., & Teregowda, P. (2011, July). Decision support tools for cloud migration in the enterprise. In *Proceedings of Cloud Computing* (CLOUD) (pp. 541-548). IEEE.

Khamayseh, Y. M., BaniYassein, M., AbdAlghani, M., & Mavromoustakis, C. X. (2013). Network size estimation in VANETs. *Network Protocols and Algorithms, 5*(3), 136–152. doi:10.5296/npa.v5i3.3838

Khan, A. U., Orioe, M., & Kiran, M. (2013b). Threat methodology for securing scalable video in the cloud. In *Proc. 8th International Conference for Internet Technology and Secured Transactions (ICITST-2013)* (pp. 428–436). Academic Press. doi:10.1109/ICITST.2013.6750237

Khan, A.R., Othman, M., Madani, S.A., & Khan, S.U. (2014). A survey of mobile cloud computing application models. *IEEE Communications Surveys & Tutorials, 16*(1), 393-413.

Khan, A. N., Mat Kiah, M. L., Khan, S. U., & Madani, S. (2013a). Towards secure mobile cloud computing: A survey. *Future Generation Computer Systems, 29*(5), 1278–1299. doi:10.1016/j.future.2012.08.003

Khan, A., Othman, M., Madani, S., & Khan, S. (2013). *A survey of mobile cloud computing application models*. IEEE Communication Surveys and Tutorials.

Khan, M. U. K., Shafique, M., & Henkel, J. (2014). Software architecture of High Efficiency Video Coding for many-core systems with power-efficient workload balancing. *Design, Automation, & Test in Europe Conference & Exhibition, 2014*, 1–6. doi:10.7873/DATE.2014.232

Kitchenham, B. A., & Taylor, N. R. (1985). Software project development cost estimation. *Journal of Systems and Software, 5*(4), 267–278. doi:10.1016/0164-1212(85)90026-3

Klein, A., Mannweiler, C., Schneider, J., & Hans, D. (2010). Access schemes for mobile cloud computing. In *Proceedings of the 11th International Conference on Mobile Data Management (MDM)*. Academic Press.

Klinger, T., Tarr, P., Wagstrom, P., & Williams, C. (2011). An enterprise perspective on technical debt. In *Proceedings of the 2nd Workshop on Managing Technical Debt (MTD '11)* (pp. 35–38). ACM.

Ko, C.-H., Huang, D. H., & Wu, S-H. (2011). Cooperative spectrum sensing in TV white spaces: When cognitive radio meets cloud. In *Proceedings of Computer Communications Workshops* (INFOCOM WKSHPS). IEEE.

Kopec, D., Kabir, M. H., Reinharth, D., Rothschild, O., & Castiglione, J. A. (2003). Human errors in medical practice: Systematic classification and reduction with automated information systems. *Journal of Medical Systems*, *27*(August), 297–313. doi:10.1023/A:1023796918654 PMID:12846462

Koponen, T., Chawla, M., Chun, B.-G., Ermolinskiy, A., Kim, K. H., Shenker, S., & Stoica, I. (2007). A data-oriented (and beyond) network architecture. *Computer Communication Review*, *37*(4), 181–192. doi:10.1145/1282427.1282402

Koslovski, G., Vicat, P., & Primet, B. (2008). VXDL: Virtual resources and interconnection networks description language. In *Proc. GridNets 2008*. Academic Press.

Kostas, K., Panagiotakis, S., Malamos, A. G., & Zampoglou, M. (2014) Special session on "3D multimedia transmission over future networks," adaptive video streaming on top of Web3D: A bridging technology between X3DOM and MPEG-DASH. In *Proceedings of2014 International Conference on Telecommunications and Multimedia (TEMU)*. Academic Press.

Kostiainen, A. (Ed.). (2014, June 19). *Vibration API*. Retrieved July 12, 2014, from Vibration API, W3C Last Call Working Draft: http://www.w3.org/TR/vibration/

Kostiainen, A., & Lamouri, M. (Eds.). (2012, May 8). *Battery status API*. Retrieved July 12, 2014, from Battery Status API, W3C Candidate Recommendation: http://www.w3.org/TR/battery-status/

Kostiainen, A., & Tran, D. D. (Eds.). (2013, October 1). *Proximity events*. Retrieved July 12, 2014, from Proximity Events, W3C Candidate Recommendation: http://www.w3.org/TR/proximity/

Koumaras, H., Negru, D., Borcoci, E., Koumaras, V., Troulos, C., Lapid, Y., & Gardikis, G. (2011). *Media ecosystems: A novel approach for content-awareness in future networks*. Springer.

Kraft, R., Maghoul, F., & Chang, C.-C. (2005). Y!Q: Contextual search at the point of inspiration. In O. Herzog, H.-J. Schek, N. Fuhr, A. Chowdhury, & W. Teiken (Eds.), CIKM (pp. 816-823). ACM.

Kremer, U., Hicks, J., & Rehg, J. (2001). A compilation framework for power and energy management on mobile computers. In *Proceedings of the 14th International Conference on Languages and Compliers for Parallel Computing* (pp. 115 – 131). Academic Press.

Kreyszig, E. (1979). *Applied mathematics* (4th ed.). Wiley Press.

Kruchten, P., Nord, R. L., & Ozkaya, I. (2012). Technical debt: From metaphor to theory and practice. *IEEE Software*, *29*(6), 18–21. doi:10.1109/MS.2012.167

Kumar, K., & Lu, Y-H. (2010). Cloud computing for mobile users: Can offloading computation save energy?. *Computer, 43*(4), 51-56.

Kumar, K., Liu, J., Lu, Y.-H., & Bhargava, B. (2013, February). A survey of computation offloading for mobile systems. *Mobile Networks and Applications*, *18*(1), 129–140. doi:10.1007/s11036-012-0368-0

Kumar, K., & Lu, Y. H. (2010). Cloud computing for mobile users: Can offloading computation save energy. *Computer Magazine IEEE*, *43*(4), 51–56. doi:10.1109/MC.2010.98

Kumbalavati, S. B., & Mallapur, J. D. (2013). A survey on 4G wireless networks. *International Journal of Cognitive Science, Engineering, and Technology*, *1*(1), 31–36.

Kuschnig, R., Kofler, I., & Hellwagner, H. (2011). Evaluation of http-based request-response streams for internet video streaming. *Multimedia Systems*, 245–256.

Kwon, J. B., & Yeom, H. Y. (2002). Providing VCR functionality in staggered video broadcasting. *IEEE Transactions on Consumer Electronics*, *48*(1), 41–48.

Labs , G. (n.d.). Retrieved July 12, 2014, from http://gearcloudlabs.com/video/

Lakhina, A., Crovella, M., & Diot, C. (2004, August). Diagnosing network-wide traffic anomalies. *Computer Communication Review*, *34*(4), 219–230. doi:10.1145/1030194.1015492

Lamouri, M. (Ed.). (2014, April 10). *The network information API, W3C working group note*. Retrieved July 12, 2014, from http://www.w3.org/TR/netinfo-api/

Lane, M. D., Scott, D., Hebl, M., Guerra, R., Osherson, D., & Zimmer, H. (2008). *Introduction to statistics*. Retrieved from http://onlinestatbook.com/Online_Statistics_Education.PDF

Lane, N. D., Mohammod, M., Lin, M., Yang, X., Lu, H., & Ali, S. (2011). BeWell: A smartphone application to monitor, model and promote wellbeing. In *Proceedings of5th International ICST Conference on Pervasive Computing Technologies for Healthcare*. Academic Press. doi:10.4108/icst.pervasivehealth.2011.246161

Lao, F., Zhang, X., & Guo, Z. (2012). Parallelizing video transcoding using map-reduce-based cloud computing. In *Proceedings of2012 IEEE International Symposium on Circuits and Systems* (pp. 2905–2908). IEEE. doi:10.1109/ISCAS.2012.6271923

Laribee, D. (2009). *Using agile techniques to pay back technical debt*. MSDN Magazine.

Lasserre, S., Le Leannec, F., Taquet, J., & Nassor, E. (2014). Low-complexity intra coding for scalable extension of HEVC based on content statistics. *IEEE Transactions on Circuits and Systems for Video Technology*, *24*(8), 1375–1389. doi:10.1109/TCSVT.2014.2305513

Lavinia, A., Dobre, C., Pop, F., & Cristea, V. (2011). A failure detection system for large scale distributed systems. *International Journal of Distributed Systems and Technologies*, *2*(3), 64–87. doi:10.4018/jdst.2011070105

Lawler, G. F. (1995). *Introduction to stochastic processes*. CRC Press.

Le Grand, T., Jones, P., Huart, P., & Shabestary, T. (2013). *RTP payload format for the iSAC codec*. Retrieved July 12, 2014, from IETF: http://tools.ietf.org/html/draft-ietf-avt-rtp-isac-04

Lefurgy, C., Wang, X., & Ware, M. (2007). Server-level power control. In *Proceedings of Autonomic Computing*. Academic Press.

Leitch, R., & Stroulia, E. (2003). Understanding the economics of refactoring. In *Proceedings of5th International Workshop on Economic-Driven Software Engineering Research (EDSER-5)* (pp. 44–49). EDSER.

Letouzey, J.-L. (2012). The sqale method for evaluating technical debt. In *Proceedings of3rd International Workshop on Managing Technical Debt (ICSE 2012)*. Zurich, Switzerland: ICSE. doi:10.1109/MTD.2012.6225997

Leung, H., & Fan, Z. (2002). Software cost estimation. In Handbook of software engineering. Hong Kong Polytechnic University.

Levy, J. (2013, February 7). *Technical debt and causes of software instability*. Retrieved April 12, 2014, from http://johnlevyconsulting.com/technical-debt-and-causes-of-software-instability/

Lévy-Leduc, C., & Roueff, F. (2009). Detection and localization of change-points in high-dimensional network traffic data. *The Annals of Applied Statistics*, 3. Retrieved July 27, 2014, from http://code.google.com/p/vmitools/wiki/LibVMIIntroduction

Li, B., Xu, J., Li, H., & Wu, F. (2011). Optimized reference frame selection for video coding by cloud. In *Proceedings of 2011 IEEE 13th International Workshop on Multimedia Signal Processing* (pp. 1–5). IEEE. doi:10.1109/MMSP.2011.6093770

Li, Q., Xiao, L., & Li, Z. (2009). Adaptive management of virtualized resources in cloud computing using feedback control. In *Proceedings of the 2009,First IEEE International Conference on Information Science and Engineering* (pp. 99 - 102). Nanjing, China: IEEE.

Li, Z., O'Brien, L., Zhang, H., & Cai, R. (2014). On the conceptualization of performance evaluation of IaaS services. *IEEE Transactions on Services Computing*, (99).

Liang, F., Peng, X., & Xu, J. (2013). A light-weight HEVC encoder for image coding. In Proc. Visual Communications and Image Processing (VCIP) 2013. Academic Press. doi:10.1109/VCIP.2013.6706448

Liang, W.-Y., & Lai, P.-T. (2010). Design and implementation of a critical speed-based DVFS mechanism for the Android operating system. In *Proceedings of Embedded and Multimedia Computing* (EMC). Academic Press.

Liang, W.-Y., Lai, P.-T., & Chiou, C. (2010). An energy conservation DVFS algorithm for the Android operating system. *Journal of Convergence*, *1*(1), 93–100.

Li, H., & Hua, X. S. (2010) Melog: Mobile experience sharing through automatic multimedia blogging. In *Proceedings of the 2010 ACM Multimedia Workshop on Mobile Cloud Media Computing (MCMC)* (pp. 19-24). ACM. doi:10.1145/1877953.1877961

Lim, E., Taksande, N., & Seaman, C. (2012). A balancing act: What software practitioners have to say about technical debt. *IEEE Software*, *29*(6), 22–27. doi:10.1109/MS.2012.130

Lin, S., Zhang, X., Yu, Q., Qi, H., & Ma, S. (2013). Parallelizing video transcoding with load balancing on cloud computing. In *Proceedings of2013 IEEE International Symposium on Circuits and Systems (ISCAS2013)* (pp. 2864–2867). IEEE. doi:10.1109/ISCAS.2013.6572476

Liu, F., Shu, P., Jin, H., Ding, L., Yu, J., Niu, D., & Li, B. (2013, June). Gearing resource-poor mobile devices with powerful clouds: architectures, challenges, and applications. *IEEE Wireless Communications*, 14–22.

Liu, C., Bouazizi, I., & Gabbouj, M. (2011a). Parallel adaptive HTTP media streaming. In *Proc. ICCCN*. ICCCN.

Liu, C., Bouazizi, I., & Gabbouj, M. (2011b). Rate adaptation for adaptive http streaming. In *Proc. ACM MMSys*. ACM.

Liu, F., Shu, P., Jin, H., Ding, L., Yu, J., Niu, D., & Li, B. (2013). Gearing resource-poor mobile devices with powerful clouds: Architecture, challenges and applications. *IEEE Wireless Communications Magazine*, *20*(3), 14–22.

Liu, H., Wang, Y., Yang, Y. R., Tian, A., & Wang, H. (2012). Optimizing cost and performance for content multihoming. In *Proc. SIGCOMM*. ACM. doi:10.1145/2342356.2342432

Liu, L., Moulic, R., & Shea, D. (2011). Cloud service portal for mobile device management. In *Proceedings of IEEE 7th International Conference on e-Business Enginering (ICEBE)*. IEEE.

Liu, X., Dobrian, F., Milner, H., Jiang, J., Sekar, V., Stoica, I., & Zhang, H. (2012). A case for a coordinated internet video control plane. In *Proc. SIGCOMM*. ACM. doi:10.1145/2342356.2342431

Liu, X., Liu, Y., Yang, W., & Yang, L. T. (2014). High-efficiency mode decision procedure for H.264/AVC under cloud computing environments. *IEEE Systems Journal*, *8*(1), 322–332. doi:10.1109/JSYST.2013.2260642

Live555. (2014). *Live555 streaming media project*. Retrieved May 22, 2014, from http://www.live555.com/liveMedia/

Li, Z., Mitra, K., Zhang, M., Ranjan, R., Georgakopoulos, D., Zomaya, A. Y., & Sun, S. (2014). Towards understanding the runtime configuration management of do-it-yourself content delivery network applications over public clouds. *Future Generation Computer Systems*, *37*, 297–308. doi:10.1016/j.future.2013.12.019

Li, Z., Wang, C., & Xu, R. (2001). Computation offloading to save energy on handheld devices: A partition scheme. In *Proceedings of the 2001 International Conference on Compilers, Architecture and Synthesis for Embedded Systems (CASES)* (pp. 238-246). CASES. doi:10.1145/502251.502257

Lodi, G., Panzieri, F., Rossi, D., & Turrini, E. (2007). *SLA-driven clustering of QoS-aware application servers*. Academic Press.

Lo, I. L., & Santano, G. S. (2014). Web-native video live streaming. In *Proceedings of the Second IARIA International Conference on Building and Exploring Web Based Environments (WEB 2014)* (pp. 14-19). Chamonix, France: IARIA.

Loreto, S., & Romano, S. P. (2012). Real-time communications in the web: Issues, achievements, and ongoing standardization efforts. *IEEE Internet Computing*, *16*(5), 68–73. doi:10.1109/MIC.2012.115

Low, Y., Bickson, D., Gonzalez, J., Guestrin, C., Kyrola, A., & Hellerstein, J. M. (2012). Distributed GraphLab: A framework for machine learning and data mining in the cloud.*Proc. VLDB Endow.*, *5*(8), 716-727. doi:10.14778/2212351.2212354

Luna, J. M., & Abdallah, C. T. (2011). Control in computing systems: Part I. In *Proceedings of Computer-Aided Control System Design* (CACSD). IEEE. doi:10.1109/CACSD.2011.6044541

Lutz Schubert, K. J. (2012). *Advances in clouds: Report from the cloud computing expert working group*. Academic Press.

Malamos, A. G., Kotanitsi, E., Sympa, P. V., Mamakis, G., Lopez, A. Z., & Crespo, A. J. (2008). *EVIE-m: Utilizing web 3D technologies in mathematics education.* Paper presented at TEMU Conference 2008, Ierapetra, Greece.

Malamos, A. G., Sympa, P. V., & Mamakis, G. S. (2009). XML annotation of conceptual characteristics in interior decoration. In *Proceedings of6th International Conference, New Horizons in Industry, Business and Education (NHIBE 2009).* Santorini: Academic Press.

Malamos, A. G., Sympa, P. V., Mamakis, G., & Kaliakatsos, Y. (2007). Evie-m (educational virtual environment mathematics): An alternative approach for an educational strategy game for mathematics. In Proceedings ofCBLIS 2007. Heraklion, Greece: Academic Press.

Malamos, A. G., Mamakis, G., Sympa, P., Kotanitsi, E., Crespo, A. J., & Lopez, A. Z. (2008). Technical aspects in using X3D in virtual reality mathematics education (EViE-m platform). In *Proceedings of the 12th WSEAS CSCC Multiconference.*Heraklion, Greece: WSEAS.

Malamos, A. G., Mamakis, G., Sympa, P., Kotanitsi, E., Kaliakatsos, Y., Kladis, D., & Lopez, A. Z. (2009). Extending X3D-based educational platform for mathematics with multicast network capabilities. In *Proceedings of WBE2009.*Phuket, Thailand: Academic Press.

Malrait, L. (2010, August). QoS-oriented control of server systems. *SIGOPS Oper. Syst. Rev.*, *44*(3), 59–64. doi:10.1145/1842733.1842744

Mann, J. (Ed.). (2012, December 17). *High resolution time.* Retrieved July 12, 2014, from High Resolution Time, W3C Recommendation: http://www.w3.org/TR/hr-time/

Mann, J., & Jain, A. (Eds.). (2013, October 29). *Page visibility* (2nd ed.). Retrieved July 12, 2014, from Page Visibility (Second Edition), W3C Recommendation: http://www.w3.org/TR/page-visibility/

Mann, J., Wang, Z., & Quach, A. (Eds.). (2013, December 12). *User timing*. Retrieved July 12, 2014, from User Timing, W3C Recommendation: http://www.w3.org/TR/user-timing/

Manvi, S. S., & Krishna Shyam, G. (2013). Resource management for infrastructure as a service (IaaS) in cloud computing: A survey. *Journal of Network and Computer Applications*, 1–17. doi:10.1016/j.jnca.2013.10.004

Mao B., Cao J., & Wu Z. (2012). *Web-based visualisation of the generalised 3D city models using HTML5 and X3Dom.* doi:10.6029/smartcr.2012.05.005

Marin, R. C., Dobre, C., & Xhafa, F. (2014). A methodology for assessing the predictable behaviour of mobile users in wireless networks. *Concurrency and Computation: Practice and Experience*, *26*(5), 1215-1230.

Marin, R.-C., Dobre, C., & Xhafa, F. (2012). Exploring predictability in mobile interaction. In Proceedings of EIDWT (pp. 133-139). EIDWT.

Marinelli, E. (2009). *Hyrax: Cloud computing on mobile devices using MapReduce.* (Master thesis). Carnegie Mellon University, Pittsburgh, PA.

Marinescu, D. (2013, October). Cloud computing: Manage your resources. *TechNet Magazine.* Retrieved June 20, 2014 from http://technet.microsoft.com/en-us/magazine/dn456533.aspx

Marin, R.-C., & Dobre, C. (2013). Reaching for the clouds: Contextually enhancing smartphones for energy efficiency. In C. X. Mavromoustakis, T. Dagiuklas, & L. Shu (Eds.), *HP-MOSys* (pp. 31–38). ACM. doi:10.1145/2507908.2507912

Marin, R.-C., Dobre, C., & Xhafa, F. (2014). A methodology for assessing the predictable behaviour of mobile users in wireless networks. *Concurrency and Computation*, *26*(5), 1215–1230. doi:10.1002/cpe.3064

Marnerides, A. K., Pezaros, D. P., Kim, H., & Hutchison, D. (2013). Internet traffic classification under energy time-frequency distributions. In *Proceedings of IEEE International Conference on Communications.* Budapest, Hungary: IEEE.

Marnerides, A. K., Watson, M., Shirazi, N., Mauthe, A., & Hutchison, D. (2013). Malware analysis in cloud computing: Network and system characteristics. In Proceedings of IEEE GLOBECOM CCSNA Workshop 2013. IEEE.

Marshall, P., Keahey, K., & Freeman, T. (2010). Elastic site: Using clouds to elastically extend site resources. In *Proceedings of Cluster, Cloud and Grid Computing* (CCGrid). IEEE. doi:10.1109/CCGRID.2010.80

Masti, S., & Raghavan, S. (2012). VNA: An enhanced algorithm for virtual network embedding. In *Proceedings of21st International Conference on Computer Communication Networks* (ICCCN). Academic Press. doi:10.1109/ICCCN.2012.6289180

Mastorakis, G., Mavromoustakis, C. X., Bourdena, A., & Pallis, E. (2013, June). An energy-efficient routing scheme using Backward Traffic Difference estimation in cognitive radio networks. In *Proceedings of 2013 IEEE 14th International Symposium and Workshops on a World of Wireless, Mobile and Multimedia Networks (WoWMoM)* (pp. 1–6). Madrid: IEEE. doi:10.1109/WoWMoM.2013.6583446

Mastorakis, G., Mavromoustakis, C. X., Bourdena, A., Kormentzas, G., & Pallis, E. (2013, September). Maximizing energy conservation in a centralized cognitive radio network architecture. In *Proceedings of 2013 IEEE 18th IEEE International Workshop on Computer-Aided Modeling Analysis and Design of Communication Links and Networks (IEEE CAMAD 2013)* (pp. 175–179). Berlin, Germany: IEEE. doi:10.1109/CAMAD.2013.6708112

Mastorakis, G., Bourdena, A., Mavromoustakis, C. X., Pallis, E., & Kormentzas, G. (2013, July). An energy-efficient routing protocol for ad-hoc cognitive radio networks. In *Future network and mobile summit (FutureNetworkSummit), 2013* (pp. 1–10). IEEE.

Mastorakis, G., Mavromoustakis, C. X., Bourdena, A., Pallis, E., & Sismanidis, G. (2013, November). Optimizing radio resource management in energy-efficient cognitive radio networks. In *Proceedings of the 2nd ACM Workshop on High Performance Mobile Opportunistic Systems* (pp. 75-82). ACM. doi:10.1145/2507908.2507920

Mastorakis, G., Mavromoustakis, C. X., Bourdena, A., Pallis, E., Sismanidis, G., Stratakis, D., & Papadakis, S. (2014). Energy-efficient routing in cognitive radio networks. In *Resource management in mobile computing environments* (Vol. 3, pp. 323–340). Springer International Publishing. doi:10.1007/978-3-319-06704-9_14

Mastorakis, G., Pallis, E., Mavromoustakis, C. X., & Bourdena, A. (2014). Efficient resource management utilizing content-aware multipath routing. In *Resource management in mobile computing environments* (pp. 389–395). Springer; doi:10.1007/978-3-319-06704-9_17

Mastorakis, G., Panagiotakis, S., Kapetanakis, K., Dagalakis, G., Mavromoustakis, C. X., Bourdena, A., & Pallis, E. (2014). Energy and resource consumption evaluation of mobile cognitive radio devices. In *Resource management in mobile computing environments* (pp. 359–388). Springer International Publishing. doi:10.1007/978-3-319-06704-9_16

Matias, J., Tornero, B., Mendiola, A., Jacob, E., & Toldeo, N. (2012). Implementing layer 2 network virtualization using OpenFlow: Challenges and solutions. In *Proceedings ofEuropean Workshop on Software Defined Networking* (EWSDN). Academic Press. doi:10.1109/EWSDN.2012.18

Matias, J., Jacob, E., Sanchez, D., & Demchenko, Y. (2011). An OpenFlow-based network virtualization framework for the cloud. In *Proc 3rd IEEE Int.Conf on Cloud Computing Technology and Science*. IEEE. doi:10.1109/CloudCom.2011.104

Matson, J. E., Barrett, B. E., & Mellichamp, J. M. (1994). Software development cost estimation using function points. *IEEE Transactions on Software Engineering*, *20*(4), 275–287. doi:10.1109/32.277575

Mavromoustakis, C. X. (2010). Collaborative optimistic replication for efficient delay-sensitive MP2P streaming using community oriented neighboring feedback. In *Proceedings of 8th IEEE International Conference on Pervasive Computing and Communications Workshops* (PERCOM Workshops). IEEE.

Mavromoustakis, C. X. (2010, March). Collaborative optimistic replication for efficient delay-sensitive MP2P streaming using community oriented neighboring feedback. In *Proceedings of Pervasive Computing and Communications Workshops (PERCOM Workshops)* (pp. 105-110). IEEE. doi:10.1109/PERCOMW.2010.5470611

Mavromoustakis, C. X., & Dimitriou, C. D. (2012, May). Using social interactions for opportunistic resource sharing using mobility-enabled contact-oriented replication. In *Proceedings ofInternational Conference on Collaboration Technologies and Systems (CTS 2012). In Cooperation with ACM/IEEE, Internet of Things, Machine to Machine and Smart Services Applications (IoT 2012)* (pp. 21-25). ACM.

Mavromoustakis, C. X., & Karatza, H. D. (2008). End-to-end layered asynchronous scheduling scheme for energy aware QoS provision in asymmetrical wireless devices. In *Proceedings of the 2008 12th Enterprise Distributed Object Computing Conference Workshops* (EDOCW '08). IEEE Computer Society. doi:10.1109/EDOCW.2008.31

Mavromoustakis, C. X., & Mastorakis, G. (2012). Using real-time backward traffic difference estimation for energy conservation in wireless devices. In *Proceedings ofthe Fourth International Conference on Advances inP2PSystems*. Academic Press.

Mavromoustakis, C. X., Andreou, A., Mastorakis, G., Bourdena, A., Batalla, J. M., & Dobre, C. (2014). On the performance evaluation of a novel offloading-based energy conservation mechanism for wireless devices. In *Proceedings of6th International Conference on Mobile Networks and Management* (MONAMI 2014). Academic Press.

Mavromoustakis, C. X., Andreou, A., Mastorakis, G., Bourdena, A., Batalla, J. M., & Dobre, C. (n.d.). *On the performance evaluation of a novel offloading-based energy conservation mechanism for wireless devices.* Academic Press.

Mavromoustakis, C. X., Andreou, A., Mastorakis, G., Papadakis, S., Bourdena, A., & Stratakis, D. (2014, August). Energy consumption optimization through pre-scheduled opportunistic offloading in wireless devices. In *Proceedings ofEMERGING 2014,The Sixth International Conference on Emerging Network Intelligence* (pp. 22–28). Rome, Italy: Academic Press.

Mavromoustakis, C. X., Mastorakis, G., Bourdena, A., & Pallis, E. (2014). Energy efficient resource sharing using a trafficoriented routing scheme for cognitive radio networks. *IET Networks, 3*(1), 54-63.

Mavromoustakis, C. X., Pallis, E., & Mastorakis, G. (2014). *Resource management in mobile computing environments* (vol. 3). Springer International. Retrieved from http://www.fp7-mobilecloud.eu/

Mavromoustakis, C., Andreou, A., Mastorakis, G., Papadakis, S., Bourdena, A., & Stratakis, D. (2014). *Energy consumption optimization through pre-scheduled opportunistic offloading in wireless devices.* Paper presented at the EMERGING 2014, the Sixth International Conference on Emerging Network Intelligence.

Mavromoustakis, C., Dimitriou, C. D., & Mastorakis, G. (2012, September). Using real-time backward traffic difference estimation for energy conservation in wireless devices. In *Proceedings of AP2PS 2012,The Fourth International Conference on Advances inP2PSystems* (pp. 18–23). Barcelona, Spain: AP2PS.

Mavromoustakis, C., Dimitriou, C. D., & Mastorakis, G. (2013). On the real-time evaluation of two-level BTD scheme for energy conservation in the presence of delay sensitive transmissions and intermittent connectivity in wireless devices. *International Journal on Advances in Networks and Services, 6*(3 and 4), 148–162.

Mavromoustakis, C. X. (2011, February). Synchronized cooperative schedules for collaborative resource availability using population-based algorithm. *Simulation Practice and Theory Journal, Elsevier, 19*(2), 762–776. doi:10.1016/j.simpat.2010.10.005

Mavromoustakis, C. X., Bourdena, A., Mastorakis, G., Pallis, E., & Kormentzas, G. (2015). An energy-aware scheme for efficient spectrum utilization in a 5G mobile cognitive radio network architecture. *Telecommunication Systems Journal.*

Mavromoustakis, C. X., Dimitriou, C. D., Mastorakis, G., & Pallis, E. (2013, December). Real-time performance evaluation of F-BTD scheme for optimized QoS energy conservation in wireless devices. In *Proceedings of 2013 IEEE Globecom Workshops (GC Wkshps)* (pp. 1151–1156). Atlanta, GA: IEEE; doi:10.1109/GLOCOMW.2013.6825148

Mavromoustakis, C. X., Dimitriou, C., Mastorakis, G., Bourdena, A., & Pallis, E. (2014). Using traffic diversities for scheduling wireless interfaces for energy harvesting in wireless devices. In *Resource management in mobile computing environments* (Vol. 3, pp. 481–496). Springer International Publishing.

Mavromoustakis, C. X., Mastorakis, G., Bourdena, A., & Pallis, E. (2014). *Energy efficient resource sharing using a traffic-oriented routing scheme for cognitive radio networks*. IET Networks.

Mavromoustakis, C. X., Pallis, E., & Mastorakis, G. (2014). *Resource management in mobile computing environments: Modeling and optimization in science and technologies*. Springer. doi:10.1007/978-3-319-06704-9

Mavromoustakis, C. X., & Zerfiridis, K. G. (2010). On the diversity properties of wireless mobility with the user-centered temporal capacity awareness for EC in wireless devices. In *Proceedings of the Sixth IEEE International Conference on Wireless and Mobile Communications* (pp. 367-372). IEEE.

Mayo, R. N., & Ranganathan, P. (2003). Energy consumption in mobile devices: Why future systems need requirements aware energy scale-down. In *Proceedings of the Third international conference on Power - Aware Computer Systems* (PACS'03). Springer-Verlag.

McAfee, A. (2011). What every CEO needs to know about the cloud. *Harvard Business Review*, *89*(11), 124–132. PMID:21370809

McConnell, S. (2007, November 1). *Technical debt*. Retrieved April 12, 2014, from http://www.construx.com/10x_Software_Development/Technical_Debt/

MCN. (2014). *EU FP7 mobile cloud networking (MCN) project*. Retrieved May 22, 2014, from http://www.mobile-cloud-networking.eu/site/

McNett, M., Gupta, D., Vahdat, A., & Voelker, G. M. (2007). Usher: An extensible framework for managing clusters of virtual machines. In *Proceedings of the 21st Large Installation System Administration Conference* (LISA). Academic Press.

Medhioub, H., Houidi, I., Louati, W., & Zeghlache, D. (2011). Design, implementation and evaluation of virtual resource description and clustering framework. In *Proceedings ofIEEE International Conference on Advanced Information Networking andApplications* (AINA). IEEE. doi:10.1109/AINA.2011.46

Mehta, M., Ajmera, I., Jondhale, R., & Sanghvi, J. (2013, October). Mobile cloud computing. *International Journal of Electronics and Communication Engineering & Technology*.

Meier, R. (2010). Professional Android 2 application development. Academic Press.

Mell, P., & Grance, T. (2011). *NIST definition of cloud computing*. National Institute of Standards and Technology, Special Publication 800-145.

Mi, H., Wang, H., Yin, G., Cai, H., Zhou, Q., Sun, T., & Zhou, Y. (2011). Magnifier: Online detection of performance problems in large-scale cloud computing systems. In *Proceedings of Services Computing (SCC)*. IEEE.

Microsoft. (2014a). *Windows Azure platform*. Retrieved from http://www.microsoft.com/windowsazure

Microsoft. (2014b). *Microsoft Hyper-V*. Retrieved from http://www.microsoft.com/servers/hyper-v-server/default.mspx

Microsoft. (n.d.). *Windows Azure platform*. Retrieved 2011 from http://www.microsoft.com/windowsazure/

Mihailescu, M., & Teo, Y. M. (2010). On economic and computational-efficient resource pricing in large distributed systems. In *Proceedings of the 2010 10th IEEE/ACM International Conference on Cluster, Cloud and Grid Computing*. IEEE.

Miller, K., Quacchio, E., Gennari, G., & Wolisz, A. (2012). Adaptation algorithm for adaptive streaming over HTTP. In *Proc. Packet Video Workshop*. Academic Press. doi:10.1109/PV.2012.6229732

Mini Page with the Use of MPEG-DASH as 3D Model's Texture for X3Dom. (n.d.). Retrieved July 12, 2014, from http://www.medialab.teicrete.gr/minipages/dash3d/

Minkov, E., Cohen, W. W., & Ng, A. Y. (2006). Contextual search and name disambiguation in email using graphs. In E. N. Efthimiadis, S. T. Dumais, D. Hawking, & K. Järvelin (Eds.), SIGIR (pp. 27-34). ACM. doi:10.1145/1148170.1148179

Mirtchev, S., & Goleva, R. (2008). Evaluation of Pareto/D/1/k queue by simulation. Information Technologies & Knowledge, 2, 45-52.

Mirtchev, S., & Goleva, R. (2012). New constant service time Polya/D/n traffic model with peaked input stream. *Simulation Modelling Practice and Theory*, *34*, 200-207.

Mirtchev, S., Goleva, R., & Alexiev, V. (2010). Evaluation of single server queueing system with Polya arrival process and constant service time. In *Proceedings of the International Conference on Information Technologies*. InfoTech.

Mirtchev, S., Mavromoustakis, C. X., Goleva, R., Kassev, K., & Mastorakis, G. (2014). Generic IP network traffic management from measurement through analyses to simulation. In *Resource management in mobile computing environments*. Springer International Publishing.

Mirtchev, S., & Goleva, R. (2009a). Discrete time single server queueing model with a multimodal packet size distribution. In *Annual proceedings of institute of matemathics* (pp. 83–101). Bulgarian Academy of Science.

Mirtchev, S., & Goleva, R. (2009b). *A discrete time queuing model with a constant packet size*. Bulgaria: Tarnovo.

Mirza, M., Sommers, J., Barford, P., & Zhu, X. (2007). A machine learning approach to TCP throughput prediction. In *Proc. ACM SIGMETRICS Mobile Cloud Networking Project*. ACM. Retrieved from http://www.mobile-cloud-networking.eu/site/

Mishra, M., Das, A., Kulkarni, P., & Sahoo, A. (2012). Dynamic resource management using virtual machine migrations. *Communications Magazine, IEEE*, *50*(9), 34–40. doi:10.1109/MCOM.2012.6295709

Mitola, J. & Maguire, G. (1999). Cognitive radio: Making software radios more personal. *IEEE Personal Communications*, *6*(4), 13-18.

Mitola, J. (2000). *Cognitive radio an integrated agent architecture for software defined radio*. (PhD Thesis). KTH Royal Institute of Technology, Stockholm, Sweden.

Mobile Cloud Computing Forum. (n.d.). Retrieved from http://www.mobilecloudcomputingforum.com/

Mobile-Web-App-State. (2014, April). *Standards for web applications on mobile: Current state and roadmap*. W3C Document. Retrieved July 12, 2014, from http://www.w3.org/2014/04/mobile-web-app-state/

Mohan, P., Padmanabhan, V. N., & Ramjee, R. (2008). Nericell: Rich monitoring of road and traffic conditions using mobile smartphones. In *Proceedings of the 6th ACM Conference on Embedded Network Sensor Systems* (pp. 323-336). ACM. doi:10.1145/1460412.1460444

Mohan, E. S., Kumar, E., & Suresh, S. (2013). Mobile cloud media computing applications: A survey. In *Proceedings of the Fourth International Conference on Signal and Image Processing 2012 (ICSIP 2012)* (pp. 619-628). ICSIP.

Mok, R. K. P., Chan, E. W. W., Luo, X., & Chang, R. K. C. (2011). Inferring the QoE of HTTP video streaming from user-viewing activities. In Proceedings of SIGCOMM W-MUST. ACM.

Mok, E. C. R., Luo, X., & Chang, R. (2012). Qdash: A qoe-aware dash system. In *Proceedings of ACM Multimedia Systems*. ACM.

Mongay Batalla, J., & Krawiec, P. (2014). Conception of ID layer performance at the network level for Internet of Things. *Springer Journal Personal and Ubiquitous Computing*, *18*(2). Retrieved from http://www.fp7-monica.eu/

Mongay Batalla, J., Beben, A., & Chen, Y. (2012, October). *Optimization of decision process in network and server-aware algorithms*. IEEE.

monitis. (2014). *IT monitoring*. Retrieved from http://portal.monitis.com/

MonPaaS. (2014). Retrieved May 25, 2014, from http://sourceforge.net/projects/monpaas/

Morgenthaler, J. D., Gridnev, M., Sauciuc, R., & Bhansali, S. (2012). Searching for build debt: Experiences managing technical debt at Google. In *Proceedings of2012 Third International Workshop on Managing Technical Debt (MTD)* (pp. 1–6). Zurich: IEEE. doi:10.1109/MTD.2012.6225994

Moscholios, I. D., Vasilakis, V. G., Vardakas, J. S., & Logothetis, M. D. (2011). Retry loss models supporting elastic traffic. *Advances in Electronics and Telecommunications*, *2*(3), 2011.

Mousicou, P., Mavromoustakis, C. X., Bourdena, A., Mastorakis, G., & Pallis, E. (2013). Performance evaluation of dynamic cloud resource migration based on temporal and capacity-aware policy for efficient resource sharing. In *Proceedings of the 2nd ACM Workshop on High Performance Mobile Opportunistic Systems* (HP-MOSys '13). ACM. http://doi.acm.org/10.1145/2507908.2507917

Mousicou, P., Mavromoustakis, C. X., Bourdena, A., Mastorakis, G., & Pallis, E. (2013). Performance evaluation of dynamic cloud resource migration based on temporal and capacity-aware policy for efficient resource sharing. In *Proceedings of the 2nd ACM Workshop on High Performance Mobile Opportunistic Systems (HP-MOSys '13)* (pp. 59–66). ACM. doi:10.1145/2507908.2507917

Müller, C., & Timmerer, C. (2011, November). A VLC media player plugin enabling dynamic adaptive streaming over HTTP. In *Proc. ACM Multimedia*. ACM. doi:10.1145/2072298.2072429

MultiCoreWare. (2014). Retrieved May 25, 2014, from http://x265.org/about.html

Murray, D. G., Yoneki, E., Crowcroft, J., & Hand, S. (2010). The case for crowd computing. In L. P. Cox & A. Wolman (Eds.), MobiHeld (pp. 39-44). ACM.

Nadella, S. (2014). *Keynote speech at Worldwide Partner Conference 2014 in Washington DC, 16/7/2014*. Retrieved July 20, 2014, from https://wpc.tri-digital.com/videoConnect.aspx?guid=9afb907f-f214-43d5-aa79-ec7872d45b99

Nagios. (2014). Retrieved May 25, 2014, from http://www.nagios.org/

Nakasu, E. (2012, April). A future TV system that conveys an enhanced sense of reality and presence. *IEEE Consumer Electronics Magazine*.

Nallur, V., & Bahsoon, R. (2012). A decentralized self-adaptation mechanism for service-based applications in the cloud. *IEEE Transactions on Software Engineering*, *99*, 1–1.

Narayanan, R. G. L. (2014). Mobile video streaming resource management. In Resource management in mobile computing environments (pp. 461-480). Springer International Publishing.

Nathuji, R., Kansal, A., & Ghaffarkhah, A. (2010). Q-clouds: Managing performance interference effects for qos-aware clouds. In *Proceedings of the ACM European Society in Systems Conference 2010*. Paris, France: ACM. doi:10.1145/1755913.1755938

NEBULA Project. (2010). *The NEBULA Project*. Retrieved July, 27, 2014, from http://nebula-fia.org/index.html

Neiger, G., Rodgers, D., Santoni, A.L., Martins, F.C.M., Anderson, A.V., Bennett, S.M., ... Smith, L. (2005). Intel virtualization technology. *Computer, 38*(5), 48-56.

Netflix Eds. (2011, December). *Netflix sees cost savings in MPEG DASH adoption*. Retrieved from http://www.streamingmedia.com/Articles/ReadArticle.aspx?ArticleID=79409

Nightingale, J., Wang, Q., Grecos, C., & Goma, S. (2013). Subjective evaluation of the effects of packet loss on HEVC encoded video streams. In *Proceedings of2013 IEEE Third International Conference on Consumer Electronics - Berlin (ICCE-Berlin)* (pp. 358–359). IEEE. doi:10.1109/ICCE-Berlin.2013.6698055

Nightingale, J., Wang, Q., & Grecos, C. (2012). HEVStream : A framework for streaming and evaluation of high efficiency video coding (HEVC) content in loss-prone networks. *IEEE Transactions on Consumer Electronics*, *58*(2), 404–412. doi:10.1109/TCE.2012.6227440

Nightingale, J., Wang, Q., & Grecos, C. (2013). Scalable HEVC (SHVC)-based video stream adaptation in wireless networks. In *Proc. IEEE 24th Annual International Symposium on Personal, Indoor, and Mobile Radio Communications (IEEE PIMRC'13)*. IEEE. doi:10.1109/PIMRC.2013.6666769

Nightingale, J., Wang, Q., Grecos, C., & Goma, S. (2014a). Evaluation of in-network adaptation of scalable high efficiency video coding (SHVC) in mobile environments. In *Proc. SPIE Conference on Mobile Devices and Multimedia: Enabling Technologies, Algorithms, and Applications 2014 (SPIE Conference 9030)*. SPIE.

Nightingale, J., Wang, Q., Grecos, C., & Goma, S. (2014b). Deriving video content type from H.265/HEVC bitstream semantics. In *Proc. SPIE Photonics Europe 2014: Real-Time Image and Video Processing (Conference EPE115)*. SPIE.

Nimmagadda, Y., Kumar, K., Lu, Y.-H., & Lee, C. S. G. (2010). Realtime moving object recognition and tracking using computation offloading. In Proceedings of IEEE International Conference on Intelligent Robots and Systems (pp. 2449–2455). IEEE.

nimsoft. (2014). *ITSM- Network monitoring and service desk management*. Retrieved from http://www.nimsoft.com

NIST. (2014). *NIST cloud definition*. Retrieved from http://csrc.nist.gov/publications/nistpubs/800-145/SP800-145.pdf

Niu, D., Liu, Z., Li, B., & Zhao, S. (2011). *Demand forecast and performance prediction in peer-assisted on-demand streaming systems*. Paper presented at the INFOCOM. doi:10.1109/INFCOM.2011.5935196

Niu, D., Xu, H., Li, B., & Zhao, S. (2012). *Quality-assured cloud bandwidth auto-scaling for video-on-demand applications*. Paper presented at the INFOCOM. doi:10.1109/INFCOM.2012.6195785

Niyato, D., & Hossain, E. (2008). Spectrum trading in cognitive radio networks: A market-equilibrium-based approach. *IEEE Wireless Communications, 15*(6), 71-80.

Nogueira, J., Melo, M., Carapinha, J., & Sargento, S. (2011). A platform for operator-driven network virtualization. In *Proc. IEEE EUROCON - International Conference on Computer as a Tool*. IEEE. doi:10.1109/EUROCON.2011.5929325

Nogueira, J., Melo, M., Carapinha, J., & Sargento, S. (2011). Network virtualization system suite: Experimental network virtualization platform. In *Proceedings of International Conf. on Testbeds and Research Infrastructures for the Development of Networks and Communities*. Academic Press.

Nogueira, J., Melo, M., Carapinha, J., & Sargento, S. (2011). Virtual network mapping into heterogeneous substrate networks. In *Proc. IEEE ISCC*. Academic Press. doi:10.1109/ISCC.2011.5983876

Nord, R. L., Ozkaya, I., Kruchten, P., & Gonzalez-Rojas, M. (2012). In search of a metric for managing architectural technical debt. In *Proceedings of 2012 Joint Working IEEE/IFIP Conference on Software Architecture (WICSA) and European Conference on Software Architecture (ECSA)* (pp. 91–100). Helsinki: IEEE. doi:10.1109/WICSA-ECSA.212.17

NSF. (2010). *National science foundation research project awards*. Retrieved July 27, 2014, from http://www.gov/mobile/news/news_summ.jsp?cntn_id=128679&org=NSF&from=news

NSTC. (2011). *Executive Office of the President, trustworthy CyberSpace: Strategic plan for the federal CyberSecurity research and development program*. National Science and Technology Council. Retrieved July 27, 2014, from http://www.whitehouse.gov/sites/default/files/microsites/ostp/fed_cybersecurity_rd_strategic_plan_2011.pdf

Nugroho, A., Visser, J., & Kuipers, T. (2011). An empirical model of technical debt and interest. In *Proceedings of the 2nd Workshop on Managing Technical Debt* (pp. 1–8). ACM. doi:10.1145/1985362.1985364

Nurmi, D., Wolski, R., Grzegorczyk, C., Obertelli, G., Soman, S., Youseff, L., & Zagorodnov, D. (2009). The eucalyptus open-source cloud-computing system. In *Proceedings of Cluster Computing and the Grid, CCGRID '09*. IEEE. doi:10.1109/CCGRID.2009.93

Nygren, E., Sitaraman, R. K., & Sun, J. (2010). The akamai network: A platform for high-performance internet applications. *Operating Systems Review, 44*(3), 2–19. doi:10.1145/1842733.1842736

O3D WebGL Implementation of O3D. (n.d.). Retrieved July 12, 2014, from https://code.google.com/p/o3d/

Oberheide, J., Veeraraghvan, K., Cooke, E., Flinn, J., & Jahanian, F. (2008). Virtualized in-cloud security services for mobile devices. In *Proceedings of the 1st Workshop on Virtualization in Mobile Computing (MobiVirt)*. Academic Press. doi:10.1145/1622103.1629656

Ong, E. H., & Khan, J. Y. (2009). A unified QoS-inspired load optimization framework for multiple access points based wireless LANs. In *Proceedings ofWireless Communications and Networking Conference*. IEEE. doi:10.1109/WCNC.2009.4917550

OpenStack. (2014). Retrieved May 25, 2014, from https://www.openstack.org/

OPNET. (2014). *Application and network performance with OPNET*. Retrieved from http://www.opnet.com

Osana, Y., & Kuribayashi, S. (2010). Enhanced fair joint multiple resource allocation method in all-IP networks. In *Proc. 24th IEEE Int. Conf. on Advanced Information Networking and Applications Workshops (WAINA)*. IEEE. doi:10.1109/WAINA.2010.33

Ott, J., Bormann, C., Sullivan, G., Wenger, S., & Even, R. (Eds.). (2007). *Request for comments: 4629. RTP Payload Format for ITU-T Rec. H.263 Video*. IETF.

Ou, S., Yang, K., Liotta, A., & Hu, L. (2007). Performance analysis of offloading systems in mobile wireless environments. In *Proceedings of the IEEE International Conference on Communications (ICC)*. IEEE. doi:10.1109/ICC.2007.304

Oza, N., Münch, J., Garbajosa, J., Yague, A., & Ortega, E. G. (2013). Identifying potential risks and benefits of using cloud in distributed software development. In *Product-focused software process improvement* (Vol. 7983, pp. 229–239). Springer Berlin Heidelberg. doi:10.1007/978-3-642-39259-7_19

Oztas, B., Pourazad, M. T., Nasiopoulos, P., Sodagar, I., & Leung, V. C. M. (2014). A rate adaptation approach for streaming multiview plus depth content. In *Proc. 2014 International Conference on Computing, Networking and Communications (ICNC)* (pp. 1006–1010). Academic Press. doi:10.1109/ICCNC.2014.6785475

Pachoulakis, I., Profit, A. N., & Kapetanakis, K. (2012). The question manager and tutoring module for the EViE-m platform. In *Proceedings of International Conference on Telecommunications and Multimedia (TEMU '12)*.Heraklion, Greece: Academic Press. doi:10.1109/TEMU.2012.6294716

Padala, P., Hou, K-Y., Shin, K. G., Zhu, X., Uysal, M., Wang, Z., … Merchant, A. (2009). Automated control of multiple virtualized resources. In *Proceedings of the 4th ACM European Conference on Computer Systems* (EuroSys '09). ACM. doi:10.1145/1519065.1519068

Pallis, G., (2010). Cloud computing: The new frontier of internet computing. *IEEE Internet Computing, 14*(5), 70-73.

Panagiotakis, S., Kapetanakis, K., & Malamos, A. G. (2013). Architecture for real time communications over the web. *International Journal of Web Engineering, 2*(1), 1–8. doi:10.5923/j.web.20130201.01

Pannu, H. S., Jianguo, L., & Song, F. (2012). AAD: Adaptive anomaly detection system for cloud computing infrastructures. In *Proceedings of Reliable Distributed Systems (SRDS)* (pp. 396-397). IEEE.

Pannu, H. S., Liu, J., Guan, Q., & Fu, S. (2012, December). AFD: Adaptive failure detection system for cloud computing infrastructures. In *Proceedings of Performance Computing and Communications Conference* (IPCCC) (pp. 71-80). IEEE.

Papadimitriou, P., Houidi, I., Louati, W., Zeghlache, D., Werle, C., Bless, R., & Mathy, L. (2012). *Towards large-scale network virtualization*. Santorini: IFIP WWIC.

Papanikolaou, K., Mavromoustakis, C. X., Mastorakis, G., Bourdena, A., & Dobre, C. (2014). Energy consumption optimization using social interaction in the mobile cloud. In *Proceedings of6th International Conference on Mobile Networks and Management (MONAMI 2014)*. Wuerzburg, Germany: MONAMI.

Papanikolaou, K., Mavromoustakis, C. X., Mastorakis, G., Bourdena, A., & Dobre, C. Energy consumption optimization using social interaction in the mobile cloud. In *Proceedings of6th International Conference on Mobile Networks and Management* (MONAMI 2014). Academic Press. doi:10.1007/978-3-319-16292-8_31

Papervision3d, Open Source Realtime 3D Engine for Flash. (n.d.). Retrieved July 12, 2014, from https://code.google.com/p/papervision3d/

Parkhill, D. (1966). *The challenge of the computer utility*. Addison-Wesley.

Parwekar, P. (2011). From internet of things towards cloud of things. In *Proceedings of Computer and Communication Technology (ICCCT)* (pp. 329-333). ICCCT.

Paul, U., Subramanian, A. P., Buddhikot, M. M., & Das, S. R. (2011). Understanding traffic dynamics in cellular data networks. In *Proceedings of INFOCOM* (pp. 882-890). IEEE. doi:10.1109/INFCOM.2011.5935313

Paulson, L. D. (2003). Low-power chips for high-powered handhelds. *IEEE Computer Society Magazine*, *36*(1), 21–23. doi:10.1109/MC.2003.1160049

PC MAG. (2014). Retrieved from http://www.pcmag.com/encyclopedia/term/39466/cdn

Peixoto, E., Shanableh, T., & Izquierdo, E. (2014). H.264 / AVC to HEVC video transcoder based on dynamic thresholding and content modeling. *IEEE Transactions on Circuits and Systems for Video Technology*, *24*(1), 99–112. doi:10.1109/TCSVT.2013.2273651

Pendyala, V. S., & Holliday, J. (2010). Performing intelligent mobile searches in the cloud using semantic technologies. In *Proceedings of IEEE International Conference on Granular Computing*. IEEE. doi:10.1109/GrC.2010.16

Peng, B. (2011). A network virtualisation framework for IP infrastructure provisioning. In *Proc 3rd IEEE Int.Conf on Cloud Computing Technology and Science*. IEEE.

Peralta, A. (2011). *Samsung, HTC And Carrier IQ face suit over logging software*. Retrieved December 2011 from http://www.npr.org/blogs/thetwo-way/2011/12/02/143051586/samsung-htc-and-carrier-iq-face-suit-over-logging-software

Pereira, R., Azambuja, M., Breitman, K., & Endler, M. (2010). An architecture for distributed high performance video processing in the cloud. In *Proceedings of 2010 IEEE 3rd International Conference on Cloud Computing* (pp. 482–489). IEEE. doi:10.1109/CLOUD.2010.73

Perez, S. (2010). *Mobile cloud computing: $9.5 billion by 2014*. Retrieved from http://exoplanet.eu/catalog.php

Persson, P. (2011, November 9). *A web RTC tutorial | Ericsson BlogEricsson research blog*. Retrieved July 12, 2014, from http://www.ericsson.com/research-blog/context-aware-communication/web-rtc-tutorial/

Pinol, P., Torres, A., Lopez, O., Martinez, M., & Malumbres, M. (2013). Evaluating HEVC video delivery in VANET scenarios. In Proc. 2013 IFIP Wireless Days (WD). IFIP. doi:10.1109/WD.2013.6686539

Poehlein, S., Saxena, V., Willis, G., Fedders, J., & Guttmann, M. (2010). *Moving to the media cloud: Available RPS toolkit*. Retrieved from http://www.cs.northwestern.edu/~RPS/

Popescu, A. (Ed.). (2013, October 24). *Geolocation API specification, W3C recommendation*. Retrieved July 12, 2014, from http://www.w3.org/TR/geolocation-API/

Portokalidis, G., Homburg, P., Anagnostakis, K., & Bos, H. (2010). Paranoid android: Versatile protection for smartphones. In *Proceedings of the 26th Annual Computer Security Application Conference (ACSAC)* (pp. 347-356). ACSAC.

Prodan, R., & Ostermann, S. (2010). A survey and taxonomy of infrastructure as a service and web hosting cloud providers. In *Proc. 10th IEEE/ACM Int. Conf. Grid Computing (Grid 2009)* (pp. 17–25). IEEE.

Project 4. (2014). *4WARD project*. Retrieved from http://www.4ward-project.eu/

Project Management Software, Online Collaboration: Basecamp. (n.d.). Retrieved from http://basecamphq.com/

Psannis, K., & Ishibashi, Y. (2008). Enhanced H.264/AVC stream switching over varying bandwidth networks. *IEICE ELEX Journal*, *5*(19), 827–832. doi:10.1587/elex.5.827

Qiang, G., & Song, F. (2013). Adaptive anomaly identification by exploring metric subspace in cloud computing infrastructures. In *Proceedings of Reliable Distributed Systems (SRDS)* (pp. 205-214). Academic Press.

Qi, G.-J., Tsai, M.-H., Tsai, S.-F., Cao, L., & Huang, T. S. (2012). Web-scale multimedia information networks. *Proceedings of the IEEE*, *100*(9), 2688–2704. doi:10.1109/JPROC.2012.2201909

Qineti. (2002). Cognitive radio technology: A Study for Ofcom. In *Proceedings ofSymposium on Electronics and the Environment*. Author.

Qureshi, S., Ahmas, T., Rafique, K., & Shuja-ul-islam. (2011). *Mobile cloud computing as future for mobile applications- Implementation methods and challenging issues*. Paper presented at IEEE CCIS2011.

Rackspace. (2014). *Cloud computing, managed hosting, dedicated server hosting by rackspace*. Retrieved from http://www.rackspace.com

Rahman, M., & Mir, F. A. M. (2007). Fourth generation (4G) wireless networks- Features, technologies and issues. In *Proceedings of the 6th International Conference on 3G and Beyond*. Academic Press.

Ranganathan, A., & Sicking, J. (Eds.). (2013, September 12). *File API - W3C*. Retrieved July 13, 2014, from File API - W3C Last Call Working Draft: http://www.w3.org/TR/FileAPI/

Rao, A., Lim, Y.-S., Barakat, C., Legout, A., Towsley, D., & Dabbous, W. (2011). Network characteristics of video streaming traffic. In Proc. CoNext. Academic Press.

Reavy, M., & Nyman, R. (2013, February 4). *Hello Chrome, it's Firefox calling! Mozilla hacks – The web developer blog*. Retrieved July 12, 2014, from https://hacks.mozilla.org/2013/02/hello-chrome-its-firefox-calling/

Red5. (2014). *Red5 media server project*. Retrieved May 22, 2014, from http://www.red5.org/

Reddy, S., Shilton, K., Denisov, G., Cenizal, C., Estrin, D., & Srivastava, M. (2010). Biketastic: Sensing and mapping for better biking. In *Proceedings of the SIGCHI Conference on Human Factors in Computing Systems* (pp. 1817-1820). ACM. doi:10.1145/1753326.1753598

Reddy, Y. B., & Ellis, S. (2013). Modeling cognitive radio networks for efficient data transfer using cloud link. In *Proceedings of Information Technology: New Generations* (ITNG). Academic Press. doi:10.1109/ITNG.2013.87

Rejaie, R., & Kangasharju, J. (2011). Mocha: A quality adaptive multimedia proxy cache for internet streaming. In *Proc. NOSSDAV*. Academic Press.

Rekhter, E., & Rosen, Y. (1999). *BGP/MPLS VPNs, RFC 2547*. IETF.

Rennolls, K. (2004). *Visualization and re-parameterization of Johnson's SB distribution*. Taiwan: Informatics, Modelling and Statistics.

Ren, S., & van der Schaar, M. (2013). Efficient resource provisioning and rate selection for stream mining in a community cloud. *IEEE Transactions on Multimedia*, *15*(4), 723–734. doi:10.1109/TMM.2013.2240673

Reservoir-FP7. (2008). *Resources and services virtualization without barriers*. Retrieved June 20, 2014 from http://62.149.240.97/uploads/Publications/Reservoir-Whitepaper_for_OGF23_-_V3.pdf

Resources, D. F. (2014). *Developerforce: Salesforce.com & force.com developer resources*. Retrieved from http://developer.force.com

RFC4347 - Datagram Transport Layer Security. (2006, April). Retrieved July 12, 2014, from IETF http://tools.ietf.org/html/rfc4347

RFC6455 - The WebSocket Protocol. (2011, December). Retrieved July 12, 2014, from Internet Engineering Task Force (IETF): http://tools.ietf.org/html/rfc6455

RFC6716 - Definition of the Opus Audio Codec. (2012, September). Retrieved July 12, 2014, from Internet Engineering Task Force (IETF): http://tools.ietf.org/html/rfc6716

Ristenpart, T., Tromer, E., Shacham, H., & Savage, S. (2009), Hey, you, get off of my cloud: exploring information leakage in third-party compute clouds. In *Proceedings of the 16th ACM Conference on Computer and Communications Security* (CCS '09). ACM. doi:10.1145/1653662.1653687

Robison, W. J. (2010). Free at what cost? Cloud computing privacy under the Stored Communications Act. *The Georgetown Law Journal*, *98*(4). Retrieved from http://papers.ssrn.com/sol3/Delivery.cfm/SSRN_ID1596975_code1461162.pdf?abstractid=1596975&mirid=2

Roettgers, J. (2011, June 30). *The technology behind Google+ hangouts – Tech news and analysis*. Retrieved July 12, 2014, from https://gigaom.com/2011/06/30/google-hangouts-technology/

Rolla, V., & Curado, M. (2013). A reinforcement learning-based routing for delay tolerant networks. *Engineering Applications of Artificial Intelligence*, *26*(10).

Rudenko, A., Reiher, P., Popek, G. J., & Kuenning, G. H. (1998). Saving portable computer battery power through remote process execution. *Journal of ACM SIGMOBILE on Mobile Computing and Communications Review*, *2*(1).

Rui, H., Li, G., Ghanem, M., & Yike, G. (2012). Lightweight resource scaling for cloud applications. In *Proceedings of 12th IEEE/ACM International Symposium on CLuster, Cloud and Grid Computing* (CCGrid). IEEE.

Ryder, J., Longstaff, B., Reddy, S., & Estrin, D. (2009). Ambulation: A tool for monitoring mobility patterns over time using mobile phones. In *Proceedings ofComputational Science and Engineering*. IEEE. doi:10.1109/CSE.2009.312

Sachs, D. G., Yuan, W., Hughes, C. J., Harris, A. F., III, Adve, S. V., Jones, D. L., . . . Nahrstedt, K. (2004). *GRACE: A hierarchical adaptation framework for saving energy*. University of Illinois Technical Report UIUCDCS-R-2004-2409.

Sagar, M. S., Singh, B., & Ahmad, W. (2013). Study on cloud computing resource allocation strategies. *International Journal (Toronto, Ont.)*, *3*, 107–114.

Saleem, Y., Salim, F., & Rehmani, M. H. (2014). Resource management in mobile sink based wireless sensor networks through cloud computing. In *Resource management in mobile computing environments* (Vol. 3, pp. 439–459). Springer International Publishing.

Salesforce, C. R. M. (2014). Retrieved from http://www.salesforce.com/platform

Samanta, R. J., Bhattacharjee, P., & Sanyal, G. (2010). Modeling cellular wireless networks under gamma inter-arrival and general service time distributions. *World Academy of Science, Engineering, & Technology*, *44*, 417.

Sánchez, Y., Hellge, C., Schierl, T., Van Leekwijck, W., & Le Louédec, Y. (2011). Scalable video coding based DASH for efficient usage of network resources. In *Proceedings of the Third W3C Web and TV Workshop* (pp. 19-20). Academic Press.

Sappington, B. (2013). *Residential gateway trends: Bringing value home*. Academic Press.

Sardis, F., Mapp, G., Loo, J., Aiash, M., & Vinel, A. (2013). On the investigation of cloud-based mobile media environments with service-populating and QoS-aware mechanisms. *IEEE Transactions on Multimedia*, *15*(4), 769–777. doi:10.1109/TMM.2013.2240286

Sarsembagieva, K., Gardikis, G., Xilouris, G., Kourtis, A., & Demestichas, P. (2013). Efficient planning of virtual network services. In *Proceedings of IEEE Region 8 EuroCon Conference*. IEEE.

Satyanarayanan, M., Bahl, P., Caceres, R., & Davies, N. (2009). The case for VM-based cloudlets in mobile computing. *IEEE Pervasive Computing*, *8*(8), 14–23. doi:10.1109/MPRV.2009.82

Satyanarayan, M. (1996). Fundamental challenges in mobile computing. In *Proceedings of the Fifteenth Annual ACM Symposium on Principles of Distributed Computing (PODC'96)*. ACM. doi:10.1145/248052.248053

Schaffrath, G., Werle, C., Papadimitriou, P., Feldmann, A., Bless, R., Greenhalgh, A., & Mathy, L. et al. (2009). Network virtualization architecture: Proposal and initial prototype. In *Proc. ACM SIGCOMM VISA*. ACM.

Schierl, T., Hannuksela, M. M., Wang, Y., & Wenger, S. (2012). System layer integration of high efficiency video coding. *IEEE Transactions on Circuits and Systems for Video Technology*, *22*(12), 1871–1884. doi:10.1109/TCSVT.2012.2223054

Schlachter, F. (2012). Has the battery bubble burst? *APSNews*, *8*(21), 8. Retrieved October 2012 from http://www.aps.org/publications/apsnews/

Schmeink, A. (2011). On fair rate adaption in interference-limited systems. *European Transactions on Telecommunications*, *22*(5), 200–210.

Schulman, A., Navda, V., Ramjee, R., Spring, N., Deshpande, P., Grunewald, C., . . . Padmanabhan, V. N. (2010). Bartendr: A practical approach to energy-aware cellular data scheduling. In N. H. Vaidya, S. Banerjee & D. Katabi (Eds.), MOBICOM (pp. 85-96). ACM. doi:10.1145/1859995.1860006

Schulzrinne, H., Casner, S., Frederick, R., & Jacobson, V. (2003). *RTP: A transport protocol for real-time applications*. IETF RFC 3550.

Schulzrinne, H., Casner, S., Frederick, R., & Jacobson, V. (2003). *RTP: A transport protocol for real-time applications*. Request for Comments: 3550. Retrieved from http://tools.ietf.org/rfcmarkup?rfc=3550

Schulzrinne, H., Rao, A., Lanphier, R., Westerlund, M., & Stiemerling, M. (2013). *Real time streaming protocol 2.0 (RTSP)*. IETF Internet Draft, draft-ietf-mmusic-rfc2326bis-36.

Schwerdel, D., Reuther, B., Zinner, T., Müller, P., & Tran-Gia, P. (2014). Future internet research and experimentation: The g-lab approach. *Computer Networks, 61*(14), 102-117.

Scott, J., & Carrington, P. J. (Eds.). (2011). *The SAGE handbook of social network analysis*. SAGE Publications.

Seaman, C., Guo, Y., Izurieta, C., Cai, Y., Zazworka, N., Shull, F., & Vetrò, A. (2012). Using technical debt data in decision making: Potential decision approaches. In *Proceedings of2012 Third International Workshop on Managing Technical Debt (MTD)* (pp. 45–48). Zurich, Switzerland: IEEE. doi:10.1109/MTD.2012.6225999

Seaman, C., & Guo, Y. (2011). Measuring and monitoring technical debt. *Advances in Computers*, *82*, 25–46. doi:10.1016/B978-0-12-385512-1.00002-5

Sebestyen, G., Hangan, A., Sebestyen, K., & Vachter, R. (2013). Self-tuning multimedia streaming system on cloud infrastructure. *Procedia Computer Science*, *18*, 1342–1351. doi:10.1016/j.procs.2013.05.301

Seo, W. C. B., & Zimmermann, R. (2012). Efficient video uploading from mobile devices in support of http streaming. In *Proc. ACM MMSys*. ACM.

Shafiq, M. Z., Ji, L., Liu, A. X., Pang, J., & Wang, J. (2012). A first look at cellular machine-to-machine traffic: large scale measurement and characterization. In *Proceedings of the 12th ACM SIGMETRICS/PERFORMANCE Joint International Conference on Measurement and Modeling of Computer Systems* (SIGMETRICS '12). ACM. doi:10.1145/2254756.2254767

Shahid, Z., & Puech, W. (2014). Visual protection of HEVC video by selective encryption of CABAC binstrings. *IEEE Transactions on Multimedia*, *16*(1), 24–36. doi:10.1109/TMM.2013.2281029

Shanableh, T., Peixoto, E., & Izquierdo, E. (2013). MPEG-2 to HEVC video transcoding with content-based modeling. *IEEE Transactions on Circuits and Systems for Video Technology*, *23*(7), 1191–1196. doi:10.1109/TCSVT.2013.2241352

Shannon, C. E. (1948). A mathematical theory of communication. *Mobile Computing and Communications Review, 5*(1), 3–55.

Sharma, M. A., & Singh, J. B. (2010). Use of probability distribution in rainfall analysis. *New York Science Journal, 3*(9).

Shen, T., Lu, Y., Wen, Z., Zou, L., Chen, Y., & Wen, J. (2013). Ultra Fast H.264/AVC to HEVC Transcoder. In *Proc. 2013 Data Compression Conference* (Vol. 92093). IEEE. doi:10.1109/DCC.2013.32

Shirazi, N., Watson, M. R., Marnerides, A., K., Mauthe, A., & Hutchison, D. (2013). A multilevel approach towards challenge detection in cloud computing. In *Cyberpatterns*. Academic Press.

Shi, Z., Sun, X., & Wu, F. (2012). Spatially scalable video coding for HEVC. *IEEE Transactions on Circuits and Systems for Video Technology*, *22*(12), 1813–1826. doi:10.1109/TCSVT.2012.2223031

Shozu. (n.d.). Retrieved from http://www.shozu.com/portal/index.do

Singh, V. P. (1998). Log-pearson type III distribution. Entropy-Based Parameter Estimation in Hydrology, 30, 252-274.

Sitaram, D., & Manjunath, G. (2012). Future trends and research directions. In Moving to the cloud. Academic Press. doi:10.1016/B978-1-59749-725-1.00010-X

Skadron, K., Abdelzaher, T., & Stan, M. R. (2002). Control-theoretic techniques and thermal-RC modeling for accurate and localized dynamic thermal management. In *Proceedings of the Eighth International Symp. on High-Performance Computer Architecture*. Academic Press.

Skicewicz, J., Skicewicz, J. A., & Dinda, P. A. (2003). *Tsunami: A wavelet toolkit for distributed systems*. Academic Press.

Skourletopoulos, G., Bahsoon, R., Mavromoustakis, C. X., Mastorakis, G., & Pallis, E. (2014, December). Predicting and quantifying the technical debt in cloud software engineering. In *Proceedings of Computer Aided Modeling and Design of Communication Links and Networks (CAMAD)*. IEEE. doi:10.1109/CAMAD.2014.7033201

Smailagic, U., & Ettus, M. (2002). System design and power optimization for mobile computers. In *Proceedings of IEEE Computer Society Annual Symposium on VLSI*. IEEE. doi:10.1109/ISVLSI.2002.1016867

Smith, D., Qiang, G., & Song, F. (2010). An anomaly detection framework for autonomic management of compute cloud systems. In *Proceedings of Computer Software and Applications Conference Workshops (COMPSACW)* (pp. 376-381). Academic Press.

Snipes, W., Robinson, B., Guo, Y., & Seaman, C. (2012). Defining the decision factors for managing defects: a technical debt perspective. In *Proceedings of2012 Third International Workshop on Managing Technical Debt (MTD)* (pp. 54–60). IEEE. doi:10.1109/MTD.2012.6226001

Snort AD. (2005). Retrieved July 27, 2014, from http://anomalydetection.info/

Soares, J., Carapinha, J., Melo, M., Monteiro, R., & Sargento, S. (2012). Resource allocation in the network operator's cloud: A virtualization approach. In *Proceedings ofIEEE Symposium on Computers and Communications* (ISCC). IEEE.

Sodagar, I. (2011). *Industry and standards*. Academic Press.

Sodagar, I. (2011, April). The mpeg-dash standard for multimedia streaming over the internet. *MultiMedia, IEEE*, *18*(4), 62–67. doi:10.1109/MMUL.2011.71

Software. P. M. (2014). Retrieved from http://basecamphq.com

Solutions, W. C. (2014). *Cloud hosting*. Retrieved from http://www.webair.com/webhosting-cloud-servers.html

Song, D. X., Wagner, D., & Tian, X. (2001). Timing analysis of keystrokes and timing attacks on SSH. In *Proceedings of the 10th conference on USENIX Security Symposium* (SSYM'01) (*Vol. 10*). USENIX Association.

Song, H. H., Ge, Z., Mahimkar, A., Wang, J., Yates, J., Zhang, Y., . . . Chen, M. (2011). Q-score: Proactive service quality assessment in a large IPTV system. In *Proc. IMC*. Academic Press. doi:10.1145/2068816.2068836

Song, C., Qu, Z., Blumm, N., & Barabási, A.-L. (2010). Limits of predictability in human mobility. *Science*, *327*(5968), 1018–1021. doi:10.1126/science.1177170 PMID:20167789

Sony Ci. (2014). Retrieved from https://www.sonymcs.com/

Southwell, R., Huang, J., & Liu, X. (2012). Spectrum mobility games. In *Proceedings of INFOCOM*. IEEE. doi:10.1109/INFCOM.2012.6195776

Stantchev, V., & Schröpfer, C. (2009). Negotiating and enforcing QoS and SLAs in grid and cloud computing. In *Proceedings of the 4th International Conference on Advances in Grid and Pervasive Computing*. Academic Press. doi:10.1007/978-3-642-01671-4_3

Sterling, C. (2010). *Managing software debt: Building for inevitable change*. Boston: Addison-Wesley Professional.

Su, A.-J., Choffnes, D. R., Kuzmanovic, A., & Bustamante, F. E. (2009). Drafting behind Akamai: Inferring network conditions based on CDN redirections. *IEEE/ACM Transactions on Networking*, *17*(6), 1752–1765. doi:10.1109/TNET.2009.2022157

Suh, K., Diot, C., Kurose, J., Massoulie, L., Neumann, C., Towsley, D., & Varvello, M. (2007). Push-to-peer video-on-demand system: Design and evaluation. *IEEE Journal on Selected Areas in Communications*, *25*(9), 1706–1716.

Sullivan, G. J., Boyce, J. M., Chen, Y., Ohm, J., Segall, C. A., & Vetro, A. (2013). Standardized extensions of high efficiency video coding (HEVC). *IEEE Journal of Selected Topics in Signal Processing*, *7*(6), 1001–1016. doi:10.1109/JSTSP.2013.2283657

Sultan, N. (2010). Cloud computing for education: A new dawn? *International Journal of Information Management*, *30*(2), 109–116. doi:10.1016/j.ijinfomgt.2009.09.004

Sun, H., & Williamson, C. (2008). Downlink performance for mixed web/VoIP traffic in 1xEVDO revision a networks. In *Proceedings of Communications*. IEEE.

Svoboda, P. (2008). *Measurement and modelling of internet traffic over 2.5 and 3G cellular core networks.* (Ph.D. dissertation). Vienna University of Technology, Vienna, Austria.

Sweeney, L. (2002, February). A model for protecting privacy. *International Journal of Uncertainty Fuzziness and Knowledge-based Systems.*

Tang, J., Musolesi, M., Mascolo, C., Latora, V., & Nicosia, V. (2010, April). Analysing information flows and key mediators through temporal centrality metrics. In *Proceedings of the 3rd Workshop on Social Network Systems* (p. 3). ACM. doi:10.1145/1852658.1852661

Tcpdump. (1987). Retrieved July, 27, 2014, from http://www.tcpdump.org/

Team, R. C. (2014). *R: A language and environment for statistical computing.* Academic Press.

Technologies, G. (2014). *Automation, orchestration, and provisioning.* Retrieved from http://www.galetechnologies.com

Teng, F., & Magoules, F. (2010). Resource pricing and equilibrium allocation policy in cloud computing. In *Proceedings of the 2010 10th IEEE International Conference on Computer and Information Technology.* Washington, DC: IEEE.

Thang, T., Ho, Q., Kang, J., & Pham, A. (2012, February). Adaptive streaming of audiovisual content using MPEG DASH. *IEEE Transactions on Consumer Electronics, 58*(1), 78–85. doi:10.1109/TCE.2012.6170058

The Economist. (2008, October 23). *On the periphery.* Retrieved June 20, 2014 from http://www.economist.com/node/12411896

The WebM Project. (n.d.). Retrieved July 12, 2014, from http://www.webmproject.org/

Theodoropoulos, T., Hofberg, M., & Kern, D. (2011). Technical debt from the stakeholder perspective. In *Proceedings of the 2nd Workshop on Managing Technical Debt (MTD '11)* (pp. 43–46). ACM.

Thomas, R. W., DaSilva, L. A., & McKenzie, A. B. (2005). Cognitive networks. In *Proceedings of New Frontiers in Dynamic Spectrum Access Networks.* IEEE.

TokBox. (n.d.). Retrieved July 12, 2014, from Add live, face-to-face video with the OpenTok platform - TokBox: http://tokbox.com/

Torres, M.E., Colominas, M.A., Schlotthauer, G., & Flandrin, P. (2011). A complete ensemble empirical mode decomposition with adaptive noise. In *Proceedings of IEEE ICASSP.* IEEE.

Turner, D., & Kostiainen, A. (Eds.). (2014, June 19). *Ambient light events, W3C last call working draft.* Retrieved July 12, 2014, from http://www.w3.org/TR/ambient-light/

Uncover and Resolve Performance Issues with Cloud Performance Monitoring. (n.d.). Retrieved from http://www.copperegg.com/product/cloud-monitoring/

Vallis, O., Hochenbaum, J., & Kejariwal, A. (2014). A novel technique for long-term anomaly detection in the cloud. In *Proceedings of the 6th USENIX Workshop on Hot Topics in Cloud Computing.* USENIX HotCloud.

Van Kesteren, A., & Çelik, T. (Eds.). (2012, July 3). *Fullscreen, W3C working draft.* Retrieved July 12, 2014, from http://www.w3.org/TR/fullscreen/

Van Wallendael, G., Staelens, N., Janowski, L., De Cock, J., Demeester, P., & Van De Walle, R. (2012). No-reference bitstream-based impairment detection for high efficiency video coding. In *Proceedings of2012 Fourth International Workshop on Quality of Multimedia Experience (QoMEX)* (pp. 7–12). Academic Press. doi:10.1109/QoMEX.2012.6263845

Van Wallendael, G., Dooms, A., De Cock, J., Braeckman, G., Boho, A., Preneel, B., & Van De Walle, R. (2013). End-to-end security for video distribution. *IEEE Signal Processing Magazine,* (March): 97–107.

Varshney, U. (2007). Pervasive healthcare and wireless health monitoring. *Journal on Mobile Networks and Applications,* March, 113-127.

Vartiainen, E., & Mattila, K. V. V. (2010). User experience of mobile photo sharing in the cloud. In *Proceedings of the 9th International Conference on Mobile and Ubiquitous Multimedia (MUM).* Academic Press. doi:10.1145/1899475.1899479

Velte, A. T., Velte, T. J., & Elsenpeter, R. (2010). *Cloud computing: A practical approach*. New York: McGraw-Hill.

Viitanen, M., Vanne, J., Hämäläinen, T. D., & Lainema, J. (2012). Complexity analysis of next-generation HEVC decoder. In *Proc. 2012 IEEE International Symposium on Circuits and Systems (ISCAS)*. IEEE. doi:10.1109/ISCAS.2012.6272182

Vinay Kumar, K., Ravi, V., Carr, M., & Raj Kiran, N. (2008). Software development cost estimation using wavelet neural networks. *Journal of Systems and Software*, *81*(11), 1853–1867. doi:10.1016/j.jss.2007.12.793

Virtual 3D Classroom. (n.d.). Retrieved July 12, 2014, from http://opencourses.teicrete.gr/index.php/el/vrclass

Viswanathan, K., Choudur, L., Talwar, V., Chengwei, W., Macdonald, G., & Satterfield, W. (2012). Ranking anomalies in data centers. In *Proceedings ofNetwork Operations and Management Symposium (NOMS), 2012 IEEE* (pp. 79-87). IEEE. doi:10.1109/NOMS.2012.6211885

VMWare vSphrere. (2012). Retrieved July 27, 2014, from http://www.vmware.com/uk/products/vsphere

VMware. (2014). *VMware vCloud director: Secure private clouds, infrastructure as a service*. Retrieved from http://www.vmware.com/products/vcloud-director/overview.html

VMware. (2014). *VMware vSphere: Private cloud computing for mid-size & enterprises businesses*. Retrieved from http://www.vmware.com/products/vsphere/mid-size-and-enterprise-business/overview.html

Vodafone Media Cloud. (2014). Retrieved from http://www.mediacloud.tv/

Volatility. (2011). Retrieved July 27, 2014, from https://www.volatilesystems.com/default/volatility

Von Kaenel, M., Sommer, P., & Wattenhofer, R. (2011). Ikarus: Large-scale participatory sensing at high altitudes. In *Proceedings of the 12th Workshop on Mobile Computing Systems and Applications* (pp. 63-68). ACM. doi:10.1145/2184489.2184503

Voznak, M., Rozhon, J., & Rezac, F. (2012). Relation between computational power and time scale for breaking authentication in SIP protocol. In *Proceedings of the12th International Conference KTTO 2012*. Malenovice, Czech Republic: Academic Press.

Wang, C., & Li, Z. (2004). A computation offloading scheme on handheld devices. *Journal of Parallel and Distributed Computing*, *64*(6), 740-746.

Wang, X. (2010). An adaptive QoS management framework for VoD cloud service centers. In *Proc.2010 International Conference on Computer Application and System Modeling*. Academic Press.

Wang, Y.C., Chuang, C.H., Tseng, Y.C., & Shen, C.C. (2013). A lightweight, self-adaptive lock gate designation, scheme for data collection in long-thin wireless sensor networks. *Wireless Communications and Mobile Computing*, *13*(1), 47-62.

Wang, Y.-K., Even, R., Kristensen, T., & Jesup, R. (2011). *RTP payload format for H.264 video*. IETF RFC 6184.

Wang, H., Wu, S., Chen, M., & Wang, W. (2014). Security protection between users and the mobile media cloud. *IEEE Communications Magazine*, *52*(March), 73–79. doi:10.1109/MCOM.2014.6766088

Wang, T., Yang, B., Gao, J., Yang, D., Tang, S., Wu, H., & Pei, J. et al. (2009). MobileMiner: A real world case study of data mining in mobile communication. In *Proceedings of the 2009 ACM SIGMOD International Conference on Management of data (SIGMOD '09)*. ACM. doi:10.1145/1559845.1559988

Watson, M., Shirazi, N., Marnerides, A. K., Mauthe, A., & Hutchison, D. (2013). Towards a distributed, self-organizing approach to malware detection in cloud computing. In *Proceedings of 7th IFIP International Workshop on Self-Organizing Systems*. IFIP/IFISC IWSOS.

Web Browsers with Real-Time Communications - WebRTC Initiative. (2014). Retrieved from http://www.webrtc.org/

Web Page for the i-Promotion Project. (n.d.). Retrieved July 12, 2014, from http://translate.google.com/translate?sl=el&tl=en&js=n&prev=_t&hl=en&ie=UTF-8&u=http%3A%2F%2Fwww.ipromotion.gr%2Findex.php%2Fhomepage&act=url

WebRTC - iLBC Freeware. (n.d.). Retrieved July 12, 2014, from http://www.webrtc.org/ilbc-freeware

WebRTC / Codelab - Bitbucket. (n.d.). Retrieved July 12, 2014, from https://bitbucket.org/webrtc/codelab

WebRTC. (n.d.). Retrieved July 12, 2014, from http://www.webrtc.org/

Websockets-Based Messenger for Text and Live Image Exchange between Browser Peers. (n.d.). Retrieved July 12, 2014, from http://medialab.teicrete.gr:8080/WebSocketsJetty/

Wei, Z., Li, J., Yang, Y., & Jia, D. (2010). *A residential gateway architecture based on cloud computing*. Paper presented at the Software Engineering and Service Sciences (ICSESS). doi:10.1109/ICSESS.2010.5552422

Weiser, M. (1991). The computer for the 21st century. *Scientific American*, *265*(3), 66–75. doi:10.1038/scientificamerican0991-94 PMID:1754874

Wenger, S., Wang, Y.-K., Schierl, T., & Eleftheriadis, A. (2011, May). *RTP payload format for scalable video coding*. IETF RFC 6190.

Werle, C., Papadimitriou, P., Houidi, I., Louati, W., Zeghlache, D., Bless, R., & Mathy, L. (2011). Building virtual networks across multiple domains. In *Proc. ACM SIGCOMM 2011*. ACM. doi:10.1145/2018436.2018495

White, T. (2009, June 5). *Hadoop: The definitive guide*. O'Reilly Media, Yahoo! Press.

Whiteaker, J., Schneider, F., Teixeira, R., Diot, C., Soule, A., Picconi, F., & May, M. (2012). Expanding home services with advanced gateways. *Computer Communication Review*, *42*(5), 37–43. doi:10.1145/2378956.2378962

Wiklund, K., Eldh, S., Sundmark, D., & Lundqvist, K. (2012). Technical debt in test automation. In *Proceedings of2012 IEEE Fifth International Conference on Software Testing, Verification and Validation (ICST)* (pp. 887–892). Montreal, Canada: IEEE. doi:10.1109/ICST.2012.192

Windows Azure. (2014). Retrieved from http://www.microsoft.com/azure

Witten, I. H., & Frank, E. (2005). Data mining practical machine learning tools and techniques (2nd ed.). Morgan Kaufmann.

Workbench for Browsers' Performance Evaluation in Terms of their Ability to Display 3D Graphics. (n.d.). Retrieved July 12, 2014, from http://www.medialab.teicrete.gr/minipages/x3domwb/

Wu, Q., Juang, P., Martonosi, M., Peh, L-S., & Clark, D.W. (2005). Formal control techniques for power performance management. *IEEE Micro, 25*(5), 52-62.

Wu, Z., & Huang, N. E. (2009). Ensemble empirical mode decomposition: A noise-assisted data analysis method. Advances in Adaptive Data Analysis, 1(1), 1-41.

Wu, W., & Lui, J. (2012). Exploring the optimal replication strategy in P2P-VoD systems: Characterization and evaluation. *IEEE Transactions on Parallel and Distributed Systems*, *23*(8), 1492–1503.

Wu, Y., Zhang, Z., Wu, C., Li, Z., & Lau, F. C. M. (2013). CloudMoV: Cloud-based mobile social TV. *IEEE Transactions on Multimedia*, *15*(4), 821–832. doi:10.1109/TMM.2013.2240670

x264. (2014). *H.264/AVC encoder*. Retrieved May 22, 2014, from http://www.videolan.org/developers/x264.html

X3Dom Website. (n.d.). Retrieved July 13, 2014, from http://www.x3dom.org/

Xen. (2003). *Citrix Systems, Inc*. Retrieved July 27, 2014, from http://www.xen.org/

Xiao, Y., Lin, C., & Jiang, Y. (2010). Reputation based QoS provisioning in cloud computing via dirichlet multinomial model. In *Proceedings of 2010 IEEE International Conference on Communications (ICC)*. IEEE. doi:10.1109/ICC.2010.5502407

Xiong, J., Li, H., Wu, Q., & Meng, F. (2014). A fast HEVC inter CU selection method based on pyramid motion divergence. *IEEE Transactions on Multimedia*, *16*(2), 559–564. doi:10.1109/TMM.2013.2291958

Xu, D., Jung, E., & Liu, X. (2008). Optimal bandwidth selection in multi-channel cognitive radio networks: How much is too much? In *Proceedings of New Frontiers in Dynamic Spectrum Access Networks*. IEEE.

Xu, D., Kulkarni, S. S., Rosenberg, C., & Chai, H.-K. (2006). Analysis of a CDN–P2P hybrid architecture for cost-effective streaming media distribution. *Multimedia Systems*, *11*(4), 383–399. doi:10.1007/s00530-006-0015-3

Yan, C., Zhang, Y., Xu, J., Dai, F., Li, L., Dai, Q., & Wu, F. (2014). A highly parallel framework for HEVC coding unit partitioning tree decision on many-core processors. *IEEE Signal Processing Letters*, *21*(5), 573–576. doi:10.1109/LSP.2014.2310494

Yang, J., Wang, H., Wang, J., Tan, C., & Yu, D. (2011). Provable data possession of resource-constrained mobile devices in cloud computing. *Journal of Networks*, *6*(7), 1033–1040. doi:10.4304/jnw.6.7.1033-1040

Yang, X., Pan, T., & Shen, J. (2010). On 3G mobile e-commerce platform based on cloud computing. In *Proceedings of the 3rd IEEE International Conference on Ubi-Media Computing (U-Media)* (pp. 198-201). IEEE.

Ye, Y., Jain, N., & Xia, L. (2010). A framework for QoS and power management in a service cloud environment with mobile devices. In *Proceedings of2010 Fifth IEEE International Symposium on Service Oriented System Engineering (SOSE)* (pp. 236 - 243). IEEE. doi:10.1109/SOSE.2010.53

Yeo, C. S., Venugopal, S., Chu, X., & Buyya, R. (2010). *Autonomic metered pricing for a utility computing service*. Amsterdam, The Netherlands: Future Generation Computer Systems.

Yin, H., Liu, X., Zhan, T., Sekar, V., Qiu, F., Lin, C., . . . Li, B. (2009). *Design and deployment of a hybrid CDN-P2Psystem for live video streaming: Experiences with LiveSky.* Paper presented at the 17th ACM International Conference on Multimedia.

Yin, Chen, & Zhang, Liu, & Li. (2012). Mining spectrum usage data: A large-scale spectrum measurement study. *IEEE Transactions on Mobile Computing*, *11*(6), 1033–1046.

Younge, A. J., Von Laszewski, G., Wang, L., Lopez-Alarcon, S., & Carithers, W. (2010, August). Efficient resource management for cloud computing environments. In *Proceedings of Green Computing Conference* (pp. 357-364). IEEE. doi:10.1109/GREENCOMP.2010.5598294

Yu, J. (2012). Solution for virtual network embedding problem based on simulated annealing genetic algorithm. In *Proceedings of the 2nd International Conference on Consumer Electronics, Communications and Networks* (CECNet). Academic Press.

Yucek, T., & Arslan, H. (2009, March). A survey of spectrum sensing algorithms for cognitive radio applications. *IEEE Communication Surveys and Tutorials*, 116-130.

Yue, H., Sun, X., Yang, J., & Wu, F. (2013). Cloud-based image coding for mobile devices — Toward thousands to one compression. *IEEE Transactions on Multimedia*, *15*(4), 845–857. doi:10.1109/TMM.2013.2239629

Zahariev, A. (2009). Google app engine. In *Proceedings of TKK T-110.5190 Seminar on Internetworking*. Helsinki University of Technology. Retrieved June 20, 2014 from http://www.cse.hut.fi/en/publications/B/5/papers/1Zahariev_final.pdf

Zampoglou, M., Malamos, A. G., Sardis, E., Doulamis, A., Kapetanakis, K., Kontakis, K., & Vafiadis, G. (2013). A content-aware cloud platform for virtual reality web advertising. In Proceedings ofWorkshop Cloud-of-Things 2013 (CoT '13). Athens, Greece: Academic Press.

Zampoglou, M., Spala, P., Kontakis, K., Malamos, A. G., & Ware, J. A. (2013). Direct mapping of x3d scenes to mpeg-7 descriptions. In *Proceeding of the 18th International Conference on 3D Web Technology.* San Sebastian, Spain: Academic Press. doi:10.1145/2466533.2466540

Zazworka, N., Shaw, M. A., Shull, F., & Seaman, C. (2011). Investigating the impact of design debt on software quality. In *Proceedings of the 2nd Workshop on Managing Technical Debt* (pp. 17–23). ACM. doi:10.1145/1985362.1985366

Zeng, L., Veeravalli, B., & Wei, Q. (2014). Space4time: Optimization latency-sensitive content service in cloud. *Journal of Network and Computer Applications*, *41*, 358–368. doi:10.1016/j.jnca.2014.02.002

Zhan, H., Kang, L., Liu, L., & Cao, D. (2013). Scalable resource aggregation service of an ErlangOTP PaaS platform. In *Proceedings of Service Oriented System Engineering* (SOSE). IEEE.

Zhang, X., Schiffman, J., Gibbs, S., Kunjithapatham, A., & Jeong, S. (2009). Securing elastic applications on mobile devices for cloud computing. In R. Sion & D. Song (Eds.), CCSW (pp. 127-134). ACM. doi:10.1145/1655008.1655026

Zhang, L., Ding, X., Wan, Z., Gu, M., & Li, X. Y. (2010). WiFace: A secure geosocial networking system using WiFi based multi-hop MANET. In *Proceedings of 1st ACM Workshop on Mobile Cloud Computing and Services: Social Networks and Beyond (MCS)*. ACM.

Zhang, S., Qian, Z., Guo, S., & Lu, S. (2011). FELL: A flexible virtual network embedding algorithm with guaranteed load balancing. In *Proc. 2011 IEEE International Conference on Communications (ICC)*. IEEE. doi:10.1109/icc.2011.5962960

Zhangwei, H., & Mingjun, X. (2010). A distributed spatial cloaking protocol for location privacy. In *Proceeding of the 2nd International Conference on Network Security Wireless Communications and Trusted Computing (NSWCTC)*. NSWCTC. doi:10.1109/NSWCTC.2010.243

Zhang, X., Kunjithapatham, A., Jeong, S., & Gibbs, S. (2011). Towards an elastic application model for augmenting the computing capabilities of mobile devices with cloud computing. *MONET*, *16*, 270–284.

Zhang, Y., Ge, Z., Greenberg, A., & Roughan, M. (2005). Network anomography. In *Proceedings of the 5th ACM SIGCOMM Conference on Internet Measurement* (IMC '05). USENIX Association.

Zhanikeev, M. (2013a). A practical software model for content aggregation in browsers using recent advances in HTML5. In Proceedings of Computer Software and Applications Conference Workshops (COMPSACW) (pp. 151 – 156). Academic Press. doi:10.1109/COMPSACW.2013.18

Zhanikeev, M. (2013b). Experiments with application throughput in a browser with full HTML5 support. *IEICE Communications Express*,*2*(5), 167-172.

Zhao, W., Sun, Y., & Dai, L. (2010). Improving computer basis teaching through mobile communication and cloud computing technology. In *Proceedings of the 3rd International Conference on Advanced Computer Theory and Engineering (ICACTE)* (pp. 452-454). ICACTE.

Zhao, Y., Song, L., Wang, X., Chen, M., & Wang, J. (2013). Efficient realization of parallel HEVC intra encoding. In *Proc. 2013 IEEE International Conference on Multimedia and Expo Workshops (ICMEW)* (pp. 4–9). IEEE.

Zheng, L., Shen, C., Tang, L., Li, T., Luis, S., & Chen, S.-C. (2011). Applying data mining techniques to address disaster information management challenges on mobile devices. In *Proceedings of the 17th ACM SIGKDD International Conference on Knowledge Discovery and Data Mining (KDD '11)*. ACM. doi:10.1145/2020408.2020457

Zhu, W., Au, O. C., Yang, H., Dai, W., Zhang, H., & Zhang, X. (2013). Simplified generalized residual prediction in scalable extension of HEVC. In Proc. Visual Communications and Image Processing (VCIP) 2013 (Vol. 16). Academic Press. doi:10.1109/VCIP.2013.6706450

Zhu, X., Uysal, M., Wang, Z., Singhal, S., Merchant, A., Padala, P., & Shin, K. (2009). What does control theory bring to system research? *Operating Systems Review*, *43*(1), 62–69. doi:10.1145/1496909.1496922

Zhu, Z., Gupta, P., Wang, Q., Kalyanaraman, S., Lin, Y., & Franke, H. (2011). Virtual base station pool: Towards a wireless network cloud for radio access networks categories and subject descriptors. In *Proc. 8th ACM International Conference on Computing Frontiers*. ACM.

Zingaya. (n.d.). Retrieved July 12, 2014, from Online call – Let the visitors call you without a phone: http://zingaya.com/

Zinner, T., Hohlfeld, O., Abboud, O., & Hoßfeld, T. (2010). Impact of frame rate and resolution on objective QoE metrics. In *Proceedings ofQuality of Multimedia Experience (QoMEX)*. Trondheim, Norway: Academic Press. doi:10.1109/QOMEX.2010.5518277

Zorrilla, M. (2012). End to end solution for interactive on demand 3D media on home network devices. In *Proceedings ofBroadband Multimedia Systems and Broadcasting (BMSB)*. IEEE. doi:10.1109/BMSB.2012.6264228

Zu, Y., Zhang-Shen, R., Rangarajan, S., & Rexford, J. (2008). Cabernet: Connectivity architecture for better network services. In *Proc. ACM ReArch '08*. ACM.

About the Contributors

George Mastorakis received his B.Eng. (Hons) in Electronic Engineering from UMIST, UK in 2000, his M.Sc. in Telecommunications from UCL, UK in 2001, and his Ph.D. in Telecommunications from University of the Aegean, Greece in 2008. He is serving as an Assistant Professor at Technological Educational Institute of Crete and as a Research Associate in Research & Development of Telecommunications Systems Laboratory at Centre for Technological Research of Crete, Greece. His research interests include cognitive radio networks, networking traffic analysis, radio resource management and energy efficient networks. He has a more than 100 publications at various international conferences proceedings, workshops, scientific journals, and book chapters.

Constandinos X. Mavromoustakis is currently an Associate Professor at the Department of Computer Science at the University of Nicosia, Cyprus. He received a five-year dipl.Eng (BSc/BEng/MEng, KISATS approved) in Electronic and Computer Engineering from Technical University of Crete, Greece, MSc in Telecommunications from University College of London, UK, and his PhD from the department of Informatics at Aristotle University of Thessaloniki, Greece. Dr. Mavromoustakis is leading the Mobile Systems Lab. (MOSys Lab., http://www.mosys.unic.ac.cy/) at the Department of Computer Science at the University of Nicosia. Dr. Mavromoustakis has extensive experience in simulation of wireless systems, MP2P and Opportunistic Systems, Mobile Computing and Web technologies. He serves as an Associate editor *International Journal of Communication Systems* (IJCS), Wiley, and editorial board member of the *Simulation Practice and Theory* (SIMPAT) *Journal*, Elsevier, and as member of Technical Program Committees for various International Conferences.

Evangelos Pallis received his B.Sc. in Electronic Engineering from Technological Educational Institute of Crete in 1994, his M.Sc. in Telecommunications from University of East London in 1997 and his Ph.D. in Telecommunications from University of East London in 2002. He currently serves as an Associate Professor at Technological Educational Institute of Crete in the Department of Informatics Engineering and acts as the Director of Research and Development of Telecommunication Systems Laboratory. His research interests are in the fields of wireless broadband and mobile networks and network management. He has more than 100 publications in international scientific journals, conference and workshop proceedings.

* * *

Haroula Andrioti received her four-year diploma in Computer Engineering in 2010 from the Department of Informatics Engineering of the Technological Educational Institute of Crete. She is currently a postgraduate student at the aforementioned department working on the implementation of a Web 3D gaming infrastructure over HTML5 and Web-based Real Time Communication (WebRTC). Her interests are extended to applied informatics and new technologies in the fields of multimedia and web-based communications.

Dimitar Kapriel Atamian received M.Sc. degrees in Telecommunications from the Technical University of Sofia (TUS), Bulgaria in 1988. He was part of the research staff of Department of Telecommunications at Technical University of Sofia (1987-1994), Assistant Professor since 1994 at the same department. His main interests are communication networks, protocols and software engineering as well as teletraffic theory and engineering, Quality of Service, simulation and network planning. D. Atamian is active in many practical, engineering, planning, design, measurements, control, and management projects. His knowledge and excellent experience is gained in more than 25 publications and more than 30 projects at national and international level.

Rami Bahsoon is a Senior lecturer in Software Engineering and founder of the Software Engineering for/in the Cloud interest groups at the University of Birmingham. The group's research aims at developing architecture and frameworks to support and reason about the development and evolution of dependable ultra-large complex and data-intensive software systems, where the investigations span cloud computing architectures and their economics. Dr. Bahsoon had founded the IEEE International Software Engineering IN/FOR the Cloud workshop in conjunction with IEEE Services. He was the lead editor of a special issue on the Future of Software Engineering for/In the Cloud with the *Journal of Systems and Software*. Dr. Bahsoon has co-edited a book on *Software Architecture and Software Quality* and another book on *Economics-Driven Software Architecture* published by Elsevier in 2014 and co-edited another book on *Aligning Enterprise, System, and Software Architectures*, published by IGI Global in 2012. He acted as the workshop chair for IEEE Services 2014, the Doctoral Symposium chair of IEEE/ACM Utility and Cloud Computing Conference (UCC 2014) and the track chair for Utility Computing of IEEE HPCC 2014. He published extensively in the area of economics-driven software engineering. He holds a Ph.D. in Software Engineering from University College London (UCL) for his research on evaluating software architecture stability using real options. He has also read for MBA-level certificates in technology strategy and dynamics with London Business School.

Vlad Barosan finished his Bachelor studies within the University POLITEHNICA of Bucharest. His main research areas are Opportunistic Networks, Large Scale Distributed Systems, and High Performance Computing.

Jordi Mongay Batalla was born in Barcelona (Spain) in 1975. He received M.Sc. degree from Universitat Politecnica de Valencia (2000) and Ph.D. degree from Warsaw University of Technology (2009), where he still works as Assistant Professor. In the past, he worked in Telcordia Poland (Ericsson R&D) and he is still with National Institute of Telecommunications, where, from 2010, he is Head of Internet Architectures and Applications Department. Dr. Jordi Mongay Batalla took part (coordination and/or participation) in 12 international ICT projects, five of them inside the EU Framework Programmes. His research interest focuses mainly on Quality of Service (Diffserv, NGN) in both IPv4 and IPv6 infrastructures, Future Internet architectures (Content Aware Networks, Information Centric Networks) as well as applications for Future Internet (Internet of Things, Smart Cities, IPTV). He is author or co-author of more than 100 papers published in books, international and national journals and conference proceedings.

Athina Bourdena received her B.Sc. from the Department of Applied Informatics and Multimedia of Technological Educational Institute of Crete, Greece in 2007. She obtained her M.Sc. in Digital Communications and Networks from the Department of Digital Systems of the University of Piraeus, Greece in 2009 and her Ph.D. diploma in the field of cognitive radio in November 2013 from the Department of Information & Communication Systems Engineering of University of the Aegean in Greece. From 2009 until now she works as a teaching assistance of the Technological Educational Institute of Crete and from 2014 until now as a post-doctoral fellow at the Department of Computer Science of the University of Nicosia in Cyprus. Her research interests are in the fields of cognitive radio networks, mobile networks and digital interactive television systems. She has published more than 35 publication articles in refereed scientific journals and international conferences.

Jose M. Alcaraz Calero is a Lecturer in Networks with the Centre of the Audio-Visual Communications and Networks (AVCN) in the University of the West of Scotland (UWS), UK. He is an Editorial Board Member in a number of international journals and special issues related to cloud computing, security, privacy, big data and wireless sensor networks, which are his main research interests. He has published more than 70 journals, books and conferences publications in these fields. He has been TPC for conferences in more than 70 times and reviewer for more than 30 high quality journals. He is an Organizing Committee Member for conferences like IEEE TrustCom, IET WSS, ICGCN, SNDS, and ATC, among others. Prior to joining UWS, he worked at HP Research Laboratories, UK and the University of Valencia, Spain, holding a post as Associate Professor. He received his PhD degree from the University of Murcia, Spain.

Radu-Ioan Ciobanu is PhD student within the Computer Science Department, in University Politehnica of Bucharest, Romania. The PhD topic is on Routing and Dissemination in Mobile Opportunistic Networks. His general interests regard distributed and collaborative systems, artificial intelligence and algorithms. His current research is focused on models and techniques for representing and reasoning on mobility support for opportunistic networking and applications.

Mihail Costea finished his Bachelor studies within the University POLITEHNICA of Bucharest. His main research areas are collaborative systems, artificial intelligence and algorithms. He is currently Software Engineer with Minato-ku, Tokyo, Japan.

Christos Damaskos was born in Athens, Greece in 1993. He graduated from Ionios Scholi high school in 2011, received his BSc degree in Computer Science in 2014 from the London Metropolitan University, Computer Science Department, and he is currently doing his Master degree in Management of Business, Innovation & Technology- MBIT in the University of Sheffield. He speaks three languages: English, German and Greek. His professional/research interests include computer science/engineering, and project/IT management. He is also aware of several programming languages such as Java, Matlab, C, JavaScript, Python, HTML, Unix, VHDL and LaTeX. He is also aware of developing and working on database systems using MySQL. Currently he is working on some self-employed IT projects like creating websites and developing applications.

George Diakoumakos was born in Athens, Greece in 1993. He graduated from Sygxroni Paideia high school in 2011, received his BSc degree in Computer Science in 2014 from the London Metropolitan University, Computer Science Department, and he is currently doing his Master degree in Management of Business, Innovation & Technology- MBIT in the University of Sheffield. He speaks three languages: English, French, and Greek. His professional/research interests include computer science/engineering, and project/IT management. He is also aware of several programming languages such as Java, JavaScript, Matlab, C, HTML, UNIX, MySQL, LaTeX, PHP, Python, HTML and VHDL. Currently he is working on some self-employed IT projects like creating websites and developing applications.

Desislava Dimitrova received her BSc in Telecommunications from the Technical University of Sofia, Bulgaria and continued to obtain her MSc in Telematics from the University of Twente, The Netherlands. She obtained her PhD degree at the same university in 2010 on the topic of scheduling in cellular networks (UMTS, LTE). From 2011 to mid-2014, she was a Postdoctoral researcher at the University of Bern, Switzerland, where she conducted research in the areas of radio localisation and mobile network virtualization. Currently, she is a Postdoctoral researcher at ETH Zurich, Switzerland on the topics of virtualization, data center modelling and management. She is a regular reviewer for journals such as *Computer Communications* and *IEEE Networks*.

Ciprian Dobre has scientific and scholarly contributions in the field of large-scale distributed systems concerning monitoring (MonALISA), data services (PRO, DataCloud@Work), high-speed networking (VINCI, FDT), large scale application development (EGEE III, SEE-GRID-SCI), evaluation using modeling and simulation (MONARC 2, VNSim). Dr. Ciprian Dobre was awarded a PhD scholarship from California Institute of Technology (Caltech, USA), and another one from Oracle. His results received two CENIC Awards, and three Best Paper Awards, and were published in 6 books, 10 articles in major international peer-reviewed journal, and over 60 articles in well-established international conferences and workshops (these articles received more than 150 citations). He is local project coordinator for national projects 'CAPIM - Context-Aware Platform using Integrated Mobile Services', and 'TRANSYS – Models and Techniques for Traffic Optimizing in Urban Environments'.

Georgios Gardikis holds a Diploma in Electrical and Computer Engineering from the National Technical University of Athens (2000) and a PhD from the same University (2004). He has been actively involved in several national and EU-funded R&D projects (IST MAMBO, IST REPOSIT, IST SOQUET, IST IMOSAN, IST ENTHRONE, ICT ADAMANTIUM, ICT ALICANTE) and he has served as Technical Coordinator of FP6/IST IMOSAN. He is currently with Space Hellas SA as R&D Project Manager, supervising a number of national and European research projects. He is Member of the IEEE/ Communications and Broadcast Technology Societies and Member of the Technical Chamber of Greece. He is the author of more than 40 publications in the field of networking in international journals and refereed conferences/workshops.

Rossitza Ivanova Goleva received M.Sc. degrees in Computer Science from the Technical University of Sofia (TUS), Bulgaria in 1982. She was part of the research staff of research Institute of Telecommunications in Bulgarian PTT (1982-1987), member of the research team of Department of Telecommunications at Technical University of Sofia (1987-1993), Assistant Professor since 1993 at the same department. Her main interests are communication networks, protocols and software engineering as well as teletraffic theory and engineering, Quality of Service, simulation and network planning. R. Goleva is also active member of IEEE section Bulgaria being correspondingly at treasurer, vice-chair and chair positions. She has more than 75 publications and supports many projects, conferences and other research activities.

Christos Grecos is a Professor in Visual Communications Standards, and Head of School of Computing, the University of the West of Scotland (UWS), UK. He leads the Centre of Audio-Visual Communications and Networks (AVCN), and his main areas of expertise are image and video compression algorithms and standards. He has more than 120 publications, and has obtained significant funding for his research from the UK EPSRC, UK TSB, European Regional Development Fund and Scottish Funding Council. He is in the international and technical programme committees of many prestigious conferences. Before coming to Scotland he worked at the universities of Central Lancashire and Loughborough. He received his PhD degree in image/video coding algorithms from the University of Glamorgan, UK.

Lubina Grigorova received her master degree in Telecommunications from the Technical University of Sofia in 2012. In 2012, she started her professional carrier in MAN design and development team of the Vivacom Ltd., Bulgaria. Her interests are in traffic engineering, traffic measurements, traffic analyses, traffic shaping, traffic management, statistical analyses, configuration management and protocols analyses. L. Grigorova has already three publications. She combines successfully practical work with her academic and research interests. L. Grigorova participated in more than five projects at national level while working for the biggest telecommunication operator in Bulgaria. She also gains international experience within the same team.

Jyoti Grover received a PhD degree in Computer Engineering from Malaviya National Institute of Technology, Jaipur (India) in 2013. Prior to this, she completed M.Tech degree in Computer Science and Engineering from G.J. University in 2004 and B.E in Computer Science and Engineering from M.D. University, Rohtak, India in 2002. Currently, she is an Associate Professor in Computer Science and Engineering department at Global Institute of Technology, Jaipur (India). Her areas of interest are Ad hoc networks security, VANET, cloud and mobile computing.

Aneliya Nedelcheva Ivanova received her bachelor's degree in Telecommunications from Technical University of Sofia in 2012. In the same year, she was hired as mobile network performance junior specialist in Alcatel-Lucent. Since 2013, she is Network Operations Centre engineer in Maxtelecom LTD. A. Ivanova has interests in traffic engineering, statistical analyses, traffic modeling, configuration management, traffic measurements, traffic control, traffic management, protocol analyses. She is focusing now on her carrier as IT manager and aims further certification as well. A. Ivanova is good in practical measurements and analyses. She combined successfully her practical work with research interests.

Kostas Kapetanakis received a B.Sc. in Applied Informatics and Multimedia (2011) and an M.Sc. in Informatics and Multimedia (2014) both at T.E.I. of Crete. Since 2008, he has been a researcher at the Multimedia Content Laboratory of T.E.I. of Crete with main interests in mobile and multimedia web applications. His recent research concerns ubiquitous devices, mobile energy consumption, multimedia content adaptation, quality of user experience and multimedia content streaming. He has published multiple peer-reviewed papers in these areas, in journals, books and conference proceedings.

Konstantinos Katzis received his BEng degree in Computer Systems Engineering and his MSc degree in Radio Systems Engineering from the University of Hull in 2000 and 2001 respectively. In 2006 he received his PhD degree in Electronics from University of York. In parallel to his PhD studies, Dr. Katzis attended a professional short-course on "Small Terminal Satellite Communications: VSAT Systems". His research involves developing highly efficient resource allocation techniques as well as handoff techniques optimised for the operation of High Altitude Stratospheric Platform communication systems (HAPs). He has also been working at the different aspects of Radio resource management, including cognitive radio, fairness in Quality of Service, dynamic spectrum sharing and coexistence. Since October 2006, Dr. Katzis has been working as an Assistant Professor at the Faculty of the Computer Science and Engineering at European University Cyprus (EUC).

Gaurav Kheterpal is a seasoned industry executive with over over 14 years of experience on cloud, telecom and mobile technologies. Gaurav currently works as the Head – Mobility at Metacube, a product engineering company based in Jaipur, India. At Metacube, Gaurav spearheads the development of several interesting native, hybrid and pure HTML5 applications across multiple industry verticals. Gaurav has spoken at leading mobile and cloud technology conferences including Dreamforce 2012, Senchacon 2013, TiConf 2014 and several others. Gaurav did BE (Computer Science) from Thapar University (2001) and M.S (Software Systems) from BITS, Pilani (2004). He has a keen interest in building mobile cloud solutions for the enterprise.

Ioannis Kopanakis is an Associate Professor and Vice Rector at the Technological Educational Institute of Crete. He holds a Diploma in computer science from the University of Crete (1998), Greece, an M.Sc. in information technology (1999), and a Ph.D. in computation (2003), both from UMIST, UK. He is the scientific Director of the e-Business Intelligence Lab (www.e-BILab.gr). His research interests include data mining, analytics, and business intelligence. He has been involved in more than twenty-five projects and research programs. He has published more than fifty papers in journals and refereed conferences and has demonstrated the results of his work in Europe and the US. He has acted as a reviewer for several international journals and member of conferences' scientific program committees. Before starting his academic career he worked in the IT industry in R&D departments.

Harilaos Koumaras was born in Athens, Greece in 1980. He received his BSc degree in Physics in 2002 from the University of Athens, Physics Department, his MSc in Electronic Automation and Information Systems in 2004, being scholar of the non-profit organization Alexander S Onassis, from the University of Athens, Computer Science Department and his PhD in 2007 at Computer Science from the University of Athens, Computer Science Department, having granted the four-year scholarship of National Centre of Scientific Research "Demokritos". He has received twice the Greek State Foundations (IKY) scholarship during the academic years 2000-01 and 2003-04. He has also granted with honors the classical piano and harmony degrees from the classical music department of Attiko Conservatory. Since 2004, he is a principal lecturer at the Business College of Athens (BCA) teaching modules related to Information Technology and Mathematics and Logic. From 2009, he has been elected as the Head of the Computer Science Department of BCA and Course leader of the respective franchised course of London Metropolitan University. He also joined the Digital Communications Lab at the National Centre of Scientific Research "Demokritos" in 2003 and since then he has participated in numerous EU-funded and national funded projects with presentations and publications at international conferences, scientific journals and book chapters. His research interests include objective/subjective evaluation of the perceived quality of multimedia services, video quality and picture quality evaluation, video traffic modeling, digital terrestrial television and video compression techniques. Currently, he is the author or co-author of more than 55 scientific papers in international journals, technical books and book chapters, numbering more than 125 non-self citations. He is an editorial board member of the *Telecommunications Systems Journal* and a reviewer of the *IEEE Network* magazine, the *EURASIP Journal of Applied Signal Processing*, the *IEEE Transactions on Image Processing*, and the *IEEE Transactions on Broadcasting*. Dr. Koumaras is a member of IEEE, SPIE, NGS, and ECPMA.

Vaios Koumaras received his BSc degree in Business Administration with major in Computer Information Systems from the American College of Greece and his MBA in Project Management from the City University, USA. Since 1997, he has worked in several positions as Computer Analyst and Software Developer, participating in major IT projects. Currently, he holds the position of senior R&D software engineer with participation and collaboration in the development and management of various R&D IT projects worldwide. In parallel, he has teaching experience of Business and IT courses in various grades since 1999. Currently, as part of his teaching activities, he is a lecturer at the Business College of Athens (BCA), at the Departments of Computer Science, Business Administration, Hotel and Tourism, teaching modules related to Information Technology, Business Administration and Mathematics. Additionally, he is part of the research team of the Computer Science Department at the Business College of Athens. He also participates, as associate R&D consultant and researcher, in several business and EC-funded projects and tasks related to IT, business planning, marketing analysis and strategy development.

Michail-Alexandros Kourtis received the Diploma in Computer Science from Athens University of economics and business, in 2011. From January 2010, he is working at NCSR "Demokritos", in various research projects. Currently, he is pursuing his PhD at Information and Communication Systems Department of University of the Aegean. His research interests include Video Processing, Video Quality Assessment, Image Processing, Network Function Virtualization, Software Defined Networks and Quality of Service.

Yiannos Kryftis holds a graduate degree in Electrical and Computer Engineering from National Technical University in Athens. He also holds an M.Sc. in Advanced Computing from Imperial College in London. Currently, he is working as a Researcher at the Department of Computer Science at the University of Nicosia. His research interests include Policy-based Network Management, Network Architectures for the Future Internet, Virtualization Information Models and Algorithms in Federated Environments, and Multimedia Services Provisioning.

Chunbo Luo is a Lecturer in Networks with the Centre of Audio-Visual Communications and Networks (AVCN), the University of the West of Scotland (UWS), UK. His research interests include wireless networks, Unmanned Aerial Vehicles (UAVs) and signal processing. He received his PhD degree from the University of Reading for his work on the study of cooperative networks. He then joined the SUAAVE project in the University of Ulster, collaborating with researchers from University College

London and Oxford University. He is leading a Royal Society funded project, which investigates oil spill detection using remote UAVs. He is also sponsored by RCUK Sustainable Society Network to study the application of UAVs for flood monitoring and disaster restoration. He is publishing top-tier papers in renowned journals and international conferences and serving as a reviewer/TPC member for academic journals and conferences such as IEEE TC, TVT, IET Communications, IEEE Globecom, and ICC.

Athanasios G. Malamos received his BSc degree in Physics from the University of Crete (1992) and his PhD from the Technical University of Crete in 2000. From 1997 to 2002 he was a research assistant and a researcher in the ICCS National Technical University of Athens. Since 2002 Athanasios is with the Technological Educational Institute of Crete at the Department of Informatics Engineering as an Assistant Professor (2002-2006) and as an Associate Professor (2006 until present). Dr. Malamos leads the Multimedia Lab. He has been granted with EU and National research funds. He has served as program committee member and reviewer for several international conferences and workshops. He is a reviewer for IEEE, Springer as other international journals. He is member of IEEE Computer Society, ACM SIGGRAPH and the WEB3D consortium. His research interests include multimedia semantics, AI, and graphics.

Radu-Corneliu Marin is PhD student within the Computer Science Department, in University Politehnica of Bucharest, Romania. The PhD topic is on Mobile Opportunistic Computing. His general interests regard distributed and collaborative systems, artificial intelligence and algorithms. His current research is focused on models and techniques for representing and reasoning on mobility for code execution in smartphone communities.

Angelos K. Marnerides is a Lecturer (Assistant Professor) in the School of Computing and Mathematical Sciences at Liverpool John Moores University, UK. His research interests include anomaly detection, network security, resilience and cloud computing. Prior to that he was a Research Associate in the department of Computing & Communications at Lancaster University (2012-2014), a Postdoctoral Research Fellow in the Carnegie Mellon University - Portugal postdoctoral scheme at IT, University of Porto (2011-2012) and an Honorary Research Associate with the department of Electronic & Electrical Engineering at University College London (UCL) (2012-2013). He obtained his M.Sc and PhD in Computer Science from Lancaster University in 2007 and 2011 respectively.

Seferin Todorav Mirtchev received his M.Sc. and Ph.D. degrees in Telecommunications from the Technical University of Sofia (TUS), Bulgaria in 1981 and 1988, respectively. In 1983 he became an Assistant Professor at the Telecommunications Department of the Technical University - Sofia. Since 1996, he is an Associate Professor at the Communication Networks Department, Faculty of Telecommunications of the Technical University - Sofia. His main interests are teletraffic theory and engineering, simulation and network planning, switching in telecommunication networks. S. Mirtchev is experiences researcher having more than 75 publications and participating in more than 30 research projects.

James Nightingale is a Postdoctoral Research Fellow with the Centre of the Audio-Visual Communications and Networks (AVCN) in the University of the West of Scotland (UWS), UK. His research interests include mobile networks, multihoming, cloud computing and video streaming techniques. He is a member of IET and IEEE. He received the BSc degree in Network Computing from Edinburgh

Napier University, UK with Distinction and as winner of the Napier Medal for Outstanding Achievement, and the BSc (Honours) degree in Computer Networks from UWS with First Class Honours and won the Best Honours Dissertation Prize. He received his PhD in video networking from UWS with Outstanding Progression Award.

Spyros Panagiotakis is assistant professor at the Department of Informatics Engineering of the Technological Educational Institution of Crete in Greece and head of the Telemetry and Industrial Information Systems Laboratory. He received his PhD in Communication Networks from the Department of Informatics and Telecommunications of the University of Athens in Greece in 2007. He is author of more than 40 publications in international refereed books, journals and conferences, which have received more than 130 citations. He also serves as peer reviewer in international conferences and journals, and member of technical programme committees of international conferences and workshops. His research interests focus on mobile multimedia technologies, communications and networking, web engineering, mobile applications, pervasive computing, sensor networks, Internet of Things and information systems in education.

Stelios Papadakis received the Diploma of Electrical and Computer Engineering and the Ph.D. degree from Aristotle University of Thessaloniki, (AUTH) Greece, in 1994 and 1999, respectively. From 2005 to 2011 he served as Associate Professor in the Department of Industrial Informatics, Technological Educational Institute (TEI) of Kavala, where the last two years he served as Head of the Department. Currently, he serves as an Associate Professor of Technological Educational Institute of Crete, at the Department of Business Administration. His expertise includes computational intelligence techniques and applications of parallel and distributed algorithms for modeling and optimization of large-scale nonlinear systems. He has participated, as a principal investigator or leader, in several research projects and has co-authored several articles in international scientific journals and conference proceedings, as well as one book and two book chapters. Additionally, He is a reviewer in several scientific journals and member of Technical chamber of Greece, IEEE, and EUCOGII.

Radu Pasea finished his Bachelor studies within the University POLITEHNICA of Bucharest. Current he is MSc student, and his main research areas cover Smart Systems and Large Scale Distributed Systems. His Master thesis topic addresses the use of context data, gathered using monitoring instruments.

Emmanouil Perakakis is a full-time Application Professor at the Department Business Administration at the TEI of Crete. He teaches courses in web design and development, social networks, e-marketing and graphic design and acts also as a member of the e-Business Intelligence Lab (www.e-bi.gr). He holds a B.Sc. degree in Computer Science from the University of Essex and a M.Sc. in Advanced Computing (Internet Technologies and Multimedia) from the University of Bristol. Since 2011 he is a part-time Ph.D. student at Brunel University, researching UX web design for the internet connected TV. Mr. Perakakis has also extended experience in the Computing and digital Marketing industry with participation to many applied projects as web designer, software/web developer, project manager and digital marketing consultant. His research interests include Human Computer Interaction, User Experience, Usability, digital Marketing, Social Media and Internet connected TV.

Zeeshan Pervez is a Lecturer in Web Technology with the Centre of Audio-Visual Communications and Networks (AVCN), the University of the West of Scotland (UWS), UK. His research interests are mainly cloud computing, data security and privacy, privacy-aware computation and encrypted data search. He has been involved in a number of research projects funded by the Ministry of Knowledge Economy (MKE), South Korea and Microsoft Asia. For his research on privacy-aware data sharing in public cloud he received 3rd Best Paper award from IEEE Seoul Section in 2010. He received his PhD degree from Kyung Hee University, South Korea.

Rosen Tsvetanov Rangelov received his master degree in Telecommunications from the Technical University of Sofia in 2013. In 2009 he was hired as an IT and Business Support Specialist in Lufthansa Technik Sofia. In 2012, he was promoted to a Central IT Support Specialist and is currently IT Products and Services Specialist in the same company. He deals with IT Infrastructure Operations, Analysis and Project Management activities. R. Rangelov has interests in traffic engineering, statistical analyses, traffic modeling, configuration management, traffic measurements, traffic control, traffic management, protocol analyses. He is focusing now on his carrier as IT manager and aims further certification as well.

Thomas Siakoulis was born in Athens, Greece in 1992. He graduated from the 2nd high school of Alimos in 2010. He is currently finalizing his Thesis towards the BSc degree in Computer Science from the London Metropolitan University, Computer Science Department. He speaks two languages: English and Greek. His professional/research interests include computer science and IT projects. He is also aware of some programming languages such as Java, Unix and HTML and he can work on database systems using MySQL.

Christos Skeberis received the Engineering Diploma Degree in Electrical and Computer Engineering in 2010 from Aristotle University of Thessaloniki and currently is a Ph.D. candidate in the same university. His research interests include design and optimization of antennas, mobile communications systems, neural networks, machine learning, radiowave propagation and ionospheric phenomena. Mr. Skeberis is a member of the Technical Chamber of Greece.

Georgios Skourletopoulos currently works as an e-Banking Platforms Use Case and Quality Assurance Analyst at Scientia Consulting S.A. in Greece. He obtained his M.Sc. in Computer Science from the University of Birmingham, UK in 2013 and his B.Sc. in Commerce and Marketing from the Technological Educational Institute of Crete, Greece in 2012, including a semester as an Erasmus student at the Czech University of Life Sciences Prague, Czech Republic and being granted a scholarship from the Greek State Scholarships Foundation (IKY). He has worked as a Junior Research Analyst at Hellastat S.A. in Greece. Mr. Georgios Skourletopoulos has publications at international conference proceedings and has also served as a reviewer of scientific papers in international conferences and journals.

Andreas Stamoulias received his four-year diploma in Computer Engineering in 2011 from the Department of Informatics Engineering of the Technological Educational Institute of Crete. He is currently a postgraduate student at the aforementioned department working on the implementation of physics support in Web3D environments. His interests are extended to applied informatics and new technologies in the fields of multimedia, web-based collaborative immersive environments and 3D realistic and interactive applications.

Dimitrios Stratakis is an Assistant Professor at the Informatics Engineering Department of Technological Educational Institute of Crete, Greece. He received his B.Sc. in Physics in 1987, his diploma degree in Electrical Engineering and his M.Sc. in Electronic Physics and Radioelectrology in 1992, as well as his Ph.D. degree in 2010 from Aristotle University of Thessaloniki, Greece. He is responsible of the Non-Ionizing Radiation Laboratory of the Technological Educational Institute of Crete, dealing with research and measurements of Non-Ionizing Electromagnetic fields at extremely low frequencies and radiofrequencies. His research interests include radiowave propagation, wireless communications systems, non-ionizing electromagnetic radiation measurements, and electromagnetic compatibility.

Ioannis Vakintis received his four-year diploma in Computer Engineering in 2011 from the Department of Informatics Engineering of the Technological Educational Institute of Crete. He is currently a postgraduate student at the aforementioned department working on the implementation of a real-time participatory sensing application via HTML5 platform including web sockets, geolocation and sensors APIS. His interests are extended to mobile and web technologies and his research activity focuses on: HTML5, JavaScript, X3D, X3DOM, WebSockets, Android development.

Qi Wang is a Senior Lecturer in Computer Networks with the Centre of Audio-Visual Communications and Networks (AVCN), the University of the West of Scotland (UWS), UK. He is the Principal Investigator of the UK EPSRC project "Enabler for Next-Generation Mobile Video Applications" (EP/J014729/1) and several industry-sponsored projects. His research interests include mobile/wireless networks, Internet protocols, cloud computing and video applications. He has published 70 papers in these areas. He was a winner of two IEEE ICCE Best Paper Awards (2012 and 2014), a finalist of the IEE 3G2003 Best Paper Award, and a recipient of a UWS 2013 STARS Award for "Outstanding Research & Knowledge Exchange" and a UK HEFCE ORS Award. He is a Regional Editor of Recent Advances in Communications and Networking Technology and a TPC member of various international conferences. He received his PhD degree in mobile networking from the University of Plymouth, UK.

Xinheng Wang is a Professor in Networks with the Centre of Audio-Visual Communications and Networks (AVCN), the University of the West of Scotland (UWS), UK. Prior to joining UWS, he worked at Kingston University and Swansea University in UK. His current research interests include wireless mesh networks, Internet of Things (IoT), converged indoor localisation, and service-oriented networks. He has authored/co-authored more than 110 journal and conference papers and filed 7 patents. He is actively engaged with industry and acting as a member of BSI (British Standards Institution) Committee in ICT, Electronics and Healthcare. In addition, he has severed as an External Expert Adviser for the National Assembly for Wales since Nov. 2009. He received his BEng degree and MSc degree in electrical engineering from Xi'an Jiaotong University, China, respectively and PhD degree from Brunel University, UK.

Thomas D. Xenos was born in Thessaloniki, Greece, in 1955. He received the Diploma in Electrical Engineering from the University of Patras, Patras, Greece, in 1978, and the Ph.D. degree in wireless communications from the Aristotle University of Thessaloniki, Thessaloniki, Greece, in 1991. Since then, he has joined the Department of Electrical and Computer Engineering, Aristotle University of Thessaloniki, where he is currently a Professor. He has participated in many national and international projects. He is the author of over 85 scientific papers. His research interests include wireless communications, radiowave propagation, nonionizing electromagnetic radiation measurements, and electromagnetic compatibility.

George Xilouris, MSc, received his BS in Physics from University of Ioannina, Greece in 1999 and his MSc in Automation Control Systems and Robotics from National Technical University of Athens in 2001. He joined the Institute of Informatics and Telecommunications of NCSR "Demokritos" in 2000 and since then, he has participated in numerous EU-funded projects, as well as in National funded projects. Currently he is the Technical Coordinator of T-NOVA FP7 project. His current research interests include, Next Generation Networks, Network Management, Network Performance, Network Security, Digital Television (DVB), Satellite Communications, Cloud Computing and IT services.

Zaharias D. Zaharis received the B.Sc. degree in Physics in 1987, the M.Sc. degree in Electronics in 1994 and the Ph.D. degree in 2000 from the Aristotle University of Thessaloniki. Also, in 2011 he obtained the Diploma degree in Electrical and Computer Engineering from the same university. From 2002 to 2013, he has been working in the administration of the telecommunications network at the Aristotle University of Thessaloniki. Since 2013, he is with the Department of Electrical and Computer Engineering, Aristotle University of Thessaloniki. His research interests include design and optimization of antennas and microwave circuits, mobile communications, RF measurements, radiowave propagation and electromagnetic scattering. Dr. Zaharis is a member of the Greek Physics Society, the Technical Chamber of Greece, and IEEE.

Index

L

M

N

O

P

Q

R

S

T

U

V

W

X

Printed in the United States
By Bookmasters